PATTERSON, D. W.

Production and Inventory Control
Systems and Decisions

Production and Inventory Control

Systems and Decisions

JAMES H. GREENE, Ph.D.
School of Industrial Engineering
Purdue University

 Revised Edition • 1974

RICHARD D. IRWIN, INC.   Homewood, Illinois   60430

Irwin-Dorsey Limited   Georgetown, Ontario   L7G 4B3

Revised Edition

5 6 7 8 9 0 MP 5 4 3 2 1 0 9

ISBN 0-256-01431-0
Library of Congress Catalog Card No. 73–93355
Printed in the United States of America

Preface

THIS BOOK, I have discovered through the years of the first edition, plays to many and varied audiences. Not only does it serve the requirements of junior-senior business and engineering students, but it also is used extensively in two-year technology and community colleges. To my pleasure, many students find it worthwhile to retain their book as a reference after graduation. In addition, many industrial people use the book as a handbook for solving day-to-day production and inventory control problems.

Some reorganization of the material has been made to suit the various needs of this wide audience. The sections and chapters have been arranged so that the book can be used to any depth desired. It can be used for an in-plant short course or an extensive graduate level course.

There are several important additions in this second edition worth pointing out. One is the emphasis on computer software packages. The background of software packaging is developed early so that each module, such as the bill of materials processor (BOMP), materials requirements planning (MRP), inventory control, and others can be developed in its appropriate chapter.

Many new subjects have been included such as materials requirements planning, which is just being introduced in industry. Inventory techniques involving exponential smoothing, part-period-lot sizing, and probabilistic models are just a few of the new additions. There are also a number of new approaches to the complex scheduling problem.

The trend towards the broader concept of materials management is recognized by the inclusion of such subjects as sales-order processing, purchasing, and capacity planning.

The material in the text is developed in seven sections with the thought that the instructor can outline his course to meet his objectives. For example, if he wishes a traditional course he may exclude the designing of a system as covered in Section Five. Or, if he is teaching an advanced group, he may wish to skip some of the basic sources of information which are discussed in Section Two.

Section One emphasizes the basics of production and inventory systems along with the logic used in developing these systems. Emphasis in computers has shifted from custom programming to pre-packaged software, and on-line terminals operating in the real-time mode. This section will give the reader a comprehensive view of this type of modern production control system.

Section Two develops all of the input information needed for a production and inventory control system. This information includes the quantities derived from sales orders or forecasts as well as the engineering, processing, and cost information required for an efficient system.

Section Three is devoted to inventory control decisions. Accounting and record keeping are not slighted in this development, which extends through practical probabilistic models to the mean absolute deviation (MAD).

Section Four is dedicated to decision making for production control. The techniques such as PERT, CPM, and critical ratio are developed along with the tools which are used to make them practical.

Section Five prepares the advanced student to be able to design production control systems. These systems range from basic manual systems to sophisticated computerized systems.

Section Six is for those who are managing, or aspire to manage, a production and inventory control system.

Man is a mosaic of his innumerable experiences. How can he recognize, let alone credit, all those who have influenced him? I recognize a debt of gratitude to too many people to list them all here. Among those are the many members of the American Production and Inventory Control Society committees with whom I have had the pleasure of working—in particular the contributors and editors who helped me put together the *APICS Handbook*.

I am deeply grateful to those at the State University of Iowa who assisted me toward my educational goals. Also, to those colleagues at Purdue who have been a constant stimulation during my teaching career. Above all, I probably owe the greatest debt for the development of this text to the graduate students whom I have supervised. I had the pleasure of being not only their teacher but also their student. In particular, I would like to thank Mamdouh Bakr, Thomas Rehg, Chandry Rao, Christian Neve, Capt. Neil Saling and Richard Scott.

Dr. Aaron Glickstein has kindly contributed the results of some of his research to the text, for which I would like to express my gratitude. Betty and Joseph Havlicek have graciously shared their knowledge in some of the technical fields.

To my wife, Barbara, goes my deepest gratitude. She had the courage to encourage me in this venture and had the foresight to prepare herself in home economics and journalism. No author could ask for more.

My objective with this book is to communicate some ideas as simply and painlessly as possible. In trying to do this, I have adhered to one of the lesser theories of Albert Einstein: Matters of elegance ought to be left to the tailor and the cobbler.

May 1974   JAMES H. GREENE

Contents

the Organization: *Inventory Control and the Accounting Function. Inventory Control and the Purchasing Function. Inventory Control and the Sales Function. Internal Organizational Control for the Inventory Function. Organizational Division of the Inventory Control Function.* Inventory Records: *Materials Budgets for Continuous Manufacturing. The Use of Bin Tags for Inventory Control. Perpetual Inventory. Flow of Information in and out of Inventory Cards. Records for Additional Information. Classifying Inventory by the ABC Technique. Physical Inventories. Difficulties Encountered in Inventory Control.* The Flow and Pricing of Inventories: *Pricing the Inventory.* Federal Government Inventory Regulations: *Valuation of Inventories.* Inventory Storage: *Systematic Storage Procedures. Complicating Aspects of Inventory Control. Inventory-Control Computer Software.*

section one

Production and Inventory Control Basics

THE PURPOSE of this section is to give you an overview of production and inventory control so that the other sections of the book may be placed in proper perspective. It emphasizes the information and decision-making process that takes place in production and inventory control, and it should give you a good insight into how it occurs in industry. If you read no further, you would have a good introduction to the subject.

Section two is devoted to the input information needed for the production and inventory control systems. These are comprehensive chapters and consequently you may find that you are familiar with the subjects. If so, you can pass over them lightly without any loss. Or, perhaps you will want to use these chapters for review.

Section three and section four are devoted to the decision processes of the production and inventory control function. If you are interested in learning only how these systems operate, you need read no further. However, if you wish to learn how to design systems, you should study section five. And if you are interested in the management of the production and inventory control functions, you must study section six.

In section one there are three chapters:

Chapter 1. Production and Inventory Control Concepts

This chapter outlines the objectives and scope of production and inventory control. A typical, and basic, production control system is illustrated. Production and inventory control operations can take on different appearances in different companies. The reasons for these differences are explained in a classification of industrial systems.

1

Chapter 2. The Logic of System Designing and Decision Making

One cannot expect to go far in the study of production and inventory control systems without a logical, global perspective of the systems concept. The logic of system designing and decision making is to help you move beyond the provincial ideas generally included in texts on this subject.

Chapter 3. Modern Production and Inventory Control Systems

Modern production and inventory control systems have developed through a sequence of steps from no documentation to handwritten documents, card data processing, and custom-made computer programs, to pre-packaged computerized systems. Since many of the chapters throughout the book will touch upon the packaged systems, a typical system will be presented. Not only will this chapter show you where production and inventory control is today, it will also give you another overview of the system.

1

Production and Inventory
Control Concepts

A TREND toward enlarging the subject of control is well established. In this text, emphasis is placed on the control problems directly related to production in a factory, but we must never forget that the methods to be discussed are equally suitable for many control problems.

Traditionally, production control texts emphasize the metal trade industries and give little consideration to the manufacture of other products, which, however, also require production control. Control problems also occur in other factory activities besides the production of goods. For example, the tooling, maintenance, materials handling, cost accounting, and personnel departments encounter control problems which are analogous to those found in the manufacture of a product.

The concepts of control can be expanded to include projects such as highways, dams, and buildings. It takes very little more imagination to apply these concepts to the design and operation of an airline ticket service, to a hotel room reservation service, or to the efficient utilization of hospital operating rooms. The methods used in designing control systems are identical, and many of the decision-making techniques are interchangeable.

Be aware of the broad spectrum of system designing and decision making for control, and apply your knowledge to any suitable problem.

Objectives of Production Control

Universally acceptable objectives for production control cannot be stated in a few words, for they are seen in the reflection of one's background. Experience with different products, markets, and plants will give different shades of meaning to the objectives.

Objectives of production control, which meet the minimum requirements, might be stated in this way: The coordination of the production facilities to produce a product at an optimum cost.

Those who would like more extensive objectives might be better satisfied with the definition of production control found in the Dictionary of Production and Inventory Control Terms:

Production control is the function of directing or regulating the orderly movement of goods through the entire manufacturing cycle from the requisitioning of raw materials to the delivery of the finished product to meet the objectives of customer service, minimum inventory investment, and maximum manufacturing efficiency. In this sense, production control includes inventory control.[1]

The literature abounds with other definitions and objectives for production control. An analysis of a few of these would illustrate the difficulty of establishing universally acceptable objectives.

In defining production control it is not uncommon to find it compared to the nervous system of the human body. This is an interesting and realistic comparison, for as the nervous system pervades the whole body, so does production control pervade the whole manufacturing organization as a comprehensive communications network. The nerve network assures conformance by many feedback links as does the production control system.

Production planning is frequently spoken of (and in the same breath) as production control. The distinction, if one is made, is that *planning* refers to establishing the requirements while production control refers to keeping production within these requirements; but most frequently production control refers to both of these activities. Recognition of the difference will be made when we discuss the planning stage, the action stage, and the compliance stage of production control.

Scope of Production Control

One difficulty in spelling out the objectives of production control occurs because different activities are combined in different organizations. These differences are caused by tradition, by variations in products and markets, and by numerous other reasons. Here is a list of activities (many overlapping) which might be included in the production control department:

Receive and record orders from the sales department.
Estimate the cost of new jobs.
Serve as a liaison between the factory and sales department or customer.
Forecast sales.
Issue purchase requisitions.

---

[1] Richard C. Sherrill, *APICS Dictionary of Inventory Control Terms and Production Control Terms*, 3d ed., American Production and Inventory Control Society, 2600 Virginia Avenue, N.W., Suite 504, Washington, D. C. 20037.

Make decisions to make or buy.
Maintain control over raw materials and finished products.
Maintain stock rooms for raw materials and finished products.
Establish inventory levels.
Determine routing of purchased material.
Determine routing of finished goods.
Determine internal transportation of material.
Control stock in branch warehouses.
Estimate manpower and machine requirements from schedules.
Make schedules and maintain production throughout plant.
Replan schedules and minimize replanning failures.
Assign jobs to men and machines.
Make product "explosions."
Dispatch production orders.
Expedite orders.
Evaluate performance.
Issue and maintain engineering prints.
Issue and maintain engineering changes.
Print and duplicate manufacturing forms.
Design and redesign data-processing systems.
Data processing.
Install data-processing systems.
Program computers.
Evaluate data-processing systems.

Production Control and the Organization

The objective of the production control department is to coordinate production facilities, and consequently numerous communication interfaces occur with the other departments. They all have a common interest in making a product on schedule at an optimum cost, but the method of doing it is at times a source of disagreement.

The sales department is interested in sales, and repeated sales. This can be accomplished only if the customer is satisfied, and he is usually satisfied if he obtains a product of the quality he desires at a reasonable cost and on schedule. Usually the delivery date becomes the point of conflict between production control and the sales department. To the sales department, the schedule is more important than living within the budget because a record of poor delivery can damage customer relations beyond repair.

The purchasing department wants requisitions placed well in advance of the time the material is needed. It also wants to purchase all material in large quantities, and to have freedom to substitute whenever this is desired.

Engineering would like to have designs accepted by the factory, regardless of the manufacturing difficulties. It would like to have any design changes made instantaneously, no matter how difficult.

The tool department wants time to design and build tools, and, if necessary, to experiment with production methods. The tool department itself is a small production facility, having many of the scheduling problems which exist in the factory as a whole.

Quality control and inspection are concerned with meeting the product standards, regardless of the production schedules to be met. This sometimes leads to open conflict, but most often production and quality control recognize their common interests and work harmoniously.

The personnel department would like to maintain a constant labor force and supply the skills from the available labor pool. Factory management is interested in long production runs with infrequent changes. They would like to keep inventories low, but at the same time keep the factory busy.

The place of the production control department in the organization will depend on many factors, but a typical structure is illustrated in Figure 1–1.

Figure 1–1
Typical Organization Chart

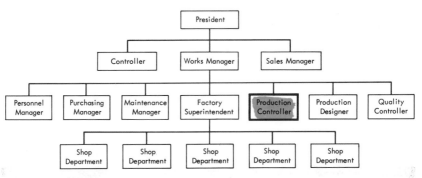

Ultimately, of course, the president of the manufacturing concern is responsible for the production control, but production control is actually the responsibility of whoever is directly charged with production: the works manager, the plant manager, or the manufacturing vice president. Except in a very small organization, this individual has many problems and therefore delegates his responsibility for the coordination of the production facilities to produce a product on schedule at an optimum cost. These responsibilities are gathered under one function under the production controller as shown on the organization chart.

Since this is a text on production control, it will be worthwhile to dwell on this part of the organization and to scrutinize the responsibilities. These responsibilities for control consist of three stages: the planning, action, and compliance stages; and each production activity is subject to these three stages of control. When an activity does not comply with the plan, the planning and action stages must be repeated; so the stages continually cycle until the activity is completed.

Four Stages of Production Control

Traditionally, the subject of production control has been so stylized that a student is led to believe that all organizations for production control are identical. The terms for the classical divisions of production control have been *routing, scheduling, dispatching,* and *expediting.* Routing and scheduling activities are contained in the planning stage, dispatching is the action stage, and expediting is part of the compliance stage.

The Planning Stage: Routing. Routing determines where the work is to be done. At times this function starts with the representation of the product as a blueprint, and every detail of how the product is to be made is decided right down to the point of designating specific machines and tools. At other times all the processing is determined by some other group, and the routing decides only which specific machine is to be used.

The Planning Stage: Scheduling. Scheduling determines when the work is to be done. It sets the timing of production control, and is not unlike the establishment of schedules for railroads, theaters, and other similar activities.

The Action Stage: Dispatching. Dispatching is the function of issuing the orders at the correct time, a function similar to the dispatching of trains in the railroad industry. In flow control, dispatching consists of notifying the production facilities of the quantity needed, while in order control it becomes a complex procedure of issuing numerous production orders to direct and indirect workers.

The Compliance Stage: Expediting. Expediting is the function of determining whether or not the work is progressing as planned. In earlier industrial history this function was called by more descriptive terms, *stock chasing* or *follow-up,* and sometimes still goes under these older names. The expeditor serves as the feedback link between the performance of work and the scheduling and routing functions of production control. In a more modern context, the work of the expeditor is minimized because it is replaced by formal progress reports which are collected and processed by automatic data processing. An excessive number of expeditors probably indicates an inefficient operation. While the expeditor can serve an important purpose in production control, he must be selected with care, because if he exceeds his authority, instead of smoothing out production, he becomes an agitating agent in what would otherwise be an efficient work situation.

The Four Stages from Two Perspectives. Because these four functions of production control—routing, scheduling, dispatching, and expediting—are referred to so frequently in the literature, the student often gets a picture something like this: There is a production control office which is centrally located in the factory, like the hub of a wheel. On the door of this office (of course) is the sign Production Control. Open this door and behind it you will find four doors leading to four equal-sized offices, each entirely divorced from the other, and inscribed Routing, Scheduling, Dispatching, and Expediting, respectively. Nothing could be further from the truth. As we shall see, in a small organization, one man, working part-time, might be doing the whole production control function. In a larger organization, we will find many people involved in one function and people handling more than one of the functions. Where specialization occurs there will have to be a great deal of communication among the groups.

The significant point is that these four activities occur in any pursuit, regardless of its importance. Even a person pursuing a hobby will go through these four steps. For example, the man who collects and refinishes antiques might progress on the restoring of a piece bought at auction as follows. First, he will plan how he is going to do the work and the tools he is going to use. This is routing. He may cut a repair part to size in his own shop, take it to his neighbor's to turn on a lathe, and return home to use his wife's vacuum cleaner to drive a paint sprayer for finishing. When the man plans to use the lathe on Saturday morning while his friend is home from work, and plans to do the painting on Sunday morning while his wife is at church (and can't object to the use of the vacuum), this is scheduling. And when he urges himself out of bed on Saturday and Sunday mornings to do the work, this is dispatching. And when the man's wife checks up to see if the refinishing will be complete by the time her sewing circle meets, this is expediting. A homely example, perhaps, and facetious, but it points up how elementary the whole production control function is and may help you to approach it with the proper perspective.

A Typical Production Control System

Now that the place of production control in the organization has been shown, this is a good point at which to introduce a typical production control system ("typical" because it would take the remainder of this text to discuss each of the variations to be found in industry). The system discussed here, and shown in Figure 1–2 is typical of an order control system to be found in the ordinary job shop that produces relatively small lots of a variety of products. Detail is purposefully left off the diagram so that it does not become too specific and so that you can observe the framework of a typical system.

The production control functions of routing, scheduling, dispatching, and expediting are shown as a box on the diagram, with the essential information inputs shown on the left. These inputs consist of the authority to manufacture the product, processing descriptions, time information, and information about the tools and machines used for production. This last input is seldom written down, but is part of the knowledge of the production control personnel.

The routing section not only determines the *route* but often prepares the numerous papers necessary for production control. The accumulation of paper forms is often referred to as the *route file*, or shop packet. In the route file will be at least some of the numerous forms listed to the right of the

Figure 1-2
Typical Production Control System

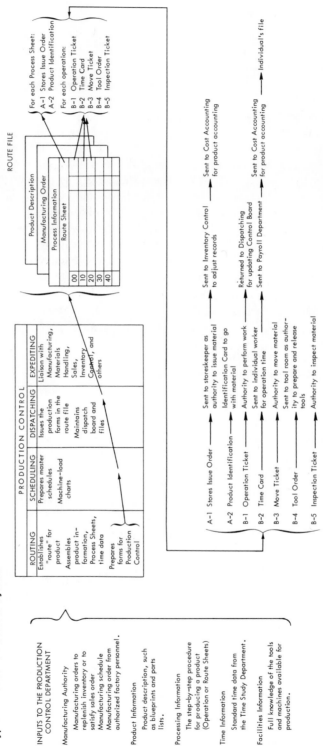

chart, and often there may be many other kinds of forms. The number and kinds of forms depend upon the type and size of the manufacturing organization.

The *stores issue* order is the authority to remove the materials from stores. It eventually will be sent to inventory control records to make the necessary adjustments, and then to cost accounting where the product costs are accumulated.

The flow of the typical forms is shown in the diagram, and it is well worth your time to follow them through carefully. The route sheet, blueprints, and manufacturing order may follow the product as it goes through the plant. When this is done, some of the other forms may be eliminated. In fact, some industries (such as manufacturers of garments and shoes) reduce their paper work to a single form designed around the route sheet. You may wish to try, as an exercise, to reduce the number of forms given in the illustration. This has been only an introduction to production control systems, and you will find a number of other typical systems in the other sections of this text.

CLASSIFICATION OF INDUSTRIAL SYSTEMS

No two manufacturing systems are identical. Not only do they have different products to process, customers to satisfy, and vendors to cope with but they also have different financing, government regulations, employees, and other qualifying factors. You should be aware of these differences and their impact upon the production and inventory control system. This section is to help you organize and visualize different production systems and their controls.

To gain an appreciation of these different systems, consider the problems of manufacturing pizza tomato sauce, working with a seasonal, highly perishable, raw material with a finished product which may be stored for months or disposed of immediately. Compare this with the problems of the can or bottle container manufacturer, or with the problems of the food-machinery manufacturer making relatively few intricate pieces of equipment out of stubborn stainless steel materials. Each of these manufacturers would have an entirely different set of production and inventory control problems. It would not make much sense to think that one system would fit all of the situations.

Each production facility will have some requirement which will make the control system unique. Yet there may be enough similarity to make it possible to use nearly the same technique.

It is not necessary to commit these systems to memory but it is desirable to get a feel for them so that you will understand why different production and inventory control systems are desirable. For example, some understanding of the systems will explain later why *finite* scheduling might be used rather than *infinite* scheduling, why materials requirements planning is the way to go rather than the conventional economic order quantities.

In cataloging the manufacturing system, it is convenient to consider it as three separate subsystems:

1. Input system.
2. Processing system.
3. Output system.

There are a number of variations of these subsystems so that when the three are combined into the manufacturing system a very large number of possibilities is obtained. Some of these systems are very common and are the cause for the complexity of some production and inventory control systems. Each system will be discussed briefly, and then some of the important combinations will be discussed.

So that these systems will leave a more lasting impression on your mind a hydraulic or fluid analogy will be used. Inventories (or stores) will be represented by tanks outfitted with valves. The processes will be represented by the impeller of a pump, which is adding some work to the fluid. Control and feedback links are represented by dashed lines. A simple code system indicating the sequence of the process and storage will be used. See Figure 1–3.

Figure 1–3
Input Systems

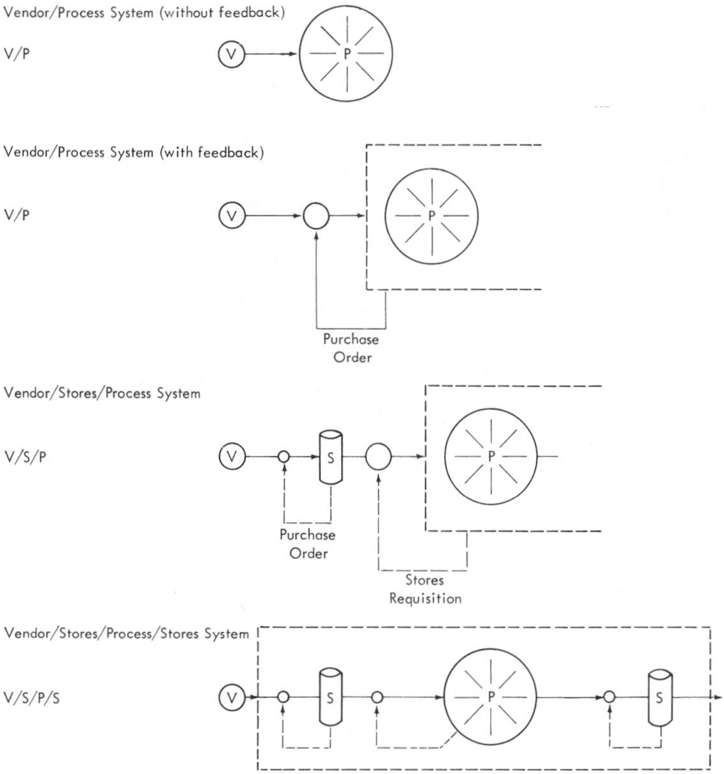

Input Systems

Vendor/Process, V/P, System (without feedback).   In some situations, such as in the canning industry, the material is processed immediately. Because the raw material is perishable it must be processed as soon as possible. The processor often commits himself to a certain quantity to keep his production uniform. There is no raw material storage to help smooth out production variations so that scheduling is at the mercy of the supplier, who is probably bringing his product to market according to the whims of nature and how it affects the growing season. Needless to say, the capital cost of equipment is as important as maintaining a stable employment for the workers. The customers downstream are also at the mercy of the vendor of the raw material. Production and inventory control as compared with other systems is elementary.

Vendor/Process, V/P, System (with feedback).   This is a more formal system than the one above and includes the purchase-order link. When the process requires materials, a purchase order is placed with the vendor.

This means that the process must be planned ahead of demand since orders cannot be filled immediately. Since there are no inventories on hand, it means that scheduling will be at the mercy of the vendor. The problems of scheduling are traded off at the costs of maintaining raw materials to be processed.

A variation on this system consists of the processor contracting with the vendor to deliver a certain quantity of material every day or other short period of time. This is not uncommon where bulky materials are used and the two plants are interlocked by ownership or a long record of cooperation. Milk might be delivered to a cheese factory every day on the basis of a contract.

Vendor/Stores/Process, V/S/P, System.   This is undoubtedly the most common way of operating a factory. The process fluctuations are taken up by the stores. When the supply reaches a predetermined order point (trigger level) a purchase order is placed with the vendor. This prevents frequent orders being placed and nearly assures that material will be available for processing. This system will probably have a more stable production rate with the inherent advantages but the problems and costs of an inventory have been added.

Vendor/Stores/Process/Stores, V/S/P/S, System.   In effect, there is often a factory within a factory. For various reasons parts or assemblies are produced and then placed in storage under control until used. Some of the reasons why this is necessary are:

1.   Parts and subassemblies which are made at a faster rate than they are used may be stored until needed. For example, manufacturers of televisions, radios, and similar complicated assemblies will often make stampings, parts such as capacitors, assemblies such as circuit boards, and store them by part number in the inventory.

2. Parts which are common to several product lines may be made in large quantities to reduce the frequency of setups.

3. Products which cannot be completed until a later date are produced and stored. For example, the same type of hydraulic pump and control might be produced for several manufacturers of road machinery and farm equipment but they must be painted to the customer's specification and must also bear his name plate with catalog and serial number. These parts will be held in inventory until the order is received at which time they are removed and processed in a relatively short time to satisfy the customer's demand for service.

4. At times the product must be interrupted in production for such reasons as lack of material, insufficient production capacity, engineering changes, and quality tests. Rather than leave the partially finished product on the manufacturing floor to be lost, stolen, or damaged, it is placed in stores. This generates one of the most difficult problems in manufacturing because it is difficult to keep track of a partially completed part which really has no specific part number. These products are frequently the useless mavericks which turn up years later during the recurring scrap drives.

The input systems have been illustrated, but this does not mean that one is used to the exclusion of the others. They are used in combinations, particularly the last two. A company may store materials which are used frequently and obtain from the vendor those which are not so common.

Output Systems

Next take a look at the output side of the system as illustrated in Figure 1–4 before considering the process itself.

Process/Customer, P/C, System (manufacturing to customer's order). The finished product in this situation is shipped directly to the customer. The shipment may be prompted by a sales order or by some other contractual relationship such as an agreement by the customer to take part or all of a process output. This system may cause extreme fluctuation in the production process but it does eliminate the problems of maintaining finished inventories. Scheduling can be extremely difficult.

Process/Stores/Customer, P/S/C, System (manufacturing to inventory). The finished product is sent to a finished inventory storage. The customer's orders are placed against this stored inventory and when they are depleted to the "trigger level" an order is placed against the manufacturing facilities. Such a system helps to smooth out the variations in production but introduces the costly finished goods inventory. The difficulty of forecasting what will or will not sell is involved in this system.

Process/Stores/Stores/Customer, P/S/S/C. It is not uncommon to find companies maintaining dispersed inventories at warehouse locations. This "cascaded" inventory system, which may have a number of levels, has

Figure 1–4
Output Systems

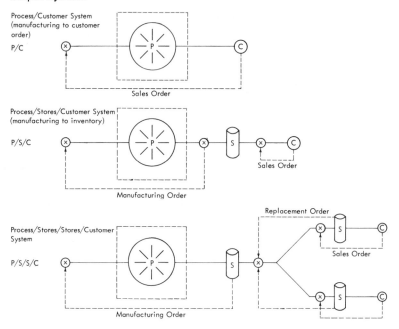

Process/Customer System
(manufacturing to customer
order)

P/C

Sales Order

Process/Stores/Customer System
(manufacturing to inventory)

P/S/C

Sales Order

Manufacturing Order

Replacement Order

Process/Stores/Stores/Customer
System

P/S/S/C

Sales Order

Manufacturing Order

an effect upon the production and inventory control system but may help improve customer service, stabilize production, and reduce inventories.

Processing Systems

In considering the process systems illustrated in Figure 1–5 the input will be designated with i and the output with o.

One-Stage Process i/P/o. This is the most fundamental of all systems and is characterized by a saw mill which transforms logs to rough boards. The problems in this process are the flow in and out of the process and scheduling the orders in the proper sequence.

Multistage Process i/PN/o. This extension of the one-stage process is hardly distinguishable from the one above because the processes are inter-locked. For example, in the forging industry the metal is heated in one process and goes immediately to the press, and then to the shear for trimming. All of these processes together perform as one with the production capacities balanced. The problems are basically the same as for the one-stage process as long as the processes remain balanced.

Unbalanced Multistage Process i/P/S/P/S/o. Typical of this system would be an assembly line for some of the complicated electronics gear. Imbalance is inherent in the system, and one of the problems is to try to obtain balance between the processes. If a balance cannot be maintained,

Figure 1–5
Processing Systems

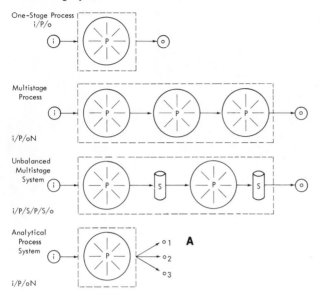

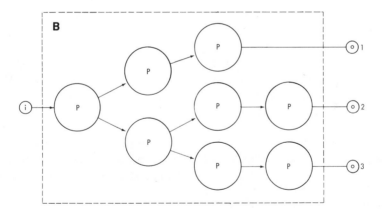

then inventories build up between processes. Balance is obtained in some cases by recycling the product through some of the process stages. Although balancing of the production line is seldom considered within the province of the production control function, it obviously has an important effect upon efficiency. Out-of-balance processes will cause inventories to build up and increase the through-put time for the product, causing schedules to break down. Inventories that build up between processes may be lost or damaged and appear in the production control office as a problem.

Figure 1–5 (continued)

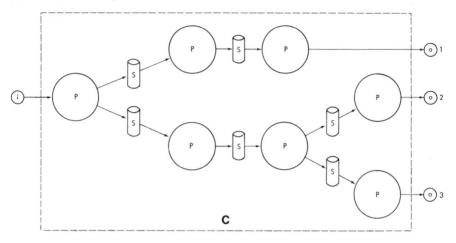

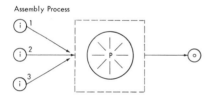

Assembly Process

Analytical Process Systems **i/P/oᴺ.** Starting with one raw material, the product is broken down into two or more products. Some chemical industries take one product, as in diagram A in Figure 1–5, and break it down to fractures which are sold directly.

Other industries may process some of the fractures further or may take a number of processes before all of the divisions are made. A real, if distasteful, example of this type of processing is to be found in the meat-packing industry, diagram B. Manufacturers in that industry are known for their skill in utilizing the entire input of raw materials. The bristles of pigs are removed and sold for brushes, and the bones are also consumed in by-products. This type of analytical process requiring more stages to complete the product is a combination of analytical and multistage process systems. It would be nearly impossible to function in a plant such as B without intermediate storages. So in reality you are going to see plants which look more like C than B.

These being complicated processing systems, one can anticipate complicated production control problems. Take for example the meat-packing problem referred to. First the raw material is constantly varying as to weight, quality, and price of the incoming product. Not only does the raw material change in price but the price of end products is also fluctuating on the market. This means that production and inventory control decisions are being constantly made in a dynamic price situation.

You should be aware that analytical-product systems also occur because of the fortuities of the process. In the production of some electrical components it is difficult to tell what the characteristics will be before the process is completed. For example, some rectifiers are sorted by their voltage range when they are near completion. So, a large quantity is started through the process with the hope that enough of the high-voltage units will be produced to meet the demand. If overproduction occurs, high-voltage rectifiers can always be used for the lower voltage applications. These types of problems make production and inventory control extremely difficult, but you should recognize them as the way of life in some industries.

Assembly Process i^N/P/o. In the simplest form, diagram A, there would be one station at which the material is assembled or synthesized into a finished product. In a more complicated assembly process the material would move along a multistage production system, B, in which the material is processed. In a still more complicated form of the assembly process, material joins the line at different stages as shown at C.

The material joining the line in the last example might simply be withdrawn from an inventory supply or it might also be supplied from other production lines which are synchronized with the assembly line. The extreme situation would exist when the components are made in some other location and the production and transportation have to be synchronized with the main production line because of lack of storage space for parts. This is not an uncommon occurrence in the automobile industry.

It is not difficult to understand how complicated this system is when you consider some electronics or mechanical assemblies. There would be no reason for starting the production without having all the parts available, and if these are not carried in stock, it means that they must be ordered with an appropriate lead time. The items must be picked from stock and *kitted* to be sent to the assembly area. Inventory records have to be reduced and orders placed with all of the accompanying problems. All of this process has come under the title of *materials requirements planning* because it seems to be a common and complex process that is worthy of consideration as a package of techniques.

In the situation as illustrated in diagram C where the material is brought into the line downstream, there are other problems to consider such as phasing production facilities, materials handling, and scheduling transportation facilities.

Job Shop Process

This is not the place to go into a long discussion of the job shop and why it is organized the way it is. For the moment be satisfied with the knowledge that it is organized with similar machines or processes grouped in one common plant area. The product then moves from one process area to another and there is no attempt to have these in a straight line. Frequently the products that go through a job shop have very little similarity. For example, a company capable of doing forging and some machining work might conceivably make cutlery, golf clubs, and some automobile and aircraft parts. Often these companies solicit work which will keep the shop busy and will take on any type of work that they can reasonably expect to do. When this occurs we get a pattern similar to what is illustrated in D. There is also a type of job shop operation in which the operations follow very similar sequences, and the product consequently moves in a standardized pattern. The manufacturing of bolts, nails, and gears is typical of this type of production. The product can only be made in one sequence, and it is moved from processing area to processing area along a fixed pattern as shown in E.

Figure 1–5 (concluded)

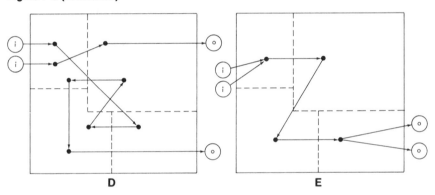

D   E

The problems in a job shop can be horrendous, and it is probably in this type of operation that good production control becomes of paramount importance. For example in the job shop, the *operation* or *routing sheet* is essential for telling the workers where the job is to be sent and in what sequence. It is really the road map which the job must follow. Feedback of information to a centralized control system is necessary so that the project may be scheduled through the shop without delay. As you probably can imagine, the scheduling of the jobs is nearly an insurmountable task.

The job shop may include just the assembly of purchased materials. These may either be assembled (kitted) before production starts or brought into the production stages downstream.

Tool Dependent Production

Before the production is started the tools have to be designed and tested. The lead time for the product must include designing the part, designing the tool, obtaining materials, testing the tool, making some products, and testing them.

A good example of this type of processing occurs in the die casting of metal parts. It is even more complicated than described above because a die has to be made to shear off the flash and sprues, but it can't be made until after the molding die is made. Often the quality has to be checked by the customer, so sample parts are shipped to him with all of the unpredictable delays. These built-in lead times make delays which are nearly impossible to avoid.

ORGANIZATION OF FACILITIES

The previous discussion gave you a structure for classifying manufacturing situations. The ensuing discussion will stress how factory facilities are organized. The type of control system depends upon the type of production facilities, so it is imperative to know something about these.

In organizing some subjects it is best to first define the two extremes and then to classify the shades of meaning in between. Things are not always black or white, but only by comprehending black and white can we sense the many shades of gray which lie between. This is the way it is in discussing types of production-facility organizations.

Two extremes which are well defined and understood in industry are:

Job Shop: A factory in which machines are grouped by the kind of work they perform.

Production Line: A factory in which machines are located by the sequence of operations required to produce the product.

The comparison between the job shop and the production line is readily made (see Figure 1–6).

Although job shop and production line classifications are generally understood in industry, synonyms are occasionally found in the literature. For example, the job shop is referred to as a *process shop* because the machines are grouped by the processes they perform. That is, all turret lathes are together and all presses are together, and so forth. They are also called *intermittent shops* because the durations of the operations are short and the machines operate intermittently. The production line is referred to at times as a *product shop* because the machines are placed in the sequence needed to produce a product.

The length of time machines are set up for a particular job is the primary reason why one arrangement of machines is chosen over another. If the processing time is short, it is usually more efficient to use the job shop, although this rule does not hold for all situations. Sometimes similar machines are grouped together because they are noisy, dirty, require special foundations, electrical facilities, or supervision.

It has been said that manufacturing to customers' orders dictates the use of the job shop layout, and manufacturing to inventory dictates the use of the production line. This is not a sufficient criterion because many factories producing to stock use the job shop layout.

Figure 1–6
Comparisons between the Two Major Types of Production

Job Shop	Production Line
1. Similar machines are grouped with common supervision.	1. Machines are located according to the sequence of operations required to produce a product.
2. The manufacturing cycles are long.	2. Manufacturing cycles are short and delivery dates are early.
3. Work loads are unbalanced, so that machines may be idle for days.	3. Work loads tend to be more balanced and every effort is made to keep the machines functioning all of the time.
4. Machine operators have extensive skills, frequently setting up their own machines.	4. Machine operators are highly skilled, but in only one type of operation.
5. Raw materials inventories may be high because of the many kinds of materials kept on hand.	5. Raw materials inventories may be high because of the quantities of material consumed. Ideally, the material is scheduled to be delivered as used.
6. Because of the long manufacturing cycle, in-process inventories are high. They are also high because the material is handled in batches.	6. In-process inventories are generally small in comparison to the large quantities produced.
7. Materials handling is more extensive in a job shop.	7. The purpose of the production line is to reduce the materials-handling costs.
8. Because there is more material handling, there must be wider aisles and other provisions for ready access to the machines.	8. Space may be utilized more efficiently.
9. Production control tends to be more complex because many jobs are in process at one time. This requires many instructions, time cards, and other forms needed to maintain schedules.	9. Production control will not be as complex because emphasis will be placed on supplying the lines with materials.
10. The output of the job shop is more flexible than that of the production line.	10. Unit costs for the production line will be lower if the production is maintained near the optimum level.

In actual practice we find plants operating between the two extremes (in the gray area) as a combination of the job shop and production line. Parts are commonly made in a job shop, while the assembly of parts is done on a production line. Some common types of production between these two extremes are worthy of their own distinct classifications, but since these are not as important, they will be discussed as minor types of production.

Erection Shop. This type of manufacturing consists of taking material and parts to one central location where the product is assembled. Usually the quantity is small and the product is not easily transported. This is the way large transformers, turbines, and similar products are produced. The production is done in accordance with blueprints, but operation sheets—common to other metal fabricating plants—are not used.

Repair Shop. This kind of manufacturing is common in the electrical equipment and appliance industry. It may be part of a large production facility or part of the service function. It can even be operated in conjunction with a district sales office. Typical repair shops are found in the railroad industry, where freight car shops approach the production line concept. Automobile generators and starters are repaired in huge quantities in shops which may be similar to job shops or to production lines, depending upon how the management chooses to operate.

Model Shops. Since these shops customarily produce small quantities, they can serve several purposes. They are used for product research and are also called upon to produce small quantities of a product for market research. In the radio business it is common to submit transformers to the radio manufacturers to test compatibility with the rest of the assembly. This calls for producing small quantities of transformers in a model shop. The model shops are informal job shops and the instructions to the workers are generally verbal because the workers are highly skilled.

Types of Control Systems

The type of control system reflects the type of production. In a job shop one can expect to find the *order control system,* but in the production line one can expect to find some form of the *flow control system.* These control systems are self-explanatory, but for a more explicit definition let us submit to the authority of the American Production and Inventory Control Society Dictionary.

> *Order Control:* Control of the progress of each customer order or stock order through the successive operations in its production cycle.
>
> *Flow Control:* A term used to describe a specific production control system that is based primarily on setting production rates and feeding work into production to meet these planned rates, then following it through production to make sure that it is moving. Flow control has its most successful application in repetitive production.[2]

It is only implied in the definitions that the material in the job shop is separated into batches or lots, while in flow control this segregation is not attempted. This leads to an intermediate situation where the material flows through the process as in a production line, but for some reason regulating it in batch quantities is desirable. This condition calls for *block control.*

> *Block Control:* Control of the production progress of groups of "blocks" of shop orders for products undergoing the same basic processes. (Appropriate to the repetitive type of manufacture.)[3]

---

[2] Ibid.
[3] Ibid.

In the clothing industry, block control may be required because of the necessity to separate different shades of cloth. In the aircraft industry, the lots must be recorded for quality control purposes. In some situations, block control is used during the transition between order control and flow control.

The size of the block is often determined by the process. For example, the block may consist of sufficient material to fill the heat treating furnace, or perhaps it may be the maximum amount which can be handled by a materials-handling truck. The block size is also determined on the basis of time, such as the quantity which can pass through the process in a half day.

One might expect job shops to use flow control, and to a degree this is true. In some job shops the flow is so standardized that, even though instruction sheets are available, the flow of the product from operation to operation is common knowledge and the routing sheets are seldom used.

Centralized vs. Decentralized Control

All of the production control activities operate out of one office in a centralized production control system. Decentralized control—in its purest sense—probably doesn't exist because it would lead to anarchy; but there are situations where all of the control activities are not centralized, and this is referred to as a decentralized production control system. Typical of such a situation would be a department which is given a schedule for completing work orders but where the foreman is left to work out the details of how the schedule is to be met.

There are both advantages and disadvantages in centralized control. Tighter schedules can be maintained with centralized control and more information is available for the customer on short notice. It has the disadvantage, however, of increasing the cost because more communications are required, more paper work is produced, and more people are needed to process it.

Perhaps the chief objection to centralized control is that supervisors lose their initiative. The foremen are not permitted to plan their work, and it is nearly an inborn instinct to want to. Because of this, the schedules are inflexible and inefficient plant operations result.

Summary

The subject is production and inventory control concepts. The first concept to understand is that production control's purpose is to direct and regulate the orderly movement of goods through the manufacturing cycle.

One difficulty in understanding production control concepts is that there are so many variations in the factory systems with different inputs and outputs. A classification system was presented so that you could see these distinctions.

Another difficulty is that factory facilities are organized in different ways.

The two major ways are the *job shop* and the *production line* with some minor ways referred to as an *erection shop, repair shop,* and *model shop.*

There are different forms of controls for these factories which include *order control* and *flow control* with an intermediate form, *block control.*

Production control is generally found on the organization chart under the supervision of the factory manager. Its organization may be centralized or decentralized depending upon the many conditions which exist in a factory.

QUESTIONS

1-1. Search the literature for three definitions of production control. Write a critical analysis of these definitions and then write your own definition.

1-2. What are the four traditional divisions of the production control function? Discuss how these are included in your activities.

1-3. How do the interests of the accounting department, purchasing department, and maintenance department respectively, conflict with the interests of the production control department?

1-4. How well equipped are you to work in a production control department? What personality strengths and weaknesses do you have for such a job?

1-5. With what you know about each of the following industries, explain what type of industrial system it is: (*a*) frozen foods industry; (*b*) metal extrusion industry; (*c*) electrical controls industry.

1-6. Choose some industry with which you are familiar. Classify it according to the industrial systems described in the text and point out the types of production and inventory control problems you could anticipate.

2

The Logic of System Designing and Decision Making

THIS BOOK is written from the design approach for those who wish to develop systems for the control of manufacturing operations. Because of this, we will dwell upon basic information and how this information can be assimilated into the design of a system.

As a bridge designer learns from a study of many bridges, so does a manufacturing control systems designer learn from studying a number of control systems. But he had first better study the components and principles which make up the system.

Since the words *system, design, production,* and *control* have significant meanings in this text, it is desirable to define them. Later on we shall combine the definitions to emphasize the objective of this book: system designing for production and inventory control. As a foundation, however, we will start with accepted definitions. For example, a system is defined as "a complex unity formed of many often diverse parts subject to a common plan or serving a common purpose."[1]

It is apparent that this definition can be extended to many design projects, such as buildings, bridges, electrical networks, and hydraulic circuits. Certainly all of these are complex unities of parts which serve a common purpose. As we shall see, it will very easily include production control.

The second word of importance is *design.* It may be of interest to note here that the material written on design has to do with either the very broad concepts of design, as considered in art, or the very narrow use of the word, as used in machine design. Here we need a different concept of the word,

---

[1] By permission; from Webster's *Third New International Dictionary,* G. & C. Merriam Co., publishers of the Merriam-Webster dictionaries.

and so we shall start again with an accepted definition of design "to conceive and plan out in the mind."[2]

It should be recognized that a design exists even though it never passes the mental projection phase. However, it would be much more systematic if the designs, at least the important ones, were recorded in one way or another. Combining the two definitions, system and design, we might come up with this definition for system designing: Conceiving and planning in the mind a complex unit of many diverse parts.

The term *parts* should not imply a static quality, for such parts might consist of manufacturing facilities, materials-handling equipment, and other factors of production.

System Design for Production Control

We are not interested in just any system design but only in one which is used for the *control* of manufacturing operations. And control, which is the next word of concern to us, means "to exercise restraining or directing influence over something."[3] The something we are concerned with is production, which is "the making of goods available for human wants."[4] So, to put it briefly, production control means: To exercise restraining or directing influence over the making of goods.

System designing for production control, the major objective of this book, can now be stated as: Conceiving and planning in the mind a complex unity of many diverse parts to exercise restraining or directing influence over the making of goods. (The reader will forgive this delay in his pursuit because he must recognize that by starting with definitions which are generally accepted we have a far greater chance of coming to a common understanding.)

The primary concern in this book is to develop the thought processes necessary to make the system design. Consequently, a number of systems will be discussed and the similarities among systems will be pointed out. Later in this section, principles for system designing will be laid down.

It is surprising to note the lack of material available on the subject of designing as it concerns the mental processes used in system designing. True, numerous books have been written on the subject of machine design, but they are primarily concerned with the application of mathematical and graphical techniques for solving specific design problems rather than with developing a technique for approaching all problems of design. But because little has been written on the thought process for designing does not mean that nothing has been done. The thought process for designing is found under such captions as Scientific Method, Engineering Mode of Analysis, Method of Inquiry, Methods, Thinking, Reasoning, and others.

---

2 Ibid.
3 Ibid.
4 Ibid.

The physiologist has tackled the problem from the mechanics of the thought process while the psychologist has approached the problem from the learning experiments of the laboratory. Philosophers have made their important contributions by going at the problem through the discipline of logic.

Physiologists' Contribution to System Designing. There is probably little light that the physiologist can shed on the subject of system designing at this time. Physiologists have made some macroscopic experiments into the way the brain works by deliberate removal of parts of the brains of animal subjects to determine how they respond. They have been able to get similar information from human beings who have had brain damage as part of an accident or illness. This has produced information concerning the function of various parts of the brain, but it leads nowhere in the study of how the brain solves problems.

The most interesting property of the nervous system is that it enables us to learn and to think, but what happens to the neurons or their synaptic connections is little more than a surmise. Many gaps in what is known about the mechanics of thinking will have to be closed before we can make any use of physiological knowledge in deliberately setting up a technique for thinking suitable for everyone.

Psychologists' Contribution to System Designing. The term *thinking* is often applied indiscriminately to a great many different kinds of psychological activities, and not just to problem solving or system designing. The restricted subject we are interested in is frequently spoken of as "reasoning" by the psychologists.

To highlight the difference between *reasoning* and *thinking*, let us point out some of the concepts that can be considered as thinking activities. One is said to be thinking when he recollects some past experience such as a travel experience, a party experience, or similar memory. One is also said to be thinking when he instantaneously recalls tables of numbers or formulas.

Imagining things which have never been brought to pass is also considered a thinking process, as when one creates in his mind a house he plans to build or a picture he plans to paint. The daydreamer is also thinking as he purposefully constructs in his mind a world which is more satisfying than the real one in which he lives.

These different types of thinking contribute to the solving of problems but they certainly cannot be construed as reasoning, problem solving, or system designing as used in this text.

What is thinking for system designing? A system design problem is a particular type of problem. A problem exists for a person when he has a definite objective or goal which he cannot reach by the behavior pattern he already has available. Problem solving comes about when there is an obstruction of some sort of the attainment of an objective. No problem exists if the path to the solution is straight and open. Only when one has to discover a means of circumventing an obstacle is the stage set for problem solving.

When one solves a problem, it is necessary to select from previous experiences those which are relevant and to organize these parts of previous experiences into the correct answer.

Deterrents and assistances to problem solving have been explored by the psychologists. One of these is *motivation*. Although little is known about how motivation is obtained, it is well known that those most productive in creating new things are highly motivated by the desire to solve challenging problems.

Habit or *set* of thinking can be helpful in solving problems and can also often delay the solution. When one practices the solving of problems, he is inclined to develop a set which makes him approach all problems in the same way. This is helpful in solving familiar problems rapidly, but when the time comes to solve new problems, the problem-solver frequently finds that it is difficult to take a new look at the situation.

Although the phenomenon of *incubation* is not well understood, many people who have been faced with problem solving are well aware of its existence. After a concentrated effort has been made to solve a problem, and a person lays it aside, the answer will frequently come to him at a time when he least expects it. Many great developments have come about in this way, and some of our greatest scientists have experienced the phenomenon of incubation to bring forth the most important developments. Incubation is no substitute for hard work, and one cannot expect to "hatch" a solution without previous sweat.

The language that we use every day is nothing but symbols, and as a man thinks he uses these symbols, whether verbal or not, as tools for the thinking process. Each individual attempts to solve problems in his own particular fashion. A person well acquainted with graphical solutions will try that method rather than a mathematical approach. One should not be bound by the pseudo-sophistry of certain methods of solving problems, for the solution is the important thing regardless of how it is obtained.

As can be seen here, the psychologist has made some important contributions to the knowledge of how man solves problems, but there is little evidence of a methodology suitable for all. On the other hand, the philosopher in his study of logic has devised methodologies; some are useful and others have outlived their purpose and are of use only to the historian of logic.

Philosophy's Contribution to System Designing. The study of control systems design is in reality a study of man controlling a small part of his environment; that part which is given to the production of goods to satisfy his needs.

Man's first attempt to control his environment was given the very general name of magic. Thus magic was for early man what the scientific method is for man today. Through the use of magical rites, man attempted (with the same sincerity of purpose as the scientist of today) to control the forces that run through nature. The second stage of man's attempt to control his environment has been referred to as uncontrolled speculation, whereby problems were solved and explanations given in terms of phenomena in the world of commonsense experience. The supernatural forces were no longer the influencing factors, but the elements of nature such as fire, air, and water became the common denominators. Explanations were accomplished not by definitely arranging experimental conditions for testing hypotheses, but by plausibility of argument alone. The flight of imagination alone was the limit, as long as the explanation seemed reasonable.

The third stage was marked by the introduction of the syllogism, a remarkable technique for testing arguments. This Aristotelian device is a common and useful thought process, although not always recognized in all its formality. The syllogism is an argument with two premises and a conclusion. To quote the classic example: "All men are mortal; Socrates is a man: Therefore Socrates is mortal."

The syllogism is frequently used today in daily discourse, but the pattern goes unnoticed because the reasoning is frequently incompletely stated. As an example: "This change in Company A's processing made a better product. Therefore this same change in Company B's processing will make a better product." Left out is that whatever processing change Company A uses can also be used in Company B's processing as an improvement.

The fourth stage utilized the syllogism for harmonizing knowledge with religious concepts. Of importance to us here is the fifth stage, which brought forth the experimental approach and the scientific method.

The Modern Logic

An understanding of some of the more important terms in the field of logic should be useful to further study of the subject. Logic itself comes from the Greek word *logos*, which means reason or discourse, and it occurs as the suffix of such words in science as geo-*logy*, bio-*logy*, and psycho-*logy*. It defines the systematic search for universal laws and principles in accordance with sound rational criteria and experimental procedures. In no facetious sense, the field of factory operations might be called industrology, for its purpose is (in part) a systematic search for universal laws and principles of industry.

The "hypothesis," which will be referred to again, is a tentative and provisional thesis put forward upon the basis of accumulated knowledge for the guidance of further investigation and research. The word is derived from the Greek word *hypo*, meaning under, and the word *tethenai*, meaning to place; and it suggests that when the hypothesis is placed under the evidence as a foundation, it will support it.

Perhaps an entirely satisfactory methodology can never be devised, for someone has compared the process of thinking to a ballgame. One can describe the game in a general way, and in considerable detail can tell how the ball should be thrown, caught, and the proper position that should be taken to bat, but one can't tell in detail the way to *play* the game. Only by experiencing the game can one really know how to play, and the same may be true of the processes of thinking. However, we will proceed to introduce a systematic method of solving problems which will serve as a useful guide.

A Guide to Logical System Designing

Probably the most comprehensive analysis of the thought process (and frequently referred to by writers in the field) has been made by Dewey.[5] The step-by-step procedure is given and should be studied extensively by anyone interested in improving his thought processes for system designing and decision making.

Step 1. Become Aware of the Problem. Although we are surrounded by problems that are unsolved, they do not become problems until we become aware of them as such. The number of problems we see, and their seriousness, depends upon our experience. The sensitivity to problems is perhaps one of the most important characteristics of the production engineer in his working with system designs.

Step 2. Define the Problem. A vague notion about the problem will lead a person nowhere, but if an effort is made to bracket the problem accurately, useful suggestions will come to mind. Often this is the most difficult part of the problem-solving procedure for the young system designer, for he is customarily given the problem—defined as such—in his academic work.

Step 3. Locate, Evaluate, and Organize Information. To prepare a hypothesis or tentative solution to a problem, it is first necessary to assemble information. This might be the information that an experienced problem-solver has at hand, or it may require the collection of additional information. No solution can be better than the facts upon which it is based, and this lack has probably been the cause of many unsuccessful system designs.

Step. 4. Discover Relationships and Formulate Hypotheses. From the data obtained, hypotheses and inferences are formed. In the actual process of thinking, however, one does not complete the definition of the problem or the location of information before he starts forming hunches, or tentative hypotheses. These two processes go on at the same time. This process of hypothesis-forming is the one about which the least is known in the process of thinking.

Although little can be said about the methodology of this step, it is known that there are certain conditions which help produce a fruitful inference. One of these is the persistence with which one attacks a problem. And, of course, this means one must be well saturated with the facts. One must be flexible in his approach and avoid the stereotyped answers which lead no-

---

[5] John Dewey, *How We Think* (Boston: D. C. Heath & Co., 1933).

where. The open mind, which is sensitive to all suggestions, is essential to the formulation of hypotheses.

Step 5. Evaluation of Hypotheses. The tentative solution must be rigorously tested in a systematic fashion. First, it should be determined whether or not the answer completely satisfies the requirements of the problem. Next, it should be determined whether or not the solution is consistent with all other facts and principles which are well established and accepted. And third, one should make a systematic search for negative exceptions which might throw some doubt upon the conclusion reached. If the hypothesis does not stand up, we must return to the hypothesis-formulating step and develop a new one, or perhaps return to the step of obtaining more information about the problem. Problem solving is not a straight-line procedure which leads directly to the answer; it is a continuously cycling procedure that requires an active mind to prevent the movement from stopping on dead center.

Step. 6. Applying the Solution. The application step is not always readily seen in some purely intellectual problems, and it is possible that it won't always be seen in the solution of a system design. However, in many important cases, the solution will be quite evident and may change the course of a whole manufacturing organization. Applying the solution in some system designs may require the expenditure of thousands and thousands of dollars and the cooperation of hundreds and hundreds of people. This is not the sort of thing that can be taken lightly, and one must develop his skill not only in obtaining the correct answers but also his skill in introducing the solutions.

The distinction between system designing and decision making will be stressed. However, you should recognize that the logic used is the same. The system decisions are made more infrequently than are the decisions which are imposed upon the system.

Since this book is dedicated to the subjects of system designing and decision making, it is essential that you have some knowledge of the logic which is used. You should make a practice of using the steps of logic described in this chapter whenever you are faced with a system design or decision-making problem.

Systems and Analogies

A system has been defined as a complex unity formed of many often diverse parts, subject to a common plan or serving a common purpose. And, as has been pointed out, this is primarily what engineers (as well as businessmen, doctors, and others) are concerned with. The professional divisions have come about by the type of system which is being emphasized. The electrical engineer works with electrical systems, the accountant works with accounting systems, and of course, the production controller works with production systems.

Problems are often solved in one field by forming an analogy with another. For example, the mechanical engineer may solve vibrations problems by forming an analogy with an electrical system. In turn, the electrical engineer might find it much easier to think of his problem in terms of hydraulics. Although it has not been exploited to any extent, it seems quite possible that the analogy will serve an increasingly important means of solving production problems.

One important aspect of the analogy is the possibility of producing models of systems which are much smaller and cheaper than a full-scale design. This technique is used extensively in the design of ship hulls, plane wings, and hydraulic systems. Since many of the relationships between the model and full-scale structure are not in direct proportion to size, an extensive knowledge of scaling has been developed. It is not difficult to imagine how important this kind of knowledge would be to the designer of manufacturing systems. By studying a small-scale operation he could predict what would happen when the operation was expanded. This technique, simulation, using mathematical analogy is now becoming important in production.

Engineers, in general, have a very good knowledge of the materials with which they work, and therefore they can quite readily design their systems. Structural engineers have gathered years of experience and information about various materials, and they can predict very closely what the responses will be to any given condition. The same is true of the electrical engineer, for he can obtain the resistance, or the capacitance, or any other characteristic of a component. If he cannot find the accumulation of this information in handbooks, he can turn to the testing laboratory to get the design information he needs. But this is not true of the designer of the industrial system, for he works with a system that includes the unpredictable behavior of human beings and many other unpredictable interactions. If the designer of industrial systems is slow in advancing the techniques of design, it can be attributed to the extreme complexity of the problems he faces compared to the design problems of others.

There are a number of ways of classifying systems, but for a quick insight into some of the problems of system design consider three different types: a static model, a dynamic model, and one with feedback (called a servo-system model).

Static Model. A bridge, or a part of a building structure, is a good example of a static system. In the case of a bridge the designer must know the distance to be spanned, the load which must be carried, and other important facts. Calling on his knowledge of statics, he knows that the sum of the forces acting parallel to an axis must be equal to zero. With this knowledge the design engineer can select the materials of the proper characteristics and design accordingly.

The industrial system designer is faced with a more or less static design when he designs an organization. The conditions under which the system is to perform are first decided, as in the bridge design; then, following certain principles of organizational design—such as the division of command, exception principles, and others—the components and the way they are to be put together are determined.

It is interesting to note the similarity of the simplifications made for the designs of the two systems. The bridge is affected not only by dead loads but also by dynamic loads, and there are some movements in the components. The organization chart also is far from static, and probably some important advances could be made in organizational designs if they were considered as being dynamic.

Dynamic Model. Many examples might be used in the study of dynamic systems, but let us select a mechanical system with which we are acquainted, the internal combustion engine. The designer wishes to know the useful output of an engine for any given input. Knowing this, he must determine how the components should be designed and how they should be put together to resist the forces and wear, all at a minimum cost. The designer does this by a well-developed theory of vector analysis, coupled with volumes of information concerning the available materials and their characteristics.

Similarly, the designer of a production system knows the input and output expected of the system, and then sets forth to make the design. He is hampered, however, by the lack of consistent knowledge of the components. He must make the best evaluation he can within the limits of his knowledge.

One can carry these analogies on to electrical systems, or fluid systems, and make some interesting observations. For example, it is known that the total resistance of a circuit connected in series, as in Figure 2–1, is the sum-

Figure 2–1
Electrical-Manufacturing Analogy

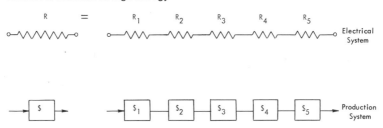

mation of the individual resistances (which can be expressed in equation form, as shown).

Similarly, the industrial systems designer might consider the cost of individual processes as "profit resistances" and add them up to find the total loss compared to profit.

It should not be overlooked that the person responsible for manufacturing-system designs is as much concerned with the relationship of input to output as is any other designer. The designer is used to discussing the ratio of output to input as "efficiency," and as we all know, the production managers have a long history of improving the efficiency of manufacturing organizations.

Servo-System Model. One of the most important and useful analogies for the industrial system designer is the servo-system.[6] The servo-system is a control system with two features, amplification and feedback. A little imagination will show that the industrial system, if properly designed, also includes these two features. The classical pyramid structure of the industrial organization, with its flow of authority—or *power of command*—flowing from the top to the bottom, shows the nature of power amplification. The output of an industrial system is evaluated by comparing it to a certain standard or objective. This serves as a motive for corrective action and reflects the feedback in the system.

Consider, for example, the steering gear of an early automobile. Probably the torque applied to the steering wheel to turn the wheels of the car is equal to the torque that reaches the wheels, causing them to turn. Power steering would be an example of amplification, while the driver's vision is comparable to the feedback.

We can simplify this illustration by using a set of conventional block diagrams, as shown in Figure 2–2. The position of the steering wheel repre-

Figure 2–2
Analogies

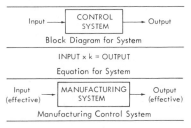

sents the input, the gears and levers the control system, and, of course, the direction of the wheels the output. Mathematically, such a block diagram can be represented by an equation, k being a constant for the system. This illustration uses the angular change as the input and the output, but it could just as well have been voltage, current, or another value.

When we talk about manufacturing systems we are frequently at a loss to quantify the values of the inputs and outputs, but for now let us call them *effective input* and *effective output* so that we have a complete analogy.

Now add the first ingredient of a servo-system to the analogy. The reason

---

[6] "An automatic device for controlling large amounts of power by means of very small amounts of power and correcting performance of a mechanism to a desired standard by an error-sensing feedback." By permission; from Webster's *Third New International Dictionary*, G. & C. Merriam Co., publishers of the Merriam-Webster dictionaries.

we don't do things for ourselves is because we want some amplification of our effective input, so we organize manufacturing industries.

Consider a very common amplification system where we have a motor which is controlled by a variable resistor, as shown in Figure 2–3. For certain

Figure 2–3
Amplification Added to System

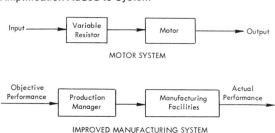

types of motors there will be a fixed relationship between the position of the resistor dial and the torque of the motor. Here it should be observed that the power available from the system is not supplied by the controlling element.

An analogy of a control system and power amplification which is a little closer to home is you and the shower you used when you got up this morning. The input is indicated by the position of the control valve, similar to that of the resistor dial; the power amplification is afforded by the water system; and the output is the water. The body's response to the temperature, which results in adjusting the controls, is the feedback link.

In the manufacturing system the input might be considered as the sales orders which need to be satisfied. The output would be the production, and the deviation would serve as the feedback in the system. Amplification will exist when the feedback induces the production manager to take some action to satisfy the objectives of the system.

It would be an oversimplification of our manufacturing system if we considered only one input, for there are many secondary inputs. It is the lack of understanding or recognition of these secondary inputs that causes all sorts of difficulties.

Consider our previous analogy of the car. Who is naive enough to believe that the car exactly obeys the driver's request? We know that the direction of the car is also influenced by the inertia of the mass, the wind pressure on the sides of the car, and the uneven friction exerted on the tires by ice, mud, and snow. Or, considering the shower analogy, one cannot forget stepping gingerly out of the shower when a disturbance to the temperature of the water was brought about by someone's turning on a faucet in another part of the house.

The secondary inputs are also in effect in the manufacturing system. The forces exerted by the supply of materials, the availability of outside capital, customers' demands, requirements by labor unions, and many others, are examples of secondary inputs.

So far we have talked only about power amplification, which is one of the important attributes of the servo-system, and the effect of secondary inputs. Now let us consider the important aspect of feedback, which gives us a *closed loop* from the output to the input.

Because of the secondary inputs mentioned above we never know what the actual output is without feedback. If you don't believe this, try driving down the street with your eyes closed when the street is covered with ice and the wind is blowing in heavy gusts. You cannot drive well because you don't have any feedback. Open your eyes and the closed loop is completed, as your eyes sense the way your car is going as opposed to the way you want it to go.

You are well acquainted with this feedback concept. The human body uses it in guiding the hands to pick up objects, and to maintain equilibrium. In fact, the common household furnace uses this concept. The controls turn on the furnace, which puts out hot air, which in turn travels to the living room and actuates the thermostat, which feeds back information to the furnace and either lets it continue to run or shuts it off.

The same thing occurs in the manufacturing system (Figure 2–4). If we

Figure 2–4
Manufacturing Feedback System

Feedback (production ticket)

don't get a feedback of some sort, we will lose control. The feedback in a factory takes the form of reports, production cards, suggestions, and the like.

With this information about the servo-system and its analogies in industry, we can go ahead and discuss some of the performance characteristics of this system.

When the input and the output of a system are constant, the system is said to be in a *steady state*, or static. But when a system receives a new input, it generally takes time to achieve a new permanent condition or steady state. During this time, the system is said to be in a *transient* condition. The various transient conditions are more conveniently shown in a graphical form (see Figure 2–5).

To make the concept of the transient a little more meaningful, let us go back to the analogy of the shower system. If you get into the shower when it is too hot or too cold, you will wish to make the proper adjustment. But

Figure 2–5
Transient Conditions

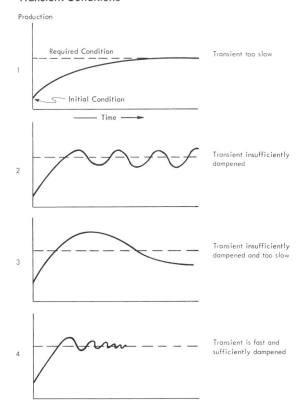

suppose the plumber has tightened the packing so that you can hardly turn the knobs; then you will have a condition similar to the first graph, and the system will be slow to respond and you will scald—or freeze.

Carrying the same situation over into the industrial system would be comparable to having a production center with a very slow response. The time it would take actual output to come up to the expected output would be long, and since it is common to pay for time expended, the cost could be prohibitive. It should be noted that this curve is somewhat comparable to a learning curve, and the slope is of critical importance. Our system is not giving the desired results.

The second graph shows that we have overcompensated. In our analogy, we have tried to get the hot water cooled off too soon, causing us to go too far. In our concern to get the temperature we want, we tend to overcompensate. All of us have experienced this sort of thing while in a shower, driving a car, bidding a bridge hand, and so on. In the industrial situation, this might be comparable to adding and removing work shifts in some production situation.

The third graph shows slowing down of the periodicity, something to be deplored. It is no doubt representative of a work system which is not properly disciplined, thus the output is erratic.

The best compromise is the last curve, in which the response is rapid, and although there is an effect of overcompensation, it is quickly dampened out. Doesn't this follow in an industrial system? You tell someone what is expected, how you wish him to comply; he does it immediately, and continues to do it with little variation from the norm.

This concept of the servo-model is not far removed from the typical organization chart hanging in many offices. Taking a typical chart, let us make the comparison. In Figure 2–6, the line leading through the boxes is the

Figure 2–6
Feedback Links Applied to the Organization

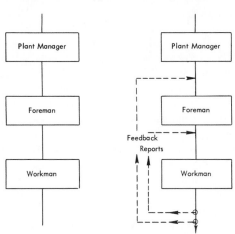

same as the input and output we have discussed. The boxes refer to the components of the system just as before, but the thing that is left out of the picture is the feedback, for it is implied. It is assumed that this is a two-way flow rather than our concept of feedback. How much better sense a chart would make if it showed the feedback lines as well. It would emphasize the necessity of communications being passed back up the line for corrective action.

One can go ahead and develop this analogy in all of its complexities. Blueprints, procedure manuals, office memos, production orders, time and quality standards are just a few examples of communication inputs in a factory system.

The feedback can take the form of time cards, quality control reports, machine downtime reports, and many other communications established upon a formal basis. On the less formal basis would be feedback in the form of general complaints, suggestion system entries, labor grievances, etc.

We will find many useful applications of the servo-system analogy, as well as the analogy of the static and dynamic systems.

The Difference between System Design and Decision Making

A sharp distinction must be drawn between system design and decision making. The decision making has to do with the signal which is imposed upon the system, and the system is the structure that carries the signal. No one should get confused between the network of telephone lines and components that carry the voice across many miles and the voice signals (suggesting decision making) that are carried along the line.

This analogy can be carried still further if we consider the internal combustion engine referred to earlier. The decision that was made and impressed upon the system was how much gas should be given to the combustion chamber by the throttle. The impulse was carried through the system more or less efficiently to the crankshaft. There is no confusion here between the signal of the decision being carried and the system that serves as the medium. Your decision to turn on a light, and flipping the switch, is certainly never confused with the design of the switch, lines, and sockets which carry your decision.

This distinction between design and decision making may appear to be so obvious as to be hardly worth mentioning. However, as we progress through the text there will be times when the distinction will be difficult to make. This confusion has caused the delay in the science of system design and decision making for production control.

Impediments in the Science of System Design and Decision Making

One of the most difficult obstructions to overcome in the development of a science of system design and decision making is the extreme complexity of the problem. This is easy to see when one considers a medium-size manufacturing plant of about 500 direct-labor workers operating in a plant with perhaps 100 indirect laborers. Each laborer may be working in a group to operate one machine, or he may be responsible for working just one machine —or even a dozen or more machines. The indirect laborers may be responsible for moving materials within the plant, keeping the work progressing, supervising, and many other jobs. All of this is influenced by unpredictable outside forces such as customer demands, labor union demands, capital available, and material shipments. It should be obvious that we have a situation which is vastly complex and innumerable interactions that are nearly impossible to isolate. Such a complex design problem would be appalling to designers of constructions, mechanical devices, and electrical networks. It is a challenge to the production manager who realizes the importance and potential of his task.

One thing which will probably delay the science of system designing and decision making is the lack of a consistent system of units. This problem has been overcome in most fields of engineering and science. Because of the physical relationship, all of the mechanical units of measure can be derived from the three fundamental units: mass, length, and time. The thermal quantities are conveniently derived from these units, plus the units of temperature. Electrical and magnetic quantities are derived from the three fundamental mechanical units and one fundamental electrical or magnetic unit. The system of units for the industrial system should be built up in this same way with modifications necessary to make the system consistent.

The convenience of using an analogy for solving problems has been pointed out, and it is apparent that the analogy gives new insights to old problems. By changing physical media it is often possible to destroy mental blocks which are delaying a solution. These similarities are pointed out in Figure 2–7.

Figure 2–7
Units of Measure

Mechanical Units		Electrical Units		Production Units
F	Force	E	Voltage	?
x	Displacement	q	Charge	?
dx/dt	Velocity	i	Current	?
d^2x/dt^2	Acceleration	di/dt	Derivative of	
M	Mass		Current	?
D	Damping	L	Inductance	?
K	Spring Force	R	Resistance	?
		I/C	Reciprocal of	
			Capacitance	?

If we can add the units for the production system, we will have made a long stride toward a system design method which will make it possible to solve many of the complex problems we have discussed. There will be some attempt to develop a consistent set of units for production and inventory control.

Summary

The distinction between system designing and decision making was stressed in this chapter. However, you should recognize that the logic used is the same. The system decisions are made more infrequently than are the decisions which are imposed upon the system.

Since this book is dedicated to the subjects of system designing and decision making, it is essential that you have some knowledge of the logic which is used. You should make a practice of using the steps of logic described in this chapter whenever you are faced with a system design or decision-making problem.

1. Become aware of the problem.
2. Define the problem.
3. Locate, evaluate, and organize information.
4. Discover relationships and formulate hypotheses.
5. Evaluate the hypotheses.
6. Apply the solution.

Students are seldom exposed to a formal study of how thinking occurs or how they can improve their thinking by a systematic process. They obtain their insight to the proper method of solving problems by the process of doing problems. In fact, the technique of learning how to solve problems is frequently the justification for many courses. But it would probably be far better for a student to first understand what is to be known about the thinking process of problem solving early in his education. He could then be aware of the process and do what he could to systematically practice the methods.

QUESTIONS

2–1. What professional group has done the most in developing a procedure for thinking? Why is this true?

2–2. Examine your own problem-solving methods. Do you believe they can be enumerated as so many steps of a procedure? Explain your answer.

2–3. What are some of the obstructions to further development in how man thinks? Will these obstructions be overcome in the future?

2–4. How important is *incubation* to your thought processes? Give an example of an *incubation* experience.

2–5. How do you use *set* in solving problems? Give a specific example. How can *set* obstruct the thought processes in solving problems?

2–6. Does the college experience teach a person to "think?" Explain.

2–7. Who, in your professional field, has contributed to an understanding of the "thinking" process? If you know of no one, choose one from another field but explain why you know of no one in your own field.

2–8. Relate system designing to what you have learned about logic.

2–9. Relate decision making to what you have learned about logic.

2–10. Is there any real distinction between the logic used in system designing and that used in the decision making which is transmitted on the system?

2–11. What can you do to further your understanding of the thought processes?

3

Modern Production and Inventory Control Systems

COMPUTER APPLICATIONS have moved into a new phase. The emphasis is no longer on the hardware of the computer and how to program it but is on complete software packages which one can buy or rent.

This new era came about for several reasons. One reason was the historical move made by the Justice Department to "unbundle" the hardware and software business. This was focused primarily on one large computer company so that it could no longer have the competitive advantage of giving away its software with its computers.

Another reason for the growth of the software business has been that the industry has come into a period of stabilization. In years past a computer no more than hit the market than an entirely new design was presented with drastic changes. For awhile it was not even certain whether the card was going to be coded short edge first or long edge first. These design changes did not permit any continuity, and every new computer meant an entirely new ball game with many adjustments to be made.

Computer languages have also stabilized. First there came machine language using the binary numbering system. Then came the period in computer history which required one to learn a new translator language every few months as a better—and still better—one came out. Just keeping up with the names of those languages, such as SOAP, SAP, MAD, was as difficult as keeping up with the current detergents that will cure all wash day woes. Today every college student and many grade and high school students are learning a fairly common type of language such as FORTRAN, COBOL, and BASIC, which are all somewhat related.

Probably a more important cause for the flurry of software activity came about because many highly skilled computer buffs recognized the similarities among solutions to problems and decided that common software packaging was one way to prevent reinventing the wheel. They are transferring all or part of programs into new applications. The more aggressive of these individuals have seen a business opportunity and set forth in the marketplaces to sell these software packages which have common applications. These common packages are to be found in many types of industries, from banks to insurance companies, to hospitals, and to factories. Unfortunately all of these programs are not as good as they might be, and customers are buying packages which are far from satisfactory.

Typical of the situation is what occurred in a large electronics company. Briefly, the situation was this. After deliberating with the factory computer experts, the production control manager purchased a particular software computer package. After many months and thousands of dollars, the system was considered to be operating satisfactorily. It was only then that he discovered that the computer package at the home plant was not compatible with the system at the company's plant a few miles away. He had the situation wherein the two computers at these two sites were strangers, having been stricken dumb and unable to talk with each other. This caused considerable anguish to the manager and undoubtedly to the corporate money counter. It is this sort of embarrassing situation that one must avoid to remain in good standing with top management.

Production and Inventory Control Packages

Industry is looking toward the day when it can have a completely integrated information system which is computer oriented. This Management Information System (MIS) has approached reality in some companies, but in others it is falling short of the desired goals. A more workable way is to develop a subsystem of the MIS which includes just the manufacturing system incorporated in production and inventory control.

One such software subsystem developed by the IBM company is referred to as the production information and control system (PICS). This system of modules has met with considerable success in industry. However, very seldom if ever will one find the entire set of modules in action. More than likely it will be that one or more modules is being applied to specific problems.

All business computer manufacturers will have software packages for production and inventory control. There are also many consulting firms who are selling a production and inventory control software package. It would be very difficult to trace the development of these programs, but in all likelihood, there is a great deal of similarity between the PICS system and the others. They are all designed to solve the same problems, and the differences are apt to be minor. Consequently, it would be desirable for you to become familiar with the rudiments of PICS so that you will know something about the other systems.

The purpose of the rest of this chapter is to give you an overview of the PICS system, which will be followed by detailed discussions in the appropriate chapters.

The Data Base

Fundamental to any MIS is a common file of information, which is used by the entire system. Instead of engineering, production control, and all of the other functions maintaining separate files, there is one computer-lodged file which is referred to as the *data base*. The data base generally includes all operational record information needed to handle a company's business. The data base is stored on computer disk files and is therefore directly on line to a computer. Because of this, "summary" and detail information can be "accessed," updated, and retrieved from multiple entry points. It is not difficult to imagine how a common data base can prevent delays, minimize filing time, and eliminate errors in transcription. The data base for PICS, Figure 3–1, consists of a number of files which are stored on disk memories within the computer for easy accessibility. The title of the file should explain its purposes and suggest the type of information that it contains.

Figure 3–1
Data Base

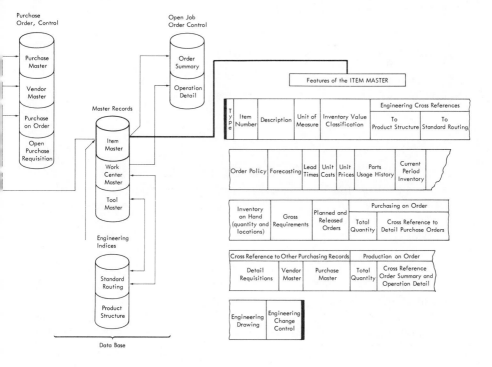

Data Base:
  Master records:
    Item master file.
    Work center master file.
    Tool master file.
    Standard routing file.   '
    Product structure file.
  Purchase order control:
    Purchase master file.
    Vendor master file.
    Open purchase order file.
    Open purchase requisition file.
  Open job order control:
    Order summary file.
    Operation detail file.

The illustration to the right of the data base shows just some of the information which is maintained in the *item-master* file.

The Production Information and Control System

The production information and control system (PICS) illustrated in Figure 3–2 is a framework for integrating the data base system for the following eight applications:

1. Engineering data control.
2. Inventory control.
3. Sales forecasting.
4. Requirement planning.
5. Capacity planning.
6. Operation scheduling.
7. Shop floor control.
8. Purchasing.

Illustrated in Figure 3–3 are these eight applications combined into a flow chart depicting the production and inventory control system. Below each of the applications, on the flow chart, is a list of the data base files which will be used.

A brief description of each function will be presented here to permit an overview of the system. However, those modules which are actively used in industry will be covered in greater detail in the course of developing the particular subject matter where they are applied. For example, the details of the bill-of-materials processor will be included in the discussion of product information.

Application 1, Engineering Data Control. This program uses the item

Figure 3–2
Production Information and Control System

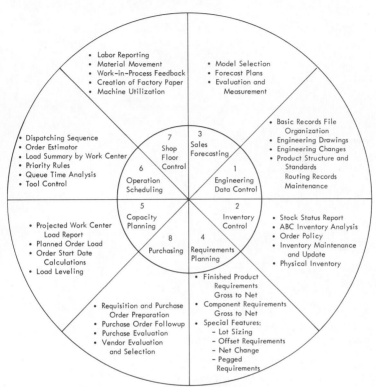

master, product structure, standard routing, and work center master files located in the data base.

Module 1 is the Bill-of-Materials Processor (BOMP), which uses the product structure information to prepare bill-of-materials in either assembly or where-used sequence.

Standard routings may be available in either the routing or work center sequence.

The maintenance section keeps the data current with these five different possible transactions:

1. Adding or removing assembly components or quantities.
2. Engineering changes which require the addition of a new item.
3. Deletion of an item.
4. Production specification changes.
5. Engineering change effectivity date.

Module 2 is for retrieval programs. The file organization provides a large variety of retrievals in the form of material lists and engineering changes.

Figure 3–3
Production and Inventory Control Flow Chart

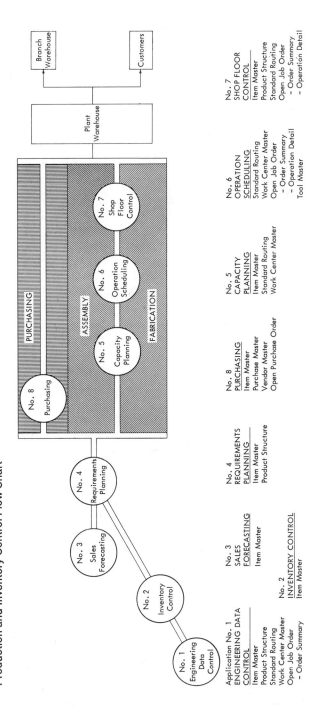

Application 2, Inventory Control Subsystem. This has the following modules:

1. An *ABC inventory analysis* which permits inventory to be handled in accordance with its value.
2. An order policy module which helps decide when and how much material is to be ordered.
3. An inventory maintenance module takes care of the day-to-day transactions.
4. A physical inventory module organizes and simplifies this time-consuming task.

Application 3, Sales Forecasting. This has two modules: One is used for examining all of the past data and selecting the appropriate model; and the other, depending upon the model selected, calculates the new average and trend.

Application 4, Requirements Planning. The function of the requirements planning subsystem is to determine the raw materials, fabricated parts, purchased parts, subassembly, and assemblies needed to meet the finished products plan that was generated by the forecasting subsystem.

Application 5, Capacity Planning. This forms the base from which a plant's detailed operational schedules can be developed.

Application 6, Operation Scheduling Subsystem. Assigns dates on which a job is expected to start and finish. The objectives are to help management meet due dates for orders, increase utilization of resources, and minimize in-process inventory.

Module 1 assigns the sequence of orders according to a priority rule, Module 2 estimates the completion time, and Module 3 is responsible for tool control.

Application 7, Shop Floor Control Subsystem. This consists of a module for releasing orders and a module for order progress.

Application 8, Purchasing Subsystem. This is responsible for the stock availability to satisfy requirements for raw materials, purchased parts, and supplies.

This has been just a global view of the Production Information and Control System. Those subsystems which have been developed to the point of being widely accepted will be included in your reading as you are introduced to the various subjects under consideration.

COPICS

An extension of the PICS system has been introduced under the name of Communications Oriented Production Information and Control System (COPICS). This is an expanded, integrated manufacturing system concept. It includes the forecast of customers' requirements through the development of a schedule to the production and shipment of the product.

A feature of the system is that it permits tactical planning by including simulation as a tool for testing decisions.

The COPICS system is terminal and communications oriented and event responsive. It functions in real-time, giving all of the information needed for immediate decisions and responses.

Summary

The move in industry is toward computer software packages which are purchased or rented from vendors. The vendors are either computer companies, software companies, consultants, or even another industry such as a bank or railroad which has developed a program. The move is away from each company developing its own programs in their entirety.

A common information system for all plant operations is desirable but difficult to install. Short of that would be an information system for the production system. The production information system, PICS, is an attempt to coordinate the production functions in one system. PICS is a collection of integrated modules working in conjunction with a data base. It is not necessary and probably not possible or desirable to install all modules. A company can choose the ones it desires to use.

The modules are too detailed to be included here. Those which are used extensively in industry will be included with the subject relating to the module. This has only been an attempt to give you an overview of the system.

With software packages comes another important decision for management to make. The rental or purchase of these packages may involve thousands and thousands of dollars. The commitment made will last for many years to come. The decisions should not be taken lightly and should include the thinking of the best brains in the company.

QUESTIONS

3-1. Discuss the antitrust laws and the current computer market.
3-2. Discuss the evolution of computer applications in industry.
3-3. What information would you expect to find in the "data base" of a manufacturing information system?
3-4. What information would you expect to find in the "item master" file?
3-5. Discuss the eight segments of the PICS system. Which would you implement first? Which would give you the greatest savings? Which would cause you the greatest difficulty during implementation?
3-6. What advantages would there be in developing software in modules?
3-7. You are confronted with the decision of which software package to buy. List and discuss five questions you would consider important.

section two

Information for Decision Making

THE PRODUCTION CONTROL FUNCTION is the nerve center of the factory and has been compared in analogies to the brain which serves the body. Like the brain, production control can only function if it receives and sends accurate information. The information required ranges from: How many have been sold? How long will it take to ship? How many should be purchased? to How many people should be hired?

The purpose of this section is to learn how to develop the information needed for an efficient production and inventory control system. You should not feel compelled to study all of the subjects in this section if you think that you have sufficient background. Some industrial engineering students, for example, will have a background in work study so that they may wish to skip that section, while students from other disciplines might find that this is new material. This book cannot be all things to all people, but it at least covers the subjects which are essential to make a production and inventory control system operate efficiently.

Chapter 4. Statistics for Production and Inventory Control

One cannot go far in modern production and inventory control without some working knowledge of statistics. It appears in inventory theory, scheduling theory, and forecasting. The statistical techniques you will be needing are discussed here in a background of industrial applications so that you will not only receive a knowledge of statistics but also how it can be applied.

Chapter 5. Sales and Forecasting Information

Sales functions for industry are like pumps which keep the profits flowing, since without profits the organization would probably cease to exist. Unless production control can assure deliveries on time, sales and profits will decrease. Production control also has the responsibility of satisfying the customers' needs for service parts. Sales and production control must work together in satisfying the customer's demand while at the same time smoothing out production fluctuations.

Chapter 6. Product and Process Information

Both the product and process description are essential inputs to the production system, for how else would the people know what and how to produce? This chapter presents a logical procedure for preparing the product and process documents for the factory.

Chapter 7. Cost Information

Buy or make? Produce by method A or method B? These are the types of questions which must be answered by production and inventory control. This chapter gives you a method of obtaining cost information with which you can make these critical decisions.

Chapter 8. Capacity Planning and Scheduling Information

Time information appears many times in the operation of the production and inventory control function. It appears in scheduling, loading, costing, inventory, plant capacity, and other decisions. How to measure the time for work is the subject of this chapter.

Chapter 9. Purchasing Information

Even if the scope of production and inventory control had not been expanded to the all-inclusive materials management concept, a knowledge of purchasing procedures would be desirable. Purchasing and production and inventory control must be geared together if material is going to move from the vendor to the manufacturing facilities on schedule.

One word, information, describes all of the chapters in this section. Without information—correct information—the production and inventory control systems will fail.

4

Statistics for Production and Inventory Control

TODAY'S PRODUCTION and inventory decisions require a good knowledge of statistics. Throughout the rest of the book will be techniques based in statistical concepts. The purpose of the present chapter is to present these concepts as concisely as possible. A person with an excellent statistical background may wish to move through the material in this chapter rapidly or even avoid it. You should be cautioned, however, that the subject is developed within the production and inventory context, and you will find many applications which will give you an insight into the subject.

The word *statistics*, as used in forecasting, has several quite distinctly different meanings. It may mean data or the collection of data, but to the more sophisticated it means the *principles of statistical inference*. Mathematical statistics can range from some very elementary ideas to extremely complicated theoretical concepts. Here we can touch only upon some of the more basic ideas, but you are urged to become acquainted with the excellent references in the bibliography.

Statistics, it should be understood, is a tool for the analysis of information and is not an end in itself. The subject will be developed with this in mind. To point the way for the discussion, the subjects will be covered in the following order:

1. Statistical sampling.
   a. Characteristics of normal distribution.
   b. Characteristics of binomial distribution.
2. Statistics of association.
   a. Regression analysis.
   b. Correlation analysis.

Language of Statistics

A person involved with the statistical literature picks up the language quickly, even though there are often several symbols for one concept. The symbols used in this chapter are listed under Symbols and Terms and will also be defined as used.

Symbols and Terms

Greek letters will be used for *parameters* of a population; Latin letters will be used for *statistics* of a sample.

a	Estimate of α, the Y intercept of a line.
b	Estimate of β, the slope of a line.
d	Deviation from a designated mean, X_d.
e	Deviation from a line.
f	Frequency.
i	Class interval.
n	The number in a sample.
N	The number in a population; in regression, the number of observations.
N^*	The number of samples.
p	The probability that a success will occur.
$\bar{p}$	The sample proportion (read "p bar").
q	The probability that a failure will occur, $p + q = 1$.
r	Coefficient of correlation.
x	The deviation of a value from the mean.
x'	The deviation of a class mid-value from the mean.
X	A value in a series of values.
$\bar{X}$	Arithmetic mean of a series of values in a sample.
$\bar{\bar{X}}$	Arithmetic mean of sample means ("X double bar").
$\bar{X}_d$	A designated mean.
Y	An observed value of Y.
Y_c	A calculated value of Y.
$\bar{Y}$	Arithmetic mean of the Y values.
S	Standard deviation of a sample.
S_x	Estimated standard deviation of a population, computed from a sample.
$S_{\bar{x}}$	Standard deviation of the sample means.
S^2_x	Estimated variance of a population, computed from a sample.
S^2_y	Total variance to be explained.
S^2_{yc}	Explained variance.
$S_{y \cdot x}$	Standard error of the estimate.
σ_x	Standard deviation of a population.
σ^2_x	Variance of a population.
$\sigma_{\bar{x}}$	Standard error of X.
Σ	Add all the values in the interval ("capital sigma"). The interval may be designated by $\sum\limits_{1}^{n}$ meaning sum the values from 1 to n.

Statistical Sampling

Sampling, to determine the characteristics of a large body of information, is an everyday experience. The preview of next week's show at the local theater is a (biased) sample to urge you to return in the near future. Glanc-

Figure 4–1
Predicting the Size of Hats

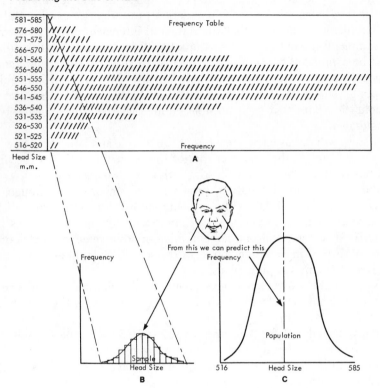

ing through the magazines on a newsstand before buying is another sampling procedure used before making a decision.

The manufacturer also uses sampling, consciously or not, to help him make forecasting decisions. For example, a manufacturer of hats is concerned about a new line for boys of a certain age group. How many should inventory control order for each size? Mindful of a boys' school nearby, permission is obtained to measure the head size of each boy in the age group of interest. This is done quickly by recording the sizes on a frequency chart (as shown in Figure 4–1A).

Plotting the frequency of occurrences on the coordinate paper for each head size in the sample will give a distribution which looks something like the diagram in Figure 4–1B. This stair-step diagram is called a *histogram*. The group of boys under observation is called the *sample*, and the potential market for boys buying the manufacturer's hats is called the *population*. We might predict the distribution of the population from the histogram (Figure 4–1C).

As the sample size gets larger and larger, one would expect the sample distribution to look more and more like the population. The problem is to predict the characteristics of the population from what we can learn about the sample. It is apparent that the statistical inference can be made from the sample. But what about this sample? Will any sample do? The sample must be a *probability sample* if it is to be used for statistical inferences. Although the simple random sample is only one form of probability sampling, our interest will be focused on this method. "Selected at random" indicates that each possible sample has the same probability of being drawn.

First we will discuss characteristics of the sample and later show how the sample can predict the characteristics of the population. This is the problem, but what are these characteristics with which we are concerned?

The symmetrical distribution, shown by the smooth line through the histogram in Figure 4–1B, is the most important distribution in statistics and is referred to as the *normal distribution* or, for obvious reasons, the *bell curve*. It is the result of a large number of additive effects and is often representative of information found in the sciences as well as in industry. It is basic to many sampling plans.

What would you want to know about the distribution of head sizes if *you* were the hat manufacturer? Certainly the average size, the largest, and the smallest sizes, and if you could have more information (which you could), you would ask for the percentage of each size you expect to sell. The arithmetic mean, often referred to as the average, is, as you know, the total of all the values of a group divided by the number in the group. This is stated by the equation:

$$\bar{X} = \frac{\sum_{i=1}^{n} X_i}{n}$$

$\bar{X}$ = Arithmetic mean of a sample
X_i = Value of the *i*th observation in the sample
n = Number in the sample

The capital sigma, Σ, means "add all the X values from 1 to n" and gives a simple way of showing the total of the values of X. No longer will the interval 1 to n, over which we are adding, be expressed; and we will always assume that we are totaling all the values in the interval.

The arithmetic mean, $\bar{X}$, (called "X bar") is only one of the measures of *central tendency*. There are others, such as the *median* (the middle number in a series of consecutive numbers) and the *mode* (the number which occurs most frequently). As you might guess, on a normal curve all these measures—mean, median, and mode—fall at the same place.

Several curves could have the same average, and be normal distributions, but look like any of the three curves in Figure 4–2. The difference is in the dispersion. The manufacturer might be satisfied by knowing the two extreme head dimensions, but there is a better measure of dispersion called the *variance*, and its next of kin, the *standard deviation*. Let us look at these together and compare them briefly before proceeding.

Figure 4–2
Distributions with Same Mean but Different
Dispersion

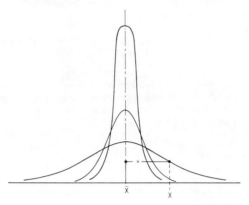

Variance of a sample size n:

$$S^2 = \frac{\Sigma(X - \bar{X})^2}{n} = \frac{\Sigma(x)^2}{n}$$

The variance, S^2, is also called the *mean square error.*

Standard deviation of a sample size n:

$$S = \sqrt{\frac{\Sigma(X - \bar{X})^2}{n}} = \sqrt{\frac{\Sigma(x)^2}{n}}$$

The standard deviation, S, is also called the *root mean square error.*

The variance and the standard deviation look alike with one exception. The standard deviation is the square root of the variance, or the variance is the standard deviation squared, whichever way you care to look at it. But one should not pull equations out of the air like this without explanation of what they measure.

As we know, $\bar{X}$ is the average value, so if we substract it from the individual X's, as shown in the previous figure, we have the differences or variability around the mean, which will be designated by small x's. Some of these will be negative, which will balance out the positive values, giving a total of zero. If negative numbers are squared, they result in positive numbers. So if we do this, $(X - \bar{X})^2$, we get positive values which are then totaled over the entire interval, as indicated by the capital sigma (Σ). This total is then divided by n. The engineer will recognize an analogy between the mean as the first moment about the origin, and the variance as the second moment about the mean.

Up to this point we have singled out the sample for discussion because we cannot conveniently obtain information about the population and must project our knowledge from a sample. Here we shall pause and compare the sample *statistic* with the population *parameter*. To minimize the confusion we shall want to use a different set of symbols for each. Here are symbols which are fairly common in the literature:

Symbols Used for Samples (Statistic)		Symbols for Samples When Used to Estimate the ,Population		Symbols for Populations (Parameters)	
S	Sample standard deviation	S_x	Estimated standard deviation of a popu- lation predicted from a sample	σ_x	Standard deviation for the population (lowercase *sigma*)
n	Number of items in the sample	n	Number of items in the sample	N	Number of items in the population
$\overline{X}$	Sample mean	$\overline{X}$	Sample mean	μ	Population mean (mu)

Notice this confusing point. The capital sigma was used for summing a series of numbers, but here the lowercase sigma, σ, indicates the *population* standard deviation. There is no relationship between the meanings of these two symbols. Also notice that S is used to indicate the *sample* standard deviation and S_x is used for the *estimated* standard deviation of a population predicted from a sample.

The population mean can be estimated by the sample mean, so the following is true:

The *sample mean* is an estimate of the *population mean*:

$$\overline{X} = \Sigma X/n \qquad \mu = \Sigma X/N$$

The greatest difficulty lies in estimating the standard deviation. To introduce sampling it was implied that the sample deviation is a good predictor of the population standard deviation. This is not a bad assumption for large sample sizes, but it introduces some error when the sample is small. The *estimated standard deviation of a population* will be designated by S_x, and the relationship between it and the population standard deviation, σ_x, is as follows:

Sample standard deviation is an estimate of the *population standard deviation*:

$$S_x = \sqrt{\frac{\Sigma(X - \overline{X})^2}{n - 1}} \qquad \sigma_x = \sqrt{\frac{\Sigma(X - \mu)^2}{N}}$$

The $n - 1$ accounts for the degrees of freedom[1] and is used instead of n so that we will obtain an unbiased estimator. That is, the estimators will not favor an incorrect answer which, in the case of using n, would on the average cause the estimate of σ_x to be small. It is obvious that the larger the sample the smaller the difference between n and $n - 1$, so it is common to use n for large samples.

---

[1] Degrees of freedom, the maximum number of mutually independent variables in a system. For example, if three items total 9 and two of them are 3 and 4, the third must be 2. For a sample size n, there are $n - 1$ degrees of freedom.

The standard deviation has an interesting characteristic. The more the X's are dispersed the greater will be the standard deviation. However, for a normal curve, the distribution of the X's will follow the pattern shown in the diagram in Figure 4–3.

Figure 4–3
Relationship between Standard Deviation and Frequency

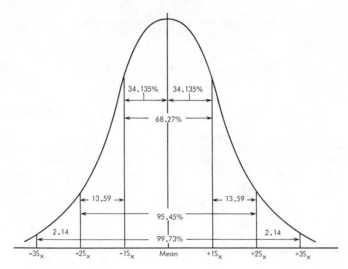

What this says is that 68.27 percent of the cases will fall within one standard deviation, either side of the mean; 95.45 percent of the cases within (plus and minus) two standard deviations; and 99.73 percent within (plus and minus) three standard deviations of the mean.

Tables are available (Figure 4–4) which give the area under the normal curve for any practical multiple of standard deviations. To enter the table, the X value is expressed in standard deviations called Z values.

$$Z = \frac{(X - \mu)}{\sigma}$$

Since population values are not known, it is necessary to estimate Z from a sample (using the following equation). This is applicable only when large samples are available and when it is known that the sample is representative of the inference population which is known to be normal.

$$Z = \frac{(X - \bar{X})}{S_x}$$

For example, if $X = 8$, $\bar{X} = 4$, and the estimated standard deviation S_x is 2, the Z value would be $(8 - 4)/2 = 2$. Entering the table, we find that 47.72 percent of the area is between X and $\bar{X}$. This is illustrated in Figure 4–4. If we were interested in the area between plus and minus X, as we might

Figure 4–4
Areas of a Standard Normal Distribution
for Z Values

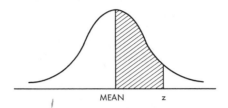

MEAN   z

Table of Areas from Mean to Distances Z*

Z	.00	.01	.02	.03	.04	.05	.06	.07	.08	.09
0.0.....	.0000	.0040	.0080	.0120	.0160	.0199	.0239	.0279	.0319	.0359
0.1.....	.0398	.0438	.0478	.0517	.0557	.0596	.0636	.0675	.0714	.0753
0.2.....	.0793	.0832	.0871	.0910	.0948	.0987	.1026	.1064	.1103	.1141
0.3.....	.1179	.1217	.1255	.1293	.1331	.1368	.1406	.1443	.1480	.1517
0.4.....	.1554	.1591	.1628	.1664	.1700	.1736	.1772	.1808	.1844	.1879
0.5.....	.1915	.1950	.1985	.2019	.2054	.2088	.2123	.2157	.2190	.2224
0.6.....	.2257	.2291	.2324	.2357	.2389	.2422	.2454	.2486	.2518	.2549
0.7.....	.2580	.2612	.2642	.2673	.2704	.2734	.2764	.2794	.2823	.2852
0.8.....	.2881	.2910	.2939	.2967	.2995	.3023	.3051	.3078	.3106	.3133
0.9.....	.3159	.3186	.3212	.3238	.3264	.3289	.3315	.3340	.3365	.3389
1.0.....	.3413	.3438	.3461	.3485	.3508	.3531	.3554	.3577	.3599	.3621
1.1.....	.3643	.3665	.3686	.3708	.3729	.3749	.3770	.3790	.3810	.3830
1.2.....	.3849	.3869	.3888	.3907	.3925	.3944	.3962	.3980	.3997	.4015
1.3.....	.4032	.4049	.4066	.4082	.4099	.4115	.4131	.4147	.4162	.4177
1.4.....	.4192	.4207	.4222	.4236	.4251	.4265	.4279	.4292	.4306	.4319
1.5.....	.4332	.4345	.4357	.4370	.4382	.4394	.4406	.4418	.4429	.4441
1.6.....	.4452	.4463	.4474	.4484	.4495	.4505	.4515	.4525	.4535	.4545
1.7.....	.4554	.4564	.4573	.4582	.4591	.4599	.4608	.4616	.4625	.4633
1.8.....	.4641	.4649	.4656	.4664	.4671	.4678	.4686	.4693	.4699	.4706
1.9.....	.4713	.4719	.4726	.4732	.4738	.4744	.4750	.4756	.4761	.4767
2.0.....	.4772	.4778	.4783	.4788	.4793	.4798	.4803	.4808	.4812	.4817
2.1.....	.4821	.4826	.4830	.4834	.4838	.4842	.4846	.4850	.4854	.4857
2.2.....	.4861	.4864	.4868	.4871	.4875	.4878	.4881	.4884	.4887	.4890
2.3.....	.4893	.4896	.4898	.4901	.4904	.4906	.4909	.4911	.4913	.4916
2.4.....	.4918	.4920	.4922	.4925	.4927	.4929	.4931	.4932	.4934	.4936
2.5.....	.4938	.4940	.4941	.4943	.4945	.4946	.4948	.4949	.4951	.4952
2.6.....	.4953	.4955	.4956	.4957	.4959	.4960	.4961	.4962	.4963	.4964
2.7.....	.4965	.4966	.4967	.4968	.4969	.4970	.4971	.4972	.4973	.4974
2.8.....	.4974	.4975	.4976	.4977	.4977	.4978	.4979	.4979	.4980	.4981
2.9.....	.4981	.4982	.4982	.4983	.4984	.4984	.4985	.4985	.4986	.4986
3.0.....	.49865	.4987	.4987	.4988	.4988	.4989	.4989	.4989	.4990	.4990
4.0.....	.4999683									

* For Z = 1.93 (illustration), shaded area is .4732 out of total area of 1.
Source: John Neter and William Wasserman, *Fundamental Statistics for Business and Economics*,
2d ed. (Boston: Allyn and Bacon, Inc., 1961), p. 809. Reprinted by permission of the publisher.

be, the area would simply be 95.45 percent. From this table it is obvious that
we can obtain information for any multiple of standard deviations.

Following the procedure just given, the hat manufacturer can forecast the quantity of each size hat he should manufacture. But can you imagine the trouble it would cause to take the sample items, subtract them from the mean, square them, add them, and extract the square root? Even the thought is fatiguing, so let us strive to find a simpler method. The evolution of reaching a practical model will be given briefly. In the following equations n will be used instead of $n - 1$ because it is assumed the samples are large, and we will start with the sample standard deviation in the form just given.

First Improvement: Rather than subtract the individual X's from the mean, $\bar{X}$, as shown in the previous equation, the following equation in terms of X's can be used:

$$S_x = \sqrt{\frac{\Sigma X^2}{n} - \left(\frac{\Sigma X}{n}\right)^2}$$

Second Improvement: By grouping data for convenience, the information can be tabulated in a frequency distribution as shown earlier. The equation can then be changed to account for the form of the data.

$$S_x = \sqrt{\frac{\Sigma f x'^2}{n}}$$

(x' is the deviation of a class midvalue from the mean; f is the frequency.)

Third Improvement: Determining x' is obviously difficult so, rather than use the average, the midvalue of any class can be used as the assumed mean. Calculations are made with the deviations around this value and then corrected:

$$S_x = \sqrt{\frac{\Sigma f d^2}{n} - \left(\frac{\Sigma f d}{n}\right)^2}$$

(d is the deviation of an X from any designated mean $\bar{X}_d$.)

The mean can be calculated:

$$\bar{X} = \bar{X}_d + \frac{\Sigma f d}{n}$$

Fourth Improvement: To shorten the process even more, the deviations can be taken in terms of classes:

$$S_x = i\sqrt{\frac{\Sigma f (d')^2}{n} - \left(\frac{\Sigma f d'}{n}\right)^2}$$

(d' is the deviation of a class midvalue from the assumed mean in terms of classes; i is the class interval.) And the mean is:

$$\bar{X} = \bar{X}_d + i\left(\frac{\Sigma f d'}{n}\right)$$

Since this fourth improvement is the most efficient, it will be used to solve the hat size problem for the inventory control department. The information for the hat size problem, shown in Figure 4–5, is given in a form that

Figure 4–5
Determination of Hat Sizes

Head Size m.m.	Fre-quency	Midvalue of Class	d'	fd'	$f(d')^2$
516–520............	2	518	−6	−12	72
521–525............	7	523	−5	−35	175
526–530............	9	528	−4	−36	144
531–535............	20	533	−3	−60	180
536–540............	38	538	−2	−76	152
541–545............	58	543	−1	−58	58
546–550............	65	548	0	0	0
551–555............	68	553	1	68	68
556–560............	54	558	2	108	216
561–565............	39	563	3	117	351
566–570............	24	568	4	96	384
571–575............	9	573	5	45	225
576–580............	6	578	6	36	216
581–585............	1	583	7	7	49
$n = \Sigma f = 400$				200	2290

$$\overline{X} = \overline{X}_d + i\left(\frac{\Sigma fd'}{n}\right) = 548 + \frac{5 \times 200}{400} = 550.5$$

$$S_x = i\sqrt{\frac{\Sigma f(d')^2}{n} - \left(\frac{\Sigma fd'}{n}\right)^2} = 5\sqrt{\frac{2290}{400} - \left(\frac{200}{400}\right)^2}$$

$$= 5\sqrt{5.725 - .25}$$

$$S_x = 11.70$$

$$\overline{X} + 3\,S_x = 585.6$$

$$\overline{X} - 3\,S_x = 515.4$$

can be readily solved by the last set of equations. As can be seen from the information, we would expect that the average hat size would be 550.5 m.m., and the two extremes would most likely be three sigma either side of the mean, which is 515.4 m.m. and 585.6 m.m. The number of hats that one would expect to sell between 566 m.m. ando 576 m.m. could be calculated in this way:

$$z \cong \frac{X - \overline{X}}{S_x} = (?) \text{ which includes } (?)\% \text{ of the area}$$

$$z_1 \cong \frac{576.0 - 550.5}{11.70} = 2.18 \text{ which includes } 48.54\%$$

$$z_2 \cong \frac{566.0 - 550.5}{11.70} = 1.32 \text{ which includes } \frac{40.66\%}{7.88\%}$$

This, of course, has been predicted on only one sample, and we would guess that there could be some differences among samples. So now we will turn to the problem of establishing confidence limits.

Confidence Intervals for Estimates

In the hat size inventory problem, the assumption of a normal population was made, which was probably not too far from the truth. Now we will turn our attention to problems where the population distribution might take practically any form, and we will be concerned with determining the average value within certain confidence limits. Before discussing how this type of problem is approached, some of the basic theory should be discussed, although we cannot digress long enough to develop proofs.

The *central limit theorem* is regarded as the most important in statistics: *If simple random samples of sufficiently large size are drawn from almost any population, the sampling distribution of the sample means, $\bar{X}$'s, is approximately normal.*

Individual sample values tend to be distributed as the population is distributed, but the distribution of sample means $\bar{X}$ takes on the form of the normal distribution.

The arithmetic mean of the sample means, $\bar{\bar{X}}$ (X *double bar*), tends to be the same as the arithmetic mean of the population, μ.

$$\mu \cong \bar{\bar{X}} \cong \frac{\Sigma \bar{X}}{N^*}$$

(N^* is the number of samples, not the number of items.) In other words, we do not need to total all the individual values, but can total the mean of the samples.

The standard deviation of the sampling distribution $S_{\bar{x}}$ is:

$$S_{\bar{x}} = \sqrt{\frac{\Sigma(\bar{X} - \bar{\bar{X}})^2}{N^*}}$$

The standard deviation, S_x, of the sampling distribution is an estimate of $\sigma_{\bar{x}}$. The relationship between the *standard error of the mean*, $\sigma_{\bar{x}}$, and the population standard deviation is given by the following for a finite population:

$$\sigma_{\bar{x}} = \frac{\sigma_x}{\sqrt{n}} \cdot \sqrt{\frac{N-n}{N-1}}$$

(N is the population size; n the sample size.)

As the population grows larger and larger, the value under the second radical, called the *finite correction factor*, approaches 1. If the portion sampled does not exceed 5 percent of the population, the equation can be simplified by dropping out the correction factor, resulting in the equation:

$$\sigma_{\bar{x}} = \frac{\sigma_x}{\sqrt{n}}$$

The tendency of the means of samples to form a normal distribution is a most convenient characteristic because we can turn to the normal distribution tables, as illustrated, and bring forth all sorts of information from which to make decisions. And this is what we will do now.

A washing-machine company, planning its future inventory of replacement parts, wishes to know the average number of years that a particular machine has been used before being serviced for the first time. It is obviously impossible for the company to obtain this information from the 10,000 customers who have bought the machines, so it must resort to a sampling technique.

The company is able to obtain information from a sample of 45 (as shown in Figure 4–6). If it were possible to get numerous samples, the average of

Figure 4–6
Time before First Service*

X	X²	X	X²	X	X²
3.5	12.25	5.5	30.25	7.0	49.00
0.0	0.0	7.0	49.00	2.0	4.00
1.5	2.25	2.5	6.25	.5	.25
5.5	30.25	1.5	2.25	1.0	1.00
4.0	16.00	8.5	72.25	6.0	36.00
7.5	56.25	0.0	0.00	.5	.25
2.0	4.0	3.0	9.00	3.0	9.00
4.5	20.25	8.5	72.25	4.0	16.00
6.0	36.00	0.0	0.00	5.5	30.25
8.0	64.00	6.0	36.00	6.5	42.25
9.0	81.00	4.5	20.25	5.0	25.00
7.5	56.25	4.5	20.25	9.0	81.00
5.5	30.25	6.5	42.25	5.0	25.00
2.5	6.25	5.0	25.00	4.5	20.25
3.0	9.00	2.5	6.25	6.0	36.00

$$\overline{X} = \Sigma X/n = 201.0/45 = 4.47 \text{ years}$$

$$S_x = \sqrt{\Sigma X^2/n - (\Sigma X/n)^2} = \sqrt{\frac{1190.5}{45} - \left(\frac{201.0}{45}\right)^2} = \sqrt{6.46} = 2.54 \text{ years}$$

$$S_{\overline{x}} = S_x/\sqrt{n} = 2.54/\sqrt{45} = 2.54/6.72 = .38$$

And since $\overline{X}$ is a good estimate of $\overline{\overline{X}}$, which is a good estimate of μ, the limits are:

Upper limit $= 4.47 + 3 \times .38 = 5.61$ years
Lower limit $= 4.47 - 3 \times .38 = 3.33$ years

* Service time ($X =$ Years to nearest one-half year).

the averages, X, of the samples would tend to be the same as the average for the population mean, μ. The problem is how far away from the sample mean is the population mean if we wish to be right in estimating μ 95 percent of the time?

The reasoning behind the solution to this problem can be shown better graphically (Figure 4–7). The diagram, Figure 4–7a represents the distribution of $\overline{X}$ values, the $\overline{\overline{X}}$ being an estimate of the true mean, μ. If our particular sample has an $\overline{X}$ value (shown in Figure 4–7b), it is possible to add confidence limits of any size to either side as shown. For a confidence interval of 95 percent, the confidence limits would be $2\sigma_x$ either side of $\overline{X}$. This

Figure 4–7
Establishing Confidence Limits

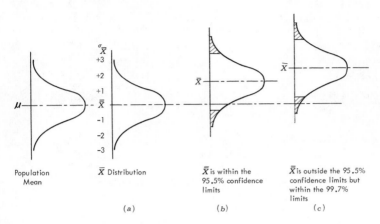

Population Mean	$\bar{X}$ Distribution	$\bar{X}$ is within the 95.5% confidence limits	$\bar{X}$ is outside the 95.5% confidence limits but within the 99.7% limits
	(a)	(b)	(c)

means that, by chance alone, we can be sure the interval $\bar{\bar{X}} \pm 2\sigma_{\bar{x}}$ includes μ 95 percent of the time and 5 percent of the time it will not. This latter situation of being outside is illustrated in Figure 4–7c.

Any confidence limits may be chosen. As you will recall, $\pm 3\sigma_{\bar{x}}$ will give a 99.73 percent confidence, and any other values can be chosen from the table of Z values.

Continuing with the data for the washing-machine inventory of replacement parts example, you will find the calculations for the sample mean $\bar{X}$, and the standard deviation of the sample, S_x, in the previous table. The sample standard deviation, S_x, is an estimate of the population standard deviation, σ_x.

We are 99.73 percent sure that the interval 3.33–5.61 includes μ. Notice that the spread depends upon the assurance desired, as expressed by 3 for the Z value, and also the size of the sample. The confidence limits decrease as the sample size becomes larger.

Statistics of Association

In production and inventory control decisions, it is frequently necessary to make predictions based on associations of data. One association of interest might be between sales and time periods. For example, the hat manufacturer is interested in the hats sold every month so that he can predict what to produce in the following month. Such an association is illustrated in Figure 4–8.

To the left of the today line, the sales are of course known. The question is what will the sales be tomorrow—and tomorrow? One way of making this prediction is to project a line through the domain that is known into the field of unknowns as illustrated. A simple way of deciding where to put the

Figure 4–8
Statistics of Association

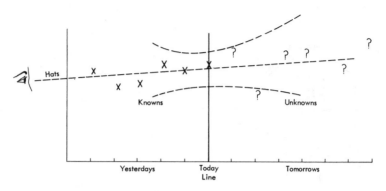

line is to "eyeball" it. When we do this we of course try to balance the plus and minus distances from the data to the line.

The vertical today axis is a moving axis that is constantly going to the right. This means that we will pay less and less attention to the information to the far left. Predicting about events to the far right is very dangerous. We have more confidence in the projection near the today line. This is illustrated by the curved lines on the chart.

Of course there are more sophisticated ways of fitting a line than using the eyeballing technique, and these will be discussed in the following paragraphs.

Statistics of Association Techniques. Up to this point we have discussed data with only one variable, commonly called *univariate* data. Next we are concerned with determining associations among things. This should not alarm you, for you probably make a number of decisions each day by association. For example, you know there is some relationship between the number of fish in a lake and the number of fish you catch, and consequently you usually try to fish in lakes where there is a large number of fish.

There are two common statistical techniques used in the analysis of bivariate data:

Regression Analysis: The derivation of a numerical relationship between two or more groups of data. The objective is to predict the value of one variable from the value of another variable.

Correlation Analysis: This is the measurement of the *degree* of relationship among the variables under consideration.

Frequently, these two subjects, regression analysis and correlation analysis, are grouped under one title, *correlation.* If the relationship is between just two sets of data, it is referred to as a *simple correlation* or *simple regression analysis;* but when more sets of variables are under consideration it is referred to as a *multiple correlation* or *multiple regression analysis.* Both regression and correlation analysis techniques will be developed in the coming sections.

Regression Analysis

In the simple regression analysis we attempt to derive a numerical relationship between two groups of matched observations, so by having information about one we can predict the value of the other. The variable to be predicted is referred to as the *dependent variable,* while the value used in predicting is called the *independent variable.*

Regression analysis is a sophisticated but meaningless name for this technique because *regress* means the act of going or coming back, which is the way a characteristic between fathers and sons behaved in an early statistical study. Since that time this word has been applied to all relationships like the one just mentioned. Meaningful or not, we are stuck with this name.

We will progress from the simplest form of regression study to relatively complicated methods. Before deriving a numerical relationship, it should be mentioned that a great deal of forecasting can be done without any knowledge of mathematical regression techniques by merely extending an appropriate line through the data by inspection (as shown in Figure 4–9).

Figure 4–9
Regression by Inspection

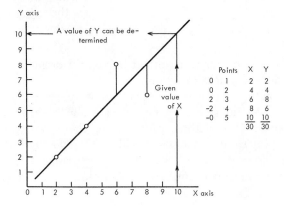

The points representing the data form a scatter diagram or *scattergram.* If the line is properly drawn, the sum of the negative vertical deviations will just equal the sum of the positive vertical deviations. Now it is apparent that we can predict the value of Y for any value of X, and we can even extend our prediction beyond the array of points, if we are willing to assume certain risks.

The Regression Equation by Inspection.   An equation for a trend line gives a concise statement of the trend, making it possible to predict values of the dependent variable without tedious plotting. This is highly desirable when you are asking a computer to do the dirty work. An equation also makes it possible to isolate and study different causes and effects.

As we determine the location of a geographical point by describing how far north and how far east it is from some known point, so can we tell the location of a point on a straight line (Figure 4–10) by describing how

Figure 4–10
Regression Equation by Inspection

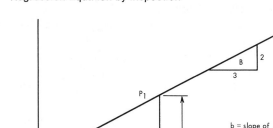

many X units and how many Y units it is from the origin. For example, P_1 is X_1 and Y_1 distances from the origin.

The equation for the line tells us the relationship between these distances as the point moves along the line. Given one value, we can solve the equation for the other. One method of developing the equation for the line is by considering the similar triangles, A and B. The short side of one triangle is to its long side as the short side of the other triangle is to its long side, which can be said more conveniently in this form:

$$\frac{Y_1 - a}{X_1} = \frac{2}{3}$$
$$Y_1 = a + 2/3\,X_1$$

It is apparent that a is the intercept of the line with the Y-axis when X is zero and b is the slope of the line. So the generalized equation can be written:

$$Y = a + bX$$

The a and b are called the *regression coefficients*.

This equation is no better than the line which we drew. We have a still better, if more tedious, way to develop the equation, which will assure the best fit, in the *least squares* sense.

Regression Equation by Least Squares.   In fitting the line by eye, remember that we tried to put the line through the scattergram so the sum of the positive deviations from the line would just equal the sum of the negative deviations.

When either positive or negative numbers are multiplied by themselves (squared), they produce positive numbers. So, if all the deviations from the line are squared, they become positive, and the problem is no longer to offset negative against positive but to minimize the total. The *least squares method*, as the name indicates, attempts to make the total of all the deviations squared, the minimum or least value. This is easy to envision, in Figure 4–11, when we observe that the objective is to minimize the areas of the squares.

Figure 4–11
Regression Equation by Least Squares

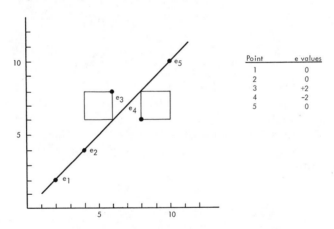

Point	e values
1	0
2	0
3	+2
4	-2
5	0

The heart of this method is to determine the regression coefficients a and b under the following conditions:

1. The sum of the vertical deviations from the regression line equal zero. That is, all the plus deviations above the line should just equal all the negative deviations.
2. The deviations, e, from the regression line, when squared, e^2, and summed, $\sum_{1}^{N} e^2$, must be less than for any other straight line that might be drawn through the points. The conditions for 1, above, are met when the condition for this part is satisfied.

As you can see on the last figure, e is the difference between the plotted value, Y, and the calculated value on the line, Y_c. Our objective, of course, is to minimize the sum of all the squares of these differences. Starting with the equation for the line, we can put it into terms of the error, e, by this method:

$$Y_c = a + bX$$

Y_c is the calculated value. Multiply both sides of the equation by -1.

$$-Y_c = -a - bX$$

Add Y to both sides:

$$(Y - Y_c') = -a - bX + Y$$

since $e = (Y - Y_c)$, and we wish to sum all of the squares of the e's.

$$\sum_1^N (e^2) = \sum_1^N (Y - Y_c)^2 = \sum_1^N (Y - a - bX)^2$$

We can minimize the value of the error term by taking the first derivative and setting it to zero,[2] first taking the derivative with respect to a:

$$\frac{\partial \left(\sum_1^N e^2\right)}{\partial a} = -2 \sum_1^N (Y - a - bX)$$

$$0 = -2 \sum_1^N (Y - a - bX)$$

The -2 can be disposed of by dividing both sides by -2. It is understood that all deviations, $e_1, e_2, \ldots, e_n$, will be considered, so we can omit the interval of the summation sign, Σ. Also, when a constant is summed over N observations, it is just the same as multiplying the constant by N. We can just say Na instead of Σa. This leads to a much cleaner way of writing the equation just given:

$$0 = \Sigma Y - Na - b\Sigma X$$

$$\Sigma Y = Na + b\Sigma X$$

The equation in this last form is called the *first normal equation*. Going through the same procedure for the regression coefficient b:

$$\sum_1^N e^2 = \sum_1^N (Y - a - bX)^2$$

$$\frac{\partial \sum_1^N e^2}{\partial b} = -2 \sum_1^N (Y - a - bX)(X)$$

$$\sum_1^N YX = a\sum_1^N X + b \sum_1^N X^2$$

$$\Sigma YX = a \Sigma X + b \Sigma X^2$$

---

[2] This method is used again in Chapter 12 for optimizing lot sizes.

This is the *second normal equation.*

We could determine the regression coefficients, and consequently the estimating equation from the normal equation above, but it would be tedious. So it is better if we have a short cut. This will be discussed by means of an example.

An Application of Regression Analysis. Before continuing with the development of statistics, an application of regression analysis will be useful to create a better understanding.

The problem is to obtain an equation for a best fit line, in the least squares sense, from which we can extrapolate information. This means finding the values for a and b for the normal equations, using the simultaneous equation solution. This is not a very enjoyable prospect when there are many large values, so let us explore a short cut and shift the axis to the mean value of X and Y.

1. Express X and Y as deviations, x and y, from their respective means:

$$\Sigma y = Na + b\Sigma x$$

$$\Sigma xy = a\Sigma x + b\Sigma x^2$$

2. The sums of the deviations from their means are zero, so:

$$\Sigma y = 0 \text{ and } \Sigma x = 0,$$

which means that these terms will drop out of the equation, and therefore the second equation becomes:

$$\Sigma xy = b\Sigma x^2$$

$$b = \frac{\Sigma xy}{\Sigma x^2},$$

which gives the slope of the line which is one of the regression coefficients.

3. For the value of a, the other regression coefficient, insert the value b in the first equation, $\Sigma Y = Na + b\Sigma X$. This can be written in a more convenient form:

$$a = \bar{Y} - b\bar{X}$$

4. Σxy and Σx^2 for determining b can be derived directly from the values of X and Y.[3]

$$\Sigma xy = \Sigma XY - \frac{(\Sigma X)(\Sigma Y)}{N}$$

$$\Sigma x^2 = \Sigma X^2 - \frac{(\Sigma X)^2}{N}$$

This short-cut method can now be used to solve a forecasting problem.

---

[3] Robert Ferber, *Statistical Techniques in Market Research* (New York: McGraw-Hill, 1949).

The information shown in Figure 4–12 is for a particular industry's domestic sales versus the disposable income.[4] With an available prediction

Figure 4–12
Domestic Sales versus Disposable Income

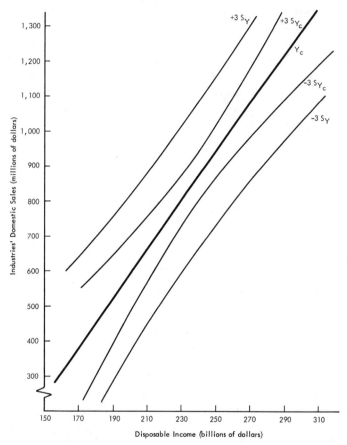

of disposable income, it is possible to predict the domestic sales. This company, knowing its share of the domestic sales, can predict its sales for any given forecast of disposable income. The information given is tabulated in the first two columns of Figure 4–13.

The method of calculating the company's sales by the short-cut method is shown at the bottom of the table in Figure 4–13.

Dispersion about Regression Line.   It is extremely doubtful that the forecasted figure will agree exactly with what actually transpires, and if it doesn't agree it would be desirable to know whether the disagreement could have come about by chance or whether it is the result of some assignable

[4] Example taken from "What Management Expects of Forecasting," B. E. Estes, Director of Commercial Research, U.S. Steel Corp., *Sales Forecasting, Special Report 16,* American Management Association, 1515 Broadway, New York 36, N.Y.

Figure 4–13
Industry Domestic Sales versus Disposable Income

Y Sales (Billion Dollars)	X Disposable Income (Bil- lion Dollars)	XY	Y²	X²
.435	181.6	78.996	.189225	32,978.6
.621	206.1	127.988	.385641	42,477.2
.819	226.1	185.176	.670761	51,121.2
.879	236.7	208.059	.772641	56,026.9
.933	250.4	233.623	.870489	62,700.2
.970	254.8	247.156	.940900	64,923.0
1.070	274.0	293.180	1.144900	75,076.0
1.180	284.0	335.120	1.392400	80,656.0
$\Sigma Y = 6.907$	$\Sigma X = 1913.7$	$\Sigma XY = 1709.299$	$\Sigma Y^2 = 6.366957$	$\Sigma X^2 = 465,959.1$
$N = 8$				

$$b = \frac{\Sigma xy}{\Sigma x^2} = \frac{\Sigma XY - \dfrac{(\Sigma X)(\Sigma Y)}{N}}{\Sigma X^2 - \dfrac{(\Sigma X)^2}{N}}$$

$$\Sigma XY = 1709.299$$

$$\frac{(\Sigma X)(\Sigma Y)}{N} = \frac{1913.7 \times 6.907}{8} = 1652.223$$

$$\Sigma xy = 57.076$$

$$\Sigma X^2 = 465959.1$$

$$\frac{(\Sigma X)^2}{N} = \frac{(1913.7)^2}{8} = 457780.9$$

$$\Sigma x^2 = 8178.2$$

$$b = \frac{57.076}{8178.2} = .0069$$

$$a = \overline{Y} - b\overline{X} = \frac{6.907}{8} - .0069 \times \frac{1913.7}{8}$$

$$= .863 - 1.670 = -.807 \text{ billion} \quad \text{or} \quad -807 \text{ million}$$

cause. This brings us to the development of a confidence interval, sometimes called a confidence band, for the calculated regression line.

The vertical distance between the actual Y value and the calculated Y value, Y_c, is $(Y - Y_c)$. These differences form a distribution about the regression line analogous to the standard deviation about the mean, but it bears the name, *standard error of the estimate*, $S_y \cdot {}_x$.

$$S_y \cdot {}_x = \sqrt{\frac{\Sigma(Y - Y_c)^2}{N - 2}}$$

The standard error of the estimate is often mistakenly used to develop confidence bands, represented by the parallel lines $Y_c \pm tS_y \cdot {}_x$. The multiplier, t, is used rather than Z because we are concerned with a small sample. This would be correct only if there was assurance that the calculated line was the true regression line. Remember, the line itself is calculated from a sample and is subject to sampling errors.

The error in the line is expressed in the variances of the two regression coefficients in the linear equation. In fact, the variance of Y_c for a given value of X, X_p, is the sum of the variances due to the coefficients in the regression model $(Y_c - \bar{Y}_c) = a + b(X - \bar{X})$.

$$S^2_{Y_c} = \frac{S^2_{y \cdot x}}{N} + \frac{S^2_{y \cdot x}(X_p - \bar{X})^2}{\Sigma(X - \bar{X})^2}$$

$$= \frac{S^2_{y \cdot x}}{N} + \frac{S^2_{y \cdot x} x^2_p}{\Sigma x^2}$$

$$S_{Y_c} = S_{y \cdot x}\sqrt{\frac{1}{N} + \frac{(X_p - \bar{X})^2}{\Sigma(X - \bar{X})^2}} = S_{y \cdot x}\sqrt{\frac{1}{N} + \frac{x^2_p}{\Sigma x^2}}$$

where:

$$\frac{S^2_{y \cdot x}}{N} = \text{Variance for the regression coefficient } a$$

$$\frac{S^2_{y \cdot x}}{\Sigma x^2} = \text{Variance for the regression coefficient } b$$

For large samples of 30 or more, any desired confidence level for Y_c can be established by multiplying S_{y_c} by an appropriate Z value (as was illustrated in Figure 4–4). Plus or minus $3S_{y_c}$ would give a confidence band of 99.7 percent, while $2S_{y_c}$ would give a confidence band of 95.45 percent. For example, the 99.7 percent confidence band for Y_c is:

$$Y_c \pm 3 S_{y \cdot x}\sqrt{\frac{1}{N} + \frac{(X_p - \bar{X})^2}{\Sigma(X - \bar{X})^2}},$$

or,

$$Y_c \pm 3 S_{y \cdot x}\sqrt{\frac{1}{N} + \frac{x^2_p}{\Sigma x^2}}$$

The x^2_p is the square of the X_p value being estimated in deviation units. The Σx^2 and N are for the whole sample and remain the same for all calculations of S_{y_c}.

The confidence band for the individual Y's is even wider, as it includes the variance $S^2_{y \cdot x}$ around the regression line. So the variance for the Y's is as shown:

$$S^2_y = S^2_{y \cdot x} + \frac{S^2_{y \cdot x}}{N} + \frac{S^2_{y \cdot x}(X_p - \bar{X})^2}{\Sigma(X - \bar{X})^2},$$

or,

$$S^2_{y \cdot x} + \frac{S^2_{y \cdot x}}{N} + \frac{S^2_{y \cdot x} x^2_p}{\Sigma x^2}$$

And it follows that the 99.7 percent confidence band for Y is:

$$Y_c \pm 3 S_{y \cdot x} \sqrt{1 + \frac{1}{N} + \frac{(X_p - \bar{X})^2}{\Sigma(X - \bar{X})^2}},$$

or,

$$Y_c \pm 3 S_{y \cdot x} \sqrt{1 + \frac{1}{N} + \frac{X_p^2}{\Sigma x^2}}$$

The development of the confidence bands, so far, has been based on a large sample, and it was appropriate to use Z values. In the example illustrated, domestic sales versus disposable income, the sample cannot be considered large, so we must modify the confidence bands to account for the small sample. This may be done by using the t distribution, which is applicable where only small samples are available. The t tables are used in a way which is similar to the table of Z values except to enter the table it is necessary to know the acceptable confidence level and the degrees of freedom in the equations. The degrees of freedom are $N - 2$ because there are two regression coefficients.

The method of calculating $S_{y \cdot x}$ has been passed over lightly but you can see that finding $(Y - Y_c)$ for all the points would be a most tedious task. Fortunately, $S_{y \cdot x}$ can be found directly from the values of Y and X:

$$S_{y \cdot x} = \sqrt{\frac{\Sigma Y^2 - a \Sigma Y - b \Sigma XY}{N - 2}}$$

For a small sample, a better answer is obtained if $N - 2$ is used in the denominator to account for the degrees of freedom lost in the regression coefficients.

The illustration of the data, domestic sales versus disposable income, with the bands for S_{y_c} and S_y, makes the difficulty of prediction appear obvious. Certainly parallel bands, $Y_c \pm 3S_{y \cdot x}$, would be of little help in a prediction. As is apparent, the farther one goes to the right of center the more questionable becomes the prediction.

Interpreting the information leads to some interesting observations. For example, the predicted value of sales when the disposable income reaches $240 billion is $868 million, with a range of plus or minus $213 million for 99.7 percent confidence. The same values for $300 billion is $1,287 million, with a range of plus or minus $251 million. It is apparent what the effect of the widening band has upon the prediction. When the band is too wide to be practical, one must work on reducing either $S_{y \cdot x}$ or the total variance of Y.

Correlation Analysis

Correlation analysis is the other commonly used technique for evaluating the relationship between two groups of data. Recall, in the regression analysis just discussed, we were striving for a graphical or numerical relationship between the variables under consideration. However, at times, we are interested only in the degree of the relationship, without regard to the quantitative aspects. In the last of the preceding section we developed the *standard error of estimate* as a measure of the closeness of the relationship. Shortcomings of that system are:

1. The standard error of estimate is an absolute measure of the relationship and has little meaning unless one is well acquainted with the data.
2. The standard error of estimate is in the same units as the data, so relationships based on units of different size or even units of different types cannot be compared.

The faults are overcome by the *coefficient of correlation, r,* or the closely related *coefficient of determination, r^2,* to be discussed in this section. These coefficients do not attempt to distinguish between dependent or independent variables, but present an abstract number. These numbers are readily explained by Figure 4–14 which illustrates that the total

Figure 4–14
Correlation Analysis

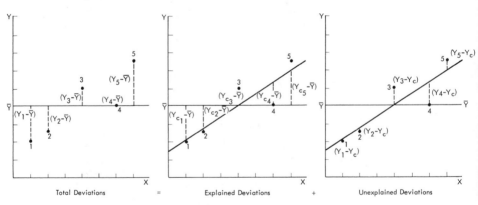

sum of the squares of the deviations is equal to the explained sum of the squares of the deviations plus the unexplained sum of the squares of the deviations.

The coefficient of determination, r^2, is defined as:

$$r^2 = 1 - \frac{\text{Unexplained sum of squares}}{\text{Total sum of squares}}$$

$$r^2 = 1 - \frac{\Sigma(Y - Y_c)^2}{\Sigma(Y - \bar{Y})^2}$$

When the difference between the calculated value Y_c and the actual value Y, for all observations, becomes zero, the ratio between the unexplained and the total sum of squares then becomes zero, thus yielding an r^2 value of 1. When X contributes no information about Y, the numerator and denominator are equal, making the ratio between the unexplained and the total sum of squares equal to 1, which results in an r^2 value of 0.

This illustration should give you some comprehension of why r^2 can range between 0, indicating no relationship, to 1, indicating a perfect relationship. Its square root, r, the coefficient of correlation, can range between $+1$ to 0, to a -1, this latter indicating a perfect inverse relationship. This explanation has been limited to the situation of predicting Y from X. As you would expect, X could have been predicted from Y, which would complicate the explanation. Probably the best-known equations for obtaining the coefficient of correlation are these:

$$r = \frac{\Sigma xy}{\sqrt{\Sigma x^2 \Sigma y^2}}$$

This can be expressed in terms of the measured values:

$$r = \frac{\Sigma(X - \bar{X})(Y - \bar{Y})}{\sqrt{\Sigma(X - \bar{X})^2 \Sigma(Y - \bar{Y})^2}}$$

For ease in computing the coefficient of correlation, the following equation might be used:

$$r = \frac{N\Sigma XY - (\Sigma X)(\Sigma Y)}{\sqrt{[N\Sigma X^2 - (\Sigma X)^2][N\Sigma Y^2 - (\Sigma Y)^2]}}$$

This correlation measure can be used when we wish to determine the degree of relationship without any concern for the functional relationship. For example, if we had wished to determine the degree of relationship for the sales to disposable income, we could have used the correlation coefficient.

Summary

Statistics is an essential tool for every modern production control manager. His knowledge should include statistical sampling and statistics of association. In production and inventory control one is frequently encountering different distributions, such as the normal and the Poisson, which must be taken into consideration. Forecasting and analysis of other data will require a knowledge of regression and correlation.

QUESTIONS

4–1. Give several examples of predictions which you make every day in which there is some uncertainty.

4–2. What is meant by a random sample?

4–3. What are the characteristics needed to describe a population?

4–4. Why is the subject of sampling statistics of importance to forecasting?

4–5. What is the difference between regression analysis and correlation analysis? When would you use each one of these techniques?

4–6. Why is the central limit theorem important in the application of statistical procedures?

4–7. Suggest some information which would be highly correlated with the sales of one of the following: household appliances, school furniture, animal vaccines, car accessories.

5

Sales and Forecasting
Information

You ARE AWARE that the systems approach is being emphasized and the system with which we are concerned is for production. This system could be isolated at the factory walls but that would give an incomplete and provincial view by ignoring some of the more important inputs. Consequently the sales department's input is going to be touched upon to emphasize how important this function is and how essential for understanding any production and inventory control system.

The customer and his demands are what production is all about. Without customers there would be no need for production and consequently no need for production and inventory control. This is ample reason for any production control book to take a good look at the sales department since it interfaces between the customer and production.

Since customers supply the money that causes our industrial processes to flow, it should be our primary concern to deliver products which they want when they want them. The importance of the customer and the sales activity is brought out clearly by the *funds flow chart* shown in Figure 5–1. This chart is a fluids analogy of what goes on in the cycle of buying material, changing it to a product that a customer wants, selling it, collecting the money, and starting the cycle over again.

The sales department is like a "pump" that keeps the whole system flowing. If there are no sales, there is no flow of funds. The rate at which the flow occurs is all important for it is that which increases the profit and it is the profit that attracts capital. Only with a flow of funds can materials be purchased, employees paid, and dividends be issued, and it is only sales that can make this possible.

There are other inputs to the system, such as capital and personnel but

Figure 5–1
Fund Flow

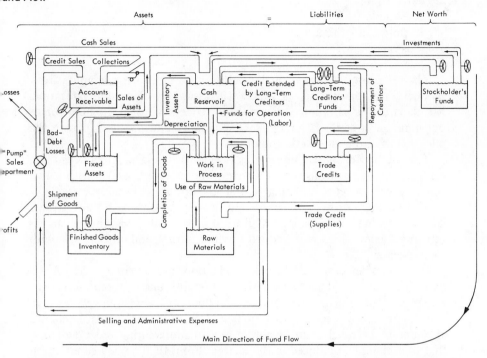

these decisions are more infrequent and are not related as often to production control. Sales information is a daily or hourly communication which must be received by production control.

ORGANIZATION OF THE SALES DEPARTMENT

In some companies you could search high and low for an office marked "sales" or even a desk with a sign on it saying "sales." This does not mean that this activity does not exist. It just means that it occurs so infrequently that it does not merit a special office. What probably occurs in this situation is that the sales are limited to just a few customers and for just a few items. It may be that the entire output of the factory is being sent to another factory to be assembled into another product. Nevertheless, there is a sales function which is being handled by the president, plant manager, office manager, or other person in the organization.

There are many ways of organizing the sales function depending upon the product being sold, the market, the people involved, and other factors. It is common to have the sales organization headed by a sales or marketing manager. If the position is important enough it will probably carry a vice president's title. Under the supervision of this manager will be an organization which might have the following sections:

1. Sales force.
2. Advertising.
3. Sales desk.
4. Inquiries and estimates.
5. Customer service.

The sales force if large enough might be organized by geographic areas, product lines, or other ways which will assure an efficient organization. Members of this sales force may make infrequent visits to the home office but maintain a contact through correspondence and phone calls with the sales manager, the sales desk, and others.

The method of marketing such as through wholesalers, direct customer contact, and other means is an interesting and extensive subject with which you may wish to become familiar as you advance in the business world.

The manager of sales will probably also be responsible for advertising. This will seldom require a large staff for it is primarily a liaison with an advertising agency which is staffed with writers, artists, and other people with specialized skills.

It is the sales desk with which production and inventory control has its major interface. The "sales desk" is in reality one or more individuals who receive the sales order either by mail, phone, or teletype, and processes it. The sales orders will come across the sales desk and be either translated into an order to be filled from inventory or a manufacturing order requiring that something be produced in the factory. From then on any communications between the customer and the factory such as schedule changes and product changes will be handled through the sales department. It is usually considered a poor practice to let the customer communicate directly with the factory or production control department. Such communications interrupt the other activities and can be the source of considerable confusion.

Inventory control will also interface with the sales department when finished inventoried products are sold. In this case the sales order is used as the basis for releasing and shipping material to the customer.

For some products the process of answering inquiries for prices and schedules can be a very extensive activity. In this situation it may be desirable to set up an entire "inquiries" subdivision of the sales department. This activity calls for good communications between it and production control, because only they know what capacity will be available in the weeks to come and whether it is feasible to bid on the requests or not.

In some industries, a company may receive only a small percentage of orders from the estimates and bids they have made. This can be very expensive, and it will take considerable judgment to decide which requests should be answered.

Customer service is another important interface between the customer and production control. Often the service department asks the factory to make special replacement parts which must be expedited through the factory. Production control will be asked to upset its schedules and rush the orders through the factory. Here is where an important interplay between the customer, sales, and factory can occur. If service is handled properly it can go a long way to enhance the reputation of the company and increase sales in the future.

Processing the Typical Sales Order

The sales desk receives orders from the salesman or directly from the customer. If enough orders come in by phone, there may be a special division to handle these.

When the order comes in by mail, it must be sorted from the other correspondence by the mail clerk. A *pre-entry sales order clerk* will then edit the order, checking such things as prices, reasonable quantities, catalog numbers, and other pertinent information. If certain sales districts or salesmen are to be given credit for the sales, the necessary information will be entered so that eventually the correct person will be credited with the order. If the customer's credit is questioned, the order might be sent to the credit department for approval.

After the initial editing the order is sent to an *order entry clerk*, where the order information is again checked. The order at this stage is commonly rewritten on a multicopy sales order form. This form bears a serial number which becomes the sales order reference number for this particular order as it winds its way through the inventory or factory. Companies keep track of their sales order numbers in various ways. Some will maintain a ledger where all orders are recorded with the serial number, customer, date, and so forth.

If a company is producing to stock, the sales order may never get to the factory floor and the sales order is used to ship material from the finished inventory. If a company is producing to customer's orders, a sales order will be converted to a *manufacturing order*. This will probably be done by the production control department.

When a sales order can be partially filled from stock but the balance must be produced, a very complicated situation occurs. Will material be shipped from stock at once or will it be held until the whole order can be shipped? Will the customer be satisfied with a partial shipment? How should the customer be billed? These are just a few of the knotty questions which can occur.

One might suspect that the paper industry is behind the development of the sales order procedure because numerous copies are produced. Here is just one way that the many copies might be distributed in the factory.

One copy could go into a file by sales order number. This will make a handy reference in case the factory, production control, shipping department, inventory control, or anyone else wishes to verify some information about the order and have the sales order number to start with.

One copy goes into a file by the customer's name. When a customer makes an inquiry, the order can be readily traced from his name and related to the order number.

One copy may be sent to the salesman and the district sales manager for their information.

One copy goes to the billing department for accounting and billing purposes.

One copy goes to the shipping department so it will have something to ship against. An extra copy may be enclosed with the material at the time of shipping to serve as a list of contents.

One copy goes to inventory control if these are stock items. This serves as a copy for picking the stock and releasing it for shipment.

One copy goes to production control if the products are to be made to order. They in turn write up a production order. The sales order may be returned to the sales department with information about the expected shipping date and other important information for the cusomer.

This is just one of many ways that copies of the sales orders might be distributed in a factory. Additional copies might be produced and distributed as needed but one should keep in mind, however, that a proliferation of paper is costly and does not always serve a useful purpose.

Phone sales, after they have been written up by the clerk, follow the same procedure as the written sales order. Depending upon the circumstances, companies might maintain a number of phone sales desks. These same people may be responsible for any inquiries that may come in regarding orders.

Production Control and Sales-Related Problems

Answering inquiries and other communications from customers may be an extensive activity for some factories. Customers make periodic inquiries regarding their orders to be sure that they do not fall behind schedule. It may be that they are coordinating their order with the construction or assembly of products and they want to make sure that it is shipped on time.

For some products the specifications may change from day to day. This is particularly true for products such as military airplanes and similar products. Some of these changes may be very critical and if not accomplished would endanger lives, while others may be trivial such as affecting the appearance of the product. Nevertheless, these changes must be worked into the production of the product. If a change is imperative it may mean closing down an entire production line while new components are made and delivered. This situation may be as difficult as any the production control department will be asked to face. Frequently the customer will have to be notified of any change in cost or scheduled shipping.

During a crisis, such as war, customer orders may be under the control of a priorities system. This has placed unusual strains on the production facilities of our country. During these times the production control department must schedule production while always considering the priority status of the order. These orders frequently change priority status during the production process, adding to the complications.

Another complication in handling customer orders is trying to predict the scrap loss which might occur during production. This can create one of the more difficult problems for production control. For example assume that a customer wishes to buy 500 finished malleable iron castings and the records on this type of casting show a maximum of 25 could be lost during the heat treating process and another 25 during the machining. If the manufacturer starts 550 into production to account for these losses, he is apt to find that he has produced more than the 500 needed to satisfy the customer's order. What does he do? Absorb the loss and junk the extra ones? He could store them hoping that the order will be repeated, in which case he will probably forget that he has them on hand and will end up junking them a number of years later after he has gone to the expense of storing them.

On the other hand, what if he decides to start only 525 and the maximum loss occurs at both processes and he has only 475 when it comes time to ship? A delay to produce the other 25 will irritate the customer and to start a new order, with all the preparation costs, may wipe out any anticipated profit.

This problem may be overcome if the sales agreement is written for 500 parts plus or minus 50. This will keep any surplus cleared out of the inventory and will still supply the customer with most of his needs. When the customer is placing orders repeatedly he probably will agree to this arrangement, especially if the price reflects the economics to the manufacturer.

If a product, such as a plastic item or aluminum extrusion, requires special tooling or dies, they will probably be built by the manufacturer and charged to the customer. These tools and dies are built and fitted to the machines of the manufacturer but are the property of the customer. When the job is completed, they may either be sent to the customer or stored by the manufacturer to be used again when an order is received.

Set-up costs incurred for preparing the machines for production may be buried in the unit costs to be reflected in the price breaks for various order quantities. Another way is to charge the set-up cost as an additional cost to the unit cost. This has a way of putting the costs in their true perspective and often encourages the customer to place larger orders as he attempts to spread this cost over more products. Manufacturers may take an advantage of these separate preparation charges by processing similar products at one time. If these products require only minor adjustments to the production machines, the manufacturer will gain.

Sales to the military and the government agencies may cause extra problems. Undoubtedly the manufacturer will have to furnish a bid for the items under consideration. After that there will probably be stringent agreements to be fulfilled regarding shipping dates and quality. For products that are in the process of development, such as airplanes and electronic gear, there may be numerous engineering changes which will have to be entered into the production process. This often makes the pricing of products especially hazardous for it is not uncommon to attach penalties for not delivering on schedule.

It is for the customers that manufacturing organizations exist. Without them there would be no manufacturing. The customer's needs are expressed by a sales order through the sales department. Strictly speaking it is by the sales order that the factory has its first contact with the customer. Since production control is responsible for adjusting the flow of the factory processes, it becomes the linkage between the customer, sales, and production. After the production process is started, there is need for communications with the customer. These also flow through the sales department to production control. So it is reasonable to say that one cannot fully understand the process of production control without understanding the contribution made by the sales department.

FORECASTING SALES

The prefix, or suffix, *fore* means *before* something, either in position or in time. In our usage, to be more specific, *fore*casting means the estimating of some quantity, stated either in numbers or value, to be produced and sold in the future.

We are all personally acquainted with forecasting and with some of its inherent dangers. For example, we are aware of the problems and results that accompany forecasting weather, baseball scores, presidential elections, or even how one's partner will bid his bridge hand. All of these forecasts, and many more, are plagued by numerous factors affecting their outcome.

Determining what will happen in the future is forecasting, and all profitable companies do this to at least some degree—although some don't put a name to it. We will first discuss the general problem of forecasting, its need and place in the organization, and then the statistical techniques which are either used extensively or hold promise of being useful.

The Problem

The problem, as stated in the definition, is to predict the sales at some future date. Designers make frequent predictions, but not always on a time scale. For example, the stress-strain curve for a sample of steel is used to predict the performance of some part of a bridge structure. The problem is to determine, with some degree of certainty, how a part under consideration, such as the cables of the bridge, will perform under certain loads. This is a prediction that uses a scale other than time, but the designer also forecasts on a time scale. The electronics designer is predicting on a time scale when he examines current or voltage variations.

Forecasting sales is similar to the example but far more complex, because there are more factors influencing the problem—which in many cases are not definable or measurable. Scientists and engineers might scoff at industrial people for not being more quantitative, but it is not the lack of ability which makes them less quantitative; rather it is the more difficult problems they need to solve. Eventually, mathematical models will be developed for business changes as they have been for engineering phenomena, but they will be much more complex.

Need for Forecasting

The sales forecast is the link between the external, uncontrollable movements of the economy and the internal, controllable affairs of the business. Therefore a sales forecast must be based on a careful analysis of external factors, as it is the foundation for planning all aspects of a company's operations. It dictates, among other things, production schedules, purchasing of inventory, capital expenditures, rental of warehouses, and budgets for labor. These activities, and many more, depend upon the sales forecast.

One might assume that forecasting is unnecessary if a company manufactures to order. To a degree this is true, but it is an oversimplification of the situation. It takes time to procure raw materials, personnel, and machines; to build parts, make them into subassemblies, and eventually into assemblies. Therefore it is essential that a company does some forecasting, especially if there is any variation at all in its output. Forecasting is no substitute for actual knowledge of a market, and subcontractors, in particular, would do well to create a close liaison with their customers and vendors.

Budgeting and forecasting go hand in hand, and the interest in budgeting during recent years has stimulated an interest in forecasting. There are a number of concrete advantages in having a good forecast:

1. Customers can be kept happy by being supplied the products they want as soon as they want them.
2. Cancelled orders, because of slow deliveries, can be eliminated.
3. A greater feeling of cooperation can be created in the factory.
4. Direct labor costs can be kept at a minimum by balancing work loads thus preventing overtime and reducing costly hiring and firing.
5. Inventories can be manipulated more efficiently.
6. Capital, in the form of both money and machines, can be used more effectively.

Forecasts are always wrong in the respect that the levels attained are hardly ever the same as anticipated. This must be understood by all those associated with the forecast. Seldom, if ever, will a guess about the future be exact—but how much better an *intelligent* estimate of the future, based on information, than a *wild* guess.

Forecasting and the Organization

The activities of a manufacturing business have been divided into three major functional groups: marketing, production, and finance. Marketing includes all the activities needed to move a product from the manufacturer to the consumer. Market research, part of marketing, is a critical and exhaustive investigation of the problems allied to getting a product to market.

Forecasting is just one activity in the market research picture, which includes studies of product acceptance, customer dissatisfaction, new uses of products, product simplification, and many other subjects which are fascinating but too extensive to dwell upon here.

Not many companies are large enough, or the sales forecasting critical enough, to warrant a market research organization. The function is usually served, in these situations, by the sales department, and the forecast may be nothing more exotic than a compilation of orders from which some idea of the trend can be gained. Even the companies with market research groups frequently delegate some of the forecasting function to the sales department.

Market research problems are often handled outside the organization, and there are a number of market research agencies available for manufacturers who do not wish to establish their own organizations. If the manufacturer passes the selling function on to other independent companies, he will probably pass on the sales forecasting. Advertising agencies have been taking on an increasingly important part of the market research function. Trade associations also serve a need in market research, for they can handle industry-wide problems which are beyond the scope of many companies. The production control function is usually not responsible for forecasting, although occasionally it is driven to it by the default of others. Its task is usually limited to analyzing forecasts made by the sales department to develop master production schedules. Forecasts must be interpreted in terms of factory capacity. Thus the problems of matching forecasts to production conditions are, within narrow limits, those of production control. Wider variations will probably be the responsibility of upper management. If the forecast does not utilize all the plant capacity, a cut may have to be made in work hours, and consequently, fewer goods will be produced; or management may decide finished goods should be stockpiled or other markets found. If the forecasts are greater than capacity, the management must be satisfied with less than the total possible sales, or must increase production capacity by adding facilities or subcontracting to other manufacturers.

Forecasting often becomes a committee activity. Such a committee might include the production manager, sales manager, and treasurer. All these individuals will be able to contribute knowledge concerning their particular areas of responsibility, although there is the danger that one may unduly influence the others. The sales manager would have the factory make immediate delivery on anything and everything without regard to cost. The production manager wants an even flow of production, just slightly below full capacity, with large inventories available to balance out fluctuations in load. The treasurer wants to retain a high cash reserve to meet all contingencies, which means he would like to have small inventories. Thus the conflicting interests within the committee are obvious.

Approaches to Forecasting

Before going into any one technique of forecasting, let us take a look at all the methods so we can see them in perspective and dispose of those which promise to be of little value.

Forecasting for New Products. Forecasting demand for products which are established can often be a routine procedure, but forecasting demand for new products is considerably more difficult. In forecasting for old products, past information is available on which the future can be predicted. This is, of course, generally not true for new products. Some of the methods used for new product forecasting are:

Direct Survey Method. The prospective customers are asked what they intend to buy. As it is nearly impossible to ask *all* the customers, it is necessary to use sampling techniques and ask only a few. From the few it is possible to predict, with some degree of certainty, how the population will respond. Since the purchaser is likely to vacillate from day to day because of economic changes, political changes, style changes, and other reasons, surveys should be tempered by factors which account for these changes.

Indirect Survey Method. Another method of forecasting demand is by asking the people who know how the customer responds. Frequently the salesman knows, but his estimates are likely to be overly optimistic. Wholesalers, jobbers, and other middlemen are also solicited, since they have their fingers directly upon the pulse of the consumers' demand.

Comparing with Established Products. At times the product under consideration is comparable to an existing product, so sales figures can be compared. If it is an outright replacement for the present product, probably little difficulty will be encountered when the new product is properly introduced. If the new product is a substitute for a competitor's product, its acceptance will depend upon the advertising program and the customers' loyalty to the present product.

Limited Market Trial. Another method of forecasting the demand for a new product is to try selling it in a limited area to see how well it is accepted by potential customers.

Forecasting for Established Products. These are the methods which are common for forecasting sales of well-established products:

Projection Method. This method is based upon the assumption that what has gone on before will continue. The relationship of sales with income, time, or other factors is projected ahead to determine what the sales will be in the future. This is illustrated in Figure 5–2. A line drawn through the known information is projected into the forecast area to predict what the sales volume will be for future periods.

Figure 5–2
Example of Projection Method

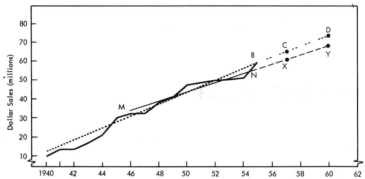

Source: "Finding and Evaluating Basic Data for Sales Forecasting," *Sales Forecasting Uses and Techniques,* by Alfred C. Scott (the Upjohn Co.) and published by the American Management Association, Special Report 16.

There are several ways of making a projection. Those techniques you will encounter here are regression, moving average, and exponential smoothing. The latter technique is especially useful for predicting the movement of stock-keeping units because the information required from period to period is minimal, making it relatively easy to store the information and make the calculations when necessary.

Related Information Method. In this method (Figure 5–3), a predictor which varies directly with the sales volume is found. In this example the Federal Reserve Board Index is used. Of course the predictor must be available well in advance of the need. This means the predictor must either lead the sales or be a forecast itself for some time into the future. For example, the actual birthrates might be used to predict the sale of baby foods, or well-established predictions of births might be used. These two techniques, the projection method and related information method, will be examined later by statistical techniques.

Examples of Correlation in Forecasting. Correlation has an interesting application where there are two series of events running side by side (as shown in Figure 5–4, top). The first might be called a synchronous series, while the second might be called a leading series.

These two relationships, where correlation can be found to be useful, are described more fully:

Synchronous Series. In this situation two series of events move together step by step. One series of events, perhaps a government index, is in itself a prediction which is available in advance of the time that the product forecast

Figure 5–3
Example of Related Information Method

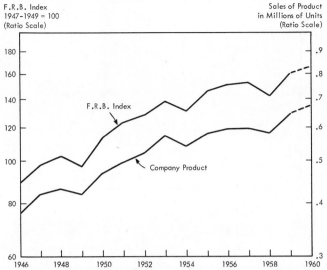

Source: John Neter and William Wasserman, *Fundamental Statistics for Business and Economics,* 2d ed., p. 809, copyright 1961 by Allyn and Bacon. Reprinted by permission of the publisher.

is needed. Relating these two values make it possible to predict sales from the index.

Leading Predictors. Frequently, a series of events leads the series being predicted (as in Figure 5–4, bottom). Croxton and Cowden[1] propose an ingenious way of solving such correlation problems:

1. Plot each of the series on separate transparent papers, making sure that the horizontal scale is the same for each.
2. Place one of the charts over another in front of a strong light. Move the leading series chart to the left until it closely agrees with the lagging series.
3. Adjust both series for trend and irregular movements.
4. Compute the r value for the best visual fit and check this against r values for shorter and longer leads.
5. If the value of r is high enough, fit a curve.

Time Series

There is one large area of statistical analysis in which the independent variable, on the horizontal axis, is time. A *time series* is chronological data

---

[1] P. E. Croxton and D. J. Cowden, *Applied General Statistics,* 2d ed. (Englewood Cliffs, N.J.: Prentice-Hall, 1955).

Figure 5–4
Application of Correlation to Forecasting

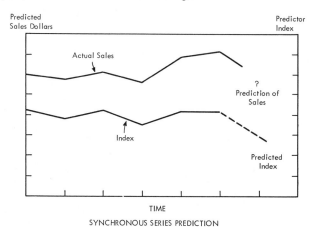

SYNCHRONOUS SERIES PREDICTION

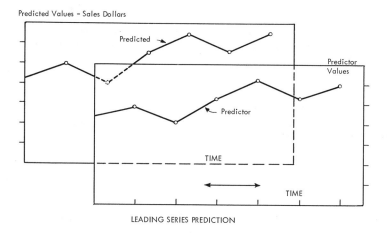

LEADING SERIES PREDICTION

which has some quantity, such as sales dollars, sales volume, or other information, as the dependent variable and units of time as the independent variable.

The movements or variations of the dependent variable can be divided into four distinct components which can be studied independently. These are called *trend, cyclical, seasonal,* and *irregular* variations. A more extensive description of the movements of the time series will be of value. Starting with the longest periods of movement:

Trend Variations. Changes which occur over a long period of years. When all the intermediate variations are not considered, a time series frequently shows a tendency to increase or decrease.

Cyclical Variations. These changes occur over a shorter period of years and show some evidence of periodicity. They can be compared with a pendulum or spring-mass system in the field of mechanics. As we all know, when a pendulum is set in motion it attempts to reach its point of equilibrium, but overshoots this position. In attempting to return to equilibrium, it again overshoots, and so goes through a series of vibrations until it finally attains the rest position. If there is an outside disturbance, this gyration can continue indefinitely. There may be several cycles with different time periods in effect at the same time, one superimposed upon the other. Industries would like to predict the cycles, and many attempts have been made to correlate them with phenomena such as weather and sun spots, but with little success.

Seasonal Variations. The most common periodic movement is the seasonal variation which occurs, with some degree of regularity, in the span of a year. These variations are caused by climate conditions, such as the effect of the sun and good weather on lawns, which in turn affects the sale of lawn mowers, fertilizers, lawn furniture, and similar commodities. Social customs have a strong influence, such as the effect of spring housecleaning on the sale of home furnishings, Christmas on the sale of toys, and Easter on the sale of hats. Attempts are made to iron out seasonal variations by building up demand for off-season use of the product or by manufacturing another product for off-season use.

Irregular Variations. These are movements which occur without any particular rhythm. They may be important enough to make a noticeable shift in the time series or they may be only temporary surges of no lasting importance. They can be correlated with some event, such as the start or end of a war, epidemic, or other crisis. They can also be caused by something as trivial as a scene in a movie, as when Clark Gable appeared in a movie sans underwear shirt, causing the sale of underwear shirts to go into a tailspin.

The four classifications of time series movements are of importance because we may wish to isolate one effect and study it alone; or we may also wish to remove one effect, such as a trend, to study the others.

The decomposition of the time series is accomplished by the model:

$$O = T \times C \times S \times I$$

where O equals the observed value, T equals the trend, C equals the cycle, S equals the seasonal, and I equals the irregular.

An additive model is used at times, but the multiplicative model is preferred because it can be used with percentage changes rather than absolute changes.

Since this is a multiplicative model, it is only necessary to divide by the appropriate factor to remove its effect. For example, to de-trend the series, we can divide by T, so $O/T = T \times C \times S \times I/T$, or, to remove the effect of the cycle, $O/C = T \times C \times S \times I/C$.

The percentages used in these models are good examples of index numbers and are worthy of a separate discussion.

Index Numbers

Index numbers are a series of percentages showing change in price, quantity, or value, with reference to a base. The choice of the base is arbitrary but should usually be selected to give an unbiased picture. Often, but not necessarily, the base is for the first period or for the average of several of the initial periods. The numbers given here illustrate the development of index numbers.

Year	1st	2nd	3rd	4th
Sales	37	39	43	47 thousand
Base		39 (an arbitrary choice)		
	37/39	39/39	43/39	47/39
Index	95%	100%	110%	120%

Indexes are classified by the way they are formed:

Simple Index. The example given is a typical simple index, one value divided by the base.

Simple Aggregate Index. Several values, such as the price of corn and wheat, are added and divided by the base period total. The result is multiplied by 100 to form a percentage.

Average of Relatives Index. Two or more indexes are added together and averaged.

Weighted Aggregative Index. In the average relative index, each component has an equal influence. In the weighted aggregative index, the statistician applies weighting factors to the components as he thinks necessary. Determining the weighting factors can be a study in itself.

The index plays an important part in forecasting as well as in the analysis of the economy. We are all aware of cost-of-living indexes, market indexes, and others. It is now time to put these concepts in their proper perspective by illustrating them with an example. The reader definitely should not confuse this example, which has time as the independent variable, with the earlier example, which has disposable income as the independent variable.

Example of a Forecasting Problem

The example will proceed in steps:

1. The long-term forecast, Y_c = Trend.
2. Forecast modified by the influence of the cycle, Y_c = Trend × Cycle.
3. Short-term forecast to account for the seasonal Y_c = Trend × Cycle × Seasonal.

Step 1. Yearly Demand Forecast, Y_c = Trend. The yearly sales for a particular pharmaceutical product are shown graphically in Figure 5–5. The

Figure 5–5
Yearly Sales of a Pharmaceutical Product

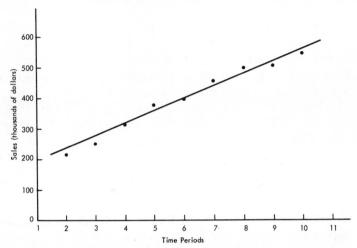

problem is to extend the information into the future and predict what the sales might be for any year. We can do this best by finding the regression equations for the best-fit line. From this can be predicted the value of Y, sales, for any value of X, years.

The solution of the problem is shown in Figure 5–6. The calculations are somewhat simplified over the previous example because any year we wish

Figure 5–6
Data for the Yearly Sales for a Pharmaceutical Product

(1)	(2) x Deviations (One-Year Units)	(3) Y Sales-TCI-$	(4) xY	(5) x^2
Year				
1	−5	204,875	−1,024,375	25
2	−4	219,190	−876,760	16
3	−3	252,324	−756,972	9
4	−2	317,258	−634,516	4
5	−1	372,356	−372,356	1
6	0	402,140	0	0
7	+1	451,020	+451,020	1
8	+2	480,010	+960,020	4
9	+3	503,060	+1,509,180	9
10	+4	543,870	+2,175,480	16
11	+5	591,200	+2,956,000	25
$N = 11$	$\Sigma x = 0$	$\Sigma Y = 4{,}337{,}303$	$\Sigma xY = +4{,}386{,}721$	$\Sigma x^2 = 110$

Calculations for a

$a = \Sigma Y / N$

$a = \dfrac{4{,}337{,}303}{11}$

$a = 394{,}300$

Calculations for b

$b = \Sigma xY / \Sigma x^2$

$b = \dfrac{4{,}386{,}721}{110}$

$b = 39{,}879$

Calculations for Y_c

$Y_c = a + bx$

$Y_c = 394{,}300 + 39{,}879x$

$x = \text{years}$

$Y = \text{dollars}$

Origin: July 1, 6th year.

may be chosen for the origin. By taking the origin as the middle year, the sum of X values becomes zero. The normal equations become:

$$\Sigma Y = Na$$
$$\Sigma XY = b\Sigma X^2$$

The yearly sales, plotted on the graph, are shown in column 3 of the table. At the bottom of the table you will see the equations needed for determining the regression coefficients, a and b. As can be seen, the value of a is 394,300. Knowing this and the value of b, it is relatively easy to predict the value of Y_c for any year in the future. For example, the forecast for the year 12 is:

$$Y_c = a + bx$$
$$Y_c = 394,300 + 39,879 \times 6$$
$$Y_c = 633,574 \text{ dollars}$$

Step 2. Yearly Demand Modified for Cycle Variation: $Y_c =$ Trend × Cycle. As we have noted, there is a cyclic variation imposed upon the long-term trend, so it would seem obvious that the value obtained for the example so far should be modified for the effect of the cycle.

If a general business forecast predicts an increase or decrease of activity, we can modify the trend by:

$$\text{Trend} \times \text{Cycle} = \text{Forecast}$$

Obtaining the value for the cycle variation is a statistical task in itself, but for the example assume the value for next year will be +4 percent:

$$633,574 \times 104\% = 658,917 \text{ dollars}$$

Step 3. Short-Term Forecast to Account for Seasonal: $Y_c =$ Trend × Seasonal × Cycle. Those responsible for the day-to-day operations of a factory will be interested in short-term forecasts for determining inventories, labor, and other needs. The monthly forecasts can be made by fitting a trend line to the monthly data, but this would be tedious and unnecessary as it is possible to adjust the yearly trend line. Starting with the trend line, $Y_c = a + bx$, developed for the yearly forecast, it can be modified for monthly forecasts:

The a value, the arithmetic mean of the annual total, is divided by 12 to obtain the mean of the monthly total.

The value of b must be divided by 12 × 12. This can be explained in this way. Dividing b by 12 reflects the annual increase in the monthly data. Dividing by 12 again, we have the monthly increase per month.

The revised equation is:

$$Y_c = a/12 + bx/12 \times 12$$

It is simple enough to calculate the monthly forecast, but there is the problem of determining the correct x value for any given month. First, examine the position of the origin.

For a trend line fitted to an *odd* number of years, the origin is *centered* on July 1st of the middle year.

For a trend line fitted to an *even* number of years, the origin is centered on January 1st, dividing the years.

An example will show how the value of x is determined. Let us assume that we wish to know the value for the month of October of the 12th year.

From July 1st to January 1st...........................	6	months
From January 1st of the 7th year to January 1st of the 12th year......................................	60	"
From January 1st of the 12th year to October 1st of the 12th year.......................................	9	"
From October 1st to middle of October.................	.5	"

$$x = 75.5 \text{ months}$$

Inserting this value of x into the equation for trend, the value for October can be estimated:

$$Y_c = a/12 + bx/144$$
$$Y_c = 394,300/12 + 39,879 \times 75.5/144$$
$$Y_c = 52.244 \text{ dollars}$$

This value for the month of October has not been adjusted for cyclical changes. Applying the cycle variation:

$$Y_c = 52,244 \times 104\%$$
$$Y_{cOct.} = 54,334 \text{ dollars}$$

Since the irregular variations cannot be forecast, it is only possible to add the seasonal variation. Obtaining a seasonal index can be done by following the steps shown in Figure 5–7. The sales for each month of the previous year

Figure 5–7
Monthly Sales Index

Month Column 1	Sales/Month (Nearest $100) Column 2	Index Column 3
1 Jan.	39,300	79.8%
2 Feb.	44,700	90.7
3 March	46,300	94.0
4 April	49,200	99.9
5 May	49,800	101.1
6 June	49,100	99.7
7 July	58,200	118.1
8 Aug.	68,100	138.2
9 Sept.	57,100	115.9
10 Oct.	58,900	119.6
11 Nov.	40,600	82.4
12 Dec.	29,900	60.7
	591,200	

Example: $\dfrac{\$591,200}{12 \text{ mo.}} = \$49,267/\text{mo.}$

$\$29,900/\$49,267 = 60.7\%$

are given in column 2. These are totaled and then averaged. The average forms the base for this index. It would be better if several years had been used in developing the index, but this will illustrate the idea. The next step is to adjust the forecast in the last example for the seasonal variation:

$$\text{Forecast} = \text{Trend} \times \text{Seasonal} \times \text{Cycle}$$
$$\text{Forecast} = 54{,}334 \times 119.6\%$$
$$\text{Forecast} = 64{,}983 \text{ dollars}$$

The example presented indicates the logic of developing a forecast by means of regression techniques and should establish in your mind a structure for approaching such problems. But do not be misled by the mathematical preciseness. There are any number of changes that could come about, such as technological advancements, consumer desires, political and economic developments, and many others which could have a profound effect upon the forecast. The unwary could make dangerously misleading forecasts with these techniques, but the astute industrialist can find them an important tool in obtaining a sales forecast with logic.

Nonlinear Trends

For short periods of time the straight line may be adequate as a predictor, but for periods of longer duration a curved line may be needed.

The straight line equation, $Y_c = a + bX$, can be expanded into a family of curves. The first, second, and third degree curves are the most useful.

First degree	$Y_c = a + bX$	Straight line (no curve)
Second degree	$Y_c = a + bX + cX^2$	One bend in curve
Third degree	$Y_c = a + bX + cX^2 + dX^3$	Two bends in curve

In fitting a first degree curve, two normal equations were used, but for a second degree curve three normal equations are needed, and for a third degree curve, four normal equations are needed, and so on.

The form of such a set of equations for a second degree curve is illustrated here:

$$\Sigma Y = Na + b\Sigma X + c\Sigma X^2$$
$$\Sigma XY = a\Sigma X + b\Sigma X^2 + c\Sigma X^3$$
$$\Sigma X^2 Y = a\Sigma X^2 + b\Sigma X^3 + c\Sigma X^4$$

The third degree set of equations includes one more equation of similar form.

In addition to these there are other nonlinear trends which have found wide application in forecasting.

Growth Curves

The long-term trend pattern for many industries and products has indicated a growth pattern not unlike that to be found in the biological sciences.

The growth is slow at first, with a gradual acceleration. Eventually, the growth starts to decelerate, and in time stops. This phenomenon (shown in Figure 5–8) is prevalent throughout the world where growth is involved, and is a valuable predictor for those responsible for forecasting.

Figure 5–8
Example of Gompertz Curve: Domestic Consumption of Rayon Filament Yarn (1920–52) and Trend

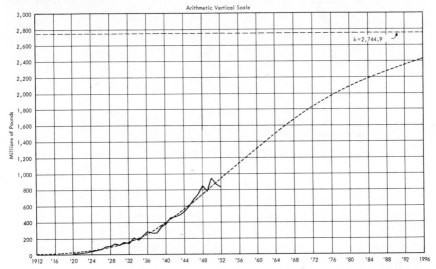

Arithmetic Vertical Scale

Frederick E. Croxton and Dudley J. Cowden, *Applied General Statistics*, 2nd ed., © 1955, by permission of Prentice-Hall, Inc., Englewood Cliffs, N.J.

Of the various growth curves, the two of greatest importance are the Gompertz curve, and the logistic, frequently referred to as the Pearl-Reed curve (shown in Figure 5–9). Both of these are S curves of similar shape (as illustrated). Other examples of these curves as prediction devices can be found in most of the statistical economic texts. These curves, like the straight line, can be fitted to data and used in forecasting in a similar if more complicated fashion.

Moving Average

The moving average is essentially a descriptive method of forecasting and does not produce a mathematical trend equation. This technique has found favor by some forecasters because of its simplicity.

The moving average substitutes the mean of a series of items for the given series of items. The mechanics are more readily understood by considering Figure 5–10. For example, consider a series of three items. These three items are added and averaged and inserted in column 2. For the next

Figure 5–9
Example of Logistic or Pearl-Reed Curve

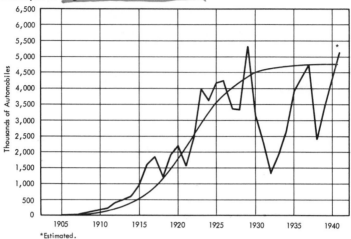

*Estimated.

Source: W. A. Neiswanger, *Elementary Statistical Methods* (New York: Macmillan Co., 1943), p. 536.

average, the first item is dropped and the fourth one picked up. If just three values are used in the moving average, one point is missing on either side of the center, and if five values are used, two points on either side of the center are lost. This indicates one of the difficulties of this method; it is always behind.

The length of the series of items averaged should be equal to the *period* of the data. For seasonal data, a 12-month period is often suitable, although, because it is an even number of items, it increases the difficulty of calculating.

A forecast is made by extrapolating the trend of the moving average into the area of prediction. This can be done by means of the chart and subjective judgment.

Exponential Smoothing

Robert G. Brown has developed the technique of exponential smoothing for forecasting.[2] Exponential smoothing is a special kind of weighted moving average which is especially suitable for data-processing applications. A new estimate is a weighted sum of the old estimate and the demand occurring in the most recent period since the last review. This estimate does not include any specific considerations for trend, but the technique can be extended to include the calculation of the trend.

---

[2] Robert G. Brown, *Statistical Forecasting for Inventory Control* (New York: McGraw-Hill, 1959), used by permission.

Figure 5–10
Moving Average

MONTH	SALES	3-MONTH MOVING AVERAGE	5-MONTH MOVING AVERAGE
1	$39,300		
2	44,700		
3	46,300		
4	49,200	$43,433	
5	49,800	46,733	
6	49,100	48,433	$45,860
7	58,200	49,366	
8	68,100	52,366	
9	57,100	58,466	
10	58,900	61,133	
11	40,600	61,366	
12	29,900	52,200	
		43,133	

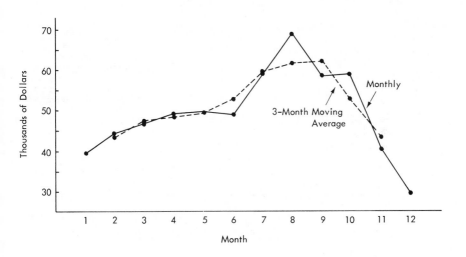

The logic is easier to follow by a series of diagrams:

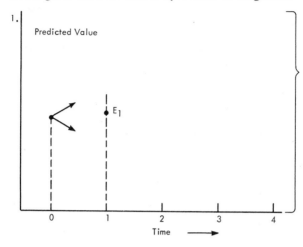

1.

The forecast must be started with some judgment value, at some instant of time, 0, as shown. Now predict the sales, E_1, that will be made through the first period. Starting with no information in the past, we can do nothing more until the end of the first period, when we will predict again.

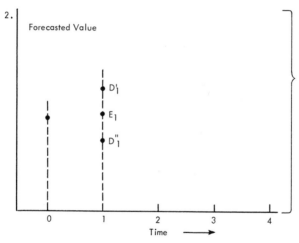

2.

We would be lucky if the demand, D_1, during the period agreed with the estimate. E_1. It is more than likely that it will be above or below the estimate, as shown in D_1' or D_1''.

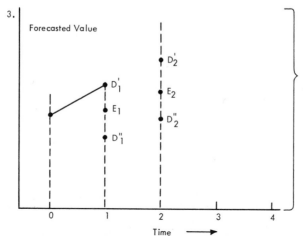

3.

To make the new estimate, E_2, start with the value of E_1 and modify it by some fraction of the amount that the demand, D_1, missed in the previous estimate. So we have:

New estimate = Last estimate + α (Current demand − Last estimate):

$$E_2 = E_1 + \alpha(D_1 - E_1)$$

Alpha, α, is called a smoothing constant and has a value between zero and one. If the value is small, in the order of .001, the response will be slow and gradual. A value such as 0.5 will cause a quick response. In actual practice, companies have found 0.1 is a satisfactory smoothing constant.

The greater the difference between the estimate made for the last period and the actual demand this period $(D_1 - E_1)$, the greater will be the adjustment for the next period. If the difference is negative, rather than positive, this change is also taken care of automatically by the equation.

We are justified in calling this estimate an average in the same sense that we use the term *moving average*. This is seen more readily by changing the previous equation:

$$E_2 = E_1 + \alpha(D_1 - E_1)$$

to:

$$E_2 = \alpha D_1 + (1 - \alpha)E_1$$

New estimate $= \alpha$(Current demand) $+ (1 - \alpha)$ (Last estimate)

As we accumulate the new estimates over a number of estimating periods, we are doing the following: The last estimate of the above equation could be replaced by the new estimate of the period before. This, of course, will include a last estimate again, which can be replaced by the appropriate new estimate, and this procedure can be carried on indefinitely:

New estimate $= \alpha$(Last demand) $+ (1 - \alpha) [\alpha$(Last demand) $+ (1 - \alpha)$ Previous last estimate]

This, continued, would become cumbersome, so we resort to the symbols; only notice now that we are extending the subscripts back in time rather than forward.

New estimate $= \alpha D_0 + \alpha(1 - \alpha)D_1 + \alpha(1 - \alpha)^2 D_2 + \ldots + \alpha(1 - \alpha)^{k-1} D_{k-1} + (1 - \alpha)^k$ [estimate made k months ago]

where:

$$D_0 = \text{Demand last month}$$
$$D_1, D_2 = \text{Demand one and two months ago}$$
$$D_k = \text{Demand } k \text{ months ago}$$

Continue this process long enough and the factors $(1 - \alpha)^k$ become smaller, and the early information has no appreciable effect on the present estimate. If the sum of the weights is equal to 1, the estimate can be called an average, and the sum of the weights $\alpha + \alpha(1 - \alpha) + \alpha(1 - \alpha)^2 + \ldots + \alpha(1 - \alpha)^k + \ldots$ does equal 1.0.

New average $= \alpha$(Last demand) $+ (1 - \alpha)$ (Old average)

This equation, which is referred to as the *first-order* system of smoothing, will respond to random changes. If there is a consistent trend, the estimates will be biased and will fall above or below the demand. Now let us see how we can account for the trend. The trend can be estimated by the following equation, which is referred to as the *second order* system of smoothing.

$$\text{Current trend} = \text{New average} - \text{Old average}$$

This trend is the amount by which the average increases in one month. The random fluctuations in demand will cause variation in the estimated average demand, and therefore the current trend. The average trend can be computed:

$$\text{New trend} = \alpha(\text{Current trend}) + (1 - \alpha)(\text{Old trend})$$

Brown has shown that this method of computing the trend is the equivalent of the least squares method, if the weights given to the demand in each previous month are the same as those used in computing the average.

The correction for the lag caused by the trend is:

$$\text{Expected demand} = \text{New average} + \frac{(1 - \alpha)}{\alpha}(\text{New trend})$$

The practical aspects of this method of forecasting are fairly obvious since it is only necessary to store the previously calculated values for the average and the trend.

Example of Exponential Smoothing.   Review for a moment what the problem is: We want to know what the demand will be for the next time period—month or other time period. Knowing this we wish to determine what the quantity will be during the lead time so that the order point can be established.

A company producing men's socks is generating an inventory record, month-by-month, as shown in the left-hand column of Figure 5–11.

Step 1.   Record demand for each month, Column 1.

Step 2.   Start with an estimate of the average and calculate the new average.
New average = α (last demand) + $(1-\alpha)$ (old average)
New average = $0.2 \times 210 + 0.8 \times 200 = 202.0$ for 2d month.
$\qquad 0.2 \times 180 + 0.8 \times 202 = 197.6$ for 3d month.

Step 3.   Calculate change for current trend.
New average. (Note sign changes.)
Change = $202 - 200 = + 2$ for 2d month.
$\qquad 202.0 - 197.6 = - 4.4$ for 3d month.

Step 4.   Calculate trend. Starting with the trend equal to zero or other initial value.
New trend = α (current trend) + $(1-\alpha)$ (old trend)
$\qquad = 0.2 \times 2 + 0.8 \times 0 = 0.4$ for 2d month.
$\qquad 0.2 \times - 4.4 + 0.8 \times 0.4 = - 0.56$ for 3d month.

Figure 5–11
Calculation for Exponential Smoothing

Item: Men's Socks—Size 11–12, Color Blue

$\alpha = 0.2$ $(1 - \alpha) = 0.8$ $\dfrac{1 - \alpha}{\alpha} = 4$ Lead time 3 months $L(L + 1)/2 = 6$

Month	Step 1 Demand (gross)	Step 2 New Average	Step 3 Change	Step 4 Trend	Step 5 Expected Demand	Step 6 Fore-cast	Step 7 Demand during L	Step 8 Error
1		200.0*						
2	(0.2 × 210) + (0.8 × 200) =	202.0	+2.0	+ .400	203.6	613.2	590	+23.2
3	180	197.6	−4.4	− .560	195.4	582.8	640	−57.2
4	190	196.1	−1.5	− .748	193.1	574.8	650	−75.2
5	220	200.9	+4.8	+ .362	202.4	609.4	670	−60.6
6	230	206.7	+5.8	+1.450	212.5	646.2		
7	200	205.4	−1.3	+ .900	209.0	632.4		
8	240	212.3	+6.9	+2.100	220.7	674.7		

* Initial estimate.

Step 5. Determine expected demand which is:

$$\text{Expected demand} = \text{New average} + \left(\frac{1-\alpha}{\alpha}\right) \text{New trend}$$

Expected demand for 2d month $= 202.0 + (4 \times 0.4) = 203.6$

Expected demand for 3d month $= 197.6 + (4 \times - 0.56) = 195.4$

Step 6. Determine the quantity used during the lead time. This is the order point.

$$\text{Forecast} = (\text{Lead time} \times \text{expected demand}) + \frac{\text{Lead time (Lead time + 1)}}{2} \text{ Trend}$$

$$= 3 \times 203.6 + (6 \times 0.4) = 613.2$$
$$= 3 \times 195.4 (6 \times - 0.56) = 582.8$$

Step 7. Determine the actual demand during the lead time—starting with the next month.

$180 + 190 + 220 = 590$
$190 + 220 + 230 = 640$
$220 + 230 + 200 = 650$
$230 + 200 + 240 = 670$

Step 8. The error may be calculated and plotted to evaluate the value of α being used.

There have been a number of methods proposed for calculating the proper value for α. However, the time and cost does not seem worth the effort, and in practice α is determined from trial and error.

Exponential smoothing is a practical method of forecasting each individual *stock-keeping unit*, SKU, on a computer. Since it is associated with each inventory item, one can ask whether this is a forecasting technique, as discussed here, or whether it should not be considered as an inventory technique. Consequently, you will encounter this subject again in the inventory subjects.

Nonstatistical Forecasting Decisions

This chapter has been primarily devoted to statistical techniques used in forecasting. Needless to say, not all forecasting questions can be answered by quantitative methods as described, so one must make decisions by other means. Such factors as the domestic and foreign political climates must often enter into forecasting decisions. Frequently, styles and fads must be considered, along with such imponderables as the weather. These subjects cannot be covered in depth, but some are worthy of mention.

The purchasing pattern of producer goods (goods used to produce other goods) often varies more drastically than consumer goods (goods used by the consumer). Anyone responsible for forecasting will naturally take this into account.

The decision process for buying producer goods is frequently considered to be more objective than the decision process for buying consumer goods. The motives for purchasing producer goods are frequently based upon economic considerations alone, and the buyers, being professionals, have greater experience and buy with less emotion.

The elasticity of demand concept isn't usually considered as a forecasting technique, but a knowledge of how price affects demand is useful in forecasting.

We all know that, generally, as the price of a product is increased, the demand will decrease, and as the price of the product is decreased, the demand will increase. This relationship can be plotted as a demand curve, as shown in Figure 5–12). Those products shown by curve (a) are little affected

Figure 5–12
Price and Quantity Relationships

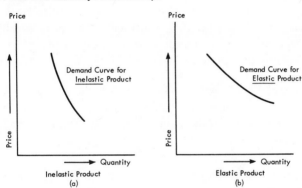

by any change in price and are said to be inelastic. Those for which the quantity varies considerably with the price change, as in (b), are said to be elastic. In other words, the demand is stretchable or not, depending upon how important the product is to the well-being of the customer.

The reason for this phenomenon is fairly obvious. As the prices are lowered for a product such as butter, people will start using it rather than a cheaper spread. If the price goes low enough, it may become the raw material from which other products are manufactured.

It is possible for a company to test the elasticity of a product by a controlled experiment. Field testing of the elasticity of consumer products is often done in cooperation with dealers. Typical of such studies would be to place a product in a store and change the price level from time to time to see how this affects the sales.

The addition of a tax to a product with an elastic demand curve could affect the demand to the extent of making it unprofitable to produce. Such changes in demand are of vital importance to the manufacturer. This is why elasticity of demand and external forces can have a profound effect upon the forecast.

These are just a few examples of the many factors to be considered when making a forecast. As illustrated, some information for forecasting can be handled analytically but other information cannot. Regardless of the source of information, the forecast serves as a link between the external environment and the internal operations of the business. It is, therefore, an important input to the system design of production control.

Summary

Sales is what makes the factory's wheels go around. Without customers and their demands, there would be no industries and consequently no production control.

The relationship between the customer and factory is so important that production control personnel should know how it functions so that they may help keep the system running smoothly and the customer happy.

The sales forecast is the link between external, uncontrollable movements of the economy and the internal, controllable affairs of the business. Although sales forecasting is an important function, its place in the organization will depend upon personnel available, type of product being sold, and many other factors.

Regardless of how forecasting is organized, the forecasting decision deserves the best information available. Statistics is an important tool for making these decisions. Of these tools, sampling, regression, and correlation present the most useful applications.

QUESTIONS

5–1. A manufacturer of plastics has sold an order for $2,000.00 worth of drill cases. Show how this affects the funds-flow chart.

5–2. Describe a sales organization and system used in some manufacturing organization with which you are familiar.

5–3. Discuss how each of the following interface with the sales department:
Manufacturing.
Engineering.
Inventory Control.
Quality control.
Customer service.

5–4. A manufacturer of bolts can ship about 75 percent of the customer's requirements from inventory. The other 25 percent must be produced to order. Discuss how you would handle this situation in writing the sales order.

5–5. A company producing ceramic insulators has an order for 10,000 special items. The scrap history has been 4 percent on these items. How would you arrange this sale to minimize your costs?

5–6. Who in the manufacturing organization should be responsible for sales forecasting? Justify your choice.

5–7. Select a company and outline a procedure for making sales forecasts.

5-8. Discuss the relationship between sales forecasting and the success of some particular manufacturing company.

5-9. What effect would good sales forecasting techniques have on the various departments of a manufacturing business?

5-10. Have you ever participated in a market survey? Explain.

5-11. What are the four components of variation in a time series?

5-12. Discuss the growth curve for one of the following products: color television, Salk vaccine, hoola hoops, bottle caps, plastic wading pools.

5-13. What are the advantages of the exponential smoothing technique used in forecasting?

6

Product and Process Information

AN ESSENTIAL INPUT to the production control system is the *product information,* for by what other means would it be known how to produce a product? The first thing that comes to mind when we consider product information is the engineering drawing used to describe metal, plastic, and some wood products. But this would be a very narrow interpretation because many products cannot be adequately described by a drawing. For example, how can one describe, by an engineering print, such a thing as a lady's garment, a pair of shoes, a can of paint, or a drug?

PRODUCT AND PROCESS DESCRIPTION

The product information is an instruction, to the worker and others, of how a product is to be produced; and it takes two basic forms:

1. The *product description* tells how the product will appear in some stage of production. It may be a drawing, a picture, a model, or a sample of the product.
2. The *process description* does not describe the product; it describes the steps needed to attain the end product. This is the method used in the production of paint, dairy products, bakery goods, pharmaceuticals, and so on.

To make the distinction clearer between the product description and the process description, consider the manufacture of an ice cream bar. The tasty slab of ice cream can be depicted as to size, flavor, and even porosity. The chocolate coating can be described, and we could say the stick is placed so it won't gag the unsuspecting customer, but all of this product description would be of little help if we wanted to produce ice cream bars. What we need is a step-by-step process description of how to make the product.

Ice cream bars are relatively simple, but consider a product such as a pharmaceutical. The description, even a chemical description, would be of little assistance in manufacturing the product. Such products require step-by-step information as to how the product is compounded, how long it is kept at a certain temperature, how it is filtered, and other necessary information.

Many industries use both the product description and the process description. In the metal trades it is common to have an engineering print and an operation sheet, which are, respectively, the product description and the process description. To bring some order to this discussion, the product description will come first, then the process description. The bill of materials which is an important part of the product description will also be included as a major portion of this chapter. Other information will be added along the way which may be useful to you some time in your career.

Product Description

Often the product description is conveyed verbally. The engineers in a model shop may confer directly with the operators, discussing what needs to be done to produce the model. This is the way exclusive garment makers work. It calls for a close liaison between designer and seamstress.

On assembly lines, the placement of a wire on a radio chassis or the location of a weldment on an automobile body might be passed on from foreman to worker or even from worker to worker. Some place there is probably a master print of the assembly, but it is not used by the individual operator to produce his part of the product. It would be far better, of course, if each operator had his own print showing how the task should be performed.

Formal product descriptions may be either pictorial or nonpictorial. Most important of the nonpictorial descriptions is the *specification*. Frequently the specification is associated only with the purchasing function, but the purchasing specification for one company may be the production specification for the vendor. A typical specification developed by an association is shown in Figure 6–1.

A good product specification for purchasing should conform to a general plan or format so those who use it may become accustomed to finding information in a familiar and orderly sequence. The important parts of the product specification, and their characteristics, are:

Heading. This should contain the specification number, the date it was issued, and an issue number. The specification number might be keyed to some established system of product numbers used for accounting purposes and shipping identification.

General Requirements. This section should give a brief description of the product and explain its uses. Of course, at times it may be desirable not

Figure 6–1
Product Specification

AEROSPACE	AMS 5609
MATERIAL SPECIFICATIONS	Issued 1/31/– –
SOCIETY OF AUTOMOTIVE ENGINEERS, Inc. 485 Lexington Ave., New York 17, N.Y.	Revised

STEEL BARS, FORGINGS, AND TUBING, CORROSION AND MODERATE HEAT RESISTANT
12.5Cr - 0.12Cb (SAE 51410 Cb Modified)
Ferrite Controlled

1. ACKNOWLEDGMENT: A vendor shall mention this specification number in all quotations and when acknowledging purchase orders.

2. FORM: Bars, forgings, mechanical tubing, and forging stock.

3. APPLICATION: Primarily for parts and assemblies requiring uniformly high room temperature properties and uniform response to tempering along with oxidation resistance up to 1000 F (540 C) where control of ferrite content is necessary.

4. COMPOSITION:

	min		max
Carbon	0.12	-	0.15
Manganese	--		0.60
Silicon	--		0.50
Phosphorus	--		0.025
Sulfur	--		0.025
Chromium	11.50	-	12.50
Nickel	--		0.75
Molybdenum	--		0.20
Columbium	0.05	-	0.20
Aluminum	--		0.05
Copper	--		0.50
Tin	--		0.05
Nitrogen	--		0.08

to divulge the usage, especially if a product is part of a newly developed machine or has military significance.

Detail Requirements. This section lists all the necessary physical, chemical, electrical, and other properties of the product specified. Everything about the product should be listed, such as the tolerance permitted on the dimensions. The performance and sale of the product should be stressed, and all extraneous characteristics should be eliminated.

Methods for Testing. For each specification of a property there should be an accompanying test for compliance. These test methods should be fully explained to avoid any errors in interpretation. If a sampling procedure is used, it should be fully explained.

Packing and Packaging. Since the method of packing is so important in the distribution and sale of goods, it should be described in detail in this section of the specification.

Another nonpictorial product description is the *standard parts index.* Frequently a company uses common parts, such as bolts, pins, and washers, so often that it is desirable to standardize on certain sizes, catalog them under part numbers, and have them available to design engineers for their selection. In this situation a company can take advantage of the simplification and standardization of products. Parts indexed may be either purchased from the outside or produced in the factory. Often there is an incentive to produce special parts by modifying standard parts, if the standard parts are readily available.

A pictorial product description may consist of nothing more than a model which shows how the product is to be produced. In the dress industry, the finished garment is available for workers to examine, and in addition, dress patterns (Figure 6–2) illustrate how paper models are used as patterns for

Figure 6–2
Product Description for the Garment Industry

cutting the material. There are numerous other instances where a model is used for describing how the product is made.

By far the most common pictorial product description is the engineering drawing, or a copy of it, made by one of the various techniques: the blueprint, ozalid, or spirit duplicating process. There are numerous books on the techniques of drawing, and not much can be added here except to reacquaint you with the basic concepts.

The Engineering Drawing

The purpose of the engineering drawing is to convey, in the most efficient way possible, information concerning a part or an assemblage of parts. The engineering drawing is the language by which designers converse with each other and with people in the factory. It is such a common language in the factory that it is highly desirable that almost everyone be somewhat acquainted with the techniques used.

Since a drawing is a language, certain symbols and conventions are followed. While there are several standardized ways of selecting the views and projecting them, the one most common in ordinary engineering practice is the orthographic. For many, this means of envisioning an object is through an imaginary glass box. Imagine a part (Figure 6–3) encased in a glass box

Figure 6–3
The Engineering Drawing

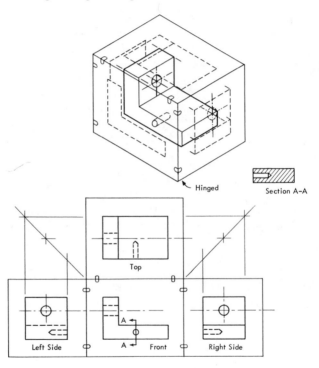

which forms planes. Now imagine looking at the part through these planes from a great distance, so that the rays of vision are parallel lines which would produce images on the glass in the true dimension. The objective, of course, is to show the three dimensions of the product on a flat sheet of paper. To do this requires the unfolding of the imaginary glass box. The standard way of unfolding the box is shown, with the top view above and the bottom view below the front view. Any face of the part can be shown as the front view, but usually that view is chosen which will reveal the most information with the least amount of drawing.

Notice that the part is the same length in the front, top, and bottom view—as you might expect. The views also agree in depth and height so that they are aligned, making it easy to move from one view to another. Auxiliary views and sectional views are frequently used to reveal some characteristics which are not shown by the projections just discussed. The sectional view is cross-hatched to make it stand out and show that this view represents a slice through the object. The point at which the cross-section is taken is indicated, as shown, by a dashed line with arrowheads at either end. The view is shown as if you were looking in the direction in which the arrows are pointing. Center lines are indicated by a dash-dot-dash line.

Good drawing practices permit making presentable product descriptions which will not be confusing to those who have to read them. In the past, drawing techniques emphasized more than the bare essentials needed for understanding. While the artistic engineering drawings are commendable, art should not be emphasized to the detriment of profits. Recently there have been several publications which emphasize simplified drawing practices which many companies could use to advantage. Drawings should be produced economically, but it should also be kept in mind that they leave an impression on the worker which may give him a clue to how he is to perform. If the drawings are slipshod, so may be the worker's interpretations.

It is often unnecessary to have a new drawing made for each product if the configuration remains the same from product to product. A standard drawing, with fill-in dimensions (Figure 6–4), can be used with considerable

Figure 6–4
Part Drawings Using Fill-in Dimensions

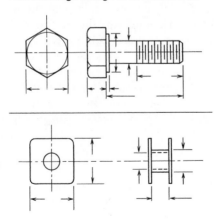

savings. One word of caution: factory personnel should not scale dimensions from a print, neither on the standard print nor on any other.

An engineering drawing may contain one part or more per sheet. The *one-part system* is favored by many companies, and for good reasons. The part number and print number can be the same, simplifying the indexing system. Drawings which have been superseded can be kept out of the files. The one-part system is simpler when a drawing change has to be made; one drawing can be rectified without disturbing a large drawing. This also simplifies drafting when several people are making changes on one large assembly. The one-part drawing will be easier to use in production as the drawings of concern to an individual need be issued only to him. This helps prevent confusion in the shop. The cost of reproduction is kept to a minimum because the prints are small, and only that part which has been changed must be reproduced. With this background in the product description, let us turn to the process description.

Process Description

The process description is a step-by-step set of instructions that indicates how a product is to be produced. This contrasts with the product description, just discussed, telling what the end product should be. Often the process description and the product description are used together, but sometimes the product defies description, in which case the process description must be used alone.

Many different industries use the process description, but the example here is in the metal working industry. From this you can understand the process description as used in other industries. The objective here is not only to acquaint you with a typical process description but also to make you aware of a logical method of developing this description.

Responsibility for the process description can be that of the production department, the design engineers, tool engineers, a special process-planning group, estimators, sales engineers, or others, depending upon the product being produced and the personnel available in the various functions mentioned. Developing the process description is often called *process planning* or *process designing*. The end product is the set of instructions, which will go by such titles as *instruction sheets, operation sheets,* and *route sheets.*

Process planning is the technique of predetermining the most suitable materials and methods to produce a product of required quality at a minimum cost. This results in a set of written instructions for the production personnel.

Scrap heaps and profit-and-loss statements bear witness to the importance of process planning, an importance which cannot be overemphasized. This means that manufacturing management should choose process planners with the greatest care. Ideally, they should have the equivalent of a college education and a number of years working on the factory floor. In addition, it is imperative that they are endowed with ingenuity and respect for cost.

The logic of process planning can be developed more concisely if some of the terms are defined.[1]

---

[1] The following material first appeared in an article written by the author and published in the April 1958 issue of *The Tool Engineer.* It is used with the permission of that publication (American Society of Tool and Manufacturing Engineers, Detroit, Mich.).

The *process* is all the work done on a product from the time it leaves a controlled storage point until the time it returns to a controlled storage. The process, a comprehensive term, is made up of building blocks which are generally called operations.

An *operation* is all the work done at one location. This applies to a single worker on an engine lathe, several workers on a press, or one worker operating several automatic screw machines. The key to whether it is an operation or not is to determine if just one instruction is needed. If so, it is an operation. To think of it another way, can it be handled by just one set of time-card entries? If so, it is an operation. As the process can be broken down into operations, so can the operations be subdivided into suboperations.

The *suboperation* is defined as work which is done without interruption. For example, drill, paint, burr, broach, and mill are all common sub-operations.

The logic of process planning can be stated as a step-by-step procedure:

First Step: Determine, by a systematic method, all the suboperations required to produce a product.
Second Step: Group the suboperations into logical operations.
Third Step: Place the operations in their proper sequence for the process.

To illustrate how this method works in actual practice, a common part—such as the fuel pin illustrated in Figure 6–5—will be used. The first step is to list every building block suboperation. It is important that every suboperation is included in this analysis because this process plan is the basis upon which costs are estimated and time studies are established. Should you miss one, it might make the difference between a profit or a loss.

Listing the suboperations could be on a hit-or-miss basis, but it is wise to use some systematic scheme. For example, all the cylindrical surfaces might be listed first—or maybe all the facing suboperations—from left to right. Here, we will work systematically from left to right, numbering the suboperations as we go.

There should be no difficulty in understanding the instructions: drill, turn, and the others. Other industries have similar terms which are just as easily understood by the experienced worker. The man in the woodworking plant knows the suboperations of rabbet and dado, and the operator in the garment plant knows the suboperations sew, buttonhole, and hemstitch.

Early in the process design, some considerations must be given to the characteristics of the material and to how it will be held while being processed. The obvious choice for the product illustrated, the fuel pin, is to make it from square bar stock of the dimension required. This material can be worked in a turret lathe or automatic screw machine by passing it through a collet in the head stock. It is held in a rack and turns freely as the suboperations are performed. The last suboperation must be the cut-off. Because of the concentric holes, it is apparent that the bar must be held as is shown on the diagram.

Figure 6–5

The Logic of Process Planning

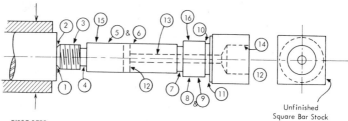

Unfinished
Square Bar Stock

FIRST STEP

List of Suboperations:

1. Face and cut-off
2. Chamfer
3. Thread
4. Neck
5. Rough turn
6. Finish turn
7. Neck
8. Rough turn
9. Finish turn
10. Neck
11. Washer face
12. Drill lateral hole
13. Drill concentric hole (small)
14. Drill concentric hole (large)
15. Grind small diameter
16. Grind large diameter

SECOND STEP

Operation Groupings:

Drill lateral hole

Grind small diameter

Grind large diameter

Face and cut-off, chamfer,
neck, rough turn,
finish turn, neck, rough turn,
neck, washer face,
drill concentric hole (small)
drill concentric hole (large)
Thread

THIRD STEP

Operation Sheet

PRODUCT NAME _Fuel Pin_		PRODUCT NO. _12-562_
MATERIAL _1020 C.R.S._		PRINT NO. _1-A-391_
PLANNER _T. I. M._	DATE _6/5/--_	REVISIONS _R. G._

OPERATION NO.	OPERATION DESCRIPTION		OPERATION	TOOLS
10	Face and cut-off, chamfer, neck, rough turn, finish turn, neck, rough turn, neck, washer face, drill large concentric hold, drill small concentric hole.	--	T.L.	_For special tools only_
15	Thread		T.L.	
20	Drill lateral hole	--	D.	
30	Grind small diameter	--	Gr.	
40	Grind large diameter	--	Gr.	

It is desirable to identify the suboperations by referring to the dimensions of the blueprint. This method has one inherent danger: shop personnel may produce the product to the specifications written on the instruction sheet, but this may not agree with the latest design change shown on the engineering print. Ideally, dimensions should not be used, but often this is the only practical method of identifying surfaces.

The next step is to group the suboperations into operations. There is no need to place the suboperations into any sequence order. Placing them in order would be meaningless where several suboperations are to be done simultaneously. Also, the sequence can be determined by the operator or set-up man.

Next comes placing the operations in sequence for the process. This is an important step because there are many factors that must be taken into consideration. Some of these general factors, or *sequence criteria*, will be considered briefly to point up their importance.

Plant Layout. The process should generally cause the product to travel the shortest possible distance. Therefore the operations sequence should adhere to the layout of the equipment.

Reference Surfaces. Where dimensions are interrelated, it is necessary to place the operations in proper sequence to attain the requirements specified on the blueprints. For example, a part may have to be milled on one surface first in order that all measurements can be made from this reference surface.

Physical Requirements. First things must come first. For example, holes must be drilled before they are tapped.

Cost of Operations. If a product is likely to be scrapped during the process, then all costly operations should be deferred to the last.

Finishing. The finish should be put on a product near the last of the process so as to prevent marring.

There are other sequencing criteria, but the preceding gives an idea of what must be kept in mind while determining the operations sequence.

The final arrangement of the operations in a process is shown as a sequence of operations on the instruction (Operation) sheet. The operations are often numbered in sequence: 10, 20, 30, etc. The reason for numbering them by tens is so that other numbers may be inserted between operations in case an operation has been left out. Some factories use the operation number to designate what department is to do the work, such as 10 for drilling and 20 for milling, but this can lead to confusion if a product has to be processed in a department more than once. Maybe a part has to be drilled, milled, then drilled again, giving operation numbers 10, 20, 10. The question may come up, Which operation 10 are you talking about, the first or second?

Process planning has been discussed as a design procedure. This should not imply that all process planners follow the logic illustrated here. Many older, experienced planners go directly to the operation sequence, but they are often guilty of making costly errors which could have been minimized by the step-by-step procedure discussed herein.

To illustrate the process plan for other industries, an example is given for the manufacture of a pharmaceutical (Figure 6–6).

Figure 6–6
Process Plan for Pharmaceutical Industry

MANUFACTURING DEPARTMENT	PRODUCT Aspirin Capsules	CONTROL NUMBER 397783
WORK SHEET	FOR Inventory	

FORMULA: /Capsule

1. Aspirin — 5 gr.
2.
3. Starch — 1 gr.
4.
5. Talc — 1/8 gr.
6.
7. Magnesium Stearate — 1/8 gr.
8.
9. Red & Blue Capsules
10.
11.
12.
13.
14.

DATE BEGAN: _____
COMPLETED: _____
YIELD:
THEORETICAL ___ 102,000 ___
ACTUAL
BULK WEIGHT:
THEORETICAL _____
ACTUAL _____ BY _____
CONTROL CHECKED:
BY _____ DATE _____
BY _____ DATE _____
MIXING CHECKED:
WEIGHTS _____ DATE _____
INGRED'S _____ DATE _____

CHK	INGREDIENTS	INV	SOURCE	LPI LOT NOS	POUNDS	OUNCES	GRAINS	CAPSULES
1	Aspirin	✓	Mall.		72.86			
2	Starch	✓	✓		14.57			
3	Talc		✓		1.82			
4	Mag Stearate		✓		1.82			
5	Blue & Red Cap.		✓					102,000
6								
7								

PROCEDURE:
1) Weigh powders
2) Mix for 20 minutes in Ribbon blender
3) Hand mix thru "Fitz" #2A sieve (40mesh)
4) Label bulk powder
5) Check bulk wt.
6) Move to encapsulation
DELIVERY DATE _____

Automated Process Planning.   There have been some successful attempts to automate the process planning. The parameters of a product such as a multidiameter shaft are fed to the computer. With the information stored in the computer a machine is selected, the operations described, and the appropriate feeds and speeds selected. It does not take too much imagination to recognize that this procedure could be extended to derive time standards and establish product costs.

Understanding the Product Information

Some aspects of product descriptions included in many products are worthy of inclusion here. You should have some acquaintance with this information, if for no other reason than to have a broader understanding and to reduce the chance of embarrassment.

Two of these concepts are *tolerances* and *allowances*. At the risk of being facetious, or being criticized for using a word to define the word itself, *tolerance* can be defined as that which is tolerated and *allowance* as that which is allowed. These are not sophisticated definitions, but they should help you keep them straight.

Tolerance: The total variation permitted for some characteristic of a product. It could be a weight variation, resistance, dimension, or other.

Allowance: An intentional difference between the maximum size of mating parts.

To illustrate these two concepts from a dimensional viewpoint, consider the shaft that fits in a bearing, as illustrated in Figure 6–7. In the first illus-

Figure 6–7
Tolerance and Allowance

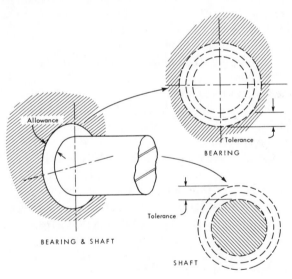

tration, assume the part is exactly the size illustrated. The space between them is what has been allowed by the designers. However, there could be no space allowance between the two parts, giving a zero allowance, or even a force-fit, which would mean a negative allowance.

It is unrealistic, because of variations in manufacturing, to expect the two parts to be exactly the sizes illustrated. Each part might vary, as is shown by the dotted lines in the second diagram. The difference between the two extreme dimensions is what can be tolerated. The variation in a part dimension is determined by the manufacturing process, while the designers specify within what limits the part will be acceptable. Hopefully, the designers' limits of acceptability will be greater than the tolerances dictated by the process. The tolerance is associated with one part, while the allowance refers to the mating of two parts. The system for maintaining quality is within the scope of this book, but the statistical applications for quality control are covered comprehensively by many excellent references and will not be included here.

Since so many products are made of iron, a few words about the characteristics and designation of this material will be included. Cast iron (*CI* on the product description) is an alloy of iron and carbon containing from 2 to 4 percent of carbon, 0.5 to about 3 percent of silicon, plus a small percentage of such elements as manganese, phosphorus, and sulphur. Its industrial importance comes from its capacity to be poured into molds of intricate shapes, thus reducing the machining time. It also has a high dampening capacity which makes it desirable for machine structures. And it has a high compressive strength, but it is not suitable for applications requiring high tensile strength.

Different types of cast iron result from different procedures of cooling the molten metal. Gray cast iron is the most common, but rapidly cooled cast iron—called white cast iron—is the basis for the very important material, wrought iron. The white cast iron castings are packed in an inert substance to prevent warping, then slowly heated and cooled for a period of several days. This changes the brittle white cast iron to highly malleable iron suitable for the agricultural, automotive, and other industries.

Mild or so-called plain carbon steels are basically alloys of iron with very little carbon and some small amounts of other elements. The low carbon steels have a carbon content between 0.05 and about 0.3 percent, while the medium carbon steels have a carbon content between 0.3 and 0.7 percent, and high carbon steels contain from 0.7 to about 1.3 percent. The low carbon steels are softer and therefore are used for such products as bolts, boiler plate, and similar products. Carbon can be added to the surface of this steel to give it a hard surface with a tough ductile interior. Medium carbon steels are used where requirements are more demanding, as for automobile crankshafts, axles, and similar parts. High carbon steel is used in tools, drills, reamers, springs, and other parts requiring a high quality.

If the steel is rolled while hot it is referred to as *hot rolled* (*HR*), and has a characteristic scaly, black surface. Cold rolled steel (*CRS*) has a smooth bright surface. Steels are designated on the product description by a code system. One common code, developed by the Society of Automobile Engineers (*SAE*), is referred to later in the chapter.

These are just a few aids to the reading of engineering prints. There are many other shorthand descriptions, such as *fao* for finish all over, with which one should become acquainted. The person working with engineering prints would do well if he obtained a copy of *American Standard Drawing and Drafting Room Practice*.

Simplification, Diversification, and Standardization

A thorough study of simplification, diversification, and standardization should precede any attempt to classify and code products, parts, and so on.

Simplification. This is the process of eliminating all extraneous or marginal product lines. For example, a manufacturer of stoves may be producing 15 different models and decide to simplify the line by producing five.

Standardization. Often confused with simplification, standardization relates to a product or very closely related products. It is a criterion of size, shape, performance, and quality. A company producing automobile engines might standardize the size of gaskets, generator mountings, or other parts. Standardization may often lead to more and different products being available. This was the case when a pump manufacturer standardized the two end plates and bearings and produced a series of spacers and impellers of various thicknesses to give a broad range of pump capacities from which to choose.

Diversification. This process, the opposite of simplification, is a trend toward even broader lines of products.

There are certain forces within industry and society that, as a whole, bring about the processes of simplification and diversification. The force to diversify producers' goods is not nearly as strong as the force to diversify consumers' goods, and here is the secret of diversification. Many people, at least in the economy of the United States, are reluctant to buy products exactly like their neighbors'—or even very similar. While this is often referred to as "keeping up with the Joneses," it should be interpreted as "being different from the Joneses." This is a powerful force and one that is expressed through the sales departments of companies by an urge to create more diversified product lines. This process is accentuated when a number of companies strive to meet the competition created by other companies' diversifications.

The force to offset diversification often comes from the manufacturing function. Simplification means that the supervisor of manufacturing can reduce his inventories and take advantage of large-purchase quantities. By having long manufacturing runs, he can install special production equipment and reduce the set-up costs. Specialization, and all of the inherent savings, are natural outcomes of simplification.

One interesting case of successful simplification is the ultrasuccessful German Volkswagen. Apparently, customers who buy the Volkswagen are more interested in the economy and quality that comes from a one-product line than they are in the fact that all the cars look practically the same.

Anyone aware of the production history of the United States must know the importance of standardization. This important contribution to our outstanding success is said to have been originated by a New England inventor, Eli Whitney, who is probably better known for having invented the cotton gin. At one time he won a large government contract for firearms by showing that they could be produced with interchangeable parts.

The success of our electrical business depends upon the fact that the important characteristics of the power supply have been standardized, as have many of the sockets, connectors, and other accessories. This means that producers can make consumers' products in huge quantities at low cost. Wherever standardization has not existed, as in some of the early machine screw threads, phonograph records, cards for data-processing, and systems for color television, confusion has reigned, and at the expense of the consumer.

There are many agencies that work on the problem of standardization, and it is a wise management that sets up a "standards" function in its organization—not only to establish internal standards but to select additional standards from outside sources. Many trade and professional societies have standards committees which continually establish better standards. The American Standards Association is composed of representatives from trade and professional organizations, and is concerned with the unification of the effort to standardize.

The Army, Navy, and other government agencies have also striven to produce standards, and any manufacturer producing for them must be well acquainted with their requirements. The National Bureau of Standards has probably made the most profound contribution to the process of standardization in the United States. The story of its achievement is too extensive to relate here, but it makes fascinating reading for anyone who is seriously interested in the details of our manufacturing history.

Classification and Identification

Many companies have found themselves in difficult times when their product line outstripped their code system and it became necessary to revise or start coding over again. This has led to confusion, not only among factory employees but also among customers, and has been reflected by a lower sales volume.

The advent of computer processing has jolted many companies into overhauling their outdated coding methods, with painful repercussions upon both personnel and budgets. For instance, one large and well-established machine tool builder decided to inaugurate a card-data-processing system in the payroll department, with the possibility of adding production control, inventory control, and other functions later. Because the coding system in use was not consistent with the card-data-processing requirements, it was essential to make some changes in the original code, which on the surface appeared to be fairly minor. Soon after the task was begun, the team processing the code changes had to be enlarged as numerous problems came up. It was discovered that the code changes had many ramifications which were not even dreamed of when the program was initiated.

Instead of some of the part numbers getting smaller under the new system, they became longer, requiring more space on the part. This meant an engineering change in the part, which in turn necessitated changes in the patterns and in the tools and fixtures. Some parts even had to be completely redesigned to give the part the proper balance. So what started out as a minor change in the system turned out to be an extensive overhauling of the entire product line. Nothing has been mentioned here about the difficulty experienced in making the changeover in the inventories, or the confusion experienced by the employees and the faithful customers.

This is just one experience of one large company. And it is true that it was a very old company, and that the founders had no way of knowing the extent of the company's growth or the impending birth of automatic data processing. However, no company devising a code system today should encounter these problems if proper consideration is given, but surprisingly enough, this subject now receives less attention in literature than it did in the early days of scientific management.

Classification is the grouping of things by common attributes. The classes are identified by symbols. This system of symbols is called the code. Classifying is an economy-of-thought process which goes on whether we put tags on the classes or not. It goes on in the mind, although the individual is hardly aware that the activity exists, and a little introspection will verify this. One is continually classifying things and even people (a source of frequently dangerous generalization), and one in fact spends a great portion of his life making or memorizing classifications.

The process consists of establishing gross groupings of these things, and each large class is then subdivided into smaller classes. These subclasses, in turn, can be divided. The following classification of materials is typical of the process.

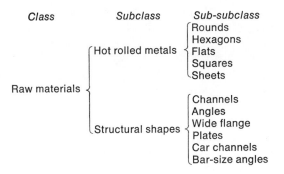

Class	Subclass	Sub-subclass
Raw materials	Hot rolled metals	Rounds / Hexagons / Flats / Squares / Sheets
	Structural shapes	Channels / Angles / Wide flange / Plates / Car channels / Bar-size angles

Economic Considerations.   Within the classification process there may be subgroups with common characteristics which could profitably be put together. Since there are rarely two things which are identical, the classifying, subclassifying, and sub-subclassifying could go on until each unit is a class by itself, but this would defeat the purpose of classifying. Our purpose is to get manageable groups which have some common meaning or purpose. If classification continues until it is no longer profitable for the purpose at hand, the returns on additional classification will start going up. The optimum point is very difficult to determine by quantitative means, but certainly an intuitive decision is close enough.

Considerations in Classifying and Coding

A symbol is one (or more) number, letter, or similar identification used to represent a class or subclass of things. It is the shorthand method used to refer to classes. So, while classification has to do with the grouping of things, symbols are used to identify the classes. Classification, by its very nature, must precede identification and symbolization.

The code is the arrangement of the symbols into some orderly structure. The symbols of the code are the "signals" which are the manifestation of the class information which is to be transmitted by the system. For example, a person wishing to convey information about a product from the sales department to the production department will write down the symbols of the code representing the product. These may in turn be translated into a set of hole symbols on a card, which will later be interpreted by machines back into a series of numbers or letters which are read by someone in the production department. By this means, a wealth of information is quickly and accurately conveyed.

Numerous ways of classifying and symbolizing have been used in manufacturing. Practically every aspect of the business of manufacturing is classified and coded, and it is not uncommon to find codes used for accounts, parts, blueprints, departments, materials, tools, and many other purposes. Some of these systems have outlived their usefulness, while some which have been discarded should probably be rediscovered. One will get a better insight into how a coding system should be developed by taking some of the following considerations into account before he studies the various codes:

Symbols Should Have Multiple Functions. The symbol, as a whole, should of course have meaning, but the parts of the symbol should be put together according to a definite method so that each part conveys a message. The set of symbols in Figure 6–8 are used in a code for grinding machines.

Figure 6–8
Code for Grinding Machines

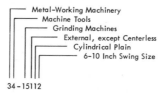

34 - 15112

Classifications and Codes Should Have an Open End. Classification and code systems should be constructed so that new classes can be added without making any changes in the basic system.

Subclasses Insertable. The system should be so designed that classes can be inserted within classes. Regardless of how a person tries to make a complete code, new divisions always develop or some are inadvertently left out. This difficulty can be overcome by leaving large "gaps" in the code.

Classification and Code Should Be Logical. This is an obvious observation yet one that is difficult to stress: The system should be thought through from one end to the other, and all possible exceptions should be taken into account. This process can frequently be pursued by means of a graphical layout of all the parts of an assembly.

Consider the Length of the Symbol. One cannot design a symbol system without considering the limitations of card-data-processing equipment. It is necessary to allocate a certain number of columns for a particular purpose, and this space cannot be enlarged at will. Since card space is usually severely limited, the number should be kept brief, but possible additions must be kept in mind. There are also certain limitations in the interpreting equipment which will be discussed under the section on card-data-processing equipment.

Brevity in a symbol is desirable because it makes remembering and reproducing easier. Not only is the time required for transferring a symbol less, but so is the chance of making errors. Often, when symbols are typed on a form, the space is limited, and this should be considered reason enough for keeping the symbol brief.

Coordinate Classification and Symbol Systems. It is desirable to keep the number of code systems to a minimum in a factory and to interlock as many as possible with common terms. Occasionally one finds a separate code system for blueprints and parts which may lead to considerable confusion. By careful planning, these two systems can be merged so that the part number serves to identify both the print and the part. This system can be extended to the patterns, tools, dies, cost sheets, and throughout the factory—whenever it is necessary to identify the part.

Consider Subcontracting and Job-Lot Requirements. Frequently, companies that do subcontracting find they are producing the same product for a number of companies. Their manufacturing costs may be reduced by pooling the requirements of all the customers, but this makes the indexing system more complex. It is frequently necessary to use a cross-indexing technique. Study of the particular problem will often result in a suitable method.

Punctuation Should Be Used with Caution. Punctuation is useful in separating one class from another, to know where one class ends and another starts. It is also helpful as an aid to memorization of numbers. Punctuation is commonly used in library work (the Dewey Decimal System) and also in some office and accounting files. However, it has been found to be less desirable in factories because the periods, dashes, or whatever get lost when marked on rough materials. It should also be remembered that there is no way to identify the period on card-data-processing equipment, for seldom would you want to give up a space for that purpose.

Some numbering systems have letters inserted between numbers to give the effect of punctuation. The letter is commonly given some significance, and in engineering blueprints it frequently refers to the print size. A would indicate an $8\frac{1}{2}$ x 11 print, B would indicate an 11 x 17 print, and so on, in multiples. The file drawers are designated by the letters and thus the prints are easy to locate. The strongest objection to using letters mixed in with numbers is the difficulty encountered when card-data-processing equipment is also used. Some operations become impossible, and even such basic operations as card punching become more difficult when letters are inserted.

Consider Aids to the Memory.   This aspect of coding has been ignored in recent years. Taylor, along with others, was concerned with how easily a code system could be associated with the item it represents. The death blow was dealt this type of symbolization by the card-data-processing systems, but in many cases this reason for leaving letters out of a symbol is not enough. There certainly will be far fewer errors if the symbols aid the memory, and it is impossible to calculate the cost of errors caused by symbols that are difficult to remember—with all the accompanying frustrations to new employees and the irritations to customers. One important advantage of a memory-aiding code is reduction in learning time while a new employee tries to absorb all facets of a new job.

Consider the Product to Be Coded.   Some products do not lend themselves to being coded by a number or letter system, and using colors is more satisfactory. This is true of some steel shapes, and we find that the bars in a warehouse are frequently marked with colors for quick identification. An excellent example of a color code, which is universally recognized is the code used for electrical resistors (shown in Figure 6–9).

Figure 6–9
Resistor Color Code

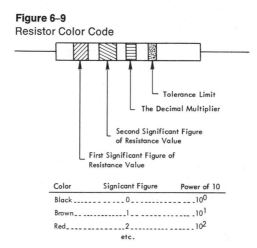

Examples of Coding Systems

Many different classification and coding systems have been in favor at different times during the history of industry. Some have not been found suitable and therefore have been short-lived; others have been discarded without ample justification. It is not our intent to claim that only one classification and code system is suitable for all purposes, but rather to select and describe those which are representative and have been accepted. Coding systems can be cataloged as alphabetic, numeric, or a combination of the two.

Alphabetic Codes. Some straight alphabetic codes are not intended to aid the memory, and some are designed to help recall the object symbolized. Probably little can be said to justify the use of straight alphabetic codes, as compared to numbers, except that a letter position can represent one of 26 classes and a number only one of 10 classes. The straight alphabetic code, if very long, is difficult to remember; but if you have need for a short code, with more than ten numbers in each class, then perhaps you should consider it. You should be sure that it probably will never have to be used with machine punched cards.

It is better to use the mnemonic code, which is intended to aid the memory. This code, which was first devised by Taylor, borrows its name from Mnemosyne, the Greek goddess of memory, and makes use of a few letters to remind the user of what the code indicates. As an example, the departments of a shop may have the code letters, *TL, CH, ASM,* meaning, respectively, turret lathe, cold heading, and automatic screw machines. Only three or four letters should be used together, or they start to lose their meaning (as anyone knows who has tried to interpret the letters designating various government agencies).

This technique of aiding the memory has been useful in designating small classification groups in industry, and it should not be overlooked by the present designer of codes, despite some of the disadvantages attributed to it.

Where space is limited for coding purposes, there are means of abbreviation which might be useful. One widely used method is consonant coding, which consists of dropping all vowels beyond the first letter. The abbreviation as *MTRL* for material is a good example.

Numeric Codes. Numeric codes are favored today over alphabetical codes, and a number of widely accepted systems have been developed by government agencies, trade associations, and professional societies. One who is given the task of setting up a code would do well to explore all available codes and perhaps adapt one to his purpose. For example, a well-known and accepted coding system for steel was developed by the Society of Automobile Engineers, the SAE series. Every manufacturer should be acquainted with this system, which is given here in a brief form (Figure 6–10).

The *sequence method* of coding consists of simply assigning numbers,

Figure 6–10
SAE Numbering System

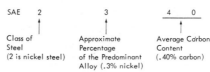

starting with 1, to a list of items arranged in a particular order. There is no provision for classifying items with this method, and it should only be used if the list is not too long to be easily memorized.

If new names are assigned to the list, they must take the next higher number, but this is awkward if the original list is in alphabetical order. This difficulty can be partially overcome by skipping numbers when originally setting up the table so that new names can be inserted later. This, of course, leaves much to be desired. Because of its simplicity, the sequence coding method has often been used, but often with drastic results. It should only be used when there is assurance that the list is static and not extensive.

The group classification code uses succeeding digits of a number to indicate major, minor, and subminor classifications. An example of this is an abridgement of the full United States Standard Commodity Classification (Figure 6–11) to suit the purpose of metal manufacturers, and its logic should be obvious. Raw materials are designated by the number 200. Thus all raw materials are prefixed with a 2. The second number, if a number 1, refers to hot rolled material; if a number 2, to cold rolled material; 3 refers

Figure 6–11
Abridged Commodity Code

200 Raw materials	350 Wood screws and nails	660 Welding and soldering
210 Metals hot-rolled	351 Wood screw flat hd	680 Miscellaneous
211 Rounds	352 Wood screw rd hd	
212 Hexagons	353 Common nails	700 Pipe and fittings
213 Flats	354 Brads	710 Pipe and flanges
214 Squares	359 Miscellaneous	711 Threaded pipe
215 Sheets	360 Nuts and washers	712 Flanged pipe
	361 Reg. C.P.S.F. nuts	713 Plain pipe
220 Metals cold-rolled	362 Slotted SAE nuts	714 Pipe nipples
221 Etc.—same as above	363 Check nuts	715 Companion flanges
230 Structural shapes	364 Lock washers	716 Blind flanges
231 Channels	365 Flat washers	717 Floor flanges
232 Angles	390 Miscellaneous	718 Common flanges
233 Wide flange	391 Rivets, rd hd	719 Other
234 Plates	392 Rivets, flat hd	720 Union and union elbow
235 Car channels	393 Keys	721 Standard union
236 Bar size angle	394 Cotter pins	722 Brass seated union
240 Metals, other forms	395 Drive screws	723 Flanged unions
241 Tubing	396 Taper pins	724 Union elbows 90°

to structural shapes, and so on. The meaning of the third number, which indicates a sub-subclassification, is evident. Codes may include one or more digits which will indicate some qualification of the product, such as weight, dimension, capacity, or other factor. For example, the code described could be extended. The symbol, 211–15, would refer to a hot rolled bar fifteen-sixteenths of an inch in diameter.

Material on classification and codes should include reference to the Dewey decimal system, widely used in libraries, and which has found its way into industry, especially for referencing files. This system, which was published by Melvil Dewey in 1876, uses a class and subclass approach. Characteristic of this system is the method of separating classes and subclasses by colons and periods. Such marks are considered too perishable to permit this code to be used universally in industry, however, because these important parts of the code are likely to be lost in the marking of steel and similar materials.

In 1967 the NIDA-SIDA Standard Numbering System was endorsed by the Council on Industrial Distribution.[2] The number consists of two sections, a manufacturer's number and an item number. The first section is a four-digit number assigned to all members of the American Supply and Machinery Manufacturers Association (ASMMA) and other prominent suppliers. The second section, made up of five digits, is an item number assigned by the manufacturer and is completely under his control.

The National Association of Electrical Distributors (NAED) announced a standard numbering system in 1965, Figure 6–12, which is exactly like the NIDA-SIDA system and which has been adopted by such prominent electrical suppliers as Westinghouse, General Electric, and Sylvania.

Figure 6–12
NAED Code

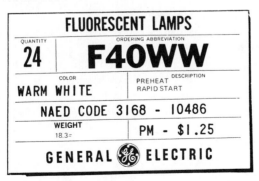

2 Modern Methods Committee, National Industrial Distributors Association (NIDA) and the Southern Industrial Distribution Association(SIDA), 1900 Arch St., Philadelphia, Pa. 19103.

One of the most significant attempts to standardize inventory items came about in 1952 with legislation directing the Department of Defense to establish the *federal catalog system*. Up to this time the Department of Defense was using 21 different numbering systems and 8 different supply classification systems.

The federal supply catalog has caused some amazing savings—for example —one third of the 25,000 hand tool items was eliminated.

Space precludes an extensive discussion of the federal catalog system, but if a company is supplying government agencies, it will want to become fully acquainted with the system.

Bill of Materials

Equally as important as the process description or the product description is the *bill of materials*, usually written B/M. It is in fact frequently included with the product description and produced as part of the engineering print.

To start with basics, the bill of materials is an itemized list of all the components that are required to produce an assembled product. There are many other names for this important document which includes parts list, where-used list, B/M, and others.

The importance of this document becomes more obvious as we note those functions which make constant use of it:

1. Engineers are responsible for putting the bill of materials together and for making any required changes. They are interested in the ease of making these necessary changes. They are also interested in developing standard-part systems which help reduce the designing time and consequently the manufacturing costs.

2. Process-planning personnel work with the bill of materials to decide how the processes will be designed and routed. They often make requests to the design engineers for changes.

3. The accounting department must keep track of the bill of materials parts to accumulate costs for the products.

4. Estimating uses the bill of materials to predict the manufacturing costs. The form of the bill of materials that helps them derive these costs will be the one they will want to use. Purchasing must use the descriptions on the bill of materials for requesting quotations or for generating purchase orders.

5. Production control finds the bill of materials extremely important for their operations. Not only can it tell them all of the items needed for production, it can also tell them the order of urgency for each product if the bill of materials is in the proper form.

6. Service departments are concerned with readily locating the correct part and making the necessary replacement and this can be found on the bill of materials.

Needless to say, it is nearly impossible to find one bill-of-material format which will satisfy all of these functions.[3] Consequently, we often find departments maintaining their own bill of materials in the format they desire. This leads to duplicate files being kept with all of the consequent costs and errors.

Ideally, at least, there should be one and only one bill of materials for each product. This should be maintained by the design engineers and kept up to date constantly with a well-contrived procedure. Unfortunately this is not always possible, and we find the various departments making up their own particular format to suit their needs. This leads to chaotic conditions which can only be stamped out by a management which understands the importance of standardized master bills of materials.

Characteristics of Good Formats:
1. Easy to extend (*explode*) product requirements.
2. Easy to determine end use.
3. Shows the "goes into" effect for production control purpose.
4. Legible and easily reproduced.
5. Easy to change and update.
6. Easy to extract common parts.

Bill-of-Materials Terminology.   Here is a survey of terminology used when discussing the bill of materials.

Graphic Bill of Materials—"Christmas Tree."   The tree or Christmas tree, shown in Figure 6–13, is not only a format which is used in industry

Figure 6–13
The A521 Assembly Example a
Christmas Tree Format

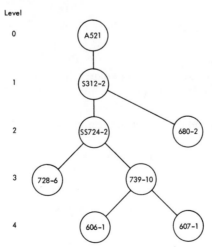

<hr />

[3] For a comprehensive treatment of this subject, see *Production & Inventory Control Handbook* (McGraw-Hill and American Production & Inventory Control Society), chap. 17, "Requirement Planning," chap. ed. Oliver B. Wight.

to display the parts needed and the way they are related, but it is also a way of thinking which is useful in less graphic bill-of-materials formats.

A *level* is a stage in assembly which can be considered as an entity. For example, the finished assembly is usually considered at the zero level, the subassemblies that make up the assembly are at the "first" level, followed by the "second" level and others as shown in the diagram. Numbers following the part number refer to quantity.

Explosion-Type Bill of Materials. An explosion-type bill-of-materials format breaks an assembly part number into its lower level components. There are several explosion-type bill of materials that will be of interest.

Single-Level Explosion. A bill-of-materials format that explodes an assembly into its direct components and quantities as shown in Figure 6–14.

Figure 6–14
Single-Level Explosion

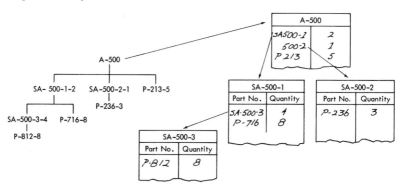

This single-level format would include all of the pertinent manufacturing information such as part number, description, quantity per assembly, and perhaps an extended quantity for a number of assemblies. This form of document is useful for sales cataloging information including different options. Service and repair departments also find this format a handy reference.

Indented Explosion. This format, Figure 6–15, consists of breaking down

Figure 6–15
Indented Explosion

A - 500	
Part Number	Quantity
SA 500-1	2
SA-500-3	4
P-812	8
P. 716	8
SA-500-2	1
P-236	3
P-213	5

Figure 6–16
Summarized Explosion

Assembly 500	
	Quantity
SA-500-1	2
500-2	1
500-3	4
P-213	5
236	3
716	8
812	8

a major assembly into its subassemblies and parts level by level. The display consists of offsetting part numbers, level numbers, or otherwise indenting to indicate levels.

This form is used by engineers to envision the whole product structure and how engineering changes may be incorporated. Production control finds this form essential for determining scheduling offsets and tracing the flow of the product through the plant. Plant layout makes use of this form in determining the flow of products.

Summarized Explosion. This is a complete breakdown of top-level assemblies into all subassemblies and parts with the quantities summarized. It is this form, Figure 6–16, which is essential for the operation of a materials-requirements system.

Implosion Bill-of-Materials Format. In the implosion type of retrieval, Figure 6–17, we obtain a direct or indirect usage of a part number on higher

Figure 6–17
Implosion Bill-of-Materials Format

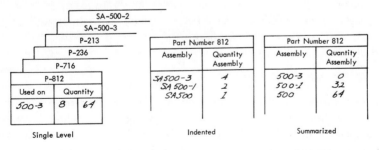

| SA-500-2 |
| SA-500-3 |
| P-213 |
| P-236 |
| P-716 |
| P-812 |

Used on	Quantity	
500-3	8	64

Single Level

Part Number 812	
Assembly	Quantity Assembly
SA 500-3	4
SA 500-1	2
SA 500	1

Indented

Part Number 812	
Assembly	Quantity Assembly
500-3	0
500-1	32
500	64

Summarized

level assemblies. In effect it is the reverse of the explosion process. The formats are similar to the ones given before. This format is useful to engineering when planning an engineering change. What parts will be affected by the change of one? might be asked. Production finds this format useful in planning production when shortages occur.

The Bill-of-Materials Processor (BOMP)

The answer to all of the confusion of having many different bills of materials distributed about the plant is the *bill-of-materials processor* incorporated in a centralized computer system.

The bill-of-materials processor is a computer *software package* which organizes disk files so that they may be linked—or chained—together in one or more logical patterns.

As you no doubt know, the software of a computer system is the programmed set of instructions for some operations you wish the computer to perform. The disk files are those spinning disks, in the computer, covered with a material which can be magnetized in a pattern to serve as records called *files*. These files are illustrated on flow charts as cylinders, but you may wish to envision them as a stack of phonograph records in a jukebox which can be accessed in a *random* pattern.

The key to the functioning of the bill-of-materials processor is the *chaining* of records so that it is possible to move back and forth from one set of records to another in a sequence of logically designed steps. The *sequence chains* are numbers carried with each record which will relate it to another record. All of this searching and transfer of information is done at the tremendously high speeds we have grown to expect from today's modern computer. How the sequence chains are used will be illustrated in the flow charts.

Advantages of the Bill-of-Materials Processor. The advantages of the bill-of-materials processor have been alluded to, but perhaps a cataloging of these would be useful:

1. It eliminates duplicate files which are costly and the source of errors and delays in a factory.
2. This procedure incorporated in an on-line computer means that information may be recorded and retrieved with a minimum delay.
3. Normally one could expect greater efficiency and reduced costs with this system as compared to all others.

Structure of the Bill-of-Materials Processing Files

Obtaining information for the various bill-of-material formats described above as well as for other purposes requires that information be stored in the computer in a particular way. This includes *two* distinct file arrays, placed on the disk files, both being directly accessible at the same time. These two files are:

Product structure record: referred to as the PSR. A listing of all active bills of materials in a form which may be retrieved in either "assembly" or "where-used" format.

Part number master record: referred to as the PNMR. This is a record for each item listed on a bill of materials. There is one—and only one—record for each part and assembly number even though it is used in many places.

This record contains all of the information about the part needed during the factory operations. For example, inventory information could be included such as part number, description, quantity on hand, requirements, lead times, cost data, low-level codes, and other information.

These two sets of records are on line and functioning in the computer at the same time. They are cross-indexed with the "linking" or "chaining" code which instructs the computer where to go for the information desired.

These two sets of records, along with the "intelligence" of the computer is all we need to illustrate how the various bills of material are produced and how they can be altered from time to time as the need occurs.

How the Bill-of-Materials Processor Functions

All of the operations of the processor will be shown as a series of steps. These steps are adjacent to a flow chart which is showing what is going on in the computer.

Inserting or Loading Information into the Computer System:

Step 1. From the engineering document, drawing, or bill of materials, a *part number master record* is produced on a deck of cards.

Step 2. Determine which part numbers are new. This can be done either by sorting on the computer or on card-data-processing equipment.

Step 3. Insert part number information in the part number master records. (The part number master record file organization and maintenance program will place one record in disk storage for each part number.)

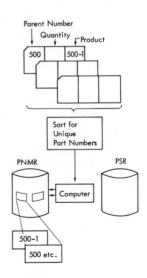

Updating. The product structure must be also updated to agree with the new assembly, and this is done in the following steps:

Step 1. Start with the same first step as given above.

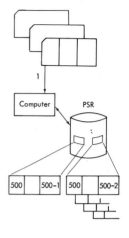

Step 2. The product structure is recorded in the product structure records (PSR). This is done by a software program called product structure record file organization and maintenance program.

Low-level codes are automatically generated and recorded for each part number in the master record. The low-level code indicates the lowest level at which a part is used. This is used to increase the efficiency of retrieval programs and also to serve to check the "product tree."

Retrieving Information. Now that the information is in the computer, let us see how it can be removed—in the format desired.

Retrieving a Bill-of-Materials Format:

Step 1. An inquiry for an assembly is made.

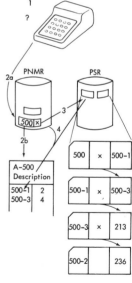

Step 2. The assembly part record is assessed and all pertinent information concerning the parent assembly is printed out in the heading.

Note: The computer processing block will be left out of the diagrams from now on to simplify the illustrations. Also the records will be blown up as shown below the disks. The component chaining is illustrated in the record blocks.

Step 3. The PNMR for the parent assembly has the address of the first assembly component.

Step 4. The PNMR indicates that the first part is 500–1. From the two records in the computer, all of the information such as the quantity per assembly, cost, and description is printed out.

Step 5.   Each product structure record contains the next-assembly item, so that the process described above is repeated until all parts are listed.

Retrieving a Where-Used Format.   Using the PNMR and the PSR, a where-used format may be derived:

Step 1.   A where-used inquiry is made for a particular part number.

Step 2.   The part number or subassembly number is accessed in the PNMR.

Step 3.   Information concerning the part number is printed out on the where-used bill of materials.

Step 4.   *a.*   The PNMR indicates one direct usage on a higher level assembly.

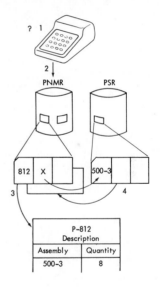

   b.   The PSR is accessed and it shows that it is used on part 500–3.

   c.   The PNR for it is accessed.

   d.   From the product structure record and the part number master record, all of the pertinent information regarding the part is printed out.

Step 5.   In each PNMR there is another address linking another direct usage of the part number on a higher level assembly.

The process described above is continued until the end of the where-used chain is recognized.

Engineering Changes.   This set of procedures illustrates what happens when an engineering change is made which will affect the records contained in the computer.

Step 1.   Starting with a bill of materials —the part to be added and the part to be deleted are determined.

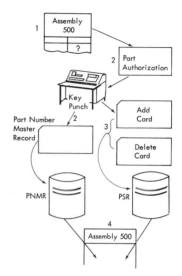

Step 2.   In case it is a new part number, a new part authorization is made out from which a new card is made out. As before, a record is created in the PNMR.

Step 3.   An add-and-delete card for modifying the product structure record is made. The program deletes the old record and adds the new record into the PSR.

This results in:

   a.   Deleting and adding links to the chain.

   b.   Low-level coding is updated.

   c.   Product structure is checked.

Step 4.   A bill of materials-revised is printed and checked by the engineer to be sure changes are made as desired.

This has been an illustration of the most basic system. There are numerous modifications which are needed for various applications. For example:

Customizing assemblies—adding different features and options to a product which requires a different bill of materials.

The complex problem of keeping track when a product change should become effective. Since the engineering change may take place over a period of time, the ability to retrieve the old and new bills of materials may be important.

Engineering Change Order (ECO).   The system of revising the product description or process description is a design problem in itself. The changes must be made in a systematic and efficient manner or all sorts of problems will occur. For example, changes might be made on the print and not on the planning sheet, and if the operator forgets and works to the planning sheet, he may be making scrap.

Figure 6–18 illustrates a typical engineering change order (ECO) form.

Figure 6–18
Engineering Change Order

										CODE IDENT 00214		ENGINEERING CHANGE ORDER	

DWG NO (1)	REV LTR (2)	DWG TITLE (3)		ASS'Y AFFECTED (4)	(5)					E.C.O. NO. (15)		SHT (11) OF
CLASS OF CHANGE (5)				RECOMMENDED INCORPORATION	YES ☐ NO ☐	MANUALS AFFECTED (13)	YES ☐ NO ☐			ORIGINATED BY (12)		DATE
ALL PARTS IN PROCESS, STOCK OR COMPLETED ASSY'S NO SHIPMENT TO BE MADE W/OUT THIS CHANGE (5.1)	4	NEXT PRODUCTION RUN (5.4)		REASON FOR CHANGE:	FACILITATE PRODUCTION ☐ PRODUCT IMPROVEMENT ☐ CUSTOMER REQUEST ☐		ERROR ☐ COST RED ☐			AUTHORIZED BY (14)		DATE
ALL-PARTS IN PROCESS AND STOCK (EXCEPT COMPLETED ASSY'S) (5.2)	5	AT CONVENIENCE OF PRODUCTION DEPARTMENT (5.3)		OTHER ☐	(7)					INCORPORATED BY (16)		DATE
ALL PARTS IN PROCESS (5.3)	6	RECORD CHANGE ONLY (5.6)								CHECKED BY (17)		DATE
EXISTING NO. IN PROCESS _____ PARTS NO. IN STOCK _____		USE AS IS ☐ REWORK ☐	SCRAP ☐ INSTRUCTIONS _____		(9)			INDUSTRIAL ENGINEER		APPROVED BY (18)		DATE
										RELATED ECO. NO. (10)		

(8)

By understanding the information on the form you will gain a better insight into the engineering change procedure.

Block 1. Drawing number: Enter the part drawing number.

Block 2. Revision letter: Each revision is given a letter, A, B, C, and so on to identify it.

Block 3. Drawing title: Enter corresponding drawing title or titles.

Block 4. Assembly affected: Enter first assembly number affected.

Block 5. Class of change: The class of change shall be completed by the originator with one of the following class of changes.

> 5.1 (Class 1). All parts in process, stock, or completed assemblies. No shipments to be made without this change.
>
> 5.2 (Class 2). All parts in process and stock (except completed assemblies).
>
> 5.3 (Class 3). All parts in process.
>
> 5.4 (Class 4). Next production run.
>
> 5.5 (Class 5). At convenience of production.

Block 6. Recommend incorporation. The originator will check this block as to his recommendations, but the drafting department may change it if desired.

Block 7. Reason for change. This block will be filled in by originator.

Block 8. Description of change. Change entries shall be shown clearly and concisely on the body of the ECO with the change from-and-to condition.

Block 9. Existing parts: This block will not be filled out prior to release and indicates how existing parts are to be disposed of.

Block 10. Related ECO no: This block shall be completed by the originator when a related drawing is affected by this change.

Block 11. Sheet number is to indicate if more than one sheet was used.

Block 12. Originated by: After an ECO has been properly filled out, the originator will sign, date, and forward to the responsible engineer.

Block 13. Manuals affected: This block shall be checked by the responsible engineer prior to approval.

Block 14. Authorized by: All ECOs shall be checked and authorized by the responsible engineer prior to release. Accuracy and feasibility of the ECOs rests with the responsible engineer. He will sign, date, and forward the ECO to the drafting checker or chief draftsman for release.

Block 15. ECO number: This block shall be completed by the drafting checker prior to release. The identifying number shall be entered on the ECO and recorded in the ECO logbook prior to release.

Block 16. Incorporated by: Original ECOs are assigned to draftsman who requests drawing from print files. The ECO is incorporated, original ECO signed and dated, and the ECO release form prepared by the draftsman. Drawing, ECO, and release forms are then forwarded to the checker.

Block 17. Checked by: The checker will check drawing for accuracy and completeness; remove recorded ECO number from the original vellum; sign ECO and obtain engineer's signature on drawing, ECO, and release form; and forward approved package to reproduction department.

Block 18. Approved by: This block shall be approved by the responsible engineer, along with the drawing and release form. The package is then forwarded to the drafting checker for release.

Not all engineering changes have the same degree of urgency, which explains the six classes of change in Block 5.

Drawings should have a block that is set aside for recording any changes which are made, and it is imperative that all changes be recorded to eliminate any misunderstanding at a later date. If the revision is minor and in no way affects the end use or the assembly of parts, it is customary simply to record the change on the print. If it is a major change, and the new and old parts are not interchangeable, the part print and number should be changed so there will be no confusion. This means the parts list and other records should also be changed to agree. A cross-indexing system may be needed between the new number and the old number in the inventory records. If the assembly bears a serial number, then it will be essential to record when the new part number went into effect. Only by this method can the customer who needs repair parts be assured of obtaining the ones he wants.

The management will be wise if it maintains a strong discipline regarding product changes. No changes of any sort should be permitted without proper written authority, which has gone through the established procedure. A checklist as presented here should help in maintaining the proper discipline:

Checklist

1. Only those responsible for the functioning of the product should be permitted to authorize changes in the product description, and this is often true of the process description.
2. Changes should be cleared with the quality control department to determine what effect the change will have on quality standards, replacement of gauges, and so forth.
3. Change suggestions should be originated by any interested person. A method for giving them propeer recognition should be devised, for by no other means can full cooperation be expected. The authority for the change must, however, come from a central function, such as the design engineer.
4. Changes should be cleared with the customer—if it is a customer's order —to see if the product will still fit his requirements.
5. Changes should be checked with the inventory control. If old parts can be used before the change goes into effect, a method of phasing from the old to the new should be arranged.
6. If the product information is retained by the foreman or others, it is essential that the old information be destroyed and the new distributed.
7. Product changes should not be made by verbal order, but should be matters of record.

Distribution of Product Descriptions

Several systems are commonly used for distributing the product description to the production personnel when needed:

1. One method is to distribute a set of prints to each foreman. The foreman in turn issues them to the operators as needed. This, however, has proven inefficient, as the foreman, with his many duties, is not inclined to keep his files current. Consequently, the department product descriptions are out of date.
2. Another method is to maintain a file of prints in the production control department, which in turn issues them with the production orders and other forms in the route file. This system often requires an excessive number of prints.
3. Another common method is to have the production control department, or others needing prints, requisition them from the engineering blueprint department. This system is efficient and conserves material, but it also has the drawback of requiring a greater lead time.

Distribution of Process Information

Once the processing is determined, it will probably remain without change. If, however, a change is needed, such as an additional operation, a request is sent to the planning department. If the requests are not sent to the planning department first, the costs are apt to increase, causing the usual repercussions from the cost department.

The process information is generally put on a master form which can be readily duplicated. This is necessary since a new set of forms will probably be needed every time an order is placed. The Ozalid process is quite commonly used for this. The master is a clear piece of plastic upon which the standard information has been printed. The information for the particular plan can then be filled in by typewriter or pen. The spirit duplicating process is also frequently used for producing process information. With both of these processes, the master can be placed back in the file and used over and over again for different orders of the same product. Certain information which might change from time to time, such as quantities and order numbers, can be easily changed.

Security of Product Information

Many product and process descriptions reveal important and secret information which a company has spent a considerable fortune to obtain by research and development. Thus, it is obvious why a strict and rigid control over the security of the product and process design must be maintained. Companies doing military contracting must be especially cautious and, consequently, restrict the circulation of the product information, storing it in vaults when not in use. Companies which have "style" products, such as automobiles, also treat their product information with care.

The product or process description is the jelling of large investments of manpower. If the descriptions were destroyed, they could probably be replaced in time, but the loss in labor hours could be tremendous. Consequently, companies go to great effort to protect these assets. Companies which are one division of a multiple-division complex will undoubtedly store each other's production information, so if one set is destroyed another set is available. Other companies send their product information to vaults. Sometimes these are storage facilities in specially air-conditioned caves. Other companies follow the practice of microfilming all the product information and storing it in a vault. This method has been found so satisfactory by some companies that they microfilm all their drawings and the engineers and production people work with the films directly by means of special readers. One by-product of this process is greater ease of sending prints through the mail.

Summary

The product information is an important input to the production control system. It is the instruction which tells the factory personnel what to produce. For some products a description of the end product, the *product description,* is all that is needed. For others, it is impossible or difficult to produce a meaningful product description, so a step-by-step *process description* is used. In many industries, the product and process descriptions are used together.

The change of the product description should follow a well-designed system, for which there are certain well-recognized criteria of design.

There is a logical procedure for the development of the process instruction, which includes determining all the suboperations, grouping these into operations, and, finally, placing the operations in a logical, efficient sequence.

Whatever the industry, there is a certain product and process information which is unique and which you will have to learn after you arrive on the job. This is something you should be aware of and look forward to with anticipation.

The production control systems are in reality communication networks of the most complicated type. If they are to be used efficiently, the messages transmitted must be received the same as sent. One of the most acceptable ways of doing this is to put the information into the form of a code. The very fact that this code is used repeatedly assures fewer errors in conveying messages. While it is difficult to say that there is one best method of classifying and coding information, there are certainly a number of distinct factors for efficient coding which should be taken into consideration.

QUESTIONS

6–1. Give an example of a company which produces a product that is not suitable for a pictorial product description.

6–2. How can a standard parts index save a company money?

6–3. Product descriptions for an assembly line are often verbal. What dangers do you see in this?

6–4. Make a sketch of a simple product, using the conventional views.

6–5. Frequently a statement is found on engineering drawings, "Don't scale the drawing." Why is this necessary?

6–6. Why does the metal working industry traditionally use both the product and process description?

6–7. Why is it undesirable to put dimensions on the operation sheet?

6–8. Consider some product with which you are familiar and for which you know the meaning of the suboperations. List the suboperations needed to produce the product. Group the suboperations into operations, and place the operations into some reasonable sequence.

6–9. Some companies identify the operation by the department number. Is there any objection to this?

6–10. Give an example of a manufacturer who could use automated process planning.

6–11. Devise a code system suitable for some product with which you are acquainted.

6–12. Discuss the effect mnemonic coding might have on training new employees and on their job satisfaction.

6–13. Design a method of distributing product and process information for a particular manufacturer. What procedure could be used for keeping this information up to date?

6–14. Briefly explain how each of the following departments uses the bill of materials.

Service department.

Estimating department.

Inventory control department.

6–15. Discuss how the bill of materials processor helps meet the needs for various B/M formats.

6–16. Explain the part that each of the following files plays in the bill of materials processor:

Product structure record.

Part number master record.

6–17. Discuss the problems a metal fabricating company could have if it had no engineering change order procedure.

6–18. Design an engineering change order procedure that could be used in a metal stamping factory.

7

Cost Information

THE USUAL OBJECTIVE of production planning and control is to minimize costs, which in turn enhances the profit of a business. This is the primary mission, and although it may be interpreted as minimizing machine downtime, limiting scrap, increasing output, and other activities, all of these can be reduced to cost as a common denominator. It is therefore important that all production control personnel have a good grasp of cost terminology and be able to interpret their day-to-day decisions in these terms.

Cost, in itself, is not important to the manufacturer, but how costs influence profit is important. So important is the generation of profit that the word should be stamped on each page of this book as a reminder to you of your purpose in studying system designing and decision making for production and inventory control.

It is true that there are other objectives of a business, such as the responsibility of furnishing an income to the employees, satisfying the ambitions of the managers, and perhaps even supplying a tax income to the government, but if a profit is not forthcoming, the capital investment will drift away to other investments where the rewards are greater. Even if you don't agree that profits are of primary importance, you will have to admit that profits are the basis for "scoring" the game. A manager, although he may have no investment in the business, is vitally interested in the profits because this is the way his success is measured, and as we move down the industrial hierarchy, the contribution to profit will still be the basis for reward.

The relationship between profit and costs can be seen on the bar chart in Figure 7–1. As is obvious, the profit can be enhanced in two ways, by increasing the price or by reducing the costs.

Figure 7–1
Profit and Cost Relationships

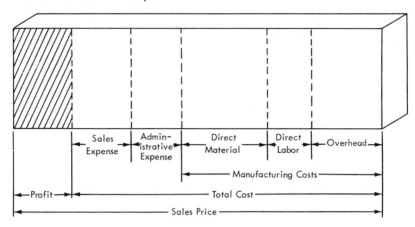

The price of a product is established by the philosophy of the management and by the environment in which the product is being sold.

1. The price of a product may be established to meet the price of similar products on the market. This means management will have little control over the price.
2. Some products are prestige items and the price is set high to accentuate that prestige. For example, fountain pens sold for the graduating senior must have a prestige price. It is difficult to imagine a loving aunt buying her favorite nephew a 39-cent pen for graduation, although it serves the same purpose (and becomes lost as quickly) as an expensive one.
3. Some companies have pursued a pricing policy of adding a fixed percentage to the cost of producing a product. These companies usually do not have a monopoly on the product and are, in effect, pricing it to conform with other companies following a similar policy.
4. Products which are made by a secret process, or are patented, can be priced for what the market will stand. If there is no substitute and the product is essential—or the public thinks it is—the price can be far beyond any reasonable figure.
5. Companies have been known to price a product according to customers' buying habits. If the product is new to the prospective customers, the price might be lowered at first, but when the inertia of buying is established, prices will be gradually raised.

The price is reflected in the gross sales on the profit and loss statement, A in Figure 7–2. From this is deducted the cost of goods sold, B, and the selling and administrative expenses, C, to arrive at the profit, D. It is evident that profit depends upon the difference between the price and the expenses.

Figure 7–2

```
                    Profit and Loss Statement
                 TROY MANUFACTURING COMPANY
                     January 1 to December 31
```

A { Gross sales		$831,600
Less: Sales returns and allowances		17,600
Net Sales		$814,000
B { Less: Cost of goods sold		
Finished goods inventory, Jan. 1 ....$119,680		
Cost of goods manufactured 579,040		
$698,720		
Less: Finished goods inventory, Dec. 31 136,400		
		562,320
		$251,680
C { Less: Selling and administrative expenses		
General office expenses ....$ 23,200		
Sales expenses 74,200		
Bad debts 8,000		
		105,400
D { Net Profit		$146,280

The selling and administrative expenses are outside the jurisdiction of the factory, and only the costs of manufacturing may be influenced. This explains why the emphasis here will be upon the *manufacturing costs*.

Job Order Costing and Process Costing

In the discussion of many manufacturing techniques, a sharp line can be drawn between those used in the job shop factory and in the production line factory.

Job order costing is used wherever it is convenient to accumulate the costs for each lot of material. For example, in the garment industry, where a limited number of each style is produced, the costs are accumulated for each *lot* or *order*. This is also the method used in the metal working industry, where the product goes through as a batch even though the batch may take considerable time to complete.

Process costing is used where one or a few different products are produced and the costs can be accumulated for each *department* over a period of time. The unit costs are obtained by accumulating the departmental costs and dividing by the number of products produced.

The objective here is not to make an exhaustive study of accounting systems, but to outline a method of obtaining cost information from which day-to-day decisions can be made. The technique used for this purpose follows, in general, the job order costing method.

The Cost Estimate for Decision Making

Referring again to the bar chart (Figure 7–3), notice that the manufacturing cost is composed of three elements: *direct labor, direct material,*

Figure 7–3
Cost Estimating

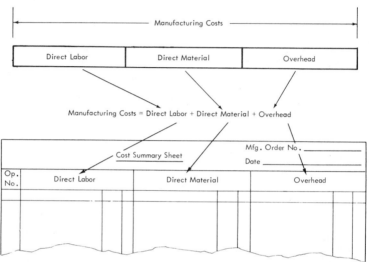

and *overhead.* This can be written as an important accounting equation, which should be committed to memory:

$$\text{Manufacturing costs} = \text{Direct labor costs} + \text{Direct material costs} + \text{Overhead costs}$$

Remember, the objective is to arrive at the manufacturing cost as directly as possible, which makes it desirable to have a *cost summary sheet* (similar to the one shown) which follows from the basic equation. Since it is necessary to obtain the data for these column entries, it is important that the three factors be defined precisely.

Direct material is all the material which can be readily charged to the product. Often this is more than the material seen in the end product, so it is of little use to use the definition of some accountants, "All of the material that can be seen in the end product." The material charged off to the product might consist of the usable material, plus stub ends of bars lost in a lathe process, the knotty pieces of wood in furniture making, the scrap from a punch press, or the broken bottles in a filling operation. As long as the costs belong to this production order, they should be charged to it. Otherwise they will be prorated throughout production.

Direct labor, like the direct material, is all the cost that can be justifiably charged to the product. Labor that cannot be charged directly to the product is caught up in the indirect labor account and, as we will see, prorated to all the jobs.

Overhead could be defined as the manufacturing costs less the direct material and direct labor costs. Since we are attempting to charge all the material and labor off to the order, we can say that the overhead is everything that is not included in these two categories. Included in the overhead expense are such items as water, electricity, coal for heating, taxes, insurance, and depreciation. How is it possible to charge these costs off to any particular product? It is done by adding them together and prorating them to the job by an elementary ratio method. Here is an example of how it might be calculated for a particular order, no. 598:

$$\frac{\text{Overhead dollars for order no. 598}}{\text{Direct labor dollars for order no. 598}} = \frac{\text{Overhead dollars spent last year}}{\text{Direct labor dollars for last year}}.$$

The unknown in this equation is, of course, *overhead dollars for order no. 598*. This would be an awkward equation for the cost clerk to use, so it is modified. The right-hand side of the equation, referred to as the *overhead rate*, is given to him as a percentage, such as 500%, which means that for every dollar of labor there are five dollars of overhead. Then, if both sides of the equation are multiplied by *direct labor dollars for order no. 598*, the equation will look like this:

Overhead dollars for order no. 598 = Direct labor dollars for no. 598 × 500%.

This is a good place to tell you that many words are synonymous with overhead, and *burden* is one of them. But you should not confuse the *overhead* with the *overhead rate*. Some of you are probably already questioning why direct labor dollars are used in the example. As you might suspect, there are other factors which could be used as long as they meet certain criteria. One obvious requirement is availability of information. As is apparent from the cost summary sheet, the *direct labor cost* and *direct material cost* are available. In addition, there is *direct labor time* and the *quantity of material used*, such as pounds or square yards. Sometimes the direct material costs and labor costs are added to form the *prime cost*, which is also used to distribute the overhead.

The second requirement is that the overhead costs and the factor used in the denominator be correlated (as is shown in Figure 7–4). As the overhead increases on a job, so should the direct labor dollars, or whatever is being used to distribute the overhead. Some prefer to think of the overhead as having fixed, semivariable, and variable components, and to treat each separately. The overhead rate, at best, is just an estimate, so many companies are negligent in keeping it up to date.

Where data processing systems are in effect, some companies derive a new burden rate every month. The other extreme is the company which will go for years without updating its rates, and does so only when it finds it

Figure 7–4
Desired Relationship for Overhead Rates

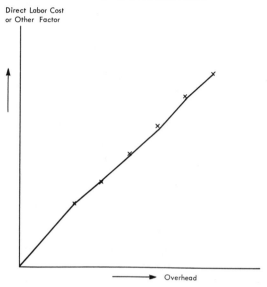

Direct Labor Cost
or Other Factor

Overhead

is out of competition or losing money. A company has been known to use a rate borrowed from another company, but with disastrous results. Overhead rates can be developed only by accumulating actual costs from company records. There is nothing sacred about certain overhead rates, and they can range from a couple of dollars per hour (or less) to more than a thousand dollars per hour.

The Danger of a Common Overhead Rate

So far, it has been assumed that the factory processes are uniform and that all operate at full capacity. This can be a dangerous assumption if the company is using a plantwide overhead rate.

The danger can be pointed out in the hypothetical factory shown in Figure 7–5. Department A has a very expensive press while Department B

Figure 7–5
The Problem of a Plantwide Overhead Rate

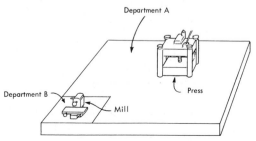

Department A

Department B

Press

Mill

has a considerably less expensive milling machine, used part of the time to process dies for the press but most of the time for subcontracting work. The overhead on these two machines accumulates at the rate of $100 per hour. Since there are two machines, it might seem reasonable to divide the $100 between the two for a rate of $50 per hour per machine, and this in fact is just what happens when a plantwide overhead rate is used.

Now assume there is another company, that owns just a milling machine, and finds its overhead rate is $20 per hour; while still another company, owning just a press, has an overhead rate of $80 an hour. It is obvious that the company with both machines won't be able to compete with its milling machine since its overhead rate is $50 an hour compared with the $20 an hour charged by the competition. However, it will have cornered the market on the press work because its overhead rate is $50 an hour rather than $80 an hour. The only difficulty is that both machines must operate to cover the $100 per hour overhead which is accumulating. You undoubtedly will read in the financial section that bankruptcy has been declared.

The solution to this problem is to have an overhead rate calculated for each department. The overhead costs for each department, or work place, can be derived by the following equation:

Overhead for department = Indirect labor for department + Indirect material for department + Indirect expenses for department.

Each of the quantities on the right-hand side of this equation requires further explanation:

Indirect labor is that labor expense which can be charged directly to the production center. The fact that it is an *indirect* charge indicates that it cannot be charged directly to the product. Such expenses as labor for machine repairs can be charged to the department, and usually such labor is charged on a different-colored time card to distinguish it from the direct labor.

Indirect material is all material, such as repair parts, cutting oil, and similar items, which cannot be charged directly to the product, but can be charged directly to the production center.

Indirect expenses are all those overhead items which are not charged directly to the department. Since this information cannot be obtained directly, it is necessary to take each expense item and prorate it in some equitable way. This can be easily explained if we consider such an expense item as taxes for the factory building. The problem is to find the tax dollars to be charged to the department.

$$\frac{\text{Tax dollars for department}}{\text{Floor area for department}} = \frac{\text{Tax dollars for factory building}}{\text{Floor area for factory}};$$

$$\text{Tax dollars for department} =$$
$$\text{Floor area for department} \times \frac{\text{Tax dollars for factory building}}{\text{Floor area for factory}}.$$

Each indirect expense item is considered and prorated on an appropriate basis to the departmental account. When all the costs—including indirect labor, indirect material, and indirect expenses—are accumulated for a department, they are divided by the direct labor dollars, direct labor hours, or other appropriate value which has been accumulated for the department to form a *departmental overhead rate*. The objective in establishing departmental overhead rates is to find true and equitable values. However, some companies adjust their cost figures arbitrarily to cover departments which are in the process of developing, or which the company wishes to justify for one reason or another. This defeats the purpose of a good cost accounting system and can have a discouraging effect on the departmental supervisors who are saddled with excessive overhead rates.

Do not lose sight of the objective in the estimating procedure. The *manufacturing cost* for a product is the desired goal, but the procedure starts way back where the indirect expenses are prorated to the departmental account. This account also accumulates the indirect material and indirect labor. If the direct labor dollar method of applying overhead rates is used, the manufacturing expense for the department is divided by the dollars of direct labor used in that department. Remember that this, of necessity, is done with past information and will not necessarily reflect conditions as they exist now, but it is the best estimate that can be made.

The overhead is applied to the cost summary sheet, along with the accumulation of direct labor and direct material costs, to complete the manufacturing cost for the product.

Sources of Cost Information

The various costs have been defined and the logic for developing the manufacturing cost has been shown. But what are the sources of these various cost data? This depends upon whether we are working before or after the fact. Working before the fact is the process of estimating, and the sources of the cost information are quite different from working after the fact. The flow of information into the cost summary sheet for *after-the-fact costing* is illustrated by Figure 7–6. The direct-labor costs are obtained from

Figure 7–6
After-the-Fact Costing

Source: Production Control Forms

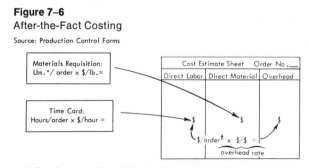

* For the example, weight has been used as the unit of measure, but it could be any other, such as board feet, gallons, or tons.

† The overhead is applied on the basis of direct-labor dollars in the example, but it could just as well have been any of the other methods mentioned in the text.

the time cards. The material costs are obtained from the materials requisitions which have gone through the stores record section to obtain both the cost and quantity. The overhead is applied using the overhead rate. The development of the overhead rate and the method of application are the responsibility of the accounting department.

The source of cost information for *before-the-fact costing* (or estimating [Figure 7–7]) is considerably different than that for after-the-fact cost-

Figure 7–7
Before-the-Fact Costing (estimating)
Source of Calculations:

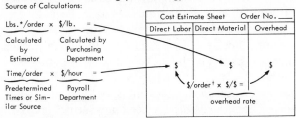

* For the example, weight has been used as the unit of measure, but it could be any other, such as board feet, gallons, or tons.

† The overhead is applied on the basis of direct-labor dollars in the example, but it could just as well have been any of the other methods mentioned in the text.

ing. Since it is of greater importance to the subject of production planning and control, more time will be spent on it.

Direct Labor Costs. The time required to do a task can be derived by one of the methods to be described in Chapter 8. For estimating, usually the more precise methods are not necessary, and tables of gross times are suitable. Metal processing companies (and others) will frequently develop their own time data from actual experience. When the elapsed time is composed of machine-dictated time and man-dictated time, these two are calculated separately and then added:

(Man time + Machine time) × Labor rate = Direct labor costs.

The labor rates are often tabulated for each production center, but the source of this information is the payroll department.

Direct Material Costs. Because the materials vary so greatly from product to product, it is difficult to generalize on the methods of calculation, but an example from the fastener industry will give you some idea of the process. Consider a small hexagonal head bolt made of brass. This could be made from a hexagon bar stock, which comes in lengths of about 15 feet. The problem is to determine the gross weight of the bolt.

Fortunately, a table in an engineering handbook will give the weight of the bar stock per inch. If the scrap is to be credited to the cost, the net weight of the bolt must also be found. This can be done quite rapidly by considering each part of the bolt as a geometric form: a cylinder, square, or hexagon. The weight per lineal inch for these forms can also be found in a table. The cost per pound of materials, including the shipping charges, can be obtained from the purchasing department. If the scrap is to be credited, it will be credited at the scrap price and not the price of the bar stock.

Overhead Costs. The overhead rate is furnished to the estimator by the cost accounting department. The way of applying, such as the direct labor dollar method or direct labor method, will not be decided by the estimator but will have been made by management at some earlier time.

Example of a Cost Estimate. How all the foregoing concepts fit together to produce an estimate is illustrated in Figure 7–8. The example is kept as simple as possible, yet it must still show the basic ideas. The cost estimating sheet, in this example, accompanies the operation sheet. This is logical since the process design must be decided before the costs can be estimated. Notice that this is just one process design, and there are probably others. For example, the number of cavities in the die might have been more or less than 16, and a different material might have been selected. All the alternatives should be considered by the process designer and should be checked by the costing methods shown. Often the costs have been previously worked out for various quantities, so decisions become automatic, and each process is not checked every time a product is made.

Our example is an actual cost estimate for a plastics company. You will notice that their cost breakdown is slightly different from the previous example. This is typical of the variation you can expect from industry to industry. In particular, you will find tooling and set-up costs handled in different ways. Some companies include these costs in the overhead while others add them to the total manufacturing costs.

Decision Making

An understanding of the cost information developed in this chapter is essential for decision making throughout production planning and control. Cost will be used for inventory control, scheduling, learning curve, and other decision-making models.

Cost is also used for the direct comparison between processes. The process planner may have to make a decision between mounting a part in a fixture for milling and mounting a part in a magnetic chuck to grind. The milling process will be much faster, but the fixture will cost more than would mounting the part in the magnetic chuck for the slower process of grinding. A quick check of the costs for both processes will tell which is the best decision. Another example might be a choice between using some old cams for an automatic screw machine (which will take longer to do the job at hand) or some new, specially designed cams. The problem is whether the reduced production rate with the old cams will be more costly than making new cams. These and many other problems can be solved by making a direct comparison of cost between the two processes.

Although cost permeates all production planning and control, there are

Figure 7–8
Example of a Cost Estimate

INDUSTRIAL PLASTICS, Inc.

Job Quotation Worksheet

Quote No. 2435

Date 12 - 16 -

Customer Keen Edge Knife Co.
Part Name Display Box Part No. —
Quote Promised 12-20-64 By TIM

MOLDS: Number of cavities 16 comb.
Machine Size
Cycle 30 sec.

COST: Hourly Production 864
Administration/hr. 4.80
Machine Overhead/hr. 3.25
Labor/hr. 4.80

MATERIAL: Type General purpose crystal
Lot Size —
Cost/lb. 1.45
Weight 50.7
Scrap 5.3
Weight-Gross 56.0

MISC. SUPPLIES:
Cartons 80
Tape 66

SUMMARY:

Raw Material	8	12		
Misc. Material	1	46		
Overhead	3	76		
Labor	5	56		
Manufacturing Costs			18	90
Administration			5	56
TOTAL PRODUCT COST				24.46
PROFIT			3	67
SELLING PRICE				28.13

DAILY PRODUCTION 20, 736

WEEKLY PRODUCTION 103, 680

some special techniques for making decisions which should be discussed.

The Break-Even Chart. The break-even chart is in reality two charts, one superimposed upon the other, and for the sake of clarity, each will be discussed separately. The expense chart (Figure 7–9A) has expenses on the ordinate (vertical) axis and production on the abscissa (horizontal) axis. In the diagram the *fixed costs* are separated from the *variable costs*. Fixed

Figure 7–9
Break-Even Chart

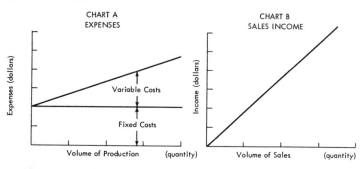

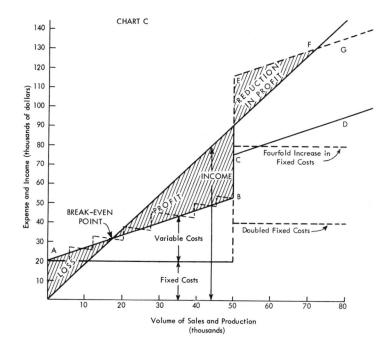

costs remain fairly constant throughout a range of output: rent, insurance, and taxes, for example. The variable costs increase with production.

You are cautioned here to consider the cost with reference to the plant and not to the product. If you consider the product, you will become confused, as the fixed and variable cost concepts will be reversed. As production increases, the fixed costs per unit will become less and the variable costs will remain fixed. The concept of fixed and variable costs used in the diagram refers to the production center or factory.

The second chart is the sales income chart (Figure 7–9B). This chart also has production on the horizontal axis, as did the expense chart, but the sales income is on the vertical axis. It is assumed that when production is zero, the sales are zero. It is further assumed that sales income will increase linearly with production, which of course is not always true. When these two charts are superimposed upon each other, we have the typical break-even chart shown in Figure 7–9C.

The reason this is called a break-even chart is apparent upon inspection. The point at which the income exceeds the expenses is called the break-even point. This chart is an oversimplification of reality. The relationships, in most cases, won't be linear but will have steps—as represented by the dashed line.

The example given here is for a small company manufacturing a livestock spray which sells for $1.80 a gallon. The fixed expense for the factory is $20,000 a year with a maximum output of 50,000 gallons. The variable expense is $0.66 per gallon. It is apparent that the company must sell a little more than $30,000 worth to break even. The profits will be enhanced as more and more is sold because the fixed costs can be spread over more items. This chart, as we will see, can reveal interesting information for decision making.

The capacity of the plant is 50,000 gallons a year, but what would happen if additional plant facilities were added to the picture? Suppose the plant were doubled in size and the fixed cost was also doubled (line AB–CD). The profits will increase, but at a lower rate.

If the plant were increased fourfold, as shown by A–B–E–F–G, there would be a loss between E–F which must be offset against the profit. Not until this point is past will profit improve. This is a condition well worth remembering when one increases the size of a processing unit. The break-even chart can be used to simulate many conditions to obtain a better grasp of what changes will do to the profit.

Process Comparison Charts.   Related to the break-even chart is the comparison chart (Figure 7–10). This chart is used for deciding whether to use one process or another. Typical of this decision is whether—for a particular product—a turret lathe, a single spindle screw machine, or a multiple spindle screw machine should be employed. The tooling costs will become progressively higher in each instance, but the labor costs per unit would be lower. The basic problem is to weigh the labor costs against the tooling costs. Below point A, it pays to use the turret lathe, and between A and B, the single spindle automatic screw machine. The point where the lines cross, at A and B, is often called a break-even point, which is undoubtedly a carryover from the previous chart. This chart can also be used for simulation by varying the data. The numerous applications of this type of chart depend upon the imagination of the person seeking the answers for decisions.

Cost Reporting Charts.   A form of cost report, which has been useful in some project work, is shown in Figure 7–11. This chart plots three kinds of information:

Figure 7–10
Process Comparison Chart

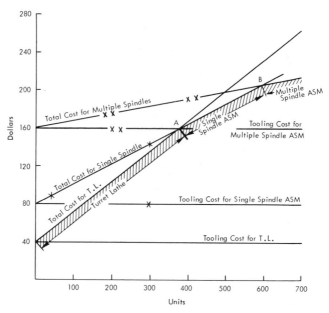

1. *Actual costs:* Those costs which have been incurred to date.
2. *Budgeted costs:* Those costs which have been anticipated.
3. *Estimated costs for performance:* Those costs which could be anticipated for the performance at this date.

Two examples are given in the chart. In the first example the actual costs
are less than what had been budgeted for the elapsed time; however, the
performance is less than had been anticipated. In the second example, the
actual costs are more than the budgeted cost, but the work performed is
greater than had been anticipated.

These are just a few of the charting techniques in which cost information
can be applied for decision making. Other techniques are included throughout the book, so it is essential that you have a comprehension of how costs
are derived.

Cost Estimating in Practice

A logic for estimating costs has been developed in this section, but not
all companies follow the step-by-step procedure illustrated. Many companies
are more likely to have someone estimating costs who has been in the business a long time. The process for estimating might go something like this:

Figure 7–11
Cost Report Chart

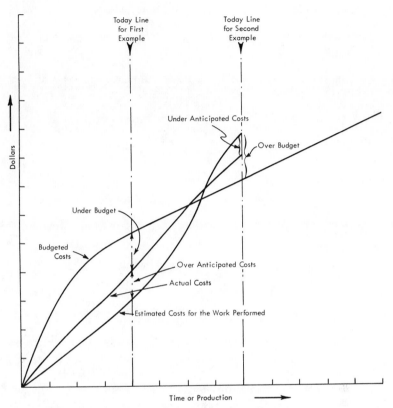

This looks like a part we made three years ago for a certain company. We lost some money on that job so we will add 15 percent in order not to lose again. In the meantime we have negotiated a new labor contract, so we will increase the price by 25 percent rather than by 15 percent. This part is a little thinner in some sections than was the other part, so we can reduce the cost by 10 percent, but there are two extra holes to drill and tap which increase the price by 20 percent. . . .

Amazingly, these estimates often prove correct to the penny, but one suspects that the factory workers *make* it come out that way. In some cases they may lose large sums of money—which are fortunately made up by some other estimate which has a compensating error. As in any process, it is well to understand the logic so as to realize the risks involved when a shortcut is taken.

Summary

The price of a product is determined by many factors which are usually beyond the realm of the factory personnel. The factory contributes to the profit by reducing the manufacturing costs. The manufacturing costs for a product can be determined by four equations which should be first-hand knowledge to at least all supervisory personnel.

(1) Manufacturing costs = Direct labor costs + Direct material costs + Overhead costs.

(2)
$$\frac{\text{Overhead costs for a job}}{\text{Direct labor costs for a job}} = \frac{\text{Overhead costs for last year}}{\text{Direct labor costs for last year}}.$$

(*The right-hand side of this last equation is known as the* overhead rate.)

If departmental overhead rates are needed instead of plantwide overhead rates:

(3) Overhead for department = Indirect labor for department + Indirect material for department + Indirect expenses for department.

The indirect expenses may be calculated by an equation similar to no. 2 above:

(4)
$$\frac{\text{Indirect expense (taxes) for department in dollars}}{\text{Floor space for department in square feet}} =$$

$$\frac{\text{Indirect expense (taxes) for factory in dollars}}{\text{Floor space for factory in square feet}}.$$

Of course, in this last equation, each indirect expense is prorated on an appropriate basis. The example has been for property tax, but it could have been for any other indirect expense, such as insurance or heating.

The objective in the estimating procedure is to obtain the manufacturing costs, which means that the equations must be solved in the reverse of the order shown. Normally the accounting department will be responsible for nos. 3 and 4 and will furnish the *overhead rate* for solving no. 2.

The costs can be obtained before the fact (estimating), or after the job is done, for cost comparison purposes. Costs are of vital importance to nearly all the activities of production planning and control—in fact this one word might be said to be the theme of this book.

QUESTIONS

7–1. Select several common products and suggest how the selling price is determined.
7–2. What are the three cost factors which make up the manufacturing cost?
7–3. Discuss how the production control department applies cost information to scheduling, expediting, and routing.
7–4. Estimate the cost of a product with which you are familiar, such as a spool of thread or a candy bar.
7–5. Why should burden rates be calculated from historical data?
7–6. Explain why burden rates are never right.

7-7. Give an example of a company which could use a uniform burden rate for an entire factory.

7-8. What could a company do about obtaining a true burden rate when it is just starting business?

7-9. Companies producing products on a production line may use job order costing systems. Explain why.

7-10. In choosing the denominator for the burden rate you should look for certain characteristics. What are they and why are they important?

7-11. Break-even charts are often drawn with straight lines. Is this realistic? Draw a chart for a particular company showing how you would expect the lines to appear.

7-12. Explain, by means of a break-even chart, why some companies find their profits reduced when they increase their production facilities.

7-13. It is not uncommon to find small industries operating out of the family garage and competing very well. When they expand to more luxurious facilities they often fail. Explain this by means of a break-even chart.

7-14. How many processes can be compared on one process comparison chart?

8

Capacity Planning and Scheduling Information

CAPACITY PLANNING and scheduling are two subjects of increasing concern to the production and inventory control manager. Basic to these activities is a knowledge of the time available to do a task and how long a time it actually takes. This chapter describes how you can determine these times for capacity planning and scheduling. If you have had a thorough background on this subject you may wish to go on to the next chapter. On the other hand, you may find that this chapter is an excellent review and puts the subject in perspective.

Since we are interested in the efficient planning and control of a factory, it is essential to know the best ways to develop the necessary time information. This subject makes up part of this chapter, but we must also know the strengths and weaknesses of these time data. In addition, you will observe the effect of learning upon time estimates. You will also become acquainted with the various *industrial calendars* found in today's factories.

Use of Time Estimates

Our major interest in time values for tasks is in their application to scheduling and capacity planning, but this is not their only use. For example, time estimates are tied directly to the wage incentive plan. They are also used in the scientific cost estimate, as we have seen. Where the activities are composed of several men or machines, the time estimates can be used to balance the loads. Motion study, which is the analysis and improvement of methods of doing work, goes hand in hand with the determination of time values, for how else could the improvement be measured?

With all the various uses for time estimates it is little wonder they do not meet all the objectives. Also, it is reasonable to expect different degrees of accuracy to be required for the various uses. This is true, and we should be able to select the proper measuring tool for the work to be done.

METHODS FOR ESTIMATING TIME VALUES

A number of techniques are used in determining the time required for factory and office activities. Some of these methods can only give crude approximations of the actual time while others can give quite accurate information. The common methods will be briefly discussed in this order:

1. Time estimates based on past experience.
2. Stop-watch time study.
3. Elemental standard data.
4. Predetermined motion-time data.
5. Work sampling.

Past Experience Estimates

Probably no self-respecting devotee of scientific management would ever recognize this method of obtaining time information. Nevertheless, the technique does exist to a considerable extent when the information is used for scheduling. This method is practiced by recording the past performance of an operation, often directly on the operation sheet. When this job, or a similar one, is to be run again, the information is pulled from the file and used with perhaps some modifications for changes in machines, operators, materials, and the other variables. Lacking this past performance record, a *guesstimate* is made using the past experience of similar projects familiar to several production people. Such estimates should not be used as a basis for wage payments, of course, but in scheduling they can be used satisfactorily if the personnel are experienced and no better information is available.

Stop-Watch Time Study

Stop-watch time study is the most common method of measuring the time that it takes to accomplish a task. Dr. Ralph M. Barnes, a pioneer developer of this tool of scientific management, defines time study thus: "Time study is used to determine the time required by a qualified and well-trained person working at a normal pace to do a specified task."[1]

The objective of the time study is to determine the *standard time*. This is defined as the time it takes to do a task, usually expressed in minutes per part. At a glance, it would appear that this can be obtained by going out on

---

[1] Ralph M. Barnes, *Motion and Time Study: Design and Measurement of Work*, 6th ed. (New York: Wiley, 1968), p. 342.

the factory floor with a watch and timing the task, but it isn't quite that simple.

First, when you time the task you have no assurance that the worker is doing the task at a *normal pace*, for he may be working faster or slower than the average. Therefore it is necessary to modify or *normalize* the task time as measured by the watch. Second, we usually cannot time the task all day,

Figure 8–1
Time Study Recording Equipment

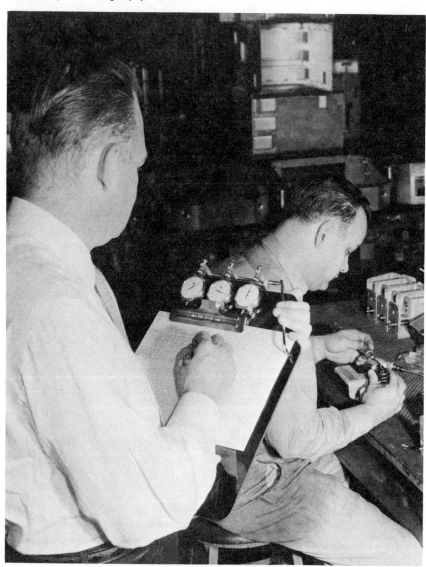

Courtesy of Meylan Stopwatch Corporation

and therefore cannot include all the additional time needed for personal needs and other delays which are inherent in the work. It is obvious that the time values we obtain during our short stay on the factory floor will have to be modified in two ways: one, to make them represent the normal pace; second, to allow for the unavoidable delays that occur during the task.

There are some variations in the way stop-watch time studies are made, but the following discussion will give a brief summary of a common method. The equipment used by the time study analyst consists of time study data sheets, conveniently secured to a clipboard to which a decimal stop watch is attached (Figure 8–1). The analyst takes up a position from which he can conveniently observe both the task being performed and the watch and board. It should be pointed out that there are other timing methods used, such as strip recorders, but the common method is the decimal stop watch.

The entire stop-watch procedure can be best understood by following it step by step. The recorded results of these steps are indicated directly on the time sheet (Figure 8–2).

Step 1. Observe and Record Job Conditions. First, the analyst should observe the job for a period of time and discuss it fully with the foreman in

Figure 8–2
Time Study Data Sheet

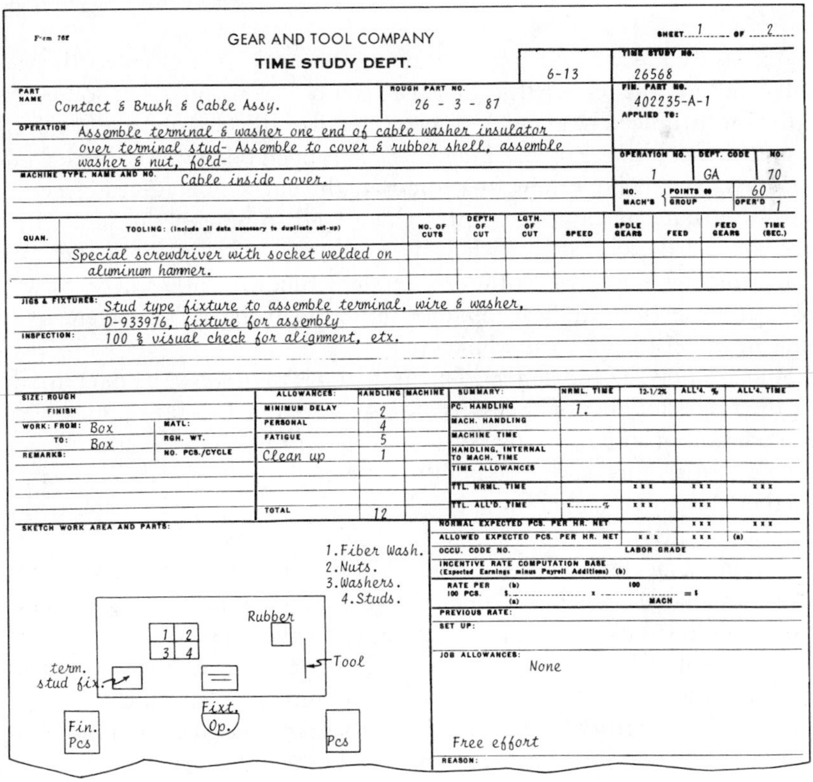
Form 762
GEAR AND TOOL COMPANY
TIME STUDY DEPT.
SHEET 1 OF 2
6-13
TIME STUDY NO. 26568
PART NAME Contact & Brush & Cable Assy.
ROUGH PART NO. 26 - 3 - 87
FIN. PART NO. 402235-A-1
APPLIED TO:
OPERATION Assemble terminal & washer one end of cable washer insulator over terminal stud- Assemble to cover & rubber shell, assemble washer & nut, fold-
MACHINE TYPE, NAME AND NO. Cable inside cover.
OPERATION NO. 1 DEPT. CODE GA NO. 70
NO. MACH'S POINTS 60 GROUP OPER'D 1

QUAN.	TOOLING: (Include all data necessary to duplicate set-up)	NO. OF CUTS	DEPTH OF CUT	LGTH. OF CUT	SPEED	SPDLE GEARS	FEED	FEED GEARS	TIME (SEC.)
	Special screwdriver with socket welded on aluminum hammer.								

JIGS & FIXTURES: Stud type fixture to assemble terminal, wire & washer, D-933976, fixture for assembly
INSPECTION: 100 % visual check for alignment, etx.

SIZE: ROUGH
FINISH
WORK: FROM: Box TO: Box
MATL:
RGH. WT.
NO. PCS./CYCLE
REMARKS:

ALLOWANCES:	HANDLING	MACHINE
MINIMUM DELAY	2	
PERSONAL	4	
FATIGUE	5	
Clean up	1	
TOTAL	12	

SUMMARY:	NRML. TIME	12-1/2%	ALL'4. %	ALL'4. TIME
PC. HANDLING	1.			
MACH. HANDLING				
MACHINE TIME				
HANDLING, INTERNAL TO MACH. TIME				
TIME ALLOWANCES				
TTL. NRML. TIME		x x x	x x x	x x x
TTL. ALL'D. TIME	x........%	x x x	x x x	
NORMAL EXPECTED PCS. PER HR. NET			x x x	x x x
ALLOWED EXPECTED PCS. PER HR. NET		x x x	x x x	(a)

OCCU. CODE NO. LABOR GRADE
INCENTIVE RATE COMPUTATION BASE (Expected Earnings minus Payroll Additions) (b)
RATE PER 100 PCS. $ (b)/(a) x 100/MACH = $
PREVIOUS RATE:
SET UP:
JOB ALLOWANCES: None
Free effort
REASON:

SKETCH WORK AREA AND PARTS:

Figure 8–2 (continued)

DATE

TIME STUDY SHEET
SHEET 2 OF 2

START	STOP	ELAPSED	PART AND OPERATION:
2:30	4:30	--	Contact & Brush & Cable Assy--

DESCRIPTION OF ELEMENT	1	2	3	4	5	6	7	8	9	10	TTL	AV.	SLCT	PERF. RTG.	Norm TIME
1. Position washer fix. stud	8	9	9	8	9	7	10	7	6	7	2.32				
pos. cable & stud - hit stud-	08	94	84	36	18	99	04	83	59	38	28	0829			
2. Pick up cable assembly, pos	13	12	16	8	9	10	13	13	10	10	3.16				
stud & bend wire down.	21	06	00	44	27	09	17	96	69	48	28	1129			
3. Pos. fiber washer over	16	12	16	8	11	19	12	13	18	17	4.03				
term.studs pos, cover over.stud-	37	24	16	52	38	28	29	09	82	65	28	1439			
4. Pick up rubber shell &	8	10	10	12	10	11	10	8	12	14	3.20				
fit washer into shell & shake to seat.	45	34	26	64	48	39	39	17	94	79	28	1143			
5. Pick up special socket wrench, position nut into socket & then to shell-	12	11	8	16	10	8	10	9	9	10	2.77				
	57	45	34	80	58	60	49	26	03	89	28	0989			
6. Position to terminal stud start nut - secure nut-	15	16	16	18	19	14	15	14	15	16	4.17				
	72	61	50	98	77	74	64	40	18	05	28	1489			
7. Pick up assembly, remove wrench. Alignment, bend wire per print.	13	14	15	11	15	20	12	13	13	14	4.95				
	85	75	65	09	92	94	76	53	31	19	28	1411			
												8429			
						.8429 X 1.10 = .9272									
						.9272 + (.9272 X 12%) =								1.0384

charge, as well as with the operator doing the work. It is essential that the task conditions be recorded so that they can be reconstructed at some time in the future if need be. Therefore, every detail of the task must be recorded.

Step 2. Establish the Cycle Elements. The operation cycle is divided into elements. This is important to assure that the entire operation is recorded and to separate machine elements, which tend to remain the same, from man-controlled elements, which may vary. As we will see later, these elements might be used to synthesize standard times for other tasks as well. Also, in some time study techniques the normalizing is done element by element rather than for the whole cycle.

Step 3. Time the Elements. The next step is to observe the operator doing the task a number of times, recording the time taken for each element. There has been some controversy as to whether the watch should run continuously, with the analyst taking the time at the end of each element, or whether the watch hands should be "snapped back" to zero at the end of each element. Both methods appear to give good results.

This phase of the stop-watch time study is a sampling procedure, and we must take a large enough sample to represent the population. This is an extensive subject, but the recognized texts in the field not only develop the statistics behind the sampling procedure, they also have tables and charts which can be used in determining the correct number of readings.

Step 4. Normalizing the Recorded Time. According to our definition, we wish to determine the normal pace needed to do a specified task. We have used the word normalize as being more descriptive, but the process is more commonly called *rating*. In the rating process the time study analyst compares the actual performance of the operator with a concept of *normal performance*. This concept of normal performance is frequently reinforced by observing rating films in which a number of levels of performance are known. The result of Step 4 is the *normal time*. There are various other ways of rating, one being *objective rating*, in which each element is rated.

Step 5. The Addition of Allowances. The normal time developed in Step 4 is usually obtained over a relatively short period, so it does not account for any rest, personal time, or other delays. Since these are to be expected, we must increase the normal time. This information is usually in a table prepared from all-day time studies.

Briefly, these have been steps in making a stop-watch time study, but the method might be more obvious if we simply state the equations used in obtaining the *standard time*.

$$\text{Selected time} \times \text{Rating} = \text{Normal time}$$
$$\text{(also called } base\ time, leveled\ \text{or } rated\ time)$$

To the *normal time* must then be added the allowance to obtain the *standard time*.

$$\text{Normal time} + (\text{Normal time} \times \text{Allowance}) = \text{Standard time}$$

To start with, we obtain the *selected time* for the task. We have divided the task cycle into distinctive, easily measured elements, and have determined the time for a number of cycles of these elements which will give a representative sample. The number of cycles must be large enough to assure that the times are representative. A common way of obtaining a representative time for the cycle is to add and average all the readings. This cycle time is referred to as the selected time.

The selected time, as we know, may not be representative of a normal pace, so the time study analyst must modify it by multiplying by a rating factor. As we will see later, it is the rating factor which might cause us difficulty in applying the standard times to scheduling. This subject is worthy of a lengthy discussion but we should first see how it is part of the other methods of estimating time values. To the normal time must be added time for rest and personal needs. This is done by the allowance, which varies from task to task, depending upon the specific requirements of that task.

Elemental Times

In certain kinds of work, such as in the metal working industry, standard times can be synthesized from the elements of previous time studies. For example, in simple drilling operations the time for loading the jig is nearly the same as for an entire family of tasks. The machine time, on the other hand, will vary from task to task because of the size and depth of the hole to be drilled. The same is true for milling operations, lathe operations, and many other tasks. Consequently, we can separate the man-time from the machine-time, calculate each separately, and then combine them into a standard time.

Man Time. Standards departments take advantage of the similarity among jobs and accumulate the times for common elements, which they then compile into a table. Lacking time study data of their own, they might resort to one of the compilations of data (Figure 8–3) available in one of

Figure 8–3
Elemental Times for Drilling*

> *Method 2.*—To be used for the drilling of one hole in bolts, small tubes or shafts, cotter-pin holes, etc. A small jig is used, and the part is held in place by one setscrew.
>
> *Minutes*
> 1. Pick up part from tote pan, and install in jig 120
> 2. Position jig and work on table under spindle 060
> 3. Advance drill to work 030
> 4. Drill, ream, tap, etc.   See Tables 69–78
> 5. Clear drill 020
> 6. Release part from jig 080
> 7. Aside with part to tote pan 050
> 8. Blow jig and table clean to receive next load 100
> 9. Unit time to check part   See Chap. IV
> 10. Unit time to sharpen drill   See Table 68
> 11. Personal allowance 5%
> 12. Fatigue allowance   See Chap. IV

* W. A. Nordhoff, *Machine Shop Estimating* (New York: McGraw-Hill, 1947).

the commercially available handbooks. This is for one simple operation, but these books cover most of the common machine tools. Other information is available for other industries as well.

Machine Time. Often the times for machine operations are compiled in a table. The time it takes for threading one inch of rod in various diameters and materials is an example. Sometimes this information is not attainable and one must work from the basic information of feeds, speeds, and depth of cut. This is a subject with which you should be familiar and one which will be discussed later in this chapter.

PREDETERMINED MOTION-TIME STANDARDS

Predetermined motion-time standards are more refined than the elemental time methods just described. In the elemental time method the units measured were gross compared with the units used in predetermined motion times. The characteristic of the predetermined motion-time standard is to consider the basic motions for which extensive time data have been obtained by such techniques as time study, frame-by-frame analysis of motion pictures, and, more recently, by electronic instrumentation.

There are a number of predetermined motion-time standard systems available which go under such names as methods time measurement (MTM), work factor plan (WF), basic motion-time study (BMT), and others. The basic motions, with their associated time values for the MTM system, are shown in the following tables (Figure 8–4). These values are all normalized but do not include any allowances. To show how quickly this system can be put to the task of calculating a standard time, observe the calculations for the illustration in Figure 8–5.

Figure 8–4
MTM Tables

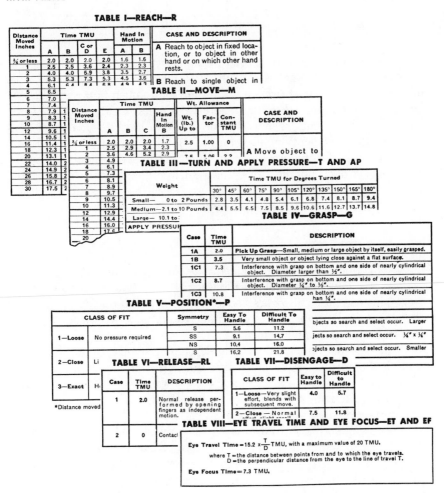

Figure 8–5
MTM Example Problem

METHODS ANALYSIS CHART					REFERENCE No. ___ _____
PART___ _"C" Clamp_____			DATE_____		STUDY No. _____
OPERATION ___ _Remove small "C" Clamp_____			ANALYST_____		SHEET No. ____OF___ SHEETS

DESCRIPTION — LEFT HAND	No.	L H	TMU	R H	No.	DESCRIPTION — RIGHT HAND
Reach for clamp		R24B	21.5	R24B		Reach to clamp handle
Grasp clamp		G1A	2.0	G1A		Grasp handle
			16.2	AP1		Loosen (apply pressure)
			9.4	T180S		Turn handle
			4.0	RL1	2	Release
			18.8	T180	2	Turn hand back
			4.0	G1A	2	Grasp handle
			18.8	T180S	2	Turn handle
Regrasp clamp		G2	5.6	RL1		Release
Remove clamp		M16B	15.8			
Lay aside clamp		M24B	20.6			
Release		RL1	2.0			
			138.7			

These motion times can be used to engineer the methods and times for tasks even before the task is actually performed by an operator. In actual practice, on highly repetitive work the time for an operation is synthesized directly from the tables shown in Figure 8–4. On less highly repetitive work, standard data elements, such as the one shown in Figure 8–5, are first built up. Then these elements are used for the establishing of methods and standards. By means of the process of building up standard elements from the basic motion data, nonrepetitive work—such as the building of an entire ship and various kinds of maintenance work—has been successfully placed on standards, even to the setting of incentive rates.

Work Sampling

Work sampling is a method of analyzing and evaluating the time used for work by a series of random observations which are extended over a period of time. This technique also goes under the name of *ratio delay* because one of the first applications was to determine the ratio between the delay and the actual work being performed.

While our main interest here is in developing standard times for scheduling, it should not be concluded that this is the only application for this technique. It is useful in determining the allowances as used in stop-watch time study, balancing work loads in multiple man-machine operations, and other instances when work is to be measured.

Work sampling has the advantage over conventional stop-watch studies in that special skill is not required for observations and a high degree of accuracy is obtained without constant observation. In fact, the answer given by work sampling might be more accurate than all-day studies.

First observe how a standard time is calculated by means of work sampling; then we shall develop more fully the logic behind this valuable measuring tool. The standard time for a task by work sampling can be calculated in the following manner:

$$\begin{array}{l}\text{Standard time}\\ \text{(min./part)}\end{array} = \frac{\begin{array}{c}\text{Total time}\\ \text{(in min.)}\end{array} \times \begin{array}{c}\text{Working time}\\ \text{(in percent)}\end{array} \times \begin{array}{c}\text{Performance index}\\ \text{(in percent)}\end{array}}{\text{Total number of pieces produced}} + \begin{array}{c}\text{Allowance}\\ \text{min./part}\end{array}$$

Information for the above equation is to be found in several places:

Total time, in minutes, can be found in the past experience of the time cards.

Working time, in percent, is to be found in the sampling technique to be discussed.

Performance index, in percent, is the same objective method as used in the stop-watch time study, for rating.

Allowances are determined in the same way as those used in the stop-watch time study. Both the rating factor and the allowances might have been the result of a work sampling study.

Total number of parts is available from the company's records.

We shall now proceed to discuss how the percentage of working time is obtained, since it is the only factor not readily available for the equation.

Work sampling is based on the laws of probability, discussed in Chapter 4. By determining the characteristics of a sample it is possible to predict the characteristics of a population. The standard time for a task extending over a long period can be obtained by merely taking a sample of data. This can be seen by means of an illustration. Assume there is some task which runs for a period of eight hours, represented by the lines in Figure 8–6. This, incidentally, could be a man and machine activity, running simultaneously, in which case we could have used one bar to represent each activity. To keep the example straightforward, consider one man working eight hours, or 480 minutes, so the bars represent 480 discrete time units.

If the man's activity was observed and recorded all day, it would be seen that he works most of the time. In fact, the example shows the man working 80 percent of the time and not working 20 percent of the time (as represented by the dark bar).

This all-day observation is too expensive and might even be impossible if we were observing a number of activities. Sampling is a better method and, strange as it may seem, can be more accurate.

The sample taken must be random; that is, every minute of the working period must have an equal chance of being the one observed. One way of doing this is to number the time increments on the chart from 1 to 480, then to take a similar amount of numbered chips, shake them in a container, and draw them at random. For example, if a sample of 40 was taken, the times indicated on the bar chart by short vertical lines might have been drawn. A

Figure 8–6
Work Sampling Example

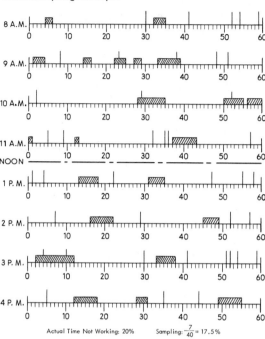

Actual Time Not Working: 20%   Sampling: $\frac{7}{40} = 17.5\%$

more sophisticated and less tedious method would have been to select numbers from a random number table (to be found in many statistical texts). The results might have been:

Number of times observed *not* working . . . . = 7⎫
Number of times observed . . . . = 40⎭ 7/40 = *p*

The ratio between the number of times observed not working and the number of times observed is a sample proportion, *p*, which is used to predict the true proportion, *p'*. The symbols in this discussion will conform to the literature of work sampling rather than to the statistics of forecasting to be found in Chapter 4. The concepts are the same, so you should encounter little difficulty in transferring your knowledge or in reading the work sampling literature.

The observations, being either yes or no, form a binomial distribution which fortunately can be approximated, in this case, by a normal distribution.[2] Consequently, we can use the normal-curve tables referred to earlier to determine the probability of obtaining any proportion, *p*, of a sample.

---

[2] Refer to Chapter 4. The normal-curve approximation is fairly good under the conditions of work sampling.

The standard deviation for a binomial distribution is:

$$\sigma_p = \sqrt{\frac{p(1-p)}{n}}$$

where

$p =$ Sample proportion of occurrences expressed as a decimal or percent
$n =$ Number of items in a sample

Pursuing the same logic used in the previous discussion of statistics, two standard deviations either side of the mean will include 95.4 percent of the occurrences. Thus we say the confidence limits are 95 percent (rounded), which means that events could occur outside these limits 5 percent of the time just by chance. The value of the standard deviation, as can be seen from the equation, is dependent upon the value of p and n, but the acceptable dispersion in terms of σ_p is established as a policy. These two viewpoints can be grasped more easily by a diagram, Figure 8–7. First, you should be cau-

Figure 8–7
Logic of Sampling for Work Sampling

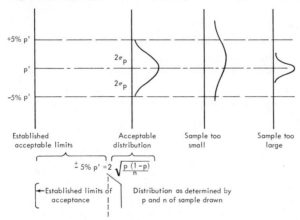

tioned that p is varying from sample to sample, and while it is illustrated on the diagram as being in one position, it is in reality constantly shifting until we zero in on the true value, p', as the sample size becomes larger.

The established acceptable limits, or accuracy, a, is often set at $\pm$ 5 percent p'. This seems to be a workable value, and for the example—where we believe the true p' is 20 percent—the limits would be established at 19 percent and 21 percent.

It is apparent that the standard deviation decreases directly with the square root of the sample size. It would not be economical to take an extensive sample if it were not needed. The problem is to solve the equation for n, but there is another unknown in the equation, and that is p. The solution to this dilemma is to first take a sample to get a rough approximation of p, insert that in the equation, and solve for n. When a sample of n has been collected, recalculate p, and from this calculate a new value of n until the $2\sigma_p$ is within the accuracy established. To get some idea of how p and n are interrelated, study Figure 8–8.

Figure 8–8
Observations Required for Work Sampling*

	Number of Observations Required 95 Percent Confidence				
	Relative Error			Absolute Error	
p \ a	1%	5%	10%	1%	3.5%
10	360,000	14,400	3,600	3,600	294
20	160,000	6,400	1,600	6,400	522
30	93,300	3,730	935	8,400	686

* Ralph M. Barnes, *Work Sampling,* 2d ed. (New York: Wiley, 1957), pp. 30, 36.

From the table it becomes obvious that the number of readings required becomes extensive if p and the limits of accuracy, a, are small. This has brought some to consider the use of an *absolute* measure of accuracy, a percent, rather than a *relative* measure, $p \pm a$ percent. Further information regarding this can be found in the work sampling references listed in the References.

The following is a step-by-step procedure for determining the standard time by work sampling:

Step 1. Policy has been established in the standards department that p will be within ± 5 percent, with a 95 percent confidence.

Step 2. An initial study shows the operator was idle 16 times out of 100, or 16 percent of the time; $p = 16$ percent.

Step 3. Determine the number of readings needed. The accuracy ± 5 percent must be included in 95 percent, or roughly $2\sigma_p$, either side of the mean.

$$0.05p = 2\sqrt{\frac{p(1-p)}{n}}$$

$$n = \frac{4p(1-p)}{0.0025p^2}$$

$$n = \frac{4 \times 0.16(1 - 0.16)}{0.0025 \times 0.16^2} = 8,400 \text{ readings}$$

Step 4. Part way through the study it appeared that the p value was nearly 20 percent rather than 16 percent, as thought at first. This is of interest because the size of the sample can be reduced.

$$n = \frac{4p(1 - p)}{0.0025p^2} = 6{,}400 \text{ readings}$$

Step 5. The p value is checked periodically to see if it is within the limits desired. It is finally determined that $p = 19$ percent. This can now be included in the standard time equation. (Note: Only the delay time, as a percentage of the entire time, has been developed here. All other information for the standard time will be found elsewhere in the standards department.)

Step 6. Calculate the standard time:

$$\text{Standard time (min./part)} = \frac{\substack{\text{Total time} \\ \text{(in min.)}} \times \substack{\text{Working time} \\ \text{(in percent)}} \times \substack{\text{Performance index} \\ \text{(in percent)}}}{\text{Total number of pieces produced}}$$
$$+ \text{ Allowance}$$

$$\text{Standard time (min./part)} = \frac{15{,}000 \text{ min.} \times (1.00 - 0.19) \times 0.95}{4{,}300 \text{ parts}}$$
$$+ 15 \text{ percent allowance}$$

Standard time $= 3.09$ minutes/part

The five ways of determining the time needed to perform a task have been developed. It is not supposed that from this you will become a proficient technician, but you should have some insight into the source of time information before discussing how it is applied to systems design.

Errors Caused by Rating

A basic difficulty in using the standard times developed by the methods described is that they are used primarily with wage incentive systems, and the objectives are somewhat different than they are for scheduling. This problem can be pointed out by means of a diagram (Figure 8–9).

An incentive is no incentive at all unless it affects most of the people. This means that both the good and the poor operators must come under the incentive system. However, there is considerable difference between the good operator and the poor operator. In fact, it has been shown that this relationship is in the order of two to one. The best worker produces two times as much as the poorest, and the workers in between these two extremes would form a frequency distribution as shown. Because most workers should make incentive pay, the standard of performance is set to the left of the average performance.

How far to the left the standard performance should be depends upon the policy of the company. The average worker is usually expected to earn 25 to 30 percent incentive, which would place the standard of performance to the left on the curve, as shown.

This means that if standard times are to be used for scheduling, they

Figure 8–9

Time Study Rating

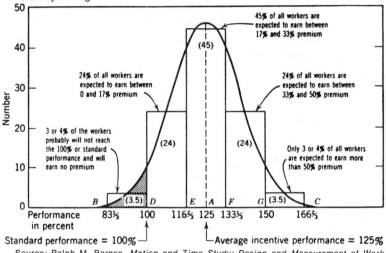

Source: Ralph M. Barnes, *Motion and Time Study: Design and Measurement of Work,* 6th ed. (New York: Wiley, 1968), p. 388.

must be adjusted. This can be done on a gross basis by multiplying the times by a factor which takes account of all discrepancies between the calculated times and the actual times. Some companies ignore this discrepancy, feeling their scheduling plan is so loose that the error makes little difference.

Determining Machine Controlled Times

Not all tasks are controlled by the movements of an operator. Consequently, it is necessary to calculate by different means the time needed for the machine time. Only metal working is discussed here, but task times can be determined for other processes, too.

The rate at which metal is removed in a cutting operation is determined by three factors:

1. *Speed:* The rate at which the tool passes the work or the work passes the tool; given as feet per minute.
2. *Feed:* The distance the tool moves in a cycle of operation; given in inches per revolution.
3. *Depth of cut:* The right angle distance between the old surface and the newly cut surface; given as inches per pass.

These three concepts become more obvious when we see them on the simple diagram, Figure 8–10. It is of interest to note that we are talking about three different movements, and this corresponds to the three dimensions of the object we wish to alter.

The optimum relationships for speeds, feeds, and depths of cuts have

Figure 8–10
Determining Machine Controlled Time

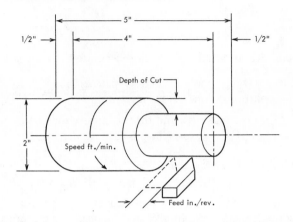

been determined for the common materials, common cutting materials, and the finish desired on the part. This information is available in many engineering handbooks. For example, to determine the time for removing the material on the simple cylinder, as shown, we could find in a handbook that the speed, feed, and depth of cut for mild steel, cut by high-speed steel, should be:

Speed: 200 ft./min.   Feed: .020 in./rev.   Depth of cut: .125 in.

From the speed and the diameter of the part, we can determine the correct rotational speed:

$$\frac{\text{Speed (ft./min.} \times 12 \text{ in./ft.})}{\text{Circumference } (\pi \times D \text{ in.})} = \frac{200 \text{ ft./min.} \times 12 \text{ in./ft.}}{2 \text{ in.} \times 3.14/\text{rev.}},$$

Since

$$12/\pi = \text{approximately 4,}$$

then:

$$\frac{200 \text{ ft./min.} \times 4 \text{ in./ft.}}{2 \text{ in./rev.}} = 400 \text{ rpm.}$$

This is a theoretical speed, and if such a speed is not available on the machine, it is necessary to adjust the theoretical speed accordingly. Whether one adjusts the speed up or down depends upon the finish desired, the capabilities of the machine, how decrepit it is, and other factors. For the example, assume 425 rpm is the nearest actual speed.

Next we need to know how many revolutions are required. Since it would be unlikely that the tool would start and end on the piece, we must add a little tool travel on each end. This is called "cutting air." Our calculations continue in this way:

$$\frac{\text{Length of part (inches)} + \text{Additional length (inches)}}{\text{Feed (in./rev.)}} = \text{Rev./part}$$

$$\frac{(4 + \tfrac{1}{2} + \tfrac{1}{2}).\text{in./part}}{.020 \text{ in./rev.}} = 250 \text{ rev./part}$$

From the above information we can determine the time per cut or pass:

$$\frac{\text{Revolutions/part}}{\text{Revolutions/min.}} = \frac{250 \text{ rev./part}}{425 \text{ rev./min.}} = .59 \text{ min./part}$$

But this is for only one pass, and for the surface desired it may be necessary to take several passes. Assume in this case we need three:

$$\text{Minutes/part/pass} \times 3 \text{ passes} = .59 \times 3 = 1.77 \text{ min./part}$$

These same basic ideas can be extended to drilling, boring, milling, planing, and similar operations. For other processes there are other ways of determining the time that it will take to do a task. For example, press times can be determined by finding the cycles per minute.

Machine controlled times are often necessary in calculating time data for scheduling as well as for estimating costs.

THE EFFECT OF LEARNING ON THE DATA

Most industries have established standards of performance, with little or no consideration for the improvement that comes about by the repeated performance of a manual task. This improvement phenomenon is such a commonly observed experience that it seems peculiar no practical use was made of it until recently. Even now it has not been universally accepted. Although a company may not wish to apply the learning curve phenomenon by using the simple logarithmic charts described here, it should be aware of the learning phenomenon in general, and take advantage of it to predict costs, estimate capital requirements, enter into contracts, and perform all the other activities which require accurate predictions of production times.

The learning curve is the graphical representation of the very well-known fact that a worker learns as he works. The more often he repeats a task, the more proficient he becomes. As he becomes more proficient, his production rate increases, which of course means that the production time decreases.

While in the past many people in industry must have been aware of this phenomenon, and perhaps occasionally took some recognition of it in their predictions, it was not until World War II that it became generally known and used to any extent.

Airframe manufacturers were one of the first to use the learning curve in predictions, probably because the large number of labor hours and consequent high costs required in constructing each frame helped to make the phenomenon so obvious. Soon the usefulness of the learning curve came to the attention of the Armed Forces and they put the Stanford Research Institute to work making a statistical study of the direct labor costs going into airplane frames. It became apparent that each type of frame—bombers, fighters, and so forth—had its own initial production time (as might be expected), but the rates of improvement for all frames were remarkably similar. In fact, they were all so similar that the industry's improvement characteristic of 20 percent has been carried over to other industries without ample proof of the similarity—and probably without adequate justification.

Construction of the Learning Curve

The first relationship which will be discussed is the cumulative average man-hours/unit as they are related to the cumulative number of units produced. The cumulative average man-hours/unit is the total number of production hours accumulated since production began, divided by the number of units produced. As the time for each succeeding unit becomes less, the cumulative average becomes smaller and smaller. It should be recognized that this average time will never become as small as the total man hours for a specific unit because it is influenced by the early, less efficient production.

As an example, consider wiring an electrical control panel, which takes 100 hours to produce the first product. Each time the production is doubled there is a 20 percent improvement. Another way of saying this is that as each time production doubles, the cumulative average man-hours is 80 percent of the previous production level. This can be seen in the following form:

		Cumulative Average Man-hours/unit
First unit takes:		100.0
First 2 units take:	$\dfrac{2 \text{ parts} \times 100 \text{ hours} \times 80\%}{2 \text{ parts}} =$	80.0
First 4 units take:	$\dfrac{4 \text{ parts} \times 80 \text{ hours} \times 80\%}{4 \text{ parts}} =$	64.0
First 8 units take:	$\dfrac{8 \text{ parts} \times 64 \text{ hours} \times 80\%}{8 \text{ parts}} =$	51.2

Before plotting this information, look at the right-hand column of the table above and predict what is going to happen as cumulative times are plotted against cumulative units. The differences between succeeding units are 20, 16, and 12.8 hours. As is to be expected, the greatest reduction of time occurs in the early stages of production and tapers off gradually as production continues. If this information shown above is placed on a chart (Figure 8–11), the change in production rate is dramatic.

The curve shown illustates the change vividly, but it makes the con-

Figure 8–11
Learning Curve

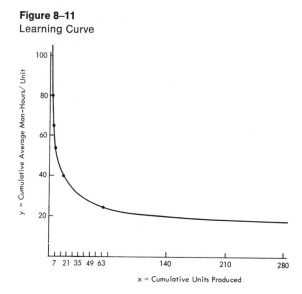

x = Cumulative Units Produced

struction and subsequent reading a little more difficult than if the equation were converted to logarithms and plotted on logarithmic paper (Figure 8–12).

Figure 8–12
Learning Curve, Log-log

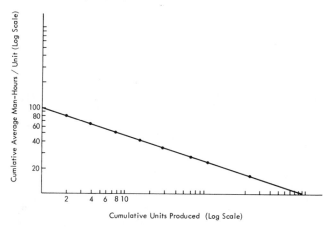

Cumulative Units Produced (Log Scale)

The equation of the curve just illustrated is given by:

$$Y = KX^{-n}$$

Y = Cumulative average man-hours/unit for any number of units, plotted on Y-axis

K = Number of man-hours to build the first unit

X = Cumulative number of units produced

n = The exponent of the curve which will, in the example, be negative

This equation, $Y = KX^{-n}$, can be restated in terms of logarithms thus:

$$\log Y = \log K + (-n)\log X$$

For those who have forgotten, the product of two numbers, K and X, is found by adding their logarithms. The logarithm of a number raised to a power, X^{-n}, is the product of $-n$ and the logarithm of the number, or $-n \log X$.

By this familiar technique of changing to logarithms we have simplified the graphic representation of the problem by putting the information in a linear form. For just a moment let us pause and interpret the above equation in terms of its graphical presentation. The first term, $\log Y$, is equal to $\log K$ when X is one. This value, $\log K$, therefore, is the intersection of the curve with the Y-axis. The letter n in the expression is the slope of the line, and will be negative because the line slopes from left to right. In addition to having a straight line, which is easier to interpret, another bonus is obtained because, as you will see, log-log paper keeps the chart within reasonable bounds.

The slope of the line, n, can be derived:

$$Y = KX^{-n}$$
$$Y = K/X^n$$
$$X^n = K/Y$$
$$n \log X = \log K - \log Y$$
$$n = \frac{\log K - \log Y}{\log X}$$

It turns out that n is the log (percent of learning curve) divided by log 2. This might be seen more clearly if we consider the equation when the production is doubled, using the previous data of 100 hours for the first unit and an 80 percent learning curve.

First doubling: $\qquad n = \dfrac{\log 100 - \log (100 \times .80)}{\log 2}$

Double production again: $n = \dfrac{\log 100 - \log (100 \times .80 \times .80)}{\log 4}$

$$n = \frac{\log 100 - \log 100 - \log .80 - \log .80}{\log 2 + \log 2}$$

$$n = \frac{-2 \log .80}{2 \log 2} = \frac{-\log .80}{\log 2}$$

This step was taken to make it apparent that doubling factors cancel out and the slope remains, log (percent of learning curve)/log 2. From this basic equation, $Y = KX^{-n}$, several other significant and useful equations can be derived.

Total Man-Hours. Many times it would be convenient to know what the total man-hours are for any level of production. This can be determined by obtaining the product of the cumulative average man-hours per unit and the number of units produced.

$$T = YX$$

$$T = \text{Total man-hours required to build a}$$
$$\text{(predetermined) number of units}$$

or we can say:

$$T = KX^{-n} \times X$$

So, in effect, we are saying only that the product of the cumulative average time for each unit, KX^{-n}, and the number of units, X, is equal to the total time it takes to produce a quantity. From this equation it is possible to go on and develop an equation for determining the time it takes to produce any one unit.

Unit Time. The unit time for any unit is derived with a little more difficulty, starting with the total time just derived. Remember that, so far, the average time, Y, for all units up to a certain point has been derived. The unit time, U, will give the time required for any one unit without including all the production which has gone before.

$$T = KX^{-n} \times X$$
$$T = KX^{-n+1}$$
$$T = KX^{(1-n)}$$

If the first derivative of the total man-hours is taken with respect to units:

$$\frac{dT}{dX} = (1 - n)KX^{-n}$$
$$U = \text{Man-hours/unit} = (1 - n)KX^{-n}$$

Since $KX^{-n} = Y$, the cumulative average man-hours per unit, we can see that the time to produce any one unit is merely the product of Y and $(1 - n)$. The values of n and $(1 - n)$ can be obtained from logarithm tables, but some common ones will be given here for convenience (Figure 8–13).

Figure 8–13
Learning Curve Values

Efficiency	Learning Curve Value	n	$1 - n$
35%	65%	.624	.375
30	70	.515	.485
25	75	.415	.585
20	80	.322	.678
15	85	.234	.766
10	90	.152	.848
5	95	.074	.926

The three important relationships of the learning curve have been given. It might be well to turn our attention back to the example problem mentioned previously for wiring the electrical control panel and see how these relationships are used.

The production control department would like to know how long it will take to produce the first 70 control panels and also the maximum time for each of the succeeding 10 panels. In brief, how long will it take to produce 70, T, and how long will it take to produce the 71st panel?

The cumulative average hours, Y, is:

	Example
$Y = KX^{-n}$	$\log 100 = 2.00000$
$\log Y = \log K - n \log X$	$-.322 \log 70 = -.59412$
	1.40588

and the number for this logarithm is 25.46 hours.

Since T equals YX,

$$\text{Total hours} = 25.46 \text{ hours/panel} \times 70 \text{ panels} = 1{,}782 \text{ hours}$$

The unit time for the 71st panel is:

$$U = (1 - n)KX^{-n}$$
$$\text{Unit time} = .678 \times 25.46 = 17.26 \text{ hours}$$

While we have shown the calculations here, it is much simpler, of course, to select the information from the curves. Check the calculations with the curve and see if they compare. The "unit times" can also be plotted on a curve for ready reference.

This is the kind of information that is needed by every production control department, as well as by other branches of management, if both are going to operate with any reasonable accuracy.

This technique has some opportunities for error and certain precautions should be taken. The relationship that has just been considered between the number of products produced and the cumulative average hours is probably not caused entirely by the worker's learning experience because there are *many* factors which could influence the curve. These factors might include improvements in production design, new tooling, innovations by the industrial engineering group, improved management, and so on. This means that the learning curve is probably not an absolutely scientific tool but has overtones of empiricism. This does not particularly matter as long as we don't accept it as being infallible. The important thing is that the curves seem to show a consistent pattern of behavior which is reliable enough to use in the production situation.

Learning curves are applicable primarily to hand and assembly operations where the learning factor is significant. Machines, by themselves, do not learn to run any faster, and as could be expected, the learning curve will be steep for manual operations and flat for machine operations. While the aircraft industry has found the 80 percent curve universally acceptable, there are other industries which would have a 90 or 95 percent curve, or an even flatter curve. Others may experience steep, 65 or 60 percent learning.

Shifts in the use of direct labor, such as the purchase of parts on the outside, can cause errors in the curves by showing abrupt declines in the labor used. A shift in the proportion of direct labor to indirect labor may also be misleading. For example, a reduction in low-cost direct labor might be made at the expense of high-cost indirect labor. Any changes in the direct labor costs at the expense, or benefit, of other costs should be handled with caution.

Innovations in the process should also be handled with caution for it is possible that they would cause a large jump in the curve, either plus or minus, with the start of a new learning curve. Of course the direct labor costs are frequently influenced by the level of production. As a productive unit operates near its maximum, the direct labor may be reduced. At least, there is some level of production which is optimum, and any variations in labor efficiency from this cause should not be interpreted as learning. If the production is intermittent, the curve cannot be expected to be smooth since there will be a certain amount of relearning every time the production is restarted.

It has already been shown how the learning curve might be used for scheduling information and advising customers of delivery dates, but this is not the limit of its usefulness—even though it is important enough to make it universally acceptable.

Instead of using units for the X-axis, it is possible to use *pounds* of material. This makes it possible to predict and compare the cumulative hours on the basis of weight of material and not on units, thus giving a broader application from product to product.

The learning curve can be used in the decision to buy or to make component parts. A contractor should consider whether or not his subcontractor has a flatter learning curve than his own. If it is flatter, even though it may start at a lower level, the alternative to make the component obviously should be considered.

In the planning of capital expenditure (Figure 8–14) the learning curve has some obvious applications. For example, the unit-cost curve will cross the cumulative average-cost curve (as shown). To the left of this intersection there is a financial drain on the business while at the right there is a financial return. Knowing this, the people responsible for the budget can do a better job of planning. The purchasing agent can also use this in his dealings with the subcontractors to advise them on costs. By using the learning curve it is possible to predict budgets and come up with reasonable data at each step; it is not necessary to wait until the end for cumulative data.

For large assemblies, where considerable area is necessary for large jigs and fixtures, the learning curve finds an application in space utilization. The

Figure 8–14
Capital Planning with Learning Curve

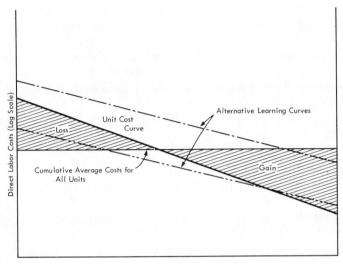

Cumlative Number of Units Produced (Log Scale)

space can be determined for each production level for different products and, consequently, building space can be used to the utmost.

As is obvious, the time—at least at the beginning of production—will have some wide variations. This makes scheduling of subsequent quantities very difficult. Therefore the learning curve is an obvious tool for smoothing out the production schedule of jobs with high percentages of learning. If the total number of employees and the hours available are known, it is possible to work backwards and determine the delivery schedule. By taking the cumulative average learning curve and projecting on it the total number of man-hours, the production schedule can be determined.

Practically any industry could use the learning curve if there are tasks which require a large percentage of man controlled operations rather than machine controlled operations, and where the product or parts of the product are being made repeatedly.

INDUSTRIAL CALENDARS

It is in keeping with industries' standardization efforts that they have frequently put into practice standardized calendars. It is nearly impossible to compare sales, costs, and other production figures without standardizing the time period for which they are being compared. It is not uncommon to hear such statements as "the sales for last month were 5,000 units," but unless we know something about the number of days in last month, the number of weekends included in the month, and the number of vacations we know very little about the sales figure. The working time might vary as much as 10 percent from month to month.

Attempts to make the industrial calendar uniform have been tried, with unusual success, for many years. There are various ways of making the calendar periods uniform, but probably the 13-period calendar has been the most successful. Companies using the "13-month" system divide their year into 13 equal periods—of 4 weeks, or 28 days, each. The year is divided into quarters of 3 "months" each, for accounting purposes, with the vacation period falling into the extra month.

Some companies have used the so-called 4-4-5 quarter plan in which the first and second month of a quarter contain 4 weeks each and the third month contains 5. Still other companies, also wishing a uniform calendar, have employed other plans.

In all these plans there is the problem of the extra days left over after the periods are made as uniform as possible. Also there is the question of the extra day occurring because of leap year. Quite commonly days are carried forward until they accumulate to a full-week period. The pros and cons of uniform industrial calendars can more readily be summarized in a list of advantages and disadvantages.

Each month is made up of exactly the same number of days, which makes it possible to compare successive months, as well as the months themselves, from year to year.

It is not necessary to keep in mind the number of days in each month and then try to make necessary adjustments. Comparisons can be made on the basis of costs, output, and other variables without considering the number of days in the denominator.

Payrolls can be closed at the end of a week, which eliminates the usual letdown in production when a pay period ends in the middle of a week. This has been an advantage to the community as well because there is a tendency for bills to be paid regularly and promptly.

It is easier for employees to determine what is required of them; it gives them a means of measuring progress; and they appreciate more uniform pay periods.

Physical inventories can be taken over the weekends without any interruptions. Since the plant will probably be closed down, it is easier to determine what material is in process and what isn't.

It becomes difficult to compare cost figures with companies not operating on the same plan.

External accounting, such as accounts receivable, will have to be carried out on a 12-month basis or other arrangements made.

Thirteen closing periods for the accounts will add to the clerical costs.

Banks and exchanges require reports on the monthly and quarterly basis.

The names of the months will have to be disregarded and numbers used for identification.

Numbering Production Days

Whether or not a company uses a standardized calendar, it can obtain considerable advantage from numbering its production days consecutively so that certain *production days* can be referred to instead of a certain month and day in the month. A calendar printed to show the number of the production days is shown in Figure 8–15. This system eliminates many misun-

Figure 8–15
Production Calendar

JANUARY

BLK.	MON.	TUES.	WED.	THURS.	FRI.
1	NEW YEAR HOLIDAY	1 **3**	2 **4**	3 **5**	4 **6**
2	5 **9**	6 **10**	7 **11**	8 **12**	9 **13**
3	10 **16**	11 **17**	12 **18**	13 **19**	14 **20**
4	15 **23**	16 **24**	17 **25**	18 **26**	19 **27**
5	20 **30**	21 **31**			

FEBRUARY

BLK	MON.	TUES.	WED.	THURS.	FRI.
5			22 **1**	23 **2**	24 **3**
6	25 **6**	26 **7**	27		
7	30				

derstandings and—best of all—gives a common time-language for the entire factory by which production goals can be set.

Four-Day Week. The four-day week and other unusual ways of scheduling the worker's time will have an important impact upon production control operations. Scheduling furnace operations working three shifts can cause almost impossible problems to overcome. Additional limitations established by unions can also help to increase the difficulties.

Summary

Time is the keystone for all factory operations. Investments must have a payoff within a certain time. Inventories must be turned over within a certain time. Labor is paid for its work on the basis of time, and customers expect their orders filled by a certain time.

The system designer measures the input to the factory in units of time.

The feedback is also recorded in units of time. Ultimately, the efficiency of the system is determined by how well time is utilized.

Since time is the common denominator of many aspects of planning and controlling factory operations, it is important that you know how time information is obtained. There are a number of common ways of developing time information; these include past estimates, stop-watch time study, elemental standard data, predetermined motion-time data, and work sampling. These methods are usually not designed for scheduling and cost estimating and, therefore, must be adjusted for these purposes.

When people repeat tasks time after time they become more proficient, which in turn reduces the time. This, in many cases, will influence the schedule and should be accounted for when establishing the time relationships among jobs.

Conventional calendars are not always the most useful media for regulating factory activities, and many companies have found that uniform calendars offer many advantages.

If you have never given consideration to the importance of time as it affects our lives, perhaps now is the time to start—using some of the many time-regulating techniques discussed in this book.

QUESTIONS

8–1. What are the applications of time estimates in a factory?

8–2. What are the strengths and weaknesses of the various methods of estimating the time to do a task?

8–3. Give an example of a job which could be estimated from:
past experience.
predetermined motion-time data.
work sampling.

8–4. In what two ways is the actual measured-time adjusted in a stop-watch time study? To what degree does this affect the objectivity of the techniques?

8–5. What advantages does the work sampling method have over the other methods?

8–6. What information would you need to determine how long it takes to turn a metal cylinder on a lathe? What is the source of this information? How does the theoretical information compare with the actual information?

8–7. In what situations would the effect of learning be important?

8–8. How does the time study analyst cope with the problem of learning?

8–9. Why is the log-log graph of the learning curve used?

8–10. Compare the advantages and disadvantages of the uniform calendar.

8–11. Discuss the problems you could anticipate by switching an aluminum extrusion plant to a four-day week.

9

Purchasing Information

PURCHASING, like production control, exists to serve the manufacturing function in the objective of transforming materials into desirable consumer products. Industrial purchasing is an integral part of the factory system designed to provide maximum profits. According to one study, the purchase of goods and services for the average industrial concern represents 56 cents of the sales dollar while profits represent 6 cents of the sales dollar. Consequently a 1 percent reduction in purchasing costs results in a 9 percent increase in profits.

The objective of the purchasing department has frequently been stated as *procuring materials of the right quality, in the right quantity, at the right time, at the right price, from the right vendor.* This is a continuous process that requires the greatest of skills.

A member of the production and inventory control department is going to work constantly with the purchasing department, and therefore it is important that he knows and appreciates its contributions. There has been a trend to integrate under a *materials manager* the activities of production control, inventory control, purchasing, and other material functions. Only by understanding the purchasing function can you realize the importance of such an organizational design.

As interest in management information systems (MIS) grows, it becomes more important that you have a global view of the entire system. Computers, with their common data base, make the integration of all functions feasible. For these reasons, you should know how purchasing and production and inventory control are integrated.

Inventory control generates the quantity and specifications for the needed purchase items from its records. Output of the materials requirements program also serves as the input for the purchasing procedure.

In turn purchase orders provide the inventory system with the information needed for updating the "on order" status of the records. When the materials are received and inspected, the inventory control department is advised of the quantity so they may update the "available" columns of their records.

Scheduling and dispatching establish production dates, but without the material, the factory cannot function because work is released to the factory based upon the availability of material. The factory must work directly with purchasing so that they can process the materials as scheduled or make the necessary adjustments.

Frequently the question comes up as to whether a product should be made or purchased. This "buy-make" decision is a question which requires assembling information and comparing alternatives. Information regarding the purchased items is best obtained through the purchasing department.

Purchasing Organization

No generalization about the purchasing department organization structure can be made because it depends upon such things as whether the department is centralized or decentralized, the product cost, tradition, and many other factors. There are enough common characteristics, however, that are worth mentioning.

The head of the purchasing function is the purchasing *agent*. This can be an extremely important position in an organization carrying a vice president's title. The purchasing agent has extreme powers of committing the company, so some companies limit the amount that a purchasing agent can buy without the approval of another officer in the company. There are all sorts of legal overtones that go with this position which should be understood by anyone accepting it.

The *buyers*, under the supervision of the purchasing agent, are the ones who actually do the buying. In a large organization it is common for the buyers to specialize in a particular product area, such as plastics, die casting, forgings, and textiles.

Follow-up or *expediting* may be a separate function in a purchasing department or it may be under the supervision of the buyers. Its purpose is of course to see that the orders are received on schedule and to expedite the orders which might be falling behind.

Record clerks are an essential part of the purchasing department. Even where the function is fully computerized there will be a need for clerical help in checking off invoices, filing orders, and similar duties.

Some companies will have a need for a *research* and *specification* section of purchasing to evaluate products and establish specifications. The traffic department for incoming shipments might also be part of the purchasing department.

Purchasing Procedure

There is a need for classifying inventories for purchasing:

Controlled or *classified* items are those which are regularly and repeatedly used in the manufacturing process. They also include office supplies and other items which are used frequently enough to require a constant control.

Uncontrolled or *unclassified* items are those which are purchased so infrequently that it is not necessary to maintain perpetual inventory records. Since no record is available for these parts, information needed for ordering will have to be generated each time a product is purchased.

Some products may fall between the two classifications so it will be up to management to decide whether they should have a record or not. The rest of the discussion about the purchasing procedure will be related primarily to controlled inventory items because they represent the bulk of those used in the manufacturing process.

There is no one standardized purchasing procedure, but there is enough similarity among companies so that examining a general procedure will be worthwhile. In any purchasing procedure the following activities can be defined:

1. Development and processing of the *purchase requisition* with a statement of quality, quantity, and delivery date.
2. Selecting the source of supply and placing the purchase order.
3. Follow-up.
4. Invoice checking.
5. Receiving and inspecting materials.
6. Completion of records.

These are not organizational divisions but activities which must be handled in the purchasing procedure. Each one will be discussed in turn.

1. Development of the Purchasing Requisition. The purchase requisition is an internal form which is issued by the person needing the material and is sent to the purchasing department. The typical requisition form will contain the following information:

Date when requisition was issued. This should be checked by the purchasing department to assure that there were no delays for which they will be held responsible.

Requisition number is a serial number by which the requisition may be quickly identified.

Name of department and individual originating the request in case there are any questions and also so it will be known where to send the material when it is received.

Account to which the purchase is to be charged. This becomes an important part of the accounting procedure.

Requested date of delivery so that the material which is to be integrated into the production schedule is received on time. Since the purchasing agent must take this into consideration, he may make a different selection of vendors and shipping carrier or ask the user for a revised date.

Description and quantity desired must be filled out in detail. The buyer may ask for revisions since he may be aware of substitute products or know of quantity discounts.

The distribution of the requisition copies will vary from company to company. Duplicate copies are typical with one being retained within the originating department and the original sent to the purchasing department.

Purchase requisitions are originated directly from the inventory records if the order point and order quantity procedures are used. However, some companies do not bother to write the requisitions but forward the inventory record cards directly to purchasing to take action and fill in the purchasing information. This system has a weakness in that the ordering procedure takes time and the records may not be returned to the inventory control section in time for frequent updating, thus resulting in inventory records that are out of date.

If production is for just a limited or experimental quantity which will probably never be repeated, the materials requisitions are written just once with a complete description of what is needed. A company using the materials requirements planning procedure will place orders according to the extended requirements generated by the procedure. The person recognizing the need must specify exactly what is wanted. It is not the business of the purchasing department to determine what is needed. However, efficient purchasing personnel are aware of what the present and future needs are so that they may suggest new products which might be desirable replacements. They communicate these finds to the users, which is extremely important and is one of the reasons why production and purchasing should work hand in hand.

As you will learn from the order quantity equations, frequent orders have an effect upon lowering the cost, but they are also disrupting to the standard procedures and clutter up the receiving dock and other areas with a constant flow of emergency materials. Rush orders can become a way of life which cost far more than might be apparent. They can be minimized by charging the responsible department with any extra cost incurred.

2. Selecting Source of Supply and Placing Order. Purchasing is responsible for locating a source of supply. They will no doubt know which suppliers can furnish the common items at the best price in the time desired. Some companies follow a policy of not permitting a *single-source supplier* because they do not want their business to be taken for granted and want to be sure of an alternate source in case something should happen to a first-choice supplier.

Some companies follow a policy of requiring bids on items which exceed a certain price. This can be a time-consuming process, but at times it pays.

These requests for quotations are usually printed *inquiry not on order* in large letters so that they do not get processed like a purchase order.

The purchase order is usually issued on a special purchase order form which contains all or some of the following information:

Date of issue.
Serial number.
Name and address of the firm issuing the order.
Name and address of the firm receiving the order.
Quantity and description of items ordered.
Date of delivery required.
Shipping directions.
Prices.
Terms of payment.
Conditions governing the order such as price discounts, shipping, quality, cancellations, under- and over-shipments, and guards against patent infringement.

The number of copies of the purchasing order will vary from company to company but here is a typical distribution:

Original is sent to the vendor.
A second copy may be sent to the vendor to be returned as an acknowledgement giving the details of delivery.
One copy is sent to the originating department to indicate that its requisition has been processed. They in turn check it against the purchase requisition. The purchase order number is entered into the requisition and the inventory records.
One copy is used as a working copy in the purchasing department.
One copy is sent to the accounting department for clearing the invoice when it is received.

3. Follow-up on the Purchase Order. This is important if the production schedules are to be kept. This function may be organized separately within the purchasing department or it can be tied in with the buyers and their areas of specialization.

The procedure can range from a simple postal card inquiry to periodic phone calls, or a visitation in the vendor's plant. The open orders are frequently filed in a *tickler file* by date and are checked regularly to be sure that the orders are delivered before an emergency occurs.

4. Invoice Checking. Invoices are claims against the buyer for the purchased material and should be handled expeditiously. They are generally received in duplicate, bearing the purchase order number of the customer as well as other pertinent information. They are stamped with a serial number, furnished by the accounting department, which corresponds to the payment voucher number. The invoice is extended and checked and any cash discount is taken. When approved, one copy is sent to the inventory-records department and another copy to the accounting department for payment. They, of course, do not make the payment until the copies which were sent to receiving have been processed and also sent to the accounting department where it is checked. This gives a three-way check which is very desirable for keeping people honest.

Checking the invoice is generally an essential part of purchasing. However, in some companies it is considered a function of accounting. When the process of paying the invoice is handled entirely by the accounting department, they must compare the information shown on the purchasing order with the information obtained from the receiving report. This method offers some safeguards, but it also requires extensive communications between accounting and purchasing, and accounting and receiving.

Under this procedure the purchasing department may miss some information which is essential for its operations. For example it will not have the information available for follow-up purposes if it is not notified that the invoice has been received. It will also miss the information needed for making vendor evaluations. Prices, terms, and discounts are all established by purchasing and it should know immediately of any changes that take place. This can be done only if purchasing receives the invoice first.

Care must be taken that invoices are paid on time to receive the discount allowed, and some protection must be set up to prevent paying the invoices twice.

5. Receiving and Inspection.   Not all receiving departments are given access to a copy of the purchasing order and probably for good reasons. For one thing, there is information on the purchasing order such as price which need not become common knowledge. Also, if a clerk is forced to identify and count the incoming material, it is more likely that the receiving reports will be correct.

The receiving report is made out in several copies. One goes to the purchasing department for checking against the invoice, two go to the inventory department where one is retained to update the inventory records and one is returned to the receiving department as proof that the copies have been processed. Other copies may be sent to accounting and the traffic department.

You have been presented with a typical purchasing procedure. Hopefully, you will have obtained enough basic information so that you can adjust to other systems if necessary.

The Computerized Purchasing Procedure

Putting the purchasing procedure on a computer yields many advantages:

Duplicate records of purchasing, inventory control, production control, quality control, and accounting may be eliminated.

Buyers will have more and better information available about products

Figure 9–1
Relationship of Purchasing Records

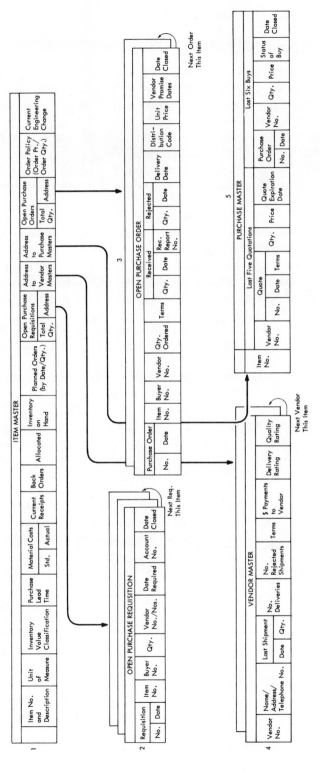

and vendors. They can have immediate access to such information as price breaks and transportation costs.

The routine paper work can be eliminated with its inherent costs and delays.

A purchasing software package consists of the records shown in Figure 9–1 which will be discussed here.

Record 1 is the *item master* which is the same one you saw in the bill-of-materials processor. This record contains the total quantity requisitioned and open purchase orders. In addition, two fields contain addresses that *point* to the *vendor master record* and the *purchase master record* for this particular item.

Record 2 is the *open purchase requisition file* which contains the requisition number, item number, information regarding the vendor, and other pertinent information as shown.

Record 3 is the *open purchase order file* which contains the information about the purchase orders which have not been filled. As you will notice it includes information to identify the purchase order, vendor, and all of the other important information.

Record 4 is the *vendor master file* which records all of the past experience with each vendor plus additional information such as vendor evaluations based on quality and delivery.

Record 5 is the *purchase master file* which is an extension of the item master and contains a history of the last few vendor quotations and purchases.

The purchasing procedure incorporating these records is shown in Figure 9–2 as four distinct modules. As you can see each one uses one or more of the five records discussed above. Requisition and purchase order preparation, module 1, incorporates all five sets of records. The buyer's process of requisitioning and ordering may tap any or all of the information available in these files while making the necessary decisions. Eventually a purchase order form is printed and the record created in the file. At the same time receiving and inspection forms may be printed for the receiving department to use when the material is received.

Purchase maintenance and update, module 2, uses requisitions and purchase orders as input to develop open purchase requisition and open purchase order files. Parts may be rejected by the system at receiving, inspection, or parts storage. A coded rejection slip is printed authorizing return to vendor, use as is, rework in plant, and other alternatives. The output of this module includes reports which will tell production and inventory control where the order is.

Purchase order follow-up, module 3, uses the vendor master file and open purchase order file to provide an automatic follow-up procedure by printing out reports listing orders that are past due as well as other problems which will delay the receipt of the materials.

Purchase evaluation, module 4, provides for a periodic evaluation of

Figure 9–2
Purchasing Systems

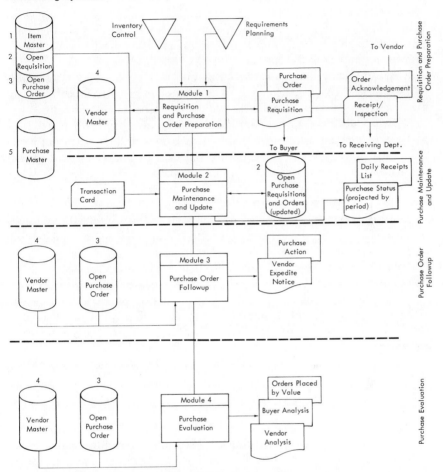

vendors. Ratings are prepared reflecting both the quality and ability to deliver on time. The method of calculating vendors' ratings is a subject covered in the next section.

Evaluation of Supplier Performance[1]

The supplier might be considered as an extension of the company's present manufacturing capabilities. Therefore, it is only good business strategy for a factory to extend the same good business controls over its suppliers as

---

[1] For a comprehensive discussion of this subject see: *Evaluation of Supplier Performance*, prepared by the Development Project Committee on Standards for Vendor Evaluation. National Association of Purchasing Agents, 11 Park Place, New York, N.Y. 10016.

it has over its own shop. The need for more effective supplier evaluation has been derived from the greater technical complexity of products as well as increased pressure on adequate inventory controls.

To improve the control over the supply of raw materials and other purchased products for the factory, giant strides have been made in recent years to evaluate and rank the suppliers. Most of these plans use price, quality, delivery, and service as a basis of appraisal.

Two of the recognized supplier evaluation plans are the categorical plan and the weighted-point plan. These two plans will be discussed briefly.

Categorical Plan. This is the simplest of the plans to be discussed. It is a qualitative system which avoids the compilations of huge masses of data. Each buyer keeps a list of his major suppliers, on which he catalogs good and bad features concerning the suppliers' services. The buyer also gathers information either directly or through quality performance and technical service reports.

Monthly meetings of all buyers are held where the notes of the previous month are compiled and evaluated on a three-point, plus, minus, and neutral basis. The supplier in turn is kept informed of his current evaluation.

Weighted-Point Plan. Keep in mind that the ultimate responsibility for choosing the supplier and placing the purchase order remains with the purchasing department, but quality control shares part of purchasing's responsibility in setting up and maintaining the weighted-point plan. A typical weighted-point plan, Figure 9–3, might distribute the available points in the following way:

Quality	40 points
Price	35
Service, including delivery	25
	100 points

The number of points given to each of the following factors would vary in importance from time to time depending upon business conditions. The example given will be for a specific period. The evaluation of each factor will be explained.

Quality control is responsible for evaluating the quality points that a vendor obtains in the rating. If all lots are acceptable, then the full 40 points are given. If they are not, the points would be reduced by some proportional amount. For example, if 60 lots have been received but only 54 are accepted, the rating would be as illustrated.

The price index is calculated on the net price for the particular product, and service is based on a straight percentage of delivery promises kept.

These are but two of the vendor rating plans available. In other plans, such costs as vendor qualifying visits, expediting costs, premium transportation, and shipping promises not kept are taken into consideration. This points out that there can be a number of rating plans but a company chooses the one which will give it the information it needs at a cost it can afford.

Figure 9–3
Weighted-Point Plan

		Lots Received	Lots Accepted	Lots Rejected	Percent Accepted	× Factor	= Quality Control Rating
Quality Rating	Supplier A ...	60	54	6	90.0	40	36.0
	Supplier B ...	60	56	4	93.3	40	37.3
	Supplier C ...	20	16	4	80.0	40	32.0

		Catalog Price	− Discount (percent)	= Unit Price	Plus Transportation Charge	= Net Price
Price Rating	Supplier A	$1.00	10	($ .90)	$.03	$ .93
	Supplier B	1.25	15	(1.06)	.06	1.12
	Supplier C	1.50	20	(1.20)	.03	1.23

		Lowest Price	÷ Net Price	= Percentage	× Factor	= Price Rating
	Supplier A	$.93	$ .93	100 percent	35	35.0
	Supplier B	.93	1.12	83	35	29.1
	Supplier C	.93	1.23	76	35	26.6

		Promises Kept (percent)	Service Factor	Service Rating
Service Rating	Supplier A	95	25	22.5
	Supplier B	95	25	23.8
	Supplier C	100	25	25.0

		Supplier A	Supplier B	Supplier C
Summary of Ratings	Quality (40 points)	36.0	37.3	32.0
	Price (35 points)	35.0	29.1	26.6
	Service (25 points)	22.5	23.8	25.0
	Total Rating:	93.5	90.2	83.6

Summary

A company can no longer consider what goes on just within the walls of its factory. It must consider how the vendor is going to affect production and delivery dates.

Materials management is a way of organizing all materials functions so that the vendor's contribution is given consideration. One way of keeping on top of the vendor problem is to establish a vendor rating system.

QUESTIONS

9–1. Discuss what effect an inefficient purchasing department could have on a company manufacturing children's toys.

9–2. Present your opinion of the materials manager concept and explain why you think it is or is not a good idea.

9–3. Design an organization chart for a purchasing department. Use a situation you know about or a hypothetical one but establish the conditions within which the department must operate.

9-4. A manufacturer of farm machinery has repeat orders for 70 percent of the items used. The other 30 percent of the items are unique. Explain what impact you would expect this to have on the purchasing department.

9-5. What advantages and disadvantages would you anticipate by having a single-source supplier?

9-6. A company has a policy that all items costing more than $500 will require more than one bid. Is this reasonable? Explain why you like or do not like this policy.

9-7. As head of the purchasing department, you are trying to persuade your management to computerize the purchasing procedure. Explain how it could be done. What records would be available? List the advantages and disadvantages.

9-8. Assume you are responsible for a purchasing department. Would you attempt to evaluate your suppliers on a formal basis? If so, which system would you use? Explain why. If not, explain why not.

section three
Inventory Control

Inventory control is one of the major subjects to which this book is dedicated. In this section you will learn how inventories are accounted for, managed, and controlled in the factory situation. Two different but related approaches to inventory control are presented. These are economic lot sizing and materials requirements planning.

The current computer software packages are constructed around probabilistic models, part-period lot sizing, and other techniques which are included in a separate chapter.

Recall that this book is organized so that you can ultimately design systems, but it also can be used to any depth desired. For an introductory course, it may be desirable to delete the last chapter of this section, while for an advanced course, the first chapter can be used as a review.

Chapter 10. Inventory Management and Control

This chapter is a comprehensive view of the accounting aspects of inventory control. The ABC technique for separating inventories into categories worthy of their control is presented.

Inventory pricing is under the influence of government regulations, and every competent inventory manager should be aware of how these regulations apply to him.

Chapter 11. Materials Requirements Planning

Order quantities are *deterministic* when they can be related to a specific demand such as a sales order. In this situation it is desirable to work backwards from a master schedule to determine when and how much material should be started into production. This way of operating has only become feasible since the development of the computer software capable of making the numerous calculations. The software and methods of *exploding* the bills of materials are presented in this chapter.

Chapter 12. Economic Lot Size Planning

If the order quantities are not deterministic, it is common to use the economic order quantity theory presented in this chapter. The background for calculating when to order and how much to order is presented without any regard for stochastic information. This chapter contains material typical of that which is covered in an introductory course.

Chapter 13. Inventory Models

This chapter presents some of the inventory models, such as LIMIT, which have had some acceptance in industry. In addition, it includes the inventory models which are to be found in software packages. The emphasis is on models which are found useful in industry, and there is no attempt to present a cataloging of all inventory models regardless of whether they are useful or not.

10

Inventory Management and Control

A DISTINCTION should be made between inventory management and inventory control. *Inventory management* pertains to the development and administration of policies as well as the systems and procedures by which they are implemented. *Inventory control* pertains to the implementing and carrying out of policies which have been established by management. The policies which have been established by management are carried out by production and inventory control.

Inventory Management Policies

Management policies for inventories are broad in scope, covering all aspects of inventories. Not all facets may be included here, but some of the more important will be touched on.

Inventories are money and consequently should work efficiently. One measure of efficiency is inventory turnover.

$$\text{Inventory turnover} = \frac{\text{Annual cost of goods sold}}{\text{Average value of inventory}}$$

While a high inventory turnover ratio does not tell the complete picture, it is at least some indication of management efficiency.

Another bench mark of managerial efficiency is the ratio of inventory to total assets, Figure 10–1. This kind of information is available to all managers, and they should be aware of the norms of their industry and how their operation compares.

Since inventories are money, management must decide where the money will be invested to do the most good. Rather than investing in inventories, it

Figure 10–1

MANUFACTURERS OF—FARM MACHINERY & EQUIPMENT 48 STATEMENTS ENDED ON OR ABOUT JUNE 30, 1972 47 STATEMENTS ENDED ON OR ABOUT DECEMBER 31, 1972						MANUFACTURERS OF—GENERAL INDUSTRIAL MACHINERY & EQUIPMENT 75 STATEMENTS ENDED ON OR ABOUT JUNE 30, 1972 167 STATEMENTS ENDED ON OR ABOUT DECEMBER 31, 1972				
UNDER $250M	$250M & LESS THAN $1MM	$1MM & LESS THAN $10MM	$10MM & LESS THAN $50MM	ALL SIZES	ASSET SIZE	UNDER $250M	$250M & LESS THAN $1MM	$1MM & LESS THAN $10MM	$10MM & LESS THAN $50MM	ALL SIZES
32	45	11	95		NUMBER OF STATEMENTS	26	64	109	43	242
%	%	%	%	%	ASSETS	%	%	%	%	%
5.2	5.2	6.1	5.7		Cash	6.2	5.8	5.3	4.6	4.8
.4	1.1	1.4	1.2		Marketable Securities	.6	.9	1.4	.6	.8
23.3	24.1	30.6	27.7		Receivables Net	26.4	31.3	28.4	27.2	27.7
47.6	38.2	38.7	38.9		Inventory Net	25.8	30.2	33.4	33.3	33.2
1.3	4.6	2.1	3.0		All Other Current	.4	2.3	2.1	2.1	2.1
77.8	73.2	78.8	76.5		Total Current	59.4	70.5	70.6	67.8	68.6
18.5	19.7	16.2	17.7		Fixed Assets Net	35.6	23.3	23.5	25.5	24.9
3.6	7.2	5.0	5.8		All Other Non-Current	5.0	6.2	5.9	6.8	6.5
100.0	100.0	100.0	100.0		Total	100.0	100.0	100.0	100.0	100.0
					LIABILITIES					
					Due To Banks-Short Term	12.0	11.9	8.6	5.1	6.2
					Due To Trade	13.8	17.0	13.2	10.8	11.6
					...me Taxes	1.5	2.2	2.2	3.1	2.8
					...as LT Debt	6.1	2.3	1.9	1.9	1.9
						10.6	11.4	8.2	5.8	6.6
						43.9	44.9	34.1	26.6	29.2
						16.6	10.9	10.6	14.9	13.7
							55.8	44.7	41.5	42.9
									2.3	1.8
										55.4

Source: Robert Morris Associates, Philadelphia National Bank Building, Philadelphia, Pa., 19107.

might be more profitable to buy capital equipment, invest outside the company, or even hold the funds in a readily available form so that they may be used for some opportunity that comes along.

Robert Morris Associates does not claim that these composite figures are representative of the entire industry because only companies are included for whom submitting banks have recent figures. No claim is made for statistical validity. Also, some companies have varied product lines so they are cataloged by the primary product. Do not automatically consider the figures as representative norms.

One way that management controls the size of inventory is by including the value of money as one of the factors in the order quantity equations to be discussed in a later chapter. Often management does not realize that its decision concerning the opportunity costs of investments affects the size of inventories.

What happens to the operating inventory as the value of money is changed in the economic ordering decision models? It is of interest to note that when the value of money is doubled, say from 5 percent to 10 percent, the inventory order quantity will be $\sqrt{\frac{1}{2}}$ or 71 percent of the original value. A 29 percent reduction in inventory results in money working 41 percent more efficiently.

There are many other inventory decisions which have to do with the value of money. For example, a company may decide to hedge against the possibility of a strike or other interruption of the flow of raw materials. A company may also wish to hedge against price changes. Management will also know of sales campaigns which might create unusual demands upon inventories.

Discussions concerning the investment alternatives always assume that alternatives are possible. This is not necessarily true as more than one company has found it necessary to operate with very small inventories so that payrolls can be met every week. More than one unethical company has been known to send customers' statements well before a product has been shipped with the hope of generating some cash for operations.

The pricing of inventories to give the best price break is a top-level management policy decision. There are also questions concerning property taxes and insurance which should be included in managerial policies.

The categorizing of inventories becomes a management decision. What are supplies and what are materials for production? What products should be logged in and out on a perpetual inventory record? How much inventory should be on hand at the time the physical inventory is taken? These are all management policies to be conveyed to inventory control.

Without customers there will be no company—and without good customer service there will be no customers. Needless to say, the number of inventory stockouts permitted is a very important management policy. The availability of service parts is a management policy decision which may cost the company a bundle of money but may have an excellent payoff in better customer relations.

It is not the purpose here to exhaust all of the inventory management policies that exist but only to point out that inventory management and inventory control are two different subjects. Most books on inventory concentrate on control techniques, while more attention should be given management policies.

The Inventory Control Function

The inventory control function should be discussed not only as an input to the production control system but also as a system in itself, for the information from the inventory system is an input to the purchasing system and the cost system, as well as to the production system. The inventory function is also a system with inputs from the production function, purchasing function, and others. Thus it might be difficult to decide where in the development of a system design this subject should appear, but since we are talking of inputs in general, the discussion of inventories and how they are controlled should come early.

The Meaning of Inventory.   The word *inventory* has so many meanings that it often leaves the new student of the subject a bit bewildered. An inventory refers to the movable articles of a business which are eventually expected to go into the flow of trade. Inventory is also used to indicate the value of these goods. Frequently it is used to designate a detailed list of the articles, with perhaps the description, identification number, quantity, and value. Inventory can also be used as a transitive verb to indicate the counting and listing of goods. We frequently hear such statements as "Companies usually *inventory* their goods on the first of January." The meaning of these different usages soon becomes apparent.

Classes of Inventory.   Industries find that it is far more convenient to establish classes of inventory rather than to throw everything together into one class. They separate those goods which have had no work done on them from those which have had some work done, and both from those which are finished. The advantages of making these classifications will be obvious as you become more aware of the problems involved.

The common inventory classifications found in industry are:

Raw materials.
Materials in process.
Finished products.
Component parts.
Supplies.

The term *raw materials* can have two quite distinct meanings to the economist. First, it can mean that the material has just been extracted from nature. For example, iron ore, crude oil, and coal would all be raw materials in this sense. The other meaning, understandable to both economist and the accountant, is that raw materials are those goods which have had no work added to them *in the plant in which they are situated.* This is the definition which will be used here.

Raw materials, then, can sometimes be considered as finished materials. For example, iron pigs are finished products for the blast furnaces, but raw materials for the foundry. Rough castings are the finished goods for the foundry, but raw materials for the machine shops. And, in turn, the finished castings may be the raw materials for a manufacturer of generators.

The relationship among the classes—raw materials, materials in process, and finished goods—can be shown more vividly by a chart of costs versus operations (Figure 10–2).

The raw material comes into the plant with an initial cost, shown on the left of the chart. As it remains in storage, it "gains" some cost, but the major cost contributions come at the various operations shown on the chart. After the material starts through the steps of the process, it is considered as material in process. Of course it eventually reaches the end of the processing and becomes a finished product.

At the end of the fiscal period the cost of the raw materials is easily obtained (for inventory purposes) from the invoices or lists of merchandise sent from the vendors. The finished goods cost is fairly easy to obtain by accumulating the labor costs, materials costs, and overhead. The real difficulty is finding the cost of materials in process at some particular stage. So, when the inventories have to be evaluated, it is more easily done in either

Figure 10–2
Relationship of Material Costs

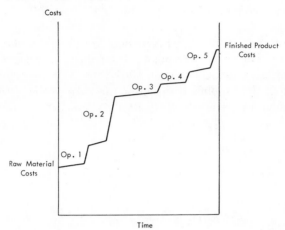

the raw materials form or in the finished product form. This is often impossible to arrange without considerable loss in production.

Component parts are either manufactured or purchased units which are carried in stock. A distinction may be needed between simple parts, such as washers and bolts, and complex items, such as motors, generators, and other subassemblies which will eventually go into the assemblies. The situation becomes more complicated because these subassembly units might be sold as replacement parts or used in the production of final assemblies. The complex subassemblies are, at times, kept in a separate inventory grouping under such a title as "Assemblies."

Supplies are items which are not included in the final product, except in a very minor way: such things as lubricating oil, repair parts for machines, cleaning and polishing materials, and similar indirect cost items.

These are the classifications, although they may have different names, which most companies find will cover their needs. A company should, however, as it thinks necessary, break its inventory down into classes.

The Importance of Inventories and Their Management

It is difficult to pick up the financial section of a newspaper without finding some reference to the status of inventories. Such a comment as the following is commonplace and typical: "Economists say that an efficient clean-up of the heavy carryover of this year's inventory of cars, and brisk early sale of next year's models, would lead to a high automobile production and would stimulate a comfortable rise in the output of steel, copper, glass, tires, textiles, and other material."

The values of inventories in an industry are watched carefully by investors and regarded as bellwethers of industry. When raw material inventories build up, it shows some optimism in the future sales of a product. Permitting inventories to become depleted is apt to indicate a pessimistic attitude by the industry.

The inventory is of such great consequence to the manufacturer that it shows up in the most important financial statements, the balance sheet and the profit and loss statement (Figure 10–3).

As shown in the simplified version of the balance sheet, the inventory value appears on the assets side. It is part of the property owned by the còm-

Figure 10–3
Balance Sheet and Profit and Loss Statement

Statement of Financial Position	May 31, 19––	May 31, 19––
CURRENT ASSETS:		
Cash	$ 6,769,180	$ 10,436,420
Temporary cash investments, at cost	14,091,774	44,494
Receivables, less allowance for doubtful accounts of $_____ and $927,000, respectively	44,179,473	40,856,243
Inventories	50,881,396	53,644,821
Advances on purchases	2,802,895	5,501,391
Prepaid expenses	1,625,947	1,969,672
Total current assets	$120,350,665	$112,453,041
CURRENT LIABILITIES:		
Notes payable	$ 11,363,198	$ 19,152,955
Trade accounts payable	22,261,720	20,141,457
Accrued liabilities and miscellaneous accounts payable	10,645,696	10,151,255
Dividends payable	930,173	899,299
Current portion of long-term debt (Note 4)	472,082	1,106,799
Taxes on income	3,907,760	3,513,450
Total current liabilities	$ 49,580,629	$ 54,965,215
WORKING CAPITAL	$ 70,770,036	$ 57,487,826
PROPERTY, PLANT, AND EQUIPMENT (Note 3)	64,211,251	65,975,109
GOODWILL ARISING UPON CONSOLIDATION (Note 1)	3,154,704	2,880,332
INVESTMENTS AND OTHER ASSETS	2,607,209	1,887,981
	$140,743,200	$128,231,248
DEDUCT:		
Deferred taxes on income (Note 5)	$ 334,944	$ 564,210
Long-term debt, non-current portion (Note 4)	38,736,752	27,512,828
Minority stockholders' interest	1,499,401	1,423,913
	$ 40,571,097	$ 29,500,951
NET ASSETS	$100,172,103	$ 98,730,297
STOCKHOLDERS' EQUITY:		
$4 cumulative preferred stock (redeemed during the year)	$ —	$ 2,539,800
Common stock (Note 6)	36,821,420	36,710,117
Accumulated earnings, retained and used in the business (Note 4)	63,350,683	59,480,380
	$100,172,103	$ 98,730,297

Statement of Earnings	19––	19––
INCOME:		
Net sales of products and services (Note 7)	$446,361,776	$419,798,321
Interest and miscellaneous income	1,728,523	1,168,545
	$448,090,299	$420,966,866
COSTS AND EXPENSES:		
Cost of products and services	$344,415,269	$326,661,702
Selling, general, and administrative expenses	81,403,139	74,972,909
Interest and debt expense	2,990,232	3,127,637
Miscellaneous deductions	1,278,632	1,268,904
	$430,087,272	$406,031,152
EARNINGS BEFORE TAXES ON INCOME	$ 18,003,027	$ 14,935,714
TAXES ON INCOME (Note 5)	9,000,000	7,113,453
NET EARNINGS	$ 9,003,027	$ 7,822,261

Cost of Products includes starting inventory plus purchases less ending inventory.

Source: *The Pillsbury Company.*

pany, and the managers—as well as the stockholders—are interested in knowing just how well this property is used. The most recent inventory value and the previous value are both shown on the profit and loss statements as a means of calculating that most important figure: the profit or the loss. There are also a number of relationships among the inventory value and other values, shown on both the balance sheet and the profit and loss statement, which indicate the efficiency of an industrial organization.

Materials in Process

Industry has emphasized control of raw materials and finished goods with little consideration being given to goods in process. This may be because goods in process is considered the responsibility of plant layout, processing, and materials handling. The production control department should realize what effects excessive work-in-process inventories have on costs and act to minimize them.

Often the production control department is guilty of releasing more material to the plant than it can use with the thought that this will smooth out production scheduling. In reality this procedure not only will increase the work-in-process inventory but also can increase the through-put time.

Stock-picking and kitting components in advance of the time they are needed for assembly will increase the materials in process. This might be minimized by better inventory and scheduling techniques, but it is nearly impossible to eliminate entirely.

Besides the cost of investment, excess goods in process may be costly in other respects. Material becomes damaged, depreciates, gets lost, is processed into the wrong order, or just stolen. Floors crowded with goods in process can be dangerous and cause delays in processing.

There is a case, on the other hand, for having large work-in-process inventories. For one thing it gives the machine operators freedom to select orders to minimize the set-up times. Production line workers get some satisfaction out of seeing the material accumulate at the end of the line, and a stockpile ahead of a line will often act as an incentive.

Importance of a Good Inventory Control System

Before we expand the subject of inventories it will be well to emphasize the importance of good control over the inventory.

1. A good inventory control system minimizes the possibility of delays in production. Depletion of an item's inventory quantity may indicate a sad and dangerous condition for a factory.

Consider what would happen if an automobile company ran out of sheet steel. The plant would have to close down, discharge its employees, stop processes (which cannot be started again overnight), advise its carriers that there would be no cars to deliver, and inform unhappy customers that they would have to wait. Probably the dividends would be lower, which would make the stockholders unhappy, and they would proceed to replace the management that let this happen in the first place. This is a black picture, but it is the sort of thing that happens to companies with poor inventory control.

2. A good inventory control system permits a company to exercise economies in many ways. It eliminates duplication in ordering and encourages a better utilization of available materials by interdepartment or intercompany transfers. Purchasing economies can be exercised by obtaining quantity and shipping discounts.

3. A good inventory control system is essential for an efficient accounting system. This is especially true for the materials aspect of cost accounting.

4. A good inventory control is a deterrent to dishonest people who might steal materials from the factory. Also, a good inventory control stimulates respect for the material, minimizing losses caused by damage in careless handling. And, of course, a good inventory control system is desirable to expedite the production of the financial statements.

INVENTORY CONTROL AND THE ORGANIZATION

The inventory control function can be in one of several places on the organizational chart. Its exact location depends upon the financial condition of the company, the product which is being produced, and, not of least importance, the people who are involved. From the manufacturing viewpoint, the best place to have the inventory function is directly under the manufacturing supervisor. It is often, however, under the supervision of accounting, and occasionally one finds it under the supervision of the purchasing agent. The purchasing agent, closely connected with the vendor, is sensitive to new products coming out and can often buy to advantage if he knows the inventory. In case a company is short of working capital, or is buying in a speculative market, the treasurer should keep a close watch on the inventory.

One possibility in organizing the inventory control function is to split it between finished goods and raw materials. The factory might have supervision of the raw materials and the sales department might take over the supervision of the finished inventory. The sales department's control should not extend back into the production function, for its objectives are frequently different and this can cause confusion.

Inventory Control and the Accounting Function

The production personnel are interested in the physical flow of inventories as it affects production, and consequently have become more and more involved in the accountant's realm of recording the value of inventories. The two areas, production and accounting, are so closely interrelated that it is well for both to be cognizant of the interests and objectives of the other.

The cost accounting department performs five principal functions in handling the details of the stores inventory.

1. It supervises the stores inventory auxiliary ledger records pertaining to the receipts, issues, and balance of all store items.
2. It maintains an up-to-date price record of all items kept in the storeroom by revising the unit prices of any items when the purchase invoice indicates the necessity for their revision.
3. It prices the stores requisition and makes the extensions and totals thereon for all items issued.
4. It prepares cost summaries showing the cost of materials and supplies consumed.
5. It prepares the factory journal or journal voucher entries for all store items issued, spilled, salvaged, and scrapped, and for the estimated shrinkage of the stores inventory.[1]

The accountant has found it necessary to improve his recording systems as industry has become more complex and demanding. He has found it necessary to divide and subdivide accounts to paint a more realistic financial picture and to cash in on the specialized abilities of various individuals.

In the most elementary form of cost accounting, all the costs of manufacturing are subtracted from the income for any period of time. Among the costs of manufacturing is the cost of material, which is obtained by adding the cost of the initial inventory to the material purchases and deducting the cost of the remaining inventory. In today's more complex accounting systems, there are numerous records in which the daily transactions are recorded. These accounts, pertaining to the control of inventories, are shown in the flow diagram of Figure 10–4.

Figure 10–4
Accounting for Inventories (dollars)

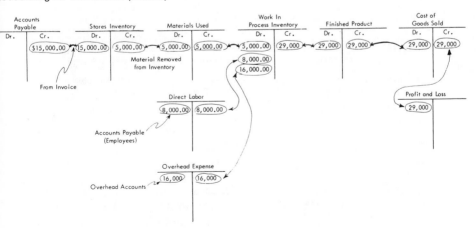

[1] Clarence L. Van Sickle, *Cost Accounting Fundamentals and Procedures*, 2d ed. (New York: Harper & Brothers, 1947).

A word about the flow of the entries shown in the diagram might be useful for those unfamiliar with accounting procedures. Most all accounting today is *double entry*, which means that two entries will be made for each transaction. The two entries which are associated on the diagram are connected by an arrow, but there are numerous alternatives to the accounting procedure shown.

The cost accounting records are affected not only by the inventory transactions but also by the general accounts, which include accounts payable and the cash account. The flow of materials into the inventory and the payment procedure are shown in Figure 10–5.

Figure 10–5
General Accounting Procedure for Receiving

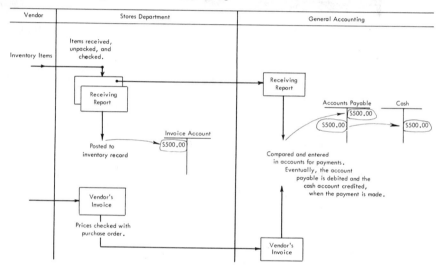

This has been a sketchy overview of the accountant's part in the inventory procedure, but if you are a serious student of manufacturing you will become thoroughly familiar with accounting, and, in particular, cost accounting. Probably no other subject can give you such an important insight into manufacturing.

Inventory Control and the Purchasing Function

Nearly everyone seems to get involved in the inventory control procedure, but the purchasing department is particularly involved. A common practice followed for the purchasing cycle is shown in Figure 10–6. The purchase requisition is initiated by a person with authority, and, most frequently, by someone involved in the inventory records.

If the order is one of high value, it is not too uncommon to request price

Figure 10–6
Purchasing Procedure

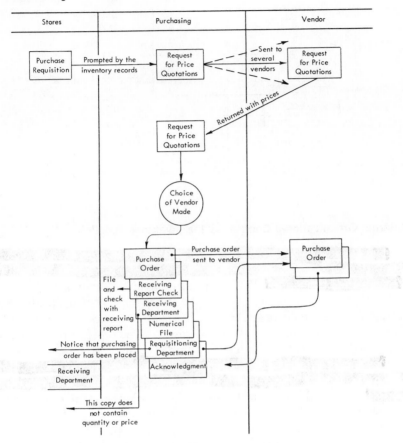

quotations from several vendors. This, however, is a slow process, and usually the purchase order is placed directly with a vendor on the basis of known quality, service, transportation cost, or other criteria.

This is not the place to study the purchasing function intensively, but probably no other function can contribute more to an efficient manufacturing operation.

Inventory Control and the Sales Function

The finished inventory is withdrawn by the authority of the *sales order*. A typical chain of events for the sales order is shown in Figure 10–7. This is a typical procedure, but there are simpler and more complex methods for consummating the sale of the product.

Figure 10–7
Sales Procedure

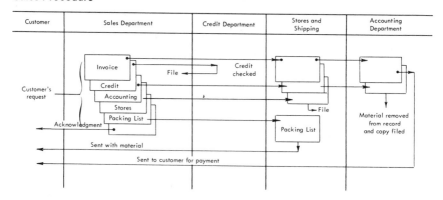

Internal Organizational Control for the Inventory Function

The physical inventory count, which must be taken once a year, is a check against errors and theft, but once a year is sometimes not often enough for keeping the best control. If there is an error in the records, it should be detected as soon as possible, before the stores run out of materials which are essential for production. On the other hand, dishonest employees in the factory should be found out as soon as possible. The very fact that inventory is checked periodically will often keep employees honest.

One way of patrolling the inventory is to set up a three-way check among the stores keeper, the inventory record clerk, and some other responsible person (such as the assistant to the works manager). At intervals, perhaps once a week, the assistant chooses some product numbers at random. He makes a simultaneous request for counts, from both the inventory record clerk and the stores keeper. If the counts do not agree, the discrepancies can be investigated and corrected at once. This three-way check minimizes any cover-up of records, which otherwise could go on year after year.

Organizational Division of the Inventory Control Function

There are three distinct functions in inventory control: the actual receiving and shipping (with the required checking of goods), the store-keeping, and the recordkeeping. All three activities can be located in one place, or they can be distributed around the plant in separate localities. If separated, more communication among the groups is necessary and the system becomes more complex. In addition to the above functions, the inventory control group frequently serves other purposes. They sometimes salvage and rework material, and often prepare material for production. This is especially common in the metal working industry, where it is necessary to cut materials to length.

INVENTORY RECORDS

Many small companies operate efficiently without any written records of their inventories. The number of items is so few and the quantities so small that one man can keep track of them. This method depends upon an occasional physical count of the items, known as a *physical inventory*. For many small companies this method is the cheapest and most efficient, and a complex and extensive system should never be imposed upon them.

Materials Budgets for Continuous Manufacturing

In continuous manufacturing, the materials needs should be budgeted on the basis of the sales forecast (which was discussed in Chapter 5). By anticipating the materials needed on a weekly or monthly basis, the shipments of materials can be kept flowing with a minimum of delay. The materials for production can be received, processed through the inventory control, and go directly to work in process without any excessive handling within the plant. The materials budget can be made a year in advance; and minor adjustments can be made throughout the year, as necessary, to meet changing demand and production.

The Use of Bin Tags for Inventory Control

The bin tag, used in two quite distinctly different systems, is found in many companies today. In the first situation, the bin tag is the only form of written record kept on the storeroom items. The tag, which is fastened to the front of each bin, has all the identification information, such as part and number and part name. In the body of the tag is space to record the withdrawals and additions. This is done at the time by the storeroom clerk. This system, however, leaves much to be desired. The clerk frequently fails to fill in the necessary information because he doesn't have a pencil, his hands are full, or he "just forgets."

In the second situation, the bin tag is used as a supplemental record to that which is kept by the inventory clerk. The record on the bin tag and the inventory record should agree. This method of using the bin tag doubles the work that has to be done and is probably not worth the effort.

Perpetual Inventory

The perpetual inventory record is a running account of the incoming materials, outgoing materials, and the balance on hand. At practically any instant one should be able to check the perpetual inventory and determine the quantity on hand and the activity of the particular item. The perpetual inventory record can take many forms which assist in the rapid transfer of information, but for simplicity's sake consider here that the inventory information is placed on a card. This card has two distinct sections: the heading, where all of the unchanging information is placed, and the body, where the changing information is to be found. A short discussion of these two sections will point out the type of information that might be needed. It cannot be stressed too strongly that information not put to useful purposes should be left off the record.

In the heading, shown in Figure 10–8, the following might be found:

Figure 10–8
Heading for Perpetual Inventory Record

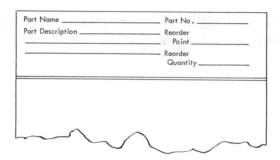

Material Designation. The part name and number should be shown clearly at a position on the form that makes it convenient to leaf through the forms and find the desired card.

Part Description and Size. A brief description of the part, with the size and any other important information, should be contained on the card.

Reorder Point. This should contain the information that will indicate the reorder time to the recordkeeper. He will be able to check the quantity on hand with the order point.

Reorder Quantity. When the clerk makes out the requisition for materials, the order quantity should be readily available; and this is a convenient place to keep the information.

Many companies have additional information on their inventory cards. For example, it might be desirable to include the reserve quantity on the card to show when the inventory goes below the danger point. When the reserve quantity is omitted, the clerk must be aware of items which should be watched carefully. The product specification, or a description of the material from which the product is made, might be carried on the inventory card. If the item is purchased from the outside, the list of vendors can be kept on the card, along with the ordering priority. The location of the material in the storeroom can be indicated as well. The record is a useful place to keep information about the product, but care should be exercised to keep the record from becoming cluttered with a lot of useless information which will lead to the introduction of errors and delays.

The essential information included in the body of an inventory record

Figure 10–9
Body of Perpetual Inventory Record

RECEIVED			ISSUED			BALANCE
Date	Order No.	Quantity	Date	Order No.	Quantity	Quantity

card (Figure 10–9) tells us about the incoming and outgoing material, and what is on hand. There are other items which we will discuss, but this is the minimum that one could expect. In each incoming and outgoing column should be sufficient information to determine the person responsible for making the entry, the date the entry was made, and the source document— such as the materials requisition, stores record, and so on. Other columns of information find their useful purpose in the inventory record, but first the flow of information into this simple record should be shown.

Flow of Information in and out of Inventory Cards

Since there is a difference in the flow of information for raw materials records and finished goods, each will be discussed separately. Figure 10–10 shows the elementary raw materials record, with the accompanying input and output information. Each of these will be discussed briefly.

Figure 10–10
Flow of Information for Raw Materials Inventory

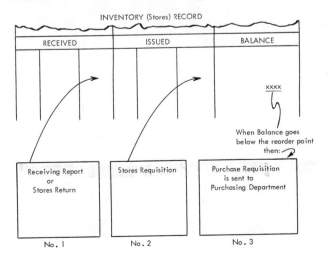

Number 1 (in the illustration) is the receiving report. The receiving department maintains a file of unfilled purchase orders against which it checks incoming shipments. The receiving report is the form which is used by the receiving clerk to notify the inventory clerk that material has been received. This should give all the pertinent information, such as the quantity, date, and rejections if any. One might ask why a copy of the purchase order should not be used for this purpose. It could, if the entire order is filled at one time. Since this does not occur frequently, separate receiving reports for each shipment must be made out. Several copies of the receiving report are made out at one time and sent to different departments for various purposes.

Number 2, the stores requisition, is an authorization to remove material from stores. One might consider that the stores clerk is responsible for all stock, and if he doesn't have the material on hand, he must have a record to show why—and where—it has gone. The stores requisition serves much as a personal check does on a bank account. This form will usually originate in the production control department. After the material is issued by the stores clerk, the quantity will be deducted from the stores record and the stores requisition will be forwarded to cost accounting for calculating the cost of the product.

Number 3, the purchase requisition, is a signal or authorization to the purchasing agent of a company to procure the goods described. This, of course, cannot be issued by just anyone but must come from an authorized person, such as the inventory clerk.

Figure 10–11 shows a set of typical forms which might be used for the receiving report, stores requisition, and purchase requisition.

The stores requisition will seldom be made out for exactly the quantity used in production; it will also take into account the quantity of material that might be spoiled during manufacturing. If this excess material is not used, or if material is returned for some other reason, there must be some provision for doing this. The "storage return" or "credit" requisition is the form that is made out for this purpose and might be considered as a stores requisition in reverse. It should contain the same information.

Before going to more complicated stores records, let us see how the stores record for finished goods would be different from the one just illustrated. In Figure 10–12 we have a flow chart that depicts the inputs and outputs for the finished goods inventory.

The forms which are used for the input and output of the finished goods inventory are the materials received from manufacture report, the sales order, and the production order. These have been numbered on the flow chart for ready reference.

Number 4, the materials received from manufacture report, is used to account for the materials coming into the finished stores. A copy of this form should be sent not only to the inventory control but also to the production and accounting departments. At times, the manufacturing order might serve the purpose of materials received from manufacture report. This

Figure 10–11
Typical Forms

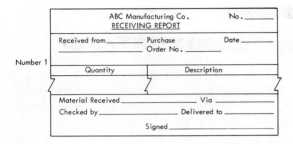

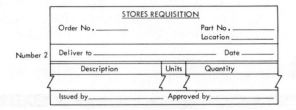

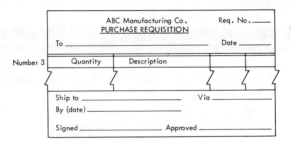

Figure 10–12
Finished Goods Inventory

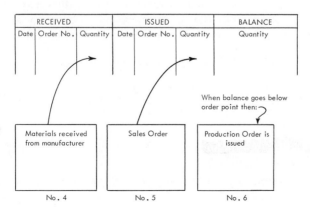

report serves the same purpose for the finished stores record as does the receiving report for raw materials.

Number 5 is the sales order, which is the authorization to remove the finished goods from the inventory.

Number 6 is a production order, or production requisition, which serves as a signal and authorization for manufacturing to produce goods to fill up the inventory which has become depleted (as shown) when the balance on hand is compared with the order point.

The component-part inventory record will be slightly different from the raw materials record and the finished goods record. If the component is a purchased component, it will have the same inputs and outputs as the raw materials record. However, if it is a manufactured component, it will differ from the finished goods inventory record in that the sales order will be replaced by the stores requisition.

Records for Additional Information

The perpetual inventory record—with its three columns, received, issued, and balance—is sufficient for many inventory systems, but occasionally more information may be desirable (as is shown in Figure 10–13).

An *ordered* column should be added to the inventory record form if the ordering cycle is so long that one or more orders might be out at one time. The purpose of this column is to prevent making repeated orders for materials when they are not needed. The input of information for this column would, of course, be the purchase order for raw materials and components and the manufacturing order for finished goods and manufactured components. The ordered column should only be added to the record when multiple orders are being made and when it is costly to have duplicate orders delivered. Adding the column may cause errors which would not occur on the illustrated, simpler form.

Similar reasoning could be used for an *apportioned* column. If the materials go directly into production after the requisition has been made, there is no need for the apportioned entry. If, however, there is a delay which would cause a serious overdraw on the materials on hand, then this column should be added. The input of the apportioned column would come from the manufacture order.

Classifying Inventory by the ABC Technique

The professional manager will expend his efforts where they will yield the greatest rewards. Fortunately he has a well-developed tool, the ABC inventory analysis technique which makes it possible for him to use this philosophy with relative ease.

The ABC analysis is a formal way of classifying inventory items so that the important ones will be given the most attention. The importance is

Figure 10-13
Records for Additional Information

Part Name __Bracket Motor Mount__   Order Point 1000   Part No. 8A-1036

Part Description __C.I. Bracket, 3" center, ½" holes.__   Order Quantity 8000

1. Ordered			2. Received		3. Balance on Hand		4. Issued			5. Apportioned but Not Issued			6. Available for New Orders	
Date	Order No.	Quantity	Date	Quantity	Date	Quantity	Date	Order No.	Quantity	Date	Order No.	Quantity	Date	Quantity
7/15	P.O.-950	8000			6/16	3000	6/20	MO-98	1200				6/16	3000
						1800	7/12	MO-127	1000				6/20	1800
						800	7/28	MO-316	600	7/22	MO-316	2400	7/12	800
		0000	8/1	8000	8/1	200						−600	7/15	8800
		8000				8200							7/22	6400

measured in terms of *annual-usage value*. The annual-usage value is determined for each inventory item by multiplying the unit cost by the quantity used or forecasted during a year. The ABC of the ABC analysis refers to three classes, A, B, and C, into which the inventory is divided when the annual usage value is considered. As illustrated in Figure 10–14 only a few

Figure 10–14
Typical Distribution of ABC Analysis

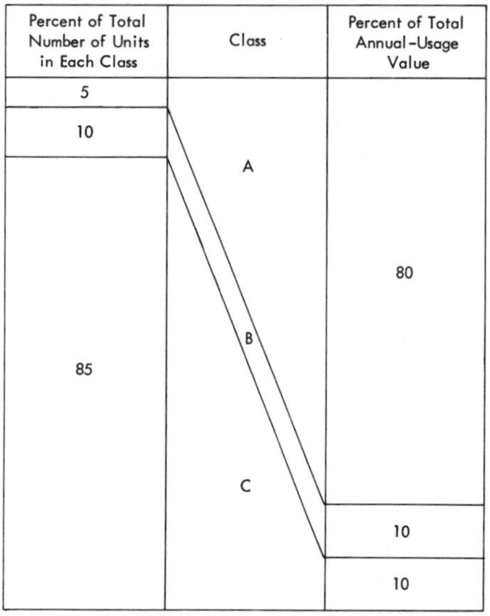

of the items in Class A account for the major portion of the annual-usage value, while many items in Class C account for very little of the total value. This is important because it shows where managers should focus their attention.

Each of the three classes should be given different treatment. Management will want to consider:

Applying occasional physical inventory counts instead of maintaining perpetual inventory records for the C items and perhaps the B items.

Different ordering procedure for the different classes. The frequency of orders, quantity ordered, safety stock permitted, and lead time should be evaluated for each of the classes.

The method of issuing stock might be more relaxed for C items than for B and A items.

In general, forecasting A items should be taken more seriously than for C items.

The ABC distribution is illustrated further in Figure 10–15 by what has become known as the typical ABC curve. You will observe that the *per-*

Figure 10–15
ABC Curve

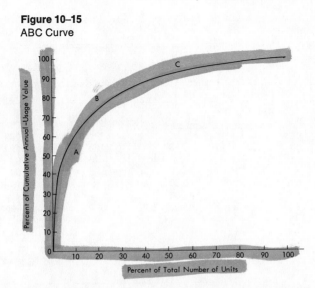

centage of cumulative annual-usage value is plotted along the vertical axis, while the percentage of the total number of units is plotted along the horizontal axis. This is the common way of displaying information for the ABC analysis, but occasionally one sees the data plotted with the total annual-usage value on the vertical axis and the percentage of the total number of units plotted on the horizontal.

The percentage of items in each inventory class is different for each situation. The divisions illustrated are typical, but each company will have to determine its own dividing line between classes of inventory items. Some companies prefer to use four classes and some only two. The class name is not important and x, y, and z have been used as well as such names as *blue chip* for A to convey the importance of a class.

Mechanics of the ABC Analysis

Step 1. Before the ABC analysis is made, a list of the inventory items as shown in Figure 10–16 must be available with the essential information.

Step 2. Calculate the annual-usage value in dollars for each item, see Figure 10–16. Annual-usage value, col. 4 = Number of items used or forecasted/year (col. 3) × Unit value (col. 2).

Step 3. Sort according to the annual-usage value and place in a descending sequence as shown in Figure 10–17, col. 4.

Step 4. Print a list for these ranked items showing:

1. Part name and number, col. 1, Figure 10–17.
2. Unit value, col. 2.
3. Units used per year, col. 3.
4. Annual value, $/year, col. 4.

Figure 10–16
Step 2 Calculations for ABC

Item	Part Name and No.		Col. 2 Unit Value ($/unit)	Col. 3 Units Used (units/year)	Col. 4 Annual-Usage Value for Each Item ($/year)
	Col. 1				
	Step 1			Step 2	
1	Union	U–83	.46 ×	1,304 =	599.84
2	Coupling	C–21	.83	1,220	1,012.60
3	Pipe	P–33	.21	1,400	294.00
4	Gasket	G–20	.08	2,500	200.00
5	Trap	T–8	5.00	102	510.00
6	Trap	T–4	4.00	211	844.00
7	Union	U–98	1.00	599	599.00
8	Valve	V–30	8.00	500	4,000.00
9	Valve	V–28	7.50	200	1,500.00
10	Pipe	P–30	.25	2,000	500.00
	Total Annual Usage Value				$10,060.24

Step 5. Starting at the top of the table, compute the cumulative annual-usage value in dollars/year, col. 5.

Step 6. Compute the cumulative *percentage* of annual-usage value, col. 7.

$$\text{Percentage, col. 7.} = \frac{\text{Figure in col. 5 for each item}}{\text{Last figure in cumulative annual usage (col. 5)}}$$

$$\text{Example 1.} = \frac{5,500.00}{10,060.24} = 54\%$$

Step 7. Starting at the top of col. 3, compute a cumulative total of units used per year, col. 6.

Step 8. Compute the percentage of cumulative annual usage.

$$\text{Percentage of cumulative annual usage} = \frac{\text{Cumulative units in year}}{\text{Last figure in col. 6}}$$

$$\text{Example 2.} \qquad \frac{700}{10,036} = 7\%$$

Step 9. Plot the values, Figure 10–18, given in col. 7 on the vertical axis and those in col. 8 on the horizontal axis. Draw in curve.

Step 10. Decide upon appropriate divisions for the ABC classes. Typical would be:

Class A— 0 to 60% annual-usage value.
Class B—60 to 85% annual-usage value.
Class C—85 to 100% annual-usage value.

Figure 10–17
Sorted Inventory Items for ABC Calculations

Item	Col. 1 Part Name and No. (Step 4)	Col. 2 Unit Value ($/unit)	Col. 3 Units Used per Year (units/year)	Col. 4 Annual-Usage Value ($/year) (Step 3)	Col. 5 Cum. Annual-Usage Value ($/year) (Step 5)	Col. 6 Cum. Annual-Usage Units per year (units/year) (Step 7)	Col. 7 x-axis Percent of Cum. Annual-Usage Value (Step 6)	Col. 8 y-axis Percent of Cum. Annual Usage
8 .... Valve	V–30	8.00	500	4,000.00	4,000.00	500	39.8	5
9 .... Valve	V–28	7.50	200	1,500.00	5,500.00	700 Ex.1	54.0 Ex.2	7
2 .... Coupling	C–21	.83	1,220	1,012.60	6,512.60	1,920	65	19
6 .... Trap	T–4	4.00	211	844.00	7,356.60	2,131	73	21
1 .... Union	U–83	.46	1,304	600.64	7,957.24	3,435	79	34
7 .... Union	U–98	1.00	599	599.00	8,556.24	4,034	85	40
5 .... Trap	T–8	5.00	102	510.00	9,066.24	4,136	90	41
10 ... Pipe	P–30	.25	2,000	500.00	9,566.24	6,136	95	61
3 .... Pipe	P–33	.21	1,400	294.00	9,860.24	7,536	98	75
4 .... Gasket	G–20	.08	2,500	200.00	10,060.24	10,036	100	100

Figure 10–18
ABC Curve Example

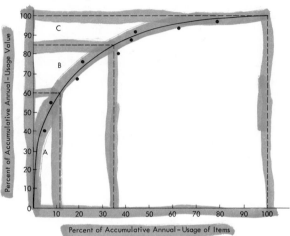

Percent of Accumulative Annual – Usage of Items

Physical Inventories

The physical inventory is an actual count of the materials on hand. This often entails considerable expense and trouble, and one might ask what is the point of keeping the elaborate perpetual inventory if periodic checks are still made by counting the goods. There are a number of good reasons why this must be done.

Operating the plant without delays is imperative to the management, which wishes to make a profit, as well as to the employee, who is concerned with his income. More than once, a plant or department has had to close down temporarily because of a lack of parts, parts which appeared on the record but could not be found in the storeroom. They had disappeared because of an error in the record, carelessness, or theft. This would be reason enough for a periodic check, but there are also many others.

One of the most important reasons for taking a physical inventory is because banks and the government will not accept a count that is taken from the record and not substantiated by a physical count. The reason for this is apparent when one realizes that the value of the inventory at the start of the accounting period and at the end of the accounting period enters into the calculation of the profit. It is quite natural that the Bureau of Internal Revenue, which taxes profit, is concerned with how these values are obtained.

Several methods are commonly followed in taking the physical inventory.

1. Whenever a requisition is placed, the material in the stores, which should be at a minimum, is checked against the record.

2. Cycle counting is evaluating the inventory material on a continuous basis. Periodically the material is counted so that during the course of a year the items will be counted once. This is the only dependable method

for keeping inventory records accurate and has the following advantages:

a. By proper timing the cycle count can be coordinated with low levels of activity in the storerooms.

b. Errors in the records may be cleared up before the information becomes ancient history.

c. Plant close-downs, with their accompanying costs, may be avoided.

d. A small group of personnel may be assigned this task, and they will be able to develop skill in their tasks.

e. The errors will be significantly less.

A disadvantage is the difficulty in manipulating records so that materials requisitions are reflected in the actual count.

3. A physical count at the end of the accounting period, of six months or a year, is the most common method. Under this plan the activities in the storeroom are suspended for a day or so while the material is counted. This means an unusual demand upon the stores and factory personnel, and frequently the manufacturing activities will have to be closed down, adding another cost to this operation.

In effect, the physical inventory should be taken instantaneously—as if a photograph of all the quantities were taken at one time. This, of course, is impossible, so activities have to be suspended while a "time exposure" is taken. There are, however, various ways that the time can be shortened. Tape recorders and photographs are methods that have been used. The inventory clerks read off the quantities stored into a tape recorder and later a secretary types off a list. The photographic technique can be used where the material can be arranged to be counted in the photograph and where nothing is hidden from view.

In any method of taking the physical inventory, the first step should be to have the stock in good condition, piled in an orderly fashion, and consolidated so it can be counted rapidly.

Probably the most common method of taking inventory rapidly is to use a serrated tag (Figure 10–19) which is fastened to each inventory item

Figure 10–19
Inventory Tags for Physical Inventory

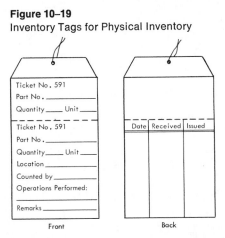

Front   Back

or group of items. This can be done well in advance of the time that the inventory is to be taken. The least active items can be tagged and counted first. Entries can be made on the card later if there are any additions or subtractions. At the instant the inventory is to be taken, the clerks can rapidly go through the stockroom and tear off the bottom half of the card, leaving the top of the tag with the item. The tags can then be checked with the inventory record and, where there are discrepancies, a recheck can be made. With the tag serial number, and the location of the material, it is quite simple to find any errors.

Physical Inventory Procedure. Taking a physical inventory has all the overtones of a small military operation and requires as much detailed planning. To be sure that all of the details have been planned, a standard operating procedure should be established and maintained from year to year. Figure 10–20 shows an actual example of part of a procedure. One person

Figure 10–20
Standard Operating Procedure for a Physical Inventory

Sept. 1	1. Order necessary forms for physical inventory.
	2. Hold first meeting with the following:
	    a. Plant superintendent.
	    b. Purchasing manager.
	    c. Inventory control manager.
	3. Obtain special scales, stamps, pencils, and so on.
	4. Establish physical inventory date.

Sept. 2	Receive items 1 and 3.
Oct. 1	Personnel department will furnish manager with a list of people in each department who can work on the physical inventory.
Oct. 25	1. After the 2d shift the assembly department may not return any unused parts to stores. 2. Scrap must be moved to scrap department. All scrap will be refused after this date. 3. Tooling and fixtures may not be returned after the 2d shift.
Oct. 28	1. Department heads notify plant manager of extra scales and recording equipment needed. 2. Personnel department notifies those people who will be working on the inventory count.
Oct. 31	Store room will close at 12 noon. All material must be withdrawn before this period. Draw only material needed.

should be made responsible for this procedure and given ample authority so that it can be carried out without delays.

This is just an example of the detailed planning needed to carry out an efficient inventory count. Each organization will have to prepare its own schedule, taking into consideration its own unique problems. Some of the things to be considered are included in this list:

1. Obtain supplies needed for taking the inventory.
2. Obtain and train the personnel needed for taking the inventory.
3. Determine the cutoff dates so that material is not counted twice in two different places or missed completely.
4. Keep to a minimum the material which has been withdrawn from stores and on the shop floor.
5. Prepare a map of the areas to be inventoried and assign responsibility for each.
6. Establish the inventory start and cutoff date. (When will the shop start producing again?)
7. Prepare the storeroom for counting. Don't have a housecleaning while counting.
8. Account for all inventory forms. Never scrap forms but mark them VOID. Cards should be placed in numerical sequence and all cards accounted for.
9. Plan the release of inventory personnel. What are their responsibilities before being released?
10. Be sure that all forms are clear and won't need interpretations which will delay the counting.
11. Audit the inventory counts by checking against the inventory records as well as running a double count on some items chosen at random. The audit may be done by an outside accounting firm.

Difficulties Encountered in Inventory Control

A difficulty is encountered in the inventory control procedures when material in process cannot be completed because of some delay in the processing. Perhaps a tool has broken down and it will be some time before it is repaired, or perhaps a rush order has come in that will delay the production of parts in process. Leaving the parts on the production floor often is not desirable because of the space they take up or because they might become damaged.

Part numbers refer to either a raw material or finished goods, so materials in process have no unique number. If the material in process is placed in storage under the finished product number, the records will be incorrect and if not numbered will become lost or forgotten. These "orphaned" materials in process should be given every consideration and adequate cross-references and codes should be set up to prevent any loss.

One knotty problem encountered in inventory control is that subassemblies carried in stock can be drained off in two directions. They can be sent into production to produce a final assembly; or they might be shipped out for replacement parts. Consequently, production of assemblies can be delayed because of a lack of subassemblies which were in the inventory when production started.

THE FLOW AND PRICING OF INVENTORIES

If inventories did not change with time, did not deteriorate, change styles, or otherwise become less desirable, there would be no problem of inventory flow. But because they do change, there is an inventory flow problem which management must face. The problem can best be described, as before, by an analogy.

In the first-in-first-out (Fifo) process, the material which flows in first is the first to flow out. It is as if a viscous fluid, which never mixes, is flowing through the tank. This is the ideal flow of inventories when such changes as the age hardening of steel or the spoilage of dairy products might occur. But, as everyone knows, excessive time delays in such inventories as dairy products can cause customer dissatisfaction. This method can cause considerable difficulty in materials handling because it is necessary to have old stock continuously accessible.

The last-in-first-out (Lifo) method is suitable for items which do not deteriorate. Pipe fittings are typical of such products which, in fact, appear to gain in value with their griminess. With such material, the new stock can be placed in front or on top of the old material, and we can expect seldom if ever to see the first material received.

While the physical flow of the inventory is obviously important, there is a closely related problem of pricing the inventory, which is also important.

Pricing the Inventory

If the material was purchased and sold instantaneously, or if the prices never fluctuated, we would not need to be concerned with the pricing of the inventory. But since it doesn't always move quickly, and prices do change, management must be concerned with the pricing of the inventory as it goes into the cost sheet for the finished product. As we will see, the profits can be understated or overstated, depending upon how the inventory is priced. And when we are tampering with profits we are awakening a whole host of interested parties, ranging from the employee working on a profit-sharing plan to the Bureau of Internal Revenue standing by to tap its share, based on the profits of the company.

Fifo and Lifo sound like the same words we used when discussing the flow of inventories. The analogy is the same, but we should recognize that the material could flow in the Fifo fashion and be priced in the Lifo fashion, and vice versa.

Since the choice of the above methods can have a profound effect upon the balance sheet and the profit and loss statement, let us take a look at the simple one-item inventory and price it under the two methods illustrated. We will first consider a case of prices increasing, and you may wish to try a similar example with prices decreasing.

Fifo Method:

In	Out	Balance	Price	Transaction
		00		
50 gal.		50 gal.	50¢	+$25.00
100 "		150 "	75	+ 75.00
	60 gal.	90 "	{ 50 at 50¢ 10 at 75¢	− 32.50

Lifo Method:

		00		
50 gal.		50 gal.	50¢	+$25.00
100 "		150 "	75	+ 75.00
	60 gal.	90 "	60 at 75¢	− 45.00

It will be worthwhile to make an analysis of this simple example, so let us look at the Fifo method first. Since the prices are going up, we can expect to pay at least the most recent price of 75¢ a gallon for the next purchase, or $45 to replace the 60 gallons sold. This same amount of material was priced out at $32.50, so we have wiped out $45 minus $32.50, or $12.50, of any profit we might have anticipated just by the act of replacing the inventory. Not a very profitable transaction, is it? So, in an increasing market, it would be wise to price the inventory on the Lifo basis rather than on the Fifo basis. What does this do to the value of the remaining inventory? It is out of date, so the inventory shown on the balance sheet will appear out of date, and the true value of the company's assets will not be revealed. One can't have his cake and eat it, apparently. Either the profit and loss statement will be accurate and the balance sheet will be out of date, or the reverse will be true.

The profit, the value of the inventory, and thus the business are strongly influenced by the method chosen for pricing the inventory. It is therefore of vital concern to the stockholders and management, but it is the Bureau of Internal Revenue of the United States Treasury Department which exercises the greatest regulatory force. They are interested because it is the profit which is taxed, and if the profit can be changed so can the taxes.

FEDERAL GOVERNMENT INVENTORY REGULATIONS

Paraphrasing the law is never a substitute for reading the actual text. When you become involved in controlling inventories avail yourself of the current regulations and become familiar with them. The following comments should not be considered as a substitute for reading the law itself.

When it is necessary to use inventories to determine the income of any taxpayer, the inventories will be taken on a basis which will conform as nearly as possible to the best accounting practices in the business that will most clearly reflect the income.

To reflect taxable income correctly, inventories at the beginning and end of each year are necessary in every case in which production, purchase, or sale of merchandise is an income-producing factor.

Inventory values should include all finished or partly finished goods. In the case of raw materials and supplies, only those which have been acquired for sale or will become a part of the merchandise intended for sale (such as containers when the title passes to the customer) are included.

Merchandise should be included in the inventory only if title is vested in the taxpayer. The seller should include in his inventory goods under contract for sale but not segregated and applied to a contract. A purchaser should include in his inventory merchandise which is purchased and to which title has passed to him even though the material may be in transit and not yet in his possession.

Valuation of Inventories

Inventory rules cannot be uniform from company to company since, as has been stated, inventory valuations will conform to the best accounting practices in the business which clearly reflect the income.

An inventory value that can be used under the best accounting practices for a balance sheet to show the financial position of the taxpayer can as a general rule be regarded as clearly reflecting his income.

Inventory practice should be consistent from year to year, and greater weight is given to consistency than to any particular method of inventory or basis of valuation as long as the method complies with the regulations. Two common methods of valuation which meet the requirements are:

1. Cost.
2. Cost or market whichever is lower.

Inventories at Cost.

1. For merchandise on hand at the beginning of the tax year, cost means the inventory price of such goods.
2. For merchandise purchased since the beginning of the tax year, cost is the invoice price less trade or other discounts. Strictly cash discounts which approximate a fair interest rate may be deducted or not at the option of the taxpayer if a consistent course is followed. To the net invoice price should be added transportation and other necessary charges incurred in acquiring the goods.
3. For merchandise produced by the taxpayer since the beginning of the tax year, the following will be used:
   a. Cost of raw materials and supplies entering into or consumed by the product.
   b. Cost of direct labor.
   c. Indirect expenses including a reasonable proportion of management expenses but not any cost of selling or return on capital whether by way of interest or profit.

Inventories at cost or market whichever is lower. Under ordinary circumstances market means the current bid price prevailing at the date of the inventory for the particular merchandise purchased in the usual volume. This is applicable in the cases of:

1. Goods purchased and on hand.
2. Goods in the process of manufacture and on hand which include the elements of cost, materials, labor, and burden. Excluded are goods in process or manufactured for delivery upon firm sales orders at fixed prices entered into before the date of inventory. These goods must be inventoried at cost.

Where inventory is valued upon the basis of cost or market, whichever is lower, the market value of each article on hand at the inventory date shall be compared with the cost of the article, and the lower of such values shall be taken as the inventory value of the article.

Last-in–First-out Inventory. This technique is covered in an extensive section of the regulations. Lifo regulations are considerably more complicated than others. For example, there are problems of identifying raw materials which go into textiles, separating costs of animal carcass derivatives, and the costs of several stage processes such as the rod and wire in a steel mill.

The Lifo inventory method may be adopted and used only if the taxpayer files a request on the appropriate form at the close of the tax year when the method is first used. This request must meet particular requirements and contain a statement of the taxpayer's election to use such an inventory method. The statement will be accompanied by an analysis of all inventories as of the beginning and end of the taxable year and also the beginning of the prior year.

When Lifo is adopted the taxpayer shall file an application which will specify the goods to which it is applied. All materials need not be on Lifo, however a taxpayer who has elected to do so may not elect to exclude any raw materials covered by a previous election. The methods for changing the method and pricing of the inventory are stated in detail in the regulations.

An election to adopt and use Lifo inventory method is irrevocable, and the method once adopted shall be used in all subsequent tax years, unless another method is required by the tax commission or authorized pursuant to a written application. If Lifo is revoked there are specific inventory pricing processes to follow.

State Government Inventory Regulations. There is no uniformity among the state income tax regulations. Therefore, it is important that a manufacturer become acquainted with the regulations in the state in which he does business.

INVENTORY STORAGE

The actual storing and moving of the materials in an inventory might be considered as analogous to the operation of a filing system. As in a filing system, we wish to place and withdraw materials as rapidly and economically as possible. More than one efficient factory has been hampered by an inefficient inventory storage system. While space does not permit an adequate discussion of the materials-handling equipment used to manipulate the materials, we can discuss some of the more efficient ways of locating materials in storage spaces. First we will discuss some of the systematic storage procedures, and then discuss the complicating aspects of inventory storage.

Systematic Storage Procedures

Storage by Part Number. In this procedure, the parts are stored in the sequence of their part numbers. This is satisfactory if all the parts are small and have similar characteristics. What do you do, however, when one part is a five-foot pulley and the next a small key that holds the pulley on the shaft? Or one part is a transformer housing, and the next part in the sequence a can of highly inflammable and messy cooling oil used in the transformer?

In general, this system of storing by part numbers is suitable for small parts where the quantity on hand remains fairly uniform. Bolts, rivets, nails, and similar items which are used in small quantities can be stored very conveniently by this method, but if we are talking about carloads of such items, then there are better storing systems.

Storage by Coordinate Index Number. In this procedure the storage area is laid out in a coordinate index system, and a cross-reference is established between the part number and the index. One way of setting up the index is to number the storage spaces, as in Figure 10–21. The aisles are numbered in sequence, as are the rows and levels of bins. A number, such as 2–4–4, would indicate the bin in the second aisle, fourth column, at the fourth level. To this could have been added a number to designate the particular storage area.

Instead of locating material by part number, the location of the material is shown on the inventory record or on a special index sheet. This requires a little more time in the recordkeeping, but it permits greater flexibility and more efficient utilization of space. If there are excess parts for a certain area, they can overflow into another space, just as long as the cross-reference is made. When the inventory is reduced, the space can be utilized for other purposes.

Storage by Serial Index Number. Rather than establish index number by coordinates, some companies prefer numbering the storage spaces in sequence. This has some advantage for areas which are not perfectly rec-

Figure 10–21
Storage by Coordinate Index

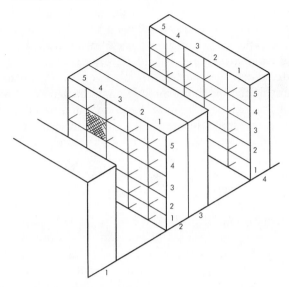

tangular, but until personnel is familiar with the locations, it might take a longer time to find any particular part. There is also some advantage in this system since the numbers need not be in blocks, as in the coordinate system.

Storage by Frequency of Use. Some organizations have made extensive studies to determine their most frequently used material. Those products which are withdrawn most often are located near storage area exits. Other companies place some of these materials near the point of use and maintain additional material in remote storage areas. This latter method is likely to make the recordkeeping somewhat more complicated. The index number method is still quite suitable for frequency-of-use storage procedures.

Complicating Aspects of Inventory Control

There are many reasons why storage of materials becomes more complicated than would appear necessary. In attempts to conserve space, inconvenient and undesirable space is often used. Frequently the space is not symmetrical, so it becomes difficult to install standard racks, and it is nearly impossible to lay out the space to take advantage of a uniform indexing system. These spaces are in out-of-the-way places, with inadequate access for the materials-handling equipment available.

Often city ordinances and fire insurance policies require that inflammable materials be placed in remote locations. Some materials have disagreeable or corrosive characteristics that make it desirable to locate them away from the usual storage area.

Heavy parts and materials that have to be handled by large materials-handling equipment should be placed in bays where the necessary moving equipment is available. Large tools and dies can often be covered with a preservative and stored in open yards. This means that equipment must be available to move the tools and dies to the cleaning area as well as to and from the production areas.

Often material can be stored at the point of use. This can save many dollars by reducing the warehouse supervision costs, but it can be done only if the value of the material is so small as to be unimportant, or its size and shape such that it cannot be carried out without being detected. Some companies, making good use of this technique, store metal bars near the work place, using a color code painted on the floor area to indicate when it is time to reorder and when the stock is dangerously low. This assumes that the material is always removed and replaced in a particular order.

Field warehousing seems to be increasingly popular with companies fabricating products out of steel. The raw materials are set aside in a restricted area under the supervision of a bonded warehouse man who represents the vendor. The material in the restricted area is the property of the vendor and does not belong to the customer until it is properly checked out by the warehouse man. For companies operating on a limited amount of capital, field warehousing offers many advantages.

Many of the storage problems encountered by factories are unique and it is impossible to delineate all of the possibilities and possible solutions. A logical, analytical approach should result in a solution satisfactory to the particular problem.

Scrap Losses. When production creates scrap parts, there is always a question of how many parts should be started into the production so that we produce just the right number—not too many and not too few.

The proper quantity to start into production can be calculated by the following equation:

$$\text{Quantity started} = \frac{\text{Quantity desired}}{1 - \text{Average percentage defective}}$$

For example, a lot of 2,700 finished parts are desired from a process that has produced 10 percent average defective in the past.

$$\text{Quantity started} = \frac{2,700}{1 - .10} = 3,000$$

Frequently this problem is misunderstood and is calculated by the following equation which will obviously give the wrong results.

$$\text{Quantity started} = \text{Quantity desired } (100\% + \text{Average percentage defective.})$$
$$\text{Quantity started} = 2,700 \, (100\% + 10\%) = 2,970$$

Notice that if the process has 10% defective, we will have 2,970 — (2,970 × 10%), or 2,673, which is not very helpful when we wanted to have a quantity of 3,000. We are just 327 parts short of our goal.

The scrap loss calculated previously is accurate, but we have considered the *average* scrap loss and this may have considerable variation. Frequently one runs into the situation that a product requires numerous very expensive set-up costs. To start a few products through again, making up for defective items, would be excessively expensive. Yet this may be a product for which there is no other customer, and it might be extremely expensive to store the excess production while waiting for the customer to place another order. In this situation one can either charge the customer enough to absorb the risk of over- or underproducing or one can contract with the customer to accept a certain percentage under or over the exact order quantity.

Inventory Efficiency. Engineers, and to some degree accountants, are used to discussing activities in terms of efficiency. They wish to know what they are getting out of a system for what they are putting in. Unfortunately, this attitude does not prevail throughout industry.

Mathematically, efficiency is expressed as *output* over *input*.

$$\text{Efficiency} = \frac{\text{Output}}{\text{Input}}$$

It would be most unusual, if not impossible, to have an output which is greater than the input. Therefore, efficiency is always one or less and is frequently stated as a percentage.

The measures of inventory efficiency are not in terms of output over input but nevertheless indicate how efficiently the inventory is being manipulated. This not only gives a measure of the probability of stockouts but also the number of lead times during which demand exceeds the reorder point.

Often the interest is not on the percentage shipped but the percentage not shipped in a period of time.

$$\text{Percentage of shortages} = \frac{\text{Number of units short} \times 100}{\text{Number of units demanded}}$$

Some inventory management decisions may be decided on the basis of stockout in days.

$$\text{Percentage of stockout days} = \frac{(\text{Number of days inventory goes to zero}) \times 100}{\text{Total number of working days}}$$

There are other measures which can be used for determining production and inventory efficiency.

Service level is of concern to the manager because in spite of methods to prevent stockouts there will probably always be some. Service level for some time period is defined as:

$$\text{Service level} = \frac{\text{Units supplied without delay} \times 100}{\text{Units demanded}}$$

For example:

$$\text{Service level} = \frac{398 \text{ units supplied} \times 100}{502 \text{ units demanded}}$$

Service level $= 69.3\%$

A more useful form of the equation is:

$$\text{Service level} = \frac{(\text{Units demanded} - \text{Units short}) \times 100}{\text{Units demanded}}$$

Stockouts in periods are also of concern to a manager.

$$\begin{array}{c}\text{Percentage of}\\ \text{stockouts}\end{array} = \frac{(\text{Number of order periods inventory goes to zero}) \times 100}{\text{Total number of order periods}}$$

Some other measures will be touched upon throughout the rest of the book. The main thing is for you to start extending your thinking to making these types of important evaluations which so often appear as ratios or ratios of ratios. You evaluate your car in terms of miles per gallon, miles per tire, or your savings account in dollars per dollar. As a manufacturing manager why shouldn't you be just as astute and form some meaningful data for measuring efficiency?

INVENTORY-CONTROL COMPUTER SOFTWARE

This section briefly describes a computer software package available for inventory control. This is an overview because of space, but this is fortunate because you will not become bogged down in details. The computer software consists of programs, subroutines, and supporting documentation which can be grouped into three phases as shown in Figure 10–22 and discussed here:

1. *Execution*—to take care of the transaction and status reporting.
2. *Planning*—which includes inventory analysis and the determination of order points and order quantities.
3. *Projection*—for editing and selection of appropriate models to update and project information.

Execution, Blocks 1. Execution includes two basic programs, *transaction processing* and *status reporting*. The first, transaction processing, A, accomplishes the day-to-day inventory transactions by updating the item master file. During transaction processing, a punched card with the item number, transaction code, and quantity is read into the computer to update the specific item master records. These transactions as illustrated in Figure 10–23 are punched into the first columns of the card and are followed by the

Figure 10–22
General Relationship of Programs

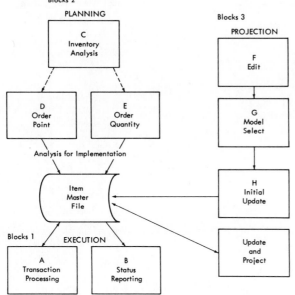

Courtesy International Business Machines Co.

corresponding changes to the item master record. For example a purchase order transaction (PO) for 500 items would increase the item master record of "on order purchase quantity" by 500. In addition to the activities listed here, the user of this software package has many options which he can use.

The transaction processing program punches an order-recommendation card when the available inventory in the item master file is reduced below the order point. If action is not taken within an appropriate time, a follow-up card is issued.

The *status reporting program*, B, prepares a *stock status report* from information in the item master file. The report has a line for each item and also includes summary information. The status reporting program can be modified to include different calculations.

Planning, Blocks 2. The planning phase includes three functions which are:

Inventory analysis, C, which separates the inventory into segments to which different levels of control can be applied. This analysis is comparable to ABC inventory control. But to accomplish this it is necessary to make four different computer runs.

Order-point program, D, contains the routines used to calculate the expected usage through lead time. It also contains several options for safety stock. The available inventory is checked against the order point to deter-

Figure 10–23
Transaction Processing Matrix

Transaction Example	On Hand	On Order Purchase Quantity	On Order Production Quantity	Allocated Quantity	Current Sum of Receipts	Current Sum of Issues	Current Sum of Issues, Transfers, and Adjustments
Work order			+				
Work order adjustment-up			+				
Cancel work order ...			−				
Work order adjustment-down ..			−				
Purchase order		+					
Receiving report (vendor)	+	−			+		
Receipt (production)	+		−		+		
Cancel purchase order		−					
Requirement				+			
Planned disbursement	−			−		+	
Inventory adjustment-up	+						+
Inventory adjustment-down ..	−						−
Miscellaneous receipt	+				+		
Assembly rework			+	+			
Store rework	−		+				
Return to stock	+			+		−	
Cancel requirement ..				−			
Issues	−					+	

Courtesy International Business Machines Co.

mine whether or not order action is indicated. In addition, the order-point program has capabilities for simulation and analysis.

Starting with a process parameter card, the item master file is searched. The searching is done on a sequential, sequential with selection, or random basis. Then the items are processed on the basis of usage during lead time, forecasting model type, and the most recent average usage. The models available range from horizontal, trend, seasonal, and trend seasonal models, or special ones designed by the user.

Within the order-point program, there are several options for calculating safety stock. These include periods of supply, as well as probabilities models or special programs designed by the user.

The value determined for usage through lead time is added to the safety stock to obtain the order point. This new value is placed on the order-point field of the item master record. The order point is compared to the available stock which has the usual definition of *on hand + on order − allocated.* Depending upon results of the comparison one of two actions is taken:

1. If available stock is below the order point an order-recommendation card is punched. The card will indicate whether cards have been punched previously and if so when. A follow-up order-recommendation card is punched after a specified number of days has elapsed.
2. If the available inventory is above the order point, an index value is computed which will estimate the number of time periods the available inventory will last.

$$\text{Index value} = \frac{\text{Available quantity} - \text{Order-point quantity}}{\text{Average demand}}$$

The new order point may be compared with the old order point. If it varies by a percentage greater than a predetermined amount, an exception line is printed out on a report.

After each order-point run is made, analysis information is printed. This *summary analysis report* contains such information as number of the item, variance check, order cards out, items with no inventory on hand, evaluation of order quantity, evaluation of old and new safety stock, and evaluation of on hand inventory.

In the order quantity, E, there are two bases available for calculating order quantities:

1. Previous usage which refers to the typical economic order-quantity models related to past experience.
2. Projection of future requirements as applied in materials requirements planning.

Since the next chapter is devoted to materials requirements planning, discussion of this technique will be delayed until that time, but the previous usage method will be discussed briefly.

The previous usage programs permit the following methods of calculating the order quantity:

Traditional economic order quantity models.
Time periods of supply.
A third option presents the user with an exit so that he may use his own equations.

These order-quantity programs use the information stored on the item master file, and the new values for order quantities are stored on the item master file.

Instructions for the order-quantity program are a parameter card which specifies the type of run and the options to be selected. The item master may be processed sequentially, sequentially with selection, and on a random basis. The latter requires input item cards for locating specific records.

The parameters for the order-quantity calculations are contained in an *order-quantity category table* and may be modified each time the program is run. A category code is used to tie the table with the inventory item. The parameters include:

Category code.
Order cost.
Carrying rate.
Calculation code.

The order costs which usually cover the paper work are added to the set-up cost to determine the preparation costs. The carrying rate is self-explanatory, and the calculation code refers to the equation to be used in making the calculations. The standard economic order quantity equation as discussed in the following chapter is used.

The program can also use *time periods* of supply. The program finds the annual usage from one of several available options and computes an average number of units per period. This average usage multiplied by the time period on the category table is stored as the order quantity. The program also in turn calculates the carrying rate which is implied by this order quantity, and this is printed out on the output report.

The order quantity developed by one of the above methods is checked against a minimum, maximum, or a multiple specification as listed here:

The calculated order quantity is rounded.

If the order quantity is less than the minimum listed, the minimum order quantity is substituted.

If the order quantity is greater than the maximum, the maximum is substituted for the order quantity.

If the minimum or maximum is substituted, an exception is printed out indicating the calculated quantity as well as the substituted value.

Projection Program, Blocks 3. The purpose of this program is to project the demand for a stock-keeping item. After screening the demand for the current period, the new average and trend are found using the appropriate mathematical model. The sum of deviations between the proposed and actual demand is stored in the item master for computing a "tracking signal" to determine if the quantity withdrawn is under control.

Although the above activities are essential there are other functions this phase performs. There is the *edit* program, *F*, which takes the user's demand data file in card, disk, or tape format and converts it to a form required for the *model select* program, *G*.

The model select program performs the following functions:

Past demand data is analyzed to determine which of four projection models (horizontal, trend, seasonal, or trend seasonal) should be used.

Calculates and includes in the output the initial values, *H*, required for the projection model.

The initial update section of the projection phase transfers the results of the model-select program to the item master record.

This concludes the overview of the inventory control software which includes an *execution* program for the transactions, a *planning* program for determining order points and order quantities, and a *projection* program for selecting the appropriate models. This has been of necessity brief, but it will give you the overall structure of a typical inventory software package.

SUMMARY

The importance of the inventory control function has been reviewed in this chapter, along with the organization and procedures required for efficient operations. The impact of pricing methods upon the financial statements was discussed, and special attention was given to efficient ways of organizing storage space.

In recent years the emphasis has been on inventory theory, the selection of the order point, and order quantity. This emphasis has come about because of the advent of the computer and the techniques of operations research.

There are savings to be made for a company in the inventory theory, but there are also savings to be made in the subjects discussed in this chapter. Do not stumble over these methods in an effort to get to the more sophisticated, but not easily applied, inventory theory.

QUESTIONS

10–1. Which is emphasized the most in the literature, inventory management or inventory control? Why do you think this is true?

10–2. What do you think of "inventory turnover" as a measure of efficiency? Explain.

10–3. Why do you think there is so much variation, from industry to industry, in the inventory-to-total assets ratio?

10–4. Purchasing agents use the "future" markets as a way of hedging against price changes. Is this a desirable procedure? Explain.

10–5. What are the classes of inventories that you might expect to find in a particular industry? Give an example of an item which might be found in each class.

10–6. Where, on the organizational chart, might one find an inventory control department? Discuss the reasons for this and the advantages.

10–7. Is it necessary for the individual responsible for the inventory control to know about the procedures and operations of the other departments? Explain your answer in full.

10–8. What purpose does each of the following serve?

a. Receiving report.
b. Invoice.
c. Purchase requisition.
d. Request for price quotation.
e. Purchase order.
f. Packing list.
g. Stores requisition.
h. Sales order.
i. Returned-to-stores record.

10–9. Is a written perpetual record of the inventory always imperative? Explain your answer.

10–10. Under what conditions would it be desirable to have an "on order" column on the inventory record? What conditions would dictate an "apportioned" column?

10–11. Outline the characteristics you would look for when hiring an inventory record clerk.

10–12. What difficulties would you anticipate in installing an ABC inventory system? What advantages can you see in such a system?

10–13. Will all inventories have the same percentages in the ABC categories? Explain.

10–14. Compare the methods of counting the physical inventory. Which do you think is the best? Explain.

10–15. Why is a physical inventory essential?

10–16. Outline the procedure for taking a physical inventory. Design the forms and explain how they will be used.

10–17. Explain why the method of pricing an inventory is important.

10–18. Explain why federal government regulations insist upon an inventory for the beginning and end of a year. Use the profit and loss statement in your explanation.

10–19. Which is given the greatest importance in accounting for inventories: consistency or particular method of costing? Why do you think this is true?

10–20. Describe a situation where storing material by part number would be suitable. What problems must you consider?

10–21. Give an example of a situation where the first-in method of handling material is suitable.

10–22. Discuss the effect of an efficient inventory control system upon the rest of the factory.

10–23. Which method of determining inventory efficiency do you consider the best? Explain why.

10–24. If you were responsible for the installation of an inventory-control software package, which module would you install first?

11

Materials Requirements Planning

MATERIALS REQUIREMENTS PLANNING (MRP) is both an inventory control and a scheduling technique. It consists of a series of steps which start by determining what finished products are needed to meet the demand by time periods and are completed with a schedule of the finished product components needed at each assembly level for each time period.

Since the assembly depends upon all parts being available, the inventories of parts are said to be *dependent*. This is in contrast to *independent* demand inventories which are influenced by random demands and should be controlled by some of the order-point and economic order quantities equations.

You might question why MRP is so much different than the other techniques as to be worthy of a separate treatment. The economic order quantity techniques to be discussed in the next chapter are associated with inventory quantities which are statistical in nature and based on predictions. In MRP the demand is known for all practical purposes and one might as well make specific plans. In the statistical technique the demand is relatively smooth, while in MRP the demand may be quite lumpy, although not necessarily so. In many systems both methods may be applicable, which may call upon judgment in deciding upon which to use.

There has been an increasing enthusiasm for this MRP technique in recent years, but this should not imply that it is new. What is new is that the common ingredients have been recognized and combined into one technique. Like many new techniques there is no agreement on names and consequently it is called *time-phased requirements planning, time series, level-by-level analysis*, and others.

The computer is the major reason why MRP has gained in popularity because the numerous calculations required for the product explosion are readily handled with the direct access capability of the disc systems. The on-line capabilities of some computers are another reason for the increased interest in MRP. The well-organized *bill-of-materials processor* introduced to you in Chapter 6 becomes an important part of the MRP software system.

Where to Use MRP

Materials requirements planning is the way of life for many industries fabricating and assembling products like automobiles and radios. It is especially suitable for situations where one or all of the following conditions exist:

The final product is complex and made up of several levels of assemblies.
The final product is expensive.
The lead times for components and raw materials are relatively long.
The manufacturing cycle is long for the finished product.
Consolidation of requirements for several products is desirable so that economic lot sizes are applicable.

MRP is a dynamic system which is constantly changing, but if changes come too frequently and involve short lead times, the system will not be able to overcome the inertia in the purchasing system. Manufacturing will also have trouble in making sudden changes in capacity, which is critical, for one cannot get more out of the factory than the capacity permits.

Understanding Materials Requirements Planning

You will probably understand MRP better if you can see how it is applied. Like so many of these techniques, they are relatively simple if applied on a small enough scale.

You are aware of those construction kits which are so popular for assembling everything from electronic pipe organs to motor scooters and hi-fi sets. With each kit comes a list of materials so you know what is included in the kit and can check off the parts. The listing of all parts that make up the finished product is called a *product explosion.*

In assembling a hi-fi set you probably would notice that the components were grouped under such headings as tuner, amplifier, and power pack. When the components are listed under their subassembly it is called a *structured* bill of materials listing the parts *level by level.*

The final assembly, consisting of the hi-fi, is designated as the *zero* level. The subassemblies going into the final assembly are at the *one* level, followed by the second level, and so forth. If the power pack in the example consisted of a sub-subassembly composed of a rectifier and heat sink, it would be designated as the second level and the rectifier and heat sink would be designated as the third level. Listing all of the parts and quantities by level would be a *level-by-level explosion.*

When you assembled the hi-fi it might be suggested that the heat sink and rectifier be subassembled some time before the final assembly. If so, this would have been a very elementary example of *time phasing.* It would have become more complicated for example if you had to order a cabinet from a different source and its delivery had to coincide with the completion of the assembly. Then you would have determined the time that it took to deliver the cabinet and ordered accordingly. This is referred to as *offsetting,* or *time offsetting.*

Now move the example into the manufacturing environment where hundreds or thousands of hi-fi sets are assembled each day and see how much more complex the problem becomes. The number produced each day will reflect the demand as stated by sales orders, forecasts, or management decisions. But do not forget that the plant capacity is a very real limitation to the number of sets which can be produced, as are such things as parts available. The demand for final assemblies is scheduled over a number of time periods and recorded on a *master schedule* as illustrated in Figure 11–1, Step 1. This master schedule can be a most important document in a manufacturing situation, for it not only serves as a schedule by time periods but is often the authority by which things are done. It is not uncommon to find a copy of this in some form hanging in the plant to indicate to all personnel what is expected of them for each time period.

Quantities that appear in the master schedule are generated from sales orders, forecasts, and management decisions. If an inventory is carried for an item, the gross requirements for each period may be adjusted up or down to build up or reduce the quantity on hand.

The bill of materials for the desired product is exploded level by level. At each level the inventory for the various items may again be checked to determine whether or not the quantity should be adjusted for the inventory on hand for that particular item. It is possible that some of the parts will be common to several subassemblies so that the quantities should be combined to avoid placing several orders.

The quantities for each assembly, subassembly, part, and raw material are not enough information to make the MRP technique work. It is necessary to establish a schedule with the appropriate lead time for each item so that they will all arrive at the assembly to be completed in time to meet the master schedule. The scheduling of all of the items, called *time phasing,* is made possible because the lead times required for each item have been recorded in the inventory files.

Multiply this simple example by the hundreds of assemblies which are produced in some factories and you will obtain some appreciation for materials requirements planning. For example, consider the manufacturing of automobiles and add the complications of making components in one city and assembling in another city many miles away. You will have to include delays in shipments caused by weather, strikes, and other unknowns.

The typical company does not attempt to schedule all parts down to the last bolt and washer as suggested by the example. Instead, they will

Figure 11–1

Flow Chart for Materials Requirements Planning

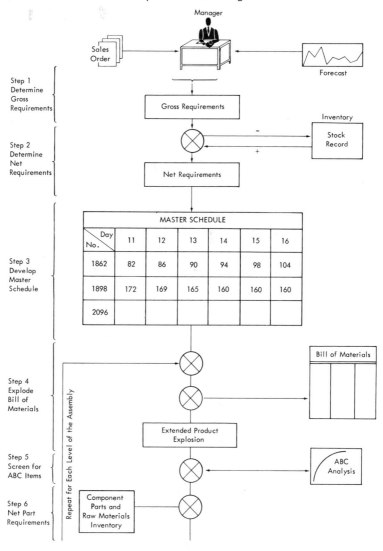

probably use some modification of the ABC inventory technique so less important items will be controlled by some common reorder rules. MRP does not rule out the use of economic order quantities (EOQs) but uses them as a supplemental technique.

Hopefully, this simple example will help you trace your way through a series of techniques which might otherwise appear very complicated.

Figure 11–1 (continued)

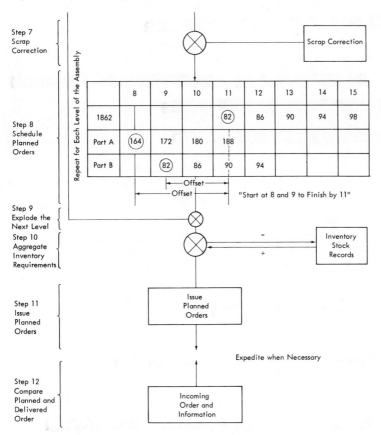

The Steps of Materials Requirements Planning

Explaining MRP is not easy because it is concerned with a number of steps for determining both quantities and times for production. To say it another way, it is concerned with both inventory control and scheduling. It is made more complex because it usually involves a long time cycle which is initiated by orders and forecasted quantities and ends with the planned purchase or manufacturing order.

Since MRP is composed of a series of steps, it will be described step-by-step as shown in Figure 11–1. It is difficult to keep the scheduling and inventory control phases in mind, but try to sort out these activities as you read the steps and you will have a better understanding of the technique.

Step 1. Determine the Gross Requirements. The gross requirement is the aggregate quantity taken from three sources: (1) The actual quantities taken from sales orders by time periods; (2) Forecasted sales quantities by time periods; and (3) Management decisions to alter the quantities derived from the previous steps. The purpose might be to smooth out production changes, adjust for vacation periods, or other reasons.

Step 2. Determine the Net Requirements. The gross requirements obtained in Step 1 are adjusted by the status of the inventory for the product under consideration.

Net requirements = Gross requirements − Available inventory

Step 3. Develop the Master Schedule. From the net requirements for each time period as determined in Step 2, a master schedule is produced.

Step 4. Explode the Bill of Materials. There will be a structured bill of materials available for each assembly on the schedule. The gross requirements for an item will be ascertained by multiplying the number of assemblies on the master schedule by the number of items per assembly as given in the bill of materials. It should be pointed out here that the computer software package to be described later does this on a level-by-level basis. One level is completed, then the next, and so forth.

If this were a purchased item, the order would be placed and this would conclude the procedure. The purchased quantity could of course be adjusted for any expected losses in scrap or rounded out for lot sizes, price breaks, car loadings, and other reasons.

Step 5. Screen for ABC Items. It may be desirable to screen out B and C items. Depending upon the situation, these items may come under the ABC order procedure and are not worthy of being included in the MRP system.

Step 6. Determine Net Requirements for Items. The previous steps developed the gross requirements for an item. This quantity should be adjusted by what is on hand or on order. It may be that a part is overstocked or a replenishment is needed.

Step 7. Adjust Requirements by Scrap or Shrinkage Factor. For some products there will be a loss during the manufacturing process which should be accounted for at the start so the correct number will be completed. Usually the percentage of loss is estimated and kept in the item file so that it may be added when material is ordered.

Step 8. Schedule Planned Orders. After the quantity for an item is determined, it will be necessary to schedule it. This process is *time phasing* and assures that the items will be ready for assembling. It is necessary to *offset* the items as shown in the diagram. The offset represents the usual accumulation of lead times needed to obtain the product on time and will be determined by some experienced individual using the experience he has obtained in ordering similar items. This offset information will have been recorded on the item record for ready reference. Notice that all items do not have the same offset. Also, as the offsetting continues for lower level subassemblies and parts their starting dates come closer to the present time. The closer they come the less time there is to respond to the demand, which can cause difficulties in adjusting factory output.

Step 9. Explode the Next Level. As mentioned in Step 4, the entire assembly is not exploded at one time but it is done level by level after all previous steps are completed. Therefore, it is necessary to repeat Steps 4 through 8 until each level has been exploded, quantities determined and time phased.

Step 10. Aggregate Demands and Determine Order Quantities. During all of the previous steps it might be discovered that one item is needed in a number of assemblies and at various levels. It would be foolish to place an order each time an item appears so we must wait until the demand is developed for all items and then aggregate this demand so just one order may be placed.

Step 11. Write and Place the Planned Orders. Writing the orders, which can be a printout from computer, is usually considered as the last step of the MRP process, but it is by no means assurance that the product will be delivered on time.

Step 12. Maintaining the Schedule. As mentioned earlier, MRP is a combination inventory and scheduling technique. The quantities and schedule have been determined from the previous steps, and from now on it will be a matter of expediting and revising schedules to meet the customer's requirements. The process is not completed until the product arrives in the customer's hands at the time he desires.

MRP Computer Software

The materials-requirements-planning computer software generates requirements by time periods for finished products, assemblies, subassemblies, and raw materials from an input of order and forecast information. To be more specific, the program will do the following:

Determine gross requirements for finished products.
Determine net finished product requirements.
Determine net component requirements.
Plan order sizes.
Offset requirements considering lead times.
Maintain and update the requirements plan (requirements alterations).
Provide a review of planned orders (interrupt) and adjustments to planned orders (reentry) which is referred to as conversational planning.
Provide management by exception.

The requirements planning computer programs are only a part of a larger system. Some parts of the system such as the bill-of-materials processor have already been discussed, but to gain an appreciation of how the various modules are interrelated you should study Figure 11–2. As is apparent, the requirements planning module depends upon the *item master* and *product structure* files developed by the bill-of-materials processor. The output interfaces with those functions related to production orders and purchase orders.

Figure 11–2

System Chart of Requirements Generation Program

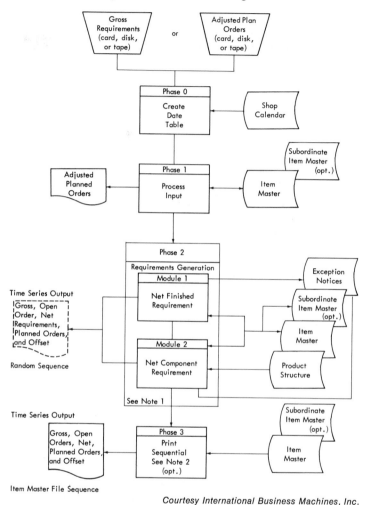

Courtesy *International Business Machines, Inc.*

Note 1: Processing routines for each module—(1) Plan orders; (2) Offset.
Note 2: If Print Sequential is elected, printing will not occur in phase 2.

A user has the option of storing gross requirements, open orders, and planned orders in the item master file if it is not overloaded or on a subordinate item master file. A linkage is made between the two files.

The requirements planning system is initiated from a card, tape, or disk containing gross requirements by shop date, calendar date, or time period. The requirements are generated manually from forecast, customers' orders, or the inventory system. The output consists of planned orders which provide input to both capacity planning and purchasing.

Software packages are often developed to satisfy many different users—each with different requirements—which means that many options must be included. To customize, the user can specify parameter values to describe contents and size of records as well as select those options desired.

There are also some choices in how the MRP program can be run which should be understood before embarking on a detailed study. These are:

Complete requirements generation starts with the forecast and sales to generate *all* requirements from level 0 to the very highest level.

Conversational planning has the same inputs as the complete requirements generation, but it interrupts after each level for any adjustments that need to be made.

Requirements alteration takes into consideration any adjustments that are made from time to time. Only the *altered* gross requirements are inputted and therefore are the only items affected.

The first and second of these three programs would be run on a scheduled basis, while the third program would be run between the scheduled runs as a means of introducing changes to previously scheduled runs.

Examining the software package itself, Figure 11–2, you will see that there are two major programs. Both of these will be reviewed here:

1. *The requirements generation program* performs the actual time-series planning.
2. *The print exception program* prints out the exceptions detected in the requirements generation program which should be brought to the attention of management.

The requirements generation program consists of four distinct phases as illustrated in the flow diagram. When one phase is completed, it is brought into the computer memory core to overlay the previous phase. These four phases and their purposes are discussed here.

Phase 0 creates a data table with individual entries for the first day of each time period within the planning horizon. The purpose of this data table is to provide an efficient use of computer core space during requirements generation. Otherwise, the entire shop calendar would be taking up computer core during the entire run.

If all dates are shop dates, a shop calendar is not needed, but if not, a shop calendar is required. The shop calendar, which is created and stored by the user, is stored in direct access memory in the format of a shop date followed by the calendar date for every shop day.

Phase 1, process input, performs the initialization of the program, including the type of processing, type of input, and functional subroutines.

The type of processing determines whether it will be a complete requirements generation, requirements alteration, or conversational planning. The type of input considers whether a complete gross requirements, altered requirements, or adjusted planned orders are used. The functional subroutines include *calculate net, plan orders,* and *calculate offset.*

Once the initialization is performed, there are two remaining functions which include processing the input and making the initial entries to the *level-activity chain*. This is done by reading the input data, retrieval of appropriate records, and posting the input to the record.

Phase 2, requirements generation, performs the actual time-series generation of requirements. This phase determines the quantity to be produced and when it should be produced. It starts with the highest level (lowest number) and completes all of the calculations and then goes to the next level and so on until all of the levels are completed. To determine the quantities, the program begins by processing the items that were inserted in the level-activity chain established in Phase 1. For each item being processed, the gross requirements stored in the item master are read into core. Net requirements are determined by reducing the on-hand inventory and open orders by the gross requirements. Gross requirements can be adjusted by a shrinkage factor.

The net requirements are those which must be satisfied by the *planned order function*. The planned order function determines the quantity and the time period that an order is needed. The *offset function* determines when the planned orders should be started by determining lead times for each item. The components of the parent assembly are retrieved through the product structure file which contains the usage per assembly. The extended requirements are posted to the component file in the item master.

This process operates level by level, starting at the top and working downwards, with each level being completed before the next.

An option available to the user inserts the logic for determining when an engineering change will take effect. Another option accounts for the scrap at each level.

Phase 3, print sequential, must be included in the customizing procedure if it is desired. Its major function is to generate a sequential detail-requirements generation. This phase will generate the report in the same sequence as the item master file. Otherwise, the report will be performed in Phase 2, and the sequence will be in reverse activity chain within low-level code.

Following the three phases of the requirements generation program is the print exception program. The purpose of this program, which probably appears obvious, is to print out the exceptions that occur during the requirements generation program.

In the design of any management information system, the objective should be to provide only that information that is important. This is done by *exception notices*. The system provides for nearly 20 different exception notices available for printout.

This is by necessity a rather cursory discussion of the typical software package used in materials requirements planning. It is intended to give you an overview so that you will be able to approach the customer's manuals in which instructions are given for installing your own materials requirements planning program.

Product Explosion Techniques

It is extremely difficult to determine the exact number of parts which are used when there are several levels of assembly. The level-by-level product explosion technique is a logical, orderly method which is readily applied in card-data procssing as well as in computer systems. The alternative is to make a detailed breakdown of the product.

Level by Level. The level-by-level requirements explosion is illustrated by Figure 11–3. In this example we are interested only in collecting informa-

Figure 11–3
Product Explosion

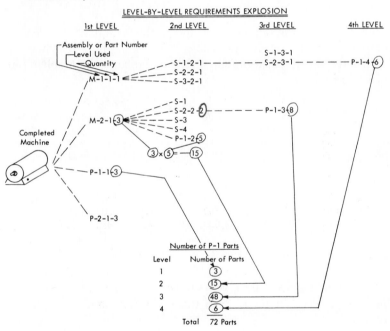

tion about part P–1 (and therefore the illustration is simplified by the omission of all information which does not lead to P–1). As indicated by the code at the head of the first column, the first number indicates the part number; the second number, the level; and the third, the quantity. This method of numbering is used primarily for illustrating the product explosion system and is not necessarily a suggested method for product numbering. The level and the quantity used for each level may be placed on the record, but not necessarily as part of the product number.

The way of accumulating the quantity of parts needed for the final assembly is illustrated in the table at the bottom of the illustration. This procedure can be used for every part and subassembly used in the completed machine.

Matrix Calculations for Explosion

Matrix manipulations are tedious to do by hand but can be done conveniently and rapidly by the computer. It is therefore reasonable to put the explosion problem in matrix form and let the computer do the calculations. The next few paragraphs explain how conveniently this can be done.

Addition. To add two matrices, they must both have the same number of rows and columns. Corresponding elements are added. This procedure is shown below:

$$
\mathbf{A} + \mathbf{B} = \mathbf{C}
$$

$$
\begin{bmatrix} 2 & 5 \\ 3 & 1 \end{bmatrix} + \begin{bmatrix} 7 & 8 \\ 6 & 2 \end{bmatrix} = \begin{bmatrix} 9 & 13 \\ 9 & 3 \end{bmatrix}
$$

Example: Table A is the shipping schedule for the first quarter of the year for Plant A, manufacturing pumps. Table B is the shipping schedule for Plant B. To determine the quantity shipped by both plants, the problem can be stated in matrix form:

	Shipping Schedule for Plant A			Shipping Schedule for Plant B		
	small	*medium*	*large*	*small*	*medium*	*large*
January	300	800	600	100	500	0
February	200	1000	500	90	700	0
March	300	850	500	120	600	0

$$
\mathbf{A} + \mathbf{B} = \mathbf{C}
$$

$$
\begin{bmatrix} 300 & 800 & 600 \\ 200 & 1000 & 500 \\ 300 & 850 & 500 \end{bmatrix} + \begin{bmatrix} 100 & 500 & 0 \\ 90 & 700 & 0 \\ 120 & 600 & 0 \end{bmatrix} = \begin{bmatrix} 400 & 1300 & 600 \\ 290 & 1700 & 500 \\ 420 & 1450 & 500 \end{bmatrix}
$$

Subtraction. Two matrices must have the same number of rows and columns if they are to be subtracted. Corresponding elements are subtracted. As you might expect, this is very similar to the rules for addition. To keep the examples consistent, observe the following example of matrix subtraction:

$$
\mathbf{A} - \mathbf{B} = \mathbf{C}
$$

$$
\begin{bmatrix} 8 & 7 \\ 6 & 2 \end{bmatrix} - \begin{bmatrix} 2 & 9 \\ 4 & 1 \end{bmatrix} = \begin{bmatrix} 6 & -2 \\ 2 & 1 \end{bmatrix}
$$

Example: The pump manufacturer referred to before may have a shipping schedule for the first quarter designated by the matrix **S**. Plant A's production is shown by matrix **A**, and it is necessary to find out what Plant B will have to ship. This can be easily done:

$$
\mathbf{S} - \mathbf{A} = \mathbf{B}
$$

$$
\begin{bmatrix} 400 & 1300 & 600 \\ 290 & 1700 & 500 \\ 420 & 1450 & 500 \end{bmatrix} - \begin{bmatrix} 300 & 800 & 600 \\ 200 & 1000 & 500 \\ 300 & 850 & 500 \end{bmatrix} = \begin{bmatrix} 100 & 500 & 0 \\ 90 & 700 & 0 \\ 120 & 600 & 0 \end{bmatrix}
$$

Multiplication (Scalar). First let us consider multiplying matrices by constants or scalars. Each element of the matrix is multiplied by the constant or scalar to form a new matrix.

Example: Assume the company producing pumps expects to double its output in the next year. This is easily determined by:

$$2 \times \mathbf{S} = 2 \times \begin{bmatrix} 400 & 1300 & 600 \\ 290 & 1700 & 500 \\ 420 & 1450 & 500 \end{bmatrix} = \begin{bmatrix} 800 & 2600 & 1200 \\ 580 & 3400 & 1000 \\ 840 & 2900 & 1000 \end{bmatrix}$$

Multiplication (Matrix). Next let us consider the multiplication of a matrix by a matrix. Multiplication of matrices is only permissible when the number of columns of the first matrix is equal to the number of rows of the second. Matrices that satisfy this condition are said to be "conformable."

Each of the ijth elements of the product matrix is the sum of the products obtained by multiplying the elements in the ith row of the first matrix by the elements in the jth column of the second matrix. The result of this multiplication is a matrix with the number of rows equal to the number of rows in the first matrix, and the number of columns equal to the number of columns in the second matrix. This can be expressed symbolically:

$$\mathbf{A}_{mp} \times \mathbf{B}_{pn} = \mathbf{C}_{mn}$$
$$(m,p) \times (p,n) = (m,n)$$

or perhaps it will be easier to see in this form:

$$\frac{\text{Number of columns}}{p \text{ in first}} = \frac{\text{Number of rows}}{p \text{ in second}} \ \& \ \frac{\text{Results in a matrix with}}{m \text{ rows and } n \text{ columns}}$$

$$m\begin{cases} 0 & 0 \\ 0 & 0 \\ 0 & 0 \end{cases} \quad p\begin{cases} 0 & 0 & 0 \\ 0 & 0 & 0 \end{cases} \quad m\begin{cases} 0 & 0 & 0 \\ 0 & 0 & 0 \\ 0 & 0 & 0 \end{cases}$$
$$\underbrace{\qquad}_{p} \qquad \underbrace{\qquad}_{n} \qquad \underbrace{\qquad}_{n}$$

The actual multiplication procedure can best be described by an illustration:

$$\mathbf{AB} \qquad = \qquad \mathbf{C}$$

$$\begin{bmatrix} a_{11} & a_{12} & a_{13} \\ a_{21} & a_{22} & a_{23} \end{bmatrix} \times \begin{bmatrix} b_{11} & b_{12} \\ b_{21} & b_{22} \\ b_{31} & b_{32} \end{bmatrix} = \begin{bmatrix} c_{11} & c_{12} \\ c_{21} & c_{22} \end{bmatrix}$$

The c_{ij} element $= a_{i1} b_{1j} + a_{i2} b_{2j} + a_{i3} b_{3j}$, so $c_{11} = a_{11}b_{11} + a_{12}b_{21} + a_{13}b_{31}$

Example: The usefulness of matrix multiplication can be cited. A manufacturer of paints wishes to determine his material needs for the next two months and has developed the following manufacturing schedule:

	Product (lots)		
	No. 1	No. 2	No. 3
Production for 1st month	5	7	10
Production for 2nd month...............	10	8	3

The material requirements for each of these lots are given in the following table:

	Drums of A	Drums of B	Drums of C
Product 1:	5	3	1
Product 2:	7	2	2
Product 3:	1	4	6

Putting this information into matrix form:

$$\begin{bmatrix} 5 \text{ lots} & 7 & 10 \\ 10 & 8 & 3 \end{bmatrix} \times \begin{bmatrix} 5 \text{ drums/lot} & 3 & 1 \\ 7 & & 2 & 2 \\ 1 & & 4 & 6 \end{bmatrix} = \begin{bmatrix} 84 \text{ drums} & 69 & 79 \\ 109 & & 58 & 44 \end{bmatrix}$$

The detailed method of determining the answer can be seen by the following:

$(5 \times 5) + (7 \times 7) + (10 \times 1) = 84$ $(5 \times 3) + (7 \times 2) + (10 \times 4) = 69$
$(10 \times 5) + (8 \times 7) + (3 \times 1) = 109$ $(10 \times 3) + (8 \times 2) + (3 \times 4) = 58$

$(5 \times 1) + (7 \times 2) + (10 \times 6) = 79$
$(10 \times 1) + (8 \times 2) + (3 \times 6) = 44$

Interpreting the answer is straightforward:

$$(5 \text{ lots} \times 5 \text{ drums/lot}) + (7 \text{ lots} \times 7 \text{ drums/lot})$$
$$(10 \text{ lots} \times 1 \text{ drum/lot}) = 84 \text{ drums.}$$

Matrix Division (The Inverse Matrix). The division of matrices is not a straightforward process and it requires some review of definitions. We describe the matrix form in a shorthand language:

$$\mathbf{Ax} = \mathbf{b}$$

where:

$\mathbf{A}$ = an $m \times n$ matrix of the coefficients of the unknowns,
$\mathbf{x}$ = a column vector of n unknowns,
$\mathbf{b}$ = a column vector of m constants.

The problem is to determine the unknown $\mathbf{x}$ quantities. To start, we might consider dividing both sides of the equation by $\mathbf{A}$, but, since division has not been defined, let us search for another method. Here is the place where the *inverse* of a matrix can be called into play. Let us see what happens if we multiply both sides of the previous equation by $\mathbf{A}^{-1}$.

$$\mathbf{A}^{-1} \mathbf{Ax} = \mathbf{A}^{-1} \mathbf{b}$$

Since $\mathbf{A}^{-1}\mathbf{A}$ is the identity matrix, $\mathbf{I}$, $\mathbf{Ix} = \mathbf{A}^{-1} \mathbf{b}$. The $\mathbf{I}$ washes out as we see:

$$\begin{bmatrix} 1 & 0 \\ 0 & 1 \end{bmatrix} \times \begin{bmatrix} x_1 \\ x_2 \end{bmatrix} = \begin{bmatrix} x_1 \\ x_2 \end{bmatrix}$$

So it seems that we can solve for the value of x_1 and x_2, if we know the value of the inverse, A^{-1}.

Let us digress a moment here to see how to obtain the inverse matrix.

Matrix Inversion. There are a number of methods for finding the inverse of a nonsingular[1] square matrix but they are all tedious and time consuming. This is the reason why the digital computer has made industrialists take a new interest in matrix algebra.

The method, discussed briefly here, consists of writing an identity matrix to the right of the matrix A. The next problem is to reduce the matrix A to an identity and at the same time perform the same operations on the identity matrix on the right. The row operations which may be performed on the matrices, and not alter their mathematical equivalence, are:

1. Any two rows may be interchanged;
2. Any row may be multiplied by a nonzero number (scalar);
3. Any multiple of a row may be added to another.

By using these rules, the appearance of the matrices will change but the mathematical equivalence will remain. In other words, the solution of a modified matrix is the same as the original. The process of inverting the matrix, step by step, is illustrated:

$$\underbrace{\quad A \quad}\ \underbrace{\quad I \quad}$$

$$\begin{matrix} x_1 & x_2 \end{matrix}$$

$$\begin{bmatrix} 1 & 3 & | & 1 & 0 \\ 2 & 3 & | & 0 & 1 \end{bmatrix}$$ Start with this.

$$\begin{bmatrix} 1 & 3 & | & 1 & 0 \\ 0 & -3 & | & -2 & 1 \end{bmatrix}$$ Rule 3: Add the product: (-2) (row 1) to row 2. Remember row 1 is not altered.

$$\begin{bmatrix} 1 & 0 & | & -1 & 1 \\ 0 & -3 & | & -2 & 1 \end{bmatrix}$$ Rule 3: Add the product: (1) (row 2) to row 1.

$$\begin{bmatrix} 1 & 0 & | & -1 & 1 \\ 0 & 1 & | & \frac{2}{3} & -\frac{1}{3} \end{bmatrix}$$ Rule 2: Multiply row 2 by $-\frac{1}{3}$.

$$\underbrace{\quad I \quad}\ \underbrace{\quad A^{-1} \quad}$$ (Only those rules were used which quickly reduced matrix A to an identity. Rule I was not needed.)

A check on the inversion process may be made if we recall $AA^{-1} = I$:

$$\begin{bmatrix} 1 & 3 \\ 2 & 3 \end{bmatrix} \times \begin{bmatrix} -1 & 1 \\ \frac{2}{3} & -\frac{1}{3} \end{bmatrix} = I$$

Multiplying as described earlier:

$$(1)(-1) + (3)(\tfrac{2}{3}) = 1$$
$$(2)(-1) + (3)(\tfrac{2}{3}) = 0$$
$$(1)(1) \;\; + (3)(-\tfrac{1}{3}) = 0$$
$$(2)(1) \;\; + (3)(-\tfrac{1}{3}) = 1$$

which is an identity: $\begin{bmatrix} 1 & 0 \\ 0 & 1 \end{bmatrix}$

---

[1] The square matrix, A, is said to be singular if $|A| = 0$, nonsingular if $|A| \neq 0$, where $|A|$ denotes the determinant of A.

Before passing on to other subjects, let us look at a real-life problem using matrix division. This will be another example taken from the paint industry, but not the same problem described before. The problem is this: The paint manufacturer has 40 drums of material A and 60 drums of material B, and he wishes to make it all up into products 1 and 2, knowing the relationships of the quantities used. This can be written into mathematical form as shown here:

$$1x_1 + 3x_2 = 40$$
$$2x_1 + 3x_2 = 60$$

A problem this size can be hastily solved by simultaneous equations with little difficulty, and $x_1 = 20, x_2 = 20/3$.

Solving this by means of the inverted matrix gives the same answers:

$$\mathbf{Ax} = \mathbf{c}$$
$$\mathbf{A^{-1}Ax} = \mathbf{A^{-1}c}$$
$$\mathbf{Ix} = \mathbf{A^{-1}c}$$
$$\mathbf{x} = \mathbf{A^{-1}c}$$

The matrix we inverted is the one associated with this problem; thus the problem can be stated:

$$\begin{bmatrix} x_1 \\ x_2 \end{bmatrix} = \begin{bmatrix} -1 & +1 \\ +\frac{2}{3} & -\frac{1}{3} \end{bmatrix} \times \begin{bmatrix} 40 \\ 60 \end{bmatrix} = \begin{bmatrix} -40 & +60 \\ \frac{2}{3}40 & -\frac{1}{3}60 \end{bmatrix}$$
$$x_1 = 20$$
$$x_2 = 20/3$$

which is exactly as we expected from the simultaneous equations solution.

By these simple examples, it has been shown that matrix algebra is a practical tool for industrial personnel to use. Bigger problems are suitable for digital computers.

The Gozinto Product Explosion Technique[2]

The *Gozinto method* is a product explosion technique using matrix algebra for determining the total number of each subassembly or detailed part going into a product. The Gozinto method is an application of matrix algebra to determine how many parts are needed.

To discuss the Gozinto method the following subjects will be discussed in turn:

1. The Gozinto graph (Figure 11–4).
2. The *next assembly quantity matrix,* called the **N** *matrix* (Figure 11–5).
3. The *total requirements factor matrix,* called the **T** *matrix* (Figure 11–6).

---

[2] The Gozinto technique illustrated here was developed by Andrew Vazsonyi and facetiously credited to an Italian mathematician Zepartzat Gozinto. For a full treatment of the Gozinto technique see: Andrew Vazsonyi, *Scientific Programming in Business and Industry* (New York: Wiley, 1958).

4.   The matrix algebra manipulations for Gozinto method.
5.   A simplified solution technique.

The Gozinto graph.   Illustrated in Figure 11–4 is a typical Gozinto graph.

Figure 11–4
Gozinto Graph

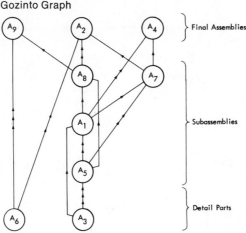

Source: Andrew Vazsonyi, *Scientific Programming in Business and Industry,* 1958. Reprinted by permission of John Wiley & Sons, Inc.

The Gozinto graph symbols are given here:

Gozinto Symbols and Definitions

Description	Symbol
Each circle represents a part, subassembly, or assembly.	
Terminal circles, A_9, A_2, and A_4 are final assemblies. All other circles represent parts or subassemblies which go into assemblies.	
Arrows indicate the direction of flow, parts to subassemblies, and to assemblies.	
The number of heads on an arrow indicates the number of items flowing into an assembly.	

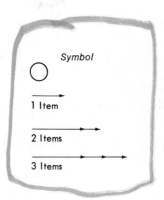

Gozinto graph.   A network of Gozinto symbols showing how many parts go into subassemblies and assemblies.

N matrix   Next assembly quantity matrix—a matrix showing how many parts or subassemblies are needed for the next subassemblies or assemblies.

T matrix   Total requirement factor matrix—a matrix showing the total number of parts and subassemblies needed for an assembly.

$\mathbf{N}_{ij}$ The number of items needed for the *next assembly*.
$\mathbf{T}_{ij}$ The total number of parts needed.

Notice that on the Gozinto graph the following situation exists: Two A_5's go into A_1 and one A_1 goes into A_8, and so on.

The question we want to answer is, "Just how many A_5's are needed?" Also, how many A_1's, A_6's, and so on are needed?

These are important questions when the number of parts is large and the set-up costs are great.

Next Assembly Quantity Matrix (N Matrix). The Gozinto graph can be organized into matrix form. Once it is in matrix form, it can be manipulated by the techniques of matrix operations which are suitable for computer operations. The next assembly quantity matrix, Figure 11–5, is the matrix representation of the graphical Gozinto chart.

Figure 11–5
Next Assembly Quantity Matrix N Table

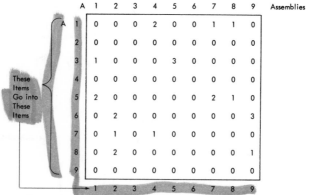

A	1	2	3	4	5	6	7	8	9	Assemblies
1	0	0	0	2	0	0	1	1	0	
2	0	0	0	0	0	0	0	0	0	
3	1	0	0	0	3	0	0	0	0	
4	0	0	0	0	0	0	0	0	0	
5	2	0	0	0	0	0	2	1	0	
6	0	2	0	0	0	0	0	0	3	
7	0	1	0	1	0	0	0	0	0	
8	0	2	0	0	0	0	0	0	1	
9	0	0	0	0	0	0	0	0	0	

(These Items Go into These Items)

Source: Andrew Vazsonyi, *Scientific Programming in Business and Industry*, 1958. Reprinted by permission of John Wiley & Sons, Inc.

Total Requirements Factor Matrix, T Matrix. Obtaining this matrix is not as straightforward as one might expect. We need a set of equations which will relate the unknown, $\mathbf{T}_{ij}$'s of the total requirements factor matrix to the known $\mathbf{N}_{ij}$'s of the next assembly quantity matrix (where i represents an item in a row and j represents an item in a column).

As an example, let us determine the number of A_5's needed for A_2:

$$(A_5\text{'s going to } A_1) \times (\text{Number of } A_1\text{'s in } A_2) = 2 \times 3 = 6$$
$$(A_5\text{'s going to } A_7) \times (\text{Number of } A_7\text{'s in } A_2) = 2 \times 1 = 2$$
$$(A_5\text{'s going to } A_8) \times (\text{Number of } A_8\text{'s in } A_2) = 1 \times 2 = 2$$
$$\mathbf{T}_{5,2} = \overline{10}$$

This placed in a more general form:

$$N_{5,1} \times T_{1,2} = 6$$
$$N_{5,7} \times T_{7,2} = 2$$
$$N_{5,8} \times T_{8,2} = \underline{2}$$
$$T_{5,2} = \overline{10}$$

or:

$$T_{5,2} = N_{5,1} T_{1,2} + N_{5,2} T_{2,2} + N_{5,3} T_{3,2} + \ldots + N_{5,8} T_{8,2} + N_{5,9} T_{9,2}$$

But, $N_5 (2,3,4,5,6,9) = 0$ (1)

$$T_{5,2} = N_{5,1} T_{1,2} + N_{5,7} T_{7,2} + N_{5,8} T_{8,2}$$

But the T's used as multipliers are unknown as is the $T_{5,2}$ for which we are searching. There is a graphical pattern behind the above equation which is shown in Figure 11–6.

Figure 11–6
Graphical Pattern

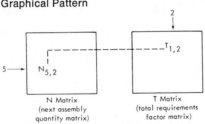

N Matrix
(next assembly
quantity matrix)

T Matrix
(total requirements
factor matrix)

Source: Andrew Vazsonyi, *Scientific Programming in Business and Industry*, 1958. Reprinted by permission of John Wiley & Sons, Inc.

By multiplication from the Gozinto graph we can obtain:

$$(A_1 \text{ to } A_8) \times (A_8 \text{ to } A_2) = 2$$
$$(A_1 \text{ to } A_7) \times (A_7 \text{ to } A_2) = 1$$
$$\overline{③}$$

which is the 3 illustrated in the **T** matrix in Figure 11–7.

Figure 11–7
Example Calculations

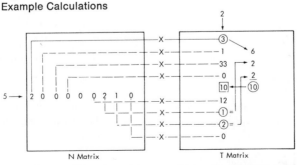

N Matrix

(next assembly quantity matrix)

T Matrix

(total requirements quantity matrix)

Remember, the only way we were able to obtain the values for the **T** matrix was from the graph. That would be very difficult to do when there are a lot of items. So apparently another way must be found.

The Equation 1 may be abbreviated:

$$T_{5,2} = \sum_k^1 N_{5,k} \times T_{k,2} \tag{2}$$

Or in a general form:

$$T_{i,j} = \sum_k^1 N_{i,k} \times T_{k,j} \qquad i \neq j \tag{3}$$

For a moment, check out this equation on one of the other values, $T_{6,2}$, which is the total number of A_6's required for each A_2 (note $i=6$ and $j=2$). (Total no. of part A_6 needed in A_2):

$$T_{6,2} = N_{6,1} \times T_{1,2} + N_{6,2} \times T_{2,2} + N_{6,3} \times T_{3,2} + N_{6,4} \times T_{4,2}$$
$$+ N_{6,5} T_{5,2} + N_{6,6} T_{6,2} + N_{6,7} T_{7,2} + N_{6,8} T_{8,2} + N_{6,9} T_{9,2}$$

This is illustrated in the following set of tables, Figure 11–8. Be sure to

Figure 11–8
Second Example Calculations

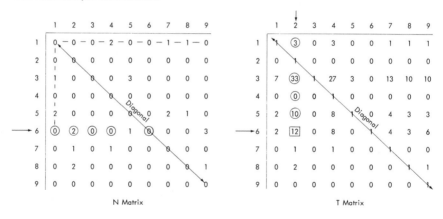

N Matrix   T Matrix

recognize that the total requirement matrix is not available at this stage, which makes explaining this Gozinto technique very confusing.

$$T_{6,2} = (0 \times 3) + (2 \times 1) + (0 \times 33) + (0 \times 0) + (1 \times 10) +$$
$$(0 \times 12) + (0 \times 1) + (0 \times 2) + (3 \times 0)$$
$$T_{6,2} = 12$$

Before going further, the convention of *one* and *zero* on the diagonal of the **N** table and **T** table should be discussed. The number of A_2's required for each A_2 for the **N** table is not meaningful. On the other hand, the *total* number of A_2's required for A_2 does not make much sense either. Since neither makes sense, a convention is used which makes the calculations work. And what makes the calculation work are the "O's" on the diagonal of the N matrix and the "1's" on the diagonal of the T matrix.

The Prohibitive Matrix Manipulation Approach. The equations represented here can be solved with matrix manipulations, but perhaps a word of explanation is needed regarding a matrix with *ones* on the diagonal. This is called the *unit* matrix and is represented by the symbol [I].

Now the equation:

$$\mathbf{T}_{ij} = \sum_k \mathbf{N}_{i,k} \times \mathbf{T}_{k,j} \qquad i \neq j$$

can be stated in matrix algebra notation:

$$[\mathbf{T}] = [\mathbf{N}] \times [\mathbf{T}] + [\mathbf{I}].$$

Notice that the unity matrix [I] imposes the ones on the total matrix [T].

This equation still causes trouble because as is obvious we are solving for the T values, the unknowns, which appear on both sides of the equation.

The problem to be solved is one of matrix inversion, the steps of which are given here:

$$[\mathbf{T}] = [\mathbf{N}] \times [\mathbf{T}] + [\mathbf{I}]$$
$$[\mathbf{T}] - [\mathbf{N}] \times [\mathbf{T}] = [\mathbf{I}]$$
$$[\mathbf{T}] \times [\mathbf{I}] - [\mathbf{N}] = [\mathbf{I}]$$
$$[\mathbf{T}] = [\mathbf{I}] - [\mathbf{N}]^{-1}\mathbf{I}$$

With problems of the size under consideration here, the solution would be prohibitive. It is therefore desirable to find an easier way.

Practical Solution Method. We are fortunate that because of the presence of those 0's and 1's on the diagonals, the problem is not as difficult to solve as it might be. Take, for example, the calculations for the T value in the first row and second column and recall the technique of matrix multiplication.

$$[\mathbf{T}_{1,2}] = [\mathbf{N}_{1,4}\mathbf{T}_{4,2}] + [\mathbf{N}_{1,7}\mathbf{T}_{7,2}] + [\mathbf{N}_{1,8}\mathbf{T}_{8,2}]$$

$$\mathbf{T}_{1,2} = 2\mathbf{T}_{4,2} + 1\mathbf{T}_{7,2} + 1\mathbf{T}_{8,2}$$

Again, it is apparent that we do not know the values for the T's on the right-hand side. Continuing with the development of all values gives us a clue to a solution, however.

$$T_{1,2} = 2T_{4,2} + 1T_{7,2} + 1T_{8,2} \tag{4}$$

$$T_{2,2} = 1 \text{ (since this is on the diagonal of the} \tag{5}$$
$$\text{total requirements factor matrix)}$$

$$T_{3,2} = N_{3,1}T_{1,2} + N_{3,5}T_{5,2}$$

$$T_{3,2} = 1 \times T_{1,2} + 3T_{5,2} \tag{6}$$

$$T_{4,2} = 0 \text{ (since the fourth row is zero in the N matrix)} \tag{7}$$

$$T_{5,2} = N_{5,1}T_{1,2} + N_{5,7}T_{7,2} + N_{5,8}T_{8,2}$$
$$= 2T_{1,2} + 2T_{7,2} + 1T_{8,2} \tag{8}$$

$$T_{6,2} = N_{6,2}T_{2,2} + N_{6,5}T_{5,2} + N_{6,9}T_{9,2}$$
$$= 2T_{2,2} + 1T_{5,2} + 1T_{9,2} \tag{9}$$

$$T_{7,2} = N_{7,1}T_{2,2} + N_{7,4}T_{4,2}$$
$$= 1T_{2,2} + 1T_{4,2} \tag{10}$$

$$T_{8,2} = N_{8,2}T_{2,2} + N_{8,9}T_{9,2}$$
$$= 2T_{2,2} + T_{9,2} \tag{11}$$

$$T_{9,2} = 0 \tag{12}$$

From the above equations it is evident that we know the values of the 2d, 4th, and 9th row of the requirements factor matrix:

$$T_{2,2} = 1 \text{ (from equation 5)}$$
$$T_{4,2} = 0 \text{ (from equation 7)}$$
$$T_{9,2} = 0 \text{ (from equation 12)}$$

Starting with these known values, first column in Figure 11–9, we can start all over, substituting these three known values where they were unknown before. This same technique could be used for each of the other columns in the total requirements tables.

Solution by a System of Triangular Equations. First switch the notation from T's to x's.

$$\begin{array}{ll} T_{1,2} = x_6 & T_{5,2} = x_7 \\ T_{2,2} = x_1 & T_{6,2} = x_8 \\ T_{3,2} = x_9 & T_{7,2} = x_4 \\ T_{4,2} = x_2 & T_{8,2} = x_5 \\ & T_{9,2} = x_3 \end{array}$$

$$
\begin{aligned}
1x_1 &= 0 \\
0x_1 + x_2 &= 0 \\
0x_1 + 0x_2 + x_3 &= 0 \\
1x_1 + 1x_2 + 0x_3 - x_4 &= 0 \\
2x_1 + 0x_2 + 1x_3 - 0x_4 - x_5 &= 0 \\
0x_1 + 2x_2 + 0x_3 + 1x_4 + x_5 + x_6 &= 0 \\
0x_1 + 0x_2 + 0x_3 + 3x_4 + 1x_5 + 2x_6 - x_7 &= 0 \\
2x_1 + 0x_2 + 1x_3 + 0x_4 + 0x_5 + 0x_6 + x_7 - x_8 &= 0 \\
0x_1 + 0x_2 + 0x_3 + 0x_4 + 0x_5 + x_6 + 3x_7 + 0x_8 - x_9 &= 0
\end{aligned}
$$

Figure 11-9
Successive Trials to Find a Solution

	Equation	1st Trial	2d Trial	3d Trial
(4)	$T_{1,2} = T_{4,2} + 1T_{7,2} + 1T_{8,2}$	Fail	**Success** $T_{1,2} = 0 + 1 + 2 = 3$	3
(5)	$T_{2,2} = 1$	Available 1	Available 1	1
(6)	$T_{3,2} = 1T_{1,2} + 3T_{5,2}$	Fail	Fail	**Success** $T_{3,2} = 3 + 3 \times 10 = 33$
(7)	$T_{4,2} = 0$	Available 0	Available 0	0
(8)	$T_{5,2} = 2T_{1,2} + 2T_{7,2} + 1T_{8,2}$	Fail	**Success** $T_{5,2} = 6 + 2 + 2 = 10$	10
(9)	$T_{6,2} = 2T_{2,2} + 1T_{5,2} + 1T_{9,2}$	Fail	**Success** $T_{6,2} = 2 + 10 + 0 = 12$	12
(10)	$T_{7,2} = 1T_{2,2} + 1T_{4,2}$	**Success** $T_{7,2} = 1$	Available 1	1
(11)	$T_{8,2} = 2T_{2,2} + 1T_{9,2}$	**Success** $T_{8,2} = 2$	Available 2	2
(12)	$T_{9,2} = 0$	Available 0	Available 0	0

If you compare this with the previous set of equations, you will observe that the values are readily obtained using a sequence of steps similar to the ones discussed.

Number of Assemblies and Parts to Ship. Up to this point the number of parts needed for each assembly has been determined. Now it will be shown how the shipping quantity may be obtained using matrix algebra for item 5. The same procedure would be used for other items.

The following notation will be used:

$s =$ The shipping requirement, $s_1, s_2, \ldots$ for each article.

$x =$ The total requirements for each article.

The problem is: Given the shipping requirement, s, what is the total requirement x?

Example: A company is shipping:

Shipping Table in Matrix Form

		0
20	A_2's	20
		0
30	A_4's	30
50	A_5's	50
		0
		0
		0
80	A_9's	80

These can be placed in a table form as shown above.

If the shipping table is combined with the total requirements matrix already presented, we have the following from which can be calculated the quantity of parts, x, required:

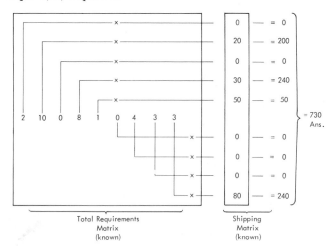

In equation form:

$$x_i = \sum_j \mathbf{T}_{i,j}\mathbf{S}_j$$

or in matrix form:

$$[x] = [\mathbf{T}][\mathbf{S}]$$

Recall that $\mathbf{T}$ can be obtained by

$$[\mathbf{T}] = \frac{[\mathbf{I}]}{[\mathbf{I}] - [\mathbf{N}]}$$

Combining, we obtain

$$[x] = \frac{[\mathbf{I}]}{[\mathbf{I}] - [\mathbf{N}]}\ [\mathbf{S}] = \frac{[\mathbf{S}]}{[\mathbf{I}] - [\mathbf{N}]}$$

This gives a concise form of the product explosion which can be manipulated on a computer.

Summary

Materials requirements planning is not a new technique but a combination of several old ones. This combination is possible because of the computer and the efficient bill-of-materials processor.

MRP is used where the final product is complex, with several levels of assembly. It is also useful for situations where the final product is expensive and long lead times exist. The two major features of the MRP technique are level-by-level explosion and time phasing.

Product explosions for complicated products are difficult to produce for which matrix algebra offers an approach.

QUESTIONS

11–1. Explain why Materials Requirements Planning is both an inventory control and scheduling technique.

11–2. Explain why some products are controlled better with Materials Requirements Planning than they are with economic order techniques.

11–3. Why is the Materials Requirements Planning technique being used more today than it was 10 or 15 years ago?

11–4. Choose an industry which would be suitable for Materials Requirements Planning and explain why.

11–5. Select some simple product such as an automatic pencil and write a structured bill of materials listing the parts level-by-level.

11–6. What information is used in producing the Master Schedule? Compare the relative importance.

11–7. Explain how the Materials Requirements Planning technique can compensate for sales variations.

11–8. Explain the purpose of the *item master file* and the *product structure file*. Explain how they are coordinated.

11–9. Define these terms:

Independent or dependent demand.   Master schedule.

Level-by-level explosion.   Gross requirements.

Time offsetting.   Net requirements.

Time phasing.   Planned orders.

11–10. What advantages do you see in the Gozinto technique?

11–11. Perform the following matrix operations:

$$\begin{bmatrix} 3 & 9 \\ 2 & 5 \end{bmatrix} + \begin{bmatrix} 6 & 2 \\ 8 & 1 \end{bmatrix} =$$

$$\begin{bmatrix} 4 & 2 \\ 6 & 1 \end{bmatrix} \times \begin{bmatrix} 8 & 9 \\ 7 & 2 \end{bmatrix} =$$

$$\begin{bmatrix} 9 & 6 \\ 8 & 2 \end{bmatrix} - \begin{bmatrix} 3 & 1 \\ 4 & 1 \end{bmatrix} =$$

12

Economic Lot Size Planning

THE STUDENT of inventory theory often fails to appreciate the development and history of this part of management. It was as early as 1912 that the H. H. Franklin Manufacturing Company was using economic order quantities. In 1915 Ford W. Harris of the Westinghouse Electric Company developed the simple lot size formula and in 1926 R. H. Wilson published a classic in the field. In 1931 Fairfield E. Raymond published *Quantity and Economy in Manufacture*. K. Arrow, T. Harris, and J. Marschak gave inventory theory a rigorous mathematical treatment in their *Optimal Inventory Policy* in 1951. T. M. Whitin developed the first stochastic treatment of inventories in 1953. Robert G. Brown's classic *Statistical Forecasting for Inventory Control* appeared in 1959.

An American Production and Inventory Control Society's study shows a surge of publication in the 1920s which disappeared in the 1930s to reappear in the 1940s and continued to expand in the 1950 and 1960s. It is interesting to try to understand these developments. The lack of interest in the 1930s probably came about because of the depression. Inventory costs were not so important at this time, and the cost of making inventory decisions was probably not worth the effort. From the 1940s on, not only were the inventories important but the computer was available to help make the decisions which were so time consuming. Along with the computers came an interest in management sciences which attempted to make management decisions more objective. Probably one explanation for the surge of literature was the rapid growth in the number of graduate students and their need for suitable research topics.

Inventory Analogy

A useful analogy can be made between a simple fluids system and the inventory system. This analogy is not too far from reality and might have an application in the storage and control of oil, chemicals, or similar fluids. Figure 12–1A illustrates a tank being filled with fluid at the top which

Figure 12–1
Inventory Concepts

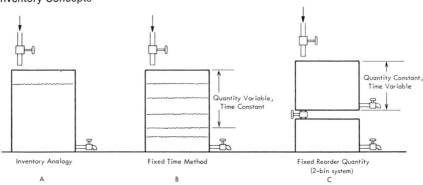

Inventory Analogy	Fixed Time Method	Fixed Reorder Quantity (2-bin system)
A	B	C

can be drawn off at the bottom. Generally, the liquid is running intermittently into the tank and is discharged intermittently. The inventory problem is to always have enough material available when it is needed, but not so much that an unnecessary and costly surplus is maintained. This might be solved in one of two ways. One is to check the level of the tank (Figure 12–1B) periodically and fill it to the top. This might require less than a gallon, or perhaps a whole tankful. Another method of solving this problem is to reorder every time the fluid gets to a certain level (as illustrated in Figure 12–1C). This might be done by setting up a reserve tank, which is drawn upon when the first tank is empty.

Checking the tank periodically is a fixed review time method of ordering, which is frequently referred to as the *ordering cycle method.* Ordering at the time the tank reaches a certain level is a fixed reorder point method, and this is frequently referred to as the *two-bin method.* The reason for it being called the two-bin method is obvious from our analogy since we have one tank or bin which holds the regular supply and another tank or bin which is drawn on after the first is depleted.

The above analogy is made clearer by a graphical description (Figure 12–2A). This is the typical saw-tooth chart used to illustrate inventory control problems. On the horizontal axis is plotted time, while on the vertical axis quantity is plotted. The withdrawal of different size lots with different time intervals is illustrated by a stepped line. If the quantity and time increments are nearly uniform from period to period, we can then, with some jus-

Figure 12–2
Graphical Inventory Concepts

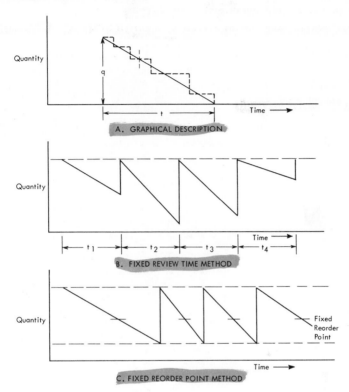

tification, smooth out the stair steps and represent them with a straight line.

The inventory starts with some quantity, q, which is gradually removed until it approaches zero in time, t. The slope of the line, q/t, shows the average quantity of inventory used per unit of time.

In the fixed review time or cyclic ordering method (Figure 12–2B) the time, t, remains fixed and the order quantity varies. The inventory items are kept under a periodic surveillance so that once a month, once a week, once a day, or some other such period, an order is placed which will bring the inventory up to the established level.

In the fixed reorder point method (Figure 12–2C) the quantity on hand is checked every time material is removed from the inventory. When it reaches a certain point, a quantity of a fixed size is ordered.

The inventory theory problem can now be summarized:

For the fixed review time method:
1. The quantity is reviewed periodically. The frequency of the review is still to be answered.
2. The order is placed for a quantity sufficient to replenish the inventory.

For the fixed quantity method:
1. The inventory is withdrawn to a point where there is just sufficient material to cover the replenishment time.
2. The order is placed for a quantity which optimizes the cost factors.

This amounts to determining *when* and *how much* to order, and we shall now proceed to study these questions in a logical order.

Fixed Review Time Method

Computers have stimulated an increasing interest in the fixed review time method because it is relatively easy to check a large number of inventory items periodically. Fixed review time can also be used in a manually operated system if the inventory consists of just a few items, or if the records can be displayed as bar charts which can be quickly reviewed.

Reviewing the inventory status by a computer, rather than manually, is still a time-consuming and costly operation. Frequently, the inventory quantities are recorded on a magnetic tape which must run from end to end checking item by item. A more efficient system would have the items grouped by optimum review times: those to be reviewed daily could be on one tape, those to be reviewed weekly on another tape, and so on.

An intuitive decision can be made concerning the length of the review period by considering the cost of short versus long review periods. As the length of the review period is increased, the clerical cost of reviewing and updating the records is decreased, because there is less labor involved (Figure 12–3). As the review period increases, the period of ignorance is increased because of the variability of demand and lead time. This means that larger reserves will be needed, which will increase the carrying costs as shown on the diagram. The total of the carrying and reviewing cost is shown as one curve on the diagram. We are, of course, interested in finding the

Figure 12–3
Cost of Review

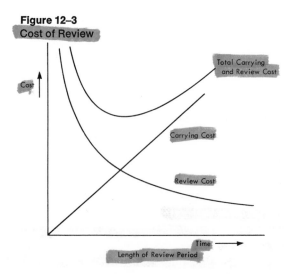

Total Carrying and Review Cost

Cost

Carrying Cost

Review Cost

Time

Length of Review Period

minimum total cost, which is obviously the lowest point on the curve. Equations have been developed along the lines described here, but probably many refinements and simplifications will have to be made before they become generally acceptable.

In actual practice there are problems which occur when the fixed review time method is used. As is apparent on the saw-tooth chart, when the time is fixed, the reorder quantity will vary, which means that it will be difficult to take advantage of economic order quantities. It is true that the person in charge of the inventory may take the option of ordering or not ordering at the review period. When only a small quantity is needed, the decision may be not to reorder, but this brings up the chance of a human error and the next review period might find the stock dangerously low.

Fixed Order Quantity Method—under Certainty

Let us expand on the fixed order quantity method, shown in Figure 12–4

Figure 12–4
Fixed Order Quantity Method under Certainty

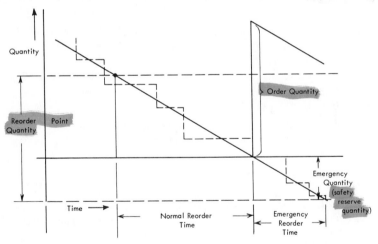

in which again the slope of the line represents the average use of material.

It would be desirable if the ordered quantity could be received at the very instant the stock was depleted, but to set up a system on this basis would be far too risky. Even if we took into account the probabilistic nature of demand, as we will do later on, we would be taking the risk of running out by failing to recognize the human element in the system.

Many inventory control models fail to take into account that even the most mechanized and computerized inventory control systems include people whose mental functions are often of a two-state nature: they either remember to do something or they forget to do something. And if they forget, they often forget forever—until reminded. These people form the numerous links between the inventory records and the production and delivery of the material. They may be the people in the inventory department, in the purchasing department, or even in some isolated railroad express office. Because of this, it is essential that some safety device be built into the system. This is the *safety reserve* shown in the diagram.

Safety Reserve Quantity. The safety reserve quantity is based on the time that it takes to obtain material in an emergency. Usually a factory knows what delay can be expected in obtaining material in the usual course of events, and it is also known that this time can be shaved considerably in an emergency by giving orders special rush priority, which may mean revising schedules, "robbing" orders, shipping by air express, and other expedients. Of course, this is very expensive and should not be permitted to occur too frequently. The emergency quantity signal may or may not be present on the inventory records, but often inventory clerks are aware of these danger points and will act "automatically."

Reorder Point. The reorder point quantity appears on the inventory record and is the "flag" for the inventory clerk, indicating when an order should be placed. If the demand is constant, as we are assuming throughout this section, the reorder point should be the safety reserve quantity plus what will be used during the time the order is being placed and delivered. In other words, it is the sum of the normal and emergency reorder time multiplied by the quantity used per day.

One obvious question: What is the normal reorder time? This, of course, will vary from vendor to vendor, and many companies prefer to use several vendors in order not to be dependent upon one. This has the advantage of making vendors more competitive. The names of the vendors can be listed on the inventory record along with typical delivery times. As you can imagine, delivery time variations among vendors can be considerable.

The best policy might be to establish the reorder point to account for the maximum reorder time, or to let the inventory clerk choose the vendor by considering the rate of withdrawal and any impending emergency. If the demand is great, the order can be placed with the vendor who can deliver the goods the fastest.

The Application of the Two-Bin System. This type of inventory control, just discussed, has been described as a two-bin system, which refers to two separate groups of inventory items. That quantity above the reorder point is the first bin and that quantity below the reorder point is the second bin. The reference to two bins might mislead the reader into thinking that there must be two distinct storage areas. This is not true, for all the material may be stored together and the only distinction between the two groups would be made on the inventory card.

On the other hand, it may actually be that the two groups are separated. For example, and especially when a perpetual inventory is not kept, it is quite common to box up a reserve quantity and set it to one side in the inventory area. When the first bin runs out and the reserve is opened, an order is placed. Some companies include a prewritten materials requisition with the reserve material. When the package is opened, the requisition is sent to the purchasing department. This same arrangement can be worked out with a bin replacing the boxed material, and from this the name of the two-bin system was derived.

The Order Quantity

Up to this point we have given our attention to the problem of *when* to reorder. Now it is time to turn our attention to *how much* to order. The fixed-order-quantity method, just described, has only one value lacking to make the picture complete. This is the *economic order quantity*, which will also be posted on the heading of the inventory record, with the reorder point quantity, for the convenience of the clerk when reordering.

The quantity that is to be ordered during a certain time can be considered as one or more *lots*. The lot is that group or batch of material that has the same identity for convenience in ordering or manufacturing. Lots are designated because of economic reasons, or for the convenience of the customer, process control department, quality control department, shipping department, or other. The *economic lot size* is that quantity which can be purchased or produced at a minimum cost.

While the method of solving the economic lot size problem is practically the same for purchased lots and manufactured lots, it should be obvious that the factors entering into the decision will be different. In purchasing from a vendor, quantity discounts should be taken into consideration as well as discounts given by transportation companies for moving large quantities.

The relationship between the lot size and the number of lots produced should be emphasized. The more often lots are produced, the smaller they need to be to satisfy the inventory requirements. Of course, the reverse is also true: large lots need be produced more infrequently. This can be easily visualized on the "saw-tooth" chart of Figure 12–5. On the left, only one

Figure 12–5
Order Frequency

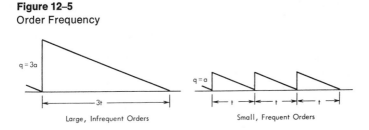

Large, Infrequent Orders   Small, Frequent Orders

large lot is made during the inventory period to last for the whole period. On the right, a number of lots are made and each one has to last but a fraction of the total time. In either case, the product of the number of lots and the lot size must be equal to the total demand for the inventory period. Be sure, when you are considering economic lot size problems, that you remember the inverse relationship between lot sizes and number of lots.

It is imperative that the manufacturing engineer fully understands the logic of the economic lot size problem and knows how it is solved. While few companies use elaborate methods of determining the economic lot size, the individuals responsible for the decision should recognize those factors that go into the elaborate formulas and how they influence the decision. The factors and logic of solving the economic lot size should be understood even though a crude rule-of-thumb method might be used.

The solution of the economic lot size problem is to minimize the inventory cost. This quickly becomes evident if one studies the two curves in Figure 12–6. No. 1 represents preparation costs plotted against lot sizes; and a curve, no. 2, represents carrying costs plotted against lot sizes.

Figure 12–6
Preparation versus Carrying Costs

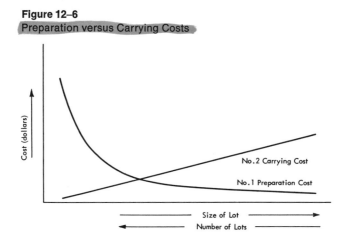

The preparation costs will include such items as preparing the paper work for the order, setting up the machine, and any other costs which are repeated every time an order is placed. The carrying costs are those costs, such as insurance and taxes, having to do with maintaining the inventory for a period of time. As you can see, on the left side of Figure 12–6, the preparation costs for many lots would be large but the carrying costs would be small. On the right, the reverse is true. So our objective in determining an economic lot size is to bring the total of these two groups of costs to a minimum and thus find the lowest possible cost per part in inventory.

The costs for economic lot size decisions can be brought into sharper focus by listing those costs which tend to make a lot size larger, and by listing separately those costs which tend to make a lot size smaller.

Those factors which tend to make a lot size large are:

1. *Preparation cost:* This includes the costs of preparing the paper work, blueprints, and so on for the order and also the set-up cost for the machines. Set-up cost is the expense of getting the machine ready for production. One question which comes up is whether or not this should include the cost of the machine's being *out* of production. This is typical of the type of question we will run into as we develop the models needed.

Those factors which would tend to make a lot size small are:

1. *Storage or warehousing charge:* This charge, which is self-explanatory, should be for the maximum space used for the items unless it is possible to utilize the space as the inventory is contracted.
2. *Interest charge:* This is the interest on the capital invested, and again we are faced with one of those inscrutable questions. Should this interest rate be what one can expect to earn in the business, or should it be the rate of loaning money or perhaps borrowing money?
3. *Insurance and tax charge:* This would include the insurance on property for both fire and theft as well as property taxes.

Developing the Economic Lot Size Model

At first we will discuss a very simple model for economic lot sizes, then progress to more sophisticated ones. The simplest model is most frequently used by industry and is the one proposed by one of the largest manufacturers of card-data-processing equipment. Although the logic of the simple formula is paved with errors and weak assumptions, it is the one which is used as a starting point for more elaborate models.

For the first model, here are some simplifying assumptions (which can be removed at a later date):

1. The order is placed so that it is received at the time the stock is depleted. In other words, we are not taking into consideration any emergency reserve.
2. The inventory carrying cost is applied to the average inventory value. This means we are not taking into account all the storage costs and the other costs which do not collapse with the decrease in the size of inventory.
3. The unit cost will remain constant throughout the range of production under consideration.

Since our objective in the determination of the economic lot size is to find the lowest yearly inventory cost, it is necessary to express the yearly cost which we intend to optimize.

The total yearly inventory cost is the total of the three costs, as illustrated on the diagram in Figure 12–7.

Figure 12–7
Economic Lot Sizes

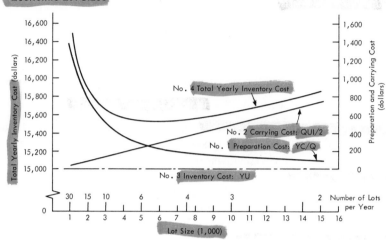

1. Cost of preparation for production
2. Cost of carrying the inventory
3. Cost of the products in inventory

Equations: 1 + 2 + 3 = 4. Total Yearly Inventory Costs

Each of these three costs, 1, 2, and 3, can be defined further:

1. **Cost of preparation for production** ($/year) equals:

$$\frac{\text{Yearly demand (units/year)}}{\text{Quantity (units/lot)}} \times \text{Cost of order preparation (\$/lot)}$$

Y = Yearly demand in units/year.
Q = Economic lot size in units/lot.
C = Preparation costs in dollars/lot.

Cost of preparation for production = YC/Q.

2. **Cost of carrying inventory** for year ($/year) equals:

Average inventory on hand during year $\times$ Cost per part $\times$ Carrying charge in percentage of part cost.

$Q/2$ = Average inventory carried during the inventory period.
U = Unit cost, which is the sum of the direct labor, direct material, and overhead, in $/unit.
I = Total of all carrying charges expressed as a percentage of the cost of the parts carried in stock for the year.

Cost of carrying the inventory = $QUI/2$.

3. Cost of inventory ($/year) equals:

Yearly demand in units/year $\times$ Cost/unit,

or, (as has been defined):

Cost of the inventory $= YU$

Expressing the total yearly inventory cost, $TYIC$, with symbols, we have:

$$TYIC = YC/Q + QUI/2 + YU$$

This gives the total yearly inventory cost; and all the items on the right side of the equation can be determined from the records (except Q). The estimate of the yearly demand, Y, is obtainable from the inventory records; the rest of the information should be found in the cost records.

The problem is still not solved, and the task of obtaining the lowest economic quantity still lies ahead. To do this we have a choice of several methods. Because it is the most revealing, let us examine the graphical solution first, using data for a typical problem.

Graphical Solution for Inventory Decisions. An electrical appliance manufacturer wishes to know what the economic quantity should be for a plastic impeller when the following information is available.

The average daily requirement is 120 units and the company has 250 working days a year, so the total yearly requirement, Y, is approximately 30,000 units a year. The manufacturing cost, U, which includes the direct labor, direct material, and overhead, is 50 cents each. The sum of the annual rates for interest, insurance, taxes, and so forth, is 20 percent of the unit cost, and the cost of preparation is $50 per lot.

$$Y = 30,000 \text{ units}$$
$$C = \$50/\text{preparation}$$
$$U = 50\cancel{c}/\text{part}$$
$$I = 20\%$$

These costs, inserted in the equation, would give the following:

$$TYIC = \frac{30,000 \text{ units/year} \times \$50/\text{lot}}{Q \text{ units/lot}} +$$
$$\frac{Q \text{ units/lot} \times 50\cancel{c}/\text{part} \times 20\%}{2} + 30,000 \text{ units/year} \times 50\cancel{c}/\text{part}$$

Figure 12–7 shows the quantity plotted on the horizontal axis, and costs, $TYIC$, on the vertical axis.

It is quite apparent that if only one lot is produced the cost for the year is very high, and that it drops rapidly as more lots are produced—until a lot size value between 5,000 and 6,000 is reached. As each additional lot is added, and the lot sizes are made smaller, the costs start to go up again. The economic lot size is, of course, where the curve dips at its lowest point, between 5,000 and 6,000.

The third factor, YU, in the equation remains constant and it is easy to see that it in no way affects the solution. All it does is to raise the base from which we start. The same solution would have been obtained if we had left out that part of the equation entirely. We could have done just as well if we had ignored part 3 of the equation and plotted only parts 1 and 2. However, it is better that you see the complete development of the equations.

The graphical solution is tedious, compared with the mathematical models which follow, but it has an advantage (which no other method presents) in that it shows the sensitivity of the costs to slight changes in lot size.

Tabular Solution.   The lowest total yearly cost can be seen by reference to the table of costs, Figure 12–8, which was assembled for plotting the

Figure 12–8
Tabular Method

Lots/Year	Q Lot Size	YC/Q Prep. Cost No. 1	QUI/2 Carrying Cost No. 2	YU Inv. Cost No. 3	Total Cost No. 4
1..........	30,000	$ 50.00	$1500.00	$15,000.00	$16,550.00
2..........	15,000	100.00	750.00	15,000.00	15,850.00
3..........	10,000	150.00	500.00	15,000.00	15,650.00
4..........	7,500	200.00	375.00	15,000.00	15,575.00
5..........	6,000	250.00	300.00	15,000.00	15,550.00
6..........	5,000	300.00	250.00	15,000.00	15,550.00
7..........	4,286	350.00	214.00	15,000.00	15,564.00

information. By observing the row showing the $TYIC$, one can see that the cost starts high ($16,550 for one lot), decreases to less than $15,550, and starts going back up again. The lowest cost is somewhere between lot sizes of 5,000 to 6,000, just as was shown on the curve.

Nomograph Solution.   Companies have found that solving the economic lot size by graphical means, by tabular solutions, or by equations has been far too cumbersome and expensive, so they have resorted to the use of nomographs. The construction of the nomograph and an example will be presented at the end of the chapter.

The Calculus Method of Solving the Economic Lot Size Problem.   The slope of a line is described by the value of a small segment of y (called *delta y*) over the small segment of x (*delta x*), as shown in Figure 12–9. Thus the value of $\Delta y/\Delta x$ is said to be the slope of the line. The slope at any point on the line can be determined as $\Delta y/\Delta x$ becomes infinitesimal. This is done by the methods of differential calculus.

We can observe that the value of the slope changes from negative to positive as we move along the curve. It becomes apparent that the lowest point on the curve—and the one we are searching for—has a slope of zero. This is found by taking the first derivative of the function $TYIC$, setting it to zero, and solving for the value of Q:

Figure 12–9
Calculus Solution

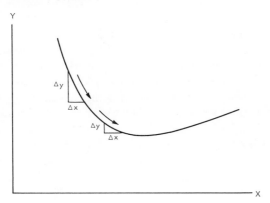

$$TYIC = YC/Q + QUI/2 + YU$$
$$d(TYIC)/dQ = -YC/Q^2 + UI/2 + 0$$
$$d(TYIC)/dQ = 0$$
$$Q = \sqrt{2YC/UI}$$

We can now solve our example by this method:

$$Q = \sqrt{\frac{2 \times 30{,}000 \times 50.00}{.50 \times .20}}$$
$$Q = 5{,}477 \text{ parts}$$

Notice that the value of YU dropped out of the solution, and remember that in our graphical solution we discovered the same to be true.

The equation, $Q = \sqrt{2YC/UI}$, states that the economic lot size varies directly with the square root of the yearly demand and preparation costs, and indirectly with the square root of the carrying costs. This leads to some interesting observations. If the yearly demand for a product went from 100 to 10,000, which would be an increase of 100 times, the economic lot size would be only 10 times larger if all the other factors in the equation remained the same. It is important to management to realize that stock need not be increased in the same ratio as sales or production. Also, as the value of I is increased from, for example, 9 to 16 percent, the economic quantity will be reduced by about 30 percent.

Another important consideration is the shape of the curve at its minimum value. Since it is quite flat near the economic lot size value, it is not critical for a considerable range of values. This indicates that the decision is not as important as one might imagine. This is a point management should keep in mind as the cost of economic lot size decisions is considered.

This equation, $Q = \sqrt{2YC/UI}$, with perhaps some slight modifications, is used by the majority of firms which use equations. One of the largest manufacturers of computer-processing equipment suggests this model to its customers. This model is also the one which pops up in the area of mathematical programming upon which more elegant models are developed. However, anyone who has had experience in factory operations must question the assumptions and factors that are used in the equation.

EOQ's Applied to Purchases. For simplicity, the examples have been chosen which would be used by a manufacturer for his own product. These are at times referred to as manufacturing order quantities, MOQ, as contrasted to purchase order quantities, POQ.

The same logic holds for POQ's as was used in MOQ's, the only difference being the cost components that are used. Preparation costs for purchased items will probably not contain a set-up cost but will be restricted to just the costs of preparing the purchase order.

In applying EOQ's to purchased items there will be price breaks to take into consideration. Price breaks refer to the better prices one can frequently obtain when buying in larger and larger quantities.

Considerations and Modifications of the Carrying Charge

The cost of the inventory carrying charge was calculated on half of the average economic lot size. This would be justifiable if the costs of carrying the inventory were to go up and down with the quantity of inventory on hand. A little consideration of the components of this cost will disclose the unreasonableness of dividing all carrying costs by two. Here are the elements of the inventory carrying costs for your consideration:

Obsolescence of the inventory items.
Depreciation of the inventory items.
Transportation and handling of the items in inventory.
Property taxes on the items in inventory.
Storage facility charges.
Insurance on the inventory.
Interest on the value of the inventory.

Each of these items must be evaluated by the company concerned; and it is probable that this is one of the most difficult aspects of the inventory control problem, and one that seems to be often totally ignored.

The obsolescence and depreciation of the inventory is peculiar to the particular industry being studied. For a company producing a high-style product, this would be appreciable, but for a company producing such items as pipe fittings it would be relatively low. These costs, as well as the transportation and handling charges, could better be associated with the total economic lot size rather than one half of it, as shown in many economic lot size formulas.

Property tax and insurance charges can be best accumulated by the accountant. These depend upon the management policies of the company as well as external forces beyond its control.

The storage charge could seldom be added for one-half the total inventory, for the space, in most cases, is not collapsed or used for something else. The bins will exist for an item whether there is 1 part or 50,000. The storage charges for a tank of chemicals cannot be reduced as the quantity is reduced. It becomes quite evident that some charges remain fixed regardless of the size of the inventory, and in reality, the value of I should be divided into two factors, I_f and I_v, to represent those charges which remain fixed and those which vary with the value of the inventory. Each item will have to be studied by both the production management and the accountant before a decision can be reached as to the approximate value.

Making this modification in the formula we have the following:

Cost of carrying inventory for year $= QUI_v/2 + QUI_f$

Thus the equation is:

$$TYIC = YC/Q + QUI_v/2 + QUI_f + YU$$
$$TYIC = YC/Q + QU(I_v/2 + I_f) + YU$$
$$d(TYIC)/dQ = -YC/Q^2 + U(I_v/2 + I_f)$$
$$Q = \sqrt{YC/U(I_v/2 + I_f)}$$

It is not easy to select the correct value for interest. One can get numerous answers to this question. The interest rate on borrowed money might be suggested or the interest rate on loaned money might be proposed. Paul T. Norton, Jr. has made extensive economic studies and suggests that it should be the minimum attractive rate of return instead of interest rate on borrowed money.[1] In other words, it should be the rate of return that the company earns in its operations, otherwise it will not account for the risks involved. A low interest rate will affect the lot size formula in such a way as to make the lot size larger than it should be.

Consideration of the Safety Reserve Quantity. On first thought it might appear that the safety reserve quantity should have been taken into consideration. We expect to replace the inventory when the level reaches the safety reserve quantity so that the economic lot size equation would pertain only to carrying the safety reserve during the inventory period. This can be written as an equation:

Carrying charge for safety reserve = Safety reserve quantity ×
Unit cost × Annual rate

If this additional carrying charge is added to the economic lot size equation it will have no influence on the final answer. This is apparent when one recognizes that the above equation does not contain Q. This is similar to the costs of the products in inventory, represented by factor 3 in the development of the economic lot size equations.

---

[1] W. Grant Ireson and Eugene L. Grant, *Handbook of Industrial Engineering and Management* (Englewood Cliffs, N.J.: Prentice-Hall, 1955), p. 143.

Consideration of Noninstantaneous Inputs. Up to this point we have considered the inventory input as being instantaneous—as exhibited by the vertical line O–A on the saw-tooth chart of Figure 12–10. Frequently, the

Figure 12–10
Noninstantaneous Inputs

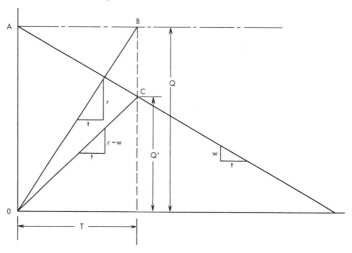

production would extend over a period of time, as shown by O–B. The slope of this line, r/t, is obviously the replenishment rate in quantity per day, week, or other unit of time. The quantity produced, Q, which should be an economic order quantity, is the product of the rate, r/t, and the time period, T, $Q = Tr/t$.

If the material is withdrawn from the inventory at a rate, w/t, while it is being replenished at a rate, r/t, we will develop a line, O–C, with a slope of $(r - w)/t$. It should be noted here that the replenishment rate, r/t, will have to be equal to or greater than the withdrawal rate, w/t, or we will run out of stock.

Since the material is running into the inventory while it is also trickling out, we will not need as large a storage space as we did when the inventory replacement was instantaneous. This results in a reduction of the inventory carrying charges, but by how much?

The maximum inventory on hand is as shown on the diagram by Q'. As is customary, the carrying charge is applied to only the average quantity on hand, $Q'/2$. Q' is the product of time period, T, and the rate, $(r - w)/t$.

Starting with $Q' = T(r-w)/t$ and $Q = Tr/t$, we can express Q' in terms of Q:

$$Q' = \frac{Q}{r}(r-w) = Q(1 - w/r)$$

Entering this quantity in the original equation for the storage carrying cost, we have:

Original Equation:

Total yearly inven- = Cost of prep- + Cost of + Cost of
tory cost   aration   carrying   inventory

$$TYIC = YC/Q + Q'UI/2 + YU$$

Revised Equation:

$$TYIC = YC/Q + Q(1-w/r)\,UI/2 + YU$$

$$\frac{d(TYIC)}{dQ} = -YC/Q^2 + \frac{UI(1 - w/r)}{2}$$

$$Q = \sqrt{\frac{2YC}{UI(1 - w/r)}}$$

It is apparent that the noninstantaneous input equation is slightly more complex than the instantaneous input equation, but probably not so much as to rule out its use. However, before making a general application of this equation, studies regarding the sensitivity should be made.

Consideration of Long Order Times. So far in our examples the order time has been less than the time it would take to use the material. This does not always occur, and frequently we find that it is necessary to have several orders in progress. This situation is more easily seen by Figure 12–11. In

Figure 12–11
Long Order Times

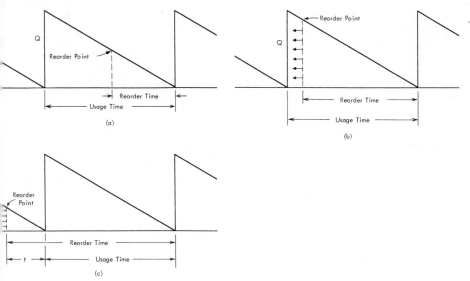

Figure 12–11A we have the situation which has been used in the previous models, in B the lead time approaches the usage time, and in C the lead time exceeds the usage time by t. Several order cycles are shown in Figure 12–12.

Figure 12–12
Several Order Cycles

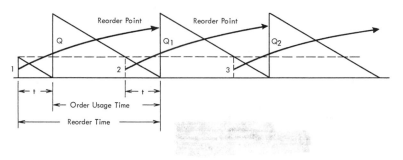

It is evident that the quantity ordered at 1 will not be delivered before the inventory is depleted, so there must be an order on its way that will build up the inventory, Q. The material ordered at 1 will be delivered to rebuild the inventory, Q_1. The material ordered at 2 will rebuild the inventory at Q_2, and so on. The reorder-point quantity is then determined by extending t to the line representing the rate of usage.

In practice, the inventory clerk must be alerted to expect more than one order out at a time. This method of development could expand through as many cycles as necessary.

Consideration for Price Breaks and Shipping Discounts. The costs that go into the price of a product can vary extensively throughout the range of possible purchased quantities. These different price levels are called "price breaks" and come about for various reasons. Price breaks occur in purchased items because the vendors frequently give quantity discounts at different quantity levels. In addition, price breaks are offered by transportation companies with carload—as opposed to less-than-carload (LCL)—prices. In manufactured products there are price breaks which are caused by differences in processing, such as the difference in costs for producing parts on an engine lathe rather than on an automatic screw machine.

Sometimes these price breaks are such that it is not easy to determine the economic lot size for any particular condition. When this is true, the best procedure is to figure the costs for several alternatives and simply choose the best.

Other Considerations. There are various combinations of the quantity constant and time constant systems. The time constant system has the inherent danger that a sudden draw on the inventory will go unnoticed and it will be too late to wait for the usual reorder time. To overcome this, a reorder point is used in conjunction with the time constant system.

In other cases a company may check its inventory items periodically but only place orders for those items which are close to the reorder point. As can be seen, many variations can be played upon these two themes.

Some Comments on Economic Lot Size Formulas

This statement will be open to criticism from those who like "elegance" of inventory models regardless of the cost. But probably economic lot decision making should itself come under the scrutiny of an economic study.

Economic lot size formulas, similar to the ones discussed, have been around since the turn of the century. After having nearly been dropped, they have recently been rejuvenated by the application of statistics and high-speed computers which make the complicated and tedious formulas more suitable for ambitious electronic slaves.

The curve of the example problem shows that it would be much better to err on the side of small lots rather than that of large lots. This is characteristic of these curves and should be taken into consideration when making the decision, with or without the aid of the economic lot size formulas. However, if the risk is high, then the decision should be made as far to the left as possible, which will also increase capital turnover. Many companies operate with so little working capital that they should not consider economic lot sizes. Also, notice how flat the curve is near the bottom. Thus, moving either way from the economic lot size has no drastic effect upon the resulting costs. Again, this should be kept in mind when making the decision.

What sense do elaborate equations make if they do not conform to the facts of life in a factory? The lot size may call for 1,000 parts as an economic lot size, but we discover that the tumbler used for polishing the parts holds just 750 parts, and to run 1,000 we would have to run a tumbler only part full. This does not make good sense, so the number should be increased or decreased to come out with even lots in the tumbler operation. Or perhaps we find this lot size would take a half hour longer than the time required for each shift. If we can reduce the time by half an hour, one of the night set-up men can make the change and the machine will not be out any productive time. This makes sense; so whenever economic lot size formulas are used, they should be tempered with good judgment.

Often the type of people who will be responsible for economic lot size decisions is forgotten. Certainly we cannot expect to use a high-level staff man for setting the numerous lot sizes; it will more likely be a clerk with perhaps less than a high school education. It would be foolish to ask him to work a complicated equation.

Also we know that no solution to a problem can be any better than the information that goes into the problem. It was evident earlier that there were some questions about some of the factors that are fed into the equations.

A good way of establishing economic lot sizes is to have a committee formed of the inventory clerk, the plant manager, foremen involved, materials handling supervisor, and other interested parties. After a full understanding of the philosophy of economic lot sizes they can progress to the establishment of economic lot sizes, taking into account the size of tote pans, set-up times, receiving methods, and other factors which bear upon the decision and to which the computers cannot possibly give attention.

Nomographs for Inventory Control

Economic lot size decisions and many other production decisions may be obtained easily from nomographs. You will probably find numerous time-saving applications of nomographs once you become aware of how easy it is to construct them. Untrained clerical personnel can learn to use them with very little difficulty. A brief discussion of their construction and an application will be presented here:

Addition. Although an addition nomograph has limited use, its construction will be illustrated so that you may more readily understand the others.

Addition

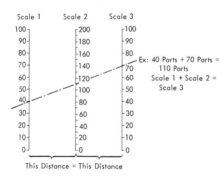

Construction:

Step 1. Draw three parallel lines equal distances apart.

Step 2. Divide lines:
Scale 1 and 3 the same.
Scale 2 (the middle one) into units one-half the size of those for 1 and 3.

Step 3. Place straight edge across lines as shown. Select numbers to be added on scales 1 and 3 and find answer on scale 2.

Subtractions. This will also have limited application but is useful in understanding nomographs.

Subtraction

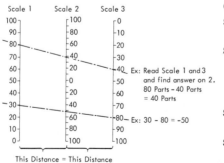

Construction:

Step 1. Draw three parallel lines equal distances apart.

Step 2. Divide line.
Scale 1 and 3 the same.
Scale 2 (the middle one) into units one-half the size of those for 1 and 3.

Step 3. Number scales as shown in example. Invert one as shown.

Step 4. Place straight edge across lines as shown. Select numbers to be subtracted on scales 1 and 3 and find answer on scale 2.

Multiplication. Multiplication is done on a nomograph by adding logarithms. The logarithms are the powers used to raise a number such as for 10^2—the 2 can be considered as the logarithm which can be added:

$$100 \times 1000 = 100,000$$
$$10^{2+} \times 10^3 = 10^5$$

The number 10 (in this system) may be raised by numbers which are not integers. For example:

$$10^{2.32} \times 10^{3.16} = 10^{5.48}$$

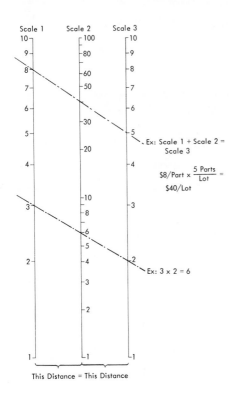

This Distance = This Distance

Multiplication

Step 1. Draw three parallel lines equal distances apart.

Step 2. Graduate the two outside scales 1 and 3 equally using a log scale (see instructions under problems of construction and scaling).

Step 3. Graduate middle scale (scale 2) with twice the cycles of the outside scales.

Step 4. Place straight edge across scales and read as shown.

Multiplication by a Constant. To multiply by a constant it is necessary to shift the middle scale, 2, as shown.

For example, if any answer from scale 1 and scale 2 is to be multiplied by 6, we start at the bottom with scale 1, starting with 1; scale 2, starting with 6; and scale 3, starting with 1. The center scale may be adjusted by a few calculations or it may be calculated.

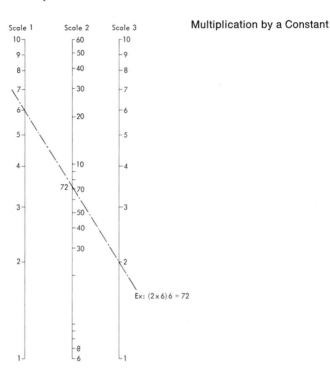

Multiplication by a Constant

Ex: (2×6)6 = 72

Division. Division is performed by the subtraction of logarithms. Consequently, it is necessary to invert the scale as shown:

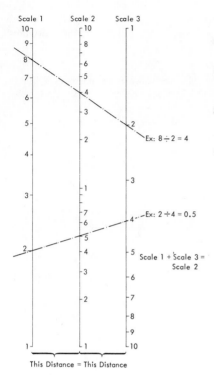

Division

Step 1.   Draw three parallel lines equal distances apart.

Step 2.   Divide lines
Scale 1 and 3 the same but invert 3.

Step 3.   Graduate middle scale (scale 2) with twice the cycles of the outside scales.

Step 4.   Place straight edge across scales and read as shown.

Ex: 8 ÷ 2 = 4

Ex: 2 ÷ 4 = 0.5

Scale 1 + Scale 3 = Scale 2

This Distance = This Distance

Three or More Variables. When three variables are used, an intermediate scale is inserted. For example, $A \times B \times C$ is constructed with an additional scale D inserted.

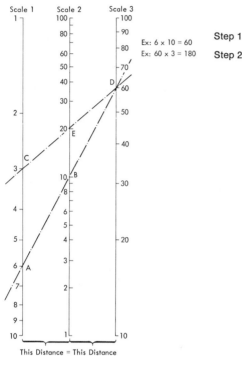

Three or More Variables

Ex: 6 x 10 = 60

Ex: 60 x 3 = 180

Step 1. $A \times B = D$

Step 2. $D \times C = E$

Mechanics of Laying Out Nomographs

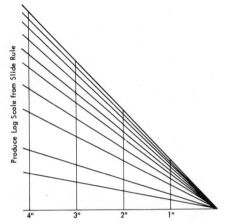

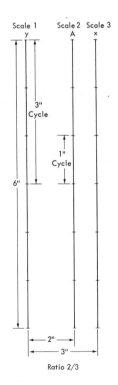

Ratio 2/3

1. *Obtaining the correct cycle length*
   Changing the cycle length is readily done using simple geometry concepts.
   a. Construct chart as shown to full scale.
   b. Select scale desired and transfer it to your nomograph.

2. *Size of scales*
   Length of scales 1 and 3.
   a. Length of line depends upon the space available and how easily it can be read.
   b. Number of cycles depends on the range of values desired.
   Length of scale 2:

$$S_2 = \frac{n_2}{\left(\dfrac{n_1}{S_1}\right) + \left(\dfrac{n_3}{S_3}\right)}$$

where:
   n_1 is the exponent for term 1
   n_2 is the exponent for term 2
   n_3 is the exponent for term 3
   S_1 is length of the cycle for scale 1
   S_2 is length of the cycle for scale 2

3. *Position of scale 2*
   The position of scale 2 stated as a fraction of the distance from scales 1 and 3:

$$= \frac{\dfrac{n_3}{S_3}}{\left(\dfrac{n_1}{S_1}\right) + \left(\dfrac{n_3}{S_3}\right)}$$

Example: $A = y\ x^2$

   A scale 2
   y scale 1
   x scale 3

Length of axis: 6″
Range 1 to 100 for y and x. This requires two cycles, 1 to 10 and 10 to 100.

Length of cycles for scale 2:

$$S_2 = \frac{1}{\left(\dfrac{1}{3}\right) + \left(\dfrac{2}{3}\right)} = 1″$$

Position of Scale 2:

$$= \frac{\dfrac{2}{3}}{\left(\dfrac{1}{3}\right) + \left(\dfrac{2}{3}\right)} = \frac{2}{3}$$

The application of the nomograph to the economic order quantity problem is illustrated in Figure 12–13. Nomographs similar to this are used throughout industry.

Figure 12–13
Nomograph Solution

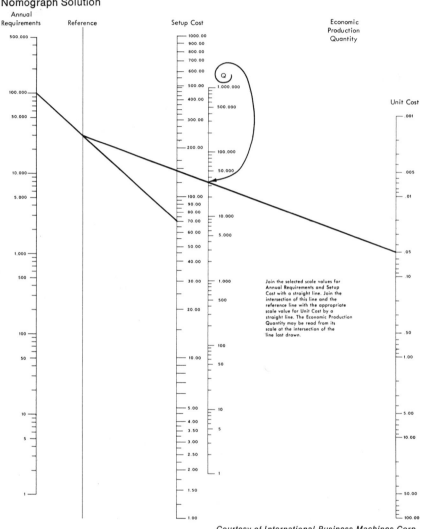

Courtesy of International Business Machines Corp.

Inventory Policies versus Theory

Modern inventory theorists often do not take into account the management policies which override some of the most elaborate models. As an example, one small manufacturer of electric measuring instruments knows that he has little to offer the customer in the way of advanced research and production facilities. He does know that one of his biggest selling points is his immediate delivery service. He therefore keeps on hand a carload of instruments so he can make shipments at once. By being able to do this he has been able to stay in business among some of the sharpest competition.

Another example of theory being overridden by practical policy is when a company is operating on little working capital. The economic lot size formulas may suggest quantities which will cause such drastic problems as making it impossible for a company to take advantage of discounts on accounts payable, or perhaps delaying the payroll. One could think of a number of examples when it is advisable to override the economic lot size decisions. One should, of course, realize that the theory is helpful in making decisions, but the cost of the inventory alone may not be the only thing to consider.

Frequently a company will install economic order procedures anticipating that inventory investments will go down only to find that they increase. This has caused some companies to drop the procedure before solving their problems. Other companies have manipulated the equations to give the answers they desired. Some, for example, have considered that I, the carrying charge in the equation, is a management factor which should be adjusted up or down to give the total inventory investment desired.

Future of Inventory Control Theory. In recent years management has learned some of the many advantages of good inventory control procedures. Efficient inventory management has been credited with playing an important role in the unprecedented and sustained prosperity of our time.

Executives will undoubtedly be exploring the possibility of applying some of the more sophisticated inventory models. Those who are developing inventory models will probably start looking more closely at the real-world conditions in which their techniques are to operate. Designing the models within the restrictions of the industrial conditions will become more important, but of greater importance will be a thorough testing to determine the efficiency of the models.

The next chapter will discuss some of the more sophisticated but useful inventory models which have been developed.

Summary

Inventory decision-making problems are of two kinds: when to order and how much to order. The decision of when to order may be based on either a constant review time or on a constant reorder quantity, the latter being favored by most companies.

The order-quantity decision is a problem of minimizing both the total costs of maintaining an inventory and the costs of placing an order.

There has been a tendency to make inventory decisions more complex than they deserve, but it is useless to be concerned about factors in equations which have little influence on the decision. It should also be kept in mind that the answer can be no more accurate than the information which is used in the model. However, the reasoning behind inventory models can be useful as a guide for day-to-day decisions of when and how much to order.

QUESTIONS

12-1. List the historical developments in inventory theory and try to explain why they occurred and what impact they might have had.

12-2. How well does the saw-tooth chart illustrate the inventory control situation?

12-3. Which is the more common system: fixed-order quantity or fixed-order time?

12-4. Which inventory system—fixed-order time or fixed-order quantity—does each of the following use: housewife, filling station owner buying gas, home-owner buying fuel oil, automobile owner buying gas?

12-5. Define the following: order quantity, reorder point quantity, safety reserve quantity.

12-6. Write a step-by-step instruction for reading the nomograph shown in Figure 12-13.

12-7. Design a nomograph to be used in a store room which will give the total weight of cartons of ball bearings. The variables will be quantity and weight of individual bearings. The bearings weigh from one pound to ten pounds and are packed from one to 100 in a box.

12-8. Discuss the dangers of both overstocking and understocking material in a manufacturing company.

12-9. Relate economic conditions to the economic order quantity.

12-10. The economic lot size attempts to minimize the total of two costs. What are they? How easy are they to obtain?

12-11. Why is it that the cost of the products in the inventory does not affect the economic lot size?

12-12. Discuss the strengths and weaknesses of the economic lot-size equations from an applied viewpoint.

12-13. A hardware company produces over 10,000 different items. Suggest how they can use economic lot-size formulas without excessive cost.

13

Inventory Models

THE PREVIOUS CHAPTER developed the basic inventory model for the reorder point and the order quantity. They are the equations which will be found in most of the companies using equations.

There is, however, a trend toward more sophisticated inventory models, and it is the purpose of this chapter to present those models which find the most frequent applications in industry. It is not intended to be an exhaustive cataloging of all models regardless of their usefulness. The models given here are the ones you are most likely to encounter in industry.

The previous chapter discussed order points first, followed by order quantities. This chapter will follow the same organization.

Background for Probabilistic Models

The models incorporating probability require some explanation and background. The next few pages will attempt to accomplish this and give you some feel for how much faith you can place in such models when you are using them in industry.

Let us briefly review the model of inventory under the conditions of certainty before exploring the application of uncertainty. In Figure 13–1 we have the typical saw-tooth chart, representing the withdrawal and replenishment of inventory, with quantity on the vertical axis and time on the horizontal axis. This is the fixed reorder quantity system which has been discussed, but it does not include an emergency quantity—which we intend to develop by a method slightly different than before.

The problem is to determine the quantity to which the inventory can be reduced before an order must be placed if it is to be received before the

Figure 13–1
Typical Saw-Tooth Chart

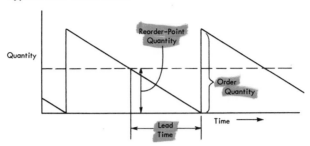

stock is depleted. Why quantity? Because this is the form of the information available in the records. This quantity must be translated eventually into time because this is the form of the replenishment information.

If the stock could be replenished instantaneously, this order point could be near the point of depletion. Since the stock cannot be obtained immediately, a *lead time* must be provided for the replenishment of stock. This conventional way of illustrating the problem can lead to some confusion and error, so a more elaborate illustration, Figure 13–2, will be developed. The part of the diagram above the horizontal time axis illustrates the with-

Figure 13–2
Withdrawal and Replenishment Cycle

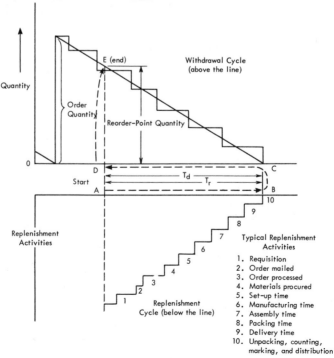

drawal cycle, as shown before, but the part below the axis illustrates the replenishment cycle.

The various replenishment activities are extended along the vertical axis, and the horizontal axis, of course, represents time. The completion of each of the various activities in the replenishment cycle is represented by a step in the line. The time to replenish the stock, either by placing an order with a vendor or with the company's facilities, is shown by T_r. The time for depleting the stock is shown by T_d.

In the first illustration we will consider the times for depletion and replenishment as being fixed or certain. In the ideal situation the time for replenishment should be exactly equal to the time of depletion, $T_r = T_d$. It should be apparent that if the material is used sooner than it is replaced—that is, T_d is less than T_r—there will not be any on hand to fill the need; but if T_r is less than T_d, we will have stock on hand before it is needed. We are assuming for the moment that the inventory can go down to zero since the problem is to eventually find the emergency stock needed under uncertain conditions.

The ideas developed here are not exotic, for this problem is no different than the one faced by a housewife. She must predict how fast the family is going to drink milk, as well as the milkman's delivery time, so that the depletion and the delivery time nearly coincide—she hopes.

We can now see that there is a sequence of steps in obtaining the reorder-point quantity. First the replenishment time, T_r, is determined, which in turn determines the depletion time, T_d, from which the reorder-point quantity can be calculated. To see this, follow the letters, A, B, C, D, and E on Figure 13–2.

$$\text{Reorder-point quantity} = \text{Replenishment time} \times \frac{\text{Quantity withdrawn}}{\text{Time}}$$

Our model does not represent the real world because, as you know, the rate of withdrawal will vary, causing the withdrawal time to vary, and the replenishment time will also be subject to variations. This is why we are interested in inventory policies under conditions of uncertainty.

We will now turn to the discussion of probabilistic models. First, we will discuss the effect of the variability in general, making some initial assumptions about the variability, and later we can discuss the variability in detail. From now on, all the stepped withdrawal and replenishment lines will be represented by straight lines to keep the illustration uncluttered. We will use our previous illustration and add the variability concept, as shown in Figure 13–3.

Not only is the average time illustrated for the depletion and withdrawal cycles, but also the minimum and maximum time for each. The frequency of the time values between the extremes can be represented by distributions which at first will be assumed to be normal. Using this assumption, three standard deviations either side of the mean will include nearly all of the

Figure 13–3
Probabilistic Model

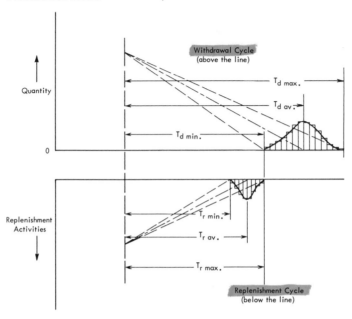

possibilities. At this point there is no reason to believe that these distributions will be normal, but it is more convenient to discuss them as if they were.

Pause for a moment and review what we are doing. It takes time to replace the stock in an inventory and we must have a signal that says, "Now is the time to start the replacement cycle, if we wish to have the material arrive on time." This signal is the reorder-point quantity.

Before going further with this model, to explore the relationship between the withdrawal and replenishment distributions, it will be worthwhile scrutinizing each distribution more carefully.

The Replenishment Distribution. This distribution is made up of a series of events which it is sometimes assumed will add together to form a normal distribution. The Poisson distribution has also been assumed to be a good model. Some samples of data, however, have exhibited distinct bimodal distributions for the total replenishment times. This might be expected because of the impact of weekends upon the series of events. But, beyond this, there are causes which could contribute to weird-looking empirical distributions, such as the effect of the heavy holiday traffic on the railroads, which in turn influences the schedules of freight and express. The coincidence of large orders arriving on the same day would have an important impact on delivery dates. These are just a couple of the causes that can affect the processing of an order—in addition to general economic conditions.

Some attempts have been made to fit the curve developed by empirical data obtained from the records, but this might lead to hazardous conclusions if the economy were to suddenly change. When business is booming, vendors will probably be slow in filling orders; during depressed periods they will not only hasten to fill orders to keep valuable customers but will also have facilities available to fill the orders. Perhaps no distribution is suitable for these changes, and we may need an elastic distribution which changes from season to season and year to year.

Including the variability of the replenishment cycle in the inventory-reorder model complicates it to such an extent that many models ignore it completely. Although the replenishment time may be extremely long, the variability for replenishment in most industrial situations is probably relatively small when compared with others.

The Withdrawal Distribution. This distribution is also suspect, as illustrated in Figure 13–4. Let us discuss withdrawals as a series of events occur-

Figure 13–4
Withdrawal Distribution

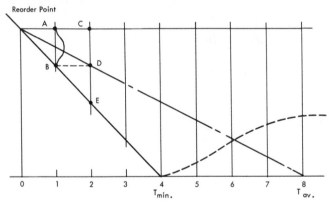

ring during time periods, such as days, as shown on the diagram. The probability of the various possible withdrawal quantities can be illustrated, for the moment, by a distribution as shown at the end of the first day. The series of events will be easier to follow if they are considered period by period:

End of the first period. It is conceivable that at the end of the first period no material will have been withdrawn, as shown at A, or the maximum quantity might have been withdrawn, as shown at B. These are, of course, the extreme conditions, and any quantity between the two could have been withdrawn, as described by the probability distribution.

End of the second period. If the first withdrawal period left the inventory at A, we can see that the second period might have left the inventory at C or D, or some place in between. If the first period had the maximum withdrawal, as shown by B, then we might have had for the second period no withdrawals, as shown at D, or some maximum value, as shown at E, or again some value in between.

Continuing this line of logic, we obtain a line with the T_d minimum intersecting the *zero* quantity line, as shown on the diagram. If the average withdrawal should occur during every time period, we can project that line to intersect with the time axis too, but what about the other extreme? The line extending horizontally is accounted for in some economic lot size models by obsolescence, and this is just what we have if the line extends as shown.

Even the distributions for each day, as shown in the illustrations, are questionable. If we were considering steel inventories, we could find the distributions skewed to the left if a steel strike were in the offing and skewed to the right if hard times were upon us. These distributions might be independent, or they might be dependent.

This situation is not unlike that faced by the owner of the local candy store. When a child, clutching a coin in his grimy little hand, gives a glance at the candy display but wanders on down the street to emerge from the ice cream store with a cone, the candy store owner knows he has lost a sale. The opportunity to fill this exact need for the child is lost forever. The child may pass this way again tomorrow, but it will not be to fill the same need—only another one. This decision depends upon the satisfactions gained for the amount of money spent. If the cost is too high, there will be substitution.

This same thing occurs in commercial buying. Steel is compared with aluminum and wood with plastic. If the price of the product is too high, and satisfaction can be gained in some cheaper way, the shelves will remain full and the withdrawal line will be horizontal. This can be a sudden change —occurring overnight—if the price of the substitute is lowered.

The decisions, on the other hand, might be dependent. It is not unusual for a customer to defer the purchase of some article because of a shortage of capital, inclement weather, or other reason and, as a result, double his purchases the following period. In other words, he lets the pipeline run low and fills it by placing one large order.

The foregoing indicates some of the difficulties encountered in describing the withdrawal cycle.

Costs of Overstocking and Understocking

Let us now take a better look at the withdrawal cycle, assuming a near-normal distribution, as shown in Figure 13–5A. This first diagram shows a situation in which there is virtually no chance of running out, if there is no variability in the replenishment cycle.

In the second example, B, with the replenishment time still fixed, there is an opportunity of depleting the stock before it is replaced. The costs of running out, which may entail shutting down production lines, air-expressing

Figure 13–5
Cost of Stockpiling Material

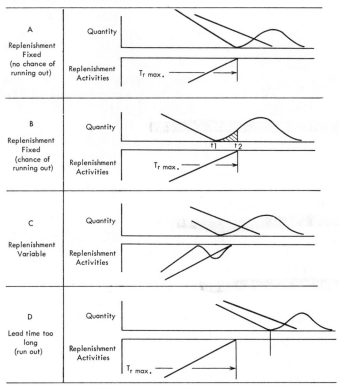

parts, and other expenses, must be weighed against the costs of maintaining an inventory for the period of time $t_2 - t_1$. This stockpiling has been the cause for some alarm, and perhaps rightly so, but it should be compared with the costs that might occur in case of a shortage.

The risk-taking problem becomes more complicated in the third illustration, C, when one tries to consider the variability both in the withdrawal and the replenishment distributions. This is especially difficult when little is actually known about each.

The fourth illustration, D, shows what can happen if the lead time is set too long, or the inventory clerk has been extremely careless in placing the order before it is signaled. The distance between the distributions would be extended, as shown, but the effect would be to increase the safety only very slightly, and at excessive costs.

Factors to Consider in the Probabilistic Model

It should be evident by now that the development of a probabilistic model is not exactly straightforward. In addition to the problems discussed, there are other factors which influence the effectiveness of any model.

The Effect of Business Trends. We have not taken into account the effect of business changes. What might be a good reorder point in one economic condition might be a poor one at another time. The Good Humor Man would be foolish to lay in a huge supply of ice cream just because he had unusually high sales on a freakishly hot day in October. Probably a good indicator would be the steepness of the withdrawal line as it passes through the reorder point. In a system using clerks, these rates are detected and taken into consideration—a computer is not programmed to judge this change and something is bound to be lost as a consequence.

Factory Scheduling and Withdrawals. The operation of the factory and the inventory are not as unrelated as might have been implied in the previous discussion. The withdrawal of raw material inventories in a job shop is at the mercy of the way the jobs are scheduled to the shop. Consequently, the withdrawal of material can be controlled by what is happening in the factory and the withdrawal distribution is not the result of chance causes alone.

Multiple Use of Inventory Items. The inventory problem is often compounded because a certain item is used in different products. While this makes it more difficult to predict withdrawals, it does permit some trade-offs to compensate for excessive withdrawals.

Cost of Not Filling an Order. There have been attempts to evaluate the cost of not satisfying a need, but we cannot forget that the customer, especially in a retail situation such as a bakery, has some opportunity to make a trade-off. Perhaps he might not get the exact item he wants from the vendor, but he will probably find an acceptable substitute. The customer's buying habits are probably not established on one item alone but upon all the items he carries out in his market basket. There is considerable inertia in a customer's buying habits, but we should remember that if we turn a customer away too often we will lose his loyalty and he will look to other vendors to satisfy his needs.

The manufacturer and the wholesaler have several means of satisfying a customer's needs. Part of an order might be back-ordered, which could be quite satisfactory to the customer since he will not have to store the material and can defer payment. He would probably just as soon fit his withdrawal cycle to the vendor's deliveries if he did not lose by doing so.

There are other trade-offs which can be made by the vendor that might be satisfactory. He might be able to rob other orders, which are not needed immediately, or he might borrow from another manufacturing unit, district warehouse, or friendly customer, and it is not uncommon to borrow from a friendly competitor. While these methods might not be the most satisfactory, they remove some of the hazards in establishing a reorder point. At any rate, the cost of not satisfying a need is probably far too complex to be answered by a single factor in an equation.

Reorder Points and People. One cannot overlook the fact that the withdrawal and replenishment cycles are under the supervision of people. In the replenishment cycle the people are naturally going to work toward the scheduled time (which they seldom will beat, but frequently go beyond). So, because of people alone, the replenishment distribution will probably tend to be skewed to the left.

There will be tendencies throughout for individuals to "pad" data for their own protection. This always makes it difficult to obtain any true picture of a time or quantity estimate.

What Is the Solution?

No case has been made for a unique method of solving the reorder-point problem under uncertainty. Rather, the complexity of the problem has been highlighted with the hope that the reader will not place false hope in a particular technique.

The quickest and easiest way of obtaining a reorder-point quantity would appear to be the product of the maximum replenishment time and the maximum usage rate. Should this give excessive inventories, it will then be necessary to reduce the quantities, realizing that a certain amount of risk is being taken.

When the savings are being considered for a certain risk, be sure to evaluate it not in abstract terms but in relationship to the cost of closing down the plant, the total plant investment, and other important cost factors.

Inventory Control and Forecasting Relationship

There is a relationship between the regression line used in forecasting and the slanting withdrawal line as used in the saw-tooth chart.

The slanting usage line of the inventory saw-tooth chart, Figure 13–6,

Figure 13–6
Inventory Control and Forecasting Relationship

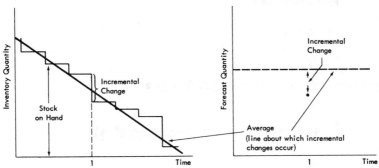

may also be considered a forecast line similar to the regression line in forecasting, the difference being that the saw-tooth chart shows total quantities under the line while the forecast illustrates incremental changes about an imposed average.

The stock on hand at the end of a period plus that which has been sold, on the left of the chart, is equal to the increment of change on the right-hand chart. This should explain why exponential smoothing is used in inventory control procedures in extrapolating the quantity to be used in future periods.

A PROBABILISTIC INVENTORY MODEL

In spite of development difficulties for probabilistic inventory models, there has been one which has had wide acceptance and is advocated by at least one computer company. This probabilistic model generates safety stocks based on the concept of service. If the customer always receives his order, the *service index* is 100 percent. Anything less than 100 percent will be a *disservice*, also called a *stock-out*. The sum of the service index and the stock-out index totals 100 percent, so the following relationship exists:

$$\text{Service index} = 100\% - \text{Stock-out index.}$$

A low stock-out index indicates a high-service index and vice versa.

The service index itself takes on several meanings depending upon whether we are concerned with the *frequency* of stock-outs during an order cycle, or during a year, or the *quantity* of stock-outs during the order cycle. Each one of these concepts will be developed but the different meanings are defined here:

Model 1. *Frequency* of service *per order cycle*. This does not tell you how *large* the shortage is but how often it will occur during an *order cycle*.

Model 2. *Frequency* of service *per year* or other period of time. This service index is more easily understood because it is concerned with service occurring during a period of time.

Model 3. The *percentage of demand* routinely filled without delay from goods in stock. The percentage is often expressed in dollars. For example 95 percent service may mean that $95 of a $100 request is shipped immediately.

The reorder point for each of these different service concepts will be developed.

Service Index: Service per Order Cycle. Figure 13–7A illustrates the typical saw-tooth inventory chart with the terms which will be used during the discussion. To the right of this conventional chart is added a distribution illustrating the *frequency of usage during the lead time.* Think for a moment how this distribution has been developed:

Line 1–2 on the diagram represents the average or "expected usage" $E(x)$ as forecast during the lead time. Note that the variability of the usage and the variability of the lead time are combined in this model.

Lines 1–3 and 1–4 represent extremes of usage during the lead time. Now think of the hundreds of times that usage during lead time could be recorded

Figure 13–7A
Saw-Tooth Chart Model

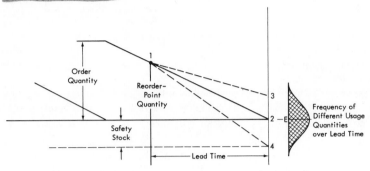

between these two extremes and how at each time the usage line would terminate at some point along the vertical line 3–4. At each time an appropriate "x" could have been filled in under the curve as shown and consequently we would develop the normal distribution illustrated.

The normal distribution has been proven by industrial data to be the most likely representation, but there are times when others, such as the Poisson distribution, might be a better description.

As would be expected, the greater the safety stock the better the service will be and the less the chance of stock-outs. The relationship between service, stock-outs, and safety stock is illustrated by Figure 13–7B. In your mind,

Figure 13–7B
Safety Stock and Service Index

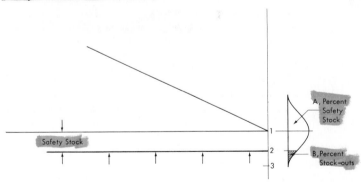

reduce the safety stock by raising the level of the bottom line in the diagram. When this is done, it means that the percentage of service represented by the area A under the normal curve is reduced at the cost of an increased percentage of stock-outs represented by the area B. From this it should be obvious that the relationship presented before holds:

$$\text{Percent of service} = 100\% - \text{Percent of stock-outs}$$

Glossary of Terms

Demand	Total requirements during a period of time for a particular item.
Expected usage during lead time	The average usage during lead time.
Forecast usage during lead time	The predicted quantity to be used during lead time.
Stock-out	Stock-out during lead time occurs when actual usage is greater than the reorder quantity.
Service level	The percentage of times the orders can be filled in a usage cycle.
Service index	The percentage of times or quantity that the inventory satisfies the customers' requirements.

$$\text{Service} = 100 - \text{Stock-out index}$$

Stock-out index	The percentage of times or quantity that the inventory cannot satisfy the customers' requirements.

$$\text{Stock-out index} = 100 - \text{Service index}$$

Safety stock	This quantity of inventory, also called "buffer stock," is used to satisfy demand which exceeds the expected demand.
Lead time	The time involved from the time a decision is made to order and when the material is received.
Order point	Anticipated demand during lead time plus reserve.

$$(\text{Lead time} + \text{Review time}) \times \text{Usage}$$

Mean absolute deviation, MAD	An approximation of the standard deviation.

Standard deviation, sigma
$$= 1.25 \text{ mean absolute deviation, MAD}$$
$$\text{MAD} = 0.8 \text{ standard deviation}$$

$$\text{MAD} = \sum_{i=1}^{n} \frac{|x - \bar{x}|}{n}$$

Steps for calculating MAD:

Step 1.   Subtract values of x from forecast during lead time.

Step 2.   Change all negative signs to positive signs.

Step 3.   Add all deviations.

Step 4.   Divide by the number of differences used in Step 1.

Recall that the area under the normal curve illustrating stock-outs during lead time may be expressed in terms of standard deviations, σ. No safety stock assures a 50 percent service as illustrated by that portion of the normal distribution above the expected usage line. This explains why the emphasis will be on "one tail" distributions.

The safety stock can be defined in terms of sigma for the one tail of the distribution:

Safety stock = Safety factor × Standard deviation

The order point is therefore:

Order point = Expected usage during lead time + Safety stock

How this can be used in practice is illustrated in Figure 13–8.

Figure 13–8
Determining Order Points with Standard Deviation

Period	Demand during Period In Units	Average $\bar{x}$	Deviation	Deviation Squared
1	120	132	−12	144
2	125		− 7	49
3	113		−19	361
4	170		+38	1,444
5	110		−22	484
6	140		+ 8	64
7	120		−12	144
8	171		+39	1,521
9	121		−11	121
10	130		− 2	4
	1,320			4,336

$$\bar{x} = \frac{\Sigma x}{n} = \frac{1,320}{10} = 132$$

$$S = \sqrt{\frac{\Sigma(x - \bar{x})^2}{n}} = \sqrt{\frac{4,336}{10}} = 20.8 \text{ or } 21$$

If management wishes to have 90 percent customer service (50% + 40%), this requires a safety factor of 1.28 (Figure 13–11)

Order point = Average usage during lead time + Safety factor × Standard deviation

Order point = 132 + (1.28 × 20.8) ≈ 159 units

A comment about the relative weights of the areas A and B in Figure 13–7B should be worthwhile. It should be apparent that adding an increment of safety stock from 1 to 2 will give greater service than adding the same increment of safety stock from 2 to 3. Customer satisfaction at a reasonable cost is what inventory control is all about. Just how great is the cost of service? You can guess that it is not something one comes by cheaply.

The graphical relationship between the service level and inventory costs might look something like Figure 13–9. As we discovered before, the last

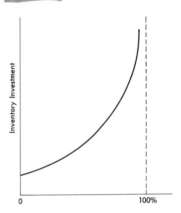

Figure 13–9
Relationship between Service and Investment

increments of service are going to cost more than the first. The problem is where to apply the brakes. When is the cost for extra service prohibitive?

MAD Simplification. Calculating standard deviations with the many numbers to be squared is tedious and not the sort of thing that even a computer would care to do for all of the stock-keeping units. Fortunately an approximation can be made of the standard deviation with considerably less effort using the mean absolute deviation, MAD. The standard deviation is equal to one and one-quarter times the mean absolute deviation.

Standard deviation = 1.25 mean absolute deviations[1]

$$\text{MAD} = \frac{\text{Standard deviation}}{1.25} = 0.8\,\text{standard deviation (normal distribution only)}$$

To calculate the MAD, follow the procedure presented below:
Step-by-Step Procedure for Calculating MAD.

$$\text{Mean absolute deviation, MAD} = \frac{\sum\limits_{i=1}^{n} |x_i - \bar{x}|}{n}$$

Step 1. Calculate mean, $\bar{x}$.
Step 2. Calculate the deviations from the mean.
Step 3. Sum the deviations without regard to the signs.
Step 4. Take the average of the number of readings.

[1] The derivation of MAD can be found on pp. 282–83 of Robert G. Brown's *Smoothing, Forecasting and Prediction of Discrete Time Series* (Prentice-Hall, Inc., 1963).

Figure 13–10 illustrates how MAD can be used to predict the order point for the same example given in Figure 13–8. Notice how closely the two compare, but the MAD procedure costs far less.

It is not necessary to convert values for MAD into standard deviations every time a calculation is made. Figure 13–11 gives the area under the normal curve in terms of MAD. An example for calculating reorder points both ways is given in Figure 13–10.

Figure 13–10
Determining Order Points with MAD

Period	Demand during Period	Average $\bar{x}$	Deviation
1	120	132	12
2	125		7
3	113		19
4	170		38
5	110		22
6	140		8
7	120		12
8	171		39
9	121		11
10	130		2
	1,320		170

$$\bar{x} = \frac{\Sigma x}{n} = \frac{1,320}{10} = 132$$

$$\text{MAD} = \frac{\sum_{i=1}^{n} |x_i - \bar{x}|}{n} = \frac{170}{10} = 17$$

Convert MAD to equivalent standard deviations:

$$17 \times 1.25 = 21.25 \text{ or } 21$$

Example 1:
  Order point = $132 + (1.28 \times 21.25) \approx 159$ parts.
  Table 13–11 presents the percentage of service directly in terms of MAD which saves time in making calculations. Using it for the previous calculation:

Example 2:
  Order point = $132 + (1.60 \times 17) \approx 159$ parts.

The service index as presented so far has been based on the order cycle. Not many managers would be satisfied with this especially as the order cycle might vary from product to product. This model, however, forms the basis upon which other more satisfactory models might be built.

Service Index: Frequency of Service per Year. The previous model would be excellent if the order quantity just lasted a year as shown in the top half of Figure 13–12. Then we could say directly what the safety stock quantity should be for some particular percentage of service during the year.

Figure 13–11

Table of Safety Factors for Standard Deviations and MAD

Percent of Service	Percent of Stock-outs	Safety Factor	
		Standard Deviation	MAD
50	50	0	x 1.25 = 0
55	45	.13	.16
60	40	.25	.31
65	35	.39	.49
70	30	.52	.65
75	25	.67	.84
80	20	.84	1.05
84	16	1.00	1.25
85	15	1.04	1.30
90	10	1.28	1.60
95	5	1.65	2.06
96	4	1.75	2.19
97	3	1.88	2.35
98	2	2.05	2.56
99	1	2.33	2.91
100	0	3.61	4.51

Figure 13–12

Comparisons of Order Quantities

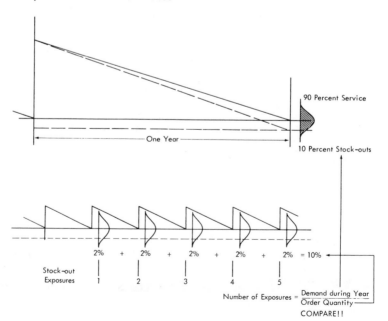

However, if the order quantity does not last for the year, there will be more than one stock-out exposure as shown in the lower half of the figure. In this case the order quantity is one fifth of that required for one order per year and there are five stock-out exposures.

If we wished to retain a 10 percent stock-out, we would divide this percentage by the number of stock-out exposures. For example, a 10 percent stock-out divided by five stock-outs gives a 2 percent stock-out per exposure. In other words a 2 percent stock-out for five stock-outs would be equal to a 10 percent stock-out for one.

Reducing the percentage of stock-outs in turn lowers the safety stock line which increases the safety stock. This illustrates that the order quantity *can* affect the safety stock.

$$\text{Adjusted percentage of stock-out} = \frac{\text{Order quantity}}{\text{Yearly demand}}$$
$$\times \text{Management's established stock-out level}$$

With this newly established stock-out percentage, we can establish safety stocks as shown by the following example.

Example:

Data: Order quantity, 1,320
       Yearly demand, 6,600
       Management-established 10 percent stock-out level

Solution:

$$\text{Adjusted percentage of stock-outs} = \frac{\text{Order quantity}}{\text{Yearly demand}}$$
$$\times \text{Established stock-out level}$$
$$= \frac{1,320}{6,600} \times 10 = 2\%$$

Two percent from Figure 13–11 gives a safety factor of 2.56.

$$\text{Order point} = 132 + 2.56 \times 18.9 = 180$$

Note how this increases the order point from 162 to 180. In the first situation, the safety stock had been based on a 10 percent stock-out for the lead time, while in the second example, safety stocks had been established on the basis of 10 percent stock-out per year.

Service Index: Percentage of Demand Filled from Stock. Often the percentage of demand filled from stock is the most meaningful service index. If the service index, for example, is 95 percent, it could be expected that $95 worth of stock would be shipped for every $100 demanded. Such statements concerning service apply of course to the inventory in the long run.

A safety factor is used as before except it is derived through an intermediate factor called a *service function*. The derivation of the service function will be discussed first and followed by an explanation of how the

Figure 13–13
Probability of a Stock-out

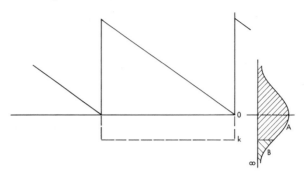

order point can be obtained when the service index, the average demand during the lead time, and the variation are known.

Derivation of the Service Function. In discussing the service function, return to the saw-tooth chart, Figure 13–14, where the area B under the

Figure 13–14
The Service Integral

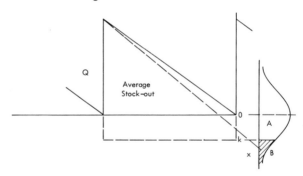

normal curve represents the probability of a stock-out and is given by the following equation:

$$\text{Probability of a stock-out,} \atop B, \text{ during an order cycle} \Bigr\} = \int_{k}^{\infty} p(x)\,dx$$

where $p(x)$ is the density function of a normal curve, and k is the safety factor for establishing safety stocks.

The expected amount of stock-out per order cycle is referred to as the service function as described by the following integral:

$$\text{Service function,} f(k) = \int_{k}^{\infty} (x - k)p(x)\,dx$$

The product of the probability and the values of each $x - k$ across the area, B, shown in Figure 13–14, represents the service function. The $f(k)$ is the average amount of stock-out expressed in units of sigma, σ. For example if $f(k)$ is 0.25 and σ is 80, the average stock-out will be $80 \times 0.25 = 20$. To obtain the *fraction* of demand unfilled, it is necessary to divide by the quantity sold, Q, during the order cycle:

$$1 - P = \frac{f(k)\sigma}{Q}$$

It is necessary to solve for $f(k)$ and then look up k in a table.

$$f(k) = \frac{(1 - P)Q}{\sigma}$$

The table was developed by rearranging the service function equation in the following way:

$$\text{Service function, } f(k) = \int_k^\infty (x - k)p(x)\,dx$$

$$= \int_k^\infty xp(x)\,dx - k\int_k^\infty p(x)\,dx$$

$$= p(k) - k\int_k^\infty p(x)\,dx$$

For any given k:

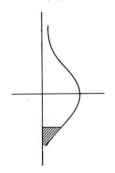

$p(k)$ may be obtained from a table of ordinates for the normal curve.

$\int_k^\infty p(x)dx$ may be obtained from a table of areas under the normal curve.

For example, assume that $k = 0.4$.

$$f(0.4) = 0.3683 - 0.4(1 - 0.6556)$$
$$= 0.2304.$$

Going back to equation (1), this says that:

$$\text{Stock-outs } (1 - P) = \frac{0.2304\,\sigma}{Q}$$

or

$$\text{Service } P = \frac{1 - 0.2304\,\sigma}{Q}$$

This discussion was based on the standard deviation because most readers are familiar with it. However, as we know, standard deviations may be expressed and manipulated more readily in MAD, and therefore these values are listed in Figure 13–15. This way of developing a reorder point is illustrated as follows.

Figure 13–15

Safety Factors and Service

Functions Using MAD*

Safety Factor	Service Function
0.0	0.4969
0.2	0.4033
0.4	0.3225
0.6	0.2539
0.8	0.1967
1.0	0.1499
1.2	0.1123
1.4	0.0827
1.6	0.0598
1.8	0.0424
2.0	0.0295
2.2	0.0201
2.4	0.0134
2.6	0.0088
2.8	0.0056
3.0	0.0035
3.2	0.0021
3.4	0.0013
3.6	0.0007
3.8	0.0004
4.0	0.0002

* Wholesale IMPACT-Advanced Principles and Implementation Reference Manual (White Plains, N.Y.: International Business Machines Corp., 1969). Courtesy International Business Machines Corp.

Example 1: Order quantity, 60; annual usage, 240; MAD of forecast error is 10. Desired service is 95 percent. Lead time is one month.

$$\text{Service function} = \frac{60}{10}(1 - 0.95) = 0.3$$

Safety factor from table $= 0.4$

$$\frac{240}{12} = 20 \text{ average usage during lead time}$$

$$\text{Order point} = 20 + 0.4 \times 10 = 24$$

Example 2: Order quantity, 80; annual usage, 240; MAD of forecast error is 10. Desired service is 95 percent. Lead time is one month.

$$\text{Service function} = \frac{80}{10}(1 - 0.95) = 0.4$$

Safety factor from table $= 0.2$

$$\text{Order point} = 20 + 0.2 \times 10 = 22$$

The two examples illustrate how the order quantity affects the order point.

Adjusting Lead Time for Forecast.   Usually forecasting will be done for all items periodically, such as every week or month, and it would be unusual if the forecast period coincided with the lead time.

Extrapolation of the expected demand is straightforward since its relationship to time is linear. For example, 1,000 units for one week may be extended to 2,000 for two weeks, 3,000 for three weeks, and so on.

The MAD on the other hand does not change in a linear fashion. The error, as you might expect, becomes larger as the time for the forecast is increased.

Tracking Signals

The purpose of a forecasting *tracking signal* is to provide a monitoring device that will:

Signal a basic change in demand pattern.
Signal that the forecasting parameters are not correct.

A tracking signal is used as a monitor to set a *limit* which if exceeded by the tracking signal will *trigger* an alarm. The technique, as shown in Figure 13–16 is analogous to the control chart used in quality control.

Figure 13–16
Tracking Signal Chart

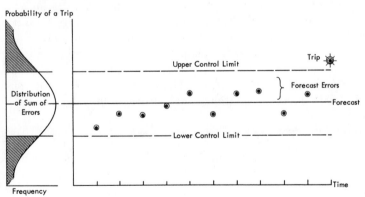

Since it is assumed that the forecast errors are normally distributed, the *sum of the errors* will also be normally distributed about the mean as shown. The upper and lower control limits may be set to make the system *trip* and issue a warning at any level desired. The probability of the trip is illustrated by the shaded areas under the two tails of the curve. To decrease the probability of a trip, it is only necessary to extend the control limit lines farther apart.

It should be obvious that if the forecasts are good estimates, the actual demand will fall above the average about half of the time. The plus and minus deviations should tend to cancel each other, and a running sum of the errors should be close to zero most of the time.

If the sum of the errors are persistently plus or minus, it would indicate that the forecasts are consistently too low or too high. In this situation the forecast is not tracking properly and should be evaluated. The sum of the errors should show no tendency of becoming large in either direction if the forecast-smoothing system is working properly.

The control limits for the tracking signal should be selected to present a balance between the desire to detect conditions causing erroneous forecasts and needless reacting to random trips. One solution is not to react against the first trip but to reset and try again. Another procedure is to set the control limits out further for the less important items.

If relatively little information is available about an item, it may be desirable to set the limits out quite a ways to eliminate a rash of trips with the hope that eventually the system will stabilize by itself. Plotting the data as shown for those items which have tripped may reveal cause and effect such as increased inventories because of sales promotions, impending strikes, and other reasons.

In the previous illustration of a control chart, we saw a distribution of the sum of the errors. Assume that it is desired to trip at a 5 percent level which would mean a $2\frac{1}{2}$ percent area under each tail of the curve. Referring to a table of standard normal distribution for Z values as shown in Chapter 4, Figure 4–4, we can find that $(100\% - 5\%)/2 = 47.5\%$, or 0.475 in the body of the table is equivalent to 1.966. This means that the upper and lower control limits should be set at plus and minus 1.966 of the sum of the errors. The problem is that the standard deviation of the sum of the errors is not readily available. So the tracking signal has to be redefined to use what is available in the record which under some conditions would be the mean absolute deviation described earlier. The method of making the translation from MAD to standard deviations is to be found in the references.

Part-Period Lot Sizing (Part-Period Algorithm)

The part-period lot sizing method[2] for determining order quantities has several advantages not to be found in the classic economic order quantity equations.

It can account for changes in demand and adjust the order quantity accordingly.
It looks ahead to adjust the order quantity and looks backward to help improve the decision.
It can be adapted to computer operations.

---

[2] J. J. Matteis, "An Economic Lot-Sizing Technique I The Part Period Algorithm," *IBM Systems Journal* 7 no. 1 (1968), pp. 30–48; A. G. Mendoza, "An Economic Lot-Sizing Technique II Mathematical Analysis of the Part-Period Algorithm," *IBM Systems Journal* 7, no. 1 (1968), pp. 39–47.

Like the traditional economic order quantity technique, the part-period method is concerned with *ordering* costs and *holding* costs. These costs are defined in the same way as they are defined in the classical EOQ equations to be found in all of the literature on the subject. As in the traditional approach, we are concerned with balancing ordering costs against holding costs and determining the quantity which minimizes the sum of these two costs.

Since the part-period term will be stressed throughout this section, you should have it defined: The *part-period* for a particular product is the number of parts held in inventory multiplied by the number of time periods over which the parts are held.

In calculating the part-period, it is assumed that no holding costs are incurred for items consumed in the period in which they are ordered. If one part is held for one period, it generates a certain holding cost which doubles when the part is held for two periods; triples, for three periods; and so forth. Two parts held for four periods generate the same holding costs as four of the same parts held for two periods.

A distinction will be made between a derived part-period value and one which is generated. The derived value expresses the holding and ordering costs in part-periods. This derived part-period value will be placed in the inventory record and needs to be calculated and recorded only once unless there is a change in some of the cost components contained in the ordering costs or holding costs. The *generated part-period value* is the accumulation of costs. This distinction between these two should be readily seen as we move along with the development of the equations.

First we will derive the part-period value. We can start with an equation which equates total holding costs and ordering costs.

$$\text{Total of all holding costs} = \text{Total of all ordering costs}$$

Using the unknown number of part-periods as a multiplier on both sides of the equation:

$$\frac{?\,\text{Part-periods}}{(\text{units} \times \text{time})} \times \frac{\text{Holding costs}}{(\$/\text{unit})} = \frac{\text{Part-periods}}{(\text{units} \times \text{time})} \times \frac{\text{Ordering costs}}{(\$/\text{unit})}$$

$$\frac{?\,\text{Part-periods}}{(\text{units} \times \text{time})} \times \frac{\text{Holding costs}\,(\$/\text{unit})}{\text{Part-periods}\,(\text{units} \times \text{time})} = \frac{\text{Ordering costs}}{(\$/\text{unit})}$$

Combining all of the known values on the right-hand side of the equation presents a derived part-period value:

$$\frac{(\text{Derived})\,\text{part-period value}}{(\text{units} \times \text{time})} = \frac{\text{Ordering costs}\,(\$/\text{unit})}{\dfrac{\text{Holding costs}/\text{One part-period}}{(\$/\text{unit})\quad(\text{units} \times \text{time})}}$$

As stated previously, this is the derived part-period value. It is the number of part-periods it takes to make the holding costs and ordering costs equal. Recall that in economic lot size theory the quantity for the minimum of the total costs coincides with the point where the ordering and holding costs are equal.

The *generated* part-period value is obtained by accumulating the part-period values for the forecasted schedule over one or more periods. To determine when to order, it is only necessary to determine when the generated part-period value equals or exceeds the derived part-period value. All of this can be more readily seen by an example:

Example:

Step 1.   Calculate the derived part-period value from available information. This would be calculated and posted in the inventory record. The ordering cost for a particular item is $95.00. The holding cost for this particular item is $.10 per period.

$$\text{Derived part-period value} = \frac{\$95.00/\text{order}}{\$.10/\text{part-period}} = 950 \text{ part-periods}$$

Step 2.   The predicted demand for a particular item during a 10-week period is as shown in row 2, Figure 13–17.

Step 3.   Determine when the cumulated part-period value, row 5, exceeds the derived part-period value shown in heading. This is illustrated at A between period four and five in the table. The new order, assuming a nearly zero lead time, should occur when the value in row five exceeds the value in row three.

Step 4.   Determine the order quantity which is the sum of the demands in the periods covered by the order. This can be readily seen in row 7 of Figure 13–17. Observe that for the example, an order is placed in periods one, five, and eight for quantities of 800, 730, and 800. The different order sizes are good evidence of the dynamic characteristics of part-period inventory methods.

Look-Ahead and Look-Backward Models

The simple model illustrated is said to work well if there are no wide variations in demand. The *look-forward* and *look-backward* modifications can improve the accuracy considerably when there are wide variations.

In the look-ahead test the model takes a look at the next periods beyond the ordering period to determine if there are any unusual demands coming. The steps of this part of the algorithm may be stated as:

Step 1.   A tentative reorder period is established previously in Figure 13–17 by the simple algorithm developed.

Step 2.   Look ahead to the demand of the next period:

a.   If the demand in the next period is less than the part-period value in the tentative reorder period, the tentative order period stands.

b.   If the demand in the next period is equal to or greater than the part-period value in the tentative reorder period, the reorder period is moved ahead a period.

Figure 13–17
Part-Period Calculations: Part No. A6832 (derived part-period value = 950)

1. Period	1	2	3	4	5	6	7	8	9	10	11
2. Predicted demand	350	200	100	150	200	250	280	200	400	200	100
3. Cumulative predicted demand	350	550	650	(800)	200	450	(730)	200	600	(800)	100
4. Generated part-period value	0 × 350*	1 × 200	2 × 100	3 × 150	4 × 200 / 0 × 200	1 × 250	2 × 280	0 × 200 / 3 × 200	1 × 400	2 × 200	3 × 100
5. Cumulative part-period value	0	200	400	A 850 < 950 < 1650	0	250	A 810 < 950 < 1410	A 0	400	A 800 < 950 < 1100	
6. Tentative order	Order now				Order now			Order now			Order now
7. How much to order	(800)				(730)			(800)			
8. Actual order	Now				Now			Now			Now

* No part-period value is generated during the period that the product is obtained.

This look-ahead feature may be invoked for two, three, or more periods in the future. Three different situations are presented in Figures 13–18, 13–19, and 13–20. Figure 13–18 illustrates a look-ahead test which failed. The predicted demand of 200 in period 5 is less than the generated part-period value of 450 shown under period 4. Figure 13–19 illustrates a look-ahead test that does not fail. Test A shows that the generated part-period value under period 4 is less than the demand shown under period 5. (The test for the next period as illustrated in Test B would have failed.) Figure 13–20 illustrates a look-ahead test for two periods which did not fail. The test shown at A indicates that the demand is greater than the generated part-period value which requires that the order period be moved ahead one period. If the test is invoked again as shown at Test B you can see that the order should be moved ahead again.

The look-back test is illustrated in Figures 13–21 and 13–22. The rule to follow is: The demand for the tentative set-up period is compared with the demand for the previous period, and if:

$$2 \times \left\{ \begin{array}{l} \text{Demand of} \\ \text{tentative} \\ \text{set-up period} \end{array} \right\} \begin{array}{l} \text{is equal to or} \\ \text{less than} \end{array} \left\{ \begin{array}{l} \text{Demand in} \\ \text{previous} \\ \text{period} \end{array} \right\} \begin{array}{l} \text{then move setup} \\ \text{back one} \\ \text{period.} \end{array}$$

LIMIT (Lot Size Inventory Management Interpolation Technique)[3]

LIMIT is a technique for obtaining the most economical lot sizes (order) when there is a limitation on the number of orders which can be processed. The limitation may be caused by the number of order-handling personnel, set-up men, or machine time available. The limitation may be expressed as: (1) A given number of orders or (2) a given number of people or hours available for set up.

LIMIT makes it possible to calculate lot sizes directly without any trial-and-error calculations and will aid in analyzing the effect on inventory of changes in setups and reduction of lot sizes. It also shows management the effect on inventory of placing restrictions on set-up times or number of orders.

An example will be used to illustrate the application of LIMIT. The calculations will be made step-by-step with a brief explanation for each step. In the course of the example, there will be two unexplained equations, but an explanation of these will be given after the example is completed.

In the course of the example we will be talking about two distinct situations, the present LIMIT situation, which will be designated by a subscript L, and the recalculated TRIAL values, designated by a subscript T. For the example it will be assumed that set-up time is the limiting factor. Calcula-

---

[3] For a comprehensive discussion of this subject, see APICS *Special Report, Management of Lot Size Inventories*, 1963, American Production and Inventory Control Society.

Figure 13–18
Look-Ahead Test That Fails: Part No. A6832 (derived part period value = 950)

1. Period	1	2	3	4	5	6	7	8	9	10
2. Predicted demand	350	200	100	150	(200)	250	280			
3. Cumulative predicted demand	350	550	650	(800)						
4. Generated part-period value	0 × 350	1 × 200	2 × 100	(3 × 150)	Test					
5. Cumulative part-period value	0	200	400	850 < 950 < 1600						
6. When to order	Tentative			Tentative						
7. How much to order	(800)									
8. Final order period	Order now				Order now					

Figure 13–19
Look-Ahead Test That Does Not Fail

1. Period	1	2	3	4	5	6	7	8
2. Predicted demand	350	200	100	50	(200)	250	280	
3. Cumulative predicted demand	350	550	650	700	(900)			
4. Generated part-period value	0 × 350	1 × 200	2 × 100	(3 × 50)	4 × 200			
5. Cumulative part-period value	0	200	400	550	Test			
6. When to order	Tentative			Tentative				
7. How much to order	(900)							
8. Final order period	Order now							

Figure 13–20
Look-Ahead Test for Two Periods:: Part No. A6832 (derived part-period value = 950)

1. Period	1	2	3	4	5	6
2. Predicted demand	350	200	100	50	200	700
3. Cumulative predicted demand	350	550	650	700	900	1600
4. Generated part-period value	0 × 350	1 × 200	2 × 100	3 × 50	4 × 200	
5. Cumulative part-period value	0	200	400	850 <950<	1650	
6. When to order	Order now					
7. How much to order	1600					

Test A (between periods 4 and 5); Test B (between periods 5, 6, 7)

Figure 13–21
Look-Back Test

Example A

1. Period	1	2	3	4	5	6
2. Predicted demand	350	200	100	150	80	
3. Cumulative predicted demand	350	550	650	800	80	
4. Generated part-period value	0 × 350	1 × 200	2 × 100	3 × 150	4 × 200 0 × 200	
5. Cumulative part-period value	0	200	400	850 <950<	1650	
6. Tentative order	Now 800			Now		
7. How much to order	Now			Now		
8. Actual order	Now					

Figure 13–22
Look-Back Test

Period	1	2	3	4	5	6
2. Predicted demand	350	350	150	70	80	
3. Cumulative predicted demand	350	700	850	(920)		
4. Generated part-period value	0 × 350	1 × 350	2 × 150	3 × 70	4 × 80	
5. Cumulative part-period value	0	350	650	860	<950<	1180
6. Tentative order	Now		Now	Now		
7. How much to order	(920)					
8. Actual order						

tions are for present LIMIT situation. See Figure 13–23 for calculations as indicated by the sequence of steps.

Figure 13–23
Calculations for LIMIT and TRIAL Solutions

LIMIT Calculations

	Col. 1	Col. 2	Col. 3	Col. 4	Col. 5
				Present Order	
	Annual	Set-up	Unit Cost	Quantity,	Present LIMIT
Item	Usage	Hours/Order	$/Piece	Piece/Order	Set-up Hours/Year
1	9,000	7	4.50	2,000	Step 2 31.5
2	5,000	9	3.00	1,500	30.0
3	24,000	10	.60	8,000	30.0
4	3,000	6	2.40	1,000	18.0

Step 1 (over Col. 1–Col. 4)

Step 3 $H_L = 109.5$ hrs.

TRIAL Calculations

	Col. 6	Col. 7	Col. 8	Col. 9
	Trial Order	TRIAL Annual	LIMIT Order	Annual Set-up
Item	Quantity, TOQ	Set-up Hours/Year	Quantity	LIMIT Hours/Year
1	Step 4 837	Step 5 75.2	Step 8 1,607	Step 9 39.2
2	866	52.0	1,663	27.0
3	4,472	53.6	8,586	28.0
4	612	29.4	1,175	15.3

Step 6 $H_T = 210.2$

Step 11 109.5 hrs.

Step 1. Accumulate the required information shown in Figure 13–23.

    Col. 1. Annual usage
    Col. 2. Set-up hours/order
    Col. 3. Unit cost, $/unit
    Col. 4. *Present* order quantity, pieces/order

Step 2. Determine the present set-up hours used per year for each individual manufacturing order.

$$\text{Annual set-up hours} = \frac{A \times SH}{OQ}$$
(for each family of items)

A = Annual usage, quantity/year
OQ = Order quantity, quantity/order
SH = Set-up hours/order

$$\text{Annual set-up hours} = \frac{9,000}{2,000} \times 7 = 31.5 \text{ hours}$$

Step 3. Determine present LIMIT of the total annual set-up time.

H_L = Total of all annual set-up times for all manufacturing orders using the limiting facility

$H_L = \overset{n}{\underset{1}{\Sigma}}$ set-up hours, n is the number of manufacturing orders

$H_L = 109.5$ hours/year (see Col. 5)

Calculations for TRIAL order quantity.

Step 4. Calculate TRIAL order quantities using the conventional equations. Since it is a TRIAL order quantity, it will be called TOQ.

$$TOQ = \sqrt{\frac{2AS}{IC}}$$

A = Annual usage, pieces/year
S = Set-up cost, dollars/order
I = Inventory carrying cost, percent
C = Unit cost, dollars/piece

If a typical inventory carrying cost of 20 percent is used for the first item and the set-up cost for this family of items is \$5.00/hour, the TOQ may be calculated:

$$TOQ = \sqrt{\frac{2 \times 9,000 \times 7 \times 5.00}{.20 \times 4.50}} = 837$$

Step 5. Calculate annual set-up hours for each item using the TOQ and annual usage for that item.

TRIAL yearly setup, hours/year (Col. 7)

$$= \frac{\text{Annual usage (Col. 1)} \times \text{Set-up Hours/Order (Col. 2)}}{\text{Trial order quantity (Col. 6)}}$$

$$= \frac{9,000}{837} \times 7 = 75.2 \text{ hours/year}$$

Step 6. Determine *total* TRIAL annual setup hours, H_T. This is the total of all values found in Step 5.

$$H_T = \overset{n}{\underset{1}{\Sigma}} \text{ (set-up hours for individual families of items)}$$
$$H_T = 210.2 \text{ (see Col. 7)}$$

Step 7. Calculate implied carrying costs for LIMIT conditions. The equation for the implied carrying costs will be explainned later but is given here:

$$L_L = L_T \left(\frac{H_L}{H_T}\right)^2$$

where:

I_L = Inventory carrying costs used in calculating the LIMIT order quantities

I_T = Inventory carrying costs used to calculate TRIAL order quantities

H_L = Total set-up hours from present order quantities

H_T = Total set-up hours resulting from trial order quantities

$$= 20\% \; (\text{Step 4}) \left(\frac{109.5 \; (\text{Step 3})}{210.4 \; (\text{Step 6})}\right)^2$$

$$= 5.47\%$$

This 5.47% is the "implied" inventory carrying cost for the LIMIT order quantities.

Step 8. Calculate LIMIT order quantities. The LIMIT order quantities are the most economical order quantities that can be produced and still stay within the present set-up hour limitations. First a multiplier, M, is calculated. The explanation of M will appear at the end of this discussion

$$M = H_T/H_L = \frac{210.4 \; (\text{see Step 6})}{109.5 \; (\text{see Step 3})} = 1.92$$

LIMIT order quantity = Trial order quantity (Col. 6) $\times$ M

$$= 837 \times 1.92 = 1{,}607 \text{ pieces}$$

Step 9. Calculate annual set-up hours for LIMIT quantities:

$$\text{Annual LIMIT} \atop (\text{set-up hours}) = \frac{\text{Annual usage (Col. 1)} \times \text{set-up hours (Col. 2) order}}{\text{LIMIT order quantity (Col. 8)}}$$

$$= \frac{9{,}000 \times 7}{1{,}607} = 39.2 \text{ hours/year}$$

Step 10. Check total of annual LIMIT set-up hours, Col. 5, with annual TRIAL set-up hours, Col. 9. They should be equal except for rounding errors.

Step 11. Compare the difference between the original and revised LIMIT value of inventory.

In Figure 13–24 the information is derived as follows:

Col. 1 from Col. 1 in Figure 13–23
Col. 2 from Col. 3 in Figure 13–23
Col. 3 from Col. 4 in Figure 13–23
Col. 4 product of Col. 2 and Col. 3
Col. 5 from Col. 6 in Figure 13–23
Col. 6 product of Col. 2 and Col. 5
Col. 7 from Col. 8 of Figure 13–23
Col. 8 product of Col. 2 and Col. 7

Figure 13–24
Savings for LIMIT Solution

Col. 1 Item	Col. 2 Unit Cost	Col. 3 Present Order Quantity	Col. 4 Present Cost	Col. 5 Trial Order Quantity	Col. 6 Trial Order Cost	Col. 7 LIMIT Order Quantity	Col. 8 LIMIT Order Cost
1	$4.50	2,000	$ 9,000.00	837	$ 3,766.50	1,607	$ 7,231.50
2	3.00	1,500	4,500.00	866	2,589.00	1,663	4,989.00
3	.60	8,000	4,800.00	4,472	2,683.20	8,586	5,251.60
4	2.40	1,000	2,400.00	612	1,468.80	1,175	2,820.00
			$20,700.00		$10,516.50		$20,292.10

The original cost of the inventory was $20,700.00; the new inventory cost is $20,292.10, revealing a savings of $407.90. Since inventory carrying costs are usually based on the average, the amount of $203.95 is of importance.

Step 12. It is possible to check different limiting values for set-up hours by changing the value of M:

$$M = \frac{H_T}{H_L}$$

Example: Assume H_L is changed from 109.5 to 200.0.

$$M = \frac{210.4}{200.0} = 1.05.$$

The total LIMIT order cost is $20,292.10, as shown in Figure 13–24. Using the new value of H_L and its associated value M, the inventory changes to $20,292.10 \times 1.05 = $21,306.71 with an average inventory of $10,653.35.

Development of LIMIT Equations

The first set of equations will produce the relationship between the inventory carrying cost, I and the set-up or ordering time, H.

Derivation of I_L.   Start with these basic relationships:

$$q = \sqrt{\frac{2as}{I}}$$

or

$$\frac{\sqrt{2as}}{\sqrt{I}}$$

$$n = \frac{a}{q}$$

where:

q = Order quantity, dollars/lot
a = Annual usage in dollars/year (for each item)
s = Set-up or procurement cost, dollars/lot
I = Inventory carrying cost percentage expressed as dollars/year
n = Number of orders placed each year

A, S, and Q are the same as the lowercase symbols except that they refer to all orders in a group having the same limiting factor. The total annual set-up costs are

$$s = n \times h \times c$$

h = Set-up, hours/order
c = Cost of set-up/hour, $/hour

For all of the n items:

$$S = \left(\frac{a_1 h_1 c}{q_1}\right) + \left(\frac{a_2 h_2 c}{q_2}\right) + \ldots + \left(\frac{a_n h_n c}{q_n}\right)$$

substituting $\dfrac{\sqrt{2as}}{\sqrt{I}}$ into the equation above:

$$S = \left(\frac{c\sqrt{I}\,a_1 h_1}{\sqrt{2a_1 s_1}}\right) + \left(\frac{c\sqrt{I}\,a_2 h_2}{\sqrt{2a_2 s_2}}\right) + \ldots + \left(\frac{c\sqrt{I}\,a_n h_n}{\sqrt{2a_n s_n}}\right)$$

Note: it is assumed that I and c are the same for all items in the family. The equation above can be arranged so that:

$$S = c\sqrt{I}\left[\left(\frac{a_1 h_1}{\sqrt{2a_1 s_1}}\right) + \left(\frac{a_2 h_2}{\sqrt{2a_2 s_2}}\right) + \ldots + \left(\frac{a_n h_n}{\sqrt{2a_n h_n}}\right)\right]$$

Square both sides and solve for I:

$$I = \frac{S^2}{c^2}\left[\frac{1}{\left[\dfrac{a_1 h_1}{\sqrt{2a_1 s_1}} + \dfrac{a_2 h_2}{\sqrt{2a_2 s_2}} + \ldots + \dfrac{a_n h_n}{\sqrt{2a_n h_n}}\right]}\right]^2$$

Simplify the equation by substituting T for the factors within the bracket, giving $I = \dfrac{S^2 T^2}{c^2}$. The total annual set-up time, H, is equal to the total annual set-up cost, S, divided by the cost per hour, c.

$$H = \frac{S}{c}$$

and

$$H^2 = \frac{S^2}{c^2}$$

Substituting H in the previous equation, we have:

$$I = H^2 T^2$$

T is constant for a group of items and is independent of I.

Assume that individual lot sizes, q, are calculated for a family of n items. For each value of I a value of H will be obtained.

$$I_a = H_a^2 T^2$$
$$I_b = H_b^2 T^2$$

This leads to a ratio:

$$\frac{I_a}{I_b} = \frac{H_a^2 T^2}{H_b^2 T^2}$$
$$I_b = I_a\left(\frac{H_b}{H_a}\right)^2$$

or in our previous example we have:

$$I_L = I_T \left(\frac{H_L}{H_T}\right)^2$$

From which can be calculated the *apparent* value of I.

Using this value of I in the EOQ equation will result in the desired value of H_T.

Derivation of M. The next set of calculations derives the value for M which can be used to simplify the calculations and eliminate the necessity of taking square roots when calculating the revised lot sizes. From

$$q = \frac{\sqrt{2as}}{\sqrt{I}}$$

for I_a

$$q_a = \frac{\sqrt{2a_a s_a}}{\sqrt{I_a}}$$

for I_b

$$q_b = \frac{\sqrt{2a_b s_b}}{\sqrt{I_b}}$$

$$\frac{q_b}{q_a} = \frac{\sqrt{2a_b s_b}}{\sqrt{I_b}} \times \frac{\sqrt{I_a}}{\sqrt{2a_a s_a}}$$

$$q_b = q_a \sqrt{\frac{I_a}{I_b}}$$

From our earlier equation,

$$\frac{I_a}{I_b} = \left(\frac{H_a}{H_b}\right)^2$$

$$\frac{H_a}{H_b} = \sqrt{\frac{I_a}{I_b}} = M$$

$$q_b = q_a M$$

This equation may be used to adjust the quantities for individual families of items.

LIMIT is an acceptable way of determining order quantities when there is some limitation such as set-up costs which must be considered. While it might seem somewhat confusing at first, it does hold some interest to those actually operating a plant under certain restricting conditions. For example, a company producing screw-machine products on an automatic screw machine would find this technique worthy of consideration. Or a pharmaceutical company with limited tablet-pressing capacity may wish to include this technique for their consideration. The calculations for LIMIT may be handled by a computer program.

Satellite-Warehouse Safety Stocks

There are many factors which enter into the consideration of how many warehouses should be used to distribute a product. Although the quantity of safety stock is not the only factor, one approach shows that one warehouse can give the same protection as several with the possible saving of cost.[4] The logic for this statement is based on the addition of variances, which is $\sigma = \sqrt{\sigma_1^2 + \ldots + \sigma_n^2}$. Figure 13–25 illustrates four warehouses located

Figure 13–25
Comparison between Warehousing Methods

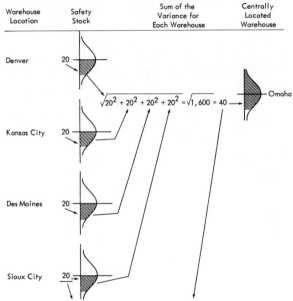

Total Safety Stock of 80 Gives the Same Safety Stock as 40 in One Warehouse

in four cities as compared to one located in a central location. The curves on the diagram are the same as those illustrated previously on the saw-tooth chart.

The safety stock for each of the satellite warehouses is given in the second column. When these safety stocks of 20 each are treated as variances and added, we find that it is the equivalent of a safety stock of 40 at one central location.

To determine whether this is a logical solution to the problem, it would be necessary to consider transportation costs. For example, it may be neces-

---

[4] For a complete development of this technique, see Arnold O. Putnam, E. Robert Barlow, Gabriel N. Stilian, *Unified Operations Management* (New York: McGraw-Hill, 1963).

sary to use air freight rather than ship by car lots or truck load lots. Of concern to the vendor and customer would be service. It may well be that a centralized warehouse will not give acceptable service compared with competition.

Critical Ratio Applied to Warehousing

The critical ratio[5] technique developed for manufacturing scheduling has been extended to the distribution problem and signals when certain items should be given shipping priority. An item with a critical ratio of less than one should be shipped on the next truck out while an item with a critical ratio of more than one may be delayed.

The critical ratio is developed here:

$$\text{Critical ratio} = \frac{\text{Days of supply}}{\text{Lead time} + \text{Lead time remaining}}$$

$$CR = DS/(LT + LTR)$$

$$DS = \text{Days of supply}$$
$$LT = \text{Lead time}$$
$$LTR = \text{Lead time remaining}$$

where DS, days of supply:

$$DS = \frac{OH - SS}{Sm}$$

OH = On-hand quantity
SS = Safety stock quantity
Sm = Smoothed usage—average quantity per unit of time

An example of calculating the critical ratio is presented in Figure 13–26.

Figure 13–26
Critical Ratio Calculations

	Quantity on Hand		Available Quantity		Days of Supply		Critical Ratio
Feb. 1	8,932–600	=	8,332 ÷ 300	=	27.8 ÷ 21	=	1.32
2	8,601		8,001		26.7		1.27
3	8,355		7,755		25.8		1.23
4	8,026		7,426		24.7		1.18
7	7,716		7,116		23.7		1.13
8	7,390		6,790		22.6		1.08
9	7,045		6,445		21.5		1.02
10	6,700		6,100		20.3		0.97

Safety stock   = 600 units   Lead time   = 21 days
Average usage = 300 units   Order quantity = 1,600

---

[5] For a more comprehensive discussion of this subject, see Arnold O. Putnam, E. Robert Barlow, Gabriel N. Stilian, *Unified Operations Management* (New York: McGraw-Hill, 1963).

In practice all the items being shipped should have the critical ratio calculated and ranked. All items with a critical ratio of less than one should be shipped on the next truck. To obtain a full truck load, the next items in order of their criticality should be shipped.

Order Quantities. Order quantities should never be less than the quantity used during the lead time. However, ordering for just lead time quantities could create excessive paper work. To overcome this, the economic order quantity equations should be invoked. When using such equations they should be suitable for warehousing situations. These would include the variable costs of ordering, paper work, picking, counting, receiving, storing, and so on.

Protecting Threatened Central Stock. An important consideration in operating a warehouse system is to not draw on the central warehouse to the extent that the satellite warehouses cannot be supplied. These warehouses may be protected by an *index* of *criticality* applied at the central warehouse.

$$\text{Index of criticality} = \frac{\text{The days of supply}}{\substack{\text{Lead time remaining to} \\ \text{replenish the central stock}}}$$
$$= DS/LTR$$

When the index of criticality is less than one, the economic order quantity is reduced by a percentage such as 50 percent. This prevents the stocks from being depleted and allows some satellite warehouse demands to be satisfied.

Summary

In presenting inventory models there is some compulsion to develop them from the most elementary to the most sophisticated. This might have been of some value to you as a learning technique, but you would have received little in how to evaluate the models in an industrial situation. The models presented in this chapter are the ones which you are most likely to encounter in industry.

The probabilistic model using MAD is too sophisticated for manual systems, but you will find it as part of software packages. LIMIT is a concept which has found some interest in production departments.

Part period lot sizing is a way of making the EOQ decisions without using up computer capabilities.

The satellite warehouse procedure extends the inventory decisions beyond the factory.

QUESTIONS

13–1.   Assume you are responsible for maintaining the inventories in a company that produces lawn furniture from aluminum tubing. What short and long term problems would you anticipate?

13–2.   Discuss how well the inventory models describe the actual situation.

13–3.   The text presents three probabilistic inventory models—frequency of service per order cycle, per year, and percentage of demand. Which one would be the most difficult to calculate? Which one would be most meaningful to management? Explain.

13–4.   What advantages are there in using the Mean Absolute Deviation? Would you consider using this in applications other than inventory control?

13–5.   As the person responsible for inventories as described in the first question you find that you are having difficulty in forecasting. Explain how you could help to solve this problem. Discuss the technique used, the inventory to which you would apply it, and add any other explanation which would make it clear to management.

13–6.   How is Part-Period Lot Sizing related to conventional economic order quantity techniques?

13–7.   What advantages does Part-Period Lot Sizing have over economic order quantity equations?

13–8.   In what situation would the "look-ahead" and "look-backward" models be useful?

13–9.   The word LIMIT refers to what? Discuss a situation in which LIMIT would be a suitable inventory technique.

13–10. A pharmaceutical manufacturer is considering the possibility of increasing the number of warehouses it maintains. Give arguments for and against taking this action.

section four
Production Control Decisions

DECISION MAKING in production control has been advancing rapidly in recent years. This has probably come about for many reasons. Management has demanded better tools by which to make decisions, and management scientists and computer scientists have been ready to satisfy the demand. This section attempts to precipitate those techniques which have moved from theory into the practical world.

The chapters are arranged to make it possible for you to select the subjects for the depth desired. Chapter 14 will take you through all of the scheduling techniques usually found in a text on this subject. However, if you wish to become more aware and knowledgeable about the techniques being used, read on to the following chapters.

Chapter 14. Capacity Planning and Scheduling

An efficient operation demands that capacity and requirement are in close balance. This chapter describes how this can be done.

Scheduling and loading as done in industry are described in this chapter. In particular, the graphical techniques such as the Gantt chart, PERT, CPM, and line of balance are presented.

Chapter 15. Scheduling Models and Techniques

The previous chapter presented graphical scheduling techniques, and this chapter is devoted to those which are not graphical. A wealth of research has been done on the scheduling subject, but this is not the place for a complete review of the literature. Just enough of the research is given to illustrate the complexity of the problem. The remainder of the chapter is devoted to practical techniques which are being used in industry with some success.

Chapter 16. Scheduling Production Lines

The problem of balancing a production line is often solved in the factory by the foreman and even occasionally by the industrial engineer.

In reality, production line balancing is just an extension of scheduling and should be included in the skills of production control personnel. This chapter presents a logical procedure for balancing lines.

Chapter 17. Queueing Theory and Simulation for Decision Making

Many problems can be framed in terms of queueing theory. If the information is available, and if the problem fits the restrictions, the queueing equations can be used. For problems which cannot be structured easily, simulation offers many opportunities. Both of these are useful tools for the professional production control man.

Chapter 18. Linear Programming for Decision Making

Linear programming is not as universally accepted as some of the scheduling techniques, but nevertheless it has many uses in production. Product mixes, process decisions, and others are suitable for linear programming decision making.

Chapter 19. Shop-Floor Control

On the shop floor is where the scheduling actually takes place. How this is done is the subject of this chapter.

An important part of shop-floor control is communications—the communication between the shop-floor and the production control department. The methods used in communicating are also presented.

14

Capacity Planning and Scheduling

BEFORE becoming involved with the many techniques of scheduling, stop for a moment to obtain a feel for the basic problems of scheduling. The basic problem is to fit the *requirements* into the *capacity* of a department or of an entire factory. The capacity of a factory may be depicted as a tank that contains not a fluid but time as shown in Figure 14–1. The amount of time

Figure 14–1
Factory Capacity and Requirements

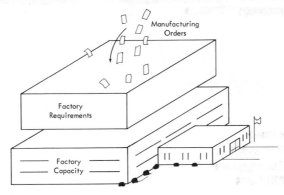

may be increased by adding more facilities or people or by working overtime. The plant requirements are determined by the manufacturing orders and how long it takes to accomplish them. The plant capacity and requirements should be nearly equal.

This is not just an academic problem, but one of vital concern to all of the people involved in a factory's operations. If the requirements exceed the capacity, customers will be unhappy as their orders go unfilled. If capacity exceeds the requirements, the costs will increase as unused capacity collects overhead. Stockholders will be unhappy with management as dividends drop. Employees will also be unhappy as they are laid off. These are real-world problems with which you will be concerned when you attempt to match requirements and capacity.

Not only is there concern for matching plant-wide capacity and requirements but also for matching capacity and requirements at the department level.

The fluids analogy can be carried further to explain some of the problems of scheduling. Consider the entire manufacturing process as a fluid system through which the orders must flow as illustrated in Figure 14–2.

Figure 14–2
Fluids Analogy of Production

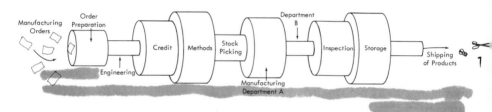

The different activities, such as sales-order processing, have a capacity through which the order requirements must pass. If the department does not have sufficient capacity, the order will be delayed. It is essential to determine the capacity of each segment and maintain a balance if an efficient operation is to be maintained. In scheduling you must consider the most restrictive department or operation. There is no use expanding Department A when Department B is the bottleneck.

Determining Plant Capacity

The capacity limit might be stated in several ways such as:

Orders per hours
Man-hours available
Factory hours available
Products produced

Some companies calculate plant capacity on a periodic basis from time study data and other sources of information, while others derive their plant capacity from history. The management knows that the plant has put out certain quantities in the past and assumes that this will continue in the future. This is the common way and is probably why one sees so little written on the subject.

Capacity figures should be reviewed from time to time since they are subject to change. Machines wear out which causes a reduction in capacity; people learn which will increase capacity. The manager should not only know what the capacity is but how much it will cost him to increase or decrease his capacity by one man, six men, or other numbers.

Excess capacity may indicate a good place to start lopping off costs. On the other hand, excess capacity may point to the possibility of building for inventory or alerting the sales department of excess capacity to be sold.

Factories, such as some chemical processors, have their capacity established when the design is made, and it is very difficult to increase or even decrease the output.

Capacity and the change of sales for a product line should be coordinated. If the sales strategy is changed, the factory should be advised immediately so that the necessary adjustments may be made in capacity.

Requirements and Capacity Planning Example. There is probably no better way to understand requirements and capacity planning than by studying an example of how a manufacturer of chain does it. A more general sequence will be presented later under loading.

Step 1.   All incoming orders are classified by:
Type of material
Cost of material
Date of manufacture
Example: $12,500 worth of orders for Class B material to be manufactured next month.

Step 2.   Convert cost of material to pounds of material for each type.

$$12,500 \times 1 \text{ lb.}/50¢ = 25,000 \text{ lbs.}$$

Step 3.   Add to pounds of materials any increase or decrease required by finished inventory.

$$25,000 \text{ lbs.} + 1,000 \text{ lbs. needed for inventory} = 26,000 \text{ lbs.}$$

Step 4.   The pounds of material by class is multiplied by a direct-labor factor as experienced by each department.

$$26,000 \text{ lbs.} \times .35 \text{ hrs/lbs.} = 9,100 \text{ hours}$$

Step 5.   The direct-labor hours determined in Step 4 is converted to number of people required. This gives the requirements.

$$\frac{9,100 \text{ hours}}{40 \text{ hours person}} = 227 \text{ people} + 20 \text{ hours}$$

Step 6.   Compare the requirements given in Step 5 with the capacity as obtained from experience. Make necessary adjustments.
Present employment 235 people.
Policy: Start working on next week's production.

Scheduling

To schedule is to make a timetable for activities which are using certain facilities. In this case the interest is in making a timetable for manufacturing orders using the production facilities in the plant. The problems, however, are not a great deal different than those encountered in setting up railroad schedules, athletic-event schedules, or class schedules. The time for each activity must be predicted by methods similar to those discussed in Chapter 8 "Capacity Planning and Scheduling Information." The activities must be coordinated to optimize investments, transportation, payrolls, or any other desired criteria.

This chapter is devoted primarily to graphical decision-making techniques, but some of them can be extended to the applications of computers. The emphasis here will be placed upon the principles, but many of these principles are applied to commercial appliances, such as the Produc-trol Board and Sched-U-Graph, which are readily available on the market. These appliances, or hardware, will be discussed.

The examples given here will be just extensive enough to make the principles clear. Nothing will put a student in shock quicker than studying elaborate scheduling charts. Before presenting the scheduling techniques, it is desirable to clarify some of the things that scheduling is not.

Master Schedule. The master schedule, introduced in Chapter 11, like the production order, is an authority to manufacture. (See Figure 14–3.)

Figure 14–3
Master Schedule

ZEPHYR MANUFACTURING COMPANY MASTER SCHEDULE						
Model Number	Date	8/9	8/16	8/23	8/30	
65 - A - 732	7-18	50	50	50	50	
65 - A - 791	7-20	80	80	30	0	
65 - A - 891 L	7-21	120	120	120	120	
65 - A - 891 S	7-28	60	60	60	60	
65 - A - 890	7-28	90	90	90	90	
66 - A - 791	8-2	3	3	40	80	

Date Aug. 1st
By T.I.M.

It is issued periodically by management to let the factory know how much of each product is to be produced in each of several time periods. The master schedule is used primarily in high production industries making a limited number of products. This important production form also goes under such names as the Manufacturing Master Schedule, Release, Manufacturing Release, and by others.

The master schedule may be considered as an order and when used also becomes a source of information for scheduling.

Loading. The schedule pertains to *when* an activity is to take place, and the load has to do with the *amount* of work to be done. The *work load* is the anticipated activity for a machine, department, or factory. The load is usually stated as being so many hours of work. A typical load chart is shown in Figure 14–4. Notice that the chart does not indicate when a task is to be performed but only how much work is ahead of each machine.

Figure 14–4
Load Chart

Machine	One day	Two days	Three days	Four days	Five days
Pratt & Whitney 12"					
Pratt & Whitney 14"					
Jones & Lamson 6"					
Warner & Swasey 12"					
B&S ASM #1					
B&S ASM #2					

Calculating the load for a load chart is an extensive problem which is more easily understood if put as a series of steps:

Step 1.   Determine the number of product assemblies to be produced, either from the master schedule or from the accumulation of manufacturing orders.

Step 2.   Adjust this quantity by any excess or shortage in finished inventory.

Step 3.   Determine the number of parts needed for each assembly by *product explosion* or similar technique (see Chapter 11).

Step 4.   Multiply the quantity of assemblies required by the number of parts required per assembly: Step 2 $\times$ Step 3 = Step 4.

Step 5.   Multiply, if necessary, by a scrap factor. If 100 is needed, and there is a loss of 15 percent in the process, then the order must be placed for at least 118: Assemblies started -15% of assemblies started = 100.

Step 6.   Adjust the number of parts by any excess or shortage in the parts inventory.

Step 7.   Determine from the time-standards records the standard time for each operation for each part. Multiply this by the number of parts found in Step 6.

Step 8.　Accumulate the time for each machine, department, or other breakdown desired.

Step 9.　Adjust the times values, found in Step 8, by an efficiency factor. This is the work load: Accumulated time/Efficiency = Work load.

The order of the steps listed above can be altered slightly and still produce the correct answer. The work load is usually shown in some graphical method, such as the bar chart. If a work load is excessive, then other arrangements will have to be made—such as shifting the work to another machine or department, or perhaps even subcontracting the work to other shops.

By proper loading, those facilities which are not active will be revealed. This permits shifting of personnel, planning vacations, scheduling maintenance, and other activities. From the information obtained by loading it is possible to make the necessary labor budgets for hiring and laying off personnel.

The efficiency factor mentioned in the last step should be determined for each department. A common efficiency factor is 80 percent, although often this is not substantiated by facts. Some factories find that the slack in the standard time just compensates for the factory inefficiencies.

Finite and Infinite Loading.　Loading a production facility as if it had unlimited capacity is referred to as *infinite loading* or loading to *infinite capacity*. If the capacity is considered as a limit for loading, it is referred to as *finite loading.*

Many companies in their enthusiasm for production use infinite loading only to find that they must disappoint their customers or meet the schedule with costly overtime or subcontracting. They just keep adding on jobs without regard for the capabilities of the production facilities.

Recently factories have been giving serious consideration to this problem, and we find that they are facing up to reality and fitting the load to the capacity available. By this way they are able to adjust the capacity and meet the customers' demands and still keep costs to a minimum.

Scheduling Requires Feedback.　In the second chapter, the need for feedback in a system with varying output was discussed. If the output is as planned, without any variation, there is no need for feedback, but this would seldom be the case because there are many unpredictable secondary inputs which are constantly changing the output from what has been planned.

The scheduling process is dynamic because conditions are changing constantly. In any good scheduling system the actual production is being constantly compared with the proposed, and necessary steps are taken to compensate for the error. This means that a feedback link is necessary to show what the actual production is.

More than one scheduling system has been devised without adequate feedback links, and the systems were soon abandoned. In the production control system the feedback link may consist of production tickets returned by the operators, showing the completion of a task; the move order, showing that the process is completed and the product has been moved; or a time card, showing that so much of the product is completed. Even a verbal report of the work completed might be suitable—if not as desirable as a written record. Some more elaborate systems have electric counters in the scheduling room which are attached directly to the machine, making a production count available every minute of the day. In some situations these counters have been tied directly to on-line computers which update the schedule constantly.

Often an employee feels that once a schedule is made it should not be tampered with. Nothing could be further from the truth. The schedule must be made to reflect reality or it is worthless, and this means that it must be adjusted periodically. How often it should be adjusted is a question of economics. Too-frequent adjustment may be wasteful, while too-infrequent adjustments may not present the information when wanted. To do scheduling efficiently requires certain kinds of personality characteristics not to be found in every individual.

Selecting Scheduling Personnel.   Frequently, education is the predominant criterion for selecting people to do scheduling. While this is important, it should not be the only consideration. Some of the desirable attributes for scheduling personnel are:

1. A proficiency in working with details.
2. A knowledge of factory activities. They can frequently detect errors or propose alternate processes if they have a knowledge of the factory.
3. A good memory is useful, as is an ability to solve the "puzzles" of scheduling.
4. Involvement in their work is important; frequently they may be called on to work overtime.
5. Since they are in contact with many of the factory workers, and even customers at times, it is desirable that they have good personal habits and get along well with people.

It is probably impossible to find personnel with all these attributes, but if they are found they contribute immeasurably to the efficient operation of a factory.

GRAPHICAL TECHNIQUES FOR SCHEDULING

Here are a number of graphical scheduling techniques. Some are not new but have proven themselves useful over the years; others are new, and appear to be important, but require further trial. As you will observe, some are very closely related while others are not.

1. Gantt chart.
2. Critical path method.

3. PERT scheduling.
4. PERT/COST scheduling.
5. Line of balancing scheduling.

Gantt Chart

"Plan your work and work your plan" has long been a byword in industry, and for many years one of the best tools for doing this has been the Gantt chart. The Gantt chart is a simple way of showing graphically both the anticipated and completed production on the horizontal axis of a chart.

Henry L. Gantt developed this charting technique as one of his many contributions to the scientific management movement, and it is probably one of the most successful devices of this type ever invented. Some modification of the Gantt chart is to be found in practically every production office, so the basic concepts of the technique should be understood by everyone in manufacturing management.

So much has been said and written about this method of planning and controlling production that the basic principles are frequently lost in a clutter of details. However, there are some real advantages in this technique which can be found in no others:

1. It forces a plan to be made, which in itself is a big step toward more efficient operations.
2. Work planned and work accomplished are easily compared; there is no need to remember a wealth of information for comparison purposes.
3. Gantt charts are compact; one chart can replace file drawers full of information.
4. Anyone can produce a Gantt chart with paper, pencil, and rule.
5. These charts are dynamic, showing a moving picture of plant activities.

Charts, you must realize, use a shorthand form of language, and to be effective, everyone using them must know the symbols. Many symbols have been used and there is nothing wrong if a company wishes to develop its own. There are some which are frequently used and a few of them (as shown in Figure 14–5) are given here to make the rest of the discussion understandable.

Figure 14–5
Gantt-Chart Symbols

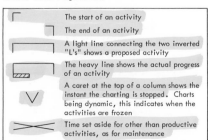

Just to show how this technique works, look at the example in Figure 14–6 for charting the manufacturing orders.

Figure 14–6
Example of a Gantt Chart

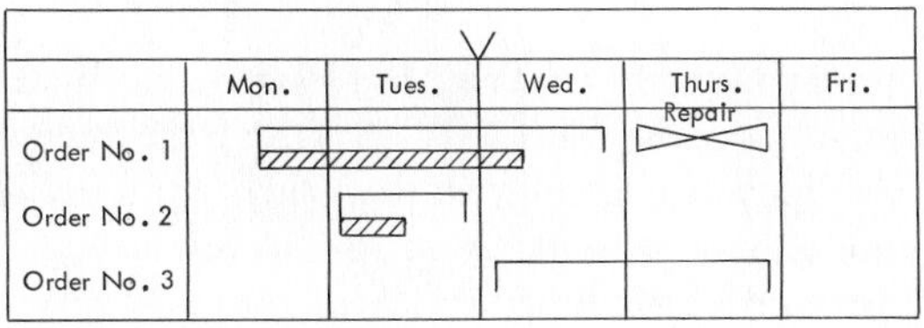

The chart was brought up to date Tuesday night, as shown by the caret, **V**. Order no. 1 was started Monday noon and is to be completed Wednesday night, as shown by the light line. The heavy line, which extends beyond the present time, shows that the order is ahead of schedule. By the same reasoning, order no. 2 is behind schedule and order no. 3 has not been started.

There are a few basic principles that must be understood before successful Gantt charting can be made. The first is that distances along the horizontal axis represent either time or production. For example, one can say that a space between two vertical lines on the charts represents one hour in which 15 parts are produced, or the space represents 15 parts which take one hour to produce. It doesn't matter which way you say it for it comes out the same. Again it should be pointed out that if production standards are in use they will have to be modified by the plant-efficiency factor to make them realistic.

Parallel to the light line, representing the proposed production, is a heavy line that shows the actual progress of production. The difference between the two lines shows how near the production is to completion.

A vertical line drawn through the caret at the top of the chart represents the instant the charting is stopped. The difference between the heavy-black progress line and the vertical line through the caret shows how far ahead or behind schedule the production is. This can be easily understood by referring to the example.

The Two Basic Charts. Although there are many confusing variations of the Gantt chart, it is possible to classify them into two basic types. For want of better names these might be called *forward* and *backward* charts. The first one is frequently called a *schedule chart* and the work is scheduled from the present date forward to determine the completion date. The backward chart, which is often called a *project chart*, is used when a completion date is known and it is desired to work backwards to find a starting date.

A simple analogy might make the distinction between these charts easier to see. Take, for example, the planning of a trip by two alternatives, either train or car. The train, as you know, goes at a certain instant, and if you are not there it goes without you. In this case it is essential to start the planning from the instant the train leaves and work backwards to fit everything into the schedule. This kind of chart would be a backward or project type of chart.

On the other hand, if you can leave by car at any time, and it doesn't matter exactly when, then you can plan your work ahead from this present moment and leave at any time you wish; and for this you need a forward or schedule chart.

Another way of saying this is that for a forward, or schedule, chart you start at the left-hand side and work to the right for the completion date. On the backward or project chart you start with the completion date on the right-hand side and work to the left. Of course, in this latter case, you would start at the bottom and work upwards so that when you read it you will be following the conventional method. Backward and forward charting are two viewpoints and both are often used on one chart.

Often the question comes up as to what to chart. Chart whatever is worthwhile charting and for which data are available. Companies are now planning and controlling workers, work centers, machines, departments, plants, parts, work orders, operations, and assemblies by this very simple device. The earlier example showed how this technique could be used for keeping track of orders, but observe here (Figure 14–7) how it might be used for scheduling machines, and also an assembly (Figure 14–8).

Figure 14–7
Machine Scheduling Chart

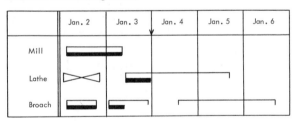

Figure 14–8
Project Chart

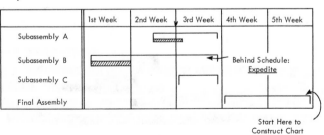

Note that this first example is usually a forward chart, for the objective is to keep the machines always loaded. Blank spaces are to be avoided for this shows when the machines are not productive. The chart should be self-explanatory if the previous symbols are understood.

Figure 14–8 is a good example of a backward or project chart. In this case it is desired not to finish before a certain date because of inventory costs and space limitations. It is easier to keep track of the necessary parts for the final assembly, and to be sure they are brought together in the final assembly on the required date, if a backward chart is used.

The methods proposed here can be used on any piece of ruled paper with the proper scale. Lines can be drawn in with pencil, crayon, or ink—although an erasable substance is preferred. One technique is to represent the lines with colored masking tape cut to length. A plastic overlay on a piece of coordinate paper makes an easily erased surface.

Several commercial applications of the Gantt chart are available and should be explored before an installation is made. One common device, the Produc-trol Board, uses spring-loaded strings to represent the bars. Another popular application of the Gantt chart is the Sched-U-Graph, a series of plastic-edged flaps mounted so that they overlap, showing a clear plastic edge. In the plastic edge can be placed cards cut to length to represent the bars. Both of the above systems have vertical dividers and methods of representing the caret.

Whatever system is used, a piece of cheap ruled paper or an elaborate commercial product, be sure the basic principles of the Gantt chart apply. One should be cautious in accepting some standard plan proposed by the vendor of a commercial product. Rather, design the method to suit the problem.

Rules for Scheduling Lots. Frequently a manufacturing-order quantity is divided into lots so that subsequent operations do not have to wait until the previous operations are completed as shown in Figure 14–9. Depending upon the time relationship for operation one and two, a forward or backward scheduling technique should be used.

Rule 1: If operation one is shorter than two, schedule forward to save delays and frequent setups.

Rule 2: If operation one is longer than two, schedule backwards to save delays and frequent setups.

Time-Cycle Charts.[1] The *time-cycle* is the time required to obtain materials and manufacture them into a product. The time-cycle chart is a technique for planning and controlling the time cycle for the many components which combine to make up an assembly.

The time-cycle chart has *two* parts imposed one upon the other.

1. A *goes-into* type of materials list—showing which parts and subassemblies go into what.

---

[1] For a comprehensive discussion of this subject, see R. L. Van De Mark, *Production Control Techniques* (Dallas, Texas: Van De Mark, Inc., 1970).

Figure 14–9
Scheduling Rules

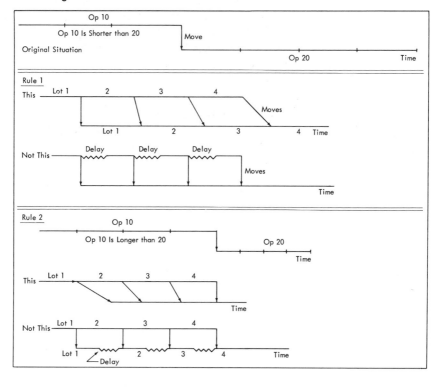

Figure 14–10
Time-Cycle Chart Developed from Revised Bill of Materials

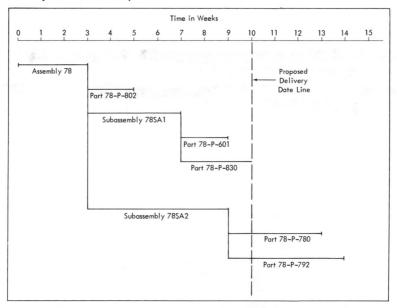

2. Superimposed on the materials list is a Gantt-type bar chart. The bars are scaled to represent the time scale for each part and assembly and are connected to form a complete time picture for the entire bill of materials, as illustrated in Figure 14–10.

The time-cycle chart is developed in the following steps:

Step 1.   Put the materials list into a goes-into form (Figure 14–11). This

Figure 14–11
Original and Revised List of Materials

Original List of Material

	Used On
Assembly-78	0
Subassembly 78SA1	1
Subassembly 78SA2	1
Part 78–P–601	1
78–P–780	2
78–P–792	2
78–P–802	0
78–P–830	1

Revised List of Material

	Time-Cycle Estimates
Assembly 78	3 weeks
Part 78–P–802	2
Subassembly 78SA1	4
Part 78–P–601	2
78–P–830	2½
Subassembly 78SA2	6
Part 78–P–780	3
78–P–792	5

may be already available or it may require that you reorganize the present list with the help of engineering and production planners.

The *Class C items,* which are not usually carried under perpetual inventory surveillance, are deleted from the list, as they would only confuse the picture and emphasize trivial parts.

Step 2.   Accumulate the time cycles required for obtaining each of the parts on the list. This time may be posted in a column along the right edge of the materials list for ready reference.

The time information, in a plant without time studies, might have to be an estimate made by a foreman, but in a well-managed plant, it will be available from the work standards department. Remember that the work cycle will be for a specific quantity, and the times will have to be developed for that quantity in mind. Several charts may be made with several different lot sizes. Be sure the most accurate estimates available are used. If the foreman supplies the times, he might be inclined to inflate them, realizing eventually he is going to live within the standards he has established.

The time increments used in laying out the chart will depend upon the way customer delivery dates are quoted and the length of the manufacturing cycle. If the predictions are by the day, then the time increments should be days. Products with long manufacturing cycles, with the predictions made on the basis of weeks or months, call for equivalent time increments.

Start with the final assembly. In doing so, follow this rule:

Align the *left* end of the goes-into part with the *right* end of the assembly or subassembly under consideration.

To the chart may be added a *promised delivery date line.* By coding, additional lines may be added to illustrate different delivery promises.

Figure 14–10 is a typical time-cycle chart, but all of its attributes are not obvious on casual observation and it is worth further discussion. Its major attributes are:

1. The production of a time-cycle chart will show that schedules are inexact because the time standards are not accurate.
2. The time-cycle chart can assist the sales department. There is little point in making delivery promises when there are bars extended to the right of the delivery promise date—unless something is done to expedite those items.
3. The time-cycle chart is especially useful in maintaining inventories. If a delivery date is promised as shown on the chart, those items with bars extending to the right will have to be carried in stock; otherwise, the delivery date cannot be kept.
4. Placing materials lists into a goes-into form will often help those responsible for releasing orders and scheduling production. They will understand which things have to be done first and give them the proper priority.

Critical Path Method

CPM and PERT (program evaluation and review technique) are just two of the newer techniques which depict activities by a network. Usually these techniques have a limited use in production but are particularly useful for projects with one terminating event. RAMP (review analysis of multiple projects) is useful for guiding the activities of several projects at one time, but it has been slow in gaining acceptance.

As in the Gantt chart, the CPM uses a set of shorthand symbols with which one must become familiar before using the method successfully. These symbols are shown in Figure 14–12.

There are several phases of the CPM and one has a choice of how far to carry it. How far to go is, of course, an economic decision and refinements should be included only on the promise of a payoff. Projects with hundreds of individual activities have been planned and scheduled by a computer. Some of the advantages of the critical path method are:

Figure 14–12
Critical Path Symbols

Symbol	Term	Comments
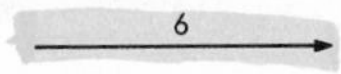	Activities	Shows an activity. No attempt is made to scale the arrow to represent time. A number over the arrow shows the time in units of hours, days, months, or other increments.
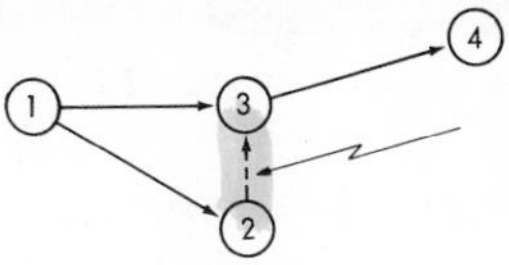	Dummy activity	Used in situations where one event takes precedence over another but there is no activity relating them. They do not require time or cost data.
	Node, event, junction	An event or node is the end of an activity. Numbers within the circle differentiate the activity from other activities. No two events should have the same numbers. The activity may be keyed with the activities such as activity 1–2 connecting events 1 and 2.
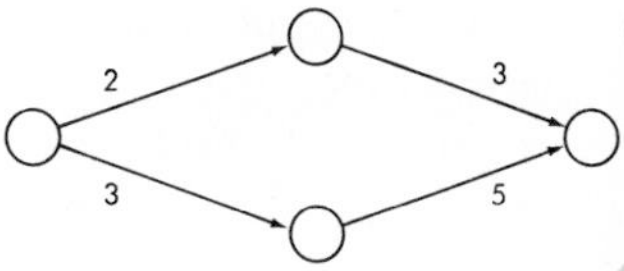	Network	Networks are composed of activities and events. Arrows terminating at a junction *must* be completed before the following activity begins.
	Critical path	The longest time path through the network is represented by a heavy line.
	Float, slack	Difference between the earliest and latest time a task can be completed and still stay on schedule. Also called "slack."
	Anchor point, objective event	Latest time on the critical path.
	Latest time	Start with anchor point and subtract each of the activity times.
	Earliest time	Sum of activity times leading to an event.
	Crash time	Fastest possible time for completing an activity.
	Crash cost	Cost of accelerating the job so that it may be completed within the crash time.

It requires the selection of specific and well-defined *events* which occur along the network of activities.

The events are linked with activities which show the interdependencies among events.

The development of a CPM chart requires an estimation of the time for all activities.

The critical aspects of each event are signaled well in advance of the occurrences.

Trade-offs between two activities may be calculated in terms of dollars, which makes it possible to decide which activities should or should not be expedited.

The critical path method is easier to comprehend if it is approached in a step-by-step procedure.

Step 1. Planning. The first step is to list all the jobs, as shown on the left of the table in Figure 14–13, in the order of their precedence. From this, an *arrow diagram* is produced as shown. Each task is indicated by an arrow, with the direction of the arrow showing the sequence of the task. The length of the arrows has no significance. The jobs are placed on the diagram one by one, keeping in mind what precedes and follows each job as well as what jobs can be done simultaneously.

Step 2. Scheduling. The task times are considered to be deterministic if there is no great variation observable in the completion times. These time elements, shown adjacent to each arrow, are determined as accurately as possible and should reflect the normal times for each job, taking into consideration the usual delivery times and applying the typical work force.

The longest time path through the network is the *critical path,* shown by the dark line on the example. Every activity on this path must be completed on time or the schedule will fall behind. But what about the other paths? Each of the other paths has some slack time (which is also termed "float"). The method of determining this slack is shown in the table. It is first necessary to calculate the earliest possible time for each event. These are the circled figures on the diagram. Then, working backwards from the longest time—determined by the critical path—find the latest possible time. These latest times are shown by the figures in the squares. The difference between the earliest and latest time, for each node, is the slack.

It is apparent that there is no slack on the critical path. In fact, one way of defining the critical path is to say it is a path with no slack. Often two or more activities lead to one node, such as 6 on the diagram. You will notice that the latest time, 29, was used in making the forward calculations.

The advantage of CPM, up to this point, has been that all critical jobs are pinpointed and the amount of slack available on all noncritical legs of the network is readily obtained. This gives one the opportunity of trading off facilities between critical and noncritical jobs.

Step 3. Cost Analysis. The CPM cost analysis step makes it possible to determine the advantage or disadvantage of making any changes in the

Figure 14–13
Critical Path Calculations

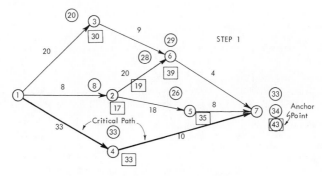

Activity	Code		Normal Time	Earliest Time		Latest Time		Float Available
	Tail	Head		Start	End ○	Start	End □	
	1	2	8	0	8	9	17	9
	1	3	20	0	20	10	30	10
List all	1	4	33	0	33	0	33	0
activities	2	5	18	8	26	17	35	9
here	2	6	20	8	28	19	39	11
	3	6	9	20	29	30	39	10
	4	7	10	33	43	33	43	0
	5	7	8	26	34	35	43	9
	6	7	4	29	33	39	43	10

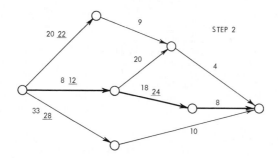

schedule. If it is necessary to compress a schedule, it is possible to determine in advance just how costly this step will be. Before looking at the application of this step, let us be sure the theory upon which it is based is understood.

In many situations management has some flexibility in determining the completion date of a task by merely adding more men and equipment. The relationship between the cost of adding facilities and the duration of a job can be illustrated by a cost-time curve similar to the one in Figure 14–14. The lowest point on the curve would be the *normal time*, T_n, and the management will undoubtedly try to work as close to this level as possible. It would not be reasonable to schedule the job for any longer than the normal time—and thus increase the cost.

Figure 14–14
Critical Path Cost Information

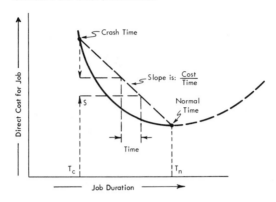

CPM Costs

Activity	Normal Days	Normal Dollars	Crash Days	Crash Dollars	Cost Slope Dollars/Day
1-2	8	80.00	7	100.00	20.00
1-3	20	150.00	18	180.00	15.00
1-4	33	400.00	30	490.00	30.00
2-5	18	250.00	16	350.00	50.00
2-6	20	400.00	20	400.00	- - -
3-6	9	120.00	9	120.00	- - -
4-7	10	150.00	8	220.00	35.00
5-7	8	160.00	6	280.00	60.00
6-7	4	120.00	3	190.00	70.00

Total 130   Total 117

Example for Job 1-2

Cost Slope, \$/Day   =

$$\frac{\text{Crash cost - Normal cost}}{\text{Normal time - Crash time}} =$$

$$\frac{\$100.00 - \$80.00}{8 \text{ days} - 7 \text{ days}} = \$20.00/\text{Day}$$

By adding extra facilities, the duration of the job is reduced and the cost is increased. The ultimate in applying extra facilities is indicated on the curve by the *crash time*, T_c. The curve between T_c and T_n can be approximated by a straight line, as shown. The slope of this line is referred to as the *cost slope* and is expressed as so many dollars per unit of time, such as \$20 per day.

Now to return to the application of this information to the network. The normal time and the crash time for each job are determined as well as the costs for these two conditions. From this can be determined the cost per unit time, as shown in the table. Now management has a tool and the information by which to make some reasonable decisions. If the cost for delaying the project is available, a comparison can be made between the cost of expediting the project and the cost of delay.

Step 4. Monitoring. Like all scheduling charts, the CPM is dynamic and is always subject to changes. The changes are dictated by a constant feedback of information. The source of the information depends upon the type of activity and could come from shipping orders, work orders, time cards, or other business forms.

If you will refer back to the second step of the critical path diagram (Figure 14–14), you can observe the changes caused by activities being ahead and behind schedule. The times for the completed activities are shown adjacent to the arrow by an underlined number. As you will observe, some of the activities were completed ahead of schedule while others fell behind. Consequently, the critical path has changed and management must turn its attention to finding ways of channeling the resources to complete the project on time. How the resources are allocated will depend upon what is a feasible schedule, as well as upon the economics of the situation as determined by the cost analysis of Step 3.

Critical Path Using Node-as-Activity Technique

A modification of the critical path method discussed in the text considers the nodes rather than the arrows as activities. The arrows only indicate precedence. This method is said to have the following advantages:

1. The network is easier to construct.
2. No "dummy" activities are necessary to show relationships.

The typical node designation and language for this node-as-activity technique are given in Figure 14–15.

Figure 14–15
Node-as-Activity Language

Symbol	Term	Comments
20 : 26 (M, 24) 44 : 50	Late Finish	
	Early Finish	
	Time t, needed for job	
	Job Identification	
	Late Start	
	Early Start	
t	Standard time	The elapsed time that it will take to do the job.
s	Start	Time or date to begin the project.
F	Finish	Completion time or date for project.
ES	Early start	Earliest possible time that a job can begin if all the predecessor jobs start at their earliest start date.
EF	Early finish	The earliest time to start a job plus the time, t, that it takes to do a job.
LS	Late start	The latest a job can be started and remain on schedule.
LF	Late finish	The late start, time for a job plus the time it takes to do the job.

This node-as-activity technique may be compared with the example in Figure 14–13 since both use the same data. First the data is reorganized as shown in Figure 14–16.

Figure 14–16
Revised Data for Node as Activity

Reference to Previous Example	Job No.	Description	Intermediate Predecessors	Time
	a	Start		
1–2	b		a	8
1–3	c	List all	a	20
1–4	d	activities	a	33
2–5	e	here	b	18
2–6	f		b	20
3–6	g		c	9
4–7	h		d	10
5–7	i		e	8
6–7	j		f & g	4
	k	end	h, i, j	

The data given in Figure 14–16 can be organized to form a network as shown in Figure 14–17. There are a couple of unique characteristics of this diagram which are worth mentioning:

Figure 14–17
Node-as-Activity Network

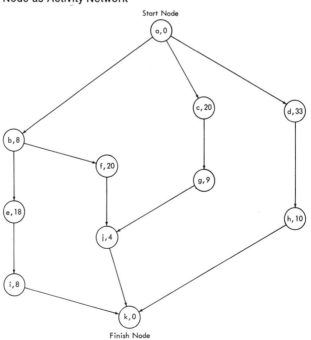

Finish Node

1. The chart is drawn with the main flow of activities vertical rather than horizontal. This makes it easier to manipulate the data but limits the size of the chart.

2. A "Start" node and "Finish" node must be included in the chart to tie the ends together. The method of determining the critical path and slack is the same as previously described but an algorithm will expedite the calculations.

Method of Determining Critical Path. Algorithm for early start and early finish times.

Step 1. Place the value of the Start on the left and right of node. See Figure 14–18.

Figure 14–18
Method for Determining Critical Path

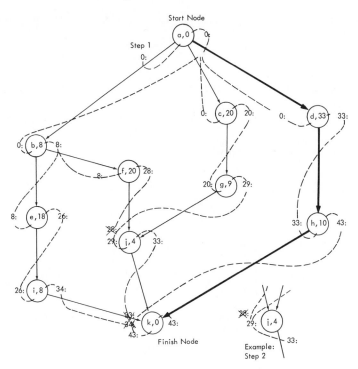

Step 2. Mark to the left of the next node the largest number to appear on the right of the previous node or nodes. Notice example for this step.

Step 3. Add to this number the value *t* to be found in the node. Place the answer to the right of the node.

Step 4. Return to Step 2 and repeat the cycle until all nodes are completed. You arrive at the finish node.

The largest value for the finish node is the time that it will take to complete the project. However, this may or may not be the *target date* that management has in mind. The target date must be equal to or greater than the finish date. The difference between the target date and the finish date is the *total slack*. The total slack will be included in all the jobs.

Algorithm for Determining Latest Start and Latest Finish Times

1. Using the target or finish date, place it to the right and the left of the node as shown. See Figure 14–19.

Figure 14–19
Method for Calculating Slack

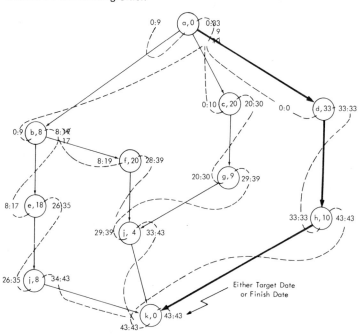

2. Place to the right of the next node under consideration the smallest number to be found to the left of a preceding node.
3. Subtract from this number the value *t* of the node. Place the results to the immediate left as shown.
4. Continue, with Step 2, until *start* is reached.

If the target date is greater than the finish date, there will be slack extending back through the network: $T - F =$ Slack.

Free slack is the amount of time that any job may be detained and still meet the schedule. The free slack equals the early finish time less the earliest of the early start times for the immediate successor.

This node-as-activity technique may simplify the diagramming procedure and add a new insight to the problem of scheduling.

The PERT Method of Scheduling

PERT is an abbreviation for Program Evaluation and Review Technique, a technique which gained acceptability in government and industry after meeting with unusual success in the Polaris ballistic missile program. In such a program innumerable parts must be brought together at the right time to produce an extremely complex product. PERT is an ideal tool for scheduling such activities.

The objective of PERT is to put planning and evaluation on an orderly and consistent basis, and also to provide an automatic device to identify potential trouble spots. The PERT technique allows some degree of simulation as well, without requiring actual changes in the project schedule.

The important points of the PERT scheduling network can be summarized as follows:

1. PERT, like CPM, requires the selection of specific and well-defined "events" that occur along the network of activities.
2. The events are linked with activities which show the interdependencies among events.
3. The development of a PERT chart requires an estimation of the time for all activities and reveals the uncertainty involved.
4. Like CPM, the critical aspects of each event are signaled well in advance of the occurrence.
5. The probability of meeting a contract date is provided.

PERT is a management-by-exception tool which is uniquely suitable for preplanning extremely involved problems where time data are not readily available, as in a research program. It is closely related to the Gantt charts, but it shows more distinctly the interrelationships of combined activities and also introduces the concept of probability by which better decisions can be made.

The PERT diagram is similar to the CPM diagram except that it will contain more information. The development of PERT will parallel CPM until the probabilistic reasoning is added. PERT is used for predicting and scheduling progress as well as for measuring compliance to plan. Sister techniques are being developed for the measurement and prediction of cost and reliability.

As with the Gantt chart—and any other similar charting techniques—it is important to understand the symbols used. Figure 14–20 presents them in table form for your convenience.

Assumptions for Times Estimates. The opportunity to determine the probability of completing a project by a certain time is a unique feature of PERT. This, however, requires a knowledge of the mean time and variance for each activity. In turn, this means that the activity supervisors must furnish three pieces of information rather than one:

1. Optimistic time, t_o: there is very little chance the activity can be completed before this time.

Figure 14-20
PERT Glossary of Symbols

Term	Symbol	Comments
PERT		Abbreviation for program evaluation and review technique.
Event	○ □ ◯⊃	Events are shown as squares or circles and indicate what has gone before. Therefore events are phrased in the past tense. Events are "checkpoints" and show that work has been accomplished up to this point.
Activity	——5—→	Activity lines represent the work needed to accomplish an event. An event is completed when the activity is accomplished. No work can start on the next activity until the preceding event is completed. The activity lines are not scaled, but the numbers over the line indicate time required.
Network (sequential flow diagram)		A web of events and activities with one starting event and one objective event.
Time estimates		Discussed more fully in text.
Optimistic time	t_o	There is very little chance that the activity can be done in less time than t_o.
Most likely time	t_m	The best guess of the time required. If only one time were available, this would be it. This is the "mode" of the distribution.
Pessimistic time	t_p	There is little chance that the task would take longer than t_p.
Expected time	t_e	There is a 50% probability that the activity completed will take less time—and 50% probability, of course, that it will take more time. $$t_e = \left[\frac{t_o + 4t_m + t_p}{6} \right]$$
Earliest expected time	T_e	The summation of all times, t_e, up to an event, staying with a single path from start to finish. When two paths lead to an event, use the one with the greatest time. For example:
Latest allowable time	T_L	The latest time an activity can start and stay on schedule.
Completion time	T_c	The instant in time that the project is scheduled for completion.
Critical path	——→	The longest time path through the network. Any delay in the critical path will cause delay in the final event.
Slack	T_s	Difference between latest allowable time and earliest expected time: $T_L - T_e$.

In the "Earliest expected time" row, the example diagram shows: $T_e = 1$, $t_e = 1$, $t_e = 3$, $T_e = 7$, $T_e = 13$, $t_e = 6$, $t_e = 2$, $t_e = 5$, $T_e = 2$.

2. Pessimistic time, t_p: at the opposite extreme of t_o is t_p. There is very little likelihood that the task would take a longer time than this.
3. Most likely time, t_m: this is the best guess of the time needed. If only one time were available, this would be it.

How well t_o, t_p, and t_m are determined depends upon the skill and experience of the person furnishing the estimate. The probability distribution of the time involved in performing the activity might be characterized by any one of the curves illustrated in Figure 14–21. It is assumed that the

Figure 14–21
Typical Distribution for PERT

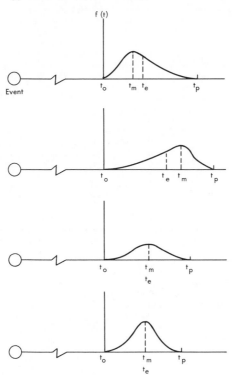

distribution is unimodal and the peak will represent the value of t_m, the most probable time for completing the activity. There is very little chance that the task can be completed before t_o or after t_p. The point, t_m, is free to move between these two, depending upon the estimator's judgment.

From these three values it is necessary to derive the expected value, t_e, commonly referred to as the average or mean. This is accomplished by an approximation developed by the originators of PERT.

$$t_e = \left[\frac{t_o + 4t_m + t_p}{6} \right]$$

Another assumption made concerning the distribution is that, for unimodal distributions, the standard deviation can be estimated roughly as one sixth of the range:

$$\sigma = \frac{t_p - t_o}{6}$$

and, of course,

$$\sigma^2 = \left(\frac{t_p - t_o}{6}\right)^2$$

From these assumptions and approximations we can proceed to discuss an example of a PERT network.

PERT Network Example. Figure 14–22 shows a very simple network, sim-

Figure 14–22
PERT Example

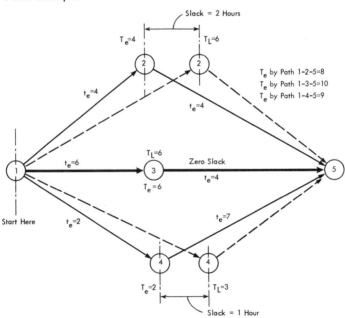

Slack = 2 Hours

$T_e = 4$ $T_L = 6$

T_e by Path 1-2-5=8
T_e by Path 1-3-5=10
T_e by Path 1-4-5=9

$t_e = 4$

$t_e = 4$

$t_e = 6$ $T_L = 6$ Zero Slack $t_e = 4$ $T_e = 6$

Start Here $t_e = 2$ $t_e = 7$

$T_e = 2$ $T_L = 3$

Slack = 1 Hour

ilar to one discussed with CPM. The starting point is at 1 with three paths showing activities required to reach objective 5. Above each activity is the previously calculated expected time, t_e. The concept of earliest expected time, latest allowable time, slack, and critical path can best be illustrated by this simple example.

The first thing we wish to learn is the earliest expected time, T_e, for each event. This is shown for each event following each path. Event 5, of course, has three time values, depending upon which path is followed. The path taking the greatest time will give the latest expected time, T_e. In our example it is obvious that this is path 1, 3, 5, which gives a total time of ten hours.

Everything up to this point must be delayed for the activities which occur on the longest path. This longest time path, as in CPM, is called the critical path.

The latest time, T_L, is the latest time a job can start and is calculated by using the latest event as an anchor point and working backwards. The earliest expected time, T_e, for the last event on the critical path became the anchor point or latest allowable time, T_L.

The T_L for event 2, 3, and 4 can be calculated by subtracting t_e for the various events from the T_L for 5.

$$T_L \text{ for } 2 \text{ is } T_L - t_e = 10 - 4 = 6$$
$$3 \qquad\qquad = 10 - 4 = 6$$
$$4 \qquad\qquad = 10 - 7 = 3$$

Probability of Meeting the Contract Date. With PERT it is possible to determine the probability of completing a contract on schedule. For example, the expected time to complete a contract is shown by T_e in Figure 14–23, but we know that only seldom will it be completed exactly as ex-

Figure 14–23
Probability of Completing on Schedule

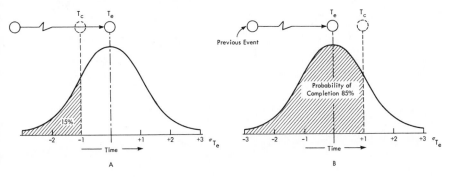

pected. We can expect to get a distribution of possible completion dates as represented by the normal curve illustrated.

The standard deviation, σ_{T_e}, of this distribution can be determined by obtaining the square root of the sum of all the variances of the activities leading up to the event under consideration:

$$\sigma_{T_e} = \sqrt{\sigma_{t_{e1}}^2 + \sigma_{t_{e2}}^2 + \sigma_{t_{e3}}^2 + \sigma_{t_{e4}}^2 + \ldots + \sigma_{t_{en}}^2}$$

Once this is obtained, we can resort to the normal statistical tables to determine the probabilities—if we know the number of standard deviations that the completion date, T_c, is from the expected date, T_e.

The probability of a task being completed at any particular time is shown on the curve by the shaded area. In Figure 14–23A, the probability of meeting the scheduled date is about 15 percent, while in B it is about 85 percent.

If the contract time is T_c, as shown in Figure 14–23A, the chances of completing the contract on time are probably too slight, while too much safety is built into a situation where the contract time is represented by anything to the far right. If T_e is equal to T_c, the probability of completing the schedule on time is 50 percent.

As in CPM, the difference between the time when an activity *can* start and when it *has* to start is referred to as the slack or float. Slack, in terms of the symbols already developed, is:

$$T_L - T_e = \text{Slack}$$

This, so far, has been an attempt to define the terms used in the PERT technique. It is now time to see an application.

A PERT Problem. The PERT techniques are best discussed by means of an example, such as is shown in Figure 14–24. The boxes indicate the

Figure 14–24
PERT Problem

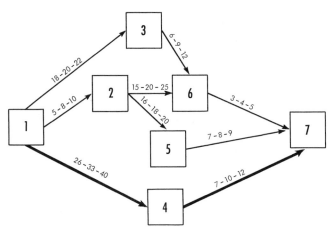

events, and the activity lines between them have three numbers above them showing t_o, t_m, and t_p.

The calculations are most readily handled if they are put in a tabular form, as shown in Figure 14–25. Each column in the table will be explained in turn.

Column 1.   Each event is listed, starting from the last (or objective) and working downward to the start.

Column 2.   Previous events: all of the events that have gone before the event listed in column 1 are listed.

Figure 14–25
Example of PERT Calculations

1	2	3	4	5	6	7	8	9	10	11	12	13
Event	Previous Event	t_o	t_m	t_p	t_e	σ^2	T_e	T_L	T_s	T_c	D	P
7	6	3	4	5	4.0	0.111				41.5		
	5	7	8	9	8.0	0.111						
	4	7	10	12	9.8	0.694	42.8	(42.8)	0.00		.52	30%
6	3	6	9	12	9.0	1.000	29.0	38.8	9.8			
	2	15	20	25	20.0	2.78						
5	2	16	18	20	18.0	0.443	25.8	34.8	9.0			
4	1	26	33	40	33.0	5.429	33.0	33.0	0.0			
3	1	18	20	22	20.0	0.444	20.0	29.8	9.8			
2	1	5	8	10	7.8	0.694	7.8	16.8	9.0			

T_c is 41.5 weeks

$$D = \frac{41.5 - 42.8}{\sqrt{5.429 + 0.694}} = 0.52 \text{ deviations}$$

Area under normal curve for 0.52 is about 30%

Column 3. The optimistic time, t_o, for an activity as determined by someone who is practiced in estimating, such as a foreman or industrial engineer.

Column 4. The most likely time, t_m.

Column 5. The pessimistic time, t_p.

Column 6. The expected time, t_e, as calculated from the three previous times:

$$t_e = \left[\frac{t_o + 4t_m + t_p}{6}\right]$$

Column 7. The variance, σ^2, for the activities calculated on the following basis:

$$\sigma^2 = \left[\frac{t_p - t_o}{6}\right]^2$$

Column 8. The earliest expected time for each event. Sum the total expected times for all activities leading to the event. When more than one activity leads to an event, the greatest T_e is chosen. For example, times leading to the event 6 from 3 and 2 are $20 + 9 = 29.0$ and $7.8 + 20.0 = 27.8$. Since we wish to choose the largest, T_e is 29.0 for 6.

Column 9. The latest time is calculated in the following manner: Start with the T_L for the last event as equal to T_e (see circled figures on Figure 14–25). Now for each path work backwards, subtracting the t_e for each activity link.

Column 10.   The slack time is the difference between the latest allowable time and the earliest expected time:

$$T_s = T_L - T_e$$

The critical path may now be determined by finding the path with zero slack. This is shown by dark lines on the activity chart. Those paths with considerable slack can now be scrutinized for "trade-offs" between facilities to reduce the overall time of the critical path. The most efficient program ·is the one with the greatest number of events having the least possible slack.

Column 11. T_c is the original contract time for the completion of an activity. We are now concerned with the probability of meeting the contract, and therefore go through the following sequence of activities.

Column 12. D indicates the distance in standard deviations that T_c is from T_e.

$$D = \frac{T_c - T_e}{\sigma_{T_e}}$$

Column 13.   The probability, P, of an event occurring at the proposed completion date can be obtained by entering a probability table (see Chapter 9) with the value of D.

This has been a relatively easy problem to solve, but you can imagine the difficulties that would be encountered if there were hundreds of different activities. These more complex problems have been programmed on a computer, but even then there are limits to the size of the problem which can be handled.

PERT/COST

An extension of PERT has been the development of PERT/COST, which not only keeps time under surveillance but also costs. Superimposed upon the usual PERT network is a cost network (Figure 14–26) consisting of cost estimates for each activity. After this planning stage is completed, control is exercised when it is discovered from the feedback of information that costs are exceeding the predictions. One way of reporting the differences between the planned and actual is shown in the PERT Time and Cost Status Reports illustrated below the network. This is just one of the many reporting forms designed to keep management informed of a project's status. Of those available, the Cost Outlook Report and the Schedule Outlook Report (Figure 14–27) are the most easily understood.

Figure 14–26
PERT Time and Cost Status Reports

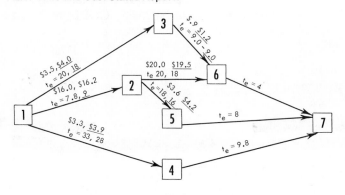

PERT/Cost Network

PERT Time = Cost Status Report												
1st Summary Report for 8/8653 Project for 7/8												
Identification			Time Status						Cost Status			
Begin Event No.	End Event No.	Account No.	Expected Elapsed Time t_e	Scheduled Elapsed Time t_s	Scheduled Completion Date	Latest Allowable Completion Date T_L	Activity Slack $T_L - T_S$	Cost Estimate ($ Thousand)	Actual Cost	Over or Under	Comments
1	3	A-160	20.0	20.0	2/22	3/3	9.8	3.5	4.00	+.5	
1	2	A-183	7.8	7.8	2/10	2/19	9.0	16.0	16.2	+.2	
1	4	A- 68	33.0	33.0	3/7	3/7	0.0	3.3	3.9	+.6	
2	5	A- 51	18.0	18.0	2/28	3/9	9.0	20.0	19.5	-.5	
2											

Figure 14–27
Cost and Schedule Outlook Reports

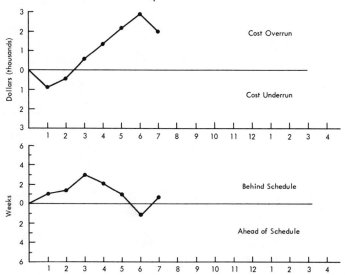

Out of PERT came a diversity of conflicting cost analysis techniques which required standardization before they could become universally acceptable. Two of these supplements to PERT/COST are discussed here:

Time-Cost Option. Most proposals require that only one cost estimate be prepared for each activity. This does not permit determining:

1. The amount of time that could be saved by spending more money;
2. The amount of money that might be saved by extending the completion date.

The time-cost option, illustrated in Figure 14–28, permits the management to make decisions on the basis of technical risks, costs, and time.

Figure 14–28
Time-Cost Option Chart

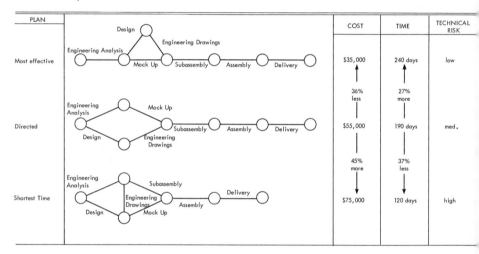

Resource Allocation. This technique is, in general, the equivalent of the cost analysis step of CPM discussed earlier. It can be explained by the series of steps:

1. The PERT/COST network is constructed as is partially illustrated in Figure 14–29.
2. Obtain alternative cost and time estimates for each activity. The number of alternatives for each activity will depend upon the nature of the activity as well as upon the available resources.
3. Select the lowest cost with its associated time for each activity.
4. Calculate the time for the critical path. If the critical path is longer than the scheduled time, recalculate a critical path using other available estimates, and making note of the time saved and the cost increase for each succeeding alternative.
5. If the critical path is less or equal to the permitted time, print-out the time and cost as a possible solution.

Figure 14–29
Resource Allocation Supplement

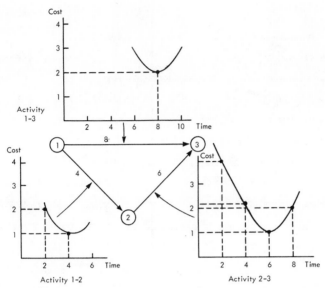

6. If the critical path is longer than the time permitted, review the activities along the critical path and select the one with the lowest cost slope. Change this activity to a shorter time.
7. Calculate a new critical path and continue with Step 6 until the critical path is less than the permitted time.
8. After the critical path has been established by Step 7, consider all of the paths with slack time. Shift activities with slack to longer time and lower cost points whenever possible. The slack points with the steepest cost-time slope should be considered first in revising the schedule.

PERT and PERT/COST have been two important developments for planning and controlling the many activities of large projects. Needless to say, only projects of a relatively small size could be handled conveniently by hand, but this difficulty can be overcome because special PERT programs are available for those companies having computer time available.

Gantt and Critical Path Charting. The network techniques devised for CPM and PERT are not so far removed from the Gantt chart. A combination of techniques worked out by one company is illustrated in Figure 14–30. On this diagram the following is indicated:

1. Completed portion of each activity is shown by shaded line.
2. Cross-hatched areas indicate slack.
3. Elapsed time is shown by a heavy vertical line.
4. Critical path, by heavy line through network.

Figure 14–30
Gantt and CPM Chart

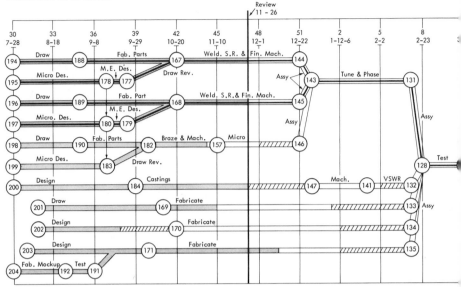

Courtesy of Purchasing Magazi

Line of Balance Technique

The line of balance technique is another method of planning and scheduling production developed by the armed forces to monitor large projects, but it is equally suitable for job shop scheduling of complex assemblies. The line of balance incorporates some of the Gantt charting method and, like it, tells how far a project has progressed as compared with where it should be. It is a management-by-exception tool which promises to find even greater use in the future.

The line of balance technique consists of three charts: the planning chart, the objective chart, and the progress chart. Each is a useful planning and scheduling device, but when used together, they yield much more information than when used alone—and with little more labor. These three charts will be described independently, and then will be combined to illustrate their maximum utilization.

Planning Chart. The planning chart is the first step in the application of the line of balance procedure. The chart in Figure 14–31 is closely related to the Gantt project chart, and as before, the horizontal scale is in units of time with the completion date shown on the right end. Charting starts at the right and is laid off to the left. Each phase of a project is shown as a scaled horizontal bar which is interconnected with the others by vertical lines to form a network. Any activity can be charted and, if necessary, can be subdivided to form monitoring points. The extent to which it is desirable to

Figure 14–31
Line of Balance Chart

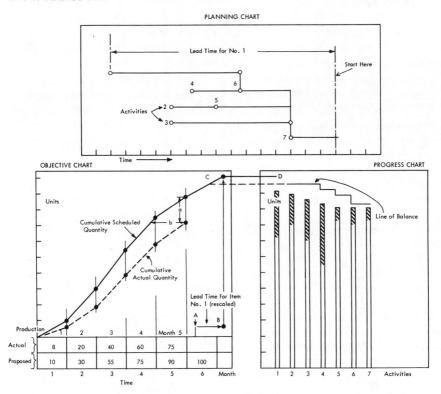

subdivided the work should be decided upon an economic basis. The jobs are numbered starting with the one which extends to the left with the earliest starting date. If two activities have the same starting date, they are numbered in order, starting with the top one first.

The Objective Chart. This chart has quantity scaled on the vertical axis and time on the horizontal axis. But, in addition, it shows—below the time scale—the quantities proposed to be delivered in each time period. At the end of each period the actual quantities delivered are also recorded. It should be pointed out that both of these are cumulative figures.

In plotting the curves the cumulative scheduled quantity is plotted immediately and the cumulative actual deliveries are plotted as the information is obtained. From these curves several pieces of important information are available:

1. The vertical distance between the two curves, a, at any instant shows what the production gap is between the actual and proposed production.
2. The horizontal distance between the two curves, b, shows how far off the schedule is in terms of time.
3. The slopes of the lines are indicative of the production rates and the

differences in slopes give some indication of whether production will eventually catch up or continue to lag behind.

The Progress Chart.   Adjacent to the objective chart is the progress chart. As you will observe, the vertical axes of each are scaled the same. However, on the progress chart the same activities as listed on the planning chart are listed from left to right. On this chart we plot two types of information. First we shall plot the progress by showing the cumulative number of units completed to date. This is done by a vertical bar, as is shown on the chart. Those activities which are nearly completed might also be shown as a phantom bar to give a little clearer picture of the progress. The second step is to draw a *line of balance* on the progress chart, which can be illustrated best by a series of steps:

1. On the objective chart the horizontal date line is scaled for the number of time periods being used. On this time scale a vertical line, A, is drawn, representing a today line. This is equivalent to the caret symbol on the Gantt chart.
2. From the planning chart the lead time for item no. 1 is determined. This lead time is rescaled and laid out on the objective chart starting at A and extending to B.
3. From the end of the lead time, a line is extended vertically to intersect the schedule line at C.
4. Point C is extended horizontally to the progress chart to intersect the projection of the activity bar, as shown at D.

This procedure is repeated for each activity and is shown by the dashed line in the example. This produces a series of lines which, when connected, comprise a stair-step—*line of balance*—on the progress chart.

The line of balance shows where each activity should be if the project is on schedule. If the line coincides with the bar, the activity is right on schedule. If the bar is below the line, that activity is behind schedule and should be expedited. If the bar extends above the line, it indicates that the activity is ahead of schedule.

By means of this technique it is possible to get an overview of a project and tell exactly where any delays might occur and what corrective action will be necessary to bring the project back on schedule.

All the graphical scheduling techniques described here have found their places in industry. One thing should be kept in mind, however: conditions change from factory to factory and even from department to department. You will be wise to learn the principles and you should feel free to adapt them to any conditions you encounter.

MECHANICAL AIDS FOR SCHEDULING

The imagination used in the development of devices for the control of manufacturing systems has known no bounds. Some of these devices have been found useful and remain important adjuncts to systems. Others have had a relatively short life and have been discarded, often to be rediscovered periodically.

These mechanical contrivances have often been plagued by overselling as well as overbuying. Often the product has been sold without concern for the design of the system. There have been cases where extensive installations were sold without adequate product descriptions and time study data being available. Elaborate mechanical aids will not overcome these shortcomings. Management also has been remiss by acquiring such equipment with the hope that managerial incompetency will be obscured.

The urge to gain status, or to have a new plaything, has often been the basis for acquiring the mechanical aid. As soon as the newness wears off, the device loses its appeal, and the aid, no matter how well conceived, falls into disrepute.

Often these aids fail to function because of personnel who may lack understanding of the necessity for the system aid, or who may be temperamentally unsuited to operate the device. Maintaining a schedule board, for instance, requires a person who likes to work with details and accepts the challenge of an ever-changing situation.

The panels discussed in this section are suitable for bar chart displays. They have been found especially suitable for displaying Gantt charts.

The Sched–U–Graph (Figure 14–32) is the Remington Rand company's

Figure 14–32
Sched–U–Graph

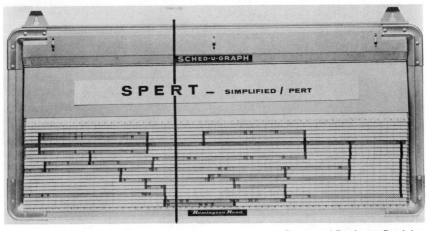

Courtesy of Remington Rand, Inc.

device for making the Gantt chart a more convenient tool. This charting device has varied applications and can be adapted to a number of uses.

The Sched–U–Graph is actually the familiar visible card file enlarged to display-board size. This type of card file consists of a number of overlapping cardboard flaps (as shown in Figure 14–33). Each flap is bound with a plastic lip on the lower edge in which a card can be filed. The flap can be raised to expose the entire card, but in its normal position only the lower margin is exposed.

Figure 14–33
Details of Sched–U–Graph

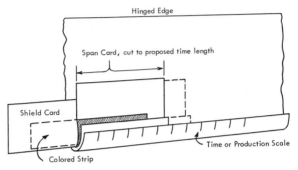

As in the Gantt chart, time or quantity is the common denominator; and in the application illustrated, a time scale—consisting of a folded date strip—is placed in the plastic pocket. The span card, which is placed behind the date strip (as shown), can be cut to any length desired, thus representing different periods of time. A colored plastic strip can be placed inside the pocket of the span card, which can be hidden behind shield cards (as shown). Signals, consisting of movable colored plastic tabs, are available for the edge and can be slid along as desired.

Figure 14–34 shows the Sched–U–Graph used for machine loading and scheduling. On the left are cards representing and describing each work center, such as the radial drill and other machine tools. In the plastic slot for each work center are placed the operation record cards for the various orders presently being manufactured. Each operation record card is cut to the proper length to represent the time it should take to complete the job. A folded "day-strip" is placed in each slot so that the dark edge of the operation record card, when placed in the slot, will appear as a bar. The white spaces indicate free time. The "today-line" is represented by the vertical tab, while progress is indicated by tabs on each plastic strip.

One obvious advantage of the Sched–U–Graph is the ease with which schedule changes can be made; it is only necessary to reshuffle the cards. This is probably one of the most practical devices for charting, and it is quite readily applied to production scheduling, graphical inventory control, and similar applications.

The Produc-trol Board (Figure 14–35) is also suitable for Gantt charting and other bar chart applications. On the left side of the illustration is shown a removable card filing system. The flaps are bound on the lower edge to hold such forms as inventory cards, operation sheets, or other manufacturing

Figure 14-34
Machine Loading and Scheduling

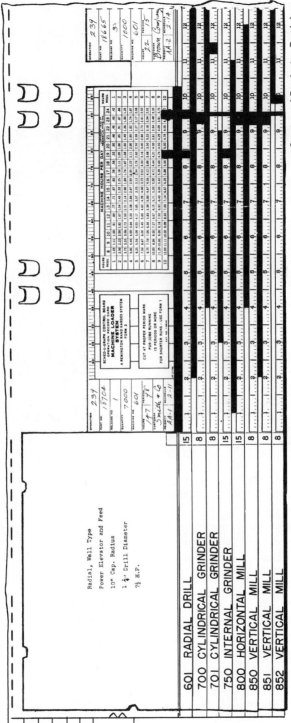

Courtesy of Remington Rand, Inc.

Figure 14–35
Produc-trol Board

Courtesy of Wassell Organization, Inc.

records. Filing information can be placed at the bottom of the form in order to be easily seen. The information on the records, as well as the records themselves, can be simply changed.

Adjacent to the card file is a board which resembles a king-size punch board. For each card in the file there are two rows of holes that extend across the board. One row is equipped with an elastic string which can be stretched across the board to form a bar. The other row of holes has a colored peg which marks off a span of holes representing time or quantity. Across the top of the board is a clip in which a paper strip can be placed, imprinted to represent time, quantity, or other desired information. A vertical, spring-loaded string can be used to indicate a today-line or, in the case of inventory applications, a reorder point.

This control panel can be used to maintain machine schedules, as previously discussed, or the individual work orders can be placed in the file card holders. When this method is used the horizontal distance across the board represents the expected and actual time for each activity. The pegs show when each individual operation will be completed, and the solid horizontal string shows what has been actually performed. A vertical string, which is moved from day to day, represents the today-line. If the horizontal strings representing the work orders are to the left of the today-line, the work is behind schedule; if they are to the right, the orders are ahead of schedule.

The board is also suitable for inventory control applications. The inventory record card can be placed in the file section where it is available for posting. The horizontal string represents the quantity on hand, while the vertical string indicates reorder and other control points. Care must be taken in selecting the units to display on the board. For example, a manufacturer of prefabricated houses would wish to reduce the component requirements to terms of houses; otherwise the record for bundles of shingles would extend off the board to the right while front doors would be hardly noticeable.

The Rol–a–Chart (Figure 14–36) offers the advantage of a continuous

Figure 14–36
Rol–a–Chart

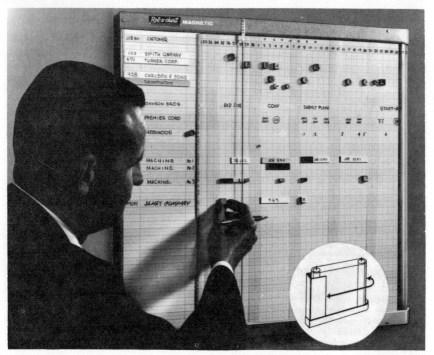

Courtesy of Wm. A. Steward Co., Rol-a-Chart Division.

charting surface in the form of a plastic belt which can be moved horizontally under a vertical, elastic, today-line. The plastic is transparent and is backed up by a permanently gridded surface which may be used to represent time or quantity units.

On the left side of the chart is a stationary section on which can be placed the items to be charted, such as work orders, work centers, and inventory items. The surface of the board accepts grease pencil markings (which are easy to erase). Eighty items can be listed vertically on this chart while the one-half-inch blocks make it possible to record 168 units on the horizontal axis. A special feature of this board allows the use of magnetic ceramic blocks and plastic strips which are also acceptable for grease pencil use. This chart is adaptable to the Gantt and other charting techniques which have been discussed.

Summary

Scheduling is probably the most difficult problem encountered by the production control department.

A production facility has a certain capacity which may be adjusted by adding facilities, working extra shifts, changing methods, and other ways which may be desirable or undesirable. Unfortunately, capacity cannot be changed quickly or without cost so to do so must be given every consideration.

If the capacity is established at a certain level, then the requirements, as expressed by work orders, should match. This balancing of capacity and requirements is an extremely difficult task requiring all of the managerial skill available.

The master schedule not only establishes the time that a task is done but also serves as authority for production. It is one of the more important manufacturing documents.

Until the advent of the computer, scheduling was primarily a graphical process. The graphical processes such as the Gantt chart, CPM, PERT, and line of balance are still important techniques and are to be found in the factory even though computers are available. Often they are more useful than the computer models and have either supplemented or replaced computerized scheduling. Along with the techniques have been developed numerous devices to assist in their implementation.

The next chapter will discuss some of the theory and models which have been developed for scheduling.

QUESTIONS

14-1. How important is it to match capacity with requirements? What would you do about having more capacity than is needed? What would you do if the requirements exceed the capacity? Is a perfect match realistic?

14-2. How would you obtain the plant capacity of a machine shop?

14-3. Where is the information obtained for a master schedule and for a load chart?

14-4. What are the arguments for finite and infinite loading?

14-5. What characteristics would you look for in a prospective employee for the scheduling department?

14-6. Often people feel that a schedule should never be changed once it is made. Why is this true? Should it be true?

14-7. Draw a Gantt chart for your activities during a day. Would this be a useful chart? Why is it difficult to draw?

14-8. Cite two factory functions which could use the Gantt charts to schedule their activities. What difficulties would you expect them to encounter in applying this technique?

14-9. Should an extremely expensive product be scheduled on a forward, or backward, Gantt chart? Explain why.

14-10. Evaluate the comparative advantages of the Gantt chart, PERT, and Critical Path techniques.

14-11. Draw a Critical Path network for some activity such as building a house.

14-12. Compare the Line of Balance technique with the Gantt chart. What advantages does the Line of Balance have?

14-13. What are the advantages of centralized dispatching? What effect will it have on the efficiency of the operations? In what type of industry would it prevail?

14-14. The horizontal bars on a Gantt chart might represent work centers or machines. What would be the advantage of one over the other?

14-15. In what particular type of industry would the Time-Cycle chart be effective? Explain.

14-16. What is essential if the various scheduling techniques are to work?

14-17. Establish a procedure for using one of the commercially available panels as a Gantt chart.

14-18. Compare the various commercially available bar charts and choose the one which you think is the best for some particular application.

15

Scheduling Models and Techniques

THERE has been no workable scheduling theory derived from the innumerable research accounts published during the past decade. The scheduling problem is a complex one which rapidly becomes more difficult as more tasks are scheduled across more facilities. Those who have attempted to solve the scheduling problem have simplified the situations by relaxing the restraints until they no longer represent the real world.

The computer which held such promise has been unable to help extensively because the scheduling problem is too big for the computer's brain and it is not agile enough to solve the problems within the time permitted. The computer has been useful in simulating and testing different scheduling rules. Even then there is some danger in not fitting the solution method to the actual problem.

There have been some practical procedures which have arrived on the scene which can help a production control department do a better job of scheduling. Some, which have become useful in industry, are described in this chapter.

Scheduling Theory

Factory scheduling can be a very complicated activity. It is so complicated that at times it is not even recognized as a problem because compensations are often made for poor scheduling. Poor scheduling might appear as excessive inventories, long lead times for customer orders, or even excessive plant investment. Many managers, in fact, will deny that they have a scheduling problem at all, not realizing the impact of scheduling on all of the other facets of the organization. When a company's scheduling is improved, the effect will appear in some of the areas mentioned before showing up on the plant floor.

Scheduling is so complicated that any practical body of knowledge has been slow to develop. Scheduling algorithms have been developed for very basic shops. But when larger plants are considered, the model soon balloons into one which would require a huge computer with many available hours. The student, however, should see some of the basic models and judge for himself how they can be applied in the real world of industry. The most common and basic algorithms will be presented.

Johnson's Method.[1] The Johnson method will develop a schedule for a basic situation under the following conditions:

1. A *two* work center *flow shop* situation.
2. All jobs have only two operations, and they must first go on work center 1 and then on work center 2.
3. The sequence of jobs on work center 1 must be the same as on work center 2.

Objectives: Determine the sequence of jobs which will minimize the total time for doing all jobs.

Step 1. List the jobs and their operation-processing times for work center 1 and work center 2, as shown in the first table in Figure 15–1.

Step 2. Scan the processing times for the smallest one as shown in Step 2.
   a. If it is in Col. 1, place that job first in the revised table as shown in Step 2A.
   b. If it is in Col. 2, place that job last in Col. 2 of the revised table as shown in Step 2B.
   In case of ties, take the one listed first.

Step 3. Check off the jobs as they are placed in the revised table.

Step 4. Repeat steps until all jobs are scheduled.

Jackson's Method. Jackson's scheduling technique extends Johnson's in that: Jobs may require just one work center or the other or both. This gives the following possibilities:

Mode 1: Work Center 1 precedes Work Center 2.
Mode 2: Work Center 2 precedes Work Center 1.
Mode 3. Only Work Center 1 is required.
Mode 4: Only Work Center 2 is required.

The procedure using Jackson's method is illustrated in Figure 15–2.

---

[1] The development of the proof for these models appeared originally in the *Naval Research Logistics Quarterly* (1954), pp. 61–68.

Figure 15–1
Scheduling by Johnson's Rule

Step 1. List the Jobs

Check-off Column	Job No.	Operation Processing Times	
		Work Center 1	Work Center 2
(Step 3) ✓	1	8 hours	9 hours
✓	2	4	(3)—(Step 2B)
✓	3	6	4
✓	4	3	7
✓	5	(2)(Step 2A)	7
✓	6	5	10

Step 2. List of Jobs in Optimum Schedule

	Operation Processing Times	
	Work Center 1	Work Center 2
5	(2)	7
4	3	7
6	5	10
1	8	9
3	6	4
2	4	(3)

Step 1.   Sequence the Mode 1 jobs by Johnson's rule.

Step 2.   Sequence the Mode 2 jobs by Johnson's rule.

Step 3.   Mode 3 and 4 jobs will have no effect on the minimum completion time.

Follow this rule:
Work Center 1:
Mode 1 before Mode 3 before Mode 2
Work Center 2:
Mode 2 before Mode 4 before Mode 1

You may find that these two simple models will have some application in a factory. But you are more likely to find that there are a number of work centers instead of two, and the orders will have perhaps 20 or 30 operations instead of two. In reality, things have a habit of not happening as planned. Tools break, materials are not delivered, processes take longer than anticipated, so that instead of a static situation we have a highly dynamic situation. It is just too complex a problem for the computer to cope with, at least yet.

Let us turn our attention to what is being done to solve scheduling problems in the factory. The ensuing discussion will present the methods which are being used in industry.

Figure 15–2
Scheduling by Jackson's Rule

		Original Schedule		
Mode	*Job No.*	*Op. No.*	*Shaper Work Center 1 (hours/job)*	*Resaw Work Center 2*
2	1	10		5 hours
		20	3 hours	
2	2	10		3
		20	2	
1√	3	10	4	
		20		1
1√	4	10	8	
		20		2
2	5	10		9
		20	7	
1√	6	10	5	
		20		3
1√	7	10	2	
		20		3
1√	8	10	8	
		20		4
1√	9	10	8	
		20		3

	Revised Schedule 1 (using Jackson's rule)		
	Job No.	*Work Center 1*	*Work Center 2*
Step 1			
	7	2	3
	9	8	3
	8	8	4
	4	8	2√
	1	4	1√
Step 2			
	2	2	3
	1	3	5
	2	7	9

Slotting Technique for Scheduling

The *slotting* technique for scheduling is more a time study substitute than a scheduling technique and is suitable for a plant with few or no job time standards. Basically, it is slotting a job into a time slot on the basis of its similarity to another job.

Time slots are based on a number of bench-mark jobs which have had times established by stopwatch time studies or predetermined times. The steps for slotting by the slotting technique are:

1. A limited number of common bench-mark jobs are measured by stop-watch time studies or predetermined times. These are used to develop a *slotting spread* sheet.
2. When a new job is to be scheduled, the time is determined by selecting the bench-mark job which most closely resembles the job under consideration. These times, with reasonable modifications, are used for scheduling purposes.

As in other methods for timing tasks, a performance rating may be obtained.

$$\text{Performance } \% = \frac{\text{Slotted hours}}{\text{Actual hours}} \times 100\%$$

This will probably not give the accuracy that time studies do, but for comparing the costs it is a very useful technique.

Short Interval Scheduling (SIS)[2]

This method of scheduling is more a philosophy than it is a technique. It is a philosophy which has been successfully employed in factories, warehouses, department stores, and offices where large clerical groups are employed.

Short-interval scheduling is a method of assigning a planned quantity of work to be completed in a specific time. It also includes a means of determining if the quantity of work has been completed within the time specified.

The important points of this technique are:

The work for one work center is scheduled by one individual.
A *reasonable* amount of work is assigned to an employee to be completed in a specified time limit.
All work loads are scheduled in advance.
Performance is checked regularly. This assures work being completed on schedule and any necessary changes can be made.

The time interval assigned is usually one hour—if a company can control the 60 minutes in an hour, it can improve its efficiency.

The first step in inaugurating an SIS system is the classification of all jobs in a department with realistic standards of hourly performance. Backorders are checked and economical lot sizes determined which will help in projecting manpower requirements for the future. The work is then assigned to the department.

If learning is involved, the quantity assigned during the first periods will be less than that prescribed by the standard. However, the supervisor works closely with the individual doing the initial work until the standard is met.

---

[2] Martin R. Smith, *Short-Interval Scheduling: A Systematic Approach to Cost Reduction* (New York: McGraw-Hill Publishing Company, 1968).

The department manager receives a report of hourly performance for all workers whether or not they fall behind schedule. This information is recorded on a *schedule control form*. This lists both the production of the individual and the department and gives the efficiency on an hourly basis and on a cumulative basis. Any time a schedule is missed, the department manager makes every effort to help the individual become proficient.

Since short-interval scheduling is a philosophy rather than a technique, each system has its unique characteristics. Distilled, the common elements appear to be:

Reduce fluctuations in the volume of work by regulating all work coming into the system, controlling the backlog of work by dispatching only the amounts of work the schedule has been planned to take, and regulating the sequence of the processing steps.

Make provision for handling nonroutine or exceptional work, because only routine work can be processed in the schedule system and exceptional cases must be handled outside it.

Identify all the operational steps of the system and change sequence to get the best possible work flow.

Do everything possible to improve methods and layout to get the best possible performance.

Time all operations and determine the capacity of each work center.

Determine the volume of work that can be done at each work center.

Determine the overall time table for the entire process.

Determine the time interval for dispatching the batches of work to the work centers.

Staff each work center so it can comfortably process all the work it receives during each interval of the schedule, and have a sufficient number of people cross-trained to staff any of the stations should any become understaffed.

Establish a central dispatching point to release work in the proper amounts at the proper time and the proper order, follow work in process to see that the schedule is being met, and place overall authority and responsibility for dispatching work according to schedule in one individual. (But reserve assignment of work to individual workers to first line supervisors.)

There are a number of advantages credited to short-interval scheduling, but probably the most important one is that the workers are assigned jobs on a short-range basis with attainable goals.

Even-Flow Scheduling Technique

The *even-flow scheduling technique*[3] takes advantage of the fact that we

---

[3] Touche, Ross, & Co., 1633 Broadway, New York City. Developed by Sanford S. Ackerman.

can estimate the *total* amount of time required for a group of operations very precisely because the errors of individual job estimates will tend to cancel out. The effect is to reduce the time allowance needed to guard against schedule interference.

In the day-to-day operations of a job shop, one can expect to find the elapsed time for a job to be highly correlated with the number of operations. The actual time that a job spends on a machine is relatively small, and the moving and waiting times are about the same for all operations.

The even-flow technique consists of designating a time period which is approximately equal to the average elapsed times required for operations, setups, and moves. These are shown as "blocks" of time on the schedule chart in Figure 15–3 and are often referred to as *time buckets*.

Figure 15–3
Even-Flow Scheduling

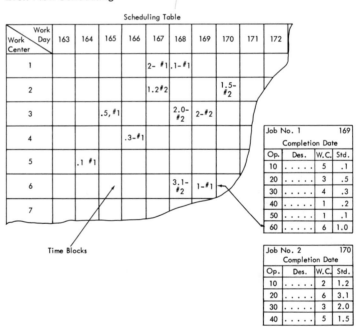

Using the data available on the operations sheet, a backwards schedule from the due date is made by allowing one time period for each operation. From this we know within which time period each operation must be performed to keep the job on schedule. This chart also shows the load for each work center for each time period.

The dispatching rule for the even-flow technique is: Any operation within a time block can be run without concern for sequence. It is just necessary for all jobs to be completed within the block to maintain the schedule.

If a job is late in arriving within the time block and has an earlier due date than the rest, it is given precedence so that it may catch up. If more than one job is running late, precedence is given to the one with the earliest due date.

Capacity planning can be visualized by a simple bar chart as shown in Figure 15–4. A time-block length corresponds to the average elapsed time for

Figure 15–4
Capacity Planning Chart

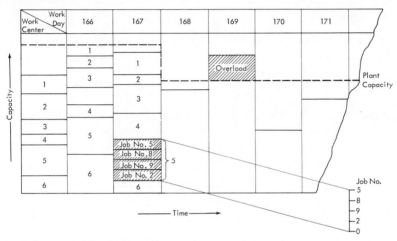

the operation, setup, and move for jobs. These blocks of time are loaded with the accumulation of jobs for each work center.

The time periods (working days) are illustrated along the horizontal axis. In each time period the blocks illustrate the time required and the capacity for each machine center. The vertical distance is scaled from the accumulation of job-times as shown at A.

If there is sufficient time, jobs will flow from one time period to another without delay. Imbalance may be compensated for by changing worker assignments and shifting of jobs to other time periods.

Critical-Ratio Scheduling

Critical-ratio scheduling[4] is a technique for establishing and maintaining priorities among the jobs in a factory. The critical ratio itself is an *index* by which the relative priorities of jobs can be determined. It is a *time* relationship between when a product is required and when it can be supplied. In its simplest form, the critical ratio may be stated:

---

[4] Adapted from material developed by Rath and Strong, Inc., Boston, Mass. Reported by Arnold O. Putnam in the 1966 *Proceedings of the American Production and Inventory Control (1) Society's Annual Conference.*

$$\text{Critical ratio} = \frac{\text{Demand time}}{\text{Supply lead time}}$$

For example:

$$\text{Critical ratio} = \frac{\text{The product is needed in 30 days}}{\text{The product will be available in 40 days}}$$

$$\text{Critical ratio} = \tfrac{3}{4}$$

It becomes obvious that the processing time must be reduced to $\tfrac{3}{4}$ of the normal expected time or the product will not be delivered on time.

The importance of the critical-ratio *value* can be summarized:

Greater than *one* means that there is ample time to finish the job ahead of schedule.

Exactly one means that the job is just on schedule.

Less than one means that the job is critical and will have to be expedited if it is to be completed on schedule.

The farther behind a job is, the *lower* the critical ratio and the more critical the job is.

Advantages of Critical-Ratio Scheduling

1. The relative priorities among jobs are established on a common basis.
2. The status of each particular job can be determined.
3. The schedule can be adjusted automatically when there are changes in demand or job progress.
4. Both stock and make-to-order jobs can be compared on a common basis.
5. A properly installed critical-ratio system, with the necessary feedback, will help to eliminate expediters and the scheduling crises of production.
6. Critical-ratio scheduling is a dynamic system.

Development of the Critical Ratio. The next objective is to develop the information for the critical ratio. The critical ratio can be expressed in a more useful form:

$$\text{Critical ratio} = \frac{\text{Date required} - \text{Today's date}}{\text{Days required to complete the lot}}$$

To keep the development of the critical ratio straight, the following topics will be discussed in this order: (1) Denominator for all critical ratios; and (2) Numerator for critical ratios, including the make-to-order situation and the make-to-stock situation.

Denominator of Critical Ratio. The denominator of the critical ratio is the standard lead time remaining for the job. This quantity, LTR, is defined as the expected elapsed time required for the job to pass through predetermined work centers from its present location until it is completed.

$$LTR = \text{Total lead time} - \text{Lead time of operations completed}$$

The lead time, LT, for a particular operation can be expressed:

$$LT \text{ (days/lot)} = SQ \text{ (days/lot)} +$$
$$\frac{SU(\text{hours/lot}) + [Q(\text{parts/lot}) \times R(\text{hours/part})]}{H(\text{hours/day}) \times E(\text{efficiency}\%)}$$

Where:

LT = Lead time for an operation in days per lot.
SQ = Standard queue allowance in days per lot.
SU = Set-up time in hours per lot.
Q = Parts per lots.
R = Standard time in hours per part.
H = Hours worked per day.
E = Efficiency in percentage.

This equation can be expanded to include the total lead time as shown by Figure 15–5.

Figure 15–5
Schedule of Activities

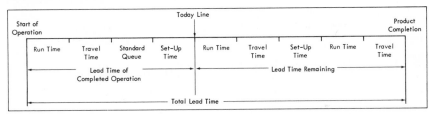

$$TLT = P + \sum_{1}^{N}\left[SQ + \frac{SU + QR}{H \times E}\right] + \sum_{1}^{N} T$$

TLT = Total lead time, days/lot.
P = Order preparation time.
T = Added allowance for transit time between operations where applicable, days/lot.
N = Number of operations.

It is possible to simplify the formula in some situations. For example, if the queue times are long compared with the set-up and run times, the equation may be simplified to:

$$TLT = 0 + \sum_{1}^{N}\left[SQ + T \right]$$

To make the critical-ratio scheduling technique function, it becomes obvious that there must be more information than is normally available. In addition to the standard times for the operations, the set-up times and the queue times must also be available.

Queues are normally found at each production center to serve as a buffer between operations and reduce the probability of shutting down because of lack of material. The queue also permits some efficiencies in arranging the work in economic sequences, consequently minimizing the set-up costs.

Numerator of Critical Ratio. The numerator for the critical ratio will depend on whether we are concerned with a make-to-order situation or a make-to-stock situation.

1. Required time for make-to-order situation is simply stated by the following expression:

$$\text{Demand time} = \text{Days remaining until the required date}$$
$$\text{Demand time} = \text{Due date} - \text{Today's date}$$

The time is measured in working days of course. The due date, although subject to change, is a firm commitment for customer's requirements or assembly requirements.

2. Required time for make-to-stock situation can be visualized easier by referring to the familiar saw-tooth chart of inventory control theory, Figure 15–6.

Figure 15–6
Make-to-Stock Situation

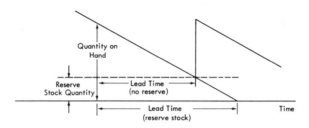

As can be seen, the time required for a make-to-stock product is the lead time, and if the management is willing to run the risk that the stock will be reduced to zero before replenishment, the lead time can be simply stated:

$$\text{Lead time} = \frac{\text{Quantity on hand}}{\text{Average quantity used/time}}$$

However, if the management does not wish to take a risk, the "base" of reserve stock may be inserted. As shown by the chart, the greater this safety stock, the greater the lead time will be.

The critical ratio can reflect the condition of stock being used faster or slower than the average and therefore becomes a dynamic scheduling technique.

Example of Critical-Ratio Scheduling. In this example, consider a small job shop with six common job routings as shown in Figure 15–7. The following paragraphs, which are keyed to the chart with letters, will explain each entry.

A.   Shown here are six common routings which range in complexity from

Figure 15–7
Example of Critical-Ratio Scheduling

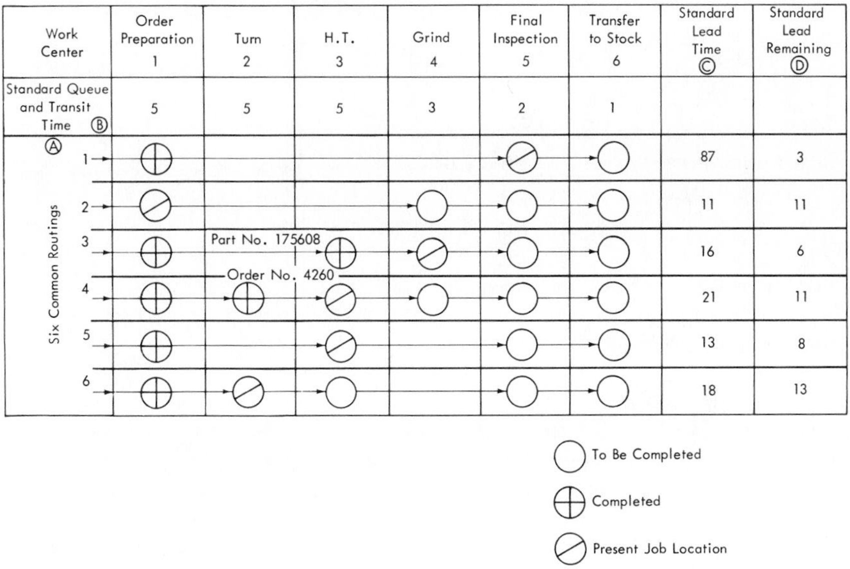

Work Center	Order Preparation 1	Turn 2	H.T. 3	Grind 4	Final Inspection 5	Transfer to Stock 6	Standard Lead Time ©(C)	Standard Lead Remaining ©(D)
Standard Queue and Transit Time (B)	5	5	5	3	2	1		

Routing		Standard Lead Time (C)	Standard Lead Remaining (D)
1		87	3
2		11	11
3	Part No. 175608 Order No. 4260	16	6
4		21	11
5		13	8
6		18	13

○ To Be Completed

⊕ Completed

⊘ Present Job Location

simple reinspection of a purchased part, no. 1, to processing in all production centers, no. 4.

B. *Standard Queue and Transit Time.* Each work center has a standard queue and transit time allowance as shown. All jobs are expected to flow through a given center within this standard time. The total amount of work at a center at one time should not exceed the standard time.

C. *Standard Lead Time.* The standard lead time for a job depends on its routing and the queue allowance for the work centers through which it passes. Standard lead times for six jobs are shown, using the simplified lead time formula.

D. *Job Progress and Lead Time Remaining.* An active job for each routing is shown with its present location indicated. Compare routings 4 and 5. Two jobs are presently located at work center no. 3. Because of the different routings, however, routing 4 has three days longer lead time remaining. All other things being equal, it should be produced after routing 5.

For the purpose of our example, we will be concerned with routing 3 where we see that part no. 175608 is being produced for job order no. 4260.

The questions which we might ask about this part are:

Is the job on time?

If behind schedule, how does it compare with other jobs at the work center?

Can it be expedited to completion on time without putting other jobs behind?

Can all jobs in queue be produced on time?

Is total shop load such that some adjustment in the production rate should be made in order to maintain standard lead times?

To do the calculations necessary for part no. 175608, which is a stock item, the following is known:

$$\text{Stock on hand} = 18 \text{ units}$$
$$\text{Safety stock} \quad = 12 \text{ units}$$
$$\text{Average daily usage} \quad = 2 \text{ units}$$
$$\text{Lead time remaining} = 6 \text{ days}$$

$$\text{Critical ratio} = \frac{\text{Demand time}}{\text{Supply time}}$$

and the demand time:

$$\frac{\text{Stock on hand} - \text{Safety stock}}{\text{Average daily usage}} = \frac{18 - 12}{2} = 3$$

and the supply time: Lead time remaining is six days.

$$\text{Critical ratio} = \% = 0.50$$

One can conclude that the usage to date since the job was started has been above average or the job has been delayed in process. In either case, progress must now be accelerated to avoid a potential stockout. The problem is, how can this be done. It can only be done by looking at the status of other jobs at work center no. 4. This is shown in Figure 15–8.

Figure 15–8
Production Schedule for Work Center 4

			November 20	
Work Center 4 Grinding			Daily Capacity 150 Hours	
		Hours of Production		Critical
Job Number	Part Number	This Job	Cumulative	Ratio
		Critical Jobs		
4592	115604	2.54	—	0.25
3654	223982	3.60	6.14	0.30
4260	175608	4.21	10.35	0.50
4109	598325	2.10	12.45	0.55
3785	600507	9.86	22.31	0.77
Total Critical 5			22.31	1.5 days
		Jobs on Time		
4465	125976	3.95	—	0.92
3987	254801	4.20	8.15	1.05
6507	739767	5.90	14.05	1.12
Total on Time 3			14.05	0.9
		Slack		
4333	439256	11.55	—	1.31
5107	157843	11.77	23.32	1.45
Total Slack 2			23.32	1.6
Grand Total 10			59.68	4.0

This schedule was produced after calculating all critical ratios and sorting them in a low-to-high sequence as shown.

Two jobs have lower critical ratios than job no. 4260. Nevertheless, the critical jobs can be produced today so this job will not sit for the normal three days. Moreover, it will automatically be produced in the proper priority sequence without detailed follow-up, because the critical ratio has slotted it in its proper place near the top of the queue. This means that it is not necessary to locate the job physically and move it to a preferred place in the shop floor queue or to locate all the related documents and change their dates or mark them "Rush."

Information for the entire plant can be organized into a total load summary as shown in Figure 15–9. A number of important relationships can be observed, such as the relationship between the critical and slack hours for a work center. Trouble is impending at A as the number of critical jobs increases for work center number one. When orders exceed production capability, trouble ahead is indicated.

While standard lead times for purchased items are generally known, there frequently is no elemental breakdown into checkpoints, comparable to production work centers, for reporting progress and determining lead time remaining. Once such a breakdown is made, the same critical-ratio formulas used in production scheduling can be applied to purchase order follow-up.

Some or all of the following checkpoints should have standard times associated with them and should have automatic feedback for status reporting:

Requisition forwarded to purchasing.
Purchase order forwarded to vendor.
Vendor acknowledgement received; promised shipping date compared
    with lead time, and LTR adjusted accordingly.
Vendor shipment made.
Order received.
Material inspected and approved.
In stock, available for use.

Of all the scheduling techniques developed in recent years, probably none promises to be as successful as the critical-ratio technique.

Scheduling One Machine for More than One Product

Work center scheduling is used to schedule *one machine* producing a *number* of different products. To place work center scheduling in its proper perspective, consider the situation of one plastic injection molding machine supplying parts for several assembly lines which produce different products. It is obvious that one molding machine could not be set up just to produce one part. The machine's production would be too great and the machine would sit idle part of the time and that would be too expensive. So, the solution is to change the mold from time to time and produce different parts.

Figure 15–9
Total Load Summary

Work Center Number	Daily Receipts		Daily Production		Standard Queue		Actual Queue			Total Load	
	This Week (hrs.)	Average (hrs.)	This Week (hrs.)	Average (hrs.)	Days	Hours	Critical	On Time	Slack	Actual	Average
1	12.0	10.0	10.0	9.5	5	47.5 A	45.0	20.0	6.0	71.0	47.5
2	22.3	21.0	15.5	20.0	5	100.0	75.6	40.2	20.6	285.7	225.0
3	26.5	24.0	19.6	21.0	5	105.0	65.7	32.7	27.3	405.2	335.0
4	19.2	16.1	16.5	15.0	5 × 3	= 45.0	22.3	14.0	23.3	322.6	270.0

Can one machine satisfy the production? How many parts should be produced at a time? And how often should the cycle of mold changes be repeated? These are the kinds of questions which cycle scheduling can answer.

The Language for Cycle Scheduling. As in all techniques using mathematics, a set of terms must be defined. Figure 15–10 shows those which will be used.

Figure 15–10
Language for Scheduling

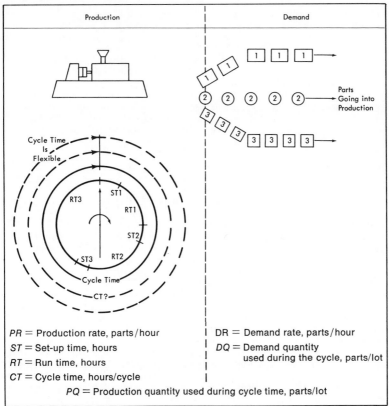

PR = Production rate, parts/hour

ST = Set-up time, hours

RT = Run time, hours

CT = Cycle time, hours/cycle

DR = Demand rate, parts/hour

DQ = Demand quantity used during the cycle, parts/lot

PQ = Production quantity used during cycle time, parts/lot

Development of Equations. It is apparent from the clock face in Figure 15–10 that the cycle time is the total of the set-up times, ST's and run times, RT's, under consideration.

$$CT(\text{hours}) = ST1 + RT1 + ST2 + RT2 + ST3 + RT3 \quad (1)$$

While this example is for three parts, it should be apparent that the equation could be generalized for any reasonable number of parts. This equation for CT presents one relationship which will be useful, but now consider another.

It does not take much imagination to recognize that whatever is *demanded* will have to be *produced*:

Production of part 1 during run time = Demand for part 1 during cycle time

$$(2a)$$

Production of part 2 during run time = Demand for part 2 during cycle time

$$(2b)$$

Production of part 3 during run time = Demand for part 3 during cycle time

$$(2c)$$

so we have:

$$PR\,1 \times RT\,1 = DR\,1 \times CT \tag{3a}$$

$$PR\,2 \times RT\,2 = DR\,2 \times CT \tag{3b}$$

$$PR\,3 \times RT\,3 = DR\,3 \times CT \tag{3c}$$

The dimensions of these equations are:

$$\frac{\text{Parts}}{\text{Hour}} \times \frac{\text{Hours}}{\text{Cycle}} = \frac{\text{Parts}}{\text{Hour}} \times \frac{\text{Hours}}{\text{Cycle}}$$

$$\frac{\text{Parts}}{\text{Cycle}} = \frac{\text{Parts}}{\text{Cycle}}$$

Can One Machine Satisfy Production?   The first question to answer is, will one machine satisfy production? The answer to this question requires substituting the running times, RT's, of equations $(3a)$, $(3b)$, and $(3c)$ into equation (1).

$$RT\,1 = \frac{DR\,1 \times CT}{PR\,1} \tag{4a}$$

$$RT\,2 = \frac{DR\,2 \times CT}{PR\,2} \tag{4b}$$

$$RT\,3 = \frac{DR\,3 \times CT}{PR\,3} \tag{4c}$$

$$CT = ST\,1 + \left(\frac{DR\,1 \times CT}{PR\,1}\right) + ST\,2 + \left(\frac{DR\,2 \times CT}{PR\,2}\right) + ST\,3 + \left(\frac{DR\,3 \times CT}{PR\,3}\right)$$

$$CT = ST\,1 + ST\,2 + ST\,3 + CT\left(\frac{DR\,1}{PR\,1} + \frac{DR\,2}{PR\,2} + \frac{DR\,3}{PR\,3}\right)$$

$$CT = \frac{ST\,1 + ST\,2 + ST\,3}{1 - \left(\dfrac{DR\,1}{PR\,1} + \dfrac{DR\,2}{PR\,2} + \dfrac{DR\,3}{PR\,3}\right)} \tag{5}$$

For CT to be positive, the sum of the DR/PR's in the denominator must be less than one. If this requirement holds, then one machine can satisfy production, and the cycle time can be calculated from equation (5), and the run times for each part are obtainable from equations $(4a)$, $(4b)$, $(4c)$, and so on.

Example of scheduling an injection molding machine. The information available for an injection molding operation is shown in Figure 15–11.

Figure 15–11
Scheduling an Injection Molding Machine

Part Number	Demand Rate DR (parts/hour)	Set-up Time ST (hours)	Production Rate PR (parts/hour)
1	600	1.25	3,000
2	500	1.25	2,000
3	200	0.75	2,000
4	300	0.25	1,000
		3.50	

Solution:

$$\frac{DR\ 1}{PR\ 1} = \frac{600}{3,000} = 0.20$$

$$\frac{DR\ 2}{PR\ 2} = \frac{500}{2,000} = 0.25$$

$$\frac{DR\ 3}{PR\ 3} = \frac{200}{2,000} = 0.10$$

$$\frac{DR\ 4}{PR\ 4} = \frac{300}{1,000} = \underline{0.30}$$

$$\text{Sum of} \left(\frac{DR}{PR}\right)\text{'s} = 0.85$$

Since 0.85 is less than one, a cycle time, *CT*, exists and should be repeated every 23.33 hours according to the following equations:

$$CT = \frac{3.50}{1-0.85} = 23.33 \text{ hours/cycles}$$

With this cycle time available, the time each product is to run can be found —which was the third question posed at the start of this discussion.

$$RT\ 1 = \frac{DR\ 1}{PR\ 1} \times CT = \frac{600}{3,000} \times 23.33 = 4.666$$

$$RT\ 2 = \frac{DR\ 2}{PR\ 2} \times CT = \frac{500}{2,000} \times 23.33 = 5.833$$

$$RT\ 3 = \frac{DR\ 3}{PR\ 3} \times CT = \frac{200}{2,000} \times 23.33 = 2.333$$

$$RT\ 4 = \frac{DR\ 4}{PD\ 4} \times CT = \frac{300}{1,000} \times 23.33 = \underline{6.999}$$

$$19.831$$
$$\text{Setup} \quad \underline{3.500}$$
$$23.331 \text{ hours/cycles}$$

Production Quantities. The quantity of pieces in a production lot, *PQ*, may be obtained from the equations. Since the quantity in a production lot, *PQ*, must equal the quantity used, *DQ*, a check on the calculations can be made quickly, as illustrated in Figure 15–12.

Figure 15–12
Quantity of Parts in Production Lot

Part		
1 .... $600 \times 23.33 = 13,998$		$3,000 \times 4.660 = 13,998$
2 .... $500 \times 23.33 = 11,665$		$2,000 \times 5.833 = 11,666$
3 .... $200 \times 23.33 = 4,666$		$2,000 \times 2.333 = 4,666$
4 .... $300 \times 23.33 = 6,999$		$1,000 \times 6.999 = 6,999$

$$PQ\frac{\text{Parts}}{\text{Cycle}} = DQ\frac{\text{Parts}}{\text{Cycle}}$$

$$PQ\frac{\text{Parts}}{\text{Cycle}} = PR\frac{\text{Parts}}{\text{Hours}} \times RT\frac{\text{Hours}}{\text{Cycle}}$$

$$DQ\frac{\text{Parts}}{\text{Cycle}} = DR\frac{\text{Parts}}{\text{Hour}} \times CT\frac{\text{Hours}}{\text{Cycle}}$$

If the production quantities are not economical or should be increased for some other reason, this can be done by increasing the cycle time.

Parts Consumed during Production. In determining the quantities required for each lot as illustrated in the previous example, it was assumed that the pieces cannot enter production until the cycle is completed. If, however, the material is being produced fast enough to overcome the demand and goes into production immediately, the lot size may be reduced as illustrated in Figure 15–13.

$$PQ1 = (CT - RT1)PR1$$

Figure 15–13
Modified Saw-Tooth Chart

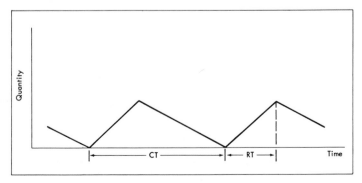

Recalculating the *PQ*'s under this condition:

1. $(23.33 - 4.67)600 = 11{,}196$ parts
2. $(23.33 - 5.83)500 = 8{,}750$
3. $(23.33 - 2.33)200 = 4{,}200$
4. $(23.33 - 7.00)300 = 4{,}899$

These quantities, calculated by either method, are in reality "banks" of material which supply production until the bank can be restored. As in any inventory situation, a reserve should be available to be used in case of production delays.

Described here has been a theoretical way of scheduling one machine. Not included in the calculations have been such unknowns as machine breakdowns, tooling failures, production of scrap parts, or operator deficiencies. It will be up to the scheduler to modify the models to fit these real-world emergencies.

Dispatching Rules

The production control manager could simplify his task as well as that of the foremen and schedulers if there were an infallible *dispatching rule* to follow. The computer could be given a rule or set of rules to follow and all schedules could be worked out in great detail. The scheduling procedure would include *local* dispatching rules for individual machines as well as *global* rules which would take into consideration the interrelationship of all jobs on the shop floor.

To develop universal dispatching rules, the simulation technique has been used. A number of scheduling simulations have been reported which attempt to evaluate different dispatching rules. As you can image, the dispatching rules can be as varied as the imagination permits. One listing of dispatching rules is shown in Figure 15–14.

To obtain some meaning from the simulation studies, you should recognize that there are three things which have to be considered.

1. The shop conditions and environment.
2. The dispatching rule to be tested.
3. The criterion by which the rule was evaluated.

Typical shop conditions and environment established for a simulation include ignoring transportation times between jobs, never interrupting jobs, fixing the plant capacity, never permitting machines to break down, and no assembly operations or jobs which can be reprocessed because of processing errors. If the average plant manager could wish away all of these problems, he would probably be so elated that his dispatching problems would seem trivial.

The criteria in the studies included mean flow time, flow time variance, meeting due dates, and minimizing inventory. Understandably one criterion may not be the one which is important at all times during the factory

Figure 15–14
Dispatching Rules

Random selection for service.
First-come, first-served.
First-in-system, first-served.
Last-come, first-served.
Shortest imminent operation (may include set-up considerations).
Static slack: Due date minus the time of arrival at the machine center.
Static slack per remaining number of operations.
Due date.
Dynamic slack: Due date minus the remaining expected flow time minus the current date.
Dynamic slack/remaining processing time.
Dynamic slack/remaining number of operations.
Two-class shortest operation: Select, first-come, first-served within each of two classes defined by operation length.
Truncated shortest operation: Jobs which have waited more than *k* units of time take precedence.
Alternate shortest operation, first-come, first-served.
Subsequent operation (look ahead): Select job which will go to a queue with less than *k* time units of work waiting. Use shortest operation among jobs for the critical queue.
Two-class truncated shortest operation: Take shortest operation within critical class based on negative dynamic slack; if critical class is empty, take shortest operation.
Cost/time: Pick critical job (negative dynamic slack) by shortest operation; for late, but not critically late, pick largest cost of lateness/operation time; for early jobs, use shortest operation.
Dynamic slack among all imminent jobs: The dynamic slack rule is applied to all jobs in the queue and also to those jobs that are in process and will join the queue after their current operation is complete.
Fewest remaining operations.
Longest imminent operation.
Least work remaining.
Most work remaining.
Greatest total work for all centers on the routing.

---

* J. M. Moore and R. C. Wilson, *A Review of Simulation Research in Job Shop Scheduling* (Washington, D.C.: Production and Inventory Management, January 1967).

operations. Economic conditions, favored customers, seasonal demands, and many other factors will influence what the managers are trying to optimize.

If you became saturated with the research being done on dispatching rules, you would probably be able to make better decisions than those that have not. It is possible that some companies through their own simulations, using their own shops as models, come up with a set of rules that suits their purposes. It is doubtful that any universal set of rules has been developed yet.

Planning Aggregate Production and Work Force

In inventory and production control we are used to working with individual decisions such as are obtained by the EOQ and scheduling models. This discussion will be about *aggregated* decisions, and the problem is one of choosing a decision rule which will minimize the expected value of the *total costs* over a large number of periods for both production quantities and labor force sizes. The production and work force decisions are not for just one product or product line but for the entire production facility.

Assuming that a factory is subject to substantial fluctuations of demand, there are several ways of responding:

1. Hire and fire the work force in response to the orders.
2. Maintain a constant work force and adjust the production rate by over- and under-time.
3. Maintain a constant work force and production rate and allow inventories and backlogs to fluctuate.

One of the most common mathematical models for finding an optimum is the quadratic equation. This equation with its highest power of two develops a bathtub curve as illustrated in the EOQ models. One fortunate thing about these curves is that they are quite flat at the bottom which means that the answers are not critical. Because they are not critical, it does not matter whether the fitting of the curve is done very well. It is this technique which is used in planning the aggregate production and work force.

The equation illustrated in Figure 15–15, along with the glossary of terms

Figure 15–15
Aggregate Production Equation

$$P_t = \begin{Bmatrix} +0.458S_t \\ +0.233S_{t+1} \\ +0.111S_{t+2} \\ +0.046S_{t+3} \\ +0.014S_{t+4} \\ -0.001S_{t+5} \\ -0.007S_{t+6} \\ -0.008S_{t+7} \\ -0.008S_{t+8} \\ -0.007S_{t+9} \\ -0.005S_{t+10} \\ -0.004S_{t+11} \end{Bmatrix} + 1.005W_{t-1} + 153.0 - 0.464I_{t-1} \tag{1}$$

P_t ↑ Production

↑ Number of employees

↑ Units of inventory

Shipments

$$W_t = 0.742W_{t-1} + 2.00 - 0.010I_{t-1} + \begin{Bmatrix} +0.0101S_t \\ +0.0088S_{t+1} \\ +0.0071S_{t+1} \\ +0.0055S_{t+3} \\ +0.0042S_{t+4} \\ +0.0031S_{t+5} \\ +0.0022S_{t+6} \\ +0.0016S_{t+7} \\ +0.0012S_{t+8} \\ +0.0008S_{t+9} \\ +0.0005S_{t+10} \\ +0.0004S_{t+11} \end{Bmatrix} \tag{2}$$

Size of work force ↓
Number of employees ↓
Units of inventory ↓

Shipments

in Figure 15–16, will give you an idea of the typical form of the equation as developed by the originators of this technique.[5]

Figure 15–16
Glossary of Terms

Aggregate production rate	Production per unit of time per week per month, and so on.
t	Time subscript t = Current month. $t - 1 =$ Beginning of current month. $t + 1 =$ End of current month and start of following month.
$c_1, c_2, \ldots, c_{13}$	Cost parameters.
c_t	Costs attributable to one month.
C_t	Expected value of the *total* cost. Sum of costs attributable to T months, expressed in dollars.
P_t	Production in gallons, pieces, and so on, per month.
I_t	Net inventory in gallons, pieces, and so on.
I_{t-1}	Number of units in inventory minus the number of units on back-order at the beginning of the month.
S_t	The forecast of units to be ordered for shipment during the current month.
S_{t+1}	The forecast for next month. Note: S_{t+2} and S_{t+3} are for the second and third month.
W_t	The number of employees required in the current month.
W_{t-1}	Number of employees in the work force at the beginning of the month. $W_t - W_{t-1}$ is the number of employees that should be hired—or fired.
O_t	Order rate.

The cost factors which are included in the planning of aggregate production and work force decisions are:

1. Regular payroll costs.
2. Hiring and layoff costs.
3. Overtime costs.
4. Inventory, back-order, and machine set-up costs.

The costs are derived for different pieces of the total cost equation. The total cost equation which was developed for this technique is:[6]

---

[5] Charles C. Holt, et al., *Planning Production, Inventories, and Work Force* (Englewood Cliffs, N.J.: Prentice-Hall, 1960).

[6] Ibid., p. 58.

$$C_T = \sum_{t=1}^{T} C_t$$

$$C_T = [C_1 W_t + C_{13}] \qquad\qquad \text{Regular payroll costs} \quad (1)$$

$$+ C_2(W_t - W_{t-1} - C_{11})^2 \qquad\qquad \text{Hiring and layoff costs} \quad (2)$$

$$+ C_3(P_t - C_4 W_t)^2 + C_5 P_t - C_6 W_t + C_{12}P_t W_t$$
$$\text{Overtime costs} \quad (3)$$

$$+ C_7(I_t - C_8 - C_9 S)^2 \qquad\qquad \text{Inventory-connected costs} \quad (4)$$

subject to the restraint:

$$I_{t-1} + P_t - S_t = I_t \qquad t = 1, 2, \ldots, T$$

which expresses the relationship for the inventory at the beginning of each month, production during the month, sales during the month, and the month-end inventory.

The following example is presented for those who might like to see how the above equation looks with real data:

$$C_T = \sum_{t=1}^{T} \{[340 W_t] + [64.3(W_t - W_{t-1})^2]$$
$$+ [0.20(P_t - 5.67 W_t)^2 + 51.2 P_t - 281 W_t]$$
$$+ [0.0825(I_t - 320)^2]\}$$

The next step in the procedure is to show the logic behind the development of the equation for *each* cost factor.

1. Regular Payroll Costs. Order fluctuations are reflected in payroll costs. These costs may be represented for a certain wage payment plan by a graph as shown in Figure 15–17 which is expressed by the equation:

$$\text{Regular payroll costs} = C_1 W_t + C_{13} \qquad\qquad (5)$$

Figure 15–17
Regular Payroll Costs

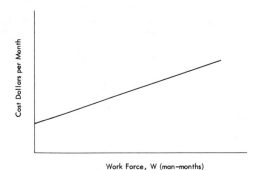

Work Force, W (man-months)

The size of the inventory is established for each time period, such as a month. This established level means that there is a certain fixed cost as represented by the C_{13}. Such a fixed cost term may be ignored unless it makes the quadratic fit better.

2. Hiring and Layoff Costs. The development of the hiring and layoff cost equation can be understood better by using some typical data: The cost of hiring and training, for example, might be \$180/man. The layoff cost—direct cost and morale for example—might be \$360/man.

Notice that these costs do not depend on the number hired or laid off. As illustrated in Figure 15–18, it is expected that future changes in the size

Figure 15–18
Hiring and Layoff Costs

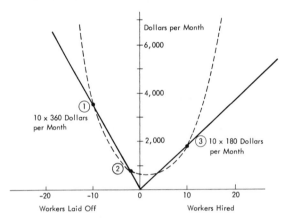

of the work force will average about 10 men per month. Seldom will layoffs exceed 20 men in any one month. The quadratic, by decision, was fitted between + and − 15 workers.

$$Hiring\ and\ layoff\ costs = C_2(W_t - W_{t-1} - C_{11})^2 + C_{13} \qquad (6)$$

Since this contains three constants, three points were plotted on the curve:

Point	Cost	Change in Work Force
1	3,600	−10
2	720	− 2
3	1,800	+10

Substituting these values in the equation above:[7]

$$3,600 = C_2[(-10)(-C_{11})]^2 + C_{13}$$
$$720 = C_2[(-2)(-C_{11})]^2 + C_{13}$$
$$1,800 = C_2[(+10)(-C_{11})]^2 + C_{13}$$

---

[7] C_{13} is added to the cost function to facilitate fitting. Being a constant, it is dropped.

Solving these equations simultaneously:

$$C^2 = 22.5$$
$$C_{11} = 2.0$$
$$C_{13} = 360.0$$

To test the values, follow these steps:

Step 1.   Plot the quadratic over the two linear equations.

Step 2.   If the fit is not satisfactory, select new points and check by Step 1.

3.   Overtime Costs.   If the work force remains stable but the production varies, the fluctuation must be absorbed by (1) overtime costs and (2) idle time costs. *Overtime costs* involve wage payments at the established premium cost which is frequently 50 percent above the regular hourly rate. *Idle time costs* are a waste of labor time which are paid for at the regular rate but include no productive activities.

The cost of overtime depends upon the size of the work force, W, and the aggregate production rate, P. The maximum number of units that can be produced without overtime is KW_t, where:

W = A given work force at time t.

K = Average worker productivity.

The straight-line relationship, Figure 15–19 will exist only if there are no

Figure 15–19
Overtime Costs for Fixed Work Force

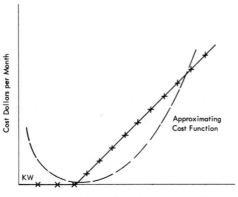

Production Rate, P (units of product per month)

discontinuities or random disturbances in the production process. These, however, are usually present and should be taken into account. The effect is to smooth the curve as shown by the dotted line.

At the first of the month it is not certain whether overtime or idle time will occur. The costs of idle time versus overtime will have to be evaluated when establishing the size of the work force.

The quadratic curve that approximates the expected costs of overtime for a given work force, W_t, and for different production rates is:

$$\text{Expected cost of overtime} = C_3(P_t - C_4W_t)^2 + C_5P_t - C_6W_t + C_{12}P_tW_t \tag{7}$$

As production, P_t, exceeds C_4W_t, a level which is set by the work force, overtime costs increase.

The linear terms, C_5P_t and C_6W_t, and the product term, $C_{12}P_tW_t$, were added to improve the approximation.

This equation has been for only one work force level, and there would of course be a whole family of curves for the different levels under consideration.

4. Inventory and Back-Order Costs. To obtain a total expected cost associated with the net inventory it was necessary to find the relationship between (1) gross inventory and net inventory, and (2) back-orders and net inventory. Data for back-orders and gross inventory accumulated for the past three years are illustrated in Figure 15–20.

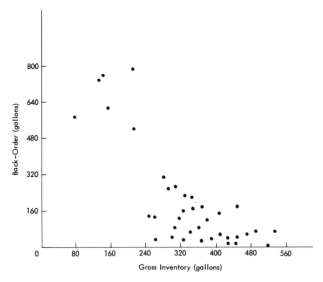

Figure 15–20
Back-Orders versus Gross Inventory

Since the relationship between *net inventories* and back-orders is required, it is derived as illustrated in Figure 15–21. This net inventory was calculated for each point by subtracting back-orders from gross inventory.

By Figure 15–20, back-orders versus gross inventory, and Figure 15–21, back-orders versus net inventory, it is possible to obtain for each month the gross inventory, the back orders, and the net inventory. The cost of holding inventories and back-orders was estimated. For the example given,

Figure 15–21
Net Inventories and Back-Orders

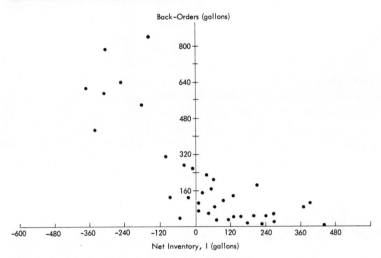

the cost of holding a gallon of gross inventory for one month was $20. The cost of holding a back-order gallon for one month was estimated at $100. The monthly total of these costs is plotted against net inventory in Figure 15–21.

It is apparent that costs rise when net inventory falls significantly below the 300-gallon level because of increasing back-order costs. Negative net inventory means that the back-orders for out-of-stock products exceed the inventory of other products. An increase in net inventory also leads to rising costs because of increasing inventory costs.

The cost function to be fitted to the curve in Figure 15–22 is given by:

$$\text{Cost of holding inventory and back-orders} = C_7(I_t - C_8 - C_9 O_t)^2 + C_{13} \qquad (8)$$

Figure 15–22
Inventory versus Inventory and Back-Order Costs

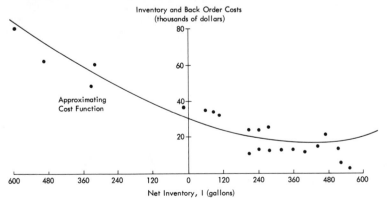

A graphical cut-and-try was used by guessing several plausible values for C_7 and substituting them into the equation:

$$\text{Cost} = C_7 x^2$$

where:

$$x = (I_t - C_8 - C_9 O_t)$$

The plot, made on thin paper, may be laid over the curve and manipulated to obtain the fit in the region of expected inventory fluctuations.

The previous discussion has shown how each component for the total cost has been developed. The originators of this system present an extensive discussion of how to minimize the costs using the techniques of equating to zero the partial derivatives of cost with respect to each of the independent decision variables. The results were presented in the first equation in this discussion.

Summary

There seem to be two bodies of literature on the subject of scheduling. One is the research literature and the other is that of the techniques which have been useful in industry. The research literature has yet to develop a universal system for solving the everyday scheduling problems in the factory, at least without simplifying assumption and exorbitant computer times. The techniques which have been used in industry often leave something to be desired, but at least they can be implemented in many cases.

Short-interval scheduling, as much a supervisory technique as a scheduling technique, has been highly successful in some industries. Scheduling with the critical ratio promises to be an understandable method of scheduling which is not beyond the possibility of calculating.

Aggregate planning has its purpose. Its purpose is the determination of production levels and work force. The costs are forced into a model which can be optimized. The model includes regular payroll, hiring and layoff, overtime, and back-order and machine set-up costs. The model presented indicates an approach to an extremely complex problem and requires more information than is generally available.

Plan your work and work your plan is still a basic tenet of scheduling and will give good results regardless of the technique used.

QUESTIONS

15–1. Why do you think that it has been difficult to develop a workable scheduling theory?

15–2. How useful would the Johnson and Jackson methods be in an industrial situation?

15–3. What are the characteristics of Short Interval Scheduling which make it suitable for warehouse operations?

15-4. What do the following terms mean when used in scheduling:
Time bucket.
Backward scheduling.
Critical ratio.
Finite and infinite scheduling.

15-5. What advantages does the critical ratio scheduling technique have over the others?

15-6. Describe a situation in which one would use the technique for "scheduling one machine for more than one product." Would you consider it worthwhile?

15-7. What objections can you see in each of the first four dispatching rules presented in the text?

15-8. Are the conditions realistic under which the dispatch rules are tested? Explain.

15-9. What difficulties would you anticipate in installing the "aggregate production and work force" procedures?

16

Scheduling Production Lines

PRODUCTION LINE BALANCING is a problem faced by many companies. The production line, as everyone knows, is characteristic of the automobile industry. Not only is it used in the major assemblies but also for subassemblies.

One subassembly, used by the thousands, is a light unit consisting of a bulb, socket, wires, and brackets. On one line producing automobile air conditioners the light bulb assemblies are used as line balancers. Whenever a foreman sees a worker idle, he puts a handful of parts in front of him with the suggestion that he fill up his time by assembling the parts. This is one way that a company can balance its production line and keep all workers productive. Other more complicated ways will be presented to do the same thing.

The highly developed production line is a characteristic of modern industry. The butt of jokes and the theme for movies, the production line is characterized by a work piece being moved along, probably by a conveyor, in an orderly sequence from worker to worker. Each worker contributes, repeatedly, the same amount of work to each work piece as it comes along. The production line, a creative milestone, has been credited to Henry Ford, but undoubtedly less sophisticated workers in a darker age found it to their advantage to divide their work and pass it from one to the next for such tasks as cleaning fish, tanning hides, or harvesting crops. It is the emphasis on the mechanized line with little or no opportunity of delaying the product between workers that makes line balancing of importance today.

Line balancing is the apportioning of the work among the workers along the assembly line with the objective of the workers being employed as efficiently as possible. In so doing, we have to work within certain restrictions as we attempt to minimize unproductive time, or delays, along the line.

Preliminary Considerations

Line balancing[1] cannot be done efficiently without considering these factors which influence the balancing decisions:

1. At what rate does the work piece have to be produced to meet the schedule?
2. How long does it take to produce each work piece?
3. How many workers and work stations are available to meet the schedule?

If the factory is working to a schedule, this will determine how fast the product must come off the line. Of course, it does not all need to come off one line. Two or more lines may be needed, or it may be desirable to use a line just part of the time.

The time to produce the work piece is obtained by some predetermined time method and will not usually change drastically after the line has been balanced. The time can change by improved methods, by different ways of dividing the jobs, or by the effect of learning. Should any of these changes come about, then a new line balance must be made.

The number of workers and facilities for work stations might be the restricting factor if employees are not to be found or additional facilities are not available. The point of mentioning these three factors is that they must be taken into account before line balancing begins. Line balancing cannot be considered just as an isolated problem to be solved in a vacuum.

The problem of balancing production lines can be summarized:

Given a production rate—or cycle time—what is the minimum number of work stations needed without exceeding the constraints of the problem?

Given a fixed number of work stations, what is the maximum production rate—or minimum cycle time?

The Language of Line Balancing

As with all techniques such as PERT, CPM, and others, a special language is used. To help you get some of the language in mind without submerging you in text, see Figure 16–1. Representation of a production line is presented along with a glossary of terms. (Notice that the terms used here were selected because they are meaningful and, hopefully, easily remembered—and not simply because they agree with any standard set of terminology.

The illustrated representation of a production line might be one with which you are familiar, such as is used for filling and labeling bottles, assembling electronic devices, or manufacturing radio cabinets.

At each work station, S1, S2, and so on, there is generally one operator, but there could possibly be more working as a team. Each operator is de-

---

[1] From *Industrial Engineering*, July-August 1961. Copyright American Institute of Industrial Engineers, Inc., 25 Technology Park/Atlanta, Norcross, Georgia 30071.

Figure 16–1
Representation of a Production Line

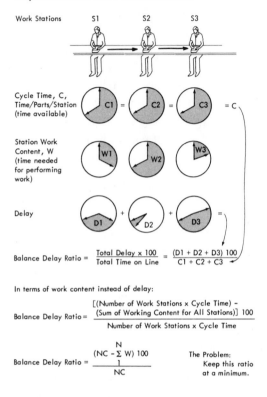

$$\text{Balance Delay Ratio} = \frac{\text{Total Delay} \times 100}{\text{Total Time on Line}} = \frac{(D1 + D2 + D3)\ 100}{C1 + C2 + C3}$$

In terms of work content instead of delay:

$$\text{Balance Delay Ratio} = \frac{[(\text{Number of Work Stations} \times \text{Cycle Time}) - (\text{Sum of Working Content for All Stations})]\ 100}{\text{Number of Work Stations} \times \text{Cycle Time}}$$

$$\text{Balance Delay Ratio} = \frac{(NC - \sum_{1}^{N} W)\ 100}{NC}$$

The Problem:
Keep this ratio
at a minimum.

pendent upon the preceding one, and there are of course no excess parts between stations. This is the characteristic of the production line balancing problem which makes it an unusually difficult one to solve. Each operator has a fixed amount of time in which to make his contribution. This fixed amount of time is illustrated by the first row of clocks in the illustration and is referred to as *cycle time*, $C1$, $C2$, $C3$, through CN. One product comes off the line at the end of each cycle time.

Ideally the *station work content*, illustrated by the second row of clocks, would about equal but not exceed the cycle time. More than likely the station work content will be different from station to station and will be something less than the cycle time. The difference between the cycle time and the station work content is defined as *delay*. It is this delay which is of concern in setting up the assembly line, and we would like to keep it at a minimum.

Balance delay is a measure of the efficiency of the balancing process and is simply the ratio, expressed as a percentage, of the total delay on the line to the total time that the product spends on the line. The development of this expression is given below the production line illustration.

Glossary of Line Balancing Terms

*Production Line.** An arrangement of machines, tools, and workers in which each worker performs a special operation on an incomplete unit, which usually passes down a line of workers until it is finished.

Production Line Balancing: Apportioning among operators on an assembly line, the work needed to produce a product.

Work Station: (In some cases, the same as "operator") An assigned location or zone where a designated amount of work is performed. A work station is usually manned by one person, but it is possible that in production runs of short duration, a person will man two or more work stations.

Station Work Content, W: The time required to perform the work at a given work station. The station work content is the total of the work elements at that station.

Work Element: The minimum rational division of the task. This is the natural minimum time unit beyond which the work cannot be logically divided. We are concerned with the time that it takes to perform a work element as well as a description. These will be listed as a "work element list."

Total Work Content: The total of all the work elements at all the stations along the assembly line, $\sum\limits_{1}^{N} W$.

Cycle Time, C: The time that the work piece spends at each work station.

Delay Time, D: (Also called idle time) The difference between the time that the part stays at a work station and the time it actually takes to perform the necessary work.

Delay time, D = Cycle time, C − Station work content, W

Balance Delay Time: The amount of productive time lost along the production line because of an imperfect division of work amongst the work stations.

Balance delay time $= D1 + D2 + D3 \ldots D\text{-}N$ or $\sum\limits_{1}^{N} D$

Balance Delay Ratio: This is the ratio of the total delay on the line to the total time on the line for a product and is of course expressed as a percentage. The equation for this is given in Figure 16–1.

Balancing Restraints: The restraints to the balancing problem may be placed in one of three categories:
1. Precedence Relations: The technical ordering of the work elements needed to produce a product.
2. Positional Restrictions: Restrictions which are imposed upon the position of the operator or product.
3. Facilities Constraints: Facility restrictions can be indicated on the diagram and described on a subsidiary list of work elements. They may also be keyed to illustrations of the restriction as shown on a schematic diagram.

Precedence Diagram or Graph: This is also called a "directed graph." A graphical display of the line-balancing situation. See Figure 16–2 for the details of this "tool" for line balancing.

Precedence Relations, r: The precedence relationship is shown by an arrow on the precedence diagram. For example: ①→② indicated that 2 *must be* preceded by 1.

Zoning: Grouping the elemental tasks into feasible combinations which take into consideration all restrictions.

* Note: *Production line* is used rather than *assembly line* because it is a more general concept. For example, in a meat-packing plant, *assembly line* would not be an appropriate term.

In the industrial situation, the desired production output and manufacturing restrictions are known, but the cycle time and number of stations are unknown. Therefore, it is necessary to determine the cycle times and number of stations for which the line delay is minimized.

The objective of the line-balancing procedure is to minimize the delay on the production line and, consequently, to improve the balance-delay factor. The techniques discussed here are for this very purpose. The development of these techniques is organized into two parts:

1. Precedence diagraming—a technique for visualizing the problem. It paves the way to a solution of the problem but does not solve the problem.
2. Work element assignment chart—a technique of grouping the elements for each work station. A *heuristic* technique is used here, but later on, modified heuristic techniques and other problem solutions will be presented.

Precedence Diagraming

The *precedence diagram* is a tool used for line balancing. With this simple graphical display of the assembly line situation, it is possible to illustrate the elements of the production line for the purpose of line balancing. It is not the purpose of the precedence diagram to give a solution but is merely an aid to the solution techniques. To this end, the precedence diagram shows:

The technical ordering of the work elements needed to produce a product.

Positional restrictions of the operator and product with respect to the assembly line.

Facility restrictions indicated on the diagram and described on the subsidiary list of work elements. They may also be keyed to illustrations of the restriction as shown by a schematic diagram.

To produce the precedence diagram, it is necessary to have the following information available:

List of Work Elements. The *work element* is the minimum rational division of the task. These elements are in the order of magnitude of suboperations and not smaller elements such as those used in predetermined time systems. The elements are listed and numbered for identification. Beside each element is a description, the time it takes to perform the element and any pertinent comments. An extraneous element such as reloading a rivet gun should be included with its appropriate element.

Schematic Drawing of the Assembly Line. This should be a dimensioned plan drawing of the assembly line with enough detail to carry out the task of assembly line balancing. It should include the main assembly and subassembly lines feeding it. The schematic drawing should also include all of the restrictive facilities.

The common language used in precedence diagraming is illustrated in Figure 16–2.

Figure 16–2
The Language of Precedence Diagraming

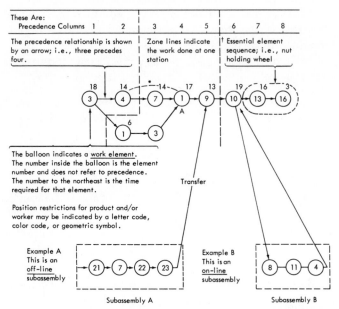

* *Precedence line rule:* No shortcut line may be drawn between two work elements if it is possible to follow an existing path. For example, the precedence relationship shown by the dotted line between elements 4 and 1 above is not permissible.
† *Essential element sequence:* This is a situation in which it is required that elements follow in a particular sequence. These are shown by encircling the elements with a dotted line.

Diagraming Procedure

Products may often be assembled in many different ways because of the *commutability* (exchangeability) relationship of the work elements. A precedence diagram should show all possible feasible ways of ordering the work elements. The steps for making a precedence diagram are shown below. These are illustrated in the example diagram of Figure 16–2 so that you can better understand the procedure.

Step 1.   First elements: The first element or elements are placed in Column 1. Usually there are very few options for the first element. Look for such elements as "place base of cabinet on the line," "place frame on skid," and so on. This element is not necessarily the first one in the list of elements.

Step 2.   Second group of elements: The elements in Column 2 are those which require those in Column 1 to be completed first. If all the elements which must precede this element are in Column 1, then this element under consideration can be placed in Column 2. Connect work elements with *precedence lines*.

Step 3. All succeeding elements: Follow the same procedure for Step 3 as was used in Step 2, and proceed to the right until all elements are included in a column.

Step 3A. Add positional restrictions: As you continue to diagram, add the appropriate positional codes to indicate any restrictions on the product or the operator.

Step 3B. Add fixed facility restrictions: Key the diagram to the work element chart and describe the fixed facilities restriction.

This completes the precedence diagram, a tool of line balancing. The next step is to determine how this tool can be used in the line-balancing procedure.

Precedence diagraming can get out of hand if done for a large complex part, so you may wish to resort to proceeding by "chunks," selecting the major subassemblies to do first.

An interesting point is that for N tasks that can be done in any order, there are N! ways of arranging the tasks. For 4, it would be 24; for 5, it would be 120; for 6, it would be 720, and so on. The various restrictions prevent this number from becoming astronomical.

Illustrating Subassemblies

Off-Line Subassemblies. These subassemblies are developed separately from the on-line operations and may be shown as in Figure 16–2, Example A, on the precedence diagram of the main-assembly line if desired and if space permits. This independent precedence diagram can be illustrated on the same sheet as the assembly line with a precedence line depicting a *transfer* connecting the two diagrams. The subassembly is enclosed with a dashed line and labeled as shown.

Elements which can be performed either on the assembly line or on a subassembly line are indicated by a circle around the balloon giving a warning that they will appear two times. If it is desirable to have them shown three times, then a third circle may be added, and so forth. When inserting the work elements in a subassembly, they should appear as they would if this were the *only* place they were displayed. If they are represented on the assembly line, they should appear in the sequence required for the assembly line.

When it comes time to balance the line and one of the options is chosen, then all the other options are deleted from the diagram and all necessary adjustments are made.

A Heuristic Method

A *heuristic* method of problem solving is characterized by an inherent self-adjusting of the method to produce successively better answers. While an algorithm for the solution of the line-balancing problem would probably be desirable, it quickly gets out of hand because the combinatorial relationships among elements increase dramatically as the number of elements increase.

First, let us discuss some general characteristics of the precedence diagram:

Notice that the work elements in any one column are mutually independent since they are not connected with arrows. This means that these elements within the column can be completed in any sequence without violating any precedence relationships.

Many of the elements may be moved to the right without upsetting the precedence relationship. If the elements are chained in adjacent rows, then the whole chain must be moved to the right.

The solution to the line-balancing problem depends upon a comprehension of the relationships among output, cycle time, and the number of stations on the line. These relationships are discussed here:

Output, O, is the number of products produced during a period of time and may be expressed in units per hour or in similar terms.

Cycle time, C, as defined in the glossary, is the time that the work piece is at each work station, minutes/unit/station.

The number of stations on the line, N, stated as stations/line.

Everytime the line cycles, there should be a product produced, so we can say:

$$O \text{ units/minute} = 1/C \text{ minutes/unit}$$

For a perfect balance, the work content at a station should equal the cycle time, and consequently, there would be no delay. Therefore, the work content for the entire production line would be:

$$\frac{\text{Work content for line}}{(\text{minutes/units/line})} = \frac{\text{Number of stations}}{(\text{stations/line})} \times \frac{\text{Cycle time (minutes/}}{\text{unit/stations})}$$

By substitution, it is possible to derive the following relationship:

$$O = N/C$$

Even without the equation, it seems obvious that the output increases with the number of stations and people working and decreases as the length of the cycle time increases.

The solution starts with knowing the desired output and from this we wish to determine the optimum number of stations and the optimum length of the cycle time. In determining the cycle time, there are two situations which should be apparent:

All the work could be done at one station so that the cycle time would include all the work elements. You'll agree, I hope, that it would be foolish to make the cycle time any greater.

The cycle time has to be larger than the maximum element time—otherwise, the part would be moved ahead before the work was completed—which is not a very desirable situation.

These two statements may be repeated in mathematical terms:

1. Cycle time $\leq$ Work content for all stations.
2. Cycle time $\geq$ Maximum work element.

Thus, it would seem that the cycle time should be someplace between these two extremes.

Next, we need to discuss the problem of determining the number of stations, and we can observe that if we had a zero delay situation, the following would be true:

Number of stations $\times$ Cycle time $-$ Work content for all stations $= 0$

$$NC = \sum_{1}^{N} W$$

$$NC - \sum_{1}^{N} W = 0$$

which can also be stated:

$$N = \frac{\sum_{1}^{N} W}{C}$$

For a given output, there may be many values which might be used for the number of work stations and cycle times. However, a discrete number of work stations is desirable because a fractional number of stations will impose some delays as some worker will only be working part time. Our next step is to find the cycle times for all the possible integer values for work stations. This can be done best by writing the total work content value as the product of prime numbers. For example, if the work content is 10.80 minutes, we can write the following expression:

$$\sum_{1}^{N} W = 1{,}080 = 2 \times 2 \times 2 \times 3 \times 3 \times 3 \times 5 \text{ (all given in hundredths of minutes)}$$

These are the possible cycle times:

$C_1 = 2 \times 2 \times 2 \times 3 \times 3 \times 3 \times 5 =$	10.80	for 1 station	
$C_2 = \not{2} \times 2 \times 2 \times 3 \times 3 \times 3 \times 5 =$	5.40	for 2 stations	
$C_3 = 2 \times 2 \times 2 \times \not{3} \times 3 \times 3 \times 5 =$	3.60	3	
$C_4 = \not{2} \times \not{2} \times 2 \times 3 \times 3 \times 3 \times 5 =$	2.70	4	
$C_5 = 2 \times 2 \times 2 \times 3 \times 3 \times 3 \times \not{5} =$	2.16	5	
$C_6 = \not{2} \times 2 \times 2 \times \not{3} \times 3 \times 3 \times 5 =$	1.80	6	
$C_7 = 2 \times 2 \times 2 \times 3 \times 3 \times 3 \times 5 \approx$	1.54+*	7	with delay
$C_8 = \not{2} \times \not{2} \times \not{2} \times 3 \times 3 \times 3 \times 5 =$	1.35	8	
$C_9 = 2 \times 2 \times 2 \times 3 \times \not{3} \times \not{3} \times 5 =$	1.20	9	
$C_{10} = \not{2} \times 2 \times 2 \times 3 \times 3 \times 3 \times \not{5} =$	1.08	10	
$C_{11} = 2 \times 2 \times 2 \times 3 \times 3 \times 3 \times 5 \approx$	.98+*	11	with delay
$C_{12} = \not{2} \times \not{2} \times 2 \times \not{3} \times 3 \times 3 \times 5$	.90	12	

$C_{13} = 2 \times 2 \times 2 \times 3 \times 3 \times 3 \times 5 \approx$ .83+*   13   with delay

$C_{14} = 2 \times 2 \times 2 \times 3 \times 3 \times 3 \times 5 \approx$ .77+*   14   with delay

$C_{15} = 2 \times 2 \times 2 \times 3 \times 3 \times \cancel{3} \times \cancel{5} =$ .72   15

$C_{16} = 2 \times 2 \times 2 \times 3 \times 3 \times 3 \times 5 \approx$ .66+*   16   with delay

$C_{17} = 2 \times 2 \times 2 \times 3 \times 3 \times 3 \times 5 \approx$ .63*   17   with delay

$C_{18} = 2 \times 2 \times \cancel{2} \times \cancel{3} \times \cancel{3} \times 3 \times 5 =$ .60   18

$C_{19} = 2 \times 2 \times 2 \times 3 \times 3 \times 3 \times 5 \approx$ .54*   19   with delay

$C_{20} = \cancel{2} \times \cancel{2} \times 2 \times 3 \times 3 \times 3 \times \cancel{5} =$ .52   20

* Note: The number of situations must be a multiple of the prime numbers. Otherwise there will be a delay.

If on checking the list of work elements it is found that the largest element is 0.60, then, of course, it would be impossible to have the line cycle on 0.54 minutes, so we can consider 0.60 as the lowest limit for the cycle time.

The cycle time will depend upon how many work stations are desired as well as the quantity which is to be produced. The calculations above determine what the cycle time can be for any number of permissible work stations. They do not indicate whether it is possible to assign the work to stations to obtain the minimum delay. This we must find out in the next step of the solution.

Assignment of Work Elements to Stations

In this step, a work element assignment chart is used as shown in Figure 16–3. The information in each column is summarized here:

Figure 16–3   Name _____
Work Element Assignment Chart for Line Balancing   Date _____

(1) Precedence Columns	(2) Element Number	(3) Transfers and Comments	(4) Work Element Time	(5) Precedence Column Total	(6) Cumulative of Precedence Column	(7) Work Column
1	1		1			
	13	→ 19	4			
	14	→ 19	4			
	15	→ 19	4			
	16	→ 19	4			
	17	→ 19	4			
	18	→	4			
				25	25	

Column 1. These are the numbers in the precedence columns shown at the top of the precedence diagram.

Column 2. Taken from the list of elements and the diagram.

Column 3. *Transfers.* Indicates to what columns of the precedence diagram the elements may be shifted and maintain their precedence relationships.

Column 4. *Work element time.* This is transferred directly from the list of work elements and is the time that it takes to perform a work element.

Column 5. *Precedence column total.* The line drawn horizontally on the chart shows the break between the group of work units performed for each precedence group.

Column 6. *Cumulative of precedence columns.*

Column 7. As stated, this is the column for making any necessary calculations.

From the choice of number of stations, choose one that will fit the requirements of management and proceed to balance the line by:

Step 1. Find the cycle time from the previous calculations.

Step 2. Go down to the point in Column 6 which approximates the cycle time.

Step 3. Adjust the choice of elements, taking into consideration the transfers given in Column 3.

Step 4. After step 3 is completed, continue down the elements until another grouping can be made near the desired cycle time.

The procedure used in Step 3 is analogous to that of packing a given number of equal-size boxes with blocks of varying sizes. The boxes represent the equal cycle times at the work stations and the blocks represent the work elements. The problem is to pack the boxes with blocks as fully as possible to minimize the total voids. As any child knows who has had to put away his own toys, it pays to put the largest blocks in the box first, then the next largest, leaving the small ones to fill in the chinks.

This concludes the heuristic procedure for balancing a production line. In brief, the procedure progressed in two steps, the precedence diagraming procedure and the development of the work assignment chart, with the consequent balancing procedure. The simple example for balancing a production line for a tube assembly will help you grasp the concepts better.

Example of Production Line Balancing

This example of production line balancing is for a tube assembly which consists of six tubes mounted in a shroud. On the aft end of the assembly are a bulkhead assembly and breechblock assemblies. On the forward end is a nose assembly. The drawing in Figure 16–4 is an oversimplified illustration of this product.

Production requirements are 250 units for each eight-hour shift. For each work shift, each operator does 450 minutes of work. The total assem-

Figure 16–4
Tube Assembly

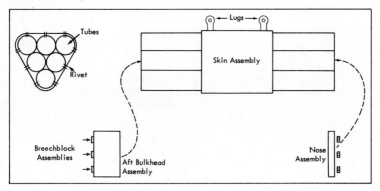

bly time is 10.2 minutes. (Note: These times are estimates and that is why they are in tenths of a minute.)

To meet production requirements:

Station		Units/Shift
1	450/10.2	44
2	450/ 5.1	88
3	450/ 3.4	132
4	450/ 1.7	264

The production line will require four stations and a cycle time of 1.7 minutes. The tables and diagrams on the following pages show:

Work elements in Tube Assembly (Figure 16–5)
Precedence Diagram (Figure 16–6)
Work Element Assignment Chart (original) (Figure 16–7)
Work Element Assignment Chart (revised) (Figure 16–8)

Figure 16–5
Work Elements in Tube Assembly

Element No.	Description	Time: .10 min.
1	Place skin assembly on line	1
2	Install fwd suspension lug	2
3	Install aft suspension lug	2
4	Insert six tube assemblies into skin assembly	8
5	Load rivet inserter tool, insert tool into tube No. 1 and eject rivets, pick up and place collars over rivets, clinch three rivets	5
6	Same as element 5—for tube No. 2	
7	No. 3	5
8	No. 4	5
9	No. 5	5
10	No. 6	5
11	Install aft bulkhead assembly	3
12	Install blkd. assembly retaining rings	12
13	Install breechblock assembly in tube No. 1	4
14	No. 2	4
15	No. 3	4
16	No. 4	4
17	No. 5	4
18	No. 6	4
19	Install nose assembly	5
20	Install six nose assembly screws	12
21	Install main wiring harness	2
22	Remove	1
	Total Work Content	10.2

Figure 16–6
Precedence Diagram

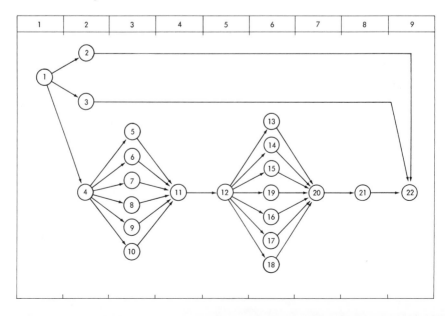

Figure 16–7
Work Element Assignment Chart (original)

Precedence	Element Number	Transfer and Comments	Work Element Time	Precedence Column Total	Cumulative of Precedence	Work Column
1	1		1	1	1	
2	2		2			
	3		2			
	4		8	12	13	
3	5		5			
	6		5			
	7		5			
	8		5			
	9		5			
	10		5	30	43	
4	11		3	3	46	
5	12		12	12	58	
6	13	→9	4			
	14	→9	4			
	15	→9	4			
	16	→9	4			
	17	→9	4			
	18	→9	4			
	19		5	29	87	
7	20		12	12	99	
8	21		3	3	102	
9	22		1	1	103	

Figure 16–8
Work Element Assignment Chart (revised)

Precedence	Element Number	Transfer and Comments	Work Element Time	Precedence Column Total	Cumulative of Precedence	Work Column
1	1		1			
	4		8			
	13		4			
	14		4	17	17	
2	5		5			
	6		5			
	7		5			
	2		2	17	34	
3	15		4			
	16		4			
	17		4			
	8		5	17	51	
4	9		5			
	10		5			
	18		4			
	11		3	17	68	
5	12		12			
	19		5	17	85	
6	20		12			
	21		3			
	3		2	17	102	
		Balance Delay Ratio	0			

This example shows how a company may actually apply the line-balancing technique which was discussed earlier.

Summary

The production line balancing technique discussed in this chapter will help determine the number of work stations needed on a line. Or given the number of work stations, it will help determine the production rate. The two tools for balancing production lines are the precedence diagram and the work-element assignment chart.

QUESTIONS

16–1. Explain in elementary terms what balancing a production line means.
16–2. Define the following terms:
      Production line.   Work station.
      Assembly line.   Heuristic.
      Balance delay ratio.
16–3. Give a step-by-step procedure for balancing production lines.

17

Queueing Theory and Simulation for Decision Making

THE TWO TECHNIQUES, queueing and simulation, are related in that they are used to solve similar types of problems. The distinction between the two is that for queueing theory you must know the characteristics of the arrival and service distributions and in simulation it is not essential to have this knowledge. Queueing theory will be presented first not only to illustrate how it can be used in production and inventory control but also to give you a framework of logic for simulation processes.

QUEUEING THEORY FOR SCHEDULING

This technique not only has direct application in production and inventory control but also is a useful framework for thinking about scheduling and other problems which cannot meet some of the rigorous mathematical restrictions of the technique.

For some reason, waiting line or queueing theory, whichever you wish to call it, can become very involved and difficult to envision. This seems particularly odd because you can hardly pass a day without becoming involved in one or more waiting line situations. Perhaps it is because it is necessary to describe a dynamic situation in which action occurs such as "things arriving" and "things being serviced." Perhaps it is because the models have been ensconced in mathematical jargon which does not convey the dynamic action of the queue. Perhaps it is one subject which should only be taught with moving pictures!

Once you become aware of the queueing mechanism, you will be able to couch many problems in terms of queueing theory. Orders are in a queue waiting to be processed. Tote pans are in a queue waiting to be processed.

Workers are in a queue waiting for materials and tools. Trucks are in queues waiting for docks. Materials handling trucks are in a queue waiting for an elevator. Workers are in a queue waiting to punch time cards. Maintenance orders are in a queue waiting to be completed. Finished goods are in a queue waiting to be inspected and on and on.

You should be aware that the description of the queueing problem can depend upon a point of view. For example, if a number of production workers are being serviced by one materials handling truck, then the workers are the waiting line and the truck is the service facility. But if several trucks are removing material from a production line, then the trucks are the waiting line and the production line is the service. Confusing? Perhaps, but it is an essential concept which you must understand if you are going to solve waiting line problems.

The kinds of questions that can be answered by queueing theory are:

How many service facilities should be available?
How long will the average customer have to wait?
What is the probability of having a certain number of customers?
What is the maximum queue length?
What is the average length of the queue?
How much idle time will there be?

The waiting line is really simple, and if you will just give it a moment of thought, you will realize that many times you have played a part in the waiting line situations to be described. It will help if you will actually try to put yourself in the situations described and that way understand waiting line theory. To become familiar with the queueing terms, a summary is presented in Figure 17–1. Pause a moment to read them.

As you think about it, you will realize that the waiting line can be broken up into zones of activity as shown in Figure 17–2, which are for *arrivals* of customers and *service* of customers—customers being people, trucks, products, and other things. The way the customers arrive and the way they are chosen for service is the waiting line *discipline*. What makes the situation really complicated is that arrivals, services, and queue disciplines may be combined in many ways as we will see.

One thing you can say right off is that the average service time must be great enough to take care of the average arrivals or there will be a queue build-up. This should not surprise you, but it does not mean there will never be a queue build-up at some time. It just will not build up indefinitely. There probably will be one at some time, and depending upon whether you are interested in the customers' waiting time or the services' waiting time, you will probably demand some action.

In discussing *arrivals* and *services* it has been customary to speak of arrival rates such as "customers per unit time," while service is described in time such as "time per customer." This convention might be a little con-

Figure 17–1
Summary of Queueing Terms

Symbol Used

Customer: Anything arriving in a waiting line for service. It is obvious from where this term was derived, and it should be apparent that the term is generalized to include anything in the line, such as trucks, tote pans, machines, and even people.

Waiting line: All of the customers waiting ahead of the service facility.

Queue: All of the customers in the line, including those being serviced.

Population: Made up of customers. Finite population: probabilities of arrival *are* affected by what went before. Infinite population: probabilities of arrival *are not* affected by what went before.

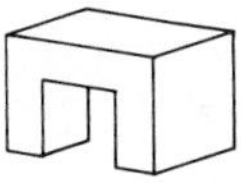

Service channel: That which satisfies the arrivals.

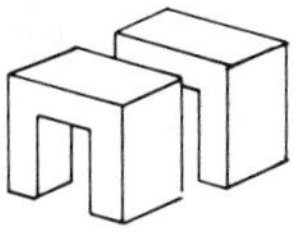

Phases: The number of channels available in *series.*

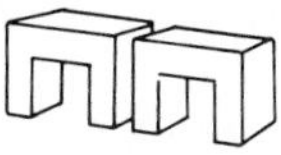

Multichannel: The number of channels available in *parallel.*

Queue discipline: How customers are chosen from arrivals: first come, first served, critical one first, random, and so on.

Figure 17–2
Basic Queueing Problems

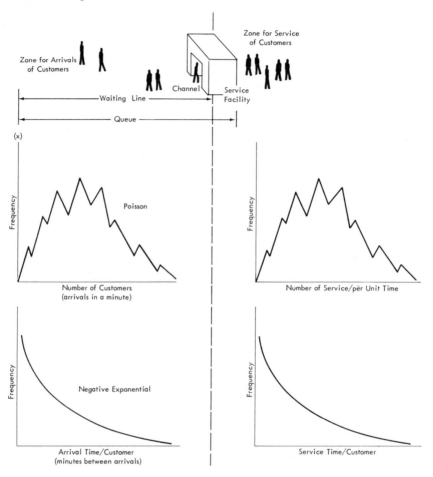

fusing but should not bother you once you realize it. Both arrivals and services rates generally follow the Poisson distribution, while times follow the negative exponential distribution illustrated.

Description of Elementary System

As pointed out there are two major activities in the elementary system—arrivals and services. We must be able to predict the characteristics of these two activities so we have two choices: either describe the activities if we can with easily manipulated equations for the arrival and service distribution or resort to the simulation technique which will be explained later. For some very elementary systems it has been found that the Poisson and negative exponential distributions are descriptive and useful in queueing problems because they are single parameter distributions with the mean and variance being equal, which simplifies the derivation of the waiting line equations. Tests have shown that the Poisson is a good model for arrivals and also fits some service situations. If in doubt, one should collect data and evaluate the fit to determine if the data behaves like a Poisson process.

The first illustration is for an elementary queueing situation. Figure 17–3

Figure 17–3
Queueing Examples

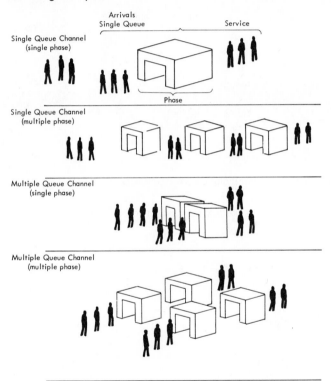

shows queueing examples which become successively more complicated. These can be further complicated by different queueing disciplines which can include such varied situations as random choice; first come, first served; basis of need; and others.

Breaking with the character of this material, the equations for the simple queueing situation are presented (Figure 17–4) without their full development. If you are applying the technique, you will probably find the conditions too restrictive for other than the basic set of equations presented. A complete development of the theory would take a number of pages for adequate treatment.

Figure 17–4
Equations for Solving Basic Queueing Problems

Conditions: Poisson arrival rates.
              Exponential service times.
              First come, first served queue discipline.
              Mean service time is greater than the mean arrival rate.

		Greek Notation
Mean arrival rate $= AR$	arrivals/time	λ, lambda
Mean service rate $= SR$	served/time	μ, mu
Load factor $= LF = AR/SR$		ρ, rho
(Utilization factor)		

	In Terms of Arrivals and Service	*In Terms of Load Factor*
Expected waiting time $=$	$\dfrac{AR}{SR(SR - AR)}$	$\dfrac{LF^2}{AR(1 - LF)}$
Expected waiting line length $=$	$\dfrac{AR^2}{SR(SR - AR)}$	$\dfrac{LF^2}{1 - LF}$

Probability of n units in the system P_n

$$\left(1 - \frac{AR}{SR}\right)\left(\frac{AR}{SR}\right)^n \qquad\qquad (1 - LF)\, LF^n$$

Expected fraction idle time $= 1 - LF$

Expected time in queue (includes one being served) $= \dfrac{1}{SR - AR}$

Expected queue length (includes one being served) $= \dfrac{AR}{SR - AR}$

An Application of Queueing Theory

A manufacturer of ice-cream items is considering changing the second step of the production of a specialty item. The item is molded, placed on a stick, and then dipped.

	Items/Hour
1st operation–molding	48
2d operation–dipping	
Process A	60
Process B	50
Process C	45

The items are molded and enter a freezing tunnel which holds 12 items. The items can only be exposed to the warm air in the plant for a maximum of 15 seconds. The first question to be asked is whether the process can keep up with the molding.

$$\text{Load factor, } LF = \frac{AR}{SR} = \frac{48}{60} = 0.8,\ \frac{48}{50} = 0.96,\ \frac{48}{45} = 1.06$$

It would not have taken the equations to decide this. But it is nice to know that it works for this situation. Process C drops out as a solution.

The second question to ask is whether the freezing tunnel is long enough.

$$\text{Expected waiting line length} = \frac{AR^2}{SR(SR-AR)}$$

$$\text{Process A} = \frac{48^2}{60(60-48)} = 3.2$$

$$\text{Process B} = \frac{48^2}{50(50-48)} = 23.04$$

The freezing tunnel will not be long enough if process B is used unless the moldings are exposed to the air beyond the time limit. The freezing tunnel holds only 12 items so Process B will not be suitable unless it is possible to have the items sitting outside at room temperature for a time.

The time that the product would be exposed to air:

$$\text{Expected waiting time} = \frac{AR}{SR(SR-AR)} =$$

Process A	*Process B*
$\dfrac{48}{60(60-48)}$	$\dfrac{48}{50(50-48)}$
0.07 min.	0.48 min.

Process B will have about 13 items exposed to the air about 15 seconds, which just meets the requirements. If the queue runs longer than average, there will be a decrease in the quality as the molds start to melt.

This has been the part of the problem which can be answered by queueing theory, but there should be many questions in your mind which relate to costs. So we leave this problem partially completed realizing that the costs of the processes will have to be collected and the different processes evaluated.

SIMULATION

Simulation is a method of solving problems by designing, constructing, and manipulating a model of the real system. Solving problems by simulation is perhaps the one thing that has distinguished the engineers and scientists from others. Since their earliest history, they have devised analogies in an effort to obtain an insight and the eventual solution to their problems.

The models may take many forms. For instance, they may be no more than scaled versions of the real thing; or they may rely on the transformation from one system to another, such as an electrical analog of a hydraulic system. Most commonplace is the symbolic model which uses mathematical and logical symbols to represent a system. The particular simulation model of interest here is a symbolic model which requires repeated solutions from which the best is chosen. This particular type of simulation has been referred to as the heuristic model because it points the way to a better solution. The reasons for resorting to simulation are numerous, but probably cost is the one which tops the list. The symbolic models are, of course, very efficient, and even three-dimensional models—such as those used in shipbuilding—are far cheaper than the real thing. Often, the symbolic model is unable to cope with the numerous interactions, so probably the only method is to work with two- or three-dimensional models. This occurs in aircraft designs when it is impossible to express mathematically all of the structural interrelationships, so a model is made and tested. The test flight of the prototype can even be considered as a full-scale model for simulation purposes.

The transformation technique, going from one system medium to another, is used both for teaching and for gaining a greater understanding. It is not uncommon to describe electrical systems by hydraulic systems, and often the mechanical system can be solved more easily and cheaply by means of an electrical system. This, in fact, is one reason for the use of the electrical analog computer. This transformation from one system to another is, in reality, a method of logic which has had a profound effect upon the scientist and engineer, making them efficient thinkers.

An extremely important aspect of simulation is that it often makes it possible to compress time. This means that costs can be reduced and decisions can be made available sooner.

Industrial Simulation

Every schoolboy knows of the automobile mock-ups which are made during the development stage of new car models. This is just one form of simulation which the industrialist uses. He also uses flow charts of the factory system in his analysis, as well as elaborate two- and three-dimensional layouts. More recently, people in industry have become interested in simulating managerial systems for determining the best operating policies.

Simulation has also had considerable impetus from the interest in management games. In the management games, business systems are simulated so that the player may whet his managerial decision-making ability, making numerous decisions in a relatively short time. Management games have been designed for hand calculations, but many of them use the computer for rapid calculations. These management or business games have enjoyed an extensive popularity, and one can find them being played in the most remote parts of the world.

The industrial simulation models which are used to optimize a system generally have variable inputs which can be changed to study the overall effect. A particular type of model which has been found useful in factory simulation uses probabilistic (or stochastic) inputs and bears the name of the Monte Carlo technique, after that renowned mecca on the Mediterranean.

Simulation Concepts

Simulation is as much art as science. So, before discussing the logic, techniques, and importance of simulation, consider an industrial example where simulation can be used.

A small job shop is having trouble meeting schedules. The manufacturing manager is urging that the shop scheduler release more work orders to the shop. Sam, the shop scheduler is reluctant to do this contending that it will only cause greater confusion and will probably slow down the jobs and increase the lead times. The plant manager is adamant and insists that, starting next week, more work orders be released.

Before doing this, Sam suggests that they attempt to use simulation to prove who is right. The plant manager replied, "This is not possible since we do not have access to a computer."

Sam said, "It is not necessary." He proceeded to clean off the top of his desk and bring out some blank cards and a couple of cardboard boxes. Sam said, "The cards can represent manufacturing orders and the boxes will be two machines, a bolt header and a thread roller." (See Figure 17–5.) "It will

Figure 17–5
The Desk Top Simulation of a Job Shop

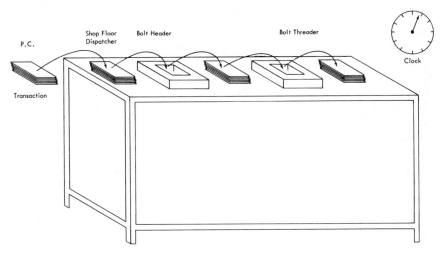

take about five minutes to shift the cards around and post the information for each move. At the end of every five minutes, the cards will have been shifted and that will represent the end of one day, so that in an hour 12 days can be represented."

Sam gloats over how he is condensing time and can tell as much about the plant in an hour as the plant manager could tell in 12 days. If he can move the cards faster, he can perhaps get each move down to two minutes and include 30 days in one hour. A computer would do these moves in a fraction of a second and therein lies the power of the computer.

Sam, the scheduler, suggests that the simulation be run for two situations, when *two* orders are released to the factory and when *ten* are released. Other rules may be used later if there are other questions which need to be answered about scheduling, but here are the rules for running the simulation as he wrote them down. (See Figure 17–6.)

Figure 17–6
Block Diagram for Simulation

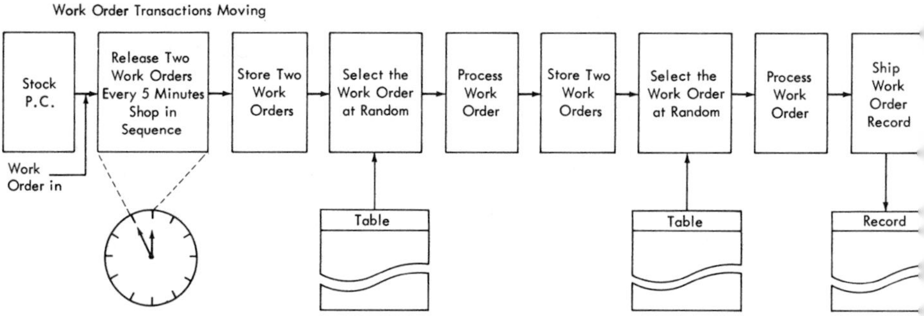

Each work order (w/o) will take exactly eight hours, and the machine loads are balanced perfectly so that the thread roller can just keep up with the header.

Reversing the order of the process is not possible because the header would ruin the threads.

One work order will be released to the factory every day.

There will be enough orders ahead of the machines to represent the situation being simulated—two work orders and six work orders.

Selecting the jobs from the ones in process for two and six is relatively easy. A coin may be used for the two orders and a die for the six orders. For other situations, numbers could be drawn out of a hat or a random number table might be used. The information in Figure 17–7 summarizes the results of the simulation for two work orders. Figure 17–8 is a summary of the six work-order simulation. If we can believe the simulations, it appears that the plant manager is wrong and releasing more jobs to the plant just adds to the time it takes for them to get through the shop and does not shorten the time as one might expect. (The second table is not reproduced in its entirety, but is summarized.)

This simple illustration has answered one condition. There are many more questions which you may want answered. For example what if the first-in, first-out method of selection had been used? What if the work orders did not take a full day and what if set-up times were included? What if more machines had been involved? What if this situation had occurred or what if that situation has occurred? Simulation is an ideal tool to use in answering the myriad of *what if* questions illustrated above which management faces every day.

Figure 17–7
Simulation for Two Work Orders

Day	w/o	In Process	Machine #1	In Process	Machine #2	w/o Com.	Days Delay
1	1	1-Blank	Blank	B–B	Blank	0	
2	2	1-2	B	B–B	B	B	
3	3	2-3	1	B–B	B	B	
4	4	2-4	3	1&B	B	B	
5	5	4-5	2	1&3	B	B	
6	6	5-6	4	2&1	3	B	
7	7	7-6	5	4&2	1	3	4
8	8	8-6	7	5-4	2	1	7
9	9	9-8	6	7-5	4	2	7
10	10	10-9	9	6-5	7	4	6
11		B-8	10	9-5	6	7	3
12		B-8	B	10-9	5	6	6
13		B-8	B	B-9	10	5	8
14		B-8	B	B-9	B	10	4
15		B-8	8	B-9	B	B	
16		B-B	B	B-9	B	B	
17		B-B	B	B-8	9	B	
18		B-B	B	B-8	8	9	9
19		B-B	B	B-B	B	B	
20		B-B	B	BB	B	8	12
							66

Figure 17–8
Simulation for Six Work Orders

Day	w/o	In Process	Machine #1 Blank	In Process	Machine #2 Blank	w/o Com.	Days Delay
1	1	1BBBBB		BBBBBB		0	
9	9	9852BB	B	7614BB	B	3	6
10	10	10–9852B	B	B761BB	4	B	
11	B	B–10–982B	5	BB61BB	7	4	7
12	B	BB982B	10	5BB61B	B	7	5
13	B	BBB82B	9	10–BB1B	6	B	
14	B	BBBB82	B	9–10–BBB1	B	6	8
15	B	BBBBB2	8	B9–10–BBB	1	B	
16	B	BBBBB2	B	8B9–10–BB	B	1	15
17	B	BBBBB2	B	BB9–10–BB	8	B	
18	B	BBBBB2	B	BBB9–10–B	B	8	
19	B	BBBBB2	B	BBBB9B	10	B	
20	B	BBBBB2	B	BBBB9B	B	10	10
29	B	BBBBBB	B	BBB2BB	B	9	20
30	B	BBBBBB	B	BBB2BB	B	B	
31	B	BBBBBB	B	BBBBBB	2	B	
32	B	BBBBBB	B	BBBBBB	B	2	30
							101

Simulation Is Not Computer Programming. Because computers have made large-scale simulation possible, it has become a common belief that they are one and the same. Not so. As you have seen by the example, simulation can be done without a computer.

Simulation has for years been a part of the professional's kit of tools for answering problems that are difficult to answer in other ways. For example, the flow of rivers is simulated by models, airplane wing models are flown in wind tunnels, and model structures are loaded with bags of sand while the deflections are studied. Simulation does not require a computer, but it can make life easier if you have one. Since simulation is not programming we will not have to confuse these two subjects, and we can go directly to the analysis of the logic used in developing the simulation model.

The Components of Simulation Models. The illustrated problem is an example of a simulation. Not a very sophisticated simulation, it is true, but one that contains all of the basic components required. To illustrate the components, the simulation will be analyzed to see the structure which is common to all simulations. The following components can be identified:

Transactions. The example had manufacturing orders which moved from place to place. These are transactions which can be created or destroyed as desired and can represent other things such as ships at a dock, trucks at a receiving department, or other entities. Each transaction has characteristics described by *parameters*. The order's parameters might be the time that it takes to complete the order, the time it has to be shipped, its weight, or other characteristics.

Facility. A facility is where the transactions are processed. Each facility can handle only one transaction at a time. The facilities in the example are the bolt header and threader, but they could be a sales clerk, a dock, or similar processor.

Storage. In the example there was a storage between the processes. As is apparent, a storage can handle one or more transactions at a time. Other storage examples would be a file of papers or parking lots.

Logic Switches. A two-state indicator which can be set "on" or "off" by a transaction to modify the flow of other transactions. Example: Traffic lights, inventory quantities, and machines operating.

Tables. Distribution tables: The flip of a coin or the shake of the die could have been represented by information which had been placed in a table. Random number tables, normal distribution tables, and other similar source data are typical of this type of table.

Collection Tables. A convenient way of accumulating information as was done in the example.

Real-time Clock. As we saw in the example, the transactions move from station to station. Each movement may be considered as an "event" which occurs at some particular instant in time.

You were probably aware that the clock was not essential in the example, but it did help count and keep track of the cycles. It will also be useful in understanding how a computer keeps track of activities in a simulation. The computer, like the example, maintains a real-time clock that records the time reached in the modeled system. This is referred to as the "clock time" and is presented in integral numbers. The clock time is related to the "system time." As in the example, five minutes is equal to one day. Any relationship between units of time may be selected, but it is important that the relationship be maintained during the entire simulation.

Simulation Modeling—Block Diagrams. The example could have been presented graphically by a block diagram which would have been more convenient than the desk-top layout. It would be especially useful if you were working toward a computer application. The block diagram, Figure 17–6 represents the entire desk-top simulation. There are transactions, facilities, storages, logic switches, and tables. Notice that there is a one-for-one relationship between the two representations. Observe that in the block diagram one of several things might occur:

A transaction is created or destroyed.
The transaction may be delayed.
The transaction may be changed in some way.
The transactions may take alternate routes.

Once the block diagram is designed to fit the situation, it is time to consider how to "code" it for the computer. One can start out with common computer language, such as FORTRAN, and build up the entire computer program. Ordinarily this would not be the most economical thing to do because there are computer software packages which are already prepared for many simulation applications.

Simulation Languages. There is no reason why the simulation cannot be written in one of the conventional computer languages such as COBOL, FORTRAN, or others. These will allow the maximum amount of flexibility in attacking different problems, formulating the model, and setting up the formats of the computer output.

The difficulties of writing simulation programs in one of the common languages can be overcome by using one of the especially prepared simulation languages. Although this is not the place to develop the intricacies of these programs, a name or two might be useful when the time comes to search out and use one of these programs: GPSS (General Purpose Simulation System), SIMSCRIPT, GASP, DYNAMO, GERT. Those wishing to have a survey of these programs shoud check the reference given.[1]

The Logic of Simulation Modeling

Although the components of the simulation model have been listed and

---

[1] Thomas H. Naylor et al., *Computer Simulation Techniques* (New York: John Wiley & Sons, Inc., 1966).

described, it may not be clear what logical procedure should be used in making the simulation: Here are steps to follow:

Step 1. Early in the procedure one should ask if the simulation is desirable. Is the answer worth the cost? Can a simulation model be made? Will the simulation give the answer in time? Why not solve the problem directly with equations?

Step 2. Describe and define the simulation by writing down:
  The purpose of the simulation.
  The boundaries of the simulation. One should not simulate an entire factory when only one line may be of interest.
  Isolate the elements of the system.
  List and describe the interactions between the elements of the system.
  Determine what the inputs to the system will be.
  Decide what kind of answers will be acceptable.
  How long will the process take to stabilize?

Step.3. Lay out the block diagram for the model. Be sure that no steps are left out and that all of the steps are fully described. This will make it easier for you to check out the model for errors and discuss it with other people.

Step 4. Code and write the computer program for the model described in Step 3. Be sure that the rules prescribed by software package are adhered to.

Step 5. Using the inputs under consideration, run the simulation and obtain answers.

Step 6. Evaluate answers. Change inputs as desired and repeat whatever steps are necessary.

Why Simulate? There are some good reasons for simulating solutions to problems:

A simulation may be much easier and cheaper to produce than the actual model.

A simulation may make it possible to experiment and test a system without interrupting the actual operations.

Modeling a simulation may reveal ways of changing the system to improve its operations.

Simulation permits the compression of time. What might take years to do on an actual system may be done in a matter of minutes on a computer.

A simulation model may reveal that some of the inputs to the system which were considered significant are in reality not important.

Simulation models may be used as training devices. For example, *management games* are used to train management personnel.

The Monte Carlo Technique. The Monte Carlo technique has become so much a part of simulation models that the terms are often assumed to be synonymous. It is, however, only a technique within simulation. Monte

Carlo is a way of selecting the variables within the simulation model and consists of the following steps:

Step 1. Determine the probability distribution of the variables under consideration. The characteristics of this distribution might be assumed from past experience. If this cannot be done with some assurance, then data should be accumulated.

Step 2. Sample the population described by Step 1, using random numbers. The random number generator creates a number which would have an equal chance of occurring in any trial.

In the illustration the random number generator was a coin for two, a die for six. It could have been numbers pulled from a hat or taken from a *random numbers table* or a random number generator in a computer.

The mechanics of this procedure may be shown by an example. Consider an inventory control problem with withdrawals per day running from zero to four with a frequency as shown in Figure 17–9.

Figure 17–9
Inventory Data

Withdrawals per Day	Frequency	Numbers in Tables
0 pounds	0.10	0–100
1	0.20	101–300
2	0.40	301–700
3	0.20	701–900
4	0.10	901–1,000

The random numbers in the right-hand column have to be distributed in the same percentage as the frequency. If one had a three-digit-table random number table running from 0 to 1,000, the range of numbers would be arranged as shown in column 3. So, if you draw a number 185, it would indicate a withdrawal of 1 pound for that day.

An Example of a Factory Simulation[2]

A part of the cheese industry in the United States is characterized by many small plants located in rural communities. The supply of labor is drawn from the community and is relatively flexible.

The milk for producing the cheese either comes from the farmer-producer or is surplus from the bottlers. Brokers and cooperatives also supply milk, but charge a slight premium. Not only is the quantity of milk variable, but so is the price.

---

[2] Material for this section is condensed from a Purdue University Agriculture Experiment Station research bulletin, No. 757, December 1962, by Aaron Glickstein, E. M. Babb, C. E. French, and J. H. Greene: *Simulation Procedures for Production Control in an Indiana Cheese Plant.* The author is especially indebted to Dr. Glickstein, for his Ph.D. dissertation was the basis for the above bulletin.

Cheese plants traditionally accept the milk as it is available from the farmer-producers. Milk, being perishable, and in spite of the improved technology for keeping it, must be manufactured into cheese in a relatively short time. This means that production is almost directly tied to the milk supply. On the average, for each 100 pounds of milk 10.7 pounds of Colby cheese are obtained.

The production level of the plant is dependent upon the supply of milk, so the quantity of labor tends to vary with the milk supply. Additional employees can be obtained during the production peaks to work for one-, two-, or three-month periods. The plant operates seven days a week, and employees work more than eight hours a day—and 40 hours a week when needed, without premium pay for overtime or for working on Saturday and Sunday. Nevertheless, efforts were made in the simulation model to limit the time for each worker to a 12-hour day.

The system is easier to visualize by a flow chart (Figure 17–10). The

Figure 17–10
Simulation Model of Cheese Plant

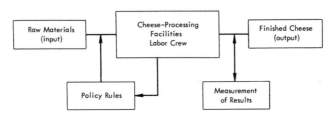

processing facilities, indicated on the model, consist of a manufacturing plant for the production of 12- to 15-pound Colby cheeses which are sold, without further processing, to distributors. Cheese making is a batch process, and in the particular plant under consideration, there are seven 15,000-pound cheese vats and such auxiliary facilities as pasteurizers, storage tanks, hoops, and other necessary equipment.

The problem is to determine the operating policy which will minimize the cost, considering the variations in the quantity and cost of raw materials. The first policy to be examined is the purchase of all milk available from the producers and none from the bottlers or other sources. To determine this cost, and costs for other production policies, it is necessary to evaluate the cost factors which make up the total. Each cost factor is given below.

1. *Fixed labor costs* include the labor used in receiving and warehousing the material as well as the labor in the office and management. These costs are assumed not to vary with the change in production. The fixed costs for the year under consideration were $45,995.

2. *Fixed plant and facilities costs* include depreciation, equipment, interest on capital, insurance, and repairs and maintenance on buildings and equipment. The sum of these costs is $35,395.

3. *Fixed services and supplies* were difficult to separate from similar variable costs. Utilities and cleaning supplies were included in this classification and totaled $10,927.75 for the year.

4. *Material costs* for any year depend upon the purchasing policy which is being pursued. In the first policy, only the milk obtained from the farmer-producer was considered. The supply of milk from this source for each day is plotted for two different years in Figure 17–11.

To determine the milk input for the simulation model, it was necessary to consider two factors: the seasonal variation and the random day-to-day variation.

The seasonal effect for each day was predicted by fitting a regression line to the data illustrated (as discussed in Chapter 4). This equation turns out to be a fourth-order *polynomial* of the form:

Figure 17–11
Milk Supply Available from Farmer-Producers for Two Years

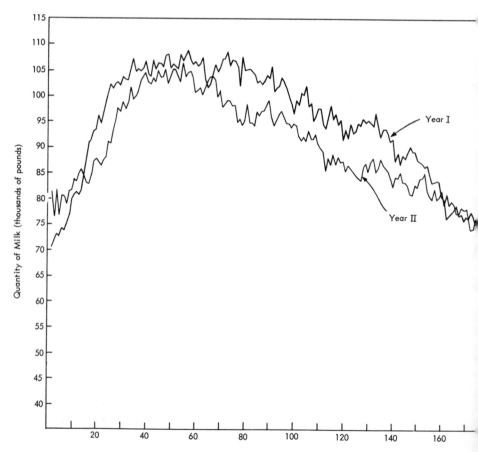

$$Y = 74{,}192 + 10{,}372X - 1{,}077X^2 + 32X^3 - .294X^4$$

In this equation, April 15th coincides with the first day. By starting with this date, the value of Y is determined for every day in the year, and column 2 of Figure 17–12 shows this value, which was calculated for the first 10 days.

The Y values obtained by regression must be adjusted for random daily variations, which are assumed to be distributed normally about the regression line. The procedure of doing this is followed more easily if it is given step by step.

Step 1. With a table of areas of standard normal distribution for Z values (as shown in Chapter 4), a series of equal Z classes is established, as shown in the first column of Figure 17–13. These classes are assigned the mid-point value, as shown in column 2.

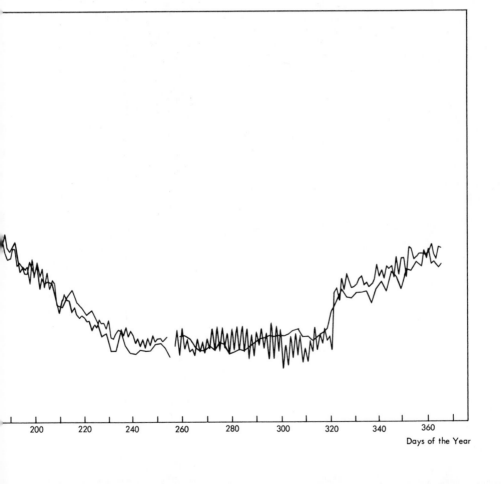

Days of the Year

Figure 17–12
Quantity of Milk Received

(1) Day	(2) Y Value (Seasonal Milk Supply)	(3) Number from Random Digit Table	(4) Z Values	(5) Z Value × Standard Error of Estimate	(6) Simulated Milk Arrivals (Col. 6 = Col. 2 + Col. 5)
				s = 3477	
1............	75,218	66,082	+ .45	+1565	76,783
2............	76,224	97,377	+1.95	+6780	83,004
3............	77,208	60,779	+ .25	+ 869	78,077
4............	78,171	63,537	+ .35	+1217	79,388
5............	79,114	65,496	+ .35	+1217	80,331
6............	80,036	69,571	+ .55	+1912	81,948
7............	80,937	12,609	−1.15	−3999	76,938
8............	81,819	20,688	− .85	−2955	78,864
9............	82,680	02,033	−2.05	−7128	75,552
10............	83,522	76,629	+ .75	+2608	86,130

Figure 17–13
Table for Determining Z Values

1 Lower class boundary of Z	2 Mid value of Z	3 Probability below class boundary
—4.00	—4.05	
—3.90	—3.95	.00005
—3.80	—3.85	.00007
—3.70	—3.75	.00011
—3.60	—3.65	.00016
—3.50	—3.55	.00023
—3.40	—3.45	.00034
—3.30	—3.35	.00048
—3.20	—3.25	.00069
—3.10	—3.15	.00097
—3.00	—3.05	.00135
—2.90	—2.95	
	⌐2.15	.98610
+2.30	+2.25	.98928
+2.40	+2.35	.99180
+2.50	+2.45	.99379
+2.60	+2.55	.99534
+2.70	+2.65	.99653
+2.80	+2.75	.99744
+2.90	+2.85	.99813
+3.00	+2.95	.99865
+3.10	+3.05	.99903
+3.20	+3.15	.99931
+3.30	+3.25	.99952
+3.40	+3.35	.99966
+3.50	+3.45	.99977
+3.60	+3.55	.99984
+3.70	+3.65	.99989
+3.80	+3.75	.99993
+3.90	+3.85	.99995
+4.00	+3.95	.99997
+4.10	+4.05	.99999

Step 2. In column 3, the probabilities below the Z boundaries are listed.
Step 3. For each day, a number is selected from a random number table. Looking in the column of probabilities, it is determined within which class the number fits.
Step 4. The mid-value of that class is then multiplied by the standard error of the estimate, 3,477 pounds (the standard error of the estimate was calculated as illustrated in Chapter 4). This product is then added to the value of Y, and the daily simulated milk arrivals are shown in column 6 of Figure 17–12.

The price of milk also varied with the season. From this data a regression line for prices was obtained:

$$Y = 3.16 - .010X + .023X^2$$

where Y is the monthly milk price and X is the month of the year. A summary of milk costs is given in Figure 17–14.

Figure 17–14
Calculations of Milk Costs

Days (1)	Equivalent period (2)	Quantity of milk (3) Pounds	Price /100 lb. milk from (4)	Cost (5) = (4)(3)
1- 16	April 15-31	1,311,604	$3.27	$ 42,889.45
17- 47	May	3,007,214	3.19	95,930.13
48- 77	June	3,121,838	3.16	98,650.09
78-108	July	3,125,515	3.17	99,078.83
109-139	August	2,824,580	3.23	91,233.93
140-169	September	2,423,819	3.34	80,955.55
170-200	October	2,093,816	3.49	73,074.18
201-230	November	1,761,685	3.65	64,301.50
231-261	December	1,631,453	3.93	64,116.10
262-292	January	1,557,040	3.75	58,389.00
293-323	February	1,463,171	3.57	52,235.20
324-351	March	1,841,273	3.40	62,603.28
352-365	April 1-14	931,350	3.27	30,455.14
Total		27,094,358		$913,912.38

Butter fat was recovered from the process which amounted to 0.5 pounds for each 100 pounds of milk received. The total quantity recovered for the period was 135,471 pounds, at 68¢ a pound, or $92,120.82. This, deducted from the cost of the milk, left a cost of $821,791.56. In addition there was the cost of rennet, salt, starter, coloring, and packaging material, which was $41,183.19 for the quantity of milk processed. The total materials cost was $862,974.75.

5. *Variable labor costs*, involving the number of people required for a particular production level, was determined by simulating the plant activities

with different size labor crews. But first it was necessary to obtain time study data to determine how long it takes to do each of the various activities. This information was put together in man-machine charts (Figure 17–15) to

Figure 17–15
Man-Machine Chart

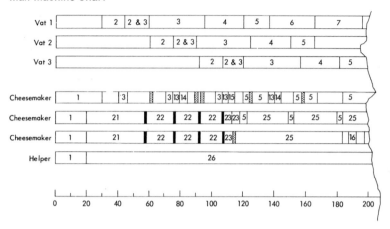

simulate work crews of various sizes. The cost of operating the plant with different crew sizes is shown in Figure 17–16. Notice that five vats can be

Figure 17–16
Crew Size and Labor Costs

No. vats per day (1)	Crew size (2)	Labor cost per day (3)	Dollars Cost per vat (4) Dollars
3	4	49.77	16.59
4	4	63.84	15.96
5	4	76.26	15.25
5	7	81.25	16.25
6	7	90.30	15.06
7	7	100.59	14.37
8	7	108.01	13.50
8	9	112.25	14.03
9	9	124.06	13.78
10	9	132.25	13.25

produced, either by a crew size of four or of seven. This is because the crew members can work longer than an eight-hour day when necessary.

The number of vats to be made each day depends upon the milk available.

Figure 17–17 shows the daily simulation for the cheese room labor costs. Column 2 indicates what has been carried over from the previous day, while

Figure 17–17
Simulation of Milk Arrivals

(1) Day	(2) Quantity of Milk Carried Over from Previous Day	(3) Pounds of Milk Received from Farmers	(4) Pounds of Milk Received from Other Sources	(5) Total Quantity Available for Manu- facturer	(6) Quantity Manu- factured	(7) Quantity Carried Over to Next Day	(8) Number of Vats Manu- factured
1.	—	76,783	0	76,783	72,500	4,383	5
2.	4,383	83,004	0	87,387	87,000	387	6
3.	387	78,077	0	78,464	72,500	5,964	5
4.	5,964	79,388	0	85,352	85,352	—	6
5.	—	80,331	0	80,331	80,331	—	6
6.	—	81,948	0	81,948	81,948	—	6
7.	—	76,938	0	76,938	72,500	4,438	5
8.	4,438	78,864	0	83,302	83,302	—	6
9.	—	75,552	0	75,552	72,500	3,052	5
10.	3,052	86,130	0	89,182	87,000	2,182	6
11.	2,182	83,475	0	85,657	85,657	—	6
12.	—	84,277	0	84,277	84,277	—	6
13.	—	84,365	0	84,365	84,365	—	6
14.	—	84,086	0	84,086	84,086	—	6
15.	—	89,699	0	89,699	87,000	2,699	6
16.	2,699	88,687	0	91,386	87,000	4,386	6
17.	4,386	88,700	0	93,086	93,086	—	7
18.	—	88,346	0	88,346	87,000	1,346	6
19.	1,346	93,190	0	94,536	94,536	—	7
20.	—	87,585	0	87,585	87,000	585	6
21.	585	89,612	0	90,197	87,000	3,197	6
22.	3,197	90,577	0	93,774	93,774	—	7
23.	—	89,092	0	89,092	87,000	2,092	6
24.	2,092	95,934	0	98,026	98,026	—	7
25.	—	98,239	0	98,239	98,239	—	7
26.	—	93,573	0	93,573	93,573	—	7
27.	—	94,106	0	94,106	94,106	—	7
28.	—	93,579	0	93,579	93,579	—	7
29.	—	89,211	0	89,211	87,000	2,211	6
30.	2,211	95,605	0	97,816	97,816	—	7
31.	—	96,073	0	96,073	96,073	—	7
32.	—	98,611	0	98,611	98,611	—	7
33.	—	100,785	0	100,785	100,785	—	7
34.	—	95,642	0	95,642	95,642	—	7
35.	—	100,567	0	100,567	100,567	—	7
36.	—	98,523	0	98,523	98,523	—	7
37.	—	104,809	0	104,809	101,500	3,309	7

column 3 shows what has been received. The total quantity available for manufacture is compared with the scheduling table to determine the number of vats which should be produced for that day.

As is apparent from the table, the number of vats for this period of time varied between five and seven. To take care of all arrivals during such a period—and not vary the labor force from day to day—the crew size would be maintained at seven. An analysis of this sort was done for the whole year. The variable labor cost was $28,861.44.

6. *Variable services and supplies* include office supplies, laboratory supplies, and laundry service. The total for the year under consideration was $5,160.34.

A summary of all the cost is given in the table in Figure 17–18. Each item

Figure 17–18
Summary of All Costs for Policy 1

Item	Total Cost (Dollars)	Cost Per Pound of Cheese (Cents)
1. Fixed labor costs	45,995.00	1.58
2. Fixed plant and facilities costs	35,395.00	1.22
3. Fixed services and supplies costs	10,927.75	.38
4. Material costs	862,974.75	29.76
5. Variable labor costs	28,861.44	1.00
6. Variable services and supplies costs	5,160.34	.18
	989,314.28	34.12

has been explained, as you will notice; but this is only one policy, and there may be many others which could be evaluated. Some that were considered are:

Policy 1. Recall that this policy permitted the purchase of raw materials only from the producers.

Policy 2. Same as Policy 1, but, in addition, surplus milk was purchased from April 15 to August 31.

Policy 3. This was an attempt to iron out the seasonal problem of the milk supply. The milk was purchased from the producers at 25¢/hundredweight, and in addition 3,000 gallons/day were purchased from an outside source during October 1 to April 14.

Policy 4. Same as Policy 3, except the premium was 50¢/hundredweight.

Policy 5. Same as Policy 3, except 51,600 pounds of milk were purchased from the outside.

Policy 6. Same as Policy 5, except the premium was 50¢/hundredweight.

Many other policies may be examined, but this will give you some idea of the procedure. A summary of costs for these various policies is shown in Figure 17–19.

Summary

Queueing and simulation are not unrelated subjects. Queueing theory is a way of solving the typical waiting line problem when it can be adequately described within the limits of the theory. Queueing theory can answer such questions as the time it takes to serve a customer, how many service facilities are needed, and how long the queue will be.

Simulation is a way of solving problems by designing, constructing, and manipulating a model of the real system. The components of simulation are transactions facilities, storage, logic switches, tables, and a real-time clock.

Figure 17–19
Comparison of Six Operating Policies

Policy number	Total pounds cheese mfd.	F. labor cost/lb.	Var. labor cost/lb.	F. plant & facilities cost/lb.	F. serv. & supplies cost/lb.	Var. serv. & supplies cost/lb.	Material cost/lb.	Av. total cost/lb.
		cents	cents	cents	cents	cents	cents	cents
1	2,899,096	1.58	1.00	1.22	.38	.18	29.76	34.12
2	3,423,190	1.34	.96	1.10[a]	.32	.17	29.80	33.69
3	3,440,174	1.34	.98	1.03	.32	.18	30.48	34.33
4	3,440,174	1.34	.98	1.03	.32	.18	30.85	34.70
5	3,981,252	1.16	.94	.89	.27	.17	31.00	34.43
6	3,981,252	1.16	.94	.89	.27	.17	31.63	35.06

[a] Plant facilities had to be expanded for Policy No. 2.

Simulation is not computer programming. The computer has just made large-scale simulation possible. It is even easier to make simulations if one of the computer simulation languages is used.

QUESTIONS

17–1. List five waiting line situations which might occur in a factory. Do you think that it would be worthwhile to apply a queueing solution to these?

17–2. Considering one of the situations described above, define the problem and describe it in terms of queueing theory.

17–3. Use one of the examples discussed in the first question and define each of the following:
   a. Waiting line.
   b. Population.
   c. Service channel.
   d. Queue.
   e. Customers.

17–4. What conditions indicate that the simulation method is the best way to solve a problem?

17–5. Explain the meaning of each of the following terms used in simulation:
   a. Facility.
   b. Transaction.
   c. Tables.
   d. Real-time clock.

17–6. What are the characteristics of simulation which makes it a useful tool for decision making?

17–7. Define *simulation* and *heuristics*.

17–8. What are the advantages and disadvantages of simulating industrial problems?

17–9. Give some examples of simulated models which are used in industry.

17–10. Discuss how simulation might be used as a method for selecting employees.

18

Linear Programming for Decision Making

THE TERM *linear programming* refers to a number of related techniques under the names of simplex method, transportation or distribution method, assignment method, and a number of others. These names of special methods should not be taken literally. For example, the transportation method can be used for problems with no physical transportation involved. Similarly, the assignment method can be used for problems other than those involving the assignment of people to tasks. In the development of the special cases the type of problem was essentially the same as the name implied, but in recent years the methods have been applied to a variety of problems.

Linear programming is a systematic, mathematical approach to a given problem to arrive at an optimal or best solution. It involves a linear objective equation and a set of linear restrictions or constraints. The objective equation of a problem may be to minimize some function, such as time, cost, or materials, or to maximize some function, such as profits. The restrictions may be due to machine capacities, available time, available raw materials, available capital for investment, and other limiting factors.

Typical of the linear programming problem is a large number of alternative choices. Initially, the problem is formulated mathematically into a set of equalities, or inequalities, with more variables present than the number of equations.

Some Uses for Linear Programming

Linear programming has been found useful in several types of production and inventory control problems which are common to many industries. To this long list of applications, new ones are being added. A brief comment about a few of these applications will give you a greater appreciation of the techniques:

Optimization of Production. Such an example will be used as an illustration in this chapter for the simplex technique. Given production time and process limitations in a linear form, along with the profit for each part, we can maximize the over-all profit or minimize costs.

Product Mix or Diet Problem. Here the linear programming technique is used to determine the right mix of such ingredients as vitamins, gasolines, and alloys to produce a product of the required specifications at a minimum cost.

Transportation and Allocation. Typical of this problem is a supply of material available at various points (warehouses) which is to be distributed to other points. Linear programming can help decide this question on a minimum cost basis.

Job and Salary Evaluation. Job evaluation has been criticized for many years because of the subjective approach of its practitioners. Linear programming has been found to be a useful tool for assigning weights to the factors in a job evaluation system.

THE SIMPLEX METHOD OF LINEAR PROGRAMMING

The *simplex method* of solving simultaneous equations, devised by G. B. Dantzig, is one of the most powerful tools developed in recent years for analyzing economic, business, and manufacturing data. It has contributed greatly to the impetus of scientific decision making which has taken hold of manufacturing engineering during recent years.

At the outset, the reader should be cautioned that the word *simplex* is not a catch word for *simple*. On the contrary, it is one of the most complicated forms of linear programming, but it is worthy of consideration because of background and the fact that it is the most general and universal method of solving the linear programming problems. *Simplex* is a mathematical term and refers, in its geometric interpretation, to an *n*-dimensional convex polyhedron having exactly $n + 1$ vertices. The linear programming model, in its geometric interpretation, is a simplex. Don't let this alarm you, but don't approach the simplex in the wrong frame of mind; it is not simple. On the other hand, it is not beyond the comprehension of anyone who has been exposed to algebra.

The simplex method will be developed with the idea of making each step understandable and logical. This is a middle ground between the two common presentations—one in which little attempt is made to make the procedure appear logical, and the other in which the procedure is bound by rigorous mathematical proofs that delay the comprehension of the simplex method. The proofs of the underlying theorems are highly desirable for one who has gained a good grasp of the technique, and it is hoped that students will learn the theory given in the reference texts.

There are several ways of approaching the simplex procedure but here we will first present a typical small-scale problem which can be manipulated as a problem in geometry. After you get some feeling of this—and more important, faith in the procedure—we will move on to a mathematical *algorithm*, which is a particular method of solving a problem.

Example Problem

The problem with which we are starting is too simple for linear programming, but it will best serve our purpose now because it is not so large that you will lose track of what we are doing.

A company is producing two aluminum forgings for the aircraft industry at a plant on the eastern seaboard. This is a small plant and has more work than it can handle, so the management has decided to produce as much as possible at this plant and to make as much profit as possible. The balance of the work will be sent to a "captive plant" in the midwest. They have decided to concentrate on two parts at the eastern plant and wish to determine how much of each they should make to maximize the profits. Part 1 is a heavy part, requiring considerable prework but very little straightening. Part 2 is

Operation Sheet

| | | Part No.: | 1 |
| | | Part Name: | *heavy forging* |
Operation No.	*Operation Description*	*Department*	*Time*
10	Upset	U	15 min./part
20	Press	P	9 min./part
30	Heat treat and straighten	S	4 min./part

Operation Sheet

| | | Part No.: | 2 |
| | | Part Name: | *light forging* |
Operation No.	*Operation Description*	*Department*	*Time*
10	Upset	U	6 min./part
20	Press	P	10 min./part
30	Heat treat and straighten	S	20 min./part

a light and intricate part which requires little prework but considerable straightening. The operation sheets for these two parts furnish us with the information we need.

This company, because of overtime costs and maintenance, has the following limitations on each of the three departments used for the forgings:

Operation	Department	Maximum Time
Upset press	U	72 hours/week
Press	P	54
Heat treat and straightening	S	80

From the operation sheets, and the available time in each department, we can see that the time used for prework in the upset press for product 1 and product 2 must be equal to, or less than, the time available on the upset press. This can be said more easily in this form where x_1 and x_2 refer to the unknown quantities of parts 1 and 2.

Dept. U: 15 min./part $\times$ x_1 parts $+$ 6 min./part $\times$ x_2 parts $\leq$ 72 hrs. $\times$ 60 min./hr. $\leq$ 4,320 min.

Dept. P: 9 min./part $\times$ x_1 parts $+$ 10 min./part $\times$ x_2 parts $\leq$ 3,240 min.

Dept. S: 4 min./part $\times$ x_1 parts $+$ 20 min./part $\times$ x_2 parts $\leq$ 4,800 min.

The subscript on the x's is used to represent the various products—rather than such terms as X and Y—because we will soon be considering other products and would run out of suitable letters.

Mathematical Interpretation of Problem

Let us digress for a moment and get a feeling for these equations and what they mean when represented geometrically. Referring to Figure 18–1, equation U, representing the upset department, is shown in two dimensions. What this means is if all the available time is used on the upset press, we can make any ratio of part 1 and part 2 which lies on the boundary represented by the line. For example, we can make no part 1s ($x_1 = 0$) and 720 parts 2s, or no part 2s ($x_2 = 0$) and 288 part 1s—or any proportion of parts 1 and 2 which is represented by the line. If we wish, we could make 220 part 2s and have enough time left to produce 200 part 1s (as shown at point a on the diagram). This upset process line divides the space into areas of permissible and unpermissible answers. Answers in the half-space below the line are permissible while those above are not.

We know from the restrictions of the problem that we cannot use the upset press for more than 72 hours. If, however, we should extend this limitation by adding overtime of perhaps 8 hours (for a total of 80 hours), the line would shift to the right (as shown by the dashed line). This, then, becomes another problem.

The lines for the equations P and S, representing the production in Departments P and S, can also be shown on the diagram (as in Figure 18–2). The limit has been set on the operations at 72 hours, 54 hours, and 80 hours; but to optimize the profit, it may be desirable for at least some department to operate at less than maximum. In fact, it may be impossible to operate all departments at their maximums.

The answer then is to the left of the lines and it might be any point, such as a, where part 1 is 90 and part 2 is 120. The area of possible solutions is

Figure 18–1
Production for Dept. U

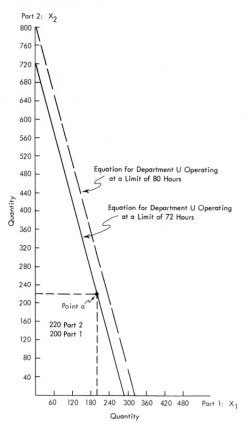

bounded by the lines as indicated by the arrows. Therefore we are not considering an equation as represented by the equal sign (=) but inequations represented by the "less than" (<) and the "more than" (>) signs. Since the departments will not exceed their limits, the problem is correct as stated before:

U: 15 min./part $\times x_1$ parts $+$ 6 min./part $\times x_2$ parts $\leq 4{,}320$ min.
P: 9 min./part $\times x_1$ parts $+$ 10 min./part $\times x_2$ parts $\leq 3{,}240$ min.
S: 4 min./part $\times x_1$ parts $+$ 20 min./part $\times x_2$ parts $\leq 4{,}800$ min.

It is worthwhile to insert a word or two about the meaning of the inequality signs. These symbols represent such restrictions as "pay no more than," "produce no more than," "stock no less than," and so on. In solving a problem containing mixed inequalities, that is, with some $<$ and some $>$, it is essential to make the system consistent. For example, if we had a set of inequalities:

Figure 18–2
Production for Three Departments

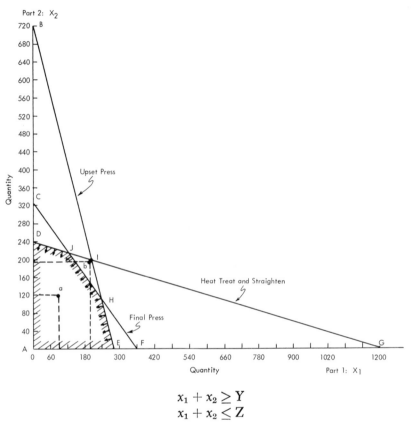

$$x_1 + x_2 \geq Y$$
$$x_1 + x_2 \leq Z$$

we can make them consistent by multiplying one of the equations by -1. The equation choice depends upon whether we wish to maximize the problem or minimize the problem:

$$-x_1 - x_2 \leq -Y \qquad\qquad x_1 + x_2 \geq \quad Y$$
$$x_1 + x_2 \leq \quad Z \qquad\qquad -x_1 - x_2 \geq -Z$$

(You should recognize that the equations on the left represent the area below the line and the equations to the right represent the area above the line.)

Returning now to our set of equations, and the way they are represented on the diagram, it is apparent that the lines for the equations bound the area containing the answers, but there might be some question about certain portions of the diagram. Let us look at one particular point on the last figure which might be confusing. Assume that 208 part 1s and 198 part 2s are made, as represented by point b. How does this affect equation P?

$$9 \, \text{min./part} \times 208 \, \text{part 1} + 10 \, \text{min./part} \times 198 \, \text{part 2} = 64.2 \, \text{hrs.}$$

This exceeds the quantity of time available by more than 10 hours, so it is apparent that the equation for P, with its 54-hour limitation, helps form the boundary of feasible solutions within the space, A, D, J, H, E, A.

This is a good place to pause for a moment and insert some of the language which prevails in the literature of linear programming to make the introduction of more complicated discussions a little easier.

A *point* is a certain position in space such as A, D, J, and so on, and a collection of such points is said to be a *set*. A straight line joining two points, as A–D, D–J, and the others, is called a *segment*. Then a *convex set* is a collection of points such that a segment joining any two points will be within the collection of points. The solution boundaries—A, D, J, H, E—are shown on the left in Figure 18–3. We can see that it is a convex set because

Figure 18–3
Convex Sets

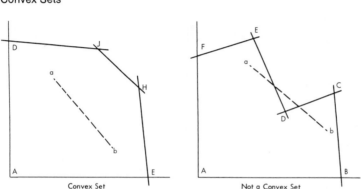

Convex Set   Not a Convex Set

any two connected points, such as a and b, will be within the collection. The diagram on the right is not a convex set.

The *vertex* is an extreme point in a convex set. It is a point in the convex set which does not lie on a segment joining two other points. A, D, J, H, E are vertices, but *no* other points are.

It is apparent, although we have not proved it, that the answer to our problem is one of the vertices. These extreme points are feasible solutions, but we are searching for the *best* feasible solution. We are searching not for any answer but for the best answer. Not only does our answer have to satisfy the restraints given, it must also maximize the profit. The profit on each part, as furnished by the cost accounting department, is:

Part 1: $10/part
Part 2: $40/part

So the total profit, Z, can be expressed:

$$\$10/\text{part} \times x_1 \text{ parts} + \$40/\text{part} \times x_2 \text{ parts} = Z \text{ dollars profit}$$

We can illustrate, by a number of lines, a series of profit values—as in Figure 18–4. Slide the line from left to right in your mind to obtain increas-

Figure 18–4
Production for Three Departments and Profit Curve

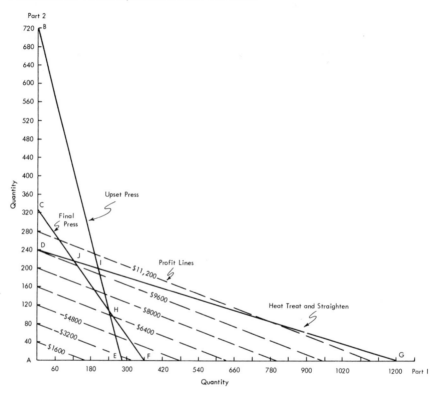

ing values of Z. We can start with producing little or no product, and make little or no profit with the line to the far left. We can keep shifting the line to the right until it intersects E to produce more profit; still farther, and the profit increases until point H is reached. Try going beyond this, and point J is reached. You cannot continue any farther without going beyond the feasible solution, as represented by the boundary of A, D, J, H, E.

Up to this point we have purposefully used a two-dimensional example because the concepts can be easily grasped. It would be a little more difficult to consider a three-dimensional problem. Instead of working with lines and intersections, we would be working with planes and the intersections of planes. We cannot extend our visual concepts beyond the three dimensions, but this does not mean that linear programming is limited to two or even three dimensions. A rigorous mathematical proof is available for the multi-dimensional problems which cannot be readily seen graphically.

The Algorithm of the Simplex

Linear programming is unlike many problems in which you close in on a solution in a predictable number of steps. It requires an unpredictable number of steps or *iterations*. Because of the sequence of steps and the number of iterations, an explanation becomes quite involved, for it is difficult to remember in which part of the cycle we are. To help overcome this difficulty a flow chart (Figure 18–5) is given here. Each step is numbered on the

Figure 18–5
Flow Chart for the Simplex Algorithm

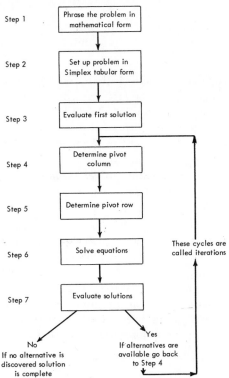

left side, and each step will be discussed in turn. Remember that this initial solution will appear long and drawn out, but this is because each step is accompanied by explanations. Subsequent solutions would, of course, be much more abbreviated as you gain confidence in what you are doing. Check back to the flow chart and occasionally see where you are, for it is there to help you. The steps will be keyed to the chart numbers.

Step 1.   Phrasing the problem in mathematical form is the most difficult part of the problem. Often, trained clerical help or a computer can handle the calculations, but the real skill lies in this first step of phrasing the problem correctly.

Step 2. Since numerous calculations are required in each iteration, it is essential that the equations be set up in a form which makes the calculations as convenient as possible. There has been a good, systematic method developed for solving the problems, which will be illustrated.

Step 3. The simplex is an iterative or cycling procedure in which new factors are added while others are removed and evaluations made at each step. The evaluation of the problem, as it is first proposed, occurs.

Step 4. In this step the new factor is selected.

Step 5. The factor to remove is selected in this step.

Step 6. The problem is actually solved here.

Step 7. The solution is evaluated to determine whether the cycling is concluded or whether it should be continued by going back to Step 4 and starting over.

It may not be apparent in the flow chart and the explanations, but there are three really distinct steps in the problem which can be repeated over and over again. The first of these is finding the *pivot column*, the second is finding the *pivot row*, and the third is to *solve the simultaneous equations*. You should keep these in mind and not run them all together. Let us now start working through the steps of the algorithm.

Step 1: Phrase Problem in Mathematical Form.[1]   Reviewing the previous example, you will observe that the problem has two distinct parts:

Constraints: The set of equations expressing the quantity of material which could be produced in the given time.

Objective function: The equation which expresses the profit.

One additional condition was implied but not expressed. This is the *nonnegative condition,* which means that the value of the quantities of production, x_1, x_2, and so on, must be equal to or greater than zero.

In a general mathematical form the problem could take the shape of a tableau (table or matrix), as has been referred to previously, and of the additional *objective function* and *nonnegative condition*.

Constraints	$\begin{aligned} a_{11}x_1 + a_{12}x_2 + a_{13}x_3 + \ldots + a_{1j}x_j + \ldots + a_{1n}x_n &= b_1 \\ a_{21}x_1 + a_{22}x_2 + a_{23}x_3 + \ldots + a_{2j}x_j + \ldots + a_{2n}x_n &= b_2 \\ \cdots \cdots \cdots \cdots \cdots \cdots \cdots \cdots \cdots \cdots \cdots \cdots \cdots \\ a_{i1}x_1 + a_{i2}x_2 + a_{i3}x_3 + \ldots + a_{ij}x_j + \ldots + a_{in}x_n &= b_i \\ \cdots \cdots \cdots \cdots \cdots \cdots \cdots \cdots \cdots \cdots \cdots \cdots \cdots \\ a_{m1}x_1 + a_{m2}x_2 + a_{m3}x_3 + \ldots + a_{mj}x_j + \ldots + a_{mn}x_n &= b_m \end{aligned}$
Objective function	$c_1x_1 + c_2x_2 + \ldots + c_jx_j + \ldots + c_nx_n = Z$
Nonnegative condition	$x_j \geqq 0$

---

[1] In the first part of the discussion "degeneracy" will not be considered.

Following the same notation used in matrix operations, the first number of the subscript gives the row and the second number gives the column. Any general a is referred to as a_{ij}. The tableau is said to be an $m \times n$ tableau, meaning that it has m rows and n columns. The c's refer to profit per unit

Since you have been introduced to the subject of matrices and vectors, either here or elsewhere, you should recognize that this tableau is a matrix, or vector problem, which could be stated:

1. Find a vector $(x_1, x_2, \ldots, x_j, \ldots, x_n)$ which maximizes the *objective function,*
2. Subject to the linear *constraints,*
3. Subject to $x_j \geq 0$.

The original example will now be restated for convenience:

Constraints:

U: 15 min./part $\times x_1$ parts +   6 min./part $\times x_2$ parts $\leq$ 4,320 min.
P: 9 min./part $\times x_1$ parts + 10 min./part $\times x_2$ parts $\leq$ 3,240 min.
S: 4 min./part $\times x_1$ parts + 20 min./part $\times x_2$ parts $\leq$ 4,800 min.

Objective function:

4. \$10/part $\times x_1$ parts + \$40/part $\times x_2$ parts = Z dollars

Nonnegative condition:

5. $x \geq 0$ for all x_j.

Before completing this step, let us consider one more aspect of the problem, that of the inequalities. The inequalities, less than ($<$) and greater than ($>$), might be disturbing, but this need not be so as we can easily make these inequalities into equalities by taking out some *slack.* These nonnegative variables, which are added as slack variables, form slack vectors which you will recognize as an identity matrix.

U: 15 min./part $\times x_1$ parts +   6 min./part $\times x_2$ parts $+ x_3$ minutes = 4,320 min.
P: 9 min./part $\times x_1$ parts + 10 min./part $\times x_2$ parts $+ x_4$ minutes = 3,240 min.
S: 4 min./part $\times x_1$ parts + 20 min./part $\times x_2$ parts $+ x_5$ minutes = 4,800 min.

The slack variables have meaning in real life and can be represented by an imaginary product with no profit. These products, which we do not produce, cause no wear on the machine, no labor costs, and use no material. Slack vectors are sometimes called *giveaway vectors* or *disposal activities.* As has been pointed out, these slack vectors form an identity or unit matrix which provides an initial *basis,* a basis being m variables which are not set equal to zero.

If the constraints are set up in the form of equalities, and an identity is not available, artificial variables can be used to provide a basis. In this case, maximizing the objective function requires associating with the artificial variables large negative "profit" values, which need not be specified, to insure that the vector does not come into the optimal solution.

Another use of the artificial variable appears when an equation contains a negative value. For example, if x_4 were preceded by a negative sign, this would be interpreted as $x_4 = -3,240$, which would make a problem impossible to solve. An initial solution of the correct form can be forced by adding an artificial variable to the second constraint. This artificial variable, x_6, will be assigned a large negative profit.

One other point should be brought up while discussing the mathematical phrasing of the problem. So far it is assumed that we are maximizing the functional, but there are also situations in which the functional should be minimized. Switching from one situation to another is easily done by merely changing the signs. For example:

$$c_1x_1 + c_2x_2 + \ldots + c_nx_n = \text{max}.$$

is the same as:

$$-c_1x_1 - c_2x_2 - \ldots - c_nx_n = \text{min}.$$

Up to this point we have discussed a typical problem and how it can be put into mathematical form, but for the repeated operations a compact form is desirable.

Step 2: Set Up Problem in Tabular Form. The simplex technique requires repeated solutions, or iterations. This means that the problem must be stated and written down time after time. This is tedious, so the problem is to simplify the mechanics of displaying the equations.

First, there is no point of stating—let alone repeating—the dimensions or the variables. As long as all like entries are placed one under the other, we can merely designate the column. Also, it is more convenient to reverse the equations and change the order slightly to put them into the conventional simplex form.

c_j					$10.00	$40.00
P_0	P_3	P_4	P_5		P_1	P_2
4320	1				15	6
3240		1			9	10
4800			1		4	20

The vertical double lines replace the equal signs, the single line replaces the plus signs, and blank spaces represent zeros. Notice that the factors for the objective function are placed above their respective P columns in the c_j row. Here is displayed, in a highly abbreviated form, all the information contained in the original equations.

It will be even more convenient to give names to the various parts of the tableau and these we will add. Some parts will be added at this point which will not make much sense but which will be explained later. You should become acquainted with these terms before you go much further.

	c_j						$10.00	$40.00	Objective Row
(Θ)	C_i 1		P_0	P_3	P_4	P_5	P_1	P_2	Variable Designations
	0	P_3	4320	1			15	6	⎫
	0	P_4	3240		1		9	10	⎬ Constraints
	0	P_5	4800			1	4	20	⎭
		z							
		$z_j - c_j$							

Minimum Ratio Column   Objective Column   Basis Variable   Constant Column   Identity (Initial Basis)   Body

Stub

Step 3: Evaluate First Solution. It is fortunate that in the way the problem is originally set up there is an initial solution. Without explaining why at this point, we set the columns P_1 and P_2 equal to zero. Thus they contribute nothing to our solution. The solution can be interpreted as producing 4,320 P_3s, 3,240 P_4s, and 4,800 P_5s. We should recall that the profit values for P_3, P_4, and P_5 are zero. The fact that these Ps are the ones used in the solution is indicated by placing the appropriate Ps in the Basis Variable column. The profit values for the products P_3, P_4, P_5 are placed for convenience in the Objective column. The total profit for this solution is given by $(4,320 \times 0) + (3,240 \times 0) + (4,800 \times 0) = Z$, which is, of course, nothing at all.

Thus what we are doing is starting with a "trivial" solution, which is point A of Figure 18–2, if interpreted in terms of the geometric presentation.

Step 4: Determine (First) Pivot Column. Since this initial solution produces no profit, it is desirable to move on to a combination which would be profitable. The question is, which combination would be the best? For a start, it would seem wise to produce the most profitable item, and by scanning the Objective row values, it can be seen that P_2 with $40 profit is the best.

Our initial Tableau A below shows what vector is to be taken out of the body and placed where it can count in the basis. The question is, which vector, P_1 or P_2, shall replace P_3, P_4, or P_5 in the variable column? (This is to be answered in Step 5.) At the end of Step 4 the tableau looks like this:

(Tableau A)

c_j						$10.00	$40.00
c_i		P_0	P_3	P_4	P_5	P_1	P_2
0	P_3	4320	1			15	6
0	P_4	3240		1		9	10
0	P_5	4800			1	4	20
	z						
	$z_j - c_j$						

Step 5: Determine Pivot Row. The decision must be made concerning which P to replace in the Objective column. The answer to this can be simply stated: Produce as many parts as possible without exceeding the time available. The number of parts which can be produced is found by dividing the time available in each department by the piece rate.

$$\text{From equation } U: \frac{4{,}320 \text{ min.}}{6 \text{ min./part}} = 720 \text{ parts}$$

$$\text{From equation } P: \frac{3{,}240 \text{ min.}}{10 \text{ min./part}} = 324 \text{ parts}$$

$$\text{From equation } S: \frac{4{,}800 \text{ min.}}{20 \text{ min./part}} = 240 \text{ parts}$$

If 720 parts were produced, the time in Departments P and S would be exceeded, and if 324 parts were produced, the time in Department S would be exceeded. Therefore it seems obvious that 240 parts is the maximum that can be produced. All the time in Department S will be used, and a surplus of time will be left in Departments U and P.

The row to replace is apparently the one with the minimum positive ratio, which, incidentally, is frequently referred to as *theta* (Θ). *Theta* can be appended to the left side of the tableau for convenience.

The old tableau, with the Pivot row and the Pivot column encircled, is shown below. The intersection of the Pivot row and Pivot column is called the *pivot*. The Θ value, for the ratio of the available time and the Pivot column, is shown at the far left.

Step 6: Solve Equations. It is now essential to lay a little groundwork because this part of the problem becomes quite involved. A discussion of solving simultaneous equations will be presented, and from this a systematic and rapid way of solving the equations in the simplex algorithm will be developed.

(Tableau A)

c_j							$10.00	$40.00	
Θ	c_i		P_0	P_3	P_4	P_5	P_1	P_2	
$\dfrac{4320}{6} = 720$	0	P_3	4320	1			15	6	Pivot
$\dfrac{3240}{10} = 324$	0	P_4	3240		1		9	10	
$\dfrac{4800}{20} = 240$	0	P_5	4800			1	4	20	Pivot Row
		z							
		$z_j - c_j$							

Pivot Column

There has been at least some indication that the feasible solutions to the problems are at the vertices where two lines cross in our two-dimensional model. While we cannot take time to prove it here, the set of all feasible solutions is a convex set and the objective function assumes its minimum or maximum at an extreme point of the convex set.

The first problem here is to solve the equations and thus find the extreme points. Later we will see how to find the optimum extreme point. Refer again to the graphical illustration of the problem, Figures 18–2 and 18–4, and take into consideration all of the lines that intersect. The lines represented by the two ordinates and the equations for U, P, and S create a boundary to the feasible solution. The vertices can be obtained by solving two of the equations involved, simultaneously. A table showing these solutions is given below. The letters refer to the intersections on the diagram. The ones enclosing the solutions are encircled.

Vertices	Ⓐ	B	C	Ⓓ	Ⓔ	F	G	Ⓗ	I	Ⓙ
x_1	0	0	0	0	288	360	1200	247.50	208.70	120.0
x_2	0	720	324	240	0	0	0	101.25	198.26	216.0

The next thing to consider is the five-dimensional problem, which has been revised to include the slack variables.

There are three equations with five unknowns, which we know from high school algebra cannot be solved simultaneously. Fortunately, there is an out. A theorem exists which states that there can be no more positive x values in a solution than there are rows. A *basic feasible* solution is a feasible solution with no more than m positive x_i.[2] This is an important theorem for

---

[2] Saul I. Gass, *Linear Programming Methods and Applications*, 2d ed. (New York: McGraw-Hill, 1964), p. 38.

our simplex procedure. We can then take the next step and set any $n - m$ coefficients equal to zero, and solve for the remaining m coefficients. These solutions are given below in table form.

$$\text{Eq. } U: \quad 15x_1 + 6x_2 + 1x_3 + 0x_4 + 0x_5 = 4320$$
$$\text{Eq. } P: \quad 9x_1 + 10x_2 + 0x_3 + 1x_4 + 0x_5 = 3240$$
$$\text{Eq. } S: \quad 4x_1 + 20x_2 + 0x_3 + 0x_4 + 1x_5 = 4800$$

Vertices	Ⓐ	B	C	Ⓓ	Ⓔ	F	G	Ⓗ	I	Ⓙ
x_1	0	0	0	0	288	360	1200	247.5	208.70	120
x_2	0	720	324	240	0	0	0	101.25	198.26	216
x_3	4320	0	2376	2880	0	−1080	−13680	0	0	1224
x_4	3240	−3960	0	840	648	0	−7560	0	620.81	0
x_5	4800	−9600	−1680	0	3648	3360	0	1785	0	0

The vertices which are encircled at the top of the table are the ones which are feasible solutions, forming the convex set A, D, E, H, J.

This pattern, with two zeros in each column, would lead one to believe that all solutions to the problem have two axes which are zero. In other words, $n - m$ of the factors is zero, and this is true. This is a fundamental theorem of linear programming which will be of help in creating solutions.

The linear programming technique is a method of searching the basic feasible solutions in an efficient way to find the optimum. It is a technique for modifying a basic solution step by step so that an optimum solution is obtained.

Now a method of obtaining feasible solutions with less energy will be developed. Start with Tableau A of the algorithm, and following it, place a revised tableau which will be called Tableau B.

(Tableau A)

	c_j						$10.00	$40.00	
⊖	c_i	P_0	P_3	P_4	P_5	P_1	P_2	Check
0	P_3	4320	1			15	6	
0	P_4	3240		1		9	10	
0	P_5	4800			1	4	20	
	z							
	$z_j - c_j$							

(Tableau B)

		P_3	2880	1		−3/10	13 4/5	0	
		P_4	840		1	−1/2	7	0	
	40.00	P_2	240			1/20	4/20	1	

The first step, shown in Tableau B, is to bring into the basis P_2 and take out another. We will want to bring in the limiting P_2 quantity of 240 parts, so that in effect we must divide both sides of equation P_5 by 20. The elements in the basis are placed on the left side under the Basis Variable column, so we can keep track of which variables are in the solution.

Notice the pattern of this first solution. There is an identity matrix and the body matrix. One of the columns will be reduced to a 1, to form a new identity matrix, while one of the 1s will take its place in the body matrix. Also notice how the dimensions of the entries change as we go from one matrix to another. Row P_5 is expressed in units of *time* in Tableau A, but when it is divided by minutes per part it is restated in number of *parts* in Tableau B.

$$240 \text{ parts} = \tfrac{1}{20}x_5 + \tfrac{1}{5}x_1 + 1x_2$$

The next problem is to remove the x_2 from the other equations:

$$240 \text{ parts} = \quad 0x_3 + 0x_4 + \tfrac{1}{20}x_5 + \tfrac{1}{5}x_1 + 1x_2$$
$$1x_2 = -0x_3 - 0x_4 - \tfrac{1}{20}x_5 - \tfrac{1}{5}x_1 + 240$$

$$3{,}240 \text{ min.} = 0x_3 + 1x_4 + 0x_5 + 9x_1 + 10x_2$$
$$3{,}240 \text{ min.} = 0x_3 + 1x_4 + 0x_5 + 9x_1 + 10(-0x_3 - 0x_4 - \tfrac{1}{20}x_5 - \tfrac{1}{5}x_1 + 240)$$

$$840 \text{ parts} = 1x_4 + 7x_1 - \tfrac{1}{2}x_5$$

$$4{,}320 \text{ min.} = 1x_3 + 0x_4 + 0x_5 + 15x_1 + 6x_2$$
$$4{,}320 \text{ min.} = 1x_3 + 0x_4 + 0x_5 + 15x_1 + 6(-0x_3 - 0x_4 - \tfrac{1}{20}x_5 - \tfrac{1}{5}x_1 + 240)$$
$$4{,}320 \text{ min.} = 1x_3 + 0x_4 + 0x_5 + 15x_1 - 0x_3 - 0x_4 - \tfrac{6}{20}x_5 - \tfrac{6}{5}x_1 + 1{,}440$$
$$2{,}880 \text{ parts} = 1x_3 + 0x_4 - \tfrac{3}{10}x_5 + \tfrac{69}{5}x_1$$

We can see that this solution gives point D. In other words, the solution calls for 2,880 part 3s and 840 part 4s (both being fictitious products) and 240 part 2s—which is a real product.

The profit has been improved, as will be seen. The profit value, c, is placed on the left side in column c_i for convenience in multiplying. The Z value, or total profit, is:

$$Z = \sum_{i=1}^{5} c_i x_i$$

What we have just developed leads us into a quick and simple method of solving the equations. As stated before, the row that is being replaced is called the *pivot row* and the column that is being replaced will be called a *pivot column*. The point at which these two intersect will be called the *pivot*.

Continuing the process which has been developed, we notice that the pivot, regardless of its original value, is changed to a 1. All the rest of the column values are zero. From this we can develop an algorithm.

Step 1.   Reduce the pivot position to 1 by dividing the old row equation by the number in the pivot:

(Tableau A—Old)	P_0	P_3	P_4	P_5	P_1	P_2
	4800			1	4	20
÷ 20						
(Tableau B—New)	240			1/20	4/20	1

The generalized statement for this is: The revised row is the pivot row divided by the pivot number. Notice that the revised row replaces the pivot row and has the same position.

Step 2.   This part of the algorithm modifies all the other rows besides the pivot row, which has just been changed in Step 1. First we will show how to do it, and then we will show how this agrees with the previous method of modifying the equations.

$$\begin{array}{c} \text{New} \\ \text{number } (a_{ij}) \end{array} = \begin{array}{c} \text{Old} \\ \text{number } (a_{ij}) \end{array} - \frac{\begin{array}{c}\text{Corresponding old}\\\text{number in pivot row}\end{array} \times \begin{array}{c}\text{Corresponding old}\\\text{number in pivot column}\end{array}}{\text{Pivot number}}$$

Let us now transform the first matrix by this method to see if it works.

(Old Tableau)

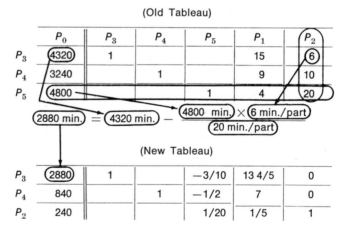

	P_0	P_3	P_4	P_5	P_1	P_2
P_3	4320	1			15	6
P_4	3240		1		9	10
P_5	4800			1	4	20

$$\text{2880 min.} = \text{4320 min.} - \frac{\text{4800 min.} \times \text{6 min./part}}{\text{20 min./part}}$$

(New Tableau)

	P_0	P_3	P_4	P_5	P_1	P_2
P_3	2880	1		−3/10	13 4/5	0
P_4	840		1	−1/2	7	0
P_2	240			1/20	1/5	1

Finishing this row, P_3, we have the following values:

$$\text{Under } P_3: \quad 1 - \frac{0 \times 6}{20} = 1$$

$$P_4: \quad 0 - \frac{0 \times 6}{20} = 0$$

$$P_5: \quad 0 - \frac{1 \times 6}{20} = -\tfrac{3}{10}$$

$$P_2: \quad 6 - \frac{20 \times 6}{20} = 0$$

$$P_1: \quad 15 - \frac{4 \times 6}{20} = 13\tfrac{4}{5}$$

Calculations for row P_4:

$$\text{Under } P_0: \quad 3{,}240 - \frac{4{,}800 \times 10}{20} = 840$$

$$P_3: \quad 0 - \frac{0 \times 10}{20} = 0$$

$$P_4: \quad 1 - \frac{0 \times 10}{20} = 1$$

$$P_5: \quad 0 - \frac{1 \times 10}{20} = -\tfrac{1}{2}$$

$$P_1: \quad 9 - \frac{4 \times 10}{20} = 7$$

$$P_2: \quad 10 - \frac{20 \times 10}{20} = 0$$

Now to see how this agrees with the original method of solving equations, as developed in the earlier method:

Original method:

$$3{,}240 = 0x_3 + 1x_4 + 0x_5 + 9x_1 + 10(-0x_3 - 0x_4 - \tfrac{1}{20}x_5 - \tfrac{1}{5}x_1 + 240)$$
$$840 = 0x_3 + 1x_4 - \tfrac{1}{2}x_5 + 7x_1 + 0x_2$$

Improved method:

$$3{,}240 = \frac{4{,}800 \times 10}{20} = 840$$

$$0 - \frac{0 \times 10}{20} = 0$$

$$1 - \frac{0 \times 10}{20} = 1$$

$$0 - \frac{1 \times 10}{20} = -\tfrac{1}{2}$$

$$9 - \frac{4 \times 10}{20} = 7$$

$$10 - \frac{20 \times 10}{20} = 0$$

Step 7: Evaluate Other Alternatives. The problem here is to determine which product should be chosen for the program. In other words, what column should be used for the pivot column? This was not a difficult decision in the simple example since all we had to do was to choose the most profitable product first, which is certainly logical. Then we had only one product left, and thus there was no choice but to put it into our solution. The decision would not have been as easy if this problem had been longer and had more choices. Therefore a method of evaluating other alternatives is needed.

Let us review what has been done up to this point. The first solution, Tableau A, indicated that no products should be made, and this would satisfy the constraints (but with a zero profit). The second solution, Tableau B, indicates that we can do $9,600 better if we make 240 light castings, P_2.

You will recall that row P_5 is expressed in units of time in Tableau A, but when it is divided by minutes per part it is restated in number of parts (Tableau B). The other rows did not change their dimensions. It is obvious that P_3 and P_4 will neither contribute nor take anything away because the coefficients are zero. Producing more of P_5 will reduce the profits by $2 a part. On the other hand, producing P_1 will improve the profits by $2 a unit. It seems obvious that it would be a good idea to bring P_1 into the production for the next program. This procedure should be continued until all difference coefficients are either zero or positive, for this is the best program that can be produced.

(Tableau A)

	c_j						$10	$40
Θ	c_i		P_0	P_3	P_4	P_5	P_1	P_2
	z_j							
	$z_j - c_j$		0				$-$10	$-$40

(Tableau B)

	($40)	P_2	($240) $-$ =			(1/20)	1/5	1
	z_j		($9600)			($2)	$8	$40
	$z_j - c_j$		$9600			$2	$-$2*	$00

* Promises the greatest improvement.

The rule for the algorithm is to program the product which shows the greatest opportunity for profit, that is, the product with the greatest negative $z_j - c_j$ difference. In Tableau A this is $-$40 for product P_2 and in Tableau B it is $-$2 for product P_1. Notice that we are searching for the largest negative number in the $z_j - c_j$ row as we are trying to maximize the profit. If costs, rather than profits, had been under consideration, and c had represented costs rather than profits, we would have been searching for the largest positive value—assuming, of course, that we desire to minimize costs.

This concludes the seventh step of the algorithm flow chart and we have seen how the no–yes decision is made. If there is a negative number in the $z_j - c_j$ row in this maximization problem, we return to Step 4 and continue the cycles until this condition does not exist.

In order for you to have a better picture of this process, the entire set of tableaus is given here and you can trace through step by step to see how the final answer is obtained.

A *check column* has been added to the tables for convenience. The entry in Tableau A for the check column is the total of the respective rows. This total is treated as another entry in the row, and if the calculations are correct, the total of each row will equal the entry in the check column. (The check column would never be used as the pivot column.)

(A)

Θ	c_i	Basis	P_0	P_3	P_4	P_5	P_1 ($10.00)	P_2 ($40.00)	Check
$\frac{4320}{6}=720$	0	P_3	4320	1			15	6	4342
$\frac{3240}{10}=324$	0	P_4	3240		1		9	10	3260
$\frac{4800}{20}=240$	0	P_5	4800			1	4	20	4825
		z_j	0						
		$z_j - c_j$					−10.00	−40.00*	

(B)

Θ	c_i	Basis	P_0	P_3	P_4	P_5	P_1	P_2	Check
$\frac{2880}{13\frac{1}{5}}=208\frac{16}{23}$	0	P_3	2880	1		$-\frac{3}{10}$	$13\frac{1}{5}$	0	$2894\frac{1}{2}$
$\frac{840}{7}=120$	0	P_4	840		1	$-\frac{1}{2}$	7	0	$847\frac{1}{2}$
	40.00	P_2	240			$\frac{1}{20}$	$\frac{1}{5}$	1	$241\frac{5}{20}$
		z_j	9600			2.00	8.00	40.00	
		$z_j - c_j$	9600			2.00	−2.00*	00.00	

(C)

	c_i	Basis	P_0	P_3	P_4	P_5	P_1	P_2	Check
	0	P_3	1224	1	$-13\frac{4}{35}$	$\frac{24}{35}$	0	0	$1223\frac{25}{35}$
	10.00	P_1	120	0	$\frac{1}{7}$	$-\frac{1}{14}$	1	0	$121\frac{1}{14}$
	40.00	P_2	216	0	$-\frac{1}{35}$	$\frac{9}{140}$	0	1	$217\frac{1}{28}$
		z_j	9840		$+\frac{19}{35}$	$+1\frac{12}{14}$	+10.00	+40.00	
		$z_j - c_j$	9840		$+\frac{19}{35}$	$+1\frac{12}{14}$	00.00	00.00	

It is evident that this solution is point J on the graphical solution, as of course it should be. The optimum production is 120 P_1's and 216 P_2's.

Degeneracy in the Simplex Problem

In Step 5 of the simplex algorithm we selected the pivot row by determining the minimum Θ value. But what if there had been a tie between two Θ values? Occasionally a tie will occur at this stage, between rows, signalling a *degenerate* condition. The wrong choice at this step could result in a solution which would cycle without reaching an optimum solution. The method proposed to resolve the tie follows:

1. Divide each element in the tied rows by the value in the pivot column for that row.
2. Compare the resulting ratios, column by column, from left to right, in the original identity, until the tie is broken. The first unequal ratio breaks the tie.
3. Select as the key row the row which had the smallest algebraic ratio.
4. Continue with Step 6 of the simplex flow chart.

The Dual Problem

Because of the dual theorem there is a choice of two problems to solve instead of just one. The linear program has two forms, the *primal* and the *dual*.

Consider, for example, a problem similar to the one just discussed. It is desired to maximize:

$$3x_1 + 1x_2 = Z$$

subject to:

$$0x_1 + 1x_2 \leq 8$$
$$1x_1 + 0x_2 \leq 6$$
$$1x_1 + 1x_2 \leq 10$$

As before, we can write these equations in this form:

	x_1	x_2	
	0	1	$\leq$ 8
	1	0	$\leq$ 6
	1	1	$\leq$ 10
Max $Z = \Sigma c_j x_j$	3	1	

Suppose now that new variables, m, are assigned to the rows and the x's are crossed out:

	x_1	x_2	
m_1	0	1	$\leq$ 8
m_2	1	0	$\leq$ 6
m_3	1	1	$\leq$ 10
Max $Z = \Sigma c_j x_j$	3	1	

These new equations are stated more conveniently if the tableau is rotated 90 degrees:

m_1	m_2	m_3	
0	1	1	≥ 3
1	0	1	≥ 1

$\text{Min } R = \Sigma g_i m_i \quad 8 \quad 6 \quad 10$

The primal and dual problems are stated graphically in Figure 18–6. As

Figure 18–6
Dual Problem: The Solution to One Is the Solution
to the Other

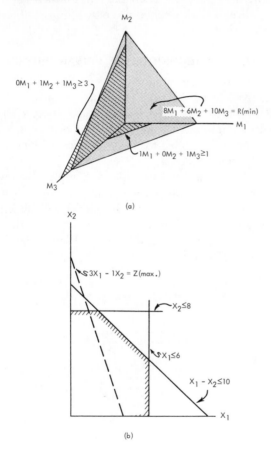

$0M_1 + 1M_2 + 1M_3 \geq 3$

$8M_1 + 6M_2 + 10M_3 = R(min)$

$1M_1 + 0M_2 + 1M_3 \geq 1$

(a)

$3X_1 - 1X_2 = Z(max.)$

$X_2 \leq 8$

$X_1 \leq 6$

$X_1 - X_2 \leq 10$

(b)

is apparent in the tableau and in the diagram, we are searching for the maximum in the primal and the minimum in the dual. The situation could have been reversed, of course.

You will obtain a better grasp of the problem and the solution if you understand the dimensions of the equations. In the first tableau we are attempting to maximize the value of Z, the profits, while in the second we would like to minimize the value of R, the cost of the resources.

$\text{Max } Z = \Sigma c_j x_j$ where:

Z is the profit of all products,

c represents the profit per unit of product,

x represents the units of product.

$\text{Min } R = \Sigma g_i m_i$ where:

R is the cost of all resources,

m represents the cost per resource,

g represents units of resources.

Because of the dual problem, one can choose which one to solve. It is possible that a judicious choice between the two forms will reduce the time expended for a solution.

THE TRANSPORTATION TECHNIQUE OF LINEAR PROGRAMMING

A special family of linear programming problems, the *transportation technique*, is derived from the simplex procedure already discussed. The word *transportation* is used because this technique is especially suitable for solving problems of minimizing transportation distances and costs, but this technique is equally suitable for other problems which fit the general terms of the transportation model.

As before, the discussion will start with an example which will give some meaning as to what we are saying, and also give some assurance of the practical use of the technique. Again, the model will be kept small and simple so that you will not get lost in the details and miss the all-important overview of the problem. As before, we shall plot our course by means of a flow chart (shown in Figure 18–7).

Figure 18–7
Flow Chart for Transportation
Technique

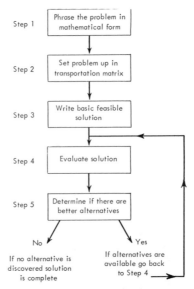

Step 1: Phrase the Problem in Mathematical Form. Assume that a meat packer has three packing plants, P_1, P_2, P_3, within a statewide area—as shown on the map in Figure 18–8. Each plant buys hogs in the city in

Figure 18–8
Transportation System

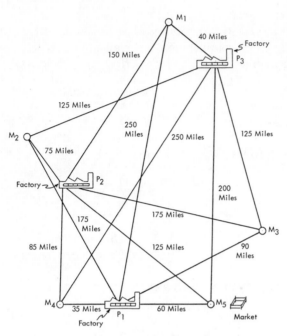

which it is located, but also buys from five auction markets, M_1, M_2, M_3, M_4, and M_5 (as shown). The distances between markets and plants are given on the map, but are also tabulated in the matrix below. The problem

	M_1	M_2	M_3	M_4	M_5
P_1	250	175	90	35	60 (miles)
P_2	150	75	175	85	125
P_3	40	125	125	250	200

is to move the hogs purchased in each market to the packing plants, according to the needs, at a minimum cost.

The type of hog being purchased on one day averaged 240 pounds. The weight loss in the hog and the transportation costs average one cent a mile per hundredweight. The mileage matrix can easily be changed to a cost matrix for 240-pound hogs.

$$\text{For } M_5 \text{ to } P_1\text{: } \frac{240 \text{ lbs./hog}}{100 \text{ lbs.}} \times \frac{1\cancel{c} \times 60 \text{ miles}}{1 \text{ mile}} = \$1.44/\text{hog}$$

	M_1	M_2	M_3	M_4	M_5
P_1	6.00	4.20	2.16	.84	1.44
P_2	3.60	1.80	4.20	2.04	3.00
P_3	.96	3.00	3.00	6.00	4.80

The matrix shows the cost of moving a hog from a market, M, to a plant, P.

On the day under consideration the company's buyers were able to buy the following number of hogs at each of the various markets:

Market:	M_1	M_2	M_3	M_4	M_5
Number of hogs:	140	180	220	250	200

Each of the plants, for the following day, accepted the following quantities:

Plant:	P_1	P_2	P_3
Number of hogs:	180	320	490

You will notice that all the hogs purchased in the markets are to be processed. This is a condition of "balance," which does not need to exist—as we will see later.

Step 2: Set Up Problem in Transportation Matrix. All the conditions of the problem can be stated very simply in one tableau:

	M_1	M_2	M_3	M_4	M_5	Receivables
P_1	x_{11} -6.00	x_{12} -4.20	x_{13} -2.16	x_{14} $-.84$	x_{15} -1.44	180
P_2	x_{21} -3.60	x_{22} -1.80	x_{23} -4.20	x_{24} -2.04	x_{25} -3.00	320
P_3	x_{31} $-.96$	x_{32} -3.00	x_{33} -3.00	x_{34} -6.00	x_{35} -4.80	490
Shipables	140	180	220	250	200	990

The costs are placed in the small corner boxes and the total quantities (*shipables*) to be moved from the markets are shown in the bottom "rim," while the *receivables* are placed in the right "rim." The x's for the unknown quantities have been placed in each box to indicate that we do not know yet what these values should be. Notice that the subscripts indicate the plant (in rows) and the markets are in the columns.

It should be noted here that costs are assigned negative signs $(-)$ and profits are assigned positive signs $(+)$. In the solution of the problem the mathematics will remain the same, whether maximizing profits or minimizing costs.

This is the problem, stated in simple form, and we will develop an algorithm for solving it. You might want to try estimating the answer before we go on to obtain a systematic method for solving the problem.

The General Form of the Transportation Problem

Now that we have discussed, but not solved, a typical transportation problem, let us outline briefly what the general form of this problem is so that you will recognize situations which fall into the transportation pattern, for this, after all, is the purpose of studying this technique.

There are markets, M_1, M_2, M_3, and so on, each having a certain amount of homogeneous products available, s_1, s_2, s_3, for shipping.

There are plants, P_1, P_2, P_3, and so on, each with a certain amount of material that it can receive, r_1, r_2, r_3.

The quantity of material which moves between a market and a factory is x_{ij}, where i designates the plant and j the market.

The cost for the product to move between a market and plant is c_{ij}. The ij's have the same meaning as those associated with the x's.

One of the conditions set up in the problem was that all that is received is to be shipped. We can overcome this condition—as will be shown eventually—but for the moment the following statement holds:

$$\sum_{i=1}^{m} r_i = \sum_{j=1}^{n} s_j$$

where m indicates all the rows, P, and n indicates all the columns, M. This restriction is reasonable for this example because holding the animals for processing would be costly and risky. This is not an essential requirement for solving the problem, however.

The transportation problem takes the following form:

Minimize:

$$\sum_{j=1,\ i=1}^{n\quad m} c_{ij} x_{ij}$$

Subject to:

$$\sum_{j=1}^{n} x_{ij} = r_i \qquad\qquad i = 1, 2, 3, \ldots, m$$

$$\sum_{i=1}^{m} x_{ij} = s_j \qquad\qquad j = 1, 2, 3, \ldots, n$$

$$x_{ij} \geq 0$$

If a problem can be written in this form, it is possible to use the trans-

Figure 18–9
Transportation Problem in Algebraic Form

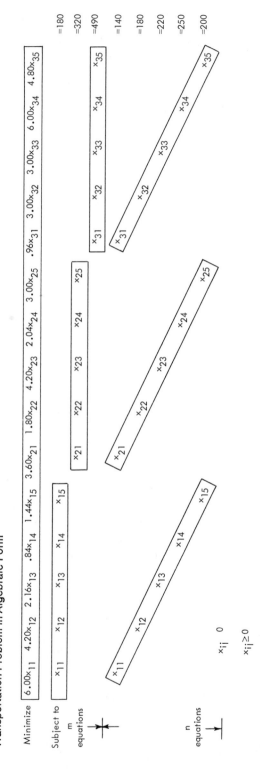

portation technique. It would be interesting now to cast our example problem into an algebraic form and notice some of the aspects which are peculiar to the transportation problem (See Figure 18–9).

This is an interesting set of equations from several viewpoints. First, all the multiples of x are either $+1$ or 0, as a negative value would have no logical interpretation. This fact, that a is either $+1$ or 0, makes the transportation equations much simpler to handle than the simplex equations. Another interesting point is that each variable appears only once in each of the m equations and once in the n equations.

If n_1, n_2, n_3, n_4, n_5 equations are added, and equations m_2, m_3 are subtracted, we will have m_1 left, which means that one equation is redundant and can be stated in terms of the others. There are then $m + n - 1$ equations in $m \times n$ unknowns.

Step 3: Write a Basic Solution. From the matrix form of the problem it is possible to derive the initial basic solution, which you will remember was our first step in solving the simplex algorithm.

	M_1	M_2	M_3	M_4	M_5	Receiv-ables
P_1	140 -6.00	40 -4.20	-2.16	$-.84$	-1.44	180
P_2	-3.60	140 -1.80	180 -4.20	-2.04	-3.00	320
P_3	$-.96$	-3.00	40 -3.00	250 -6.00	200 -4.80	490
Ship-ables	140	180	220	250	200	990

It is apparent that each column must have at least one value in it to satisfy the bottom rim conditions. The same is true of the rows; at least one value must be placed in each row to satisfy the right-hand rim condition. This is a backward way of saying that the conditions of the problem will not be satisfied if we leave a column or row blank. For example, if column M_1 and row P_1 were left blank, the shipping conditions of 140 hogs and the receiving cond: ons of 180 would not exist.

On the other hand, all the blanks cannot be filled in; there cannot be an x value for each position in the matrix. As has been learned from the simplex model, the basic feasible solution has, at most, as many x_{ij} values as there are rows. So we have as a limit $m + n - 1$ positive x_{ij}s.

A popular method for obtaining the first basic solution is the *northwest corner rule*, which leads automatically to $m + n - 1$ positive x values in the matrix—and also at least one value in each row and in each column. The logic of the northwest corner rule is easier to follow if it is presented as a series of stages (see previous tableau).

Stage 1.   Start in the upper left-hand corner, x_{11}—which is the northwest corner of the conventional map and the reason we borrowed the name. P_1 has a need for 180, and M_1 can deliver 140. All of M_1's supply will be used and 40 more from M_2.

Stage 2.   The 140 left over at M_2 are used to partially satisfy P_2's need, along with 180 from M_3.

Stage 3.   The balance of M_3's supply, 40, is sent to P_3, and all of M_4's and M_5's supply is sent to P_3.

Notice there is at least one x in each column and row, and also that we have $m + n - 1 = (3 + 5 - 1)$ positive x's, which is our assurance of a basic solution.

This method of solving the transportation problem has become known as the "stepping stone" method. Each of the x's forms stepping stones across the "water area," where no stones exist. We will be less facetious and refer to the matrix squares as being filled or not filled.

Step 4: Evaluate Solution.   This initial solution, of course, gives us one solution, which is: the product of the x's of the filled square and the cost factors shown in the small square:

Box 1-1	140 hogs × $6.00/hog	= $	840.00
1-2	40	4.20	168.00
2-2	140	1.80	252.00
2-3	180	4.20	756.00
3-3	40	3.00	120.00
3-4	250	6.00	1,500.00
3-5	200	4.80	960.00
			$4,596.00

Up to this stage we have produced an initial basic solution somewhat similar to the simplex solution, and we could continue the solution along the lines of the simplex form illustrated; however, there is a more common way of looking at the problem, which seems to be favored, and we will use it.

Step 5: Determine if There Are Better Alternatives.   The problem is to check each of the blank squares to determine if a quantity shipped from that M to the corresponding P would be more favorable than the solution of Step 3. You can memorize a procedure for this, but we prefer to present a logical method of changing the tableau. Let us start out by checking the blank square, P_2, M_1, which we will refer to as 2-1, and, for convenience, reproduce the initial solution here:

	M_1	M_2	M_3	M_4	M_5	
P_1	(140−1)—(40+1)					180
P_2	(+1)—(140−1)	180				320
P_3			40	250	200	490
	140	180	220	250	200	990

The method is to add one unit at 2–1 and see what happens. If the rim conditions are to be maintained, we cannot add one at 2–1 without making an adjustment in column M_1 and in row P_2 to compensate for the gain. Adding one at 2–1, we will move to the right and deduct one from 140 at 2–2. This will throw column M_2 out of balance, and we will have to add one to 40 at 1–2. This, in turn, will require an adjustment to the 140 at 1–1, which closes the circuit. This makes an interesting pattern with plus signs, indicating the addition of a unit at two opposite corners and negatives at the other two.

Now see what adding and subtracting these units has done to the solution:

Costs Added			Costs Removed	
2–1	−$3.60	1–1	+$6.00
1–2	− 4.20	2–2	+ 1.80
	−$7.80		+$7.80

It is obvious that there is no advantage in adding one at 2–1, but this may not be true for all unfilled squares. The procedure for checking the other squares is to form the shortest closed loops from the unfilled square back to the unfilled square. Right-angle turns are permitted only at the filled squares, and it is possible to skip over any filled squares to produce the loop. The costs are alternately added and subtracted. The value for each square is placed in the upper right-hand corner of the block, as you will notice.

Be mindful of how the signs are being used. Costs have a negative sign (−) and profits a positive sign (+), so that the costs added and subtracted (as shown in the diagram) will have the negative values for costs added and positive signs for costs removed. Since the difference between the two values will bear the sign of the larger, the alternatives with negative signs are not as good as the original solution. The alternatives with positive signs are better. The largest positive number is, of course, the best available alternative.

The largest positive number is found by finding the advantage or disadvantage of bringing into the solution all of the blank squares. The calculation for each of these squares is shown below Tableau I, and it would be advisable to calculate these values on your own to be sure you understand the procedure.

(Tableau I)

	M₁	M₂	M₃	M₄	M₅	
P₁	140 / −6.00	40 / −4.20	+4.44 / −2.16	+8.76 / − .84	+6.96 / −1.44	180
P₂	00 / −3.60	140 / −1.80	180 / −4.20	+5.16 / −2.04	+3.00 / −3.00	320
P₃	+1.44 / − .96	−2.40 / −3.00	40 / −3.00	250 / −6.00	200 / −4.80	490
	140	180	220	250	200	990

$$
\begin{aligned}
2\text{-}1 \quad & -3.60 + 1.80 - 4.20 + 6.00 = .00 \\
3\text{-}1 \quad & - .96 + 3.00 - 4.20 + 1.80 - 4.20 + 6.00 = +1.44 \\
3\text{-}2 \quad & -3.00 + 3.00 - 4.20 + 1.80 = -2.40 \\
1\text{-}3 \quad & -2.16 + 4.20 - 1.80 + 4.20 = +4.44 \\
1\text{-}4 \quad & - .84 + 4.20 - 1.80 + 4.20 - 3.00 + 6.00 = \boxed{+8.76} \\
2\text{-}4 \quad & -2.04 + 4.20 - 3.00 + 6.00 = +5.16 \\
1\text{-}5 \quad & -1.44 + 4.20 - 1.80 + 4.20 - 3.00 + 4.80 = +6.96 \\
2\text{-}5 \quad & -3.00 + 4.20 - 3.00 + 4.80 = +3.00
\end{aligned}
$$

The next question is: How shall we alter this initial solution to give us a better answer? First, it would seem logical to change the problem in favor of the most profitable change, which is $8.76 (in position 1–4). If we add one unit of this box to the solution, the answer is improved by $8.76, and if we add two, it is improved by $17.52. But how far can we go in this direction? Let us retrace our path to see if this gives us any clue:

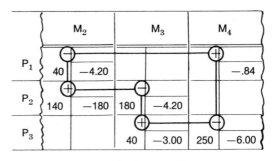

The smallest quantity at a negative spot limits the change that can be made. In this example, the 40 at 1–2 is the limiting number, for if we changed it any more, this number would become negative, creating the impossible (if amusing) situation of the hogs going from the packing plant to the markets.

Adding 40 to 1–4 and removing 40 from 1–2 will result in the rim conditions not being satisfied. It is necessary to retrace the path, adding and subtracting quantities until the rim conditions are satisfied. After each iteration it is essential to scrutinize each unfilled block to see if there is a better solution, as indicated by plus signs.

The improved solutions are shown in the following tableaus. (There is no need to rewrite the tableau each time, but it will be easier to follow the changes if we do.) It is obvious that the second solution to the tableau gives a better solution than the first. How do these answers compare with your early estimate?

(Tableau II: $4245.00)

	M$_1$	M$_2$	M$_3$	M$_4$	M$_5$	
P$_1$	140 / −6.00	−8.76 / −4.20	−4.32 / −2.16	40 / − .84	−1.80 / −1.44	180
P$_2$	+8.76 / −3.60	180 / −1.80	140 / −4.20	+5.16 / −2.04	+3.00 / −3.00	320
P$_3$	+10.20 / − .96	−2.40 / −3.00	80 / −3.00	210 / −6.00	200 / −4.80	490
	140	180	220	250	200	990

(Tableau III: $2817.60)

	M$_1$	M$_2$	M$_3$	M$_4$	M$_5$	
P$_1$	— / −6.00	— / −4.20	— / −2.16	180 / − .84	— / −1.44	180
P$_2$	— / −3.60	180 / −1.80	140 / −4.20	+5.16 / −2.04	+3.00 / −3.00	320
P$_3$	140 / − .96	— / −3.00	80 / −3.00	70 / −6.00	200 / −4.80	490
	140	180	220	250	200	990

(Tableau IV: $2456.40)

	M$_1$	M$_2$	M$_3$	M$_4$	M$_5$	
P$_1$	— / −6.00	— / −4.20	+ .84 / −2.16	180 / − .84	+3.36 / −1.44	180
P$_2$	— / −3.60	180 / −1.80	70 / −4.20	70 / −2.04	+3.00 / −3.00	320
P$_3$	140 / − .96	— / −3.00	150 / −3.00	− / −6.00	200 / −4.80	490
	140	180	220	250	200	990

(Tableau V: $2221.20)

	M₁	M₂	M₃	M₄	M₅	
P₁	— / −6.00	— / −4.20	— / −2.16	110 / −.84	70 / −1.44	180
P₂	— / −3.60	180 / −1.80	— / −4.20	140 / −2.04	— / −3.00	320
P₃	140 / −.96	+.96 / −3.00	220 / −3.00	— / −6.00	130 / −4.80	490
	140	180	220	250	200	990

(Tableau VI: $2115.60)

	M₁	M₂	M₃	M₄	M₅	
P₁	— / −6.00	— / −4.20	— / −2.16	0 / −.84	180 / −1.44	180
P₂	— / −3.60	70 / −1.80	— / −4.20	250 / −2.04	+.60 / −3.00	320
P₃	140 / −.96	110 / −3.00	220 / −3.00	— / −6.00	20 / −4.80	490
	140	180	220	250	200	990

(Tableau VII: $2103.60)

	M₁	M₂	M₃	M₄	M₅	
P₁	— / −6.00	— / −4.20	— / −2.16	— / −.84	180 / −1.44	180
P₂	— / −3.60	50 / −1.80	— / −4.20	250 / −2.04	20 / −3.00	320
P₃	140 / −.96	130 / −3.00	220 / −3.00	— / −6.00	— / −4.80	490
	140	180	220	250	200	990

Zero Evaluations in Optimum Solution

In the example just given, all the evaluation figures in the final optimum tableau turned out to be negative numbers. It is possible, however, that some of the evaluation numbers might have turned out to be zero, in which case there are alternative solutions. This is something that the management must be aware of, for it gives an opportunity to make decisions by criteria other than those given in the requirements of the problem.

The only change in our procedure is that zeros which appear in the optimal solution are treated just the same as the most positive value—that is, in the same way as the square which will make the greatest contribution. The next solution is worked out accordingly.

Unequal Supply and Demand

Our example was neater than could possibly be expected in an actual situation for it is doubtful that the supply and demand would ever be equal. Unequal supply and demand is not difficult to overcome if we are willing to insert fictitious plants or markets in the tableau.

First let us see what would have occurred if the supply had been less than the demand:

	M_1	M_2	M_3	M_4	M_5	
P_1	130	50				180
P_2		130	190			320
P_3			30	250	200	Not equal to 490
Supply	130	180	220	250	200	

It is apparent that the northwest corner rule, which was used for the initial solution, works on a first-come-first-served basis—so that P_1 and P_2 get all they want in this solution, but P_3 is shorted. We cannot make up the shortage out of thin air, but on the other hand, it may not be profitable to always short the same factory. There is a way of letting the mathematics decide to which plant it is best to ship. This is done by including in the problem a mythical *dummy* market which ships at higher but equal costs to all than any other market. These shipments would be the last to enter the solution, and their transportation cost can be subtracted from the total. This technique has been used in the following initial solution.

By following the technique for obtaining improved solutions, the shortage is distributed to the plants by cost, which is as it should be. It is worth observing that this makes it possible to stay within the requirements of the rim conditions. In this example the demand was greater than the supply. Should the supply be greater than the demand, the procedure is altered and a dummy factory (instead of a dummy market) is added.

	M_1	M_2	M_3	M_4	M_5	M_{Dummy}	
P_1	130	50					180
P_2		130	190				320
P_3			30	250	200	10	490
	130	180	220	250	200	10	990

This has been the complete transportation solution, using the northwest corner rule to obtain an initial solution. If you have followed the solution in detail, you have probably been impressed by the number of calculations needed. An easier solution is needed.

The Vogel Approximation Method

The northwest corner rule leads to an initial feasible solution but usually does not yield the optimum solution since no consideration is given to costs. A technique for obtaining a better initial solution was developed by William Vogel, and is referred to as the Vogel approximation method—or VAM.[3] The stages for this initial solution are given along with a tableau illustrating each stage for the example problem:

Stage 1.   Consider each row and each column separately, and for each one compute the difference between the two lowest cost values. These are shown adjacent to the tableau.

Stage 2.   Select the row or column with the greatest *difference* value (see circled figure on the tableau marked Stage 2).

Stage 3.   Determine the lowest cost in the row or column selected in Stage 2.

Stage 4.   Assign as much as possible to the square determined in Stage 3.

Stage 5.   Whenever a row or column rim condition is satisfied, fill in the remaining squares in that row or column with crosses.

Stage 6.   Return to Stage 1 and repeat the sequence of stages until all squares are filled with either an assignment or cross.

In the example, the difference values for each iteration are shown. It is not necessary to repeat them time after time, for as you will notice, some remain the same. If a column has the highest difference value, then the other columns will remain the same for the next iteration; and if a row has the highest difference value, the other row values will remain the same for the next iteration. Knowing this should save you some unnecessary work. Ties between two difference values may be broken by making a random choice. This may not give the most efficient solution but an error in choice will be rectified in the steps to come.

---

[3] See Nyles V. Reinfeld and William R. Vogel, *Mathematical Programming* (Englewood Cliffs, N.J.: Prentice-Hall, 1958).

Step 3: The VAM Method for Obtaining the Initial Solution

	M₁	M₂	M₃	M₄	M₅		0	1	2	3	4	5
		1.20	1.20		1.80 ⃝							
		1.20	1.20		1.80							
			1.20	3.96 ⃝	1.56 ⃝							
		1.20	.84	1.20	1.56							
	2.64 ⃝	1.20	.84	1.20								
P₁	x ⎸—6.00	x ⎸—4.20	x ⎸—2.16	x ⎸—.84	180 ⎸—1.44	180	.60	.60				
P₂	x ⎸—3.60	50 ⎸—1.80	x ⎸—4.20	250 ⎸—2.04	20 ⎸—3.00	320	.24	.24	.24	1.20		
P₃	140 ⎸—.96	130 ⎸—3.00	220 ⎸—3.00	x ⎸—6.00	x ⎸—4.80	490	2.04	.00	.00	1.20	2.40 ⃝	
	140	180	220	250	200	990	.00	.00	.00	.00	.00	.00

Stage 5 Stage 4 M₁ M₂ M₃ M₄ M₅ Stage 3

Stage 2 → 2.64

Stage 1

Step 4: $2103.60.
Step 5: See upper right-hand corner of each box.

This has been the *initial* solution, but we must move on to Step 4 to evaluate the solution and to Step 5 to determine if there are better alternatives. The results of Step 4 are shown on the tableau, and the negative signs in the upper right corner of each square show that an optimum solution has been found.

Fortunately—or unfortunately—in this example the initial solution turned out to be the optimum solution. This, of course, does not always occur, and the problem solution could have continued through a number of iterations before the optimum solution was obtained. However, this rapid converging upon the solution points up the superior efficiency of the VAM technique over the northwest corner rule.

Degeneracy in the Transportation Model

Degeneracy can occur in the transportation model just as it can in the simplex model. If less than $m + n - 1$ positive values occur in the tableau, the problem becomes *degenerate* and the common method of solving for the optimum solution will not work. If more than $m + n - 1$ values occur, there has been an error.

Of course, degeneracy can occur because an error has been made in the calculations, and a quick check back through the tableaus should be made to be sure that this is not the case. If there is no error, techniques for overcoming degeneracy should be used. The method discussed here involves *perturbing*, or adding a small amount in the square which is causing the difficulty. When we add a small amount to one square it will affect some of the others, and one must account for this. Let us discuss a particular situation: One of the shipping and receiving schedules for the packing plant looks like this:

	M_1	M_2	M_3	M_4	M_5	
P_1	70	90	1			160
P_2		?	120			120
P_3			50	40	80	170
	70	90	170	40	80	450

Look for a moment at 1–3 and 2–2. There is no way of closing the path in the usual way of determining a better alternative. If, however, a small amount is added to each market (even though we recognize we cannot add a fraction of an animal), the usual approach can be made. When the solution is concluded, these small amounts may be disposed of by simply rounding off all the answers, as we know they must be integers.

	M_1	M_2	M_3	M_4	M_5	
P_1	$70+.1$	$90-.1$				160.0
P_2		$+.2$	$120-.2$			120.0
P_3			$50+.3$	$40+.1$	$80+.1$	170.5
	$70+.1$	$90+.1$	$170+.1$	$40+.1$	$80+.1$	$450+.5$

THE ASSIGNMENT METHOD

The assignment method is used to distribute n things to n requirements. The "things" may be jobs to machines, trailers to shippers, people to machines, or similar distributions.

Each requirement can be satisfied by any of the facilities available, but not more than one facility can be assigned to a requirement. This becomes apparent when one studies the *assignment matrix* illustrated in Figure 18–10. A facility assigned to a requirement is indicated by a 1 appearing at the intersection of a row and column, as at 3–D.

Since each requirement must be satisfied with one facility, no more than one figure may appear in any row or column in the assignment matrix. All others will appear blank in the final solution.

Figure 18–10
The Assignment Method

Jobs (Requirements)

	A	B	C	D
1	1			
2			1	
3				1
4		1		

Machines (Facilities)

Assignment Matrix

Jobs (Requirements)

	A	B	C	D
1	30	40	50	80
2	40	70	20	60
3	50	40	30	20
4	60	40	80	50

Machines (Facilities)

Cost Matrix

	A	B	C	D
1	00	10	20	50
2	20	50	00	40

Step 1

This is an $n \times n$ matrix. When $x_{ij} = 1$, the ith requirement is being met by the jth facility. Said in equation form this is:

$$\sum_{i=1}^{n} x_{ij} = 1 \qquad j = 1, 2, \ldots, n$$

$$\sum_{j=1}^{n} x_{ij} = 1 \qquad i = 1, 2, \ldots, n$$

Next, consider the cost relationships between the facilities and requirements. While any facility may be used to satisfy a requirement, the cost might vary considerably from assignment to assignment. A *cost matrix* is shown just below the assignment matrix.

The cost for any assignment, c_{ij}, is shown at the intersection of i and j. The problem is to minimize the total cost, C.

$$C = \sum_{i=1}^{n} \sum_{j=1}^{n} c_{ij} x_{ij}$$

Solving this problem follows basic investigations made by König; and one solution technique, the *Hungarian method,* bears the name of his nationality. If a constant is added or subtracted from all elements in a row or a column of the cost matrix, the optimal solution remains the same as the optimal solution for the original matrix (Step 1, Fig. 18–10).

To make an optimum assignment, it makes sense to first assign the lowest cost facility, A, to requirement 1. This is illustrated by subtracting $30 from all elements in the first row. The row values change to $00, $10, $20, and $50. Zero in the A–1 position means that an assignment has been made. This is the equivalent of the 1 appearing in the assignment matrix. So now it appears that one and only one zero must appear in each column and row in the final solution. Verification of an optimal solution can be determined by observing the matrix, but an easier accounting method is to *cover* all the zeros with the minimum number of lines drawn through the rows and columns. If the number of lines is equal to n, an optimal solution has been obtained. (Rows and columns having lines are shown by arrows.)

While the solution is optimal when there are n lines, there may be a choice of two or more assignments available in a row or column. This problem is overcome by first assigning those facilities for which there can be no other choice, and then continuing this process until each row and column has one and only one assignment.

A flow chart for the assignment algorithm is given in Figure 18–11, and three different example problems are illustrated in Figure 18–12. The reason three different examples are given is to illustrate what happens when a problem terminates at one of the various intermediate steps. The initial matrices shown are similar (with the exception of the numbers marked with asterisks).

It is not necessary to elaborate upon the numerous applications suitable for the assignment model. It is a technique which can be used with hand calculations or can be adapted to computer operations.

Figure 18–11
Flow Chart for the Assignment Method

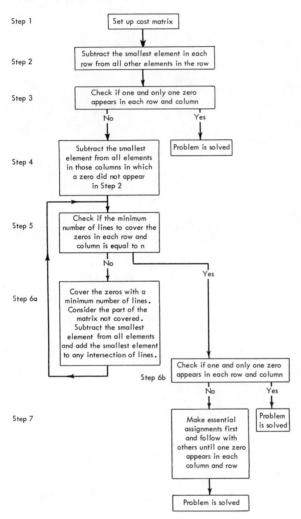

Summary

This has been only an introduction to linear programming, an introduction which has attempted to teach the logic rather than to demand an acceptance on faith.

Only some of the common forms of linear programming problems have been discussed, but the knowledge is expanding rapidly and you should become acquainted with some of the excellent references and the professional journals on the subject.

In general, theory of linear programming has outdistanced practice. This

Figure 18–12
Three Examples of the Assignment Method

EXAMPLE I

	A	B	C	D	E
1	30	60	70	80	90
2	40	70	20	60	80
3	50	60	40	20	60
4	60	40	80	50	70
5	110	80	90	100	70

Step 1

A	B	C	D	E
00	30	40	50	60
20	50	00	40	60
30	40	20	00	40
20	00	40	10	30
40	10	20	30	00

Step 2

A	B	C	D	E
00				
		00		
			00	
	00			
				00

A	B	C	D	E
1				
		1		
			1	
	1			
				1

Assignment

EXAMPLE II

	A	B	C	D	E
1	30	60	70	80	90
2	20*	70	40*	60	80
3	50	60	40	20	60
4	60	40	80	50	70
5	110	80	90	100	70

Step 1

A	B	C	D	E
00	30	40	50	60
00	50	20	40	60
30	40	20	00	40
20	00	40	10	30
40	10	20	30	00

Step 2

A	B	C	D	E
00	30	20	50	60
00	50	00	40	60
30	40	00	00	40
20	00	20	10	30
40	10	00	30	00

Step 3

A	B	C	D	E
(00)				
X		(00)		
		X	(00)	
	(00)			
		X		(00)

Steps 5, 6 & 7

A	B	C	D	E
1				
		1		
			1	
	1			
				1

Assignment

EXAMPLE III

	A	B	C	D	E
1	30	60	70	80	90
2	20	70	80*	60	80
3	50	60	40	20	60
4	60	40	50*	50	70
5	110	80	90	100	70

Step 1

A	B	C	D	E
00	30	40	50	60
00	50	60	40	60
30	40	20	00	40
20	00	10	10	30
40	10	20	30	00

Steps 2 & 3

A	B	C	D	E
00	30	30	50	60
00	50	50	40	60
30	40	10	00	40
20	00	00	10	30	←
40	10	10	30	00

Steps 4 & 5

A	B	C	D	E
00	20	20	50	60
00	40	40	40	60
20	30	00	00	40
40	00	00	20	40
40	00	00	30	00

Step 6a

A	B	C	D	E	
00	00	00	30	40	
00	20	20	20	40	
50	30	00	00	40	←
40	00	00	20	40	←
60	00	00	30	00	←

Steps 5 & 6b

A	B	C	D	E
X	(00)	X		
(00)				
		X	(00)	
	X	(00)		
	X	X		(00)

Step 7

A	B	C	D	E
		1		
1				
			1	
	1			
				1

Assignment

is probably as it should be; but soon, people like you will have the knowledge to apply the methods. Probably no technique has held out such great opportunities to improve the decision-making processes.

Many attempts to put linear programming into practice have failed because the problem was not fully understood at the outset. Just as often, the necessary information for the linear programming model was not available, or the method was too complicated for a clerk to use. In this latter case, the results of the linear programming model might have been tabulated or put in nomograph form. In any event, one must always ask: Is the information costing more than it is worth?

QUESTIONS

18–1. What is the *objective equation?* What is the *set of linear restrictions?* Give an example of each.
18–2. Suggest some industrial applications of the linear programming technique.
18–3. What is a *set,* a *convex set,* a *point,* and a *vertex?*
18–4. Describe, in your own words, and with a sketch if necessary, how the linear programming technique works.
18–5. What is an *algorithm?* Give an example of one.
18–6. What is the purpose of the *dummy* in the Transportation model?
18–7. What advantage does the VAM technique have over the Northwest Corner rule?
18–8. What requirements have to be filled when using the Assignment method?
18–9. What should you consider before making an application of one of the other linear programming techniques?
18–10. Compare the cost and value of making a decision using linear programming. What does this mean when applying it in industrial situations?

19

Shop-Floor Control

THE SHOP FLOOR referred to is the entire manufacturing facility—including the people, machines, inventory, materials-handling equipment, and whatever else is needed in the production process. Shop-floor control is bringing all of these factors into an optimum relationship for:

Meeting the customer's time and quality requirements.
Keeping the cost to a minimum by assuring that machines, people, and facilities are productive.
Keeping the inventories to a minimum.

Accomplishing all three of these at once is difficult for they seem to be in conflict:

Customer's requirements could be met if there were an unlimited number of machines and people.
The machines and people would be busy if there were unlimited inventories.
To keep the machines busy all of the time, the schedules would probably have to be juggled so that consequently the customer's demands would not be met.

Probably no two shop-floor control systems are the same because there are different processes, different dispatching rules, different feedback links, and different management objectives. There are enough similarities, however, that they can be shown by a flow chart, Figure 19–1. The objective of shop-floor control is to maintain the shop order schedule as released to the factory. The factory, unfortunately, is subject to many "disturbances" which cause the production output to fluctuate. This means that the feedback in-

Figure 19–1
Shop-Floor Control

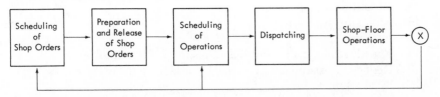

formation must be available so that the inputs can be varied to the extent necessary to maintain control.

Shop-floor control is often just associated with job shop factories, but you should not be mislead, for all factories must have shop-floor control. Chemical, pharmaceutical, and similar manufacturers monitor their processes constantly. The people on the floor might actually spend most of their time controlling the process rather than producing. Often these processes will employ electronic and mechanical devices to maintain the process in control, and the people in turn just supervise these devices for any exceptions that might appear. The high-production lines used to produce appliances and automobiles have a need for a shop-floor control system to be sure that parts are fed to the line and that products keep moving as scheduled. So while these factories have control problems, they just do not look the same as those in a job shop.

Shop-floor control becomes in some respects more complicated when a job-shop layout is used. The paper work is more extensive as materials must be scheduled to keep machines and people busy to produce the products when desired. While the emphasis here may appear to be on the job shop, you should not assume that this is the only place that shop-floor control prevails.

Purpose of Shop-Floor Control. Depending upon the production facilities and communications available, one should expect the efficient shop-control system to do most of the following:

1. Keep track of the work as it progresses through the shop.
2. Update the open order records and report progress.
3. Update the master schedule.
4. Indicate if work stations are available.
5. Indicate when personnel is or is not available.
6. Check material availability before releasing work to plant.
7. Change order quantities to compensate for scrap.
8. Assign work to the operators and work stations.
9. Check the quantities of parts from work station to work station and initiate the necessary revised orders.
10. Help expedite the materials movement through the plant by move orders.

11. Maintain work-efficiency statistics.
12. Check tool availability before releasing work to departments.
13. Record the use and cost of materials.
14. Maintain attendance records for the workers for pay and incentive purposes.
15. Expedite the quality control and inspector's function.
16. Reduce the manufacturing cycle by producing the material to schedule.

Dispatching

Dispatching is an important part of shop-floor control activities. It is the sequencing of orders on a short-term basis. The American Production and Inventory Control Society's Dictionary[1] defines dispatching this way:

> The selecting and sequencing of available jobs to be run at individual work stations and the assignment of these jobs to workers. In many companies, dispatching is done by the actual shop foreman, set-up man or lead man. A dispatcher is usually a representative of the Production Control Department who handles the job assignment task.

Dispatching—Centralized versus Decentralized. Dispatching has been classified as centralized and decentralized. In centralized dispatching the function is carried out from one location. This requires extensive communications between dispatching and the manufacturing facilities. Even with extensive communications it is difficult to maintain the tight control desired.

Decentralized dispatching requires that this service be performed at the manufacturing department. Needless to say, things are seldom black or white, and often you will find combinations of centralized and decentralized dispatching. Where the jobs are dispatched to departments rather than work centers, the supervisors are given some discretion in assigning jobs just as long as they meet the time requirements set up by the schedule.

At various times in the evolution of a factory there will be tendencies toward centralization and at other times toward decentralization. For example, when a small factory begins, the plant manager will dispatch jobs to the worker. This he will do effectively because he knows the characteristics of the workers and the machines.

When the organization gets larger, the dispatching will probably revert to a foreman-type of dispatching. Then as the organization grows even more, there will probably be a tendency to centralize the dispatching with the hope of gaining better control again.

Frequently companies have moved away from tightly centralized control because they discovered that they were losing some flexibility. But beyond that they discovered that they were losing the valuable participation of the

---

[1] Richard C. Sherrill, *APICS Dictionary of Inventory Control Terms & Production Control Terms,* American Production & Inventory Control Society, 2600 Virginia Avenue, N.W. Suite 504, Washington, D.C. 20037.

foreman in making decisions which could help to smooth out complicated production problems.

Recent developments in computer terminals which make real-time computer systems feasible have caused a return to a tight centralized control system.

Conflict in Centralized-Decentralized Control. A characteristic of the scientific management movement was centralization of the planning and control function. This was suitable a half century ago, but changes in the factory environment as well as the factory worker have made a drastic change in management's thinking. Today, factory management gives more consideration to the worker as an individual, believing that he is better motivated if he is given responsibility for decisions. Centralized control as done in a computerized system leaves little room for initiative. Management will have to find a balance between the forces involved and only then decide how much authority should be centralized.

What Is Dispatched? To control the progress of an order through a factory, it is necessary to know:

The route of the product through the shop.
The availability of inventories.
The time that each operation will take.
The tools and set-up services needed.

The route of the product through the shop, you will recall, follows the sequence of operations on the operation sheet. This manufacturing form goes by many names, such as a route sheet, factory order, instruction sheet, fabrication order, shop traveler, and others. Whatever the form is called, it will generally contain other information besides the sequence of operations needed for processing the order. Some of this information is listed here:

The work centers, departments, or other locating information.

Special tools are recorded. This information is used during production to locate, prepare, and deliver the tools to the place they will be used.

The standard times for each operation are recorded on the operation sheet. This is used for making out time cards and schedules.

The materials needed for the production of the product.

Manufacturing order.

Identification information.

The operation sheet is the source of the information needed to print the various manufacturing forms. Issuing the manufacturing forms to the factory is called a "release" or "factory release." The accumulation of materials released is the "factory packet," Figure 19–2. The factory packet will ordinarily travel with the materials through the shop.

Dispatching Boards

Dispatching is the process of issuing the necessary orders for production at the scheduled time. In the classical approach dispatching is considered

Figure 19–2
Factory Packet

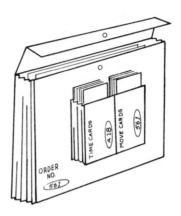

as a subject separate from scheduling. In actuality, dispatching and scheduling are bound together so that it is difficult to treat them separately, for as an order is issued a worker is told *what* work to do as well as *when*.

In the evolution of a factory, dispatching and scheduling were combined in the early stage. The owner-manager verbally told each worker what he was to do and when. The next step was probably to have a clerk issue written orders made up in advance. It is not difficult to imagine this system, with the foreman carrying these written orders around in his vest pocket. In fact, this is probably the reason why the vest became a status symbol for supervisors in the earlier days. It was probably the time that the vest remained at home with an overindulgent foreman that a more formal system of dispatching became essential. The more formal system probably consisted of filing the orders in a cigar box or perhaps in a more elegant wire basket. Even today one can find production tickets filed in this fashion in some out-of-the-way nook in the factory, but to which all employees have access for picking and choosing their jobs.

A more formal system, and one found in common practice, involves a *dispatch board*. This can take various forms, depending upon the ingenuity of the company's handyman or upon the funds available in the treasury.

The typical dispatch board consists of a piece of plywood fastened to the wall at some convenient location in the factory. The board is equipped with a number of equally spaced hooks. Each set of three, as shown in Figure 19–3, represents one work station. It is on these hooks that the production form, such as the operation ticket or time ticket, are filed. Each hook position for each work station has a significant meaning:

For machine: The bottom hook in each set of three hooks is used to file all the operation tickets for work that is to be performed at this work station.

At machine: When the work has been moved to the work station, the ticket is moved up to the *at-machine* position.

Figure 19–3
Dispatch Procedure

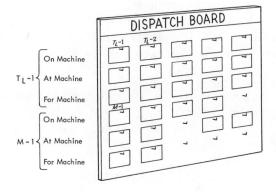

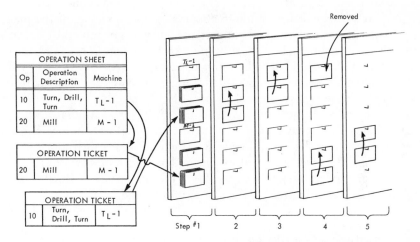

On machine: When the work is actually placed on the machine, the ticket is moved from the *at-machine* position to the *on-machine* position.

When the tickets are on the *for-machine* hook, work can be rescheduled if there are machines available. It is more difficult to reschedule when the work has been moved to the work station.

Just how the board functions will be shown by following one order through the procedure.

Step 1.   When orders are released to the factory, the operation tickets are placed on their proper *for-machine* hook, as shown.

Step 2.   When the material is sent from the stores to the first operation, the operation ticket is moved to the *at-machine* position.

Step 3.   Eventually, when the jobs ahead of this one are completed, the operator is told to do this one, and the ticket is moved up to the *on-machine* position.

Step 4.   When the work is completed, it is moved to the second operation, and the second operation ticket for the milling machine work station is moved to the *at-machine* position.

Step 5.   As before, the card is moved from the *at-machine* position to the *on-machine* position. If there had been more operations they would have followed similar sequences until the whole order was completed.

This has been just one simple order with two operations. Imagine the complexity of having several hundred jobs going through the factory, each with a number of operations. It is obvious that to make all these jobs dovetail, so that the machines are running near full capacity, is a difficult undertaking requiring a great deal of skill.

The dispatch board can show information other than production conditions. For example, a red ticket on the board might indicate that the machine is not manned, or an orange ticket might indicate the machine is down for repair. At a glance, it is possible to obtain a complete picture of the plant. A visual display may not seem important, but it is not unusual to have a machine out of production for a number of hours before it comes to the attention of the supervisor so he can take action.

The dispatch board is frequently used as a substitute for a load chart. By looking at the thickness of the stack of cards, it is possible to get some idea of the load of work ahead of each machine. If the jobs have drastically different durations, it may be necessary to scan the length of time needed for each job. At times the scheduling board (Figure 19–4) is used for dispatching as well. The cards are lined up on the board to represent the bar of a Gantt chart, and as the jobs are completed, they are removed. Rescheduling can be done conveniently by shifting the cards around.

Figure 19–4
Scheduling and Dispatch Board

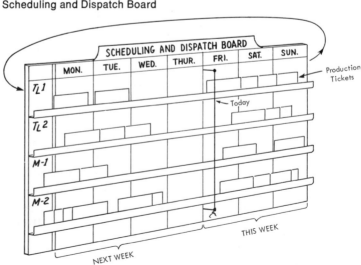

The location of the dispatching board is an important policy decision for management. In some situations it may be desirable to maintain a highly centralized control while in other situations this may not be desirable.

The feedback of information is important to the efficient operation of a dispatch board. In the decentralized system this is not important because the supervisor can maintain a close contact with the machine operator. In some situations the work tickets for the task being performed are displayed at the work stations on a convenient clip board. When this is done, it may replace the form shown on the dispatch board for *on-machine*. Usually, when the operator completes his job, he returns to the dispatcher where he turns in the card for the work completed and picks up another; so the problem of feedback is not difficult.

With this general background of dispatching, the following discussion will be focused on different means of obtaining and sending information to the shop floor.

Manual Shop-Floor Control

In discussing a manual control system, one may either generalize or discuss a specific situation. With all the opportunities to present all variations of a system, to generalize would be confusing. A specific system will show you at least how one company, an electronics manufacturer, functions.

The company has a small sheet metal and machine shop where the chassis and similar parts are produced, and an extensive assembly area where a very complicated product is put together for both the domestic and the military market.

Production control is centralized and is located adjacent to the store room and the production area. Production control is manned by three clerks and a manager who have the necessary office and duplicating equipment to handle their work. Located in their area is a large scheduling board for the active work orders. In each of the manufacturing areas, next to the foremen's offices, are dispatch boards. The dispatch boards are filled by the scheduler from the production control department. The foreman in turn issues the orders from the board following as closely as possible the sequence given, but he is at liberty to adjust the schedule slightly when unusual conditions dictate. The foreman and the dispatcher work together for the highest efficiency possible. The procedure follows these steps:

Step 1.   Orders are initiated by a shop schedule which has been developed from sales order requests, from finished inventory, or by requests from the plant manager. All of these inputs are used to develop the *build schedule* for several months in advance. When this information is received, the production order number is placed on the schedule board.

Step 2.   Production control, working from the manufacturing schedule, proceeds to prepare the necessary paper work for processing the order.

Product prints and bills of materials are requested from the engineering department.

When they are received, a colored marker is placed on the schedule board.

Operation sheets are requested from the industrial engineering department, and when they are received, another marker goes on the board.

From these forms, a packet of materials is produced which contains the engineering prints, bills of material, operation sheets, and time cards. No materials-handling cards or inspection cards happen to be used in this system.

Step 3.   An extended bill of materials is sent to the combination inventory control and stores department. They remove the items from the record and order those items which are not in stock. All items are accumulated and placed in a tote pan. When the order is completed, the production control department is advised, and another marker is placed on the board showing that the order is ready to be released.

Step 4.   The shop packet in the meantime has been placed in a rack by release date according to the schedule.

Step 5.   When the day comes for releasing the order, the inventory, engineering print, and operations sheet markers are checked. If they are not on the board, inquiries are sent out to determine the cause of the delays. If any special tooling had to be produced, a tool order would have been placed and a marker placed on the board when word was received that it was completed.

Step 6.   When the shop order is released to the factory, the packet is taken out of the "hold" rack and placed in the "active" rack. The schedule board is prepared with operation markers. The space between the markers will indicate the scheduled times as extended from the operation sheet information.

Step 7.   The time cards are distributed to the appropriate department's dispatch boards. They will be placed on the work center positions in accordance with their priority, which is determined by customer requirements, material and machine availability, and many other considerations.

Step 8.   When an operator completes a job, he is given another one by the foreman. He proceeds to clock in on the job, selects the work from the area where it has been stored, reads the operation sheet and print, prepares his machine, and starts the work.

Step 9.   When the operator has completed the work, he moves it to a pick-up area for the materials handler, making sure that the shop packet is easily visible. He then clocks the time off on the job and clocks the time on to the next job. His completed time card is placed in the rack where it can be picked up by the dispatcher when he makes his rounds.

Step 10. The time card is returned to the production control department where it is used immediately to update the schedule board and is sent on to the payroll department. If a job is still being worked on at the end of the day, a separate time card will be filled out and sent to the dispatcher. If for one reason or another there is a delay, the foreman is told at once. He in turn relates this to production control so that they may reschedule the work.

The order moves from department to department under the supervision of production control. It is the feedback that comes from the time cards, the stock clerk, drawing department, and others that makes the system work. If this system permits too many errors, it is possible to make it more formal with written records replacing the verbal orders.

Step 11. When the work has been completed, it is sent on to finished inventory where it is recorded in under the manufacturing order number. It may bypass this stage and be sent directly to the shipping department where it meets the appropriate shipping instructions.

Step 12. All of the paper work is collected in the packet and filed for further reference.

One problem encountered in this type of manufacturing is how to control parts like the chassis which is made in the machine shop and requires a long lead time. Sometimes these parts may be controlled as an inventory item using the appropriate lot sizes. This is not always possible, and the order will encounter long lead times which means that the other parts which had been removed from inventory may have to sit an excessively long time. One solution is to release one order for the parts to be made and later to release another order for the assembly parts.

This is an adequate and common shop-floor control system for a company of small size, building the type of product described. There are better ways of organizing the system and probably poorer ways.

Shop-Floor Control by Computer

There should not be any differences between files used for a manual system and those used in a computer system. However, because information is current and easier to handle, there are more extensive files for the computer system. The following files are used in a computer installation, and you will notice that these are the same files presented as part of the data base.

Shop Status File. The shop status file is in reality four records which are: the machine record, the employee record, the shop-order master record, and the work-center queue record. Each of these will be described briefly:

The *machine record,* Figure 19–5, contains all of the information pertaining to each machine. The current assignment section, as shown, tells on which order the machine is running, or whether it is being set up or just sitting idle. The *next assignment* section shows the next order which is ready to go on the machine.

The *employee record,* Figure 19–6, is maintained for each worker. The job classification code indicates the type of work which the worker can perform. A status code shows whether he is direct or indirect labor, also if he is present or absent and if so, why. If the worker is assigned to a particular work center, this can be indicated on the employee record.

The *shop order master record* is illustrated in Figure 19–7. Before the order is released to the shop, a shop order master record is created to keep track of the order as it travels through the shop.

The shop master record has three sections: (1) a heading section to describe the order; (2) a current operations section, showing the operation being performed; and (3) a routing section which contains the details of all operations both completed and performed.

Work center queue record, Figure 19–8, reveals the present and projected load scheduled for each work center, and the orders are arranged by a priority code sequence. A status field indicates whether or not the order is in the work center or not.

Reporting Shop Status

There are three different ways of collecting information from the shop floor for reporting shop status: plant mail pickups, data collection equipment, and on-line data collection. Each of these systems will be described briefly. The inventory stores and tooling procedures will be deleted to concentrate on the operator and production control relationship.

Plant Mail Pickup. The information to and from the centralized control is handled by the regular plant mail system. This means data is being received at least once a day and probably much more frequently, such as every hour or so. This is not as fast as the systems described later but is adequate for many factories. The step-by-step procedure follows:

Step 1. At the time the computer creates the shop order master record, it will also punch one card for each operation on the routing sheet and one move-card for each time the order moves from work center to work center. These computer cards, along with the engineering prints, will become part of the shop packet.

Step 2. The shop packet is placed in a file by date to be released to the shop.

Step 3. The shop packet is released to the first work center.

Step 4. The assigned employee takes the correct operation card from the shop packet. Before he begins, he enters his employee number, date, start time, number of pieces received, and machine number.

Figure 19-5 Machine Record

Heading				Current Assignment						Next Assignment				
Machine No.	Dept. No.	Work Center No.	Current Status	Order No.	Order Qty.	Piece Count Partial Completion	Pre Start Time	Job Stand-ard	Emp. No.	Next Order No.	Order Qty.	Job Stand-ard	Emp. No.	Miscellaneous Data

Figure 19-6 Employee Record

Heading					Current Assignment					Next Assignment				
Emp. No.	Employee Name	Job Class-ification	Status	Custom-ary Mach. No.	Work Center No.	Machine No.	Order No.	Operation No.	Job Start Time	Next Order No.	Next Order Qty.	Op. No.	Work Center No.	Machine No.	Job Stand-ard	Miscellaneous Data

Figure 19-7 Shop Order Master Record

Heading

Order No.	Part No.	Part Class	Priority Code	Stock Date	Qty. Ordered	Qty. Available from Last Oper.	Work-in-Process Value	Release Date	Raw Material Confirmation	Tool Confirmation

Current Operation

Operation No.	Dept. No.	Work Center No.	Machine No.	Alternate Machine No.	Job Stand-ard	Set-Up Allow.	Bypassed Operation	Start Date	Tool Require-ments	Qty. Com-pleted	Status

Routing

Operation No. 1	Dept. No.	Work Center No.	Machine No.	Alternate Machine No.	Job Stand-ards	Set-Up Allow.	Start Date	Tool Require-ments	Operation No. 2

Tool Requirements

Figure 19-8 Work Center Queue Record

Work Center No.	Order No.	Start Time	Priority Code	Operation No.	Status	Set-Up Requirement	Machine No.	Load Hrs.

Courtesy: International Business Machines, Inc.

Step 5.   When the operation is completed, the operator enters the time, number of pieces completed, and date. If the number of pieces received is greater than those completed, a scrap report is made on the operation card. If a set-up man prepares the machine, this information is also filled in on the operation card.

Step 6.   The card is returned by plant mail pickup to central control for updating the record.

Step 7.   The material is sent to the next operation. The move card is filled out by the materials handler and sent to the central control so that the location of the order is known.

Step 8.   The sequence repeats itself until the job is completed.

If the job spans more than one shift, an additional card could have been made up at the time of processing or extra cards may be made available in the departments and filled out as needed.

If the job is worked on by more than one man, a group labor card containing the payroll numbers of all the operators is filled out, and central control in turn adjusts the time-card records of the individuals. This gives you in general how a plant mail pickup system functions.

Data Collection Equipment.   As you can imagine, a plant mail system is slow. An improvement is a data collection system consisting of computer-card readers, located at strategic places in the plant and connected with the control center. Entry to the reader is in the form of a punched card, an employee's badge, and a keyboard.

Cards or tapes are produced in the central control center which in turn are entered into the computer for updating the data-base files and generating reports for planning further operations. There are a number of data collection systems available. The operation of one system is presented here as step-by-step procedure. Again inventory control and tooling will not be included in order to focus attention on the operator and computer relationship.

Step 1.   Before the worker begins the first operation, he removes the operation card and places it along with his personal badge in the data collection unit. At the same time, the machine number and job code are keyed into the data collection unit. At the central control a card is produced with the operator's information to which the clock time is added.

Step 2.   The completion of the job is recorded in the same way as the starting procedure. A card is again punched with the recorded information and clock time. A group uses a group badge number which corresponds to a number file in the computer for crediting the individuals.

Step 3.   When material is moved from one location to another, the material handler reports in to the computer by reading in the move card and his personal badge.

Step 4.   The sequence of steps is repeated until the order is completed and released to inventory control. If an operation is not completed at the end of the shift, the worker reports to central control using the data collection system. He transmits his badge and job card information, and a code number indicates that the job is only partially completed.

The cards or tape which have been punched at the central control unit are entered into the computer for updating the various files and generating the reports from which plans for future operations may be made.

On-line Shop Status Reporting.   Rather than have the intermediate step of developing cards or tapes which must in turn be fed to the computer, the terminals can be on line directly with the computer. By this means the shop status files are constantly updated, and there is no delay caused by plant pickups and batch data processing. With on-line shop status reporting, the computer and consequently the production control personnel know at any time what each person and machine is doing.

The terminals are used for both input and output so that inquiries may be sent from the factory floor to the computer. The shop order and the move order are each represented by *one* card which goes with the material. Using one card is possible because of the immediate response available from the computer which contains the necessary sequence of operations for the order. When an operation is completed, the employee—using the data collection equipment—reports that the work is finished. The computer finds the employee's record and updates the current assignment section. The machine and shop order files are also updated.

When the material handler completes the movement of a shop order, he reports it to the computer via the data collection system. This is used to update the next-operation section of the shop order in the master records. The next assignment is then made by means of the terminal in the appropriate department.

Exception reporting is a key feature of on-line data collection. Whenever a piece of data is sent to the computer, it is compared with the record. If there is a discrepancy, it is immediately brought to the attention of the individual who can make the correction.

Tool control can also be handled by the computer data collection system. As the completion notices are processed, the shop order master record is brought up to date. The computer can be programmed to check if tools are needed and, if so, to request them from the tool crib using their terminal.

Move orders for rush orders may be handled on the exception basis. The computer can be programmed to print out move orders for the materials handlers when the ordinary sequence of operation will not work.

The on-line, shop-status reporting is an important improvement over the previous methods discussed. It should be apparent that this method can

Figure 19–9
Shop-Floor Terminal

go a long way in making it possible to satisfy customer's demands, keep the factory operating efficiently, and reduce the inventories, which are the objectives of any good shop-floor control systems.

Shop-Floor Communications

This next section will illustrate some of the devices used in shop-floor communications.

Computer Terminals. Illustrated in Figure 19–9 is a computer terminal which may be incorporated in the systems discussed in the previous section. These terminals have different capabilities. For some, the information is keyed in on a device similar to some telephones. Others accept cards or badges from which information is read. Interactive inquiry stations will give readouts either printed in hard copy or as a display on a cathode-ray tube, CRT.

Mini-Computers. There is a trend toward using small computers which are dedicated to the shop-floor control problems. These stand-alone systems permit operating on line at all times without any delays caused by batch processing. A typical system with the operator's station is illustrated in Figure 19–10.

Pneumatic Tube Communications. The pneumatic tube is an excellent way of communicating between remote points in a factory or even between buildings in a factory complex. It is especially useful when it is necessary to move papers, such as production orders, or even small parts required for quality control checks.

This system, which you see in large metropolitan department stores, carrying sales slips and cash to a centralized accounting office, can serve an important function in industry as well. The carrier consists of a capsule-like device (Figure 19–11) which moves through the tube by a difference in air pressure. Where a number of lines are used it is quite common to have a centralized dispatcher, but there is a system which makes it possible to dial the destination on the capsule and send it directly without further handling or delay.

Transacter. The Stromberg Transacter System is representative of an automatic data collection and transmission system which is suitable for the internal communications encountered in control. In its basic form it consists of a transmitting unit, the transacter, and the receiving unit, called a compiler.

As many as 36 transmitting units can be connected to one compiler, which means that transmitting units can be located throughout the plant wherever data are being generated. The compiler, on the other hand, is located at the nerve center of operations and will frequently be found in the data processing center.

The input unit, or transacter, is illustrated in Figure 19–12. Fixed information is entered by punched cards placed in the slot on the top of the

Figure 19–10
Mini-Computer and Operator's Station

Figure 19–11
Pneumatic Tube

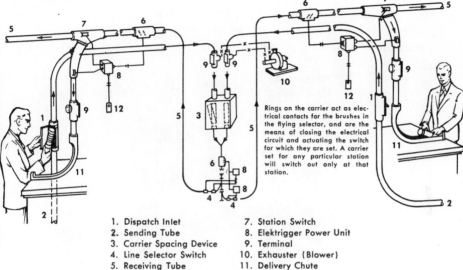

Rings on the carrier act as electrical contacts for the brushes in the flying selector, and are the means of closing the electrical circuit and actuating the switch for which they are set. A carrier set for any particular station will switch out only at that station.

1. Dispatch Inlet
2. Sending Tube
3. Carrier Spacing Device
4. Line Selector Switch
5. Receiving Tube
6. Flying Selector
7. Station Switch
8. Elektrigger Power Unit
9. Terminal
10. Exhauster (Blower)
11. Delivery Chute
12. Power Outlet

Figure 19–12
Transmitting Unit

Courtesy of General Time Corporation, Stromberg Division.

Figure 19–13
Receiving Unit

Courtesy of General Time Corporation, Stromberg Division.

console. This slot will accommodate several cards at one time. For example, the employee card, job card, and a prepunched variable card can be placed in the slot together, and all the related information will be conveyed at one time to the compiler where it is punched into paper tape. For variable information, the transactor has dials which can be set. Location codes and programming instructions are contributed by the transacter's self-contained plug board.

The compiler (Figure 19–13) has built-in checking circuits to insure that the message received is what has been sent. These messages are punched in paper tape at the rate of 60 characters per second. The tape can then be used with tape-to-punched-card converters, automatic typewriters, tape-to-tape converters, and for direct input into computers.

The versatility of the transacter system is extended by additional pieces of equipment, and one is an automatic badge reader (Figure 19–14). This

Figure 19–14
Time Clock

Courtesy of General Time Corporation,
Stromberg Division.

is an automatic time clock which uses the employee's badge as a time card. The card or badge, with prepunched information, is inserted in the clock and the information is instantaneously transmitted to the compiler, where the exact time and code number are punched into data processing tape. This information is entered into the data processing system to complete the payroll, thus eliminating all human operations and errors. These badge readers can also be used for other applications, such as document control. Also available with the transacter equipment is a high-speed read-out unit which can be used for listing information.

The transacter system eliminates many handwritten documents and presents information in a ready-to-use form to data processing systems. It is applicable to scheduling, payroll, quality control, inventory control, and other systems in a factory where high-speed communications are important.

Telecontrol. Telecontrol is another means of communicating between the activities on the factory floor and a central control point. All production information can be fed into the centralized control from remote stations, reducing the paper work involved in timekeeping, scheduling and rescheduling, dispatching, and other activities which are primarily communications.

This system has a control box (Figure 19–15) located at each production machine and work station. These boxes are linked electrically to a control panel (Figure 19–16) in a central control room. An actuator at the work station, consisting of a switch, is connected from the production activity, through the control box, and to the centralized control panel, where production is counted automatically. The control box at the machine is also equipped with switches, signal lights, and a phone jack which are connected with the central control panel.

Figure 19–15
Control Box

Figure 19–16
Control Panel

Courtesy of Hancock Telecontrol Corp.   *Courtesy of Hancock Telecontrol Corp.*

In the control room there is an individual display on a panel for each control box. The display has a holder for the job card and red and green lights which correspond to those on the control box, as well as time clocks and counters. The time clocks will register elapsed productive time and downtime. The counters record the units produced and the balance. In addition, there is a jack in which an operator key is placed which closes the circuit between the control box and the control panel so that production will be registered.

A green light on these control units indicates that production is progressing, while a flashing green light shows that the production order is nearing the end. A toggle switch on the control box turns on a flashing red light which warns the central dispatcher of trouble. He, in turn, can call the foreman by means of a public address system. The foreman carries a phone headset with him at all times and can communicate with the dispatcher through a phone jack on the control box. If the foreman authorizes downtime, he places a key in the lock switch for that machine, which immediately turns on the red light in the control panel and starts the downtime clock. A reset button on the control box is used to stop the recording of downtime and to clear the red light.

We have described only one manufacturer's version of this type of communications system, but other versions have also been widely accepted.

TELautograph. Perhaps you have stood around a railroad station schedule board and watched a small machine pen information regarding the arrival of trains. This machine, the TELautograph (Figure 19–17) obeys

Figure 19–17
TELautograph

Courtesy of TELautograph Corp.

perfectly the handwriting that is taking place on another machine in some remote location. The sender writes with an attached pen on a flat, horizontal surface, and the message is conveyed to the receiver where the information is written automatically on the horizontal surface of the receiving board. It not only conveys the message but develops a permanent record. The problems of scheduling both trains and production are similar, and so it is natural that the TELautograph has been applied to production control tasks.

Summary

Shop-floor control exists in all manufacturing. But efficient shop-floor control becomes most difficult to obtain in the job shop environment.

Shop-floor control runs the gamut from manual control systems using plant mail systems to highly sophisticated computerized systems.

Dispatching, which is an important part of shop-floor control, may be centralized or decentralized. Centralized control gives a tighter control but does not permit foremen and others the possibility of making on-the-spot decisions which may make the factory more efficient.

The number and urgency of the shop-floor communications make real-time data processing highly desirable. Real-time computer systems incorporated in a network of shop-floor terminals will undoubtedly be commonplace in the factory of tomorrow.

QUESTIONS

19-1. Discuss how shop-floor control can be used to make a Materials Requirement Planning system more efficient.

19-2. Dispatching is defined as "sequencing orders." Explain why this is not considered as part of scheduling.

19-3. List and discuss the pros and cons of centralized dispatching.

19-4. What forms will have the information needed for the dispatching operation?

19-5. How would the dispatch board be used to indicate when a machine is down for repair, or the worker is absent? Would this have any value to management?

19-6. In the example of the electronics firm, the assembly items were stock-picked at Step 3. What complications could this cause in inventory control?

19-7. Shop floor should incorporate tool control. Explain how this could be done.

19-8. The Shop Floor Control computer system consists of four records. What are they and explain why they are essential to the system.

19-9. List the advantages and disadvantages of the three ways of reporting shop status.

19-10. What advantages and disadvantages would a shop-floor dedicated computer have over a centralized computer system?

section five

Designing the Production and Inventory Control System

THE FIRST SECTIONS of the book gave you some basic information about production and inventory control. If you are interested in just operating a system, you have probably gone far enough. However, this book is written for those who wish to design and eventually manage the system. It is designing which these next chapters stress.

Chapter 20. Design of Organization and Physical Facilities

This may appear as an unusual subject for the introduction to the design of systems. However, remember that the system must operate in an environment of people and facilities. If these are not organized efficiently, then the system will operate inefficiently. This chapter presents check lists and other ways to improve the organization and physical facilities.

Chapter 21. Design of Manual Control Systems

The number of manual production and inventory control systems far surpasses the number of computerized systems when one considers every independent shop in the country. Even large plants may have some of their systems functioning by manual methods. The material presented in this chapter gives you a way of logically analyzing and describing manual systems. More than one company has used this type of material to reduce costs by thousands of dollars.

Chapter 22. Design of Machine Data Processing Systems

There is no longer any excuse for a system designer to imply that computer knowledge is not necessary. It is as basic to his needs as a knowledge of material characteristics is to a product designer. It is the substance of his design. This chapter should give you adequate background, but you should anticipate continued study if you wish to stay abreast of current developments.

Chapter 23. Programming and Software Packages

Programming may not be essential for operating a system, but it is necessary when designing and developing one. If need be, you can program your system or at least you will be able to converse with those who are programming it for you. This chapter will give you a skeleton of programming logic so that you may readily move on to more detailed studies.

The production control manager will be faced with decisions concerning software packages. These decisions may be placed in a logical structure for evaluation. This chapter presents such a structure.

20

Design of Organization and Physical Facilities

BEFORE CONSIDERING the design of a production system, it is essential to take into consideration the organization and physical facilities of the factory, for frequently the system design is limited by the characteristics of these two factors. The system may not need improvement at all, but the organization or physical facilities might need drastic overhauling. At any rate, the system designer will be wise to become well acquainted with the standards of acceptable organizations and facilities. That is the purpose of this chapter.

THE ORGANIZATION

Organizations are living dynamic organisms. Parts of the organism are growing and expanding while other parts are dormant, or even dying. As the organization grows, there are separations not unlike those that occur in the reproducing process of the cell. There is a time aspect of the organization's growth as different parts play important roles at different times during the life span. It is this dynamic aspect of an organization which makes it as difficult to deal with as to describe. One way of getting a grasp of the entire operation is by means of the organizational chart.

The Organizational Chart

The organizational chart is a symbolic method of representing the organization. Usually a "box," or rectangle, is used to represent a function performed by the plant manager, secretary, foreman, production control supervisor, and others. These boxes are interconnected to designate their relationship. The lines of authority and responsibility are inferred by the level of the boxes, as indicated on the diagram.

Before going further, you should have some idea of what a full-fledged organization looks like, but how can one observe anything as nebulous as an organization? Our only method is through the organizational charts shown in Figure 20–1. Here is a chart showing most of the major functions to be found in a manufacturing concern, but to say this is the way the organization actually functions would be extremely naïve.

Other sets of symbols have been used, such as circles instead of boxes, and occasionally we find a chart inverted so that those functions with the least authority are shown at the top, giving the effect of an inverted pyramid.

Organizational charts are desirable for any organization, but they do not tell all the story. There is no way of showing the channels of communications which exist as a result of empathy, union leadership, sports activities, and family ties, but the charts do serve as a basic structure and enforce a certain degree of discipline—which would not otherwise exist—upon an organization.

Organizational Dynamics

Before launching into a discussion of the principles involved in designing an organization, it is well to become aware of the growth of an organization. Very frequently an organization starts with just one man (Figure 20–2) who wants to go into business. More often than not, he has a limited amount of capital, and so is an inventor, engineer, capitalist, manufacturer, and salesman all at one time. This puts a strain on his abilities, and as he is able to afford the luxury of more help, he adds people to his organization. Perhaps he hires a salesman, a bookkeeper, and a production worker or two. So he has the first organization representing the factory's major functions. As growth continues, additional workers are added, which increase the owner's headache as he attempts to communicate with more and more people.

It won't be long before he sheds all these individual communications and delegates one person to take all the communications in finance, another person all the communications in sales, and another person for manufacturing. These groups will not all grow at the same rate, so eventually some individuals will have more employees reporting to them than others. Such would be the case in production, and it may be desirable to establish another layer of centralization.

This organization, responsible for production, is called the *line organization*; it is typified by authority extending down through the organization from the president, and responsibility reaching back up through the organization from the lowest level to the president. This, however, is a rather limited usage of the term *line organization*, and it is frequently used to refer to any organization within which authority and responsibility exist.

Figure 20–1
Factory Organizational Chart

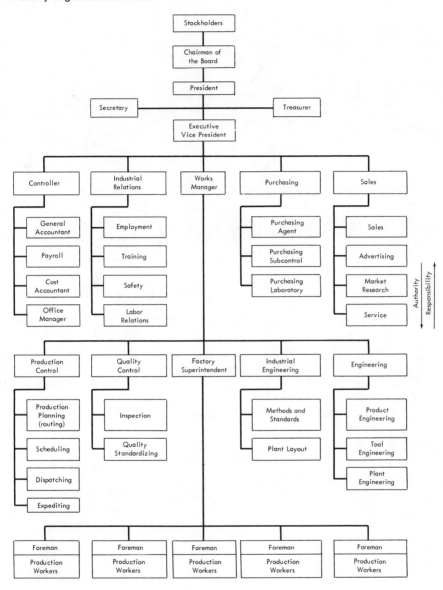

As an organization grows, it is apt to come under the influence of another growth formation. For example, in our earlier illustration the president-owner might have hired someone to help him, perhaps a typist-secretary, who would have no authority except as it was relayed through the president. The position of the typist-secretary, who is only advising, is that of *staff*. A better example might be the factory manager, who, finding that he was

Figure 20–2
The Development of an Organization

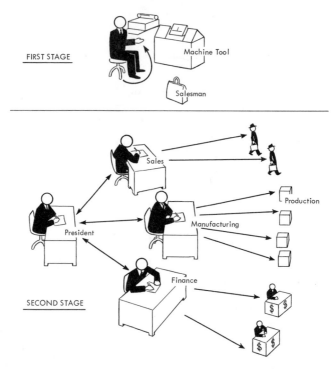

overloaded with detail, hired a person to take over the paper-work necessary for controlling production. The factory manager still maintains complete control and the staff worker merely advises him in which order the work should be performed.

Within the structure of an organization, as in many other things, it is difficult to find situations which are either black or white. And one seldom finds a staff position, for example, which is purely advisory. The line function, associated with the staff position, is often quite willing to give up or delegate some of its authority to the staff, at least as far as routine problems are concerned. This is what happens with the production control function. The production control function belongs with the factory manager, but the detail work would load him down to the extent that he would be unable to accomplish anything else. So he sets up a special group to take care of this area of activity. The factory manager will have to act only when something unusual comes up and the production control manager's authority is challenged. In time the area of authority will become well defined, so that the factory employees will know the realm within which the production control manager operates.

When a staff position has some area of authority, it is described as a *functional staff position*. Most staff positions come under this description because they exert some authority—if for no other reason than being at a higher level than some other positions.

Organization Design Principles

This being a book on the design of systems, it would be highly desirable if material of a quantitative nature could be furnished for designing an organization. Regrettably, this type of information is not available, but there are some acceptable principles of design which one should use. Some of these principles are obvious while others are intuitive, but they seem to have produced exceptional results. These principles and a brief statement about each will be given in this section.

Apply Analytical Techniques. The organization is a system, and therefore the method of logic discussed in Chapter 2 is a very useful tool in designing the organization. This, of course, includes obtaining all the facts about the problem and pursuing the same step-by-step procedure of logic as used in any other type of system.

Too frequently, organizational changes are made hastily, without due consideration for all the side effects. Remember, the organizational changes under consideration might have an impact upon other parts than the ones you wish to change. This might be checked by simulating the changes.

Define Objectives. The objectives of an organization, be it an entire factory or just a small department, should be stated and well known to all the employees. The top management should state the objectives in writing, in broad terms; while at each level below, the objectives should be restated in greater detail, as they affect the group.

If the officials of a company have decided they will produce only a high-quality product without regard to cost, this should be known up and down the organization. It would be most inefficient, if, by not stating the objectives, some employees thought that the emphasis should be placed on quality while others thought the emphasis should be placed on price. It is obvious there would be no end to the conflicts that would arise.

Design around Functions, Not People. Organizations should be designed around the essential functions and not around the available people. Ideally, the organizational structure should be designed without regard to individuals so the system remains stable, regardless of how people are moved from position to position. On the organizational chart it is best if the names of individuals do not appear at all.

We are, of course, speaking of the ideal organizational design, and seldom will it be possible to design the organization without giving some consideration to the individuals available. In the long run, however, designing around people is dangerous and leads to empire-building and too great a dependence upon certain key individuals.

Define Lines of Authority and Responsibility. Basic to the design of an organization is the fact that authority extends downward through the organization while responsibility extends upward, as has been illustrated on the charts. Each echelon is responsible for the activities of the echelons below and has authority over those echelons, for it is basic to the design of an organization that an echelon should not be responsible for the actions of a group if it does not have authority over it also. Responsibility and authority must be well defined, and one must not have responsibility over something for which he does not have authority.

Strive for a Balanced Organization. An old truism in engineering design is: *If it looks right, it is probably designed right,* and the same follows for an organizational structure. It should be well balanced, and one should look for inefficiencies where the organization appears to be overbalanced. A company which uses a large number of expediters for the size of the production force is suspect, and a close scrutiny will undoubtedly show an inefficiency in the production control department.

Policies Should Be Established. One would not consider designing a structure without dictating the specifications of the components making up the whole. In the same way, the functional components of an organization must have specifications laid down. The policies indicate the limits of response for a part of the system. As in any design, these should be written down clearly and specifically so they can never be misinterpreted. In a well-designed organization this is done by a policy manual. The company, as well as each department, should maintain a policy manual, to be referred to at any time.

Include Exception Principle. No competent designer would design a system without taking into consideration the possibility of an overload, and the same should be true in an organizational design. There are times when the problems just do not fit the routines covered by the policy manual, so provisions must be made for these condtions. This is commonly called the "exception principle."

This might be illustrated by functions 1, 2, 3, and 4, coming under A's authority and responsibility. These four functions normally operate within the limits of the policy established for them. If something unusual comes up, an *exception,* it is referred to A. This chain extends on up through the organization and can account for the highly efficient way some organizations operate. In contrast to this system, we have situations where a large share of the questions filter up through the organization for decisions, with resulting inefficiencies.

Allow for Growth. All organizations are dynamic and are usually expanding if they are healthy. This means that an organization cannot just be designed for today; every possible direction for expansion must be taken into consideration. Bridge designers take into consideration the advent of heavier vehicles and increased volume to the extent of providing for the addition of roadbeds and even double decks. The same philosophy must follow in the design of an organization. Today, a manufacturing organization must consider that production control might grow through the card-data-processing stage into extensive computer processing. This can result in radical changes in the organizational structure as the functions become more centralized.

Span of Control.   This idea, probably first defined by Henri Fayol, pioneer organizational theorist, has a close analogy in engineering systems. It is essential that any one component of a system be able to withstand all the inputs leading to it. One circuit feeding several circuits must be able to handle the flow of current of all the individual circuits. A beam supporting others must be able to support the sum of the loads.

In an organization, the individual in a function must be able to exercise authority and accept responsibility for the aggregate of functions below him on the organizational chart. Standards have been established for the *span of control* for an individual, but it is doubtful that they are meaningful, the reason being that we actually do not have any specifications for the individual. What might be a light load for one could be a heavy load for another. In any case, the span of control should be kept at a workable and efficient level.

Strive for Simplicity.   The organization should be designed as simply as possible to perform the function it is to serve. Any frills will undoubtedly affect the function in an adverse manner and will add to the overhead.

Minimize Costs.   As in every design, cost should be taken into consideration. The cost of a design improvement must be compared with the value of the improvement. Not only must the increase in cost and value be considered, but the cost of increasing the reliability of the system must also be taken into consideration.

Standardization.   In all designs we try to get the highest efficiency by standardizing the components. This concept can be carried over into the organizational design by having the functions standardized. People filling these functions can then be readily shifted as desired. This tends to develop experts in these activities with extensive knowledge and skill. This may be seen on a production line, where one job is the tightening of a bolt, and may also be found in the controller's office, where one job is taking care of a certain part of the accounts payable. One danger of this policy, if carried to the extreme, is that no individuals are trained in breadth to fill the higher echelons.

Departmentalization.   The design of the organization should include well-defined departments with established and recognized boundaries. This is helpful in developing team spirit, an essential ingredient in any organization. Where departmental boundaries are not well defined there is apt to be a shifting of responsibility and unbalanced work loads. Energetic workers will constantly increase their work loads while departments with lazy people will constantly do less.

We know it is efficient to group similar things into classes, and this follows in the organizational design. Similar activites should be grouped under one function.

Keep Lines of Communication Short. The lines of communication should be just as short and direct as possible. The more times a communication has to be repeated, the more possibilities there are for errors to occur. Long lines of communication also account for unnecessary delays.

No set of principles will account for all the design problems you will encounter in industry. Often an organization grows up not knowing exactly what its final objective is. People are hired at levels beyond their abilities, or they do not continue to produce; but rather than replace the people in the function, the function is isolated by establishing a duplicate or similar function. This is especially typical of a family-owned business where a home must be found for some of the more ineffective members of the clan. Often members of an organization collect a political power which would cause a disturbance if they were replaced. Instead of being replaced, these individuals are merely sealed off and left to wither. This is not unlike the growth of any other organism which becomes infected: the diseased portion is isolated.

The Organization and System Designing

There is little doubt that the factory organization is a system; and the production control function within the organization is just a subset of the larger system. Since it is a system, the method of logic for designing a system is a suitable approach for designing and redesigning the organization.

You are studying system designing so that eventually you will be able to put your knowledge into practice by developing improved control systems. Often the efficiency of the control system depends upon how well the organization is designed. It is therefore imperative for you to learn how to analyze and improve the organization. At least you should be aware of structural weaknesses if redesigning the organization is not permissible.

The organization is a complex system about which little is actually known. Contrary to the knowledge available in many physical systems, we are never quite sure what effect the changes made on one part of the system will have on others. Eventually, we can hope to have such useful design information, but not in the present state of the art. Now, we must depend upon *design considerations*, which are hardly more than rules of thumb for designing the organization.

THE PHYSICAL FACILITIES

Routing the product through the processes of an existing plant is part of the *process designing* activity. However, modifying the plant facilities to conform to the process is the *plant layout* activity. These two approaches are merely different ways of attacking the same problem.

If the production set-up times are short, it will generally pay to route the product from one machine to another. However, if the production set-up times are long, and if it is otherwise feasible, the equipment should be arranged so the materials flow directly from one operation to the next.

Because of these two facets of the same problem, we find factory facilities organized in the two distinctive patterns of a job shop and a production line. There are several reasons for making the decision, one way or the other, but the important one is the length of the set-up time—or how long the machines will be doing a particular job. If the machines are to be used for just a short time for a particular job, and the flow pattern will change drastically from job to job, then it is probably desirable to group the machines by the kind of work they perform.

The type of layout should not be associated with the quantity of product alone. For instance, nails are produced in large quantities in plants laid out as job shops. Why? Because the headers, which produce the nail heads, are noisy, and the plating processes have disagreeable fumes.

There are other reasons, besides the length of set-up time, which dictate a job shop layout. In some cases the process may require air-conditioning, or the process may be screened from public view because it is secret, or perhaps the layout is dictated by the weight of the product or by machines which might overstress the floor in some areas.

It is not intended to imply that a factory must be either a job shop or a production line, for it is frequently a combination of both. It is common to find a factory producing parts in a job shop but assembling on a production line. In this case, the parts are produced at such a high rate it does not pay to maintain production lines for them. Occasionally, a job shop finds that a certain sequence of operations occurs so frequently it is desirable to put several machines together in a line, such as placing a drilling machine in the lathe department for the frequent drilling jobs that need to be made on turned spindles.

The Tools of Plant Layout

The many excellent references to plant layout furnish adequate descriptions of the various tools for improving the plant layout design. Space will permit only a brief coverage of the subject here.

Process Chart. As shown in Figure 20–3, the process chart is a quick way of analyzing the process. Starting with the operation sheet, or with the actual flow of the product on the floor, a chart is made which shows every step of the process. A well-accepted set of symbols for charting has been established which represents operation, move, storage, and inspection. Others might be added as needed. And this chart is, of course, not the final objective of this technique.)

The next step is to analyze the flow for any unnecessary delays, operations out of sequence, or other signs of inefficient operation. From this analysis a new and improved chart is drawn, as shown in Figure 20–4. This now becomes the model for the improved plant layout. It should be apparent that this is a far more efficient way of analyzing and improving the factory layout, as compared with actually moving the machines about on the factory floor.

Figure 20–3
Process Chart (original)

INDUSTRIAL ENGINEERING DIVISION

SUMMARY	
OPERATIONS	7
TRANSPORTS	0
TEM. STORAGE	8
PER: STORAGE	1
INSPECTION	1
VERT. DISTANCE	–
HORIZ. DISTANCE	44
TIME	1.01

PROCESS CHART

OPERATION ASSEMBLE DEMONSTRATION
_____ PACKAGE
PRODUCT CONSUMER PACKAGE

DEPARTMENT ASSEMBLY
PRESENT ___X___ PROPOSED _____

BINDER	37X-4
CHART	1
SHEET 1	OF 1
CHARTED	
James Jones	
DATE	3/22/--
CHECKED	GCH
APPROVED	GCH

NO.	DIST. IN FEET	TIME IN HOURS	OPER'N	TRANSP.	PERM.ST	INSP'N	DESCRIPTION
1.	2	.12	①				Pick up bindings – dispose to tote box.
2.	2						Storage prior to next operation.
3.	2	.14	②				Assemble bindings, holders, and tapped bearing insert into outer container using special pliers – dispose to tote box.
4.	2						Storage prior to next operation.
5.	4	.15	③				Fasten container to body with screw.
6.	4						Storage prior to next operation.
7.	4	.27	④				Insert holding screws, attach advertising and place outer cover on container at work place 1 or 2 – dispose to tote box.
8.	4						Storage prior to next operation.
9.	3	.10	⑤				Seal rip string to cover – dispose to tote box.
10.	3						Storage prior to next operation.
11.	2	.09	⑥				Notch container – dispose to tote box.
12.	2						Storage prior to next operation.
13.	2	.07				1	Inspect container – dispose to tote box.
14.	2						Storage to next operation.
15.	2	.07	⑦				Label container – dispose to tote box.
16.	4						Accumulate packages.
17.							Storage prior to packing.

△ TEMPORARY STORAGE CAN BE DENOTED BY

KP6 340818

Figure 20–4
Process Chart (revised)

INDUSTRIAL ENGINEERING DIVISION

PROCESS CHART

SUMMARY	
OPERATIONS	5
TRANSPORTS	0
TEM. STORAGE	4
PER: STORAGE	1
INSPECTION	1
VERT. DISTANCE	–
HORIZ. DISTANCE	24
TIME	.60

OPERATION ASSEMBLE DEMONSTRATION PACKAGE

PRODUCT CONSUMER PACKAGE

DEPARTMENT ASSEMBLY

PRESENT _____ PROPOSED ___X___

BINDER 37X-4
CHART 1
SHEET 1 OF 1
CHARTED
James Jones
DATE 3-27--
CHECKED GCH
APPROVED GCH

NO.	DIST. IN FEET	TIME IN HOURS	OPER'N	TRANSP.	PERM.ST.	INSP'N	DESCRIPTION
1.	1	.12					Pick up bindings – dispose to special holder.
2.	2	.11					Assemble bindings, holders and key slot bearing and insert into container using special pliers – dispose to tote box.
3.	2						Storage prior to operation.
4.	2	.13					Insert holding screws, attach advertising and place outer cover on container – dispose to tote box.
5.	2						Storage prior to next operation.
6.	7	.13					Seal rip string to cover and notch container – dispose to tote box
7.	2						Storage prior to next operation.
8.	2	.11					Inspect and label container – dispose to tote box.
9.	4						Accumulate packages.
10.							Storage prior to packages.
11.							
12.							
13.							
14.							
15.							
16.							
17.							

TEMPORARY STORAGE CAN BE DENOTED BY △

KP4 34001B

Flow Process Diagram. As illustrated in Figure 20–5 the flow process diagram is related to the charting technique just discussed, but it has the advantage of showing the flow of the product on the floor diagram. Long hauls of materials and points of traffic congestion will show up more quickly on the diagram than on the chart. A disadvantage is that the floor diagram has to be made, but frequently this can be just a rough sketch.

Figure 20–5
Flow Process Diagram

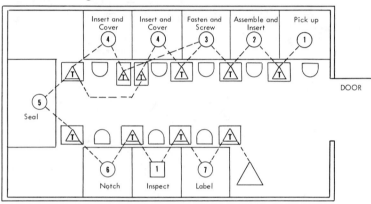

PRESENT METHOD

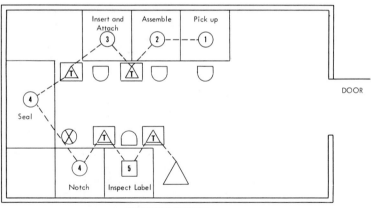

PROPOSED METHOD

Courtesy of Eastman Kodak Company.

Two-Dimensional Layouts. This tool of plant layout consists of the floor plan with templates of the production equipment placed in the proper positions. The templates can be homemade or purchased, of heavy paper or plastic. They can be shifted to represent various layouts. Obviously, it is easier to envision the plant and flow of materials with this type of layout than it is with the flow process diagram.

Three-Dimensional Layouts. These layouts are made with models which are easily produced in a model shop, or purchased. They are usually made to the scale of one-half inch equals one foot. The advantage of this layout (Figure 20–6) over the previous method is the ease of envisioning all the

Figure 20–6
Three-Dimensional Layout

Courtesy of General Motors Engineering Journal.

details, including the inferences that might be caused by machines and materials. These model layouts are also used for such a purpose as introducing new employees and visitors to the complexity of the factory.

Mentioned here are the most important tools of plant layout, and with them remarkable savings can be made in the plant operation. There are other techniques, and refinements of the methods discussed here, with which everyone interested in the efficient operation of a factory should become familiar.

Plant Layout Design Principles

As in organizational design, it is difficult to state any quantitative design criteria for plant layout, but there are a number of well-accepted design principles. Some of the most important ones are:

Material Flow Should Comply with the Steps of the Process. The most efficient way to manufacture a product is to organize the machines so that the material flows the shortest possible distance, directly from one machine to the other, with little or no delay.

Move Material at a Minimum Cost. It is an old cliché that the best solution to a materials-handling problem is not to move the material. If this is impossible, then move it by gravity. And if this is not possible, usually the next best way is to move it by power. If people must move the material, it should be moved by the cheapest labor possible.

Minimize All Production Delays. Production delays should be minimized for several reasons. They are the source of customer dissatisfaction. Inventories will increase with the consequent costs of warehousing and large investments. The smooth flow of material at a constant rate will have a favorable effect upon the morale of the factory personnel.

Utilize Space for Production. The primary purpose of the factory is to produce goods. Any space that is not used for this purpose should be suspect. Of course there must be space for storage, aisles, and service areas; and the plant personnel should not feel crowded, but steps should be taken to make as much of the space as productive as possible.

Provide for Adequate Storage. Often unexpected production delays occur. When possible, these should be predicted and provision made for storing the material. The stored material should be protected and out of the way of normal production.

Maintain Material Identification. In many situations it is essential that the material be moved through the factory without losing its identity. This is especially true when material is not easily recognized as belonging to a particular product or order. It is also true when the quality record must be maintained for some time in the future, as for aircraft components. But identification is also important for production control in a job shop, where parts are moved through the factory in lots. Periodic scrap drives are the costly result of not placing enough emphasis upon this design consideration.

Keep Direct Labor Productive. It is not uncommon to find direct laborers moving material, running errands, and other nonproductive activities. Direct labor should be kept productive, and actively producing the product.

Keep Machine Loads Balanced. On the production line, it is desirable to keep the work loads balanced from machine to machine so that each is operating near its full capacity. When several machines are being operated by one person, an effort should be made to arrange the work so that the machines and the individuals are as productive as possible.

Minimize Capital Investment. This design consideration appears at many points in the plant design, as when machines have been overdesigned and when idle machines and idle inventory are permitted—all indications of poor utilization of capital investment.

Design for Flexibility. Seldom would a plant be designed and built without the consideration of future alterations. Changes in volume, changes in product design, the addition of new and better processes, all these indicate the necessity for a flexible design.

Maintain Quality Standards. A product can lose its value as it travels through the plant because it becomes contaminated, deteriorates, or is just shopworn. Every effort should be made in the layout of the plant to maintain the quality of the product and not decrease its value.

Apply Methods Improvement to Work Center. The plant layout design is not completed until each work center is carefully scrutinized and improved, for here is a point that will yield a big payoff.

Consider the Employees' Safety and Comfort. Safety measures can be directly reflected by the reduction of insurance premiums, but there are also indirect rewards that can be gained by a company practicing good safety rules. Delays in production can be kept at a minimum, and morale can be markedly improved if personnel realize that their safety is of importance to the management. The OSHA standards have given a new importance to factory safety.

Provide for Efficient Supervision and Control. Departments should be of a size that can be efficiently supervised, and the processes should be grouped to offer the best supervision possible. Control offices and dispatch boards should be conveniently located to eliminate any undue delays and reduction in production time. *Feedback links* to the production control system should be immediate and accurate.

Physical Facilities and System Designing

Recalling the definition of a system, there is little doubt that the factory facilities form a system. A very complex system it is, of machines and other physical facilities which function together for a common purpose. Therefore the steps of logic used in system designing are applicable to the design of the physical facilities:

1. Become aware of the problem.
2. Define the problem.
3. Locate, evaluate, and organize information.
4. Discover relationships and formulate hypotheses.
5. Evaluate the hypotheses.
6. Apply the solution.

The objective in *system designing for production control* is usually the imposition of control on the present layout of the physical facilities, however it does not rule out the design or redesign of the physical facilities to meet the control requirements. Usually, books and college courses which emphasize the physical facilities come under the subject of *plant layout*. Production control and plant layout are highly correlated and are two different ways of looking at similar problems.

Summary

The design of a system cannot be considered without taking into account the environment within which it is to operate. In the factory the environment consists of the organization and the manufacturing facilities. Often any system imposed upon this environment will fail because of these two factors.

Organizations are depicted by charts, but these often tell only part of the story. The sciences of organization and facilities design have not matured to the point where all the numerous relationships can be described by equations, but as in other disciplines, this has not prevented us from designing. The designing is facilitated by a number of well known and accepted design considerations which are practiced by competent designers.

QUESTIONS

20–1. Is the organizational structure for a factory likely to change as it matures? Explain your answer. If the organization does change, where would you expect the greatest change?

20–2. How efficiently does an organizational chart explain an organizational structure?

20–3. As related to the organization, define:
  a. Line.
  b. Staff.
  c. Functional staff.

20–4. Which organizational design consideration do you consider the most important? Explain why.

20–5. In what type and size plant will the plant layout function play an important part? Explain your answer.

20–6. What advantage does a three-dimensional layout have over a two-dimensional layout?

20–7. Does a manufacturing plant ever include both job shop and production line layouts?

20–8. Job shop layouts are associated with what type of product? Production line layouts are associated with what type of product?

20–9. Which plant layout design consideration do you consider the most important? The least important? Explain why.

20–10. Draw an organizational chart for a company with which you are acquainted. Redesign the organization and explain how you have used the *design considerations*.

21

Design of Manual Control Systems

IN MANY RESPECTS, all that has gone before is culminated in this chapter. You will remember that system designing was defined as: conceiving and planning in the mind a complex unity of many diverse parts to exercise restraining influence over the making of goods.

The emphasis now will be upon how the systems are analyzed and synthesized to fit the various components together in an efficient system. Again it should be stressed that the signal and the system are two separate things: the system is being discussed and not the decisions that are imposed upon the system. The system might carry the signals perfectly, but if the signals are imperfect, the message will be imperfect.

The following chapters will cover the entire gamut of manufacturing-control system designing, from the simplest flow of paper work for manual systems to the more complicated computerized systems. Discussion of computer programming in these surroundings should not be startling if one considers the basic problem of assembling a group of components for conveying information and carrying out instructions. In a noncomputerized system, people are asked to follow the system that has been established. In a card-data-processing system, the instructions are given to the personnel in the data processing center, who in turn give them to the machines by instructions wired on the panel. In electronic data processing the instructions are also carried out by the personnel as well as by the computer which is instructed by its program.

In an era of electronic gadgetry, the computers have gained an aura of exotic mystery, but in reality they are not as complex as the human being. The computer is more predictable since it interprets instructions only as written. It can only make the logical decisions which are given to it in the computer program. This is not true for the human being, who, fortunately, or unfortunately, makes decisions on his own.

SYSTEM DESIGNING FOR MANUAL METHODS

Factory managers are accustomed to thinking of the step-by-step process needed to produce their products and constantly look for means of improvement in order to reduce direct costs and thereby increase profits. A parallel can be drawn between the product process and the paper-work procedure; the procedure being a *series of related clerical steps used to process a business form*. Improvements here are revealed in the reduction of both direct and indirect costs, which also increase profits; and profits produced in this way are just as good as those produced by process improvement. Since more companies have given less attention to their procedures than they have to their processes, the opportunities for profit-hunting by procedure analysis usually are excellent.

Some of the numerous opportunities for improvements and savings are: savings in costs by a reduction in the number of business forms and by elimination of unnecessary steps in their processing; improved customer relations by a reduction in the order processing time and by more efficient handling of the customers' inquiries; and improved employee relations by well-outlined methods and fixed responsibility.

Steps of the Systems Analysis

Systems analysis consists of three steps:

1. *Paper-Flow Charting.* This step consists of showing the flow of the paper work by some schematic arrangement. After a suitable chart is drawn, the flow is analyzed for possible improvements and a new improved procedure is developed.

2. *Design of Forms.* All the forms are designed, or redesigned, so that they can be used efficiently. This means forms must be designed to satisfy a well-thought-out set of criteria for efficiency.

3. *Procedures Manual.* Step-by-step instructions must be written to show how the improved procedure is to be operated. This could be considered as the rulebook by which the procedures are played. Changes can and should be made, but only after adequate consideration.

Preceding any attempt at paper-flow charting, the procedures analyst should become acquainted with the organization. If a chart of the organization is unavailable, one must be produced which will assist the analyst in getting orientated. The analyst should accept some responsibility in suggesting changes which will make a more efficient organizational structure.

The Paper-Flow Charting. After an overall view of the organization is obtained, it is essential to produce a detailed picture of the present system. To do this it is necessary to interview each employee involved and to record his part in the procedure. This is not always easily done, for employees frequently find it difficult to relate everything they do. The analyst must be patient in his endeavors to draw out the necessary facts and must be skilled in separating fact from fiction. He must also take care not to become involved in the personal problems of the employee. Several interviews are sometimes necssary before the information chinks are filled.

A verbal description alone is confusing to analyze, so the acceptable method is the graphic paper-flow chart, an example of which is shown in Figure 21–1.

Figure 21–1
Paper-Flow Chart

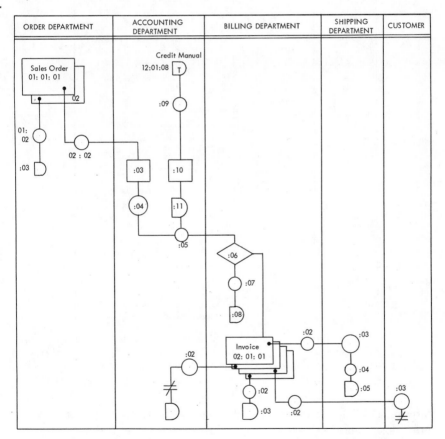

To explain the chart one must know the language. There are many languages, or sets of symbols, to be found in the literature, but a useful code is the one shown in Figure 21–2. Since this code is just a tool, you should feel free to alter or add to it to serve your purpose.

As with any language there must be rules, such as: Charting should start

Figure 21–2
Paper-Flow Charting Symbols

SYMBOL	NAME	DESCRIPTION
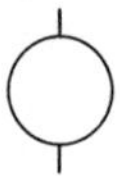	Operation	Work being done on a form: information being added, balance being extended, etc.
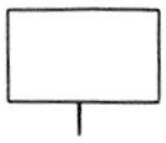	Origin Operation	Operation when it is the origination of a form.
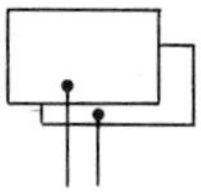	Origin Operation	Operation when it is the origination of more than one form.
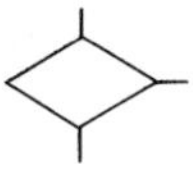	Operation Take-off	Operation when information is transcribed to another form. Horizontal line connects the two forms.
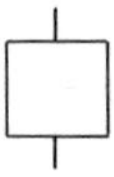	Inspection	Determination of the correctness of information.
	Move	Form is moved from one location to another.
	File	Form is placed in an organized filing system.
	Temporary File	Form awaiting to be moved for further work.
	Disposal	Form is destroyed.
	Break	A break in the procedure analysis indicating something that is not pertinent to the study.

in the upper left-hand corner and progress downward and to the right. The vertical axis shows the sequence of chronological events, with the first events at the top. Columns on the chart may be used to represent different forms or, as in the example, different departments through which the paper forms flow. Charting only the paper flow would serve little purpose; it is necessary to analyze the flow for possible improvement. This can best be done by asking questions such as:

System Design Checklist

_____ Can any forms be eliminated?
_____ Can any step be eliminated?

_____ Can any other person do the operation better?

_____ Can any steps be combined to advantage?

_____ Can any steps be subdivided to advantage?

_____ Can the sequence of steps be improved?

_____ Can spot checks be substituted for 100 percent inspection?

_____ Can the originator of a form furnish more information, and on a better form?

_____ Are work loads balanced?

_____ Could a lower paid employee do the operation?

_____ Can delays be eliminated or utilized for other operations?

_____ Can the travel distance be reduced?

_____ Can bottleneck operations be scheduled better?

_____ Can forms be presorted while completing an operation?

_____ Can any filing operation be eliminated? Why save this form?

_____ Is a record being kept in more than one place?

_____ Can any employee offer suggestions to improve the procedure?

There are other questions the inquisitive mind must ask (make a practice of it) for no checklist will ever supplant the curiosity of the good analyst. Of course, asking the questions is not enough; a new chart must be developed showing the improved method, and getting the improved method into use is the ultimate goal.

During the analysis one should see many opportunities to improve the design of the form used. Frequently the type of form will be abandoned in favor of a form which can be handled more easily or which will present information in a more vivid fashion.

Design of Forms. The design of business procedure forms is merely applied-common-sense. In general, the thing to keep in mind is how easy it is to add or remove information, whether this be by hand or by machine. But since it is difficult to keep all the numerous considerations in mind, a checklist is the best approach.

Form Design Checklist

_____ Is this form necessary, or is its purpose served by another form?

_____ Does this form have a title which really describes its purpose?

_____ Are there adequate instructions on the form for its general use?

_____ Are sorting symbols in the most convenient place?

_____ If the form is a traveler, does it need a space for addressor and addressee?

_____ Is the form of a suitable size for filing?

_____ Are there adequate margins for binding?

_____ Can both sides of the form be used?

_____ Will the forms get dirty? If so, how should they be protected?

_____ Is common information grouped in blocks? Is all the information used by one person or department placed in one location?

_____ Are data which could cause serious transcription errors separated on the form?

_____ Is the information in convenient sequence for transcription?

_____ Can more common information be printed on the form, rather than filled in?

_____ Are spaces adequate for the information to be filled in?

_____ Do the printed lines conform to typewriter spacing?

_____ Is print arranged for a minimum number of typewriter stop settings? (Stop settings should conform to other business forms in use.)

_____ Would horizontal or vertical lines help reduce errors?

_____ Can check boxes be used as a substitute for written-in information?

_____ Can any wording be misinterpreted?

_____ Can a common sketch, with fill-in spaces for specifications, be substituted for blueprints or other descriptive material?

_____ Is all the information necessary?

_____ Does the form create a good appearance? Would it create a good mental attitude in the user?

_____ Will colored paper help in identification or filing?

_____ Can the employee who uses the form suggest improvements?

Written Standard Procedure.   Improved procedures and new forms will be worthless unless the employees accept them as their own and follow them to the letter. The only thing to do is to freeze the system in a *Written Standard Procedure*. The Written Standard Procedure includes simple direct instructions in how the forms are to be used. It offers many advantages by serving as an instruction to new employees: they can see the whole picture as well as their own small part. It also prevents conflicting procedures from being inaugurated, and it presents a basis for job descriptions and disciplines.

The method of writing a Written Standard Procedure is simple. For each symbol on the chart there should be a short imperative statement. The instructions should be direct, care being taken not to insult the reader but leaving no question in his mind regarding his duty. The steps in the procedure should be indexed in some organized fashion. A simple, convenient way of doing this is to use a sequence of three numbers, both on the chart and on the Written Standard Procedure; for example:

$$01:02:04.$$

The first two digits represent the form number: *01*, in this case, represents the sales order, while the second set of digits, *02*, refers to the copy in the set, and the third set of digits, *04*, refers to the step in the procedure. The two first digits find a useful place in the organization as an index number for forms, and they should be printed on the forms. The paper-flow chart should be numbered so that the standard operations are keyed to it for ready reference. A skeleton form of the Written Standard Procedure is shown in Figure 21–3.

Figure 21–3
Written Standard Procedure

Sales Order 01
Form 01 Sales Order, Copy 01
01:01:01   Write up sales order
:02   Move to file
:03   File in numerical order
Form 01 Sales Order, Copy 02
01:02:01   Write up sales order
:02   Move sales order to accounting department
:03   Check sales order with credit manual
:04   Fill in accounting information
:05   Move second copy of sales order to billing department
:06   Remove information for invoice
:07   Move to files
:08   File
Form 02, Invoice Copy 01
02:01:01   Write up invoice from sales order
:02   Move to shipping department
:03   Fill order
:04   Move to file
:05   File

All the procedures should be kept in manuals, which are distributed to responsible people in the organization. The procedures should be reviewed periodically, and the revisions distributed.

This step-by-step method of squeezing profits out of paper work is one that can be successful for anyone, and with very little practice. One thing that cannot be taught is how to acquire an inquisitive mind; this you *must* have, and this, used with the tools discussed here, will pay big dividends. There are many other approaches to the procedure analysis which will give good results. The symbols given should serve you well, but remember that the objective is to communicate with people. If they understand another set of symbols, then by all means use them.

Travel Charting of Forms

An efficient method of analyzing the flow of charts is illustrated in Figure 21–4. This chart which is similar to the mileage charts to be found on road maps shows how two departments in an organization are related. Instead of distance at the intersection, the two related departments are indicated. This form combined with a verbal description makes an efficient way of seeing how two functions are interrelated.

Figure 21–4
Travel Charting

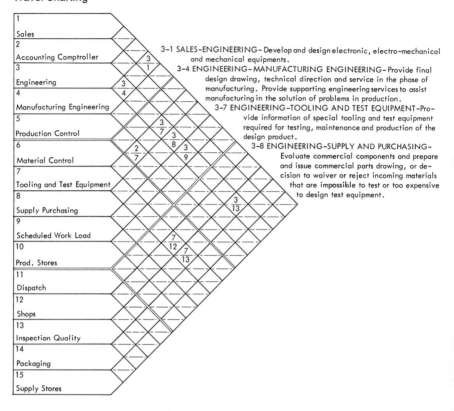

3-1 SALES-ENGINEERING-Develop and design electronic, electro-mechanical and mechanical equipments.

3-4 ENGINEERING-MANUFACTURING ENGINEERING- Provide final design drawing, technical direction and service in the phase of manufacturing. Provide supporting engineering services to assist manufacturing in the solution of problems in production.

3-7 ENGINEERING-TOOLING AND TEST EQUIPMENT-Provide information of special tooling and test equipment required for testing, maintenance and production of the design product.

3-8 ENGINEERING-SUPPLY AND PURCHASING- Evaluate commercial components and prepare and issue commercial parts drawing, or decision to waiver or reject incoming materials that are impossible to test or too expensive to design test equipment.

1 Sales
2 Accounting Comptroller
3 Engineering
4 Manufacturing Engineering
5 Production Control
6 Material Control
7 Tooling and Test Equipment
8 Supply Purchasing
9 Scheduled Work Load
10 Prod. Stores
11 Dispatch
12 Shops
13 Inspection Quality
14 Packaging
15 Supply Stores

DESIGN AND REDESIGN EXAMPLES

A system design and redesign examples, preceded by some general information about the company, the product, and whatever is necessary to give you an insight to the example, will be presented. After the brief introduction, the system will be isolated and presented. As you would anticipate, this is an improved design, but not a perfect design. There is always the possibility of further improvement. In fact, you might look for ways of improving the system presented. The possibility of improvement is what makes system designing so challenging.

Not only will you obtain some insight into system analysis but you will also become familiar with some real systems which work. A methodical approach to designing a system will be used. It is a method you may wish to follow when you become involved in similar problems during your industrial experience. These steps are:

1. Record and analyze the structure of the organization. Often the organizational chart has not been drawn, and consequently the areas of authority and responsibility are not known.

2. Make a flow chart of the present system, for this is the only way to visualize it clearly. A chart helps to draw out conflicting viewpoints and gives an opportunity to obtain and record the information in a short time. You can then remove yourself from the distracting factory environment to consider any improvements.

3. Redesign the system and describe it with a revised flow chart. This is the "thinking" step. It gives the designer an opportunity to experiment with several designs. Do not forget that there will be other people who can contribute worthwhile ideas on how the system should be designed. Explore all possibilities, but give credit to all those who contribute.

4. During and after the redesigning step the forms should be analyzed to determine their efficiency. The check list presented earlier is useful in this step.

5. All of the work done in the previous steps culminates in the Standard Operating Procedure. This set of written instructions explains to each individual involved in the system what he must do to make the system function.

The redesigned system should be prepared and presented, either in a written or oral form, with all the persuasive skill available.

In a book such as this, a certain degree of poetic license must be exercised to delete repetitious material. Also, in many cases the identity of the company in the example cannot be divulged. Therefore, companies will be given fictitious names and conditions will be altered slightly.

One word of caution. Often students are shocked by the inefficiencies of some real-world systems. They will wonder why companies have overlooked obvious improvements. They should not forget that the companies have probably been successful and the management has been often too busy to keep the control systems up to date. The student should be prepared to cope with introducing changes and not become too impatient if every one does not see what to him may seem obvious.

The Redesign of a Hand-Data Processing System

Industrial finishes such as enamels, lacquers, and varnish are produced by the Alpha Paint Company for manufacturers of such varied products as automobiles, Christmas tree ornaments, machine tools, and caskets. Alpha is a relatively small manufacturer of paint in a field dominated by giants. This has not been a deterrent to the company, however, because it has specialized in customer service.

The Alpha Paint Company maintains two manufacturing plants. One on the east coast serves that area, while the other in the midwest serves the midwest and western part of the United States. Each plant operates independently and has its own sales force. The two plants exchange and store each other's paint formulas to safeguard against loss by fire.

The manufacturing in the midwest plant is done on a job-lot basis, with the minimum lot size being maintained at 30 gallons. Raw materials are purchased from vendors and are ground, blended, and packaged in this factory. The lots are manufactured to standard formulas or specifications presented by the customer. Specifications may be nothing more than a chip of paint from a used piece of machinery.

Excluding the sales staff, there are between 60 and 70 regular employees organized into purchasing and accounting, laboratory, production control, manufacturing, filling, and shipping.

The problem of interest here is the present production control system, which starts with the sales order and terminates with the invoice. It consists of the following forms:

1. *Sales order:* This form initiates the sales transaction. It is a specially designed multiple-copy, multiple-colored form, typical of those used for this application.
2. *Master formula card:* This is used for processing information and instructions needed to produce a particular batch of material.
3. *Formula requirement sheet:* This denotes characteristics of the paint, such as luster, color, and method of application, as well as how it is to be used and tested in the laboratory. This form is used only with new orders.
4. *Invoice:* Like any invoice, this form serves notice that the material has been shipped, and it also states the terms of the sale.

The analysis of this system is given in the same series of steps discussed before, so you should have little difficulty following the developments.

Record and Analyze the Organizational Structure. This is a relatively small organization, which includes chemists and other highly specialized personnel. Consequently, there is little opportunity to improve upon the organizational structure.

Make a Flow Chart of the Present System. The flow chart could be drawn to show the entire system under consideration, but it would be too cluttered with details for practical purposes. Therefore it was divided into three separate flow charts. Figure 21–5 shows the present and revised system for the sales order. Notice that the formula requirement sheet has been combined with the sales order.

Redesign the System with a Revised Flow Chart. Following the original flow chart can be seen the redesigned system, also represented by a flow chart. Positioning the charts this way should make it easier to compare and study the changes which will be discussed.

Redesign of Forms. The forms were redesigned and will be discussed in detail. The checklist was used to make sure that all of the possible changes were included.

Record the New System in a Standard Operating Procedure. The Standard Operating Procedure for the new system is illustrated in Figure

Figure 21-5

Present System for Sales Order

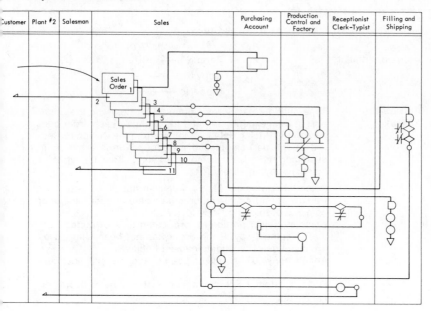

Revised System for Sales Order

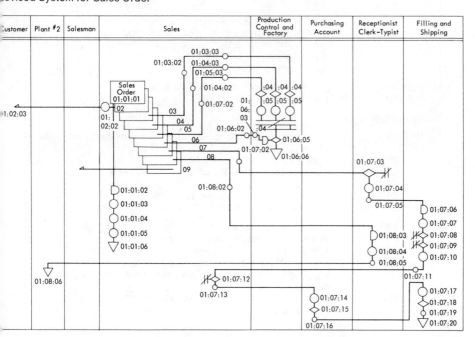

Figure 21–6
Standard Operation Procedure

:01 Sales Order

Sales Department

Form No.
Copy No.
Step No.
XX: XX: XX:

01:01:01 thru 01:09:01	Type multiple part form. Complete all items on the upper part of form except "Shipped to." Number each order consecutively. Pricing data is obtained from the Customer Record or will be computed if no information is available in customer record. Place no more than three (3) types of finish on any one order form.
01:01:02	Place form in tickler file by promised date.
:03	Remove form from file on promised date or upon receipt of completed Shipping Copy (01:07).
:04	Complete lower portion of form using data extracted from the Shipping Copy. If the order has not been shipped by promised date investigate cause of delay.
:05	Attach copy :03 of Bill of Lading and original customer order.
:06	File in Customer File alphabetically by name of customer.
01:02:02	Mail to customer.
01:03:02 *	Enter suggested basic formula information on lower portion of form.
:03 *	Send form to Production Department.
01:06:02	Send form to Production Department.
01:07:02	Send form to receptionist (clerk-typist).
:12	Extract quantity shipped and date shipped and enter on lower portion of Sales Copy (01:01). Initial form to indicate posting.
:13	Send form to receptionist.
01:08:02	Send form to receptionist (clerk-typist).
01:09:02	Mail form to salesman.

Production

01:03:04 *	Extract formula data for the preparation of the Batch Data Sheet (02:02).
:05 *	Attach form to Batch Data Sheet.
:06 thru :23 *	Form accompanies Batch Data Sheet. See 02:02:03 thru 02:02:20.
:24 *	Attach form to Expedite Copy (01:06).
:25 *	File in Production Record File (see 01:06:06).
01:06:03	Extract order information and record in Order Log.
:04	Place form in tickler file by date promised.
:05	Remove from file on date promised or upon return of Filling Copies (01:03 thru 01:05). Attach Filling Copies. If Filling Copies not available by date promised, investigate cause of delay.
:06	File form plus attached Filling Copies in Production Record File for two years.

Figure 21–6 (continued)
Standard Operation Procedure

Accounting	
01:07:17	Verify information contained on Invoice (03).
:18	Extract cost data for Accounts Receivable.
:19	Detach Invoice and Copy :01 of Bill of Lading.
:20	Send form to Shipping Department.
Shipping	
01:07:06	Place form in tickler file by date promised.
:07	Upon receipt of order from Filling remove form from file. Attach Filling Tag(s) form 12 to form :07.
:08	Extract information from form and attached tags for preparation of Bill of Lading form L–9.
:09	Extract information from the form and attach tags for Gallonage Report entries.
:10	Attach copies :01 and :03 of Bill of Lading to form.
:11	Send form with attachments to Sales Department.
:21	Place form in Shipping File for two years.
Clerk-Typist	
01:07:03	Type labels from information extracted from form.
:04	Attach labels to form.
:05	Send form with attached labels to Shipping Department.
:14	Extract information from form and attached Bill of Lading for the preparation of Invoice (form 03).
:15	Attach completed invoice to form.
:16	Send form with attachments to Accounting Department.
01:08:03	Place in temporary file.
:04	Remove from file upon receipt of proofread invoice from Accounting. Attach Storage Copy of Invoice (03:07) and Copy 01 of Bill of Lading to form.
:05	Mail form with attachments to Plant No. 2 for file storage.

* Follow same procedure for 01:04 and 01:05.

21–6. You will notice that this follows the same general format discussed earlier. A number of improvements were made to the system, which should be pointed out.

Changes Made in the Sales Order System. The information contained on the formula requirement sheet has been included in the lower portion of each filling copy of the sales order. This eliminates the formula requirement sheet and places the information where it can be used conveniently.

Portions of the filling copy of the sales order are blocked out to prevent errors, and lines were added to assist in making out the form.

Blanks for certain shipping data were added to the lower portion of the sales copy, 01:01. The entry of data in this section assures that all the necessary information is contained in the customer's file without the necessity of filing the shipping copy, 01:07.

Two copies of the original sales order—the traffic and accounting copies —have been eliminated. The checking of the accounting copy is eliminated, although a spot check with the shipping or storage copies is possible when they are in the hands of the clerk-typist.

The sales department, in the revised system, will use the sales copy, 01:01, for its tickler file and also, with the shipping data added, this copy can be used for the permanent customer's file. Shipping will use the shipping copy, 01:07, for its tickler file and place it into a permanent file upon its return from the accounting department. This will eliminate the need for the traffic copy.

Card Redesign

Without reconstructing the forms used in the system, the changes made will be listed. The important change on the formula card was the way the information was grouped. The master formula data are separated from the batch data information. The worker now concentrates his attention on the lower portion of the card while the standard data are available for reference at the top of the card. Columns have also been added for check marks by the purchasing and manufacturing departments to avoid confusion.

The statements of the conditions of the sale appearing at the bottom of the invoice form have been deleted from all copies except the customer's copy. In addition, copy titles, such as sales copy, statistical copy, and so on, have been moved from the top of the page to the lower margin where they can be easily seen when filed.

The district sales manager's copy has been eliminated. This copy, which was formerly filed for income tax purposes, has been replaced by the statistical copy, 03:05. Information from the statistical copy is extracted by both the statistics clerk and the tax record clerk, but is filed in the income tax record file. The formula requirement form is no longer necessary in the system, for, as you will recall, this was combined with the filling copy of the sales order.

Even though this is a relatively small company and the system is simple, some important and worthwhile improvements were made. These are typical rewards which can be gained by some elementary tools of system analysis.

DUPLICATING EQUIPMENT FOR MANUAL SYSTEMS

Communications is the one word which best describes the production control function of a factory, and paramount is the communication of the written word. So important is this today that practically every plant, be it large or small, contains a miniature printing plant for the production of the many forms needed in the course of today's business. Some member of the factory must take the responsibility for knowing something about the methods of printing. Because it is such an important function it is desirable for all factory management personnel to have some general knowledge of the important duplicating processes.

Raised-Type Reproduction

Among the raised-type methods, the typewriter is by far the most common for plant work. The attribute of the electric typewriter, which is of the greatest importance in the production control procedure, is the heavy force that can be applied by the type bars on the platen. If carbon paper is used, 20 copies can be produced. This is important when the alternative might be a time-consuming second operation.

For other raised-print methods, reference is limited here to the embossed-plate addressing machines as used in producing the familiar credit card. These find their place in manufacturing control for the production of tags, addressed envelopes, and similar items. The embossing plate is made of thin ductile material which is placed in a special machine—similar to a typewriter, which embosses the desired printing on the plate. The metal plates are used in a printing Addressograph machine, which will produce tags at a rapid rate. The printing machines are designed to select and to eject unwanted plates in any stack.

Hectograph

The spirit hectograph (Figure 21–7) has found an important place in plant communications. The schematic shows how the master is fastened around the drum.

Figure 21–7
Spirit Hectograph Schematic

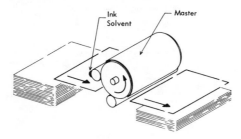

The master is a hard-surfaced paper which comes packed with a carbon paper and a light, removable insert to keep the carbon from smudging. When an impression is made on the master with a typewriter, pencil, or similar method, the ink is picked up from the carbon paper in a thick layer by the master sheet. This produces a reversed, or mirror, image on the back of the master sheet. The carbon paper is removed and destroyed before the master is placed in the machine.

As the cylinder is revolved, the master comes in contact with a roller that is slightly moistened with an ink solvent. This loosens just enough of the ink to make a proper impression on the paper as it is rolled in contact with the master. The master produces a mirror image of itself on the copy paper, which gives a readable form.

The life of the master depends upon how much carbon is placed on it by the impression of the typewriter—as well as how fast the material is removed by the fluid. A common estimate of the number of good copies is 500, but this depends upon how dim the copies can be before they become worthless for your application.

The versatility of the spirit hectograph has been expanded for manufacturing control purposes by several techniques. One improvement is a method of blocking out areas or replacing portions with a variable master. "Shingled" slips (Figure 21–8) also add to the ease of producing manufac-

Figure 21–8
"Shingled" Slips

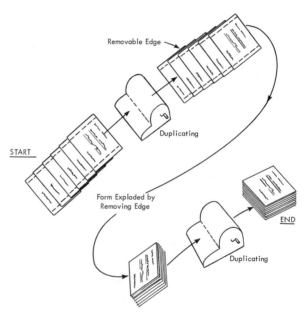

turing forms. These come bound on the edge so that they can all go through the machine at one pass, picking up the specific information from the master. They are then "exploded" and passed through the machine to pick up the common information for the heading. This is an important time-saving device in the preparation of instruction cards and time tickets.

The azograph resembles the spirit hectograph, both in appearance and method, except that the transfer sheet is covered with a layer of golden brown wax. When the wax has been moistened with a colorless fluid it leaves a blue image on the paper. This process has the advantage over the spirit hectograph in that it does not use staining aniline dyes, which are difficult to clean off.

A duplicating machine which is especially designed for production control purposes is shown in Figure 21–9. On this machine it is possible to

Figure 21–9
Versatile Duplicating Equipment

Courtesy of ORMIG.

select lines which are to be duplicated without moving or masking the master. The heading and one to three lines of an operation may be extracted from the master and printed on schedules, traveler forms, material requisitions, operations, and move tickets. From a control panel located near the operator, it is possible to add variable information such as order numbers and quantities from an optional numbering attachment. Such a machine as this may be the center of an efficient production control system.

Stencil Copying

The stencil copying machine, as can be seen in the schematic, Figure 21–10, is similar to the spirit duplicating machine, with one exception. The

Figure 21–10
Stencil-Copying Schematic

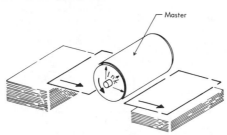

ink is not picked up from the master but is forced through from the back side. This is possible because the master is made of a fibrous paper covered with an impervious plastic coating which permits ink to flow through only where the plastic has been cut by type or a stylus. Since a quantity of the ink is squeezed through the master, it is desirable that the copy paper should be fairly porous, which would in general rule out slick card stock.

The master can be prepared by any skilled typist, but the quality of the final copy is dependent upon how well the original is prepared, and an electric typewriter with its uniform stroke is an important aid. If the stencil masters are thoroughly cleaned they can be used over and over, with only a slight decrease in the quality. These stencil machines also come equipped with attachments which make multiple-copy work for production control easier to handle.

Offset Printing

Offset printing, like many other products, has taken on the trade name of the manufacturers, which makes recognition of the process difficult. The key to the offset process is the aversion that water and oil have for each other. The ink, which is oily, will not adhere to a dampened surface but will be attracted to surfaces which are also oily.

The offset method is "flat printing," which means that it does not have the raised print of a typewriter or the "set-up" type used in printing books.

In the modern offset press a metal or paper plate is fastened to a drum, as shown in Figure 21–11. The plate does not roll in direct contact with

Figure 21–11
Offset Printing Schematic

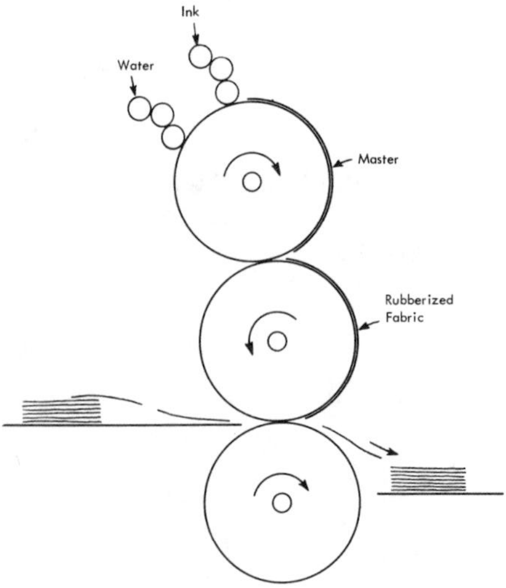

the paper as in lithography, but is in contact with a rubberized fabric on a drum which "offsets" the printing to the copy paper. It is this last cylinder which actually does the printing on the offset press. The third cylinder presses the paper against the rubber surface. These three cylinders are basic to nearly all offset presses.

The advantage of the offset technique, as compared with direct printing of lithography, is that the quality of printing is improved considerably and that the master is protected because it does not come in contact with the printed paper. The output of the offset press is about 3,000 to 6,000 copies per hour. Ordinary office help can produce typewritten masters, but beyond this the skill necessary to make photographed masters increases rapidly. The number of copies that can be produced from one master for office use is practically unlimited.

Lensless Copying

The lensless copying method requires the original document to be placed in close contact with a sensitive material while the exposure is made. There are two basic ways of exposing the sensitized paper. The light either passes through the master to expose the paper (as shown in Figure 21–12A),

Figure 21–12
Lensless Copying

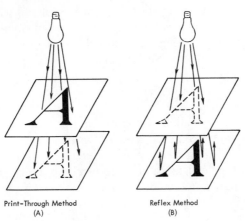

Print–Through Method
(A)

Reflex Method
(B)

with the "print-through" method; or the light is reflected from the master (Figure 21–12B), with the "reflex" technique.

Of the print-through methods, the one used in the production of engineering drawings is probably the best known. The copying paper is covered with a light-sensitive material which can be destroyed by the light in the Pyrex cylinder (Figure 21–13). The remaining chemical turns to a dye when developed either by liquid or ammonia fumes within the machine.

This type of machine produces in dye the undestroyed area under letters and lines. The result is a copy practically identical with the original

Figure 21–13
A Common Print-Through Method

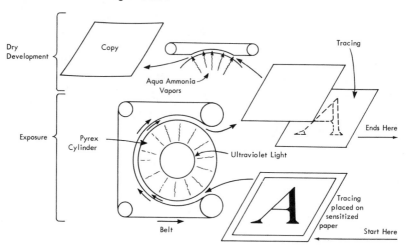

without any intermediate steps. Because of this, and because of its relatively low cost, it has found an important place in the production of materials for manufacturing control and other purposes.

Familiar to many is the engineering print machine, which, at a fairly low cost, produces copies in volume from translucent originals. The image is produced by passing a strong light through the translucent master, which is in direct contact with the copying paper. The light causes a chemical change on the copying paper, which is later brought out by a wet chemical bath to the characteristically blue color of the blueprint. Dark lines of the original show up as white lines against the blue overall background.

In production control applications the master route sheet is preprinted on plastic upon which common data is typed. The changeable information can be inserted with a special pencil which makes it possible to erase.

One common type of lensless copying machine is a modification of the familiar photographic process which uses a silver-sensitized paper. This paper is placed in contact with the original and is exposed to a strong light. The sensitized paper is "developed," which brings out the image, and it is then placed in a "hypo" which washes away the undeveloped silver compound. This method produces a copy which has opposite tones to the original; thus it is necessary to use this copy as a master and repeat the process.

At least one popular reproduction machine makes use of radiant energy rather than light. A controlled beam from a tungsten filament lamp is used as the activating source. This source sends rays through the copy paper to the typewritten original. The dark areas of the original absorb the energy and convert it into a pattern of differential temperatures. This pattern acts on the temperature-sensitive copy paper to reproduce the original. All this

Figure 21–14
Essential Steps of Xerography

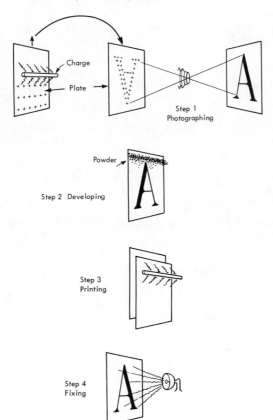

1. Photographing

   A special xerographic plate is charged electrostatically, and shielded from light until it is placed in the camera. Exposure discharges the plate where light is transmitted through the lens of the camera, leaving the image area charged. The light shield is then placed over the plate and removed from the camera for developing.

2. Developing

   A developing powder of an opposite charge to that charge placed on the plate is tumbled over the plate and attracted by the remaining charged portions to form the image. The plate now contains the mirror image of the picture photographed.

3. Printing

   The image may be transferred to paper, vellum, or to an offset master. The transfer sheet is placed facedown on the Xerox plate in contact with the image. Then both are exposed to the same electrical charge of the photographic processor. When the paper is peeled from the plate, most of the powder stays with the paper, causing a good image to remain.

4. Fixing

   The last step consists of putting the paper or master in a fuser, which heats and fuses the resinous developing powder.

occurs in a fraction of a second. The process behind this product is an instantaneous one-step method of making copies of operation sheets, bills of materials, and other production forms. Copies may be made from opaque or translucent originals, printed on one or both sides, since this is basically a reflex process. Copy papers are also available for direct-through copying techniques.

Xerography

Xerography is a printing-like process basic to a variety of copying and reproducing equipment. The secret of this process is that an electrically charged plate, when exposed to light, will lose its charge and will not attract the printing medium of the opposite charge in the exposed areas. For a more detailed description of how this machine works, a step-by-step procedure is outlined for the basic "flat-plate" machine (Figure 21–14). The four essential steps of the process are: (1) photographing, (2) developing, (3) printing, and (4) fixing.

More sophisticated Xerox machines produce copies at a high rate in a continuous process, rather than in the step-by-step procedure. The machines also produce—from microfilm images—such things as engineering drawings and other large documents. The Xerography family also contains efficient and compact office models.

Which Duplicating Method?

It would be extremely difficult to set up a decision table (Figure 21–15)

Figure 21–15
Decision Table for Duplicating

	Suitable for Short Runs (0–10 copies)	Suitable for Medium Runs (100)	Suitable for Long Runs (1,000 and over)	Investment			Quality of Print		
				Low	Medium	High	Poor	Average	Good
Hectograph	?	X		X	X		X	X	
Stencil		X	X	X	X				X
Offset		?	X			X			X
Lensless	X			X	X			X	X
Xerography	X	?							X

for deciding which duplicating process to use under all conditions. For example, you might choose a hectograph for reproducing 50 copies and find out that the labor cost of preparing the master was greater than the material cost of lensless copying. Also remember that duplicating processes for production control purposes have other requirements than those listed. For example, can the master be stored and used over and over again? Can portions of the master be changed from time to time? These are just a few of the questions to be asked.

Hand-Sorted, Edge-Notched Cards

In the order of subjects, it is difficult to decide whether hand-sorted, edge-notched cards should fall in the manual systems or in the far more sophisticated card-data-processing subjects. The gap between the manual systems and the computer system is growing so rapidly that it seems more reasonable at the moment to classify this important subject of hand-sorted, edge-notched cards with manual systems.

The edge-notched cards (Figure 21–16) are sorted by the presence or

Figure 21–16
Sorting Hand-Sorted Cards

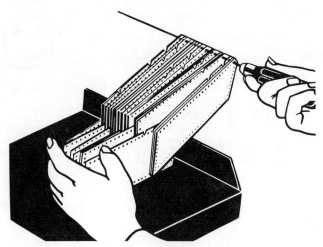

absence of a notch on the edge of the data card, as shown. The cards are supplied with prepunched holes around the periphery, to which information can be assigned. By merely notching or not notching the hole to the edge, as shown, a yes or no condition can prevail. When a needle-like tool is passed through any particular hole in a stack of cards, those which are notched will shake free from those being held by the needle.

The cards are available in various sizes, but the one that is the most popular for production purposes conforms to the card used in other card-data-processing systems. Since the center of the card is not used in the sorting process, it can be used for a written record, and standard information can be printed on the card according to what is required. Master cards for spirit duplicating are also available, so that cards with common information can be reproduced at one time.

Coding. The marginal holes on the hand-sorted card are known as "code positions" when assigned to a letter, number, or word. One or more code positions relating to a single subject is a "code field," and a "code section" is one or more fields relating to the same subject.

Direct coding is used when a specific classification, such as a first or second work shift, is assigned to a hole position.

Numerical coding is not usually done directly. To save time and space a special numerical code system is in common use. Only four holes are used for each set of numbers 0 through 9. These four hole positions are assigned the values of 7, 4, 2, and 1, as shown in Figure 21–17. By notching either a single number or the combination of two numbers, any digit from 1 through 9 may be expressed. Zeros are not notched. A number such as 653 would re-

Figure 21–17
Edge-notched Card Code

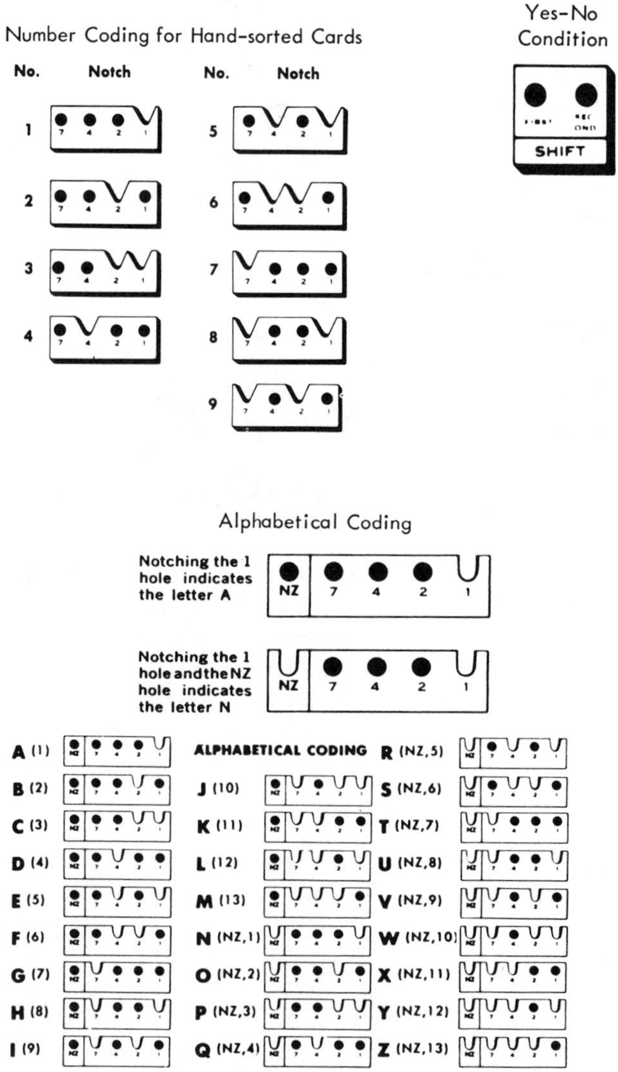

Courtesy of Royal McBee Corp.

quire three four-hole fields, one field for each of the numbers 6, 5, and 3. It is possible to increase the coding capacity of a four-hole field to include numbers from 10 to 14, if desired, for such entries as the months of the year.

To code the alphabet, each letter is numbered, but since there are more than 14 letters, the alphabet must be divided into two parts, A to M and N to Z. Each part is indicated by a separate punch position, as shown in Figure 21–17. If a letter from A to M is being punched, then the separate punch position is not notched. However, if the letter is between N to Z, the extra position is notched as shown.

Equipment Used with Edge-Notched Cards. A simple hand-operated paper-punch is available for notching the cards. This would be suitable where the volume of cards being processed is small and speed is not important, or for making occasional corrections in other, more rapid processes. The card groover is a high-speed device for notching common information in a stack of cards. As many as 50 cards can be positioned in the machine and notched simultaneously.

For high-speed notching, a keyboard keypunch is available. This machine will notch one edge of a card at a time. This keypunch can be set to repeat any columns desired, while the unset keys will be restored to their original position after each operation.

One machine performs two operations simultaneously. It will print from an embossed plate and notch the edge of the card with a single pull of a lever. Such a machine is ideally suited to the production of operation tickets or time cards (Figure 21–18) at the work location. It assures a legible, ac-

Figure 21–18
Operation Ticket

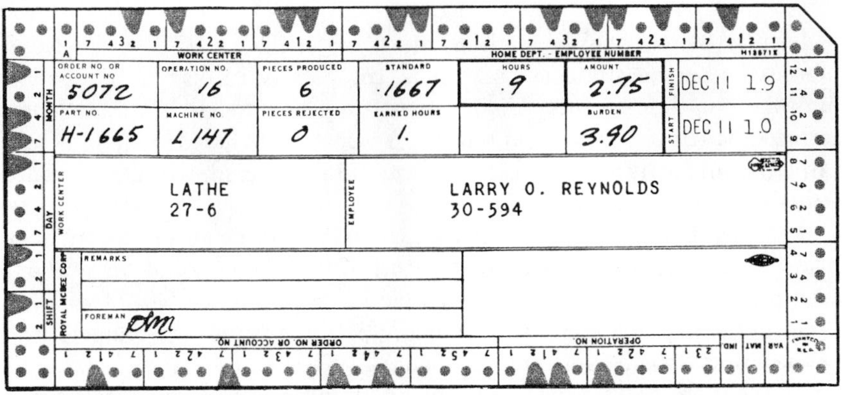

Courtesy of Royal McBee Corp.

curate, and clean card for data processing. As illustrated, a production ticket is produced with interchangeable plates for employees and work centers.

The basic tool for sorting the edge-notched cards is a screw-driver-like sorting needle. This is frequently used in conjunction with an alignment block, which increases the speed and ease of sorting.

The tabulating machine, basically an adding machine with a tape print-out and facilities for printing and reading cards, extends the versatility of the edge-notched card. For *punching and tabulating*, the card is fed in and figures are—simultaneously—punched into the card, printed on the tape, and accumulated in the register.

For *reading and tabulating*, the sorted cards are fed through the sensing track; the machine automatically reads the cards and simultaneously accumulates the figures in the register and prints out on the tape. A summary card can be placed in the punching track, and the total is automatically punched into the card and printed on the tape.

The edge-notched cards find many applications wherever records are kept. They are suitable for production control in both small and large firms, depending upon the type of product and other conditions. Companies using extensive machine-processed card systems have found edge-punched cards suitable for certain auxiliary applications, such as maintenance records and tool control.

RECORD HANDLING

The innumerable transactions that occur in production planning and control systems have made the development of rapid record handling imperative. The ones illustrated will give you some idea of the diversity of products available.

Visible Display Panels

Display panels may be nothing more exotic than a piece of plywood mounted in some strategic position in the factory to display production information. Refinements might consist only of gridded boards or cork-surfaced panels to accept thumb tacks. A display panel made by the factory carpenter might turn the trick, but if not, numerous commercial devices are available.

The board, Figure 21–19, provides visual control of all operations in a plant. Long magnetic card holders permit quick change of all data about each order. Colored cards and arrows permit easy coding of rush work.

Spring clips for holding various manufacturing forms are characteristic of the display board illustrated in Figure 21–20. Behind the surface might be one or more pockets for filing forms pertaining to the one posted under the clip.

These display boards are frequently used with specially designed systems and duplicating processes which minimize the amount of writing and posting. They have been used satisfactorily in a number of applications, such

Figure 21–19
Visible Display Panel

Courtesy of Methods Research Corporation.

Figure 21–20
Industrial Control Panel

Courtesy of Victor Comptometer Corp.

as tool control, project control, and inventory control—as well as in production control. A typical production control application is shown in Figure 21–21.

The work order for the job, along with the material requisition, is filed in the far left position. To the right, posted by operation sequence, are the productive time tickets. Either the time ticket or the move order can be used as feedback to update the productive time ticket, as shown in the bottom portion of the card.

The Flexoline display (Figure 21–22) consists of a panel which holds plastic strips. Reference material can be printed or typed directly on the plastic material, which comes in one piece and in a variety of colors. To remove a strip it is only necessary to break it loose along a serration. The stand illustrated is only one of several designs for specific purposes.

Vertical Visible File.   Figure 21–23 shows a vertical visible card file that has many applications in industry. The merit of such a system is that the cards are readily removed for posting. The card number is always visible on the mitered edge and any one that is missing is indicated by the "flag" of the card underneath.

Exposed Bottom Margin File.   A typical file system, which exposes the pertinent filing information on the bottom edge of the card, is illustrated in Figure 21–24. The cards lie flat in the tray, taking up very little room. They are hinged at the top edge to be easily exposed for changing or modifying. The card trays can be removed from the cabinet and the files can be

Figure 21-21
Application of Visible Control System

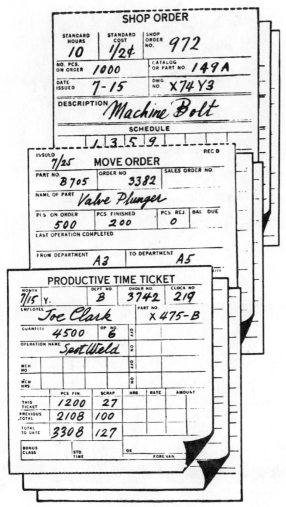

Courtesy of Victor Comptometer Corp.

Figure 21–22
Display Panel

Courtesy of Acme Visible.

Figure 21–23
Vertical Visible File

Courtesy of Acme Visible.

Figure 21–24
Exposed Bottom Margin File

Courtesy of Acme Visible.

worked on with ease. The edge of the card, besides holding the important filing information, can also be used as a bar chart to indicate quantities or time. Signal flags are available which slide along the edge of the card to indicate these values.

Microfilming and Aperture Cards. Miniaturization, which has had its effect upon many products in recent years, has also had an impact upon manufacturing planning and control systems. Many companies have found it profitable to reduce the bulk of their business and engineering files by placing them on microfilms. The sorting difficulties inherent in microfilming have brought forth another development, aperture cards (Figure 21–25), which are designed to hold the microfilm and are sorted by modified card-data-processing equipment.

A typical application of the aperture card is found in many busy engineering departments. Their product drawings, which may amount to many thousands, are photographed and filed as cards. When the drawings are needed they are easily sorted out, and if necessary, enlarged copies can be made. Often, however, the engineering and production people work directly from the microfilm by means of a special enlarger (as illustrated).

Figure 21-25
Aperture Card and Microfilm

Courtesy of Recordak Corp., subsidiary of Eastman Kodak.

These cards require considerably less space than the full-size drawings, and they last longer and are easier to send through the mail. The equipment required for the microfilming and embossing process has been highly developed and is virtually automatic.

Flexowriter. The Flexowriter, an electric typewriter, is illustrated in Figure 21-26. In addition to the document that can be typed out in the

Figure 21-26
Flexowriter

Courtesy of Friden, Inc.

usual manner, the machine will also produce a coded and punched paper tape. The tape can be run back through a Flexowriter to reproduce the document either in part or in whole. A tape reader is available which will control the input of two tapes so that fixed and variable information may be used as input to the Flexowriter as desired. The Flexowriter is one of the more versatile devices and can be used extensively in control systems.

Tag Production. Some production and inventory control systems require innumerable tags for marking and controlling production. Figure 21–27 illustrates a versatile machine which will print tags or labels from

Figure 21–27
Tag Machine

Courtesy of Dennison Manufacturing Company.

continuous strips or rolls of stock. The machine prints a full line of alphabetical and numerical characters at the rate of 165 impressions per minute. The characters in the line of print are easily set up by the dial shown on the machine. Later, if it is necessary, one or more of the characters can be changed without destroying the whole line. More than one line can be printed on the form by merely sending it through the machine again. A counter keeps track of the number of tags which have been printed and an automatic knife separates the tags as needed. For tags which are to be numbered consecutively, there is an automatic serial imprinting device.

An even more versatile tag-imprinting machine will accomplish as much as the previous one. It will imprint two lines of numbers and will punch holes in the card which can be interpreted for card-data and computer processing. The total maximum capacity of this card is 47 columns of printing, of which 25 columns can be punched.

These tag-punch machines are applied in diverse control systems. They are to be found in inventory control, production control, cost control, labor control, and quality control systems, as well as in many others.

Summary

Many thousands of organizations use manual control systems which can be analyzed and improved by the techniques discussed in this chapter. For a complete analysis, the following steps should be performed:

1. A complete flow chart of the present system should be made which can be studied to reveal any inefficiencies in the system. After the original flow chart is studied, an improved flow chart should be made showing the system as it is to function.
2. All the forms in the system should be analyzed and redesigned for greater efficiency.
3. Finally, the improved flow chart is "frozen" in a Written Standard Procedure. This Written Standard Procedure has many uses in the organization besides serving as a written statement of the flow chart. It can be used for instruction and to discipline personnel, as well as to improve the general efficiency of an organization.

The manual method must lean heavily upon the duplicating methods available. The methods discussed are the most important to be found in today's businesses. What the future holds is difficult to anticipate. It has been said that in 1900 only two out of every 100 employees handled paper; today it is 16 out of 100. The copying business, a $60 million infant in 1950, will surpass $500 million today. Such a thriving business cannot help but have some influence on our industries.

One of the most important parts of the production planning and control function is communication, and in any communications system we look for mechanical aids to store and convey information. The mechanical aids discussed in this section were designed for this purpose.

Representative devices were discussed, but the system designer should watch for new and better developments which more nearly fit the needs.

The economic considerations for selecting mechanical aids are important. No amount of money spent for these will overcome a poorly conceived system or one which lacks adequate input information.

Personnel available for the system is important. For some, the system may need to be detailed, but for others this would be frustrating. Some people are temperamentally suited for one system while others are suited for another. A good selection of equipment takes this into consideration.

QUESTIONS

21–1. Discuss the relative importance of the three steps of the systems analysis for manual methods.
21–2. What advantage does the paper-flow chart have over the procedures manual when considering a change in the system?

21-3. Show how the three steps of the manual method could be applied to some simple procedure, such as checking out books in a library.

21-4. Redesign the system discussed in the previous question, using the System Design Checklist.

21-5. Redesign some business or government agency form, such as the Bureau of Internal Revenue's form for income taxes. Use the Form Design Checklist.

21-6. As a new employee of a company, would you consider the Written Standard Procedure important or not? Explain your answer in full.

21-7. Which duplicating technique would you choose for:
   a. Engineering prints?
   b. Producing 10,000 blank operation sheets?
   c. Producing five completed operation sheets?
   d. Making one copy of a sales order?

21-8. Often the master of a form (such as the operation sheet) is retained in the files for many years and is used only occasionally for producing a few copies. Which duplicating processes would be suitable for this application? Explain your choice.

21-9. Often the master requires frequent but minor revisions. Which duplicating process would you choose to meet this requirement?

21-10. Why has a knowledge of duplicating techniques become more important in recent years?

22

Design of Machine Data Processing Systems

Some people become preconditioned to computers in a way that makes it difficult for them to understand data processing applications in industry. They use the computer to solve mathematical problems such as determining the unknown side of a triangle or fitting a line to an array of points.

The application of concern to production and inventory control emphasizes sorting and filing huge quantities of information with a few insignificant calculations. This is an entirely different world than the one which is encountered in education.

The computer did not arrive on the scene fully developed. It has evolved in a series of progressively sophisticated machines. The *unit-record systems*, which did not include the computer, was the forerunner of our present machines which have gone through many phases of improvement. The unit-record systems stood by themselves as complete production control systems. Later on the unit-record machines became *peripheral* equipment for the computers. Punching and print-out units, which stood by themselves, became the components of computer systems. Today these peripheral devices are used for off-line applications. Slower machines are giving way to faster machines developed for computer application.

Developments in Data Processing. Anyone working with computers and data processing should have some appreciation of the rapid development of these remarkable devices which are making such radical changes in science and industry. Figure 22–1 presents some highlights of their history with approximate dates.

Figure 22–1
Developments in Data Processing

Time	Event
?	Man's earliest attempts to devise a computer go back to the abacus. The first evidence of this important tool in commerce can be found in ancient Egyptian history. It is very common throughout the Orient, and improved models can be found in the Chinese laundry around the corner. This simple device uses beads to represent "place," such as units, tens, hundreds, and so on. In the hands of a competent operator, this primitive device can compete very favorably with a modern desk calculator.
1642	Blaise Pascal, of France, invented the first calculating machine along modern lines, using numbered wheels.
1671	Gottfried Leibnitz, in Germany, developed the stepped cylinder calculator.
1812–30	Charles Babbage, in England, designed (but was unable to build) a computer which is said to be the forerunner of the modern digital computer.
1880–90	Dr. Herman Hollerith, in the United States, working for the Census Bureau, devised the punched card, which was to be the start of our modern punched-card processes. This development was prompted by the fact that the census was becoming a huge task beyond the ability of the conventional methods.
1884	Dorr Felt, in the United States, designed the calculator, which is the predecessor of the present-day "comptometer."
1944	Harvard University and International Business Machines Corporation cooperated, under the direction of Howard Aiken, to build a general-purpose machine, the Mark I. Cards were used to feed the information to the machine, while relays were used in the computing process.
1947	The Moore School of Engineering, University of Pennsylvania, completed an all-electronic digital computer, the ENIAC: Electronic Numerical Integrator and Automatic Computer.
1949	Maurice Wilkes, in England, developed the first stored-program computer.
1949	International Business Machines Corporation made available the first automatic computer type of machine, the CPC.
1951	Remington Rand Company made available the UNIVAC I, which was the first large-scale automatic computer available commercially.
1952	Princeton University's Institute for Advanced Studies developed the IAS computer. This computer, designed by John von Neumann, A. W. Burks, and H. H. Goldstine, has been the basis of many other computers because of its simplicity and speed.
1955	International Business Machines Corporation developed the first commercially available automatic computer with variable word lengths.
1964	IBM System/360—a series of computers ranging in size from the small card oriented Model 20 to the very large Model 92 used for scientific problems. The System 360/30 is the most common configuration in industry.
1969	IBM System/3—a card-oriented computer system which uses a small 90-column card.
1970	IBM System/370—a larger and faster improvement of the IBM/360.

The Data Processing Card

Probably the most important innovation in production control system designs has been card-data processing. Information with which to make decisions and take action is essential in any kind of control system. Frequently, this information is kept in the mind of the individual, but as the systems become more complex it is imperative to have information recorded and available for a number of people with different needs. Writing, reading, sorting, and filing all the information needed is a time-consuming, costly operation. It is because of this that the idea of recording information by holes in cards was developed. Once the information takes the form of holes in a card, it can be sorted, filed, manipulated, and reproduced without error.

The common card is made of high-quality card stock of uniform thickness. It is about $3\frac{1}{4}$ inches wide by $7\frac{3}{8}$ inches long. One corner is cut off for convenience in filing. Any card not in the correct position can be found readily because its corner will protrude.

The general purpose card has 80 vertical columns, as shown in Figure 22–2. In each column there are 12 punching positions. The 0 through 9

Figure 22–2
General-Purpose Card

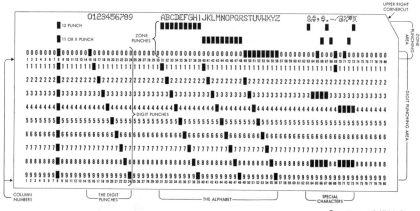

Courtesy of IBM Corp.

holes can be used to represent any number. In addition, there are two positions at the top of the card, called the 12 and 11 (or the Y and X) positions, which are used for coding the alphabet, for indicating the sign of a number, or for controlling the machine. Seldom would the 12 and 11 positions be used for the numbers 12 and 11. The 12 and 11 and 0 are called zone punches, and are used along with the numbers to indicate letters in the alphabet.

The code used for the alphabet is shown on the card. The letters of the alphabet are automatically coded and punched in the columns. The reader is cautioned to remember that it takes only one column for each letter, not three, as it might appear.

There are other ways of coding cards, but this is the accepted way for the usual unit-record applications. Later on you will see that the computer programming techniques restrict the fields of the cards to certain types of information.

Some applications are found for mark-sensed cards, Figure 22–3, in

Figure 22–3
Mark-Sensed Card

manufacturing. A graphite pencil is used to make short marks directly on the cards to represent data. The cards can then be passed through a machine which interprets the marks and punches holes in the cards.

The 96-Column Card. Not so familiar is the 96-column card as shown in Figure 22–4. This card, used with the IBM System/3, is approximately one third the size of the 80-column card but can hold 20 percent more business information. The size of card permits the use of new card-handling techniques which have resulted in smaller, simpler equipment at a lower cost.

The 96-column card is 3¼ x 2⅝ inches. Its columns are arranged in three tiers of 32 columns. A 6-row or 6-bit coding structure as illustrated provides for the punching of 64 different characters. Four 32-character lines can be printed at the top of the card—either by a data recorder when the cards are being punched and/or by a multifunction card unit during the processing run.

Figure 22–4
The 96–Column Card

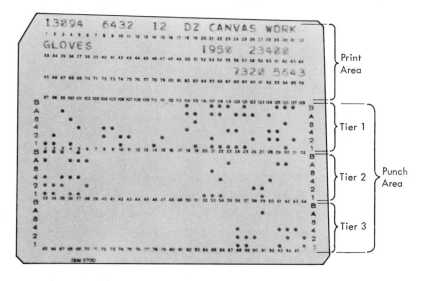

Card Layout. For any particular application, the card must be laid out into fields. A block of one or more columns having a specific meaning is called a "field." For example, the labor distribution card shown in Figure 22–5 has one column reserved for the month of the year, two for the day

Figure 22–5
Typical Card Layout

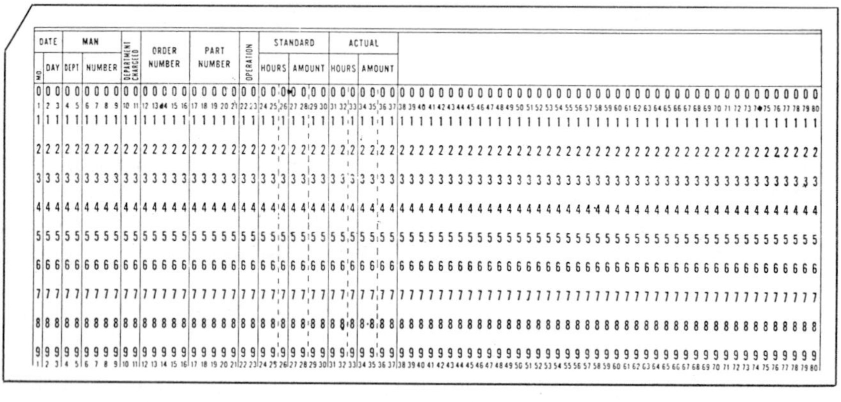

in the month, two for the department, and so on. The order number field runs from column 12 to column 16. This task of laying out the fields must be done with care and forethought, for frequently the space must be used efficiently to record all the information desired.

Peripheral and Unit-Record Processing Machines

Often the novice confuses unit-record processing with computer data processing. This is understandable since computers often use cards as the input-output medium, and at least some card-data-processing equipment is used as peripheral equipment for the computer. In this part, the computer which uses data and instructions stored in its memory will be excluded, and only unit-record processing will be discussed.

It is difficult to have an understanding of system designing for card-data processing without first having a preview of the equipment. After the preview, the techniques for system designing will be discussed.

Before discussing each machine, it will be more efficient to discuss briefly the components which are common to many of the machines. This will give you a better understanding of the processes, and then, when each machine is discussed, it will not be necessary to delay progress while digressing into some detailed function of a part.

Card Reading. The card, previously described, passes between an electrically charged brush and roller, as shown in Figure 22–6. The card, being

Figure 22–6
Card Reading

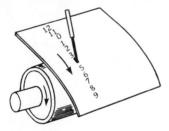

made of paper, serves as an insulator *except* where the holes have been punched. Where the brush drops into a hole and makes contact with the roller, a flow of current or "impulse" occurs, which in turn actuates some function of the machine.

The machine recognizes the number punched in the card by the elapsed time between the instant the leading edge passes the brush until the hole is sensed. In most of the machines to be discussed, there are 80 brushes, so that all columns may be read at the same time. Some computer-oriented machines scan the cards by means of *electric eyes*, which avoid the mechanical wear and consequent failure of mechanical brushes.

It is important to consider the timing of the card-data-processing machines if one is to understand how they function. There is not a constant flow of current available through the brush contacts; rather, the current is available in 12 bursts, corresponding with the number and zone positions on the card. For example, when the 8 hole passes under a brush, it is referred to as the *8 time* in the machine, and because of this the machine punches or prints an 8.

The Control Panel. In most cases the machines are not permanently wired for just one task but are designed so the operator can have some choice as to how they will perform. This choice is often exercised through a control panel, as shown in Figure 22–7. The control panel is similar to a

Figure 22–7
The Control Panel

Courtesy of IBM Corp.

telephone switchboard since circuits may be directed in many ways. Wires from the brushes and other functional components of the machine are brought out to rows of jacks. The panel board itself is a separate unit and can be replaced in the machine at will. This affords a great deal of flexibility because a number of control panels for different applications are quickly available when desired. Since it is not always convenient to work directly with the control panels when planning the circuitry, charts are available which represent the panel. One should not be dismayed by the number of *hubs* (terminals on the panel) because many of them are merely a repeat —80 times—of the same function.

Punching. As we know, the information on a machine-processed card is shown by holes. These holes are punched in the cards by magnet-actuated punches. Some machines, such as the card punch, have these punches lined up so they punch column by column, while in other machines they are lined up to punch row by row.

Emitting. Often it is desirable to place information (which is not available in the cards being fed into the machine) on a card, either in printed form or punched-hole form. For example, a deck of cards may need a manufacturing order number inserted.

The emitter device, Figure 22–8, serves as a rotary switch, producing

Figure 22–8
Digit Emitter

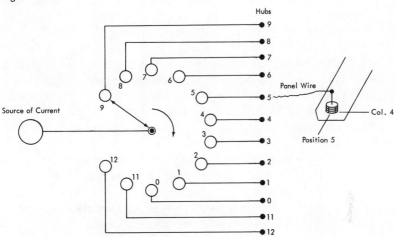

an impulse for each position on the card. These impulses are available on the control panel and, when wired to other functions of the machines, have the same effect as if they came from a card. Alphabetical information can be emitted and punched by wiring both a zone and a digit impulse to the same punching position. However, precautions must be taken to prevent back-circuits, which will cause incorrect punching. The *column split* is a means of preventing back-circuits.

Column Splits.   Before exploring the need for the column-split mechanism, it is best that we see what it is. *Splitting* the column is separating the 0–9 punches from the 11 and 12 punches. The column-split mechanism consists of a magnet, armature, and switch, as shown in Figure 22–9. The magnet, which is impulsed only during the 11–12 time, lets the current flow from the common hub on the panel through the 11–12 hub.

Figure 22–9
Column Split Prevents
Back-Circuits

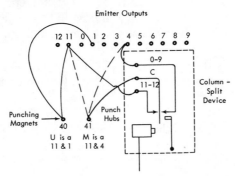

This is referred to as being *transferred*, while during the 0–9 portion of the cycle, the armature is *dropped out* and the current can flow from C (common) through the 0–9 hub.

If you trace out the dotted-line circuit, you will see that three holes (11, 1, and 4) would be punched in each column if the emitter was not used.

Normally two holes in a column would indicate a letter of the alphabet. However, it may indicate a number and a zone punch for control. The column split can be wired in the circuit to switch the zone punch impulse to where it can be used for control purposes.

Comparing.   Comparing is checking two things to see if they are alike or different, and this is an important function of data processing machines. This ability of a machine serves a very important purpose in the verification and control of the machine. Verification is the process of testing to see if the holes have been punched correctly, while control is directing the machine to perform specific operations, such as making the machine stop when cards are out of sequence or forcing the machine to print out totals when different account numbers are recognized.

The cards to be compared are fed under two sets of brushes, as shown in Figure 22–10. The cards are synchronized so the left-hand brush is reading the same hole position as the right-hand brush. The impulses from these two brushes are fed to two *comparing magnets*, as illustrated. The armature will remain in the neutral position if no impulse is fed to the magnets or if they both receive an impulse at the same time.

For example, assume the conditions shown in the illustration. In the first figure, both magnets get the same signal at the same instant, so the magnets are unaffected. In the other two examples, the signals are out of phase, and the magnets affect a switching circuit, which stops the machine or causes some other action to take place in the machine.

Sequence Checking.   Closely related to the comparing magnets are the sequence-checking magnets which determine the order of a deck of cards. It is obvious that there are three orders in which cards might be: they can all be equal, they might increase in order, or they might decrease in order. These comparing magnets are so connected to indicate a *hi*, *lo*, or *equal* condition in a series of cards.

Printing.   The card-data-processing machines not only produce information in the form of holes but will also interpret the holes and print out the information. These printing facilities, when on a machine, are available through entry hubs on the control panel.

A printing unit is shown in Figure 22–11. The paper is passed under a ribbon and around the platen, the same as in a typewriter, but the printing mechanism is entirely different. There is a bank of type bars, one for each printing position on the paper, so it is not necessary for the carriage to be moved back and forth as in the conventional typewriter. It should be apparent that this way of printing is much faster than the conventional typewriter's, which must peck out letter by letter, and it is one reason why auto-

Figure 22-10
Comparing

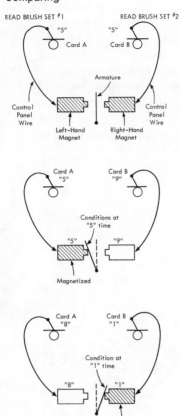

Figure 22-11
Printing Bars

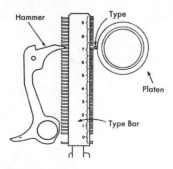

matic data processing is supplanting manual card-processing techniques. Other, and faster, printers will be discussed more fully in the computer section.

Peripheral & Unit-Record Machines

With this overview of the components, it will be easier now to move on to the machines themselves and understand how they function.

Card Punch Machines. Card punches are used for translating written documents into punched-card form. Cards are fed into the machine automatically and are moved forward, column by column, under 12 punches which can be actuated either by a keyboard or by brushes (which are sensing the preceding card). The card is moved forward either by the manual control or by a programmed card which tells the machine to skip fields, repeat what was in the previous card, or shift to alphabetical coding from numerical coding.

An illustration and schematic of the machine are shown in Figure 22–12.

Figure 22–12
Card Punch

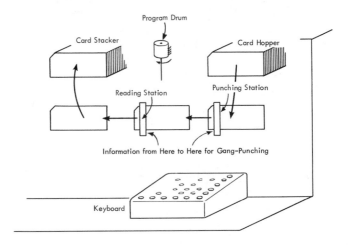

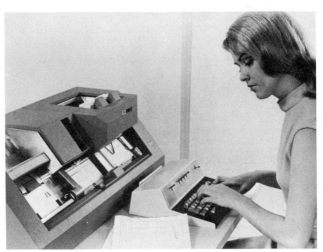

The path of the card, as shown on the schematic, is from right to left, passing under the 12 punches, the 12 reading brushes, and eventually to the card stacker. The function of each important part will be discussed.

Keyboard. Several different keyboards are available, depending upon the capabilities of the machine. The machines are designed for punching numeric and alphanumeric information, and for typing out the information as it is punched.

Punching Station. The cards are fed from the card hopper, either automatically or by depressing a feed key. The card, controlled by the program card or the keyboard, then passes under the 12 punches.

Reading Station. A set of 12 reading brushes are located about a card's length ahead of the punching station so that two cards may move in step through both and so the information on the leading card can be fed back to the following card in a gang-punching operation. The completed cards are placed in the card stacker in their original sequence.

Programming. Some of the operations of the machines are controlled by a prepared program card that is wrapped around a cylinder which rotates in step with the card being punched. The four functions which can be programmed are readily summarized with their appropriate punching positions:

Code	Function
12	*Field Definition* tells the machine how long the following functions (11, 0, and 1) should be performed.
11	*Start Automatic Skip* carries over a field which (for some sufficient reason) is not to be punched at this time.
0	*Start Automatic Duplication* actuates the machine for gang-punching information.
1	*Alphabetic Shift* makes it unnecessary for the operator to shift from numbers to alphabet on the keyboard—something he might easily forget to do.

As in other machines, there are a number of adaptations of the basic machine for specialized purposes.

Verifier. After the cards have been punched, it is usually desirable to check them in some way to be sure that they have been punched correctly. This can be done visually, but it is much faster and more convenient to place the cards in a machine which will automatically check the information as it is typed out again, preferably by another operator.

The verifying machine looks very much like the key punch, except that it has a verifying station (which is a set of brushes) instead of a punching station. The operator verifies information by depressing the keys, as in the original operation, and also verifies the gang-punching operations executed under the automatic control of a programming card. Any error is detected by a discrepancy between the digit punched and the key depressed, or between the digit punched and the digit in the preceding card. Provisions are made for three trials, so if the verifier operator makes an error there are two more opportunities to make the correction. If the third attempt to punch the correct information in the card fails, the card is "error notched" in the column where the error occurs. When the cards pass through "correct," a notch is made on the end of the card to indicate that it has been verified.

Sorters. One of the major purposes of punching information into cards is to make the information available for sorting and classifying, and for this reason the sorter is one of the most important machines in card-data processing.

The sorting operation is relatively simple. The cards are placed in the feed hopper, shown on the far right of the machine illustrated in Figure 22–13. A brush, shown in the schematic, is adjusted over the column being sorted to detect the impulse and actuate the sorting mechanism. There are 13 pockets into which the cards are sorted, one for each position in a column, plus one additional pocket for rejects. Sorting is done at the incredible speed of 2,000 cards per minute.

Figure 22–13
Sorter

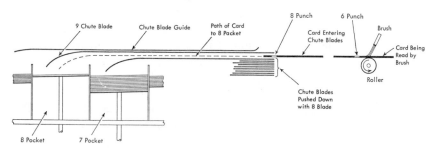

Courtesy of IBM Corp.

The card is conveyed over the pockets by rollers, but the guiding of the cards into the proper pocket is done by chute blades, as shown. The card is fed 9-edge-first and, when the hole is sensed, the magnet is actuated to pull down the corresponding blade. For example, in the illustration the 8 punch is detected, which causes the magnet to pull down the 8-chute blade (and, incidentally, all those before it: 7, 6, 5, 4, 3, 2, 1, 0, 11, and 12), leaving a gap between the 8 and 9 through which the card can pass and be guided to its proper bin. The alphabet, of course, requires two sorting operations.

Reproducer. The reproducer is one of the most versatile of all card-data-processing machines. It can reproduce and gang-punch decks of cards, and also check the work as it goes along. The numerous functions are listed below:

Reproducing is sensing any or all of the information in one deck of cards and punching it into another deck of cards (see Figure 22–14).

Figure 22–14
Reproducing and Gang-Punching

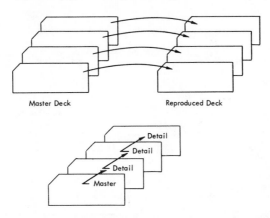

Master Deck   Reproduced Deck

Detail
Detail
Detail
Master

Gang-punching is the sensing of information in a master card and punching it into the detail cards which follow as is illustrated.

Comparing is done to check the agreement between the source and the resulting punched holes.

End printing features permit the printing of up to 16 numbers across the end of a card, such as might be done with time tickets that are stored in pockets with just the number showing.

Double-punch blank-column detection can be done (if this special device is installed on the machine).

Mark-sensing, also a special device, translates into punched holes the information which is placed on the card in the form of a pencil mark.

Summary punching can be done with this machine when it is properly equipped. This means that it can take the information prepared by some other machine, such as an accounting machine, and punch it out on cards.

The Operation of the Reproducer. The reproducer is illustrated in Figure 22–15, and the schematic shows how it operates. Notice the agree-

Figure 22–15
The Reproducer

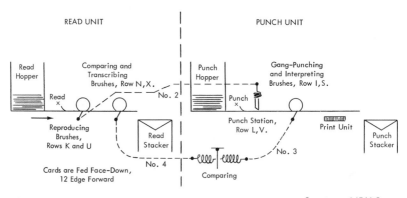

Courtesy of IBM Corp.

ment between the two; for example, the two card hoppers and the two card stackers.

On the front of the machine is the control panel, which is illustrated in more detail in Figure 22–16. Those areas which are shaded are the hubs for the more uncommon devices which can be added, but the discussion will be limited to the unshaded areas. On the schematic you will find letters (adjacent to the brushes and punches) which indicate in which rows on the control panel the hubs are to be found. You should not have any qualms about the complexity of the panel for many of the hubs are repeated 80 times, once for each column on the card. Also notice that the

Figure 22–16
Control Panel for the Reproducer

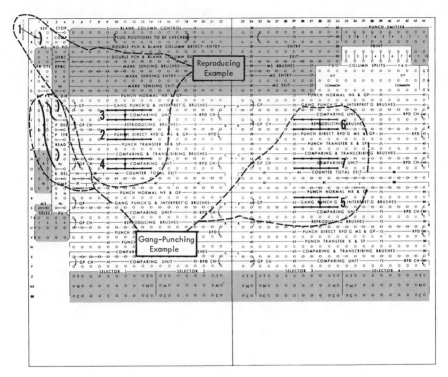

first 40 hubs are placed in the top half of the panel and the second 40 are in the bottom half, so that rows H and R perform the same function with different columns.

As is obvious from the schematic, the reproducer has two distinct units, the read unit and the punch unit. The feeds of these two units may operate separately or they may function together by jack-plugging the "reproducer on" at A–B under 1 on the panel. To reproduce all or part of the information in one deck of cards into another deck of cards is the problem of *reproducing*. We should also like to take advantage of the machine at the same time to determine whether or not the reproducing has been done correctly. This operation can be seen on the schematic and on the control panel, for reproducing columns 5 through 11. The original information file is placed in the read unit on the left while the deck to be produced is placed in the punch unit on the right.

The reproducing brushes and the punch direct hubs are connected (wire 2) on both the schematic and control panel to do the punching operation. To check the cards, the comparing and transcribing brushes are connected to one side of a comparing unit (wire 4) while the other side of the comparing unit is connected to the gang-punch and interpreting brushes (wire

3). Notice that it does not particularly make any difference which comparing units are used, but naturally both hubs of any one unit must be used. It will make some difference when one interprets information on the comparing indicator seen on the front of the machine illustrated, which tells the operator in which column an error in comparing occurred.

In the gang-punching operation the cards to be gang-punched are placed in the right-hand punch unit, and the impulses read by the gang-punching and interpreting brushes are fed back to the punch station. This is illustrated on the control panel, Figure 22–17, by wire 5. The cards are com-

Figure 22–17
Gang-punching

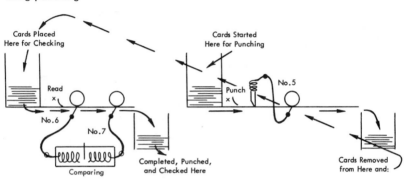

pared by placing them in the read unit after they have been punched. The read unit is wired as shown by the dotted lines on the panel and the accompanying schematic for columns 25 through 30.

Since we are gang-punching cards which have the master card interspersed in the detail cards, it is necessary to suspend punching when the master card goes under the punch (otherwise information in the previous detail card will be punched in the master card, which of course we do not wish). The same problem arises on the read unit side. This difficulty is overcome by identifying either the master or detail cards with an X punch in one of the columns. These are detected by the punch–X and read–X brushes, which cause punching and reading to be suspended by jack-plugging the correct hubs at H–I, 3–4, and M–N, 3–4 on the control panel.

Collator. There are many sorting operations for which the sorter is not as suitable as the more versatile collator. This machine is capable of performing the many operations described here.

Card Selection. The control panel of the machine can be wired to select X cards, select non-X cards, the first card in a group, the last card in a group, a single card group, a zero balance card, a card with a particular number, or a card out of sequence.

Checking Sequence. The control panel of the machine can be wired to determine if cards are in proper numerical sequence.

Merging. If two decks of cards are in the same sequence order, they can be merged into one deck with all cards in the proper sequence.

Matching. The control panel can be wired to compare two decks of cards so that for each card in one deck there is a card in the other deck.

Editing. The cards in a deck can be checked for accuracy of punching. A double-punch or blank column can cause the machine to stop.

You will notice the agreement between the configuration of the collator and the schematic shown below it in Figure 22–18. The cards to be

Figure 22–18
Collator

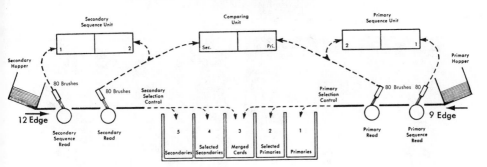

processed are placed in the left- or right-hand hopper of the machine and are fed toward the center, under two sets of brushes, where the choice of receiving bins is made. All cards may be merged into bin 3, with each feed having two additional options (as shown by the dotted lines).

Frequently it is desirable to merge two decks of cards of different colors, which have yet to be punched. Such a case might be the tool orders and operations tickets for a manufacturing packet. One deck of cards is placed in one feed and the other deck in the other feed, so that, as long as the machine is running, the cards are being alternately merged in pocket 3.

The merging operation consists of combining two files of cards, already in sequence, into one file which will still be in sequence. To do this, one file is placed in the primary feed of the collator and the other file is placed in the secondary feed. The machine is designed so that the primary feeds first. Primary and secondary sequence units are used, as well as the comparing unit, to detect the different conditions which can exist as the cards pass through the collator and cause the machine to merge the two decks in proper sequence.

Accounting Machine.   The accounting machine (Figure 22–19) is a

Figure 22–19
Accounting Machine

Paper Carriage

Tape Control

Reprinted, by permission from IBM Reference Manual: Operator's Guide, *Form No. A–24–1010.*

versatile machine, having the basic function of printing out information from punched cards, but it can also perform the elementary arithmetic operations of addition, multiplication by multiple cycling, and subtraction. Other convenient operations can be performed by this machine, such as consecutive numbering. The card-feeding mechanism is to the far left of the machine and the paper carriage is in the middle, while the control panel can be seen on the left end of the machine.

The feeding and spacing of the print-out form is under the control of a paper tape, illustrated. Punched holes in the narrow paper tape cause the form to skip, or to stop, when it reaches any predetermined position.

Interpreter. The basic purpose of the interpreter is to sense the holes punched in a card and translate this information into print on the card which can be read. However, additional features on the machine can make it a versatile servant that is capable of doing many other tasks.

With the basic unit it is possible to print out information on any of 25 lines across the card, suppressing zero printing if desired. Column splits and selectors are available for controlling the machine, such as suppressing printing when cards have an X mark. Using special features, the machine can do card-to-card comparisons, select cards and stack them in one of four stacks, find and post the next line on a card, plus a number of other useful operations.

A Unit-Record Processing System

Although unit-record systems are rapidly giving way to computer systems, it will be worthwhile to see how they operate.

With the basic symbols shown in Figure 22–20, we can develop flow

Figure 22–20
Symbols for Card-Data Processing

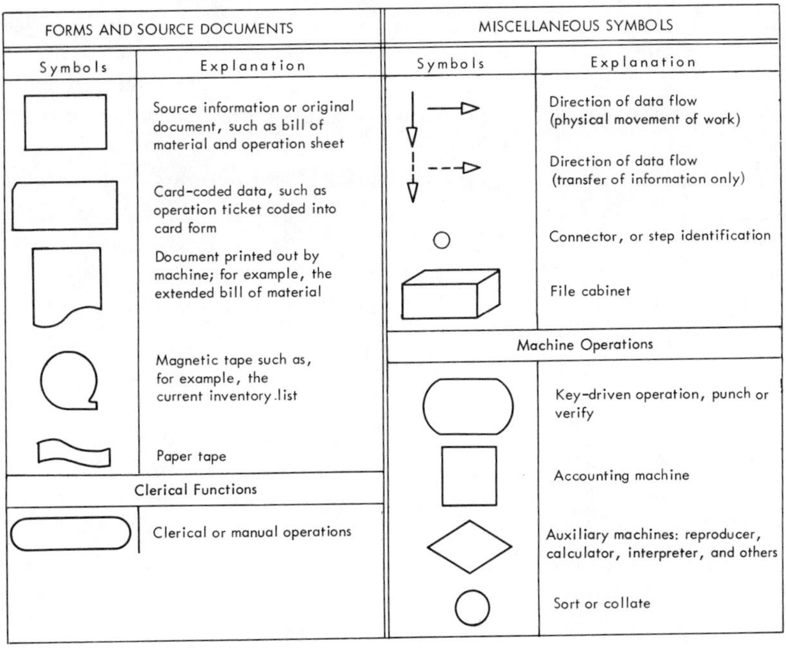

FORMS AND SOURCE DOCUMENTS		MISCELLANEOUS SYMBOLS	
Symbols	Explanation	Symbols	Explanation
	Source information or original document, such as bill of material and operation sheet		Direction of data flow (physical movement of work)
	Card-coded data, such as operation ticket coded into card form		Direction of data flow (transfer of information only)
	Document printed out by machine; for example, the extended bill of material		Connector, or step identification
	Magnetic tape such as, for example, the current inventory list		File cabinet
		Machine Operations	
	Paper tape		Key-driven operation, punch or verify
Clerical Functions			Accounting machine
	Clerical or manual operations		Auxiliary machines: reproducer, calculator, interpreter, and others
			Sort or collate

diagrams for various functions within the factory as they will be executed by card-data-processing equipment. There is no better way of doing this than to illustrate a typical system. The ones included here are part of the production control function. The illustration shows the form or operation, and directly adjacent is an explanation. The first chart shows the system for determining the material requirements for a group of orders. Before going into that, it would be desirable to review some of the basic information which must be fed into such a system.

Into any control system must go the basic data on which the system operates. In the example given here, the basic data—which will be referred to later as master files or master cards—are bill-of-material forms, order forms, and process design forms. The bill-of-material form goes hand in hand with the blueprints or product description, and contains a listing of all the material that goes into a specific product. From this original list, individual cards are made for each item on the list. These cards may eventually be grouped by final assembly, by accessory groupings, or by any other convenient arrangement. Each card would bear such information as part name, part number, and quantity. Order forms may either originate with the customer's order, or within the company's inventory control, when a balance drops below the order point. This form is the order to produce, and contains such information as order quantity, name of customer, time needed, and so on.

The process design form goes by such names as process sheet, instruction sheet, route sheet, and others. This form supplements the blueprint by giving operation-by-operation instructions of how the product is to be produced to conform to the engineering requirements shown on the print. This form contains information concerning work to be included at each work station, machines to be used, standards of performance, and, of course, the part name, number, material used, and any other pertinent information.

From these basic forms, which are usually handwritten or typed, punch cards are produced. For example, for each part on the bill of materials a corresponding card would be made; for each operation on the processing form, a card would be made; and the order-form information would also be reproduced in card form. All this is shown in two illustrations. Figure 22–21 shows how the material requirements are determined by card-data processing, while Figure 22–22 shows how the labor requirements are calculated.

These two flow charts are typical of those used in manufacturing industries. A little familiarization with the symbols and their meanings should make it possible to follow the diagrams and the verbal explanations. The next step is to take a company's routines and follow them or, better still, try to design (and eventually improve) a system. Only by this procedure can you become completely fluent with the card-data-processing language.

Figure 22–21
Material Requirements Flow Chart

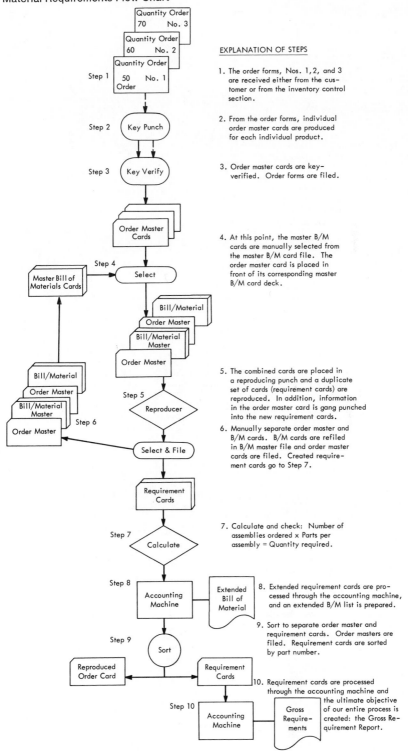

EXPLANATION OF STEPS

1. The order forms, Nos. 1, 2, and 3 are received either from the customer or from the inventory control section.

2. From the order forms, individual order master cards are produced for each individual product.

3. Order master cards are key-verified. Order forms are filed.

4. At this point, the master B/M cards are manually selected from the master B/M card file. The order master card is placed in front of its corresponding master B/M card deck.

5. The combined cards are placed in a reproducing punch and a duplicate set of cards (requirement cards) are reproduced. In addition, information in the order master card is gang punched into the new requirement cards.

6. Manually separate order master and B/M cards. B/M cards are refiled in B/M master file and order master cards are filed. Created requirement cards go to Step 7.

7. Calculate and check: Number of assemblies ordered x Parts per assembly = Quantity required.

8. Extended requirement cards are processed through the accounting machine, and an extended B/M list is prepared.

9. Sort to separate order master and requirement cards. Order masters are filed. Requirement cards are sorted by part number.

10. Requirement cards are processed through the accounting machine and the ultimate objective of our entire process is created: the Gross Requirement Report.

Figure 22–22
Labor Requirements

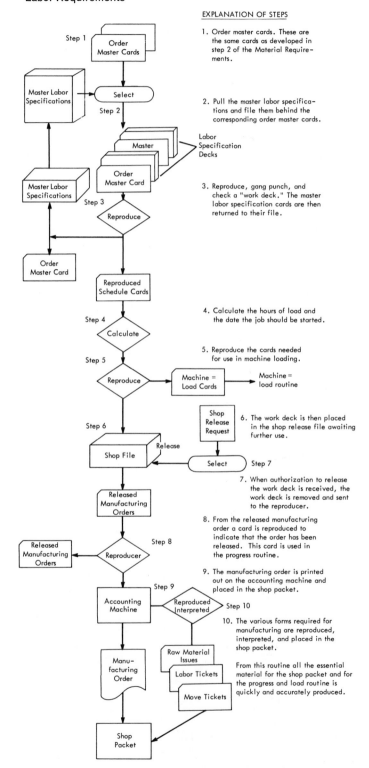

EXPLANATION OF STEPS

1. Order master cards. These are the same cards as developed in step 2 of the Material Require-ments.

2. Pull the master labor specifica-tions and file them behind the corresponding order master cards.

3. Reproduce, gang punch, and check a "work deck." The master labor specification cards are then returned to their file.

4. Calculate the hours of load and the date the job should be started.

5. Reproduce the cards needed for use in machine loading.

6. The work deck is then placed in the shop release file awaiting further use.

7. When authorization to release the work deck is received, the work deck is removed and sent to the reproducer.

8. From the released manufacturing order a card is reproduced to indicate that the order has been released. This card is used in the progress routine.

9. The manufacturing order is printed out on the accounting machine and placed in the shop packet.

10. The various forms required for manufacturing are reproduced, interpreted, and placed in the shop packet.

From this routine all the essential material for the shop packet and for the progress and load routine is quickly and accurately produced.

COMPUTER SYSTEMS

A computer is a device which carries out logical and mathematical operations either mechanically or electrically. These mechanical and electrical components form the hardware to be discussed in this section. The computer program used to control the hardware is called software and will be discussed in the following chapters.

There are two distinct types of computers, the *analog* and the *digital*, which have become important tools in science and industry. In the analog computer numbers are represented by a continuously variable physical quantity, such as an electrical voltage, a change in shaft rotation, and so forth. The answer is obtained as a measure of these physical quantities. The digital computer, on the other hand, deals directly with the digital form or with discrete items, such as counting the number of teeth on a gear or the number of electric pulses in a circuit. Neither type of computer can be said to be superior to the other. Each type has its place, and occasionally one complements the other.

Since digital computers are far more useful in manufacturing applications, this is where the emphasis will be placed. Analog computers have been used in some preliminary studies of simulation, but for the immediate future the emphasis will be on digital computers in the operation of manufacturing enterprises. Since all large digital computers of any consequence are electronic, this term will not be stressed in the definitions.

Computers are said to be in the third generation. In the first generation vacuum tubes with their heat and other inherent objections were used for switching circuits (Figure 22–23). The second generation arrived with the development of the transistors. The third generation has many transistors, diodes, and components combined in an extremely small package. One such package has over 600 transistors and other components placed on a silicon chip less than one eighth of an inch square. One model of the IBM 370 series has over 1,400 transistors, diodes, and resistors integrated into circuits on silicon chips less than one-eighth-inch square.

Computer Language

Before discussing the computer, it is desirable to have some knowledge of the internal language used by the computer to communicate among the various components. These are primarily internal languages because the operator addresses today's modern computer using the conventional number and alphabet system.

Binary. It is not difficult—although perhaps somewhat fanciful—to imagine that our timeworn, 10-digit numbering system began with some caveman sitting by his fire, counting wolf pelts (or wives) and, finding the customary pebbles out of reach, or too hot, started counting on his toes. Having 10 of them, it was natural that he should use this as the basis

Figure 22–23
Computer Hardware

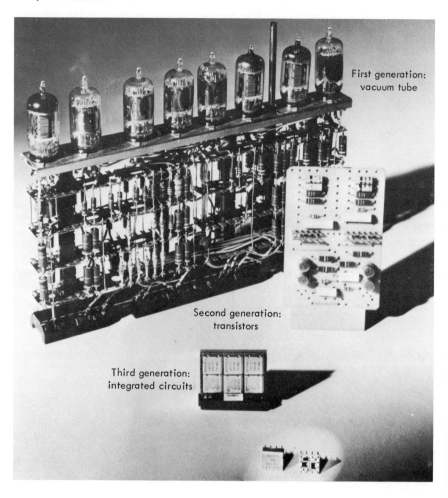

First generation:
vacuum tube

Second generation:
transistors

Third generation:
integrated circuits

of his counting system. The mathematician would say that this system, with its base of 10, had a *radix* of 10. There are other systems with other radices; but the one discussed here has a radix of two.

What is wrong with the old 10-radix system? After all, we have lived with it for many years. The trouble is that an electronic computer finds it difficult to recognize each of the 10 different conditions or states required for a 10-radix number. This is easy to understand when we remember that, because of the electronic age, we are living more and more in a "two-condition" world. Either things are on, or they are not.

For example, the furnace is on or off, the lights are on or off; and this is extended to the paper tapes and data cards for computers: there are holes or there are no holes. It is difficult for the modern machine to work with shades of meaning: everything must be either black or white, and this calls for a new numbering system, one with only two numbers. In referring to a two-number system, the *one* state is referred to as a *bit* (binary digit). This two-number idea is about as disquieting, on first thought, as the mirror room in a house of horrors; it is not bad, however, when one gets used to it.

There is a standard form by which any numbering system can be expressed. This is a series which has the general form:

$$A \times r^0 + B \times r^1 + C \times r^2 + D \times r^3 \ldots$$

or, for the ten-radix system:

$$A(10)^0 + B(10)^1 + C(10)^2 + D(10)^3 \ldots$$

For example, consider the number 1,978:

$$
\begin{aligned}
A \times 10^0 &= 8 \times 1 = & 8 \\
B \times 10^1 &= 7 \times 10 = & 70 \\
C \times 10^2 &= 9 \times 100 = & 900 \\
D \times 10^3 &= 1 \times 1000 = & \underline{1000} \\
& & 1978
\end{aligned}
$$

It is obvious that the numbers 1, 9, 7, and 8 are the coefficients D, C, B, and A.

Now that the system is apparent in our customary 10-digit numbering systems, see how the binary system can be developed. The series can be written:

$$A(2)^0 + B(2)^1 + C(2)^2 + D(2)^3 \ldots$$

$$
\begin{aligned}
A \times (2)^0 &= 0 \times 1 = & 0 \\
B \times (2)^1 &= 1 \times 2 = & 2 \\
C \times (2)^2 &= 0 \times 4 = & 0 \\
D \times (2)^3 &= 1 \times 8 = & 8 \\
E \times (2)^4 &= 1 \times 16 = & 16 \\
F \times (2)^5 &= 1 \times 32 = & 32 \\
G \times (2)^6 &= 0 \times 64 = & 00 \\
H \times (2)^7 &= 1 \times 128 = & 128 \\
I \times (2)^8 &= 1 \times 256 = & 256 \\
J \times (2)^9 &= 1 \times 512 = & 512 \\
K \times (2)^{10} &= 1 \times 1024 = & \underline{1024}
\end{aligned}
$$

The number (in binary) 11110111010 = 1978

(the-bottom-to-top sequence of column 3).

If the number had not been a whole number, for example, 19.5 (with a decimal point between 9 and 5), no particular trouble would have been encountered.

$$a \ (2)^{-1} = 1 \times 2^{-1} = \quad .5$$
$$A(2)^0 \ \ = 1 \times 2^0 \ = \ 1.0$$
$$B \ (2)^1 \ \ = 1 \times 2^1 \ = \ 2.0$$
$$C(2)^2 \ = 0 \times 2^2 \ = \ 0.0$$
$$D(2)^3 \ = 0 \times 2^3 \ = \ 0.0$$
$$E \ (2)^4 \ = 1 \times 2^4 \ = \ \underline{16.0}$$

The binary number $10011.1 = 19.5$ in decimal form.

A convenient way of converting decimal whole numbers from base 10 to another base is to divide by the base and tabulate those numbers remaining. For example using the previous example:

	11110111010
$\dfrac{0}{2\overline{)1}}$	1 remaining
	1
$2\overline{)3}$	1
$2\overline{)7}$	1
$2\overline{)15}$	0
$2\overline{)30}$	1
$2\overline{)61}$	1
$2\overline{)123}$	1
$2\overline{)247}$	0
$2\overline{)494}$	1
$2\overline{)989}$	0 remaining
$2\overline{)1978}$	

The arithmetic of adding, subtracting, multiplying, and dividing can be carried out in the binary system the same as in the 10-digit system. For convenience in checking results, the conversion table is inserted first:

Conversion Table

Ten	Binary	Ten	Binary	Ten	Binary
0	0	8	1000	14	1110
1	1	9	1001	15	1111
2	10	10	1010	16	10000
3	11	11	1011	17	10001
4	100	12	1100	18	10010
5	101	13	1101	19	10011
6	110				
7	111				

Examples

Addition		Subtraction		Multiplication		Division	
9	1001	9	1001	6	110	$6/3 = 2,$	$\dfrac{110}{11} = 10$
$+6$	110	-6	110	$\times 3$	11		
$15 = 1111$		$3 =$	11		110		
					110		
				$18 = 10010$			

The scheme is obvious when it is observed that $1 + 1 = 2$, but in the binary system, $1 + 1 = 10$. The number to the left is carried as in the conventional system.

Not only is the electronic computer a near-illiterate with its "bi-syllable" language, it is also unsophisticated in arithmetic, for all it can do is add. So, if the computer wishes to do any of the other grade-school exercises, such as subtracting, multiplying, or dividing, it must do them—in a roundabout fashion—by addition. The computer's secret of success is that it can add extremely fast.

The necessity and mystery of a two-state numbering system should be acceptable now, but an obvious drawback to this system should have attracted your attention. How can a person be expected to become familiar with this system? The memory of man seems quite capable of remembering long decimal numbers, but binary numbers—of any length—are quite meaningless.

Octal System. Because of the difficulty of renumbering long strings of binary numbers, the *octal* system with a base of eight is used. The relationship between octal and decimal is presented here:

$$12 \text{ (octal number)} = 1 \times 8^1 + 2 \times 8^0$$

12 in octal

10 in decimal

Conversion from decimal to octal is done in the same way that we converted from decimal to binary.

$$
\begin{array}{l}
0 \quad \text{with remainder of } 1 \\
8)\overline{1} \quad \text{with remainder of } 4 \quad \text{octal} \\
8)\overline{12}
\end{array}
$$

which agrees with the value given in Figure 22–24.

Hexadecimal System. Another shorthand numbering system uses the hexadecimal system of 16 symbols which includes 0 through 9 and A through F. Computers which use four bits can readily convert to hexadecimal, Figure 22–25.

Computer Codes

Before discussing various codes, it is desirable to explain the code checking technique which will be included with the code description. Although the processing components are highly reliable, they do on occasion make errors for which safeguards must be established.

The codes to be discussed are made up of *bits*. In some codes there are an even number of bits, called *even parity codes*, while in other codes there are an uneven number of bits, called *odd parity codes*. The use of these codes will become evident as we move through the subject of codes. These

Figure 22–24
Octal System

Decimal	Octal	Binary	
0	0	000	
1	1	001	
2	2	010	
3	3	011	
4	4	100	
5	5	101	
6	6	110	
7	7	110	

Since this is the end
of the octal system, a
carryover to the next
number takes place.

Decimal	Octal	Binary	
8	10	001	000
9	11	001	001
10	12	001	010
11	13	001	011
12	14	001	100

Figure 22–25
Hexadecimal System

Binary System Bit Values				Hexadecimal System	Decimal System
8	4	2	1		
0	0	0	0	0	0
0	0	0	1	1	1
0	0	1	0	2	2
0	0	1	1	3	3
0	1	0	0	4	4
0	1	0	1	5	5
0	1	1	0	6	6
0	1	1	1	7	7
1	0	0	0	8	8
1	0	0	1	9	9
1	0	1	0	A	10
1	0	1	1	B	11
1	1	0	0	C	12
1	1	0	1	D	13
1	1	1	0	E	14
1	1	1	1	F	15

codes do not prevent errors from being punched, but they do help prevent errors after processing begins. To overcome this and other problems, various codes have been established.

Binary-Coded Digit Code. The six-bit or binary-coded decimal (BCD) code is illustrated in Figure 22–26. The C position is the *odd* parity bit for

Figure 22–26
BCD Code

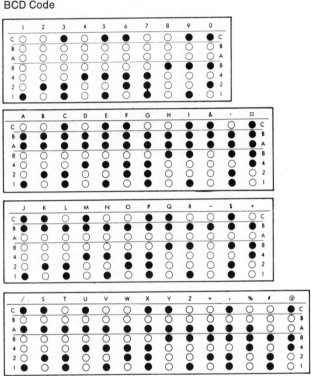

checking. Various combinations of 8–4–2–1 are used to form digits. The B and A, which are 00 when numeric characters are presented, become *zone* bits for coding the alphabet and special characters as shown. Note that a zero is represented by 00 1010 and not by a blank column. The parity check bit is shown in the check row C.

Extended Binary-Coded Decimal Interchange Code. The BCD code is limited to 64 characters, which causes some restrictions. Consequently, the eight-bit code called extended binary-coded decimal interchange code, EBCDIC (pronounced Eb-see-dick) has been devised. The code can accommodate upper- and lowercase alphabet characters and special characters which are meaningful to some peripheral devices, as well as additional characters which have not been assigned.

American Standard Code for Information Interchange. A seven-bit code designed to facilitate the communications between computer systems is the American Standard Code for Information Interchange, ASCII (pronounced As-key). A modification of ASCII is ASCII–8 which is compatible with 8-bit memory units.

Computer Words.   A group of characters treated by the computer as a unit is called a *word*. The word may be a piece of information, *data*, or an *instruction*. There is no way of telling one from the other except by the storage position, for in the computer the instructions are stored along with the data.

In fixed-word-length computers, the analogy has been made between the post office box system and the memory of computers, for it is essential not only to know what is in the box but also to know where the box is located. In a fixed-word-length computer there is a limit to the length of a word that can be placed in the box or *cell*: the computer memory is designed for only so much information, and no more can be placed in the cell.

In the computers designed for variable word lengths, there are no cells designated, but the memory is subdivided into individual character positions. Words are stored in successive character positions, with an *end of word* mark placed at the end of the series.

ORGANIZATION OF THE DIGITAL COMPUTER

The casual reader of computer literature is frequently overawed by the science-fiction implication that computers are magic brains. In order that you do not become one of these overly impressed readers, the description of the computer will start with a very basic analogy.

The computers you see shrouded in slick, metal cases, purring away in air-conditioned rooms, can be readily compared to a student working at his desk with his slide rule. If you understand this analogy, you will be a long way on the road to understanding the mysteries of the computer. Five major sections of the computer are shown in Figure 22–27. Notice that the heavy lines show the paths for numerical or logical information flow. This flow of information is controlled by the *control unit*, through "gates," as indicated by the circled X's. Each unit is, of course, a very complex organization of electrical and mechanical components, but for our purpose of the moment, the boxes can serve.

In the desk calculator, you, the human control, replace the control unit of the computer. The calculator, or slide rule, is the arithmetic unit. Your work sheet, where you jot down information, or your memory is the memory storage. The input is the problem information taken from the work sheet, and the output is the problem information placed on the work sheet. The analogy is more readily followed by the table at the bottom of the illustration.

Central Processing Unit

The *central processing unit* (CPU) supervises and controls the whole computer system, performing the arithmetic, editing, and logic, and neces-

Figure 22–27
Computer Organization

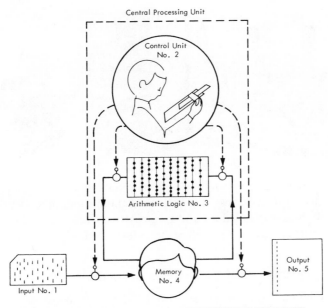

No. on Figure	Calculations	Computer Calculations
1	Input from work sheet	Input from cards
2	You, the human operator	Control unit
3	The calculator or slide rule	Arithmetic unit
4	Your memory or work sheet	Memory storage
5	Output onto work sheet	Output: cards, print-out device, etc.

sary control. Regrettably, it is impossible to discuss this part of the computer comprehensively in the short space available. However, the student, especially the engineering and science student, should enjoy further explorations into the subject. Several of the references in the bibliography should make rewarding reading excursions.

The central processing unit has two major sections:

Control Unit. Under the instructions of the stored program, the control unit directs and coordinates all operations. It controls the input/output units and the arithmetic logic operations.

Arithmetic/Logic. This not only performs the common operations such as addition, subtraction, multiplication, and division but also the operations of moving, shifting, and comparing data.

A typical CPU console with a printer is shown in Figure 22–28. The characteristic flickering lights on the console show, in code form, what information is available in the "registers." A register is a small memory unit which is capable of receiving, holding, and transferring information

Figure 22–28
Typical Computer Console

as directed by the control circuits. The register in the machine is named for the function it performs. If it is to hold the information regarding the location of data, it is called an *address register*; and an *instruction register* holds the instructions while they are being executed.

Computer Storage or Memory

One of the most important features of the modern computer, especially those used in industry, is their ability to store or "remember" large quantities of information.

Computer memory is referred to as:

Main memory, usually core, which is internal to the computer.

Auxiliary memory which is external to the main unit and is contained in a separate unit.

The auxiliary memories can, in turn, be classified by whether they have to be searched for information from one end to the other in a sequential fashion or whether the information is addressable and can be directly accessed by address.

The sequential storage includes the common tape units and also cards when used as a memory. Direct access includes data cells, drums, core memory, and disk memories.

In the course of developing the electronic computer, numerous devices have been developed and tried as storage devices. These include such designs as ultrasonic delay lines, composed of cylinders of mercury in which vibrations are cycled until needed. Those discussed here have survived the developmental stage and are actually in modern computers.

There are a number of devices or media which can be used for both memory and input/output. This will cause some overlap and perhaps some confusion for the reader. To minimize the confusion, the exclusively memory devices will be discussed first, followed by those devices which serve both as memory and input/output, and last by those which are just input/output.

Magnetic Core Memories

The magnetic core memory appeared in the first machines in the early 1950s. Although it is expensive to construct, it offers the advantages of being a nonmechanical, reliable memory that occupies a small space and consumes little power.

The heart of the core memory is a small toroid- or doughnut-shaped magnet, 30 to 50 thousandths of an inch in diameter, pressed out of ferric oxide powder and other materials and then sintered at a high temperature. The memory depends upon the two stable states of the magnet induced by a grid or matrix of wires upon which the magnets are strung like so many tiny beads (Figure 22–29A). When a current of sufficient magnitude is

Figure 22–29A
Magnetic Core Memories

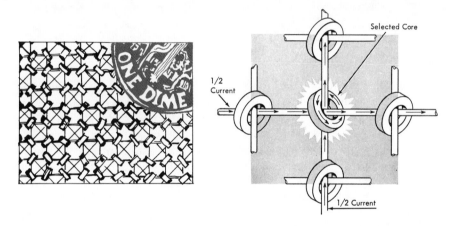

passed in one direction through the core, it is magnetized in one direction (Figure 22–29B). When the current is reversed, and is of sufficient magnitude, the magnetism of the core is in the opposite direction. It is apparent that there are two states available which can represent the binary numbering system.

Since the magnet must have two definable states which must be retained indefinitely, the magnetic material must be chosen with care.

These cores are strung in a coordinate system, with the address of any bit of information being the intersection of two wires. Each of the wires, which intersect at the address, will carry only a fraction of the current required to make the core change its magnetic direction, but the two wires intersecting at this point will carry, when combined, enough current to change the direction of the polarity. Since one wire alone does not carry enough current to change the polarity of the magnet, only the one at the intersection will be changed.

Figure 22–29B
Magnetic Core Operations

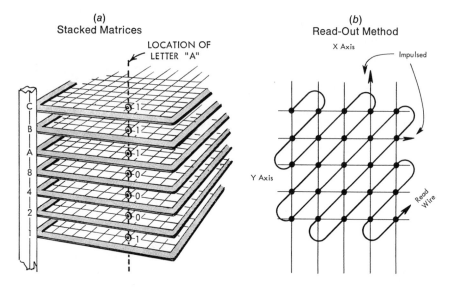

(a)
Stacked Matrices

(b)
Read-Out Method

The cores in their stacked matrices form a three-coordinate system. The X and Y coordinates represent the address of the character, while the Z coordinate represents the character. A single column of cores, all with the same X and Y coordinates, represents a single character in the memory (shown in Figure 22–29B[a]). Notice how the matrix presents a coded binary system, as discussed before. For variable word lengths there is an additional matrix for *end of word* designations.

Now that we see how information is read into a core memory, let us observe how this information may be read out. The matrix is laced by another wire (Figure 22–29B[b]) called the sense wire. If the coordinate wires are impulsed, in turn, with a negative impulse, the core magnets which are zero with a negative state will not be influenced. Consequently, there will be no signal imposed upon the sense wire. But if a core magnet had a "one" of positive state when it received the impulse, it would "flip" to the zero state. This change in the magnetic field around the sense wire would induce a voltage which would be read out of the memory.

This process of reading obviously destroys the information in the memory, and it is essential to regenerate the information and return it to the storage. This is done electronically, as is the switching required for the matrix. Magnetic core memories are ideally suited for parallel arithmetic operations, which makes them especially desirable for high-speed operations.

Magnetic core continues to be popular, but there are many other promising techniques waiting to be perfected before they are fully accepted. These include thin film and plated wires which are readily manufactured.

Monolithic circuits appearing in some present-day computers are much smaller than magnetic cores and promise to provide more and faster storage in less space.

Magnetic Drum Storage. The *magnetic drum storage* is a cylinder machined to a very high degree of accuracy which is mounted in bearings that permit constant rotation at a high speed. The drum is coated by plating or by spraying on iron oxide or a similar material. Information is stored on the drum's magnetic surface in the form of small magnetized spots, as if thousands of small magnets were imbedded in the surface of the drum. The two states of the binary digits are represented by the polarity of the magnetized spots. This polarity is retained indefinitely, or until the polarity is deliberately changed by the controls of the machine.

To read and write the magnetic spots on the drum, a magnetic head is located extremely close to the surface. Usually the same magnetic head is used for reading and writing. In reading, the lines of force of the magnetized bit induce an electrical current in the coil in much the same way that electricity is generated in a magneto. It is obvious that the movement of the drum is essential to the production of a signal.

The surface of the drum is divided into imaginary strips called tracks or bands. Each track has a read-write head rigidly mounted adjacent to it. The tracks are, in turn, divided into sectors, so there are hundreds of addressable sectors—which might be considered as analogous to files where information is kept. These locations are systematically numbered and can be selected instantaneously by the computer.

A typical drum rotates at 3,500 rpm, has 800 tracks, with a total capacity of nearly 4 million bytes.

The memory drum which played an important role in the early development of the computer has been relegated to serve as an intermediate storage device called a *buffer*.

Magnetic Disk Storage. The magnetic disk storage uses thin metal disks which are coated on both sides with ferrous oxide. These two surfaces serve the same purpose as the outside surface of the drum. The disks are spaced on a vertical shaft which rotates. Forked reading arms traverse the disks to magnetically print and retrieve information. Data is stored as magnetic spots in tracks which form concentric circles on the surface of the disk. Because these thin disks are bound to wobble as they rotate, the surfaces must be protected from being marred by the writing heads. This is done by air jets at the point of contact which produce an air-float, resulting in a small but relatively constant space between the disk and the magnetic head.

These storage units are direct access units, with all information readily available. The data can be read from the disk repeatedly, but when data is read in, it replaces any data that might be on the disk. The access mechanisms vary in design, but the comb-type as illustrated in Figure 22–30 is typical. Each arm has a read-write head, but only one head can

Figure 22–30
Magnetic Disk Storage Schematic

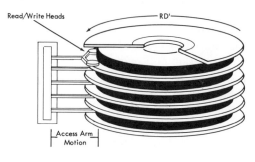

Disk Storage

operate at a time. The heads move back and forth on the radius of the disk.
An extension of the disk memory is the *disk pack* (Figure 22–31). A

Figure 22–31
Disk Pack

number of disks is packaged as a unit and the unit can be added to or removed from the computer system. This means that disk packs can be
treated as separate account categories, such as accounts receivable, inventory items, and so forth. This adds considerably to the versatility of the
computer, especially when it is used in the retailing and banking businesses.

The disk pack is mounted in a *disk drive* unit, Figure 22–32. Some disk
drives hold only one disk pack, but some hold eight plus an extra one for
maintenance.

The efficiency of the disk memory is affected by the time it takes the
arms to travel from one location to another. This can be reduced by considering the *tracks* on the stack of disks as a series of concentric drums. If
there are 10 disks with 203 tracks per surface, they can be organized as
203 concentric cylinders, which will speed up the recording and retrieval of
information.

Data Cell Drive. This carrousel-like memory device (illustrated in Figure
22–33) may contain as many as 10 data cells. The data cells are removable

Figure 22–32
Disk Drive

and interchangeable, permitting an open-ended capacity. Each data cell contains 20 subcells of 10 magnetic tape strips each. Each strip is 2¼″ wide by 13″ long.

Upon activation, the data cell drive rotates its circular array of data cells and positions one of the 200 subcells beneath an access station. When the addressed subcell is in position, separation fingers draw the addressed strip from among the 10 strips in the subcell. The strip is rapidly wrapped around a small drum, rotated past a read/write head, and returned to its subcell.

Each strip has 100 tracks in five groups of 20 each. The read/write head, composed of 20 elements, can be moved to any one of the five "cylinder positions."

Figure 22–33
Data Cell Drive

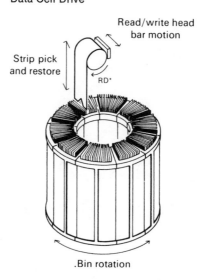

Access time can be as great as 0.650 seconds or as little as 100 microseconds. This is slower than some other memories, but it does have the advantage of large capacity.

Virtual Memory.   Industrial applications frequently overtax the memory capacity of computers. This problem can be overcome by using *virtual memory* which is a technique for managing a limited amount of high-speed memory and a much larger amount of lower speed memory in a way that the distinction is not obvious to the programmer and operator.

The technique entails some means of shifting segments of program and data, called pages, from the lower speed memory, such as drums or disks, into the high-speed memory where it can be operated on.

Normally there will be several segments of a program in high-speed memory at one time, while other segments will be in the slow-speed memory simultaneously. The high-speed memory from which instructions are executed is the real memory, and the lower speed memory is called the virtual memory.

Input, Output, and Memory

Magnetic tape serves the multiple purpose of input, output, or memory, but regardless of its application, the equipment and tape are the same.

The tape itself is plastic, coated with a magnetic substance, and is similar to the tapes used in home recording machines. Various widths of tapes have been used, from a fraction of an inch to several inches, but the most common width is one-half inch. The tape is purchased on 10½-inch reels that hold 2,400 feet.

Information is recorded on the tape as magnetized spots, or bits, by magnetic read-write heads (Figure 22–34). The information is recorded in chan-

Figure 22–34
Magnetic Read-Write Heads

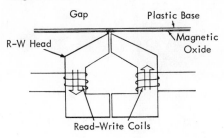

nels, as shown in Figure 22–35A. The code illustrated conforms to the one

Figure 22–35A
Coded Magnetic Tape

Figure 22–35B
Record Blocks

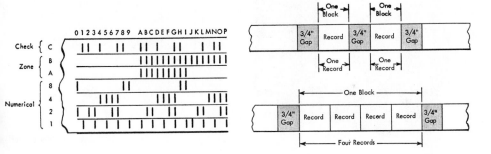

discussed previously, and as you might expect, other coding systems can also be used. Information is usually recorded in blocks (Figure 22–35B). The size of the recorded blocks can be fixed or variable, depending upon the characteristics of the machine. The tape comes to rest with the magnetic head in the middle of the "gap." The gap is essential for the acceleration and deceleration of the tape and for the proper functioning of the machine. It is apparent that gaps are an inefficient way to use the tape; therefore, it is desirable to run as many records together as is feasible.

The reading process is nondestructive, so the information remains indefinitely. Writing, of course, destroys the previous information. To prevent accidental writing, which would destroy records, reels are equipped with a safety ring. Only when the ring is in place can writing occur.

Figure 22–36A shows a typical magnetic tape unit, and the schematic is shown in Figure 22–36B. The tape feed mechanism is complicated by the need to move the tape from reel to reel rapidly and to stop it quickly. This is made more difficult because of the inertia of the reels and the fragility of

Figure 22–36A
Typical Magnetic Tape Unit

Figure 22–36B
Schematic of Tape Unit

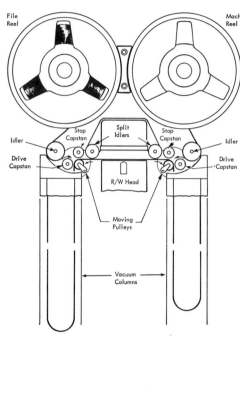

Courtesy of IBM Corp.

the tapes. The tape is moved across the magnetic heads when forced against a rotating drive capstan, and is stopped when it is forced against a stop capstan. The loops of tape which are stored in the vacuum columns act as buffers between the movement of the reels and the sensitive movement of the tape over the magnetic head.

Magnetic tape has become a well-accepted form of storage and input-output media because of its large storage capacity, which can be added to easily by using more reels. A number of magnetic tape units can be under the command of one processing unit, extending the storage capacity and contributing to the versatility of the installation.

The major disadvantage of tape is its long access time. Since the information is placed on the reel in sequential order, it requires a long time to search along the length of tape to find the required information. In addition, it is difficult to update records when they need to be changed.

Hypertape drives have extra performance characteristics and can read tape at rates of over 300,000 bytes per second. One feature is that the tape can be read backwards. Some tapes are available in cartridges which do not require rewinding.

Input-Output Devices

Printer Keyboard. The typewriter-style keyboard and printing function can be used independently: the keyboard for input to the system and the printer as an output. The machine has a stationary carriage and an interchangeable moving, spherical printing unit. The printer-keyboard is used for such applications as program checking and job logging. One printer keyboard is standard for each computer console.

Punched Card Input and Output. It would be highly desirable if the input media could be the by-product of some operation, such as typing a document or billing a customer. Often this is impossible, and the information for the computer must be produced by card-punch machines from handwritten documents. However, producing the input as a by-product is a goal for which to strive, and it is being done successfully by means of special time clocks, scales which have a card output, and cash registers which have paper tape output.

If the information is transmitted to the computer as it is produced, it is said to be an *on-line* operation. It is more common to feed the information into the computer through an auxiliary operation in batches.

The punched card described is the most common form of computer input. The cards are read by machines which operate on the same principles as those discussed in the earlier chapter. In fact, some of these machines discussed have been attached to computers to function as the reading, punching, and print-out units.

Card Read-Punch. A typical card read-punch is illustrated in Figure 22–37A. The card is conveyed under two sets of reading brushes, Figure 22–37B, where the holes are interpreted as electric pulses and stored in the computer memory. Some card readers use photoelectric cells instead of brushes.

As shown in Figure 22–37C, the card output passes under a punching and sensing unit where it can be checked. The card reader and card punch may or may not be contained within one peripheral unit.

The cards in some machines are read in the conventional, long-edge-first *parallel* mode. A *serial* mode card reader operates on a column-by-column basis.

Card Substitutes. Most entry into the computer has been through the punched card, but there are other methods becoming acceptable:

Verified keypunching is initiated in the usual manner, but instead of each key-stroke punching a hole in the card, the data is entered into core storage. During verification just the variable information is read in, and if it is correct, the verified card appears in the card stacker. It is not necessary to

Figure 22–37
Card Read-Punch

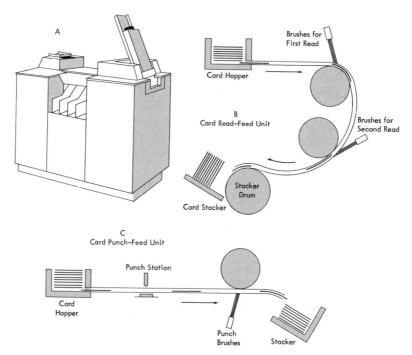

retype a card if it is in error, because it may be corrected before it is punched.

Key to cassette uses the cartridges which are so popular in home recording. The data is either keyed directly on the tape or keyed to a memory and then dumped to the tape. The system in turn uses a *pooler* to transfer the information from the cassette to computer-compatible tape.

Key-to-disc systems have 8 or 10 or more key-punch stations which enter information into a disc memory which is in turn used by the computer.

Paper Tape Input/Output. Paper tape, which was originally applied to transmitting messages over telegraph wires, has been extended to include computer applications. Not only is it used to communicate between data processing units in remote locations, it is also used as a main input or auxiliary input for computers.

Paper tape may be the by-product of a typing operation. Very effective production control systems have been developed using a tape which is punched during the sales order typing process. The tape is used for stock picking, invoicing, and so on.

Magnetic-Ink Character Readers: Input. Another means of input which is of growing interest, especially in the field of commercial banking, is the magnetic-ink character, which can be read both by man and machine. The characters on the bottom of your personal check is a typical application of the magnetic ink, with the figures at the bottom inscribed by a special electric typewriter. Later, these forms may be handled directly by a sorter, converted to magnetic tape, or fed on line directly to a computer.

Printers: Output. The electric typewriter is often used as an input-output device, especially in computers for engineering applications. Because of the single action of each individual key, the typewriter is a relatively slow output device.

Line-at-a-time printers are capable of printing much faster than the typewriter, and one which uses a series of type bars raised to the correct position before imprinting was discussed in the card-data-processing section. This device, however, is too slow for modern applications.

The chain printer (Figure 22–38A) can print up to 132 positions on a line at the rate of 600 lines per minute. This printer uses engraved type assembled in a chain which travels horizontally (Figure 22–38B). The paper is pressed against one piece of type in the moving chain by a magnetically actuated hammer.

Figure 22–38A
Chain Printer

Figure 22–38B
Print Chain

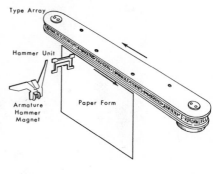

The wire matrix printer prints the characters as an array of dots formed by a rectangle of 5 dots by 7 dots (illustrated in Figure 22–39). The dots are formed by the ends of wires, extended to form the proper patterns, which are pressed against an ink ribbon in contact with the paper. The characters can be printed 120 to the line at a rate of 500 or 1,000 lines per minute.

Figure 22–39
Wire Matrix Print

ABCDEFGH

123456789

—„ :8 *#%@=

There are a number of nonmechanical printers on the market. Because these devices do not have to contend with the inertia of heavy parts, they are capable of printing at unbelievable speeds. The television-like display units have a cathode-ray tube, CRT, as their principal component, on which alphanumeric or graphic information is displayed at high speeds, which is in turn photographed.

Display Units.   Display units, Figure 22–40, are available with special

Figure 22–40
Display Unit

features. Some of these include ways of displaying vectors at any angle and special programs which will produce, at the touch of a button, the schematic figures in a design such as electrical resistors. *Light pens* guided by the operator can tell the computer where to make any necessary changes. Self-contained memories called buffers can contain diagrams which reduce the demand on the computer storage capacity.

Computer Output Microfilm, COM.   COM, a replacement for line-printing of paper forms, produces an output on 16 or 32 mm. film or on the highly condensed microfiche.

COM is a microfilm camera operating as the read-out unit for a computer. The unit may operate on line with the computer or, as more common, off line with a tape unit as shown in Figure 22–41.

Figure 22–41
Computer Output Microfilm, COM

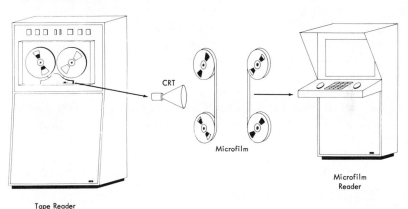

Tape Reader   CRT   Microfilm   Microfilm Reader

The COM is applied in many business situations, such as banks, insurance companies, and credit bureaus, but it is also gaining wider acceptance in industry for listing inventories, bill of materials, and similar applications. One company is using COM to list all of the active manufacturing orders on the shop floor. These manufacturing orders which include the operation sheets show the status and location of each job. The supervisor who receives the read-outs daily can refer to them by using a microfilm reader, which is conveniently located on the shop floor. The advantages of COM are that it reduces the cost of handling and storing large quantities of paper work.

Connecting Input/Output Units.   The transfer of data within the computer is extremely fast, but the communication between the computer and the input/output device is slow—so slow that it delays the whole computer operation. To alleviate this problem, the computer designers have included *channels.*

The channels' primary purpose is to direct input/output operations, and they may be either included within the console of the CPU or stand alone as an extra unit connected between the main storage and the input/output units. There are two types of channels:

Selector channels are used with input/output units which operate at high speeds, such as magnetic tapes, disks, and drums. The computer is interfacing with these devices one at a time and transfers all information in one record in what is called the *burst mode.*

Multiplexor channel units may operate in a burst mode but more frequently operate in the *byte mode*. Since it is attached to a number of slow input/output devices, it serves first one and then another.

Buffering. It is not efficient to suspend operations during the input/output process. To overcome this delay, a *buffer* is used where data is stored until it is requested. This memory device can dump its information in much less time than would be required by the input/output device itself.

Peripheral Operations. Another way of reducing the computer time involved is to use peripheral equipment. For example, cards are slow to read so that transferring card data to tape is desirable, or at other times to transfer tape data to cards or printouts. To control these units off line from the main computer, some installations have added another computer of smaller size —sometimes referred to as a *mini-computer*.

Data Transmission. In organizations with widespread activities it may be faster and more convenient and economical to centralize such activities as inventory control, production control, and payroll. A centralized data system requires transmission from many localities to a central organization.

Several systems are available which can be used in conjunction with commercial telephone and telegraph lines and with microwave and short-wave radio circuits.

The schematic in Figure 22–42 shows the typical flow of information.

Figure 22–42
Schematic of Flow of Information

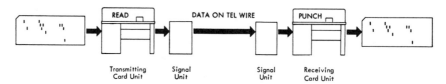

The transmitting and receiving units are identical, so only one machine is required at each end of the line.

Further applications of data transmission include remote inquiry stations, on-line with computers, so that inquiries can be directed to—and answered by—a typewriter. Refinements include data transmission units connecting two or more computers. Other common data transmission methods use paper tape, so that cards are converted to tape, and transmitted, and then converted back to cards.

Typical System Configuration. There is probably no typical system configuration, but perhaps you would like to know what to expect to see when a company is using the software packages to be described throughout the rest of the chapters. You can expect to see something like this:

Computer central processing unit, 32K bytes.
Card reader.
Printer.
Printer-keyboard.

Disk storage drives.
Key punch for system preparation.
Tape drive for system preparation.

Summary

You should now have a broad comprehension of any data processing system you encounter, and you should be able to decipher or code any data processing card you are using. Whether you are working with a highly sophisticated on-line computer, or working with a system oriented toward units-record equipment, you should feel perfectly at home.

Data processing systems are being improved rapidly so that you may expect many innovations. With the background obtained in this chapter, you should find it easy to keep up with the current literature.

QUESTIONS

22–1. What are the differences between the uses of business computers and the uses you make of the computers in school?

22–2. Define the following as applied to a computer card.
   a. 12 edge.
   b. 9 edge.
   c. 80 column.
   d. Field.
   e. Zone punch.
   f. Tier.
   g. Punch area, print area.

22–3. Compare "programming" of unit record systems with that used for computers.

22–4. What is done in data processing to assure correct operations?

22–5. Select the correct unit record machine for the following applications:
   a. Preparing cards from written documents.
   b. Checking the above cards.
   c. If you dropped the above cards and wanted to put them in sequence by clock number.
   d. Duplicating an extra set of the cards made in the first step.

22–6. Discuss why the development of the computer was so slow in coming.

22–7. Why is the binary system important in the development of computers?

22–8. Compare the binary coded digit with that used on the System 3 Computer.

22–9. What are the comparative advantages and disadvantages of the various computer memories?

22–10. What economies would you anticipate from Computer Output Microfilm?

22–11. Define the following terms:
   a. Buffering.
   b. Register.
   c. Virtual memory.
   d. CPU.

23

Programming and Software Packages

DESIGNING SYSTEMS for computers requires the knowledge of both hardware and software. Since you now have a background of how the hardware functions in the computer, we can move on to making the computer your willing servant by the appropriate software.

The subject of system designing for computers will progress in three stages. First you will be introduced to flow charting for computer systems, next to the "machine languages" of the computer which are used to address the machine directly, and finally to the more sophisticated compiler languages.

FLOW CHARTING

Flow charts, as you have discovered, are just a method of distilling and conveying ideas. There is nothing sacred about the form of the chart or the symbols which are used. Consequently, programmers have improvised methods which reflect their ingenuity and analytical abilities. Any set of symbols can be used for these flow charts, but there is something to be said for a universal language understood by all. Those symbols illustrated in Figure 23–1 are the ones most universally accepted.

The flow-chart symbols are available as a template which makes it easier to draw the flow charts. Another aid to the computer programmer is the flow-charting work sheet illustrated in Figure 23–2. These convenient forms, $11'' \times 16\frac{1}{2}''$, have guide lines which are printed in light blue ink which will not reproduce and consequently brings out the flow chart. The coordinate system makes a ready reference when describing the system.

Figure 23–1
System Flow-Chart Symbols

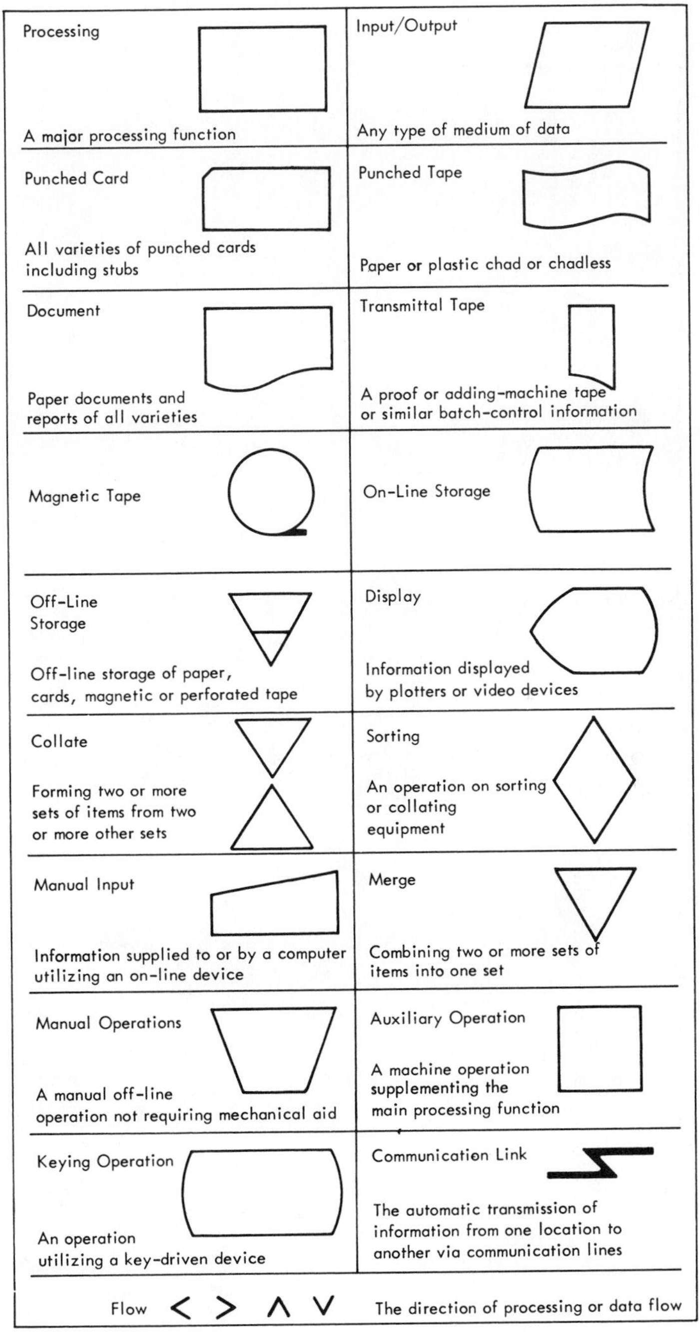

Processing A major processing function	Input/Output Any type of medium of data
Punched Card All varieties of punched cards including stubs	Punched Tape Paper or plastic chad or chadless
Document Paper documents and reports of all varieties	Transmittal Tape A proof or adding–machine tape or similar batch–control information
Magnetic Tape	On–Line Storage
Off–Line Storage Off–line storage of paper, cards, magnetic or perforated tape	Display Information displayed by plotters or video devices
Collate Forming two or more sets of items from two or more other sets	Sorting An operation on sorting or collating equipment
Manual Input Information supplied to or by a computer utilizing an on–line device	Merge Combining two or more sets of items into one set
Manual Operations A manual off–line operation not requiring mechanical aid	Auxiliary Operation A machine operation supplementing the main processing function
Keying Operation An operation utilizing a key–driven device	Communication Link The automatic transmission of information from one location to another via communication lines
Flow < > ∧ ∨	The direction of processing or data flow

Figure 23–2
Flow-Charting Work Sheet

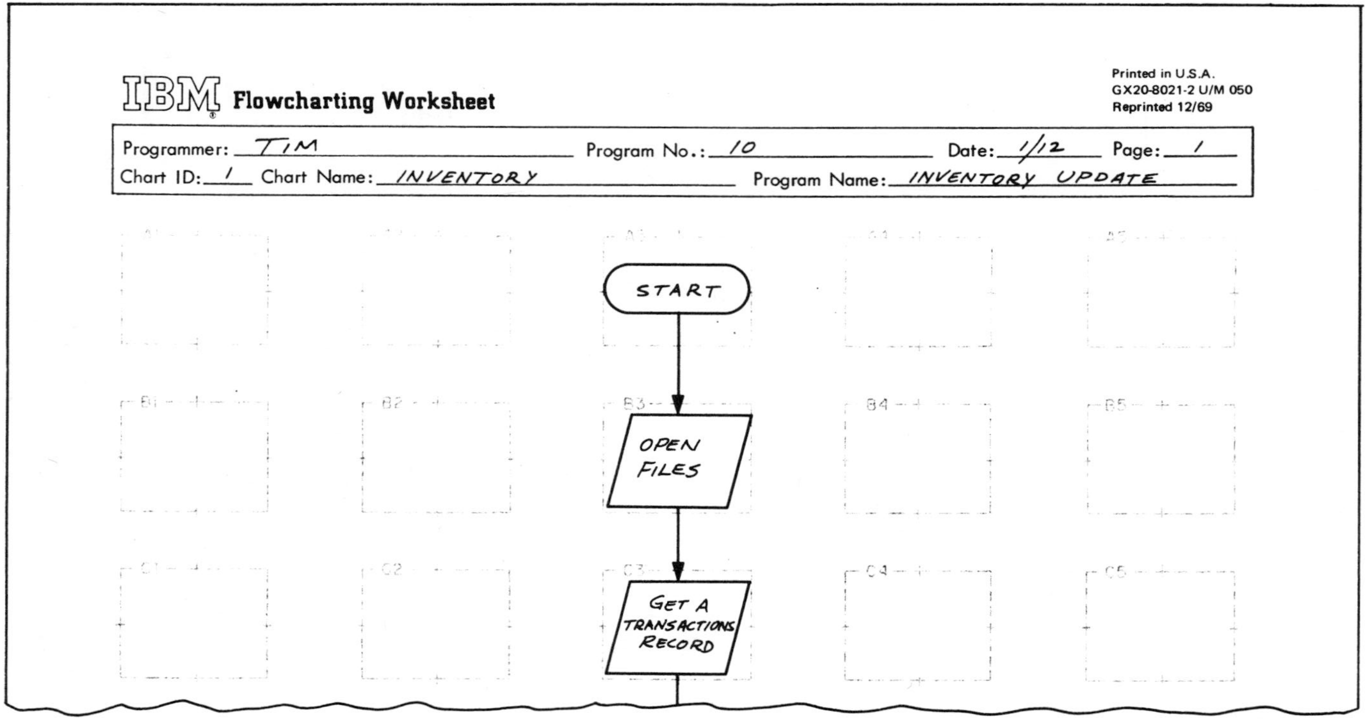
IBM Flowcharting Worksheet
Printed in U.S.A.
GX20-8021-2 U/M 050
Reprinted 12/69
Programmer: TIM
Program No.: 10
Date: 1/12
Page: 1
Chart ID: 1
Chart Name: INVENTORY
Program Name: INVENTORY UPDATE
B1
B2
B3
B4
B5
C1
C2
C3
C4
C5
START
OPEN FILES
GET A TRANSACTIONS RECORD

Programming the Computer

Programming refers to writing the instructions for the computer to follow. The resulting program is called the *software*, as compared to the computer itself which is called the *hardware*.

One has to understand the history of the computer to appreciate software developments. Programming has had three distinct stages of development:

Machine language, which came first, consisted of the symbols originated by the computer designers to instruct the computer what to do. The programmer has to address the machine in its own tongue, the binary language, and keep track of all of the information as it passes from one memory to another. This language will be described very briefly, not because you will probably ever use it but because it will give you a greater appreciation of how the computer functions.

Symbolic language rescued the programmer from the tedious, detailed operations required by machine language. In symbolic language the programmer uses an easily remembered mnemonic code. The problem of keeping track of storage spaces is taken over by the computer itself, which also translates the symbolic language to the machine language which the computer can understand. You may never have to program in symbolic language, but you should know that it exists and that it is used extensively in *software packages* where computer efficiency is important.

Each computer company has its own unique symbolic language so that learning one before it is actually needed would be most inefficient. Therefore, just a very basic example will be given.

Compiler languages are written in near-English form and take over many of the problems that one experiences in less sophisticated languages. These popular languages, such as COBOL and FORTRAN, are efficient for the programmer but not for the computer. Since you will at least be seeing one, COBOL, in industry, you will be introduced to its structure so that you will have some familiarity with it.

Machine Language. As was observed, computers were extremely tedious to program when they were first developed. One had to know the code for a hundred different operations, ranging from simple arithmetic to moving information in registers when overflows occurred or suppressing zeros when not desired. This probably would not have been so bad if it did not need to be done in binary. So as you read these paragraphs, be grateful to those who have gone before you to prepare the many sophisticated languages to which you are being exposed.

Your computer language, whatever it is, will be translated for you into machine language, so there is really no need to learn machine language except that an example will give you some insight into how the computer operates and an appreciation of the translation process.

The execution of an instruction requires two separate cycles. First, an *instruction cycle* occurs which is followed by an *execution cycle*. The time for the instruction cycle is referred to as *I time,* and the execution cycle occurs during the *E time.*

To comprehend what is happening in the computer, look at Figure 23–3 and follow the steps given here:

Figure 23–3
Data Flow Using Machine Language

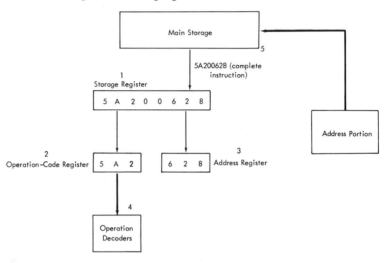

Instruction Cycle. The instruction is moved from main storage to the *storage register,* no. 1.

The operation code field is sent to *operation code register,* no. 2.

The address is sent to *address register,* no. 3.

A decoding network interprets the operation code and establishes the necessary circuit paths, no. 4.

The location of the next instruction is determined, and the *instruction counter* is updated, no. 5.

Execution Cycle. The execution or *E* time follows the *I* time, and it is during this time that the operation is performed. This may require a number of machine cycles.

The operation code register is in control of the storage register and the accumulator as shown in the illustration.

The operation code instructs the computer: "Whatever is in the storage register must be added to the accumulator register."

As pointed out in the section on number systems, computers do all of their operations by addition—addition which is done extremely fast. Computers use either *serial* or *parallel* mode addition. Usually you and I add by the serial method by carrying numbers over. This is slow, but some faster computers add numbers in parallel as we might do when we do something as familiar as counting out pocket change.

Symbolic Language. A coding sheet with typical information for programming the IBM System/360 in assembler language is illustrated in Figure 23–4. These explanations will illustrate how the coding sheet is used.

Each line on the coding sheet indicates what will be punched into one data processing card, and you will notice that there are 80 columns to correspond with the columns on a card. None of the information in the heading of the form will appear on the card.

There are two fields as illustrated:

1. Identification sequence field from column 73 through 80. The use of this field is optional for the operator. If desired, it can be used as a place to indicate the sequence of operations.
2. Statement field extends from column 1 through 71 and may contain one to four different entries:
   a. Name is an optional eight characters starting with column 1 and is used to identify a statement. The operator uses a name when he wishes to refer to this line at a later date.
   b. Operation is mandatory and tells what is to be done.
   c. Operand specifies data to be operated on.
   d. Comments are descriptive information about the program.

The casual reader will probably understand little of what is shown on the coding form. Only practice with an assembler language will give you the knowledge required to use it. An important point for you to understand is that the assembler program is passed through the computer where it is translated into the machine language of the computer.

Compiler Languages. To most students *compiler languages* will be a familiar subject, for you have undoubtedly been introduced to one such as BASIC, FORTRAN, or COBOL. If you are not acquainted with the names and purpose of some of the current compiler languages, you probably should be:

FORTRAN   FORmula TRANslator. Largely a mathematical notation, this language is used primarily for numerical computations by engineers, scientists, and mathematicians.

COBOL   COmmon Business-Oriented Language. COBOL is based on English, making it unnecessary to memorize long lists of symbols.

PL/1   Programming Language I. Designed for a large variety of computer procedures.

BASIC   A language designed for *time sharing systems* through a terminal. It is *interactive* in that the operator and computer can interact together to make changes in the program.

RPG   Report Program Generator is a symbolic language used for developing programs to generate reports. Many companies use this program for producing reports as well as for file maintenance.

Figure 23-4
Symbolic Language Coding Form

PROGRAM PROGA
PROGRAMMER J. J. JONES

PUNCHING INSTRUCTIONS — GRAPHIC — PUNCH
PAGE ___ OF ___
CARD ELECTRO NUMBER
DATE
STATEMENT
Identification-Sequence

Name	Operation	Operand	Comments
PROGA	START	256	
BEGIN	BALR	11,0	
	USING	*,11	
* THIS PROGRAM		COMPUTES TWO VALUES	
	L	2,DATA	LOAD REGISTER 2
	A	2,CON	ADD 10
	SLR	2,1	THIS WAS EFFECT OF MULTIPLYING BY 2
	S	2,DATA+4	NOTE RELATIVE ADDRESSING
	ST	2,RESULT	
	L	6,BIN1	BEGIN SECOND PROBLEM
	A	6,BIN2	
	CUD	6,DEC	CONVERT TO DECIMAL
	EDJ		END OF JOB
DATA	DC	F'25'	F RESERVES ONE FULL WORD
	DC	F'15'	
CON	DC	F'10'	
RESULT	DS	F	
BIN1	DC	F'12'	
BIN2	DC	F'78'	
DEC	DS	D	D RESERVES ONE DOUBLEWORD
	END	BEGIN	

RPG is not used to write statements in the conventional way of programming. *Specifications* are written on special forms provided for input data, output data, input/output devices, and the calculations needed.

Figure 23–5 illustrates the difference between using machine language and compiler language. At first glance, a compiler language would appear to consume more time, but this is not true. They can usually reduce preparation time considerably.

Figure 23–5
Compiler Programming

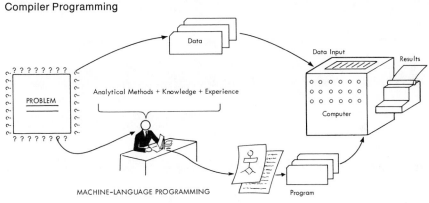

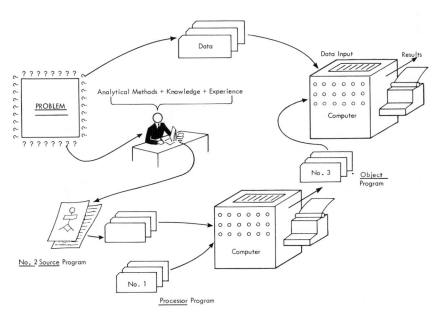

Note: Usually the same computer would be used; two are used to illustrate the steps.

In the illustration of automatic programming, it should be pointed out that three programs are involved. In the order of their development, these are:

1. *Processor program.* This (also called the translator or compiler) consists of a list of instructions which tells the machine what to do with the source program to produce the object program. The processor programs are supplied by the manufacturers of the computers.
2. *Source program.* This is the set of basic instructions, written by the programmer, which follows the rules of the specific programming method used.
3. *Object program.* This is a machine-language program developed by the computer from instructions given by the source program and the processor program. It is the one used to read the data, process it, and produce the answer.

When one speaks of COBOL, FORTRAN, or other translating systems, he means both the source program and the processor program. The source program must be written to a set of rules so that the processor program can make the necessary translation.

DEVELOPMENT OF COBOL PROGRAMMING

The COBOL compiler language was the first large-scale effort to design a single computer language which permitted writing programs adaptable to many computers. It is designed for maximum compatability among the many different computers on the market.

The proliferation of innumerable compiler programming systems caused alarm in both industry and government as there was little opportunity to transfer knowledge among the languages of different computers. Consequently the Conference on Data Systems Languages (CODASYL) was called at the Pentagon in 1959. This committee, representing computer users in government and industry (as well as computer manufacturers), set in motion several subcommittees which had as their final objective a COmmon Business Oriented Language for computers. This, shortened to COBOL, was published by the Government Printing Office in 1960 with plans to publish revisions annually. The COBOL manual is the authoritative reference, and the contents of this chapter are intended only as an introduction.

The philosophy of the COBOL system is easier to grasp when you see that it has four distinct divisions, three of which are independent of the computer being used.

1. The IDENTIFICATION DIVISION names the source program, the date the program was written, individuals involved, and other pertinent information. It is independent of the computer.

2. The ENVIRONMENT DIVISION outlines the equipment used for compiling and running the object program and is dependent on the computer.
3. The DATA DIVISION gives the file and record descriptions or data which the object program is to use. The data are described in terms of a standard data format which makes this section nearly *independent* of the computer being used.
4. The PROCEDURE DIVISION specifies the steps that the computer must take in solving the problem. The procedure is given in near-English and is independent of the computer.

These divisions, with the exception of the ENVIRONMENT DIVISION, are independent—or nearly independent—of the computer used. Only in this division is the program dependent upon the computer. So, theoretically at least, a universal program may be written and used on many common computers by merely changing the ENVIRONMENT DIVISION.

Reference Format

COBOL has a standard reference format which takes precedence over all other rules. The sequence of the program divisions must be IDENTIFICATION, ENVIRONMENT, DATA, and PROCEDURE DIVISIONS.

The COBOL *Coding Sheet* is illustrated in Figure 23–6. Pause now and explore the layout of this sheet and the explanations concerning the sequence numbers, margins, and other information given on the form.

It will help you understand the COBOL logic if you are aware that it is somewhat analogous to outlining. Figure 23–7 shows the COBOL outline with the four major divisions in their proper sequence. Under each division heading you will see subheadings for information which may or may not be added. Each of these divisions, with the detailed sub- and sub-sub-headings, will be discussed in turn.

Before going too far in the discussion of COBOL, you deserve an explanation about some slight changes in the writing style in this part of the chapter. All words which are *reserved* for precise meaning in COBOL programming (listed in Figure 23–8) are in capital letters. In the instruction format, those uppercase words which are underlined are required, while those which are not are optional—optional only in the sense that they may be deleted. (Misspelling of an optional word, or replacement by another word of any kind, is not permitted.) This writing style has been used in the government COBOL manual, as well as in a number of textbooks, so you should not find it difficult to refer to them if you wish.

Incidentally, this short chapter cannot include all the many detailed facets included in the COBOL programming, and you are urged to supplement your knowledge with one of the excellent references listed. The objec-

Figure 23-6

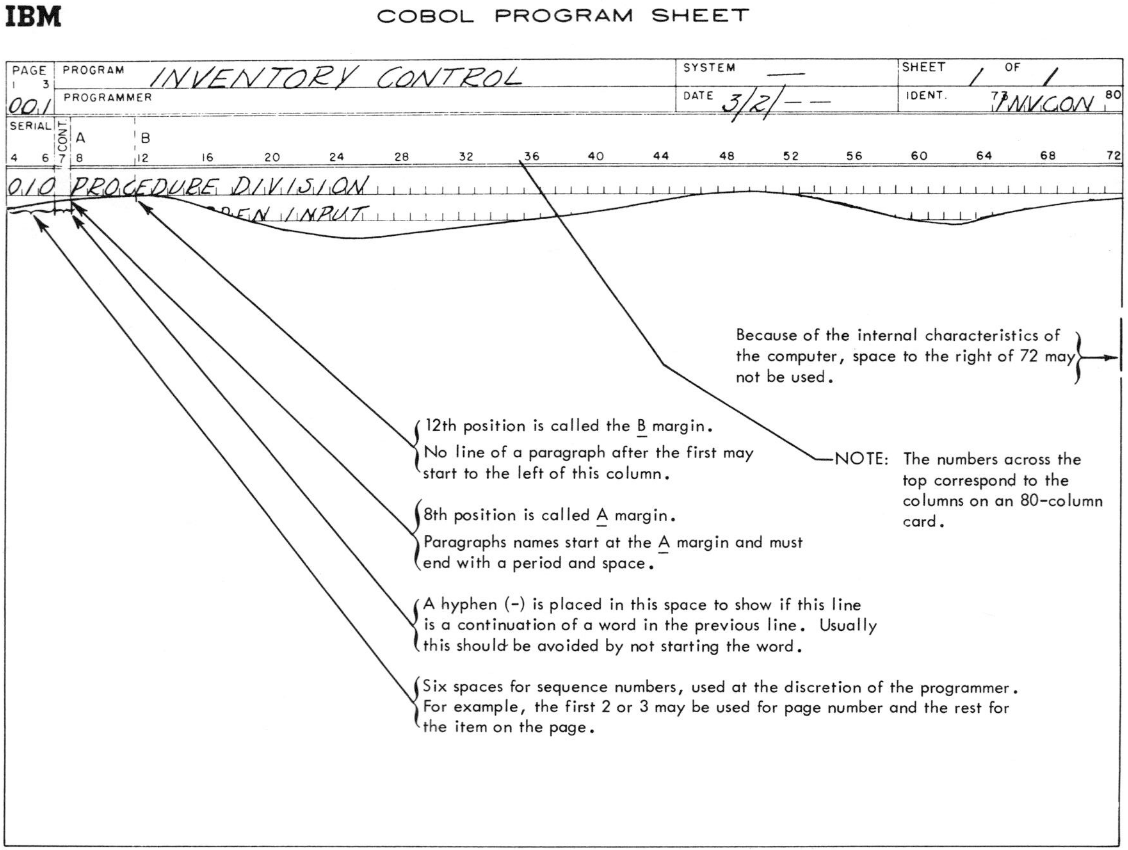

IBM

COBOL PROGRAM SHEET

PROGRAM _INVENTORY CONTROL_   SYSTEM ____   PAGE 3   SHEET 1 OF 1

PROGRAMMER ____   DATE 3/2/__   IDENT. _PNNYCON_

```
SERIAL    CONT   A   B
001   010 PROCEDURE DIVISION
          OPEN INPUT
```

Column markers: 4 6 7 8 12 16 20 24 28 32 36 40 44 48 52 56 60 64 68 72 80

12th position is called the B margin.

No line of a paragraph after the first may start to the left of this column.

8th position is called A margin.

Paragraphs names start at the A margin and must end with a period and space.

A hyphen (-) is placed in this space to show if this line is a continuation of a word in the previous line. Usually this should be avoided by not starting the word.

Six spaces for sequence numbers, used at the discretion of the programmer. For example, the first 2 or 3 may be used for page number and the rest for the item on the page.

Because of the internal characteristics of the computer, space to the right of 72 may not be used.

NOTE: The numbers across the top correspond to the columns on an 80-column card.

Figure 23–7
Outline of COBOL Structure

	L	A B
Identification Division	001010	IDENTIFICATION DIVISION PROGRAM-ID. (Inventory Control) AUTHOR (TIM) DATE-WRITTEN (Jan 10 196–) DATE-COMPILED (Jan 20 196–) REMARKS
Environment Division		ENVIRONMENT DIVISION. CONFIGURATION SECTION. SOURCE-COMPUTER. OBJECT-COMPUTER. SPECIAL-NAMES. INPUT-OUTPUT SECTION. FILE-CONTROL. I-O-CONTROL.

Data Division		DATA DIVISION.
		FILE SECTION.
		FD XXXXXXXXXXXXXXXXX
		01 XXXXXXXXXXXXXX
		    02 XXXXX
		        03 XXXXXX
		
		Note: This is a general form using indentation. Indenting is optional but if used each step must be set over four spaces.
		
		WORKING-STORAGE-SECTION.
		
		77 XXXX
		
		CONSTANT-SECTION.
		
		    XXX

Procedure Division		PROCEDURE DIVISION. XXXXXXXX (paragraph name) XXXXX (sentences)

Figure 23–8
COBOL Has a List of Reserved Words

ABOUT	DOLLAR	MEMORY	REPLACING
ACCEPT	ELSE	MEMORY-DUMP	RERUN
ADD	END	MEMORY-DUMP-	RESERVE
ADDRESS	ENDING	KEY	REVERSED
ADVANCING	ENDING-FILE-	MINUS	REWIND
AFTER	LABEL	MODE	RIGHT
ALL	ENDING-TAPE-	MODULES	ROUNDED
ALPHABETIC	LABEL	MOVE	
ALPHANUMERIC	END-OF-FILE	MULTIPLE	
ALTER	END-OF-TAPE	MUL	
ALTERNATE	ENTER		
AN			UPPER-BOUNDS
AND			UNTIL
		PROTECT	UPON
	LABEL	PROTECTION	USAGE
ING	LEADING	PURGE-DATE	USE
	LEAVING	QUOTE	VALUE
DATE-WRITTEN	LEFT	RANGE	VARYING
DECLARATIVES	LESS	READ	WHEN
DEFINE	LIBRARY	RECORD	WITH
DEPENDING	LINES	RECORD-COUNT	WORDS
DIGIT	LOCATION	RECORDING	WORKING-
DIGITS	LOCK	RECORDS	STORAGE
DISPLAY	LOW-VALUE	REDEFINES	WRITE
DIVIDE	LOW-VALUES	REEL	ZERO
DIVIDED	LOWER-BOUND	REEL-NUMBER	ZEROES
DIVISION	LOWER-BOUNDS	RENAMING	ZERO

tive is to familiarize you with the system and not to make you an expert COBOL programmer. This would probably require far more space and time than is available here. While an effort has been made to give a complete coverage of the system, it is impossible to guard against all the exceptions. This does not matter, however, for if you are going to do programming you will want to obtain the excellent, detailed government manual. The material presented here is intended to bridge the gap between having no knowledge of programming and becoming an experienced programmer.

Syntax

To understand a language one must know something about the sentence structure. This is called syntax, but the meaning will be stretched slightly to include the whole language structure. In COBOL, as in any language, we start with characters, the basic building blocks, and go on to the more complex words, statements, sentences, paragraphs, sections, and other combinations.

Characters. These are the basic elements of the COBOL language. Not all characters are used to form words; they are also used for punctuation and logical operations. The COBOL characters, with their uses, are illustrated in this resumé:

COBOL Characters

Used in relations:
> Greater than
< Less than
= Equal to

Used in Editing:
$ Dollar sign
* Check protection symbol
, Comma
. Decimal point

Used for Words:
0 through 9
A through Z
and the hyphen, or minus sign.

Used for Punctuation:
" Quotation mark
(Left parenthesis
) Right parenthesis
  Space or blank
. Period
, Comma
; Semicolon

Used in Formulas:
+ Addition
— Subtraction
* Multiplication (**Exponentiation)
/ Division
= Equality

Words. Words are composed of a combination of not more than 30 characters taken from the set of characters just given. Words must end with a space. For example, INVENTORY REPORT is two words, but INVEN-TORY-REPORT is considered as one word.

For convenience, words may be classified in the COBOL language as *nouns* or *verbs*. The nouns in turn may be classified such as: data names, condition names, procedure names, literals, special registers, and others.

Verbs are single words, appearing in the PROCEDURE DIVISION, which specify an action such as ADD, SUBTRACT, MOVE, and so on, and they will be discussed extensively when we dig deeper into the PRO-CEDURE DIVISION.

Statement. After the word, the next classification is the statement. The statements in the PROCEDURE DIVISION which require action are of three types: imperative statements, conditional statements, and compiler directing statements.

Sentences. Superior to the statement is the sentence, which consists of a sequence of one or more statements. There is a parallel between the classification of statements and sentences for there are also imperative, conditional, and compiler directing sentences. The sentence must be terminated by a period. Separators may be used between statements within the sentence, to improve the readability, but their use is optional. The allowable separators are the semicolon and THEN. Of course, one separator cannot follow another. Other rules for the use of the separator in the conditional statement are to be found in the COBOL manual.

Paragraphs. Paragraphs have been included in COBOL so that the source programmer may group several sentences to convey one idea in a procedure. The paragraph begins with a name and is the smallest grouping in the PROCEDURE DIVISION which requires a name.

Section. A section consists of one or more successive paragraphs, and when designated, must be named. The name is followed by the word SEC-TION. Section divisions are not essential for the operation of a program.

Procedure. The procedure is the largest grouping.

For a moment, review the structure of the COBOL language. Characters are used in words, words are used in statements, statements are used in sentences, which in turn are used in paragraphs, and these make up the sections which are included in the procedure. Most of the emphasis on programming logic is in the PROCEDURE DIVISION, and it is here that the higher classifications, statements, and sentences are most meaningful.

Rules of Punctuation

Splitting Words, Literals, and Paragraphs. Any paragraph occupying more than one line is split by starting the second line under B on the format. Any word or numeric literal can be split by placing a hyphen in the seventh-column position on the second line. A nonnumeric literal may be split, but any spaces appearing at the end of the line are considered as part of the literal. Continuation of nonnumeric literals must be preceded by a quotation mark.

Spacing. There must be at least one space between words, except in nonnumeric literals. Two or more spaces are treated as one space. The arithmetic operators *, $-$, /, ** must be preceded by and followed by a space.

Periods. Division titles are ended by a period and nothing else appears beyond the period on that line. Paragraph names and sentences must end with a period, followed by a space.

Commas and AND. Commas and AND may be used in the PROCEDURE DIVISION to clarify meaning in a series of operands.

Parentheses. Parentheses are used where needed in arithmetic and conditional statements to make the meaning clear.

Qualifiers and Subscripts

In the COBOL source program, names must be unique either because of spelling or because the name exists within a hierarchy of names such that the name can be made unique by mentioning one or more of the higher levels of the hierarchy. The qualifiers appear in ascending order and are appended by using the prepositional phrase containing IN or OF, depending upon the readability. As an example, DAY OF LAST-TRANSACTION-DATE OF MASTER would refer to the labeled transaction in the following list:

```
                    1  MASTER.....
                       2  CURRENT-DATE.....
                          3  MONTH.....
                          3  DAY.....
                          3  YEAR.....
                       2  LAST-TRANSACTION-DATE.....
                          3  MONTH.....
         Labeled     → 3  DAY.....
         Transaction    3  YEAR.....
```

There is a distinct difference between qualifiers (just mentioned) and subscripting. Qualification is necessary when the same data-name is used for several different items of data, and subscripting is necessary when some of the elements of a table or list have not been assigned individual names.

A subscript is an integer whose value determines which element is being referred to within a table or list of like elements. The subscripts may be represented either by a literal, which is an integer such as 40, or by a data-name, such as AGE, which has an integral value. The subscript represented by a date-name must be described by a Record Description entry in the DATA division. In both cases the subscript is enclosed in parentheses which appear immediately after the terminal space of the name of the element referenced, such as RATE (40).

The maximum number of levels which can be subscripted in a table is three. Multilevel subscripts are always written in the order: major, intermediate, minor. For example, a three-level subscript might appear as: RATE (REGION, STATE, CITY).

Detailed Discussion of Divisions

Now that you have had some introduction to the COBOL format, rules of syntax, and punctuation you are ready for a more extensive explanation of each division. The divisions, recall, are identification, environment, data, and procedure. In the discussion of the divisions, a particular notation will be introduced which is used universally throughout COBOL references. It is this:

a. All underlined uppercase words are required when the functions of which they are a part are used.

b. All uppercase words not underlined are used for readability only. They may or may not be present.

c. All lowercase words represent generic terms which must be supplied by the user.

d. Material enclosed in braces { } indicates that a choice from the contents must be made.

e. Material enclosed in square brackets [ ] represents an option and may be included or omitted.

f. When two or more nouns are written in a series, commas are shown as connectives. Where a comma is shown in the format it may be omitted or replaced by either AND or ,AND .

IDENTIFICATION DIVISION. The purpose of the IDENTIFICATION DIVISION is to identify the source program and the outputs of a compilation. In addition, the user may include such information as the date the program was written, date of compilation, and other pertinent facts.

Fixed paragraph names are used as keys in this division to identify the information contained in the paragraph. The program name must be given in the first paragraph which is PROGRAM-ID. Other paragraphs which may be included in this division are author, installation, date-written, date compiled, security, and remarks.

ENVIRONMENT DIVISION. This division must be written every time the program is run on a different computer, for the ENVIRONMENT DIVISION provides the link between the logical concepts of data and records and the physical aspects of the files on which they are stored. It is the division where all the computer-dependent information is centralized. The ENVIRONMENT DIVISION is divided into two sections.

CONFIGURATION SECTION. This section deals with the overall specifications of the computer or computers and, in turn, is divided into three paragraphs:

1. SOURCE-COMPUTER: This paragraph defines the computer on which the COBOL compiler is to run.
2. OBJECT-COMPUTER: This paragraph defines the computer on which the program produced by the compiler is to run.
3. SPECIAL-NAMES: This paragraph relates the actual names of the hardware used by the COBOL compiler to the names used in the program.

INPUT-OUTPUT SECTION. This section deals with the most efficient handling between the media and the object program and it consists of two paragraphs:

1. I-O-CONTROL which defines special input-output techniques.
2. FILE-CONTROL which names and associates the files with external media.

DATA DIVISION. COBOL makes the distinction between the *what* of processing and the *how* of processing. The what is included in the DATA DIVISION and the how is included in the PROCEDURE DIVISION. Although these two divisions are separate, they are interrelated. This separation is an important attribute of COBOL for it makes it possible to change from computer to computer without drastic revisions in the program. This is not true of many other computer languages.

The DATA DIVISION describes the files of data that are to be manipulated by the object program. Since a standard data format is used, the DATA DIVISION is to a large extent computer independent. Careful planning of the DATA DIVISION will permit the same data descriptions, with but minor modifications, to apply to more than one computer. Each item of data in the PROCEDURE DIVISION must be mentioned in the DATA DIVISION.

The DATA DIVISION is structured in three sections:

1. FILE section
2. WORKING-STORAGE section
3. CONSTANT section

Each of these will be discussed in turn, but first it should be mentioned that this division does not follow the paragraph, sentence, statement structure used in the PROCEDURE, ENVIRONMENT, and IDENTIFICATION DIVISIONS.

The basic unit in the DATA DIVISION is the entry. The entry consists of a level number, a data-name, and a series of independent clauses which may be separated by semicolons. The entry is terminated by a period. The section consists of a series of related or unrelated entries. A *File Description* consists of a single entry while the *Record Description* consists of one or more entries.

Level numbers for entries deserve extensive discussion at this point. Assigning level numbers is analogous to the outlining you have been exposed to in grammar school; it is inherent in any logical record system and comes from the need to identify subdivisions of records. To observe this analogy:

Outlining	*Programming*
I. Major topic	FD. Topic
A. Minor topic	01. First subtopic
1. First subtopic	02. First sub-subtopic
a. First sub-subtopic	03. First sub-sub-subtopic
b. Second sub-subtopic	03. Second sub-sub-subtopic
2. Second subtopic	02. Second sub-subtopic
a. First sub-subtopic	03. First sub-sub-subtopic
b. Second sub-subtopic	03. Second sub-sub-subtopic
c. Third sub-subtopic	03. Third sub-sub-subtopic

In COBOL, the various levels are indicated by a two-digit number, but the FD, standing for the File Description, does not have a number. Rather than follow the conventional numbering system, observe that all items on the same level have the same number. One level is contained within another if the second item has a higher level item and follows the first item; and there are no level numbers lower than the second number in between the first and second.

With this explanation of level numbers, which are used in the whole DATA DIVISION, it is time to look at each individual section.

The FILE section contains two elements, File Descriptions and Record Descriptions, of both label records (tapes) and data records:

1. The File Description refers to the physical aspect of the file.
2. The Record Description must follow the File Description for any particular file and refers to the conceptual characteristics of the data contained in the file.

The formats of the File Description and Record Description are shown in Figures 23–9 and 23–10, and explanations are given below the format for each.

Figure 23-9
File Description

Option 1: FD file-name COPY library-name.

This option is used when the COBOL library contains the entire File Description entry.

Option 2: (a) FD file-name   (b) [; RECORDING MODE IS mode]   (c) [; FILE CONTAINS ABOUT integer-1 RECORDS]

(d) $\left[\text{; BLOCK CONTAINS [integer-2 } \underline{\text{TO}} \text{] integer-3 } \left\{ \begin{array}{l} \underline{\text{RECORDS}} \\ \text{CHARACTERS} \end{array} \right\} \right]$

(e) $\left[\text{; RECORD CONTAINS [integer-4 } \underline{\text{TO}} \text{] integer-5 CHARACTERS]} \right]$ (f) $\left[\text{; LABEL } \left\{ \begin{array}{l} \underline{\text{RECORDS ARE}} \\ \underline{\text{RECORD IS}} \end{array} \right. \right.$

$\left. \left\{ \begin{array}{l} \underline{\text{STANDARD}} \\ \underline{\text{OMITTED}} \\ \text{data-name-1} \\ \text{library-name-1 } \underline{\text{IN}} \text{ LIBRARY} \end{array} \right\} \left[, \left\{ \begin{array}{l} \text{data-name-2} \\ \text{library-name-2 } \underline{\text{IN}} \text{ LIBRARY} \end{array} \right\} \right] \right]$

(g) $\left[\text{; VALUE OF data-name-3 IS } \left\{ \begin{array}{l} \text{data-name-4 [HASHED]} \\ \text{literal} \end{array} \right\} \text{[data-name-5 IS . . .]} \right]$

(h) $\left[\text{; DATA } \left\{ \begin{array}{l} \underline{\text{RECORD IS}} \\ \underline{\text{RECORDS ARE}} \end{array} \right\} \text{data-name-6 [, data-name-7 . . .]} \right]$

(i) $\left[\text{; } \underline{\text{SEQUENCED}} \text{ ON data-name-8 [, data-name-9 . . .]} \right]$

Note: The letters ( ) are not part of the program but a key to the explanations given below:
(a) File description.
(b) Specifies the format or organization of data on external media. When computer has only one mode this clause is not needed.
(c) Indicates the approximate number of logical records in a file and serves as an aid to optimization of the object program.
(d) Specifies the size of a physical record, that is, the block size.
(e) Specifies the size of data records.
(f) Used to cross-reference the descriptions of label records with their associated files.
(g) Particularizes the description of an item in the label records associated with a file.
(h) To cross-reference the description of data records with their associated files.
(i) Indicates keys on which data records are sequenced.

Figure 23–10
Record Descriptions

Option 1: level-number data-name [; REDEFINES]; COPY . . .

Option 2: (a) level-number $\left\{\begin{array}{l}\text{data-name} \\ \underline{\text{FILLER}}\end{array}\right\}$ (b) [; REDEFINES . . .] (c) [; SIZE . . .] (d) [; USAGE . . .] (e) [; OCCURS . . .]

(f) [; SIGN . . .] (g) [; SYNCHRONIZED . . .] (h) ; [POINT . . .] (i) [; CLASS . . .] (j) [; PICTURE . . .]

(k) [; JUSTIFIED . . .] (l) [; RANGE . . .] (m) [; editing clauses . . .] (n) [; VALUE . . .]

Note: The letters ( ) are not part of the program but a key to the explanations given below:
(a) Shows the hierarchy of data written in a logical record.
(b) To allow the same computer storage area to contain different data items.
(c) To specify, in terms of the number of standard data format characters, the size of an item.
(d) To specify the dominant use of a data item.
(e) To eliminate the need for separate entries for repeated data and to supply information required in the application of subscripts.
(f*) To specify the operational sign of an elementary item.
(g*) To specify positioning of an elementary item within a computer word or words.
(h*) To define an assumed decimal point or binary point.
(i) To indicate the type of data being discussed: alphabetic, numeric, or alphanumeric.
(j*) To show a detailed picture of the standard data format of an elementary item.
(k*) To align, either right or left.
(l*) To specify the potential range of the value of an item.
(m*) The edit clause permits suppression of nonsignificant zeros and commas; permits floating dollar signs and blanking of zeros.
(n) To define value of constants.
* SIGN, SYNCHRONIZED, POINT, PICTURE, JUSTIFIED, and RANGE, as well as the editing clauses, must not be specified except at the elementary item level.

The word PICTURE, appearing in the Record Description, is worthy of more discussion. It is used to dictate a detailed picture in the Standard Data Format of an elementary item. This is done by symbols listed below, and the general structure of the PICTURE clause is:

$$\left[\underline{\text{PICTURE IS}} \left\{ \begin{array}{l} \text{any allowable combination} \\ \text{of the characters and sym-} \\ \text{bols described below.} \end{array} \right\} \right] \quad [\underline{\text{DEPENDING ON}} \text{ data-name}]$$

Data characters:

9   represents a numeric character. For example, PICTURE 999 or PIC-TURE 9 (3) indicates three positions set aside for numbers.
A   represents an alphabetic character. For example, PICTURE AAAA or PICTURE A (4) indicates that four positions have been set aside for the alphabetic characters.
X, in the same way, represents an ALPHANUMERIC character.

There are other characters available for zero suppression, for insertions—such as dollar signs—and for operation symbols.

The FILE section of the DATA DIVISION, just discussed, dealt with the requirements for the storage of each record of the files. The WORK-ING-STORAGE section of this same division has to do with that part of the computer memory set aside for the intermediate processing of data.

The WORKING-STORAGE section is different from the FILE section because it has only Record Descriptions rather than a File Description *and* a Record Description. Therefore it begins with a section-header, followed by a period, which in turn is followed by Record Description entries.

Items in WORKING-STORAGE which have no relationship to each other (noncontiguous) need not be grouped into records, provided they need no further subdivisions. Instead, they are classified and defined as non-contiguous items and each is given a separate Record Description which begins with the special level-number 77. Level-number, data-name, and CLASS or PICTURE, or SIZE (when PICTURE is not specified) are required in each entry.

Data elements in the WORKING-STORAGE section which bear a definite relationship to each other follow the general rules of the DATA DIVISION—as discussed for Record Descriptions.

The CONSTANT section of the DATA DIVISION is organized in the same way as the WORKING-STORAGE section. The concept of literals and figuratives permits the programmer to specify the value of a constant by writing its actual value. Often it is desirable to name the value and then refer to it by name. For example, a $2.25 per hour wage rate may be named WAGE-RATE and then referred to by its name WAGE-RATE and not by its value.

In review, the DATA DIVISION describes the files of data which are to be manipulated by the object program. It consists of the FILE section, the WORKING-STORAGE section and the CONSTANT section. In the FILE section there are the File Description of the physical files and the Record Description of the conceptual files. In the WORKING-STORAGE and the CONSTANT section only the Record Description exists.

PROCEDURE DIVISION.   The PROCEDURE DIVISION contains those instructions needed to solve a given problem. It follows the syntax rules given earlier in that statements form sentences, which are combined to form paragraphs, which in turn may be combined to form sections. Recall that in the discussion of syntax it was also noted that at the statement level there are three different classifications:

Imperative statements, which consist of a verb (excluding compiler-directing verbs) and its operands.

Conditional statements, which may take the form:

$$\underline{\text{IF}} \text{ condition} \left\{ \begin{array}{l} \text{statement-1} \\ \underline{\text{NEXT SENTENCE}} \end{array} \right\} \left\{ \begin{array}{l} \text{OTHERWISE} \\ \underline{\text{ELSE}} \end{array} \right\} \left\{ \begin{array}{l} \text{statement-2} \\ \underline{\text{NEXT SENTENCE}} \end{array} \right\}$$

Compiler-Directing statements, which consist of a compiler-directing verb and its operands.

Recall that a statement or series of statements terminated by a period becomes a sentence, so there are imperative sentences, conditional sentences, and compiler sentences. In COBOL, imperative and conditional sentences describe the procedure to be accomplished. The sentences are written successively, according to the rules of the reference format, and establish the sequence in which the object program is to execute the procedure.

In the PROCEDURE DIVISION names are used so that one procedure can refer to another. In this way the sequence in which the object program is to be executed may be varied simply by transferring to a named procedure. The name consists of a noun, which is followed by a period, preceding the procedure it names.

In executing procedures, control is transferred only to the beginning of a paragraph. Control is passed to a sentence within a paragraph only from the sentence written immediately preceding it. If a procedure is named, control can be passed to it from the sentence immediately preceding it, or can be transferred to it from any sentence which contains a GO TO or PERFORM, followed by the name of the procedure to which control is to be transferred.

Conditional procedures, mentioned above, add immeasurably to the versatility of the computer program. COBOL conditionals generally contain the key word IF, followed by the conditions to be examined, followed by the operations to be performed. The flow chart for a simple conditional is shown below. Conditionals are classified as simple for two alternatives—or compound, consisting of two or more simple conditions which are interrelated.

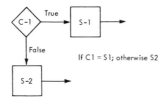

Formula Operations. Before writing a program that includes algebraic expressions it is necessary to understand how they are manipulated in the program.

1. Exponentiation is done first;
2. Multiplication and division are done next;
3. Addition and subtraction follow.

Parentheses are used to eliminate ambiguities, and the computer operates from the innermost set outward. For any one precedence level, and if no parentheses are present, the operations occur from left to right.

Subscripts are integers whose values determine which element is being referenced in a table. The tables may have a maximum of three levels, such as this example of sales information:

An Outline Form	*Computer Language*
District	01 SALES-TABLE USAGE IS COMPUTATIONAL
State	02 DISTRICT SALES OCCUR 8 TIMES
City	03 STATE SALES OCCUR 5 TIMES
City	04 CITY SALES OCCUR 25
⋮	TIMES: PICTURE IS 99999 9
City	
State	

In working with tables, two things are needed: a specification of size in the DATA DIVISION, and a means of referencing a specific item in the table—which is done with subscripts in the PROCEDURE DIVISION. The entries in the DATA DIVISION are shown on the right. In referring to the table, a reference such as SALES (2, Georgia, Macon) would refer to the entry in the DATA DIVISION.

Verbs. The detailed discussion of the verbs, which make up the important part of the PROCEDURE DIVISION, is long overdue and will be taken up immediately. The verbs, remember, are single words, appearing in the PROCEDURE DIVISION, which specify an action.

The verbs may be catalogued as:

Arithmetic verbs, such as ADD, SUBTRACT, MULTIPLY, and DIVIDE.

Input-output, as represented by READ, WRITE, and DISPLAY.

Procedure branching, as illustrated by GO.

Data movement, depicted by the word MOVE.

Ending, by STOP.

Compiler-directing verbs, represented by EXIT and INCLUDE.

Compiler-directing declaratives, such as DEFINE, USE, and INCLUDE.

To give you some feel for how these verbs are used in statements, some examples will be given here:

The ADD verb has several forms, but two common ones are:

$$\underline{\text{ADD}} \begin{Bmatrix} \text{data-name-1} \\ \text{literal-1} \end{Bmatrix} \underline{\text{TO}} \ \text{data-name-2}$$

$$\underline{\text{ADD}} \begin{Bmatrix} \text{data-name-1} \\ \text{literal-1} \end{Bmatrix} \begin{Bmatrix} \text{data-name-2} \\ \text{literal-2} \end{Bmatrix} \underline{\text{GIVING}} \ \text{data-name-3}$$

The READ verb is used to make the next logical record available from an input file. A common form of the sentence is:

$$\underline{\text{READ}} \ \text{file-name RECORD} \ [\underline{\text{INTO}} \ \text{data-name}] \ [; \text{AT} \ \underline{\text{END}} \ \text{any}$$
$$\text{imperative statement}]$$

The CLOSE verb terminates the processing of input and output reels and files, with optional rewind and/or lock:

$$\underline{\text{CLOSE}} \ \text{file-name-1} \ [\underline{\text{REEL}}] \left[\text{WITH} \begin{Bmatrix} \underline{\text{NO REWIND}} \\ \underline{\text{LOCK}} \end{Bmatrix} \right] [, \text{file-name-2} \ldots]$$

Application of COBOL

You are probably not an expert programmer now—at least not from the knowledge you have gained from this short introduction to COBOL. Hopefully, you have some feel for the subject and are able to understand a prepared program when you read it. To check this understanding, read through the example program which is presented in Figure 23–11.

COBOL in Review

It is impossible to cover, within these few pages, all of the many details of COBOL included in the extensive government manuals and other programming books which deal exclusively with the subject. You have obtained a mountain-top view of COBOL logic, and you have been properly impressed, so that when the time comes for you to discuss programming—or even write a program—you will have a structure upon which to build.

The straightforward logic of COBOL is evident in its standard format. Its versatility is enhanced by the four IDENTIFICATION, ENVIRONMENT, DATA, and PROCEDURE divisions, of which only the ENVIRONMENT division is computer-dependent. It is this feature which makes COBOL one of the most important events in computer history.

Figure 23–11

COBOL Example

```
PROG.1          JOB 326          DATE 01/22/65        TIME 03.029        PAGE  1

        0000 $IBCBC PRCG.1.

        0001        IDENTIFICATION DIVISION.
        0002        PRCGRAM-ID. PAYROLL-MASTER-FILE. PROG.1. FOR CS 580.
        0003        AUTHORS. H.M. SETHNA + D. WATANAPCNGSE.
        0004        DATE-WRITTEN. JAN 1C,1965.
        0005        REMARKS. DESIGNED FOR WEEKLY PAYROLL COMPUTATION.
        0006        ENVIRONMENT DIVISION.
        0007        CONFIGURATION SECTICN.
        0008        SOLRCE-COMPUTER. IBM-7094.
        0009        OBJECT-COMPUTER. IBM-7094.
        0010        INPUT-OUTPUT SECTION.
EN0224  0011        FILE-CONTROL.   SELECT INPUT-FILE ASSIGN TO SYSIN1.
EN0228  0012                        SELECT OLTPUT-FILE ASSIGN TO SYSOU1.
        0013        DATA DIVISION.
        0014        FILE SECTION.
        0015        FD   INPUT-FILE
ENC234(0015)
        0016             LABEL RECORDS ARE OMITTED
        0017             DATA RECORD IS DATA-CARD.
        0018        01   DATA-CARD.
ENC235(0018)
EN0237  0019             02 NAME            PICTURE X(30).
EN0238  0020             02 PAY-RATE        PICTURE 99V999.
EN0239  0021             02 FILLER      SIZE 5.
ENC240  0022             02 HRS-WORKED      PICTURE 99V99.
        0023        FC   OUTPUT-FILE
EN0241(0023)
```

```
EN0262  0045             02 FILLER      SIZE  4      VALUE 'NAME'.
EN0263  0046             02 FILLER      SIZE 26      VALUE SPACE.
EN0264  0047             02 FILLER      SIZE  8      VALUE 'PAY-RATE'.
EN0265  0048             02 FILLER      SIZE  5      VALUE SPACE.
ENC266  0049             02 FILLER      SIZE 10      VALUE 'HRS-WORKED'.
EN0267  0050             02 FILLER      SIZE  5      VALUE SPACE.
EN0268  0051             02 FILLER      SIZE  9      VALUE 'GROSS-PAY'.
EN0269  0052             02 FILLER      SIZE  5      VALUE SPACE.
ENC270  0053             02 FILLER      SIZE  7      VALUE 'FICATAX'.
EN0271  0054             02 FILLER      SIZE  5      VALUE SPACE.
EN0272  0055             02 FILLER      SIZE  7      VALUE 'NET-PAY'.
EN0273  0056             02 FILLER      SIZE 40      VALUE SPACE.
        0057        CONSTANT SECTION.
EN0275  0058        77  FICATAX-RATE  PICTURE 99V99       VALUE .18.
        0059        PRCCEDURE DIVISION.
        0060        BECIN.
ENC278(0060)
        0061             OPEN INPUT INPUT-FILE OLTPUT CUTPUT-FILE.
        0062             WRITE OUTPUT-RECORD FROM HEAUING.
        0063        REAC-DATA-CARC.
ENC279(0063)
        0064             READ INPUT-FILE RECCRD
        0065                  AT ENC GO TC END-OF-JOB.
        0066             MOVE CORRESPONDING DATA-CARD TO PAY-TABLE.
        0067             COMPUTE TEMP-2 ROUNDED = PAY-RATE OF CATA-CARD * HRS-W
        0068        -    ORKED OF CATA-CARD.
        0069             MULTIPLY TEMP-2 BY FICATAX-RATE GIVING TEMP-1 ROUNDED.
        0070             COMPUTE NET-PAY ROUNDED = TEMP-2 - TEMP-1.
        0071             COMPUTE FICATAX EQUALS TEMP-1.
        0072             COMPUTE GROSS-PAY EQUALS TEMP-2.
        0073             WRITE OUTPUT-RECORD FROM PAY-TABLE.
        0074             GO TO REAC-DATA-CARD.
        0075        ENC-OF-JOB.
EN0280(0075)
        0076             CLOSE INPLT-FILE   OUTPLT-FILE.
        0077             STOP RUN.
        0078 $CBEND
```

The syntax of COBOL is well organized, with characters building words, words statements, and so on. The only difficulty you will encounter is adhering to the detailed rules. The list of reserved words, with their strict interpretation, is typical of one of the sets of rules you must learn to live by.

COBOL's near-English statements, its universal acceptance by most computers, and its logical structure make it the computer language which promises to take a prominent place in industrial applications.

Usually the initial step is to make a flow chart which expresses your interpretation of how the system should function. This flow chart may show only the gross steps, but eventually it will be refined to a block diagram showing (in detail) the steps which must be taken in the program.

After diagraming the flow of information, the information is coded. This can either be done directly with machine language or by putting it in a form suitable for translation to machine language by one of the various translators, such as COBOL.

You now have a basic knowledge of computer hardware and software, but do not let this lull you into inactivity. Knowledge is expanding in this area and new equipment and techniques are being introduced daily. Form the habit of keeping up with these innovations.

Evaluating Software Packages

It is how to make rational purchasing decisions for software packages that this discussion is all about. When you are involved with this decision, you will become aware that a selection must be made from among hundreds of software packages without standards or even criteria.

During the past few years, more than one attempt has been made to answer these questions. For example, several data processing publications devote sections each month to the review of software packages. The typical review is a paragraph or two long, which has often been written by the vendor, giving an all too brief and glowing description of the package with none of its shortcomings.

Other attempts to evaluate packages have been made by some management consulting firms. There are also "software services" which sell publications containing evaluations of software packages. They must evaluate hundreds of packages because they cover the entire industry which produces hospital, insurance, and other software. These services obviously cannot do a thorough enough evaluation upon which you can stake your reputation and your company's investment of thousands of dollars.

The decision is complicated because there are so many facets that they all cannot be kept in focus at once. For just a moment let us pause to list some of the areas to be considered.

First, of course, is the necessity of really expressing the need for the software package. This is the difficult logic step of stating the problem. Knowing this, it is next necessary to search for all of the packages which are applicable.

This should bring up the names of a number of vendors, which opens up a whole set of new questions.

Evaluating a vendor is not as simple as picking a drugstore or even a car dealer. This is a relationship which is going to last for many years and will involve many thousands of dollars. You will want to know just how well the vendor is prepared to support the product he is selling.

Cost is of prime consideration, and one will probably have to weigh the advantages of buying, renting, leasing, or some combination of these methods. One should be sure that the vendor has the legal right to the package and no litigations will ensue.

The hardware requirements for running the software package are of greatest concern to the customer. Does he buy new equipment? More memory? Does he need more peripheral equipment? Can he get rid of the old equipment without a loss? All of these are important questions having to do with potentially costly decisions.

Then of course one must look at the software package itself. First one might study the history of the package and whether or not there are any satisfied customers. One should not just take the vendor's word for this but contact the users. The new software package will have to live with the present systems whether they are manual or computerized, so there are many questions concerning compatibility. For example, is the new package compatible with the present data base or will some expensive revisions have to be made?

Another set of questions which will be of interest to management has to do with the personnel. Do the present personnel have the knowledge? Do they have the proper skills? If they do not, they will have to be trained or new personnel obtained. These are time-consuming and costly moves to make.

The language of the program, whether it be COBOL, FORTRAN, or another, is important, for it will affect the efficiency of the program. Unless it is written in a language understood by the programmers, the customer may be in for additional retraining costs.

Documentation of the software package is important, and the vendor should furnish this at no additional cost. Often a customer can use a module of the program for other applications. This might not be possible unless the package is built up from the modules which have their details revealed by flow charts and complete documentation.

If the information is not reported in the form desired, the program may be useless. The report generator should be flexible enough to overcome any difficulty.

One should decide if the old and new systems will run in parallel for a trial period or whether a "quick change" procedure should be used. The costs and risks involved in both methods should be given very careful consideration.

Not all of the decision factors listed above can be answered in dollars and cents, but those which can should be put in a form to be analyzed. Obviously the obtaining of a software package is not a decision which should be taken lightly and requires very careful analysis.

Summary

As you might expect, system designing is more complicated for computers than it is for either manual methods or card-data processing. Making an efficient computer program requires sufficient knowledge of computer hardware as well as software. As in solving any problem, there is a logical approach, and this can be summarized in the following steps:

1. Make a statement of the problem.
2. State the problem with a flow chart:
   a. A work-flow chart to show what is to be done.
   b. A detailed block diagram to show how the work is to be done.
3. Code the block diagram in the language of the computer program.
4. Convert the source program when necessary.
5. Debug the program when necessary.
6. Place the program and data in the computer and solve.

QUESTIONS

23–1. Which is the most efficient: machine language, symbolic language, or compiler language? Explain.

23–2. Explain why compiler languages are simpler than machine languages.

23–3. Compare COBOL with any other languages you have learned in school.

23–4. Define the following terms:
   a. Syntax.
   b. Reserved words.
   c. Environment division.
   d. Literal.
   e. Qualifier.

23–5. How important is it for production control personnel to know how to program a computer?

section six
Management of Production and Inventory Control

By NOW you have learned how production and inventory control systems operate and how they can be designed. You have learned, hopefully, how to make some of the difficult decisions as well as how to make the computer your obedient servant. Now you should learn how to sell and manage the systems.

Chapter 24. Introducing the New System

It is not easy to change to a new system. There are many real and imagined hazards which must be met. Even if there were no hazards of changing over, there is always the problem of selling people on new ideas. These difficulties may be overcome by the proper application of the methods described.

Chapter 25. Managing for Production and Inventory Control

There is a large body of management literature, and there is no way that this book could cover it all. It does attempt to give you the basics of management as they apply to production and inventory control.

24

Introducing the New System

THE CONVERSION from one system to another can be one of the most traumatic experiences for a manager and the other employees.

Computer systems always take longer to install than anticipated, much to the distress of top management. Probably one reason for the delay is the fear that people have of a failure. As long as they put off the changeover, they do not know if they have a failure or not. They find excuses for not making the conversion just to avoid the possibility of a failure. This should be considered as a psychological failure and not one involved with the system.

Training. If the conversion is going to be extensive, a training program may be necessary. Such a program may be as extensive as a complete production and inventory control course or something as simple as teaching all of the plant personnel how to use a computer terminal.

Whatever the program, it should be well planned and taught by competent personnel. This may require the employment of a consulting firm or an upgrading of the present members of the staff. Often a company selling a software package will include this with its services. If so, it should be written in the contract and include the hours to be spent, the number of employees, where the training will be done, and the proficiency expected.

It may be necessary at times to send personnel away from the plant for training programs. The lead time and costs for such programs can become important factors to consider in the installation of a new system.

Do not expect too much from factory employees. A procedure on a terminal may seem very elementary because you have been working with them, but how does the machine operator feel about them? If they feel at all threatened by the new system, they will get some satisfaction out of seeing it fail. So, be sure they are secure and ready to help make the system a success.

System Changeover

There are several plans which can be used during a system changeover, and all of them have their good and bad points. The plan which has the maximum amount of security is to run the new and old system in parallel. This also gives the greatest amount of comparative information. It is costly to run the two systems in parallel, and it often serves as a crutch which people are reluctant to discard. The additional manpower required may be a burden which a company cannot afford.

The method of total conversion, often referred to as "cold turkey" is dangerous. If the new system does not work, it means some hasty patching up or reconversion to the old system. It has all of the good and bad attributes of throwing a child into deep water and telling him to swim. This can be a traumatic experience and occasionally one might lose a child. This method has been used by management when the system designers have been reluctant to make the change. The manager merely sets a date and says that the system will be operating by then or else. This has worked very satisfactorily at times, while at other times it has been disastrous.

One method of conversion, which would be taking the middle of the road, would be a *pilot study*. A small portion of the system is operated like a controlled experiment on a pilot plant. Bugs can be worked out and different systems tested until there is complete assurance that the system will work. After this the system can be extended to larger and larger segments of the organization.

There is probably no one best way of making a system conversion, and only experience will teach you what you should do. A schedule established at the beginning will give you bench marks by which to measure your progress. However, there is a time that comes in the development of the system when you must say that it must go on its own. There are probably more failures caused by lack of faith and courage to implement than there are caused by lack of knowledge.

Record Integrity. The conversion period will cause enough problems without having to worry about the integrity of records. Before the system conversion is started, every effort should be made to be sure that the records are debugged and ready to be used.

Record integrity is a process which should be pursued at all times. It is too easy to let down when concerned with some of the difficult problems of making a changeover. An individual should be charged with record integrity and should institute a program of recording errors as they appear in the system. These errors may be plotted so that the results can be traced and hopefully reduced over a period of time.

Selling the System. Nothing can be more devastating to the ego of the system designer than to present a system improvement which goes unnoticed—unnoticed not because of faulty design but perhaps because it was not properly presented. It would be better not to initiate a system study than to let it fail in this final step.

The objective in the presentation of a new system is to transfer the idea in your mind to the audience with such ease that it will be accepted as a course of action. This type of persuasion is not an activity peculiar to the system designer; it is found in every profession where creative efforts exist. You will soon be using your persuasive abilities in industry, and undoubtedly your income will reflect, to some extent, your ability to persuade. Do not object to the extra effort necessary to prepare and present your ideas in a manner which will assure their acceptance.

Organizing for System Designing

The impetus for a new or revised system may come from any number of sources. The system manager may sense the need for changes because of increases in production, replacement of personnel, or improved system equipment. He may have time to introduce these revisions himself, or he may resort to using a staff assistant.

Often the need for a change is recognized by someone who is in a higher position than the system manager. In this case the system manager may be directed to make the necessary revisions or, if necessary, call in outside help.

For minor changes it is best that one man with the time and ability consult with others and implement the necessary revisions. For major system overhauls, probably the best plan is to establish a special committee representing all interested groups. For a production control system this would mean at least one representative each from product design, production, accounting, payroll, inventory control, and purchasing. In such a committee all interested parties have an opportunity to air their views and, hopefully, no one will dominate at the expense of the others.

No committee can function without strong leadership. This leadership may be exercised by someone from top management who sees the "big picture," or by someone appointed because of his outstanding performance on similar tasks. Frequently, the leadership will be exercised by an outside consultant who has been selected because of his wide experience. A full understanding of the methods of approaching the problem and of what information is needed are essential before the committee leader can perform satisfactorily.

Setting the Stage for System Designing

Introducing the system design assumes that a logical sequence of activities has preceded the final report. This book is dedicated to those activities which can be used for the logical design of systems. So important are the steps of logic stated in Chapter 2, that it is worthwhile to review them briefly.

1. Become aware of the problem.
2. Define the problem.
3. Locate, evaluate, and organize information.
4. Discover relationships and formulate hypotheses.
5. Evaluate the hypotheses.
6. Apply the solution.

Assuming that the committee has become aware of the problem, and that the problem has been defined, it is then necessary to collect information which will help produce an optimum design. The following are examples of information which should be available to all members of the committee:

Product Information. Is the product perishable or fragile? Does it require special handling? Is it a style product which is likely to be dated? Is it small or large? Does it require high-quality workmanship? Has the product been standardized?

Raw Material. What are the raw materials? What are their costs? Are there any substitutes? What are the sources? What is the nature of the markets for these products? Is the source of raw material monopolized by any one vendor?

Plant Facilities and Processes. Is the plant a job shop or production line? Is this going to change in the future? What are the plans for expansion? How are materials handled? Does the process require special-purpose tools? How old are the tools? What are the machine capacities?

Personnel. Is there an organizational chart? Should it be revised? Are the employees on incentive? Are they skilled or unskilled? What personality conflicts exist which might make it difficult to introduce a new system?

The Present System. It is nearly impossible to consider a new system without knowing what has gone before. A complete picture of the present system should be produced. The decision must then be made to modify the present system or to abandon it and start anew. In either case the new system may be introduced piece by piece, ironing out the problems as they occur in each stage before going on to the next.

The Timetable. A timetable for introducing the system should be established and adhered to (if possible). Schedules for intermediate steps and the final installation should be established in advance.

Presenting the System Design by Means of a Written Report

Probably no stage in the life of a system design is as critical as its presentation to those who have the power to accept or reject it. It is probably also one of the most critical times in your career as a system designer: Your whole future may depend on how well the system is accepted. Often the written report is practically the only way of communicating with the people above and below you in the organizational structure, and it is therefore not surprising that many industrialists' careers have hinged on a well-written report.

Before the report is written, the ideas should be clearly outlined and committed to paper. If, in the course of writing the report, you find you are using excessive explanations, it is probably because the ideas have not been clearly outlined. Do not let this delay you, for just putting ideas down on paper will help clear away the fog. Sometimes, if you let the report "jell" for a few days at this stage, the ideas will become clearer. Many people stumble at this initial stage; they cannot put down the first word of the first paragraph. Start writing, even if it is in the middle of the report. You can always go back and fill in parts which are missing.

It is usually best if the report contains a single, main idea. This is true from an efficiency as well as a strategy viewpoint. One idea will get your reader's attention in the shortest possible time. He also is likely to accept ideas one at a time. More than one good idea has been lost because the reader took exception to some of the minor ideas included in a report.

In industry, brevity is important because "time is money." If you do not "sell" your idea in the first few minutes of reading, you probably will not sell it at all. This is a key point in the organization of the written report, as you will see in the following outline.

Typical Outline for the Written Report.   The ideal written report is economical of the reader's time, clear as to meaning, precise in its recommendations, and unambiguous. The outline proposed here will help you meet these objectives.

Outline for the Written Report

1. Preface
   A. *Title page.* Contains the name of the report, and the authors; date; and any other information necessary to tie down the report subject in time and place.
   B. *Table of contents.* Here is a place to stir the interest of the prospective reader, for often he will turn to this section first. Do not kill his interest by having obscure or too brief or too extensive titles. Make a good first impression here.
   C. *Letter of transmittal or forward.* This gives your report additional authority if it is used correctly.
2. Abstract. Should give enough information for a decision. Often the reader will go no further than the abstract. If he is to go further, you must get him involved here. He will want to read on if the idea you are conveying is important enough to become operational. Work this part over carefully, and make it *concise.*
3. Main Discussion
   A. *Background of study.* This part of the report should be treated with care for often there is a tendency to build volume regardless of

the contribution to the report. Only pertinent background should be included.

B. *Need for study.* Be sure your points will be meaningful to all. Your close association with the problem may make you tend to gloss over the need for the study. On the other hand, do not point out every trivial need or you will downgrade the importance of the report.

C. *Procedure.* This section should outline, in detail, the procedure used in the study. It should be outlined in sufficient detail so that any experimental work could be repeated at some future date.

D. *Important data and results.* The main emphasis in this section should be on the development of results. If the data do not lead directly to the results, but are important for a full understanding, they should appear in an appendix. Make specific recommendations in this section and be sure no questions are left unanswered.

E. *Appendix.* Sections A through D should be kept to a moderate size; therefore much of the supporting material should be placed in appendices, where it can be referred to as needed.

This is an acceptable outline for a written report, but effective reports have been written which deviated from this form. Variation may be the very thing which will bring your report to the attention of your reader.

Principles of Report Writing.   No number of principles of report writing will make you a good report writer without practice. However, a few good principles can well be kept in mind as you practice.

1. Write for your audience. If your audience has a technical vocabulary, you too may use a technical vocabulary. Remember, you are trying to convey an idea which you wish to have accepted, so use examples which coincide with your reader's experience.

2. Use simple, familiar words. Some of the most effective writing of all time has been in simple words simply put.

3. Keep sentences short. Short sentences are easier to read, but vary their lengths or your report will appear choppy.

4. Discard unnecessary words. Everyone tends to use more words than he needs. If a word does not add meaning, discard it. Use a newspaper style.

5. Let your personality show through. Write the same way you talk, otherwise you will sound stilted and affected. It is no crime to let your personality show—as long as it is the *most favorable* side of your personality.

6. Make your writing live. Use active verbs. In many situations using the first person will add life to your writing. Do not hesitate to refer to people by name. Do not use terms or phrases which will "date" you.

7. Point the way. Make sure there is no doubt in the reader's mind about

what you think is important. This can be assured if you work from an outline and give the most important points the most weight.

8. Create a good first impression. Be sure the report has a suitable cover, for this is your introduction to the reader. It is his invitation to read your ideas and be convinced.

9. Conform to style standards. Often the first draft of a report should be done by double-spacing the typewritten page. This permits editing. In the final draft single spacing is often preferred. Your typist can advise you about the style used in the company; listen to her.

10. Abbreviate and symbolize with care. Remember you are trying to convey ideas; do not lose your reader with abbreviations or symbols with which he may not be familiar. If there is any question, use a glossary of terms.

11. Paragraph with care. The first sentence should tell what is coming and be followed by several explanatory sentences. Cover only one idea per paragraph.

12. Be brief, but not so brief the reader misses the point.

13. Use visual aids. The old cliché about a picture being worth a thousand words is equally true in report writing. Use charts, diagrams, and pictures with care, and place them in the text where they will do the most good.

14. Be accurate. In an engineering or cost report accuracy is paramount. One error can discredit all your work. Check and double-check.

15. Write to express, not to impress. If you write to express your ideas, and to persuade people to use them, you will not have to try to impress them. They will be.

Presenting the System Design by the Conference Method

When ideas are presented orally instead of by a written report, it is usually because two-way rather than unilateral communications are needed. The need for two-way communications may come about for several reasons. It may be necessary to get the group together to agree on something as simple as an appropriate time for action. The system designer might convene the members of the committee to obtain their ideas. Often there are faults in the proposed system that can only be brought to light by the members' focusing their attention on the problem as a group.

Of greatest importance, the conference offers the opportunity to obtain participation. Only by involvement will you be able to tap all the resources of the personnel, and only by involvement will they accept the system and make it work. If it is this objective of group involvement for which you are striving, you will have to become aware of—and practice—the art of conference leadership. This is an activity which has been given considerable attention in recent years, and you will be wise to supplement the conference outline below by exploring some of the references listed in the bibliography.

Typical Outline for the Conference Procedure. Like the written report, the conference also has an approved form; and, like the report outline, it is only a recognized guide, and one should feel free to deviate from it as necessary.

1. ADVANCE PLANNING FOR THE CONFERENCE
   A. Decide what the objectives are.
   B. Be sure the topic is suitable for a conference solution.
   C. Prepare a conference agenda with time schedule and key questions.
   D. Prepare visual aids and assemble any references and other information needed for the conference.
   E. Be sure conferees are invited well in advance so they will have the opportunity to arrange their schedules.
   F. The conferees should be told the subject of the conference well in advance.
   G. Prepare the meeting place: Consider noise, temperature, seating, and other factors that will affect the physical setting of the conference.

2. OPENING THE CONFERENCE
   A. Start on time; this can set the tone for the entire conference.
   B. Introduce conference members who are not known to all.
   C. Establish a friendly atmosphere.
   D. Review the background of the problem and relate it to the conference theme.
   E. Present the conference theme in a way that will interest the conferees and so that they will wish to discuss and contribute.
   F. Use illustrations to point up the importance of the problem and write the problem on the board.

3. DIRECT THE DISCUSSION
   A. Direct the discussion to draw out the conferees' viewpoints. Ask key questions.
   B. Encourage participation by directing questions to those who are not participating.
   C. Do not make a practice of answering questions, but redirect them to conferees.
   D. Write the pertinent decisions of the group on the board.
   E. Keep the conference moving, but do not display a feeling of impatience.
   F. Be alert and take advantage of every break in the conference.

4. SUMMARIZE
   A. Obtain agreement upon points along the way.
   B. Obtain final agreement and formulate a plan of action before the end of the conference.

5. FOLLOW-UP
   A. After the meeting, write up a brief report or minutes.

B.   Send each member a copy to reinforce any action that was taken.

Twenty "Don'ts" for the Conference Leader

1.   Don't discuss personalities.
2.   Don't permit arguments.
3.   Don't answer questions if you can redirect them to other conference members.
4.   Don't let the conference drag; keep it on schedule. Quit when the work agenda is finished.
5.   Don't let the discussion wander from its objective.
6.   Don't be sarcastic or use a patronizing attitude.
7.   Don't lose control of the conference.
8.   Don't monopolize the conversation.
9.   Don't let any member, or group of members, monopolize the conference time.
10.   Don't play the role of an expert.
11.   Don't let the shy conferee escape fielding a question; encourage involvement.
12.   Don't let an important point of agreement go by without recording it.
13.   Don't accept agreement on the basis of deference to authority. This will kill the voluntary contributions you want.
14.   Don't dampen the enthusiasm of the conferees.
15.   Don't forget to use visual aids when they can be effective.
16.   Don't take credit when it can be given to someone else.
17.   Don't let the meeting break up on an unfriendly note.
18.   Don't forget to summarize.
19.   Don't lose the confidence of the conferees.
20.   Don't neglect to issue a report of minutes.

Visual Aids for the Conference.   Often the entire tone of the conference can be set by the use of visual aids. If they are thoughtfully prepared and well done, the conferees will take the meeting seriously and put their minds to the objectives. Some of the various visual aids which can be found in a well-run conference are discussed briefly here.

Blackboards are still one of the best devices for conferences. Be sure they are clean and you have plently of space. Needless to say, there should be an ample supply of chalk and erasers. A little practice in drawing on the board will help. Develop your discussion by writing on the board from left to right just as you write on a page. Solving the problem of writing on the board while talking to the audience takes practice.

Flip charts are large tablets hung on an easel. The charts may be prepared in advance or developed in a manner similar to the blackboard technique. Charts need not be prepared by an artist; they are quite effective even if crudely drawn. Develop one point per sheet, and don't forget the man in the back row who does not have 20/20 vision.

Flannel or magnetic boards are covered with cloth, such as outing-flannel, that has a nap. Cutouts, mounted on sandpaper, adhere to the nap. The cutouts may be words or illustrations which can be placed on the board during the development of the presentation. The magnetic board uses small magnets, instead of sandpaper, which adhere to an iron-surfaced board. Both techniques are effective, and impressive displays can be prepared by a resourceful conference leader. They are, however, expensive displays and should be used only when the cost is warranted.

Overhead projectors are used with slides or larger transparencies. The image is projected over the head of the conference leader onto a screen in back of him, but in full view of the audience. This permits the leader to face the audience as he discusses the material. An objection to this device is that the room must be slightly darkened.

Slides and moving picture films are useful for presenting some types of material. Films take some lead time and expense to prepare. Also, the room must be darkened and some members may be overcome by the urge to sleep.

Opaque projectors are excellent devices for presenting printed material to a small audience. The efficiency of the projectors is not great, so the print must be large and the picture must be shown on a good screen in a darkened room.

Printed handouts are convenient for developing discussions, but they must be used with caution. The members of the conference are apt to be distracted by reading ahead. The material should not be handed out before time of use. They do serve as excellent take-home material.

Summary

Any presentation such as this concerning written reports and conference leadership is superficial, to say the least. The real effectiveness of these techniques depends upon you and who you are. This chapter cannot train you to be honest, to be courteous, to have insight to problems, and all the other numerous characteristics required for success. You must work on developing these attributes yourself, every day.

A system design is an idea or group of ideas. The idea should be acceptable to those who must use it. This means that persuasion must be employed. Today's system designer has numerous devices for persuasion. Some of these methods are the product of extensive research. Become acquainted with them and make the greatest possible use of them to insure your success.

QUESTIONS

24–1.   Outline a schedule for converting a manual system to a computer system.
24–2.   How could you set up a program to assure record integrity?
24–3.   Why should every system designer know the fundamentals of persuasion?
24–4.   What are the advantages and disadvantages of having a committee responsible for a system design?

24-5. Outline the way you would approach and complete the task of redesigning a system.

24-6. Which principle for report writing do you consider the most important? In your own writing, which is the most difficult to master?

24-7. How can practice in report writing help you in presenting better oral reports?

24-8. Write a report on some selected industrial subject following the principles given.

24-9. Present an oral report of the above subject and have the members of your class evaluate your presentation. Are you guilty of any "don'ts" for the conference leader?

24-10. Compare the advantages and disadvantages of the various visual aids which can be used in presenting a system.

25

Managing for Production and Inventory Control

THE PRODUCTION and inventory control manager is a manager in two respects. First, he is the *functional* manager of the plant's production facilities just as if he were the plant manager. He is, in effect, the plant manager as far as the production control function goes. He must assure that shipments are made on schedule, that inventories are maintained at optimum levels, and that men and machines are productive. This, as you can imagine, is a large task in itself.

In the second place, he serves as a manager of his department and has all of the management responsibilities that go with it. He also has the responsibility of maintaining a viable system. This means monitoring it constantly and keeping it up to date by incorporating new developments. Not only must the manager be aware of the innovations in decision making, but he must also be aware of the computer and hardware developments. This is no small responsibility.

There is no doubt that the production and inventory control (P&IC) manager has extensive management responsibilities and should avail himself of every opportunity to become a better manager. Needless to say, it is impossible to more than touch upon how he can accomplish this so he would do well to obtain a library of management literature and study and practice it constantly. The astute manager will take advantage of the wealth of literature, seminars, and other methods available to perfect his skills.

The P&IC Job Description. A job description, Figure 25–1, is for the production control manager. Listed separately is the job description of the inventory control manager. Not only is this a definitive list for describing the manager's job, it also serves as an overview for anyone considering employment in this field.

Figure 25–1
Job Description of the Production Control Manager

The Production Control Manager—
1. is to maintain and direct an organization which is adequate for the performance of the production control function.
2. develops and maintains master schedules and shop schedules which coordinate engineering, manufacturing, and sales.
3. develops lead time estimates and establishes delivery dates.
4. recommends changes in work force, hours and/or machine utilization to meet changing conditions.
5. dispatches and expedites production.
6. has the responsibility for reports and records.
7. establishes machine and equipment loading.
8. must see that all shop orders, move orders, and so on are issued.
9. must see that actual time expended is properly recorded on job time cards and factory work cards.
10. recommends to the vice president of manufacturing revisions in department policies and procedures when advisable to achieve more effective production control.

Inventory Control may be a function of the production control department or it may be a separate function, but closely allied to production control.

The Inventory Control Manager—
1. controls the delivery of material requirements as to the time and requirement.
2. provides records for in-process and stored inventory.
3. determines the order points for materials.
4. provides internal transportation.
5. must be constantly alert for opportunities to improve methods, materials, and procedures which would affect economy in the department and the division.
6. insures that stocks of goods are adequate but not excessive for operating requirements.
7. is to promote rapid inventory turnover and minimize the investment in inventory in order to reduce taxes, insurance, and handling expenses; minimize losses from obsolescences and physical deterioration; and minimize the cost of the idle time, yet provide service to customers.

Management of the P&IC's Function. The management *functions* have been studied for a number of years and a cataloging of those which have been universally accepted is given here. These functions are: planning, organizing, staffing, direction, control, and innovation. Each of these is worthy of a brief discussion.

Planning. First, the manager must decide what he wants done by establishing both short- and long-range objectives and by planning the means of reaching them.

To the P&IC manager this means that he must translate and interpret business conditions in terms of his operations. If business is expanding, he may need to add more employees, reorganize those he has, and improve the systems. Verbal communications, which have worked well for a small system, may have to be replaced with a computerized system.

Organizing. In the organizing function, the manager must decide on the skills needed to meet the planning phase. He decides upon the position to be filled and the duties and responsibilities of each. Not only must he decide on how the organizational position should be filled but also on how the positions are coordinated.

Staffing. In organizing, the manager decides on the requirements for each position. Staffing is matching people to these organizational slots. This is a continuous job because the organization will change and there will always be attrition.

Direction. The manager must supply the day-to-day direction for his subordinates. Although he can outline the broad objectives for continuous operations, there will also be day-to-day guidance needed. He must let his staff know what is expected of them and help them improve their skills.

The P&IC manager must establish standards of accuracy and help train people to attain his goals. Working efficiently is also an important consideration for all of the departmental employees.

Control. Control in mangement consists of finding out how efficiently the tasks are performed and what progress is being made in obtaining the objectives. The manager must know how well the organization is functioning so that he can intercede and make necessary corrections. Control is an important function for the P&IC manager and is one of the major subjects included in this chapter.

Innovation. Many managers end their managerial obligations by serving only the functions mentioned above. They simply continue to do what has been done. The additional qualification required of an excellent manager is *innovation*. This is especially true for the P&IC manager. He will be exposed to numerous opportunities to improve procedures as well as processes.

Representation. The last of the list of functions is representation—representation of the production control department to all of the other branches of management. Many P&IC managers have not represented their department's importance to management, and therefore it is held in low esteem. Consequently, their share of the budget is not what it should be, which in turn results in having to hire less than qualified personnel. The process continues to spiral downward.

The P&IC manager is responsible for maintaining good relationships between his department, the factory, the order department, and others. In this process he must honestly represent his department and protect his people. In representing P&IC he is responsible for knowing in detail what is going on in his department in order to furnish with a great degree of assurance answers that may be needed by others.

These functions, which exist in all organizations, appear to take on unusual importance when discussing the P&IC managers.

Principles of Management

Reference is frequently made to principles of management as if they were some common body of laws known to all who are managers. Frequently a person will refer to a management principle and never bother to name it or its source. But at this stage of management history, there does not appear to be a universally accepted set of principles which are as laws obeyed by the industrial structure.

The nearest thing to a set of principles was developed at the turn of the century by a French industrialist, Henri Fayol. Some of these will sound like truisms which are hardly worth putting down on paper; others will seem dated and no longer serviceable in our sophisticated world. Remember, however, that these were developed long before the electronic and aerospace age and appreciate Fayol's insight into the world of industry.

These are *principles of management*[1] abbreviated somewhat:

1. *Division of work.* Specialization belongs to the natural order of things, and the objective of specialization in industry is to produce more and better work with the same effort.

2. *Authority and Responsibility.* Authority is the right to give orders and the power to exact obedience. Responsibility is to one's superior.

3. *Discipline.* This is in essence obedience, application, energy, behavior, and outward marks of respect in accordance with standing agreements between the firm and its employees.

4. *Unity of Command.* For any action, whatsoever, an employee should receive orders from only one superior.

5. *Unity of Direction.* There should be one head and one plan for a group of activities having the same objective.

6. *Subordination of Individual Interest to General Interest.* This principle calls to mind the fact that in a business the interest of one employee or group of employees should not prevail over that of the industrial concern.

7. *Remuneration of Personnel.* It should be fair and, as far as possible, afford satisfaction both to employee and employer.

8. *Centralization.* Centralization is always present to a greater or lesser extent. It is just a question of proportion.

9. *Scalar Chain.* Rather than communicate up and then down the organizational chart, a "gang plank" effect should be encouraged so that horizontal communications exist. This assumes that subordinates advise their superiors about the communications.

10. *Order.* A place for everything and everything in its place is a cliché which can be extended to employees—the right man in the right place.

11. *Equity.* For personnel to be encouraged to carry out their duties they must be treated with kindliness. According to Fayol, *equity* results from a combination of kindliness and justice.

12. *Stability and Tenure of Personnel.* Instability of tenure is at one and

---

[1] Principles of management adapted from Henri Fayol, *General and Industrial Management* (Paris: Dunod, 1925).

the same time cause and effect of bad management. Time is needed for a person to get to know a job and settle in. Nevertheless, changes are inevitable so stability of tenure is a matter of degree.

13. *Initiative.* The power of thinking out and executing a plan is referred to as initiative and is one of the greatest satisfactions for an intelligent person. This is a great source of strength to a business and should be encouraged.

14. *Esprit de Corps.* Harmony and union among personnel add strength to an organization.

These are the principles developed by Fayol. As previously mentioned, some of these seem to be dated and not in agreement with some modern management codes. They seem, however, to have merit and are worthy of consideration.

Management by Objectives. Probably no management philosophy has had a greater impact than management by objectives. Basic to this philosophy is the establishment of specific accomplishments expected of each individual in a specified time period. They are set for personnel all of the way up and down the organizational ladder, from the foreman to the accountants, industrial engineers, and so forth.

Management by objectives may be contrasted with management by job description where the list of duties is important. In management by objectives, it is *results* which are stressed and not duties.

Management by objectives encourages responsibility and consequently develops more valuable employees. Planning is encouraged which results in major contributions to the organization.

This philosophy is in step with the personality of the people in industry today. They are given a chance to use their extensive education and become important contributors. Any professional production control manager will become aware of this way of managing and use it to the utmost.

The Exception Principle. Students of organizational theory will recognize the application of the *exception principle* in the feedback concept. In this principle, routine decisions are made without reference to higher authority. Those decisions which are not routine are an exception, and require further attention. The same idea is applied in the feedback concept, because it is only necessary to take action when information fed back indicates that the system is not conforming to what is desired.

The fact that routine decisions are handled automatically does not mean that no decision has been made. It *has* been made, but since it works for a number of repetitious problems, it can be used over and over again. This is analogous to a gauge which is used for checking parts. The gauge itself is used repeatedly to check parts, but the gauge dimensions were decided only once. If the parts are outside the gauge tolerance, a higher authority must make the decision as to whether or not the parts are acceptable.

Expanding Your Management Knowledge

Many publications contain information about production planning and control. Some of these are commercial publications, sponsored by publishers for financial reasons. Often these articles will be of the how-to-do-it variety and will contain few if any sophisticated ideas. They will give you confidence in making applications.

Another important source of information is to be found in the publications of various professional societies. It would be difficult to classify these societies, or even to be sure of having an up-to-date listing, but look to groups representing these areas to publish useful information:

Production and inventory control	Systems and procedures
Accounting and cost accounting	Operations research
Management	Industrial engineering
Economics	Computers

The publications put out by these groups will range all the way from how the Sew and Sew Garment Company redesigned its production forms to scheduling models which will require computer facilities more costly than the manufacturing facilities they are intended to schedule.

More specifically there are several societies which can help the P&IC manager. The American Institute of Industrial Engineering may be of particular interest because it has an active production control section.

The American Production and Inventory Control Society, APICS, is endeavoring to extend the knowledge of its members by many means. Its meetings are well organized and always well attended. The society has sponsored a number of self-study aids in addition to monthly and quarterly publications. It has sponsored the Production and Inventory Control Handbook, published by the McGraw-Hill Book Company, which is the definitive publication on the subject.

Among APICS' more important activities is an educational and certification program, designed to help educate its membership through a self-improvement program in which members obtain recognition by a certification.

One of the most valuable services that the APICS has performed is the survey taken in cooperation with *Factory* magazine.[2] This well-conducted survey, which has been taken twice and will be taken again, gives the production control manager real data from similar companies which he can use for comparison. The latest information from this study is referred to several times in the remainder of this chapter. This information can be very useful to the operating production control manager.

APICS Checklist.[3]   One way of evaluating management performance is

---

[2] *Factory* is now *Modern Manufacturing*, published by McGraw-Hill.

[3] G. Jerome Tabern, *APICS Checklist*, A. T. Kearney & Co., Chicago, Illinois.

Figure 25-2

YOUR PERSONAL
APICS CHECKLIST

FOR EVALUATING PRODUCTION AND
INVENTORY CONTROL EFFECTIVENESS

Designed as a self-appraisal by Production and Inventory Control Supervision. Check appropriate answer.

TYPE OF INDUSTRY (*Check one in each category*)

1. ☐ Heavy 2. ☐ Processing, ☐ Fabrication,
   ☐ Light**
   ☐ Assembly, ☐ Fabrication & Assembly, ☐ Other (Indicate)
   ☐ Production Line, ☐ Job Shop (Primarily)

SIZE OF PLANT OR DIVISION (*Check one*)
☐ Under 200, ☐ 200-500, ☐ 501-1,000 ☐ 1,001-2,000,
☐ 2,001-3,000, ☐ 3,001-5,000, ☐ Over 5,000.

**SIZE OF PRODUCTION AND
INVENTORY CONTROL DEPARTMENT** (*Check one*)
☐ Under 5, ☐ 5-10, ☐ 11-20, ☐ 21-30, ☐ 31-50,
☐ 51-100, ☐ Over 100.

YES NO PARTLY

I. CONTROLLING SERVICE TO CUSTOMERS

1. Are lead times or delivery schedules:
   (a) Published
   (b) Realistic?
   (c) Competitive in the industry?
2. What is your delivery performance goal (_____%)?
   (a) Do you meet it?
   (b) What is the maximum margin by which delivery schedules are missed? (_____ days)
3. Do you keep your customers informed?
4. Do you lose sales because of stock-outs or poor delivery performance?
5. Do you know the cost of a lost sale?
6. Does your company enjoy a good reputation for good customer service?

**Characterized by one or more of the following: light manufacturing equipment, bench or hand operations, products handled in small to medium sized containers.

CONTINUED ON NEXT PAGE

YOUR PERSONAL APICS CHECKLIST

YES NO PARTLY

7. Is your service on sample orders good?
8. Are you convinced that the orders which Sales labels as urgent are truly urgent?

II. CONTROLLING PRODUCTION PLANNING

1. Do you participate in preparation of, or prepare your own sales forecast?
2. Do you establish production levels?
3. Do you have prepared and at your finger-tips the capacity of your critical lines or machines?
4. Have you recently (within the last year) determined your most economical production plan? (fluctuating inventories, versus fluctuating work forces versus use of overtime)
5. Do you have an overtime (hourly) goal?
   (a) Is it met?
6. Are priorities and lead times scheduled for:
   (a) Engineering?
   (b) Industrial Engineering?
   (c) Tooling?

III. CONTROLLING INVENTORY LEVELS AND STORAGE

1. Are inventory level goals determined by:
   (a) Executive opinion?
   (b) Over-all financial considerations?
   (c) Employment level and seasonal fluctuations?
   (d) Production plan related to forecast?
   (e) Reorder point–EOQ?
   (f) Optimum inventory calculation? (Such as ABC)
   (g) Inventory turnover?
   (h) Other calculations?
2. Are your inventory level goals met?
3. Do you consider your inventory balanced?
4. Do you compute and report your ratio of inactive to active parts and act to improve it?
5. Is your actual stock-out frequency compatible with target?
6. Do you work to a known stock-out risk?
7. What is your requirement for on-time vendor performance? (_____%)
   Is this requirement met?
8. Is it used to control or select vendors?
9. Is corrective action taken when a vendor:
10. (a) Ships early?

CONTINUED ON NEXT PAGE

YOUR PERSONAL APICS CHECKLIST

YES NO PARTLY

   (b) Ships late?
   (c) Overships?
11. Are purchasing lead times reviewed regularly?
12. Does Purchasing transmit price break and other economical buying information to Production Control?
13. Is storage space adequate?
14. Are storage areas well protected, orderly and clean?
15. Are the following items stored and identified separately:
   (a) Rejected Material?
   (b) Returned goods?
   (c) Slow moving items?
   (d) Obsolete items?
   (e) Stock?
   (f) Non Stock?

IV. CONTROLLING PRODUCTION OPERATIONS, COSTS

1. What is your factory production schedule performance goal? (_____%)
   (a) Do you meet it?
2. Is labor utilization:
   (a) Regularly reported?
   (b) Optimum?
3. Is machine utilization:
   (a) Regularly reported?
   (b) Optimum
4. Does scheduling contribute all possible to labor efficiency?
5. Is production control concerned with shop set up costs?
   (a) Are they optimum?
6. Is there a report giving reasons for late production to pin-point recurring problems?
7. Are prototypes processed through a short run shop?
8. Are less than 5% of orders expedited?
9. Does the shop:
   (a) Produce only specified quantities?
   (b) Follow Production Control dates?
10. Are all necessary parts, materials, tools, and drawings on hand before an order is released to the shop?
   (a) Initially?
   (b) When dispatching in the shop?
11. Is the feedback of information from the shop:
   (a) Factual?
   (b) Meaningful?
   (c) Current?

CONTINUED ON NEXT PAGE

YES NO PARTLY

6. Is there a specific program (short and long range) to improve the system?
7. Are lines of communication good?
8. Is creation and obsolescence of parts under control?
9. Is there a good engineering change procedure?
10. Do you have procedures for determining when item inventory status changes? (For instance from non-stock to stock.)

VII. CONTROLLING THE SITUATION

1. Is the stature of the Department all that it might be?
2. Are relationships with other departments good?
3. Does the Production and Inventory Control Department receive top level support?
4. Does the "plan" prevail over would-be crash programs such as the "$ billing evil"?
5. Are production processing problems in control or adequately compensated for?
6. Has there been a promotional meeting in the last six months in which the purposes and problems of P&IC were conveyed to supervision of other functions?
7. Are all of the basic functions performed:
   (a) Forecasting and planning
   (b) Scheduling, loading and dispatching
   (c) Reports and controls
   (d) Raw material control
   (e) In-process control
   (f) Finished goods control
8. Is there a program to schedule and combine shipments to obtain optimum transportation costs?
9. Does the Production and Inventory Control Department effectively sell management on what is best from an over-all standpoint?
10. Does your boss concern himself only with overall measures of Production and Inventory Control Department performance? (As contrasted with asking you about the status of particular orders?

APICS INTERNATIONAL

330 S. WELLS STREET • CHICAGO, ILL. 60606

A/C 312 - 939 - 4956

YES NO PARTLY

(d) Adequate for scrap control?
(e) Adequate for cost control?
(f) Enough but not too much?
(g) Used to take action?
12. Are shipments relatively level through the week or month?

V. CONTROLLING INTERNAL OPERATIONS

1. Do you have a formal organization chart?
2. Is there a job description for each job?
3. Is the Production Control Manager a planner rather than a fire fighter? Does he spend the equivalent of five hours per week planning departmental operation?
4. If your department performs a stockroom kitting operation, what is your performance goal? (_____)
5. Do you have written policies and procedures covering all phases of departmental operations?
6. Do you meet your departmental budget objective?
7. Do you have and meet some objective regarding size of the department such as number of people per 100 direct labor employees or number of people per 100 orders processed?
8. Do you have a goal for departmental overtime and is it met?
9. Are absenteeism records maintained and is the level normal?
10. Have all of the departmental employees received some off-the-job training in the last year?
11. Is the department fluid rather than static regarding promotions inside and outside the department?

VI. CONTROLLING THE SYSTEM

1. Does the system provide the right degree of sophistication at the right cost?
2. Does the system employ the newest and best applicable tools and techniques?
3. Are forms simple and paperwork at a minimum?
4. Have unnecessary perpetual inventory records and visual charts been eliminated?
5. Is exception reporting employed wherever possible?

CONTINUED ON NEXT PAGE

PRINTED AND DISTRIBUTED THROUGH COURTESY OF

AKRON CHAPTER

American Production & Inventory Control Society

Courtesy of G. Jerome Tabern, principal, A. T. Kearney & Co., Chicago, management consultant.

to use a checklist against which to compare performance. A checklist developed by members of the American Production and Inventory Control Society is presented in Figure 25–2. This makes an excellent assessment technique. It could be even more useful if several managers from different companies would compare answers to the ones posed in the questionnaire.

Staffing the P&IC Department

Production control impinges upon practically every other department, and its personnel are in contact with other people inside and outside the factory. Thus it is understandable that personnel relations are considered of utmost importance.

An organization with few disturbances reaches a state of "equilibrium" in which each person knows what is expected of him. Personnel become familiar with their surroundings and know how their fellow workers are going to react under certain conditions. When changes occur, the individual must make adjustments, and these adjustments may involve many distressing decisions. Production control is responsible for making many of these changes which the factory personnel may find so distressing. Every change in production quantity or methods may upset the organizational equilibrium. Members of the production control department must be aware of this possible problem and strive to alleviate the difficulties.

Because relations with others are so important, the staff of the production control department should be selected with care:

They should know the work they are directing and be well-acquainted with advanced methods.

Production control personnel operate in a no-man's-land between staff and line authority. Consequently, they should be aware of their position and of the source of their authority. They must exercise, but not usurp, authority.

Since production control personnel are often in direct contact with customers, they must present a good company image.

They must be friendly and enthusiastic.

They should have perseverance, but not be stubborn.

They have many opportunities to show favoritism; this, however, is not permissible, and they must be fair and unbiased.

They should be tactful and cooperative.

They should have excellent personal habits so that they will not offend those with whom they have contact.

They should be educated and trained in the subjects related to production control: statistics, economics, data processing, and others.

These are only a few of the important characteristics that should be looked for when hiring personnel for the production control department.

A production control manager might reasonably ask, "How many people are needed to staff my department?" The answer to this will depend upon the product and how it is manufactured. A job shop could expect to use more people than a continuous process, and the scope of the production control function will also determine the size of the department. The APICS survey shows that the norm is between 3 percent and 4 percent of the total employment. The survey also shows that as the departments improve their operations this percentage drops.

Management and the Computer

Along with the greater efficiencies of the computer have come some management difficulties. Because of the high cost of the computer and the specialized personnel, the computer becomes a centralized function as illustrated in Figure 25–3.

The application of the computer has had a strong influence upon the design of the organization. Frequently the first computer application is made in the payroll department where it can be quickly adapted and will show cost savings in a short time. From this application, it is often used in other accounting applications such as accounts receivable, purchasing, and so on. Consequently, the computer and data processing center are under the supervision of the accountant or the treasurer. This can cause some difficulty for the production control manager who must have time on the computer at scheduled intervals or his operations will fall apart.

Frequently production control applications come last. By that time accounting and data processing personnel are well entrenched. This can lead to the production control function being usurped by people who know little or nothing about production control and the factory operations.

A typical development was illustrated in a company which hired a data processing technician who had been trained by and later released from the armed forces. Because of his specialized knowledge, he was hired by a large job shop to help develop its data processing system. Eventually, he became responsible for scheduling although he knew practically nothing about the people and machines in the factory. Needless to say this was disastrous.

To avoid such a situation requires a strong production control manager who understands the computer and can demand his share of the computer's time. The trend appears to be to place the computer in a separate function under top management to serve all departments. This trend could change as mini-computers become more commonly used.

It is not necessary for all production control personnel to know how to program computers, but there should be some staff who know. Beyond being programmers, they should be system designers and know what the computer can and cannot do.

The thrust toward computer applications in production control has certainly accelerated in recent years. The APICS-factory survey available probably does not tell the entire story, and we will have to wait for a new

Figure 25–3

A Comprehensive Factory Data System

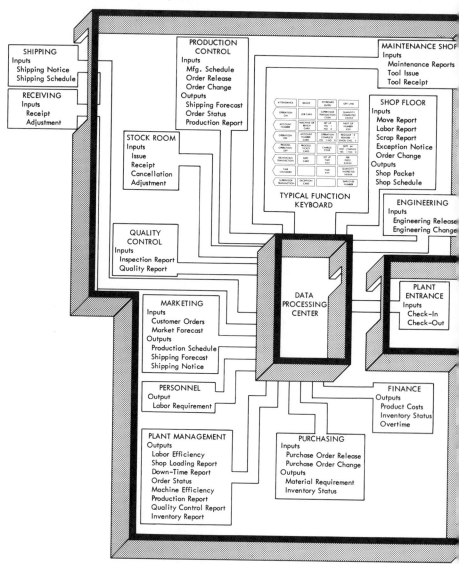

Courtesy of Computer Decisions, *March* 1

one to be made. However, the trend was indicated by the study as shown in Figure 25–4. The surprising thing is the number of companies that will still be anchored to the manual systems, as shown in the chart.

Figure 25–4
How Information Is Processed: 1961 versus 1966

Percent of plants using these methods

TYPE OF INFORMATION	Manual Systems 1961	Manual Systems 1966	Control Boards 1961	Control Boards 1966	Edge-Notched Cards 1961	Edge-Notched Cards 1966	Punched Cards (Tab) 1961	Punched Cards (Tab) 1966	Stored Program Computer 1961	Stored Program Computer 1966	Desk* Calculator 1966
Customer delivery schedules and order backlog	58	53	7	10	2	1	27	16	10	23	5
Production orders: quantity and timing	66	59	8	12	1	1	15	13	11	24	9
Preparation	67	69	3	3	2	1	15	11	8	17	7
Detailed schedules for production departments	69	58	11	12	1	1	11	10	5	12	6
Follow-up reporting of progress on schedules	68	57	7	8	1	1	14	11	5	14	3
Inventory records for: finished goods	56	40	1	2	1	2	34	18	15	27	4
Work in process	59	44	3	3	3	2	24	15	9	21	4
Raw materials	67	50	1	1	1	1	23	14	10	20	5
Order entry*		51		5		1		24		27	5
Machine loading*		45		9		1		8		11	4

* Not surveyed in 1961.

Control in the P&IC Department

Perhaps control cannot be said to be the most important function of the manager for all functions are essential. However, it is the one to which managers seem to pay little attention. It is not unusual to ask a production control manager or even a plant manager what his plant's efficiency is and have him reply that he does not know. Or one might get a similar response to such questions as, "What is your scrap rate?" or "What is your inventory turnover rate?" or "What percentage of errors do your inventory clerks make?"

To have control, it is essential to know where you have been, where you are now, and where you want to be in the future. All of this requires a feedback of information in the system and some way of measuring change. This points up some basic ideas which are often forgotten.

In the control function, one must have more than just a number. For example, if someone said to you the number 365 you might immediately jump to the conclusion that he was talking about the days in a year when in reality he might be telling you the number of guppies in an aquarium. There is considerable difference. Thus, it is apparent that just a number is worthless unless it includes a description and is expressed as a rate—such as 365 days in a year, or 365 guppies in an aquarium.

Not only are there simple rates, but there are rates which involve other factors or other rates. One with which you are familiar is acceleration, which is the rate by which velocity (a rate) is changing with time.

It is not unusual to find many sophisticated techniques being used in a factory, but this simple concept of a rate is being forgotten. It is especially strange when one considers how sensitive people are to rates outside the industrial environment. They can undoubtedly tell you how many miles to the gallon they get with their car and how many quarts of oil between oil changes but they will not have the vaguest idea of how many orders they receive for the number bid. Accountants and engineers are trained to use ratios to measure efficiency but often fail to use them in their factory operation.

The production control manager should start developing meaningful ratios to measure performances of importance as this is the only way he can exercise control. Some of the measures are discussed in ensuing pages. This does not mean that these are the only ones of importance.

One of the manager's problems is finding the information he needs to develop ratios. Many of the useful rates are developed within the factory, and he uses them from day to day in making his evaluations.

The manager may wish to have some outside figures to compare. These can be found in various government bulletins, financial services, and business publications. Some of these are loose-leaf records that are kept up to date by a librarian. The manager's best sources for comparative data may be the local librarian. It may be that colleagues in other plants will be willing to help by divulging some of their information. Not all companies will permit this, but if it is done on a mutual exchange basis it may be useful. Of course, one of the most useful sources of information is the professional society. The services furnished have already been referred to.

More than one company has "controlled itself" out of existence. Therefore one of the most important considerations is how much control is necessary. Poor control can ruin a company by causing unnecessary set-up costs, excessive delivery times, excessive overtime costs, and many other unnecessary expenses. These expenses must be weighed against the cost of tighter control, which might lead to hiring more people and buying additional equipment. Part of this text is dedicated to decision making and one of the most important decisions is just how much control is desirable.

Management of Techniques

A P&IC's manager who has kept up to date may be concerned about whether his department is making use of all the latest techniques. The APICS' survey of companies using operations research techniques, Figure 25–5, might be useful. The chart can be interpreted in several ways. For example, EOQ being an older technique than simulation has caught on. On the other hand, it may indicate that EOQ's have shown signs of the greatest payoff. Anyway, the chart says that more people are using the

Figure 25–5
Plants Using Operations Research Techniques

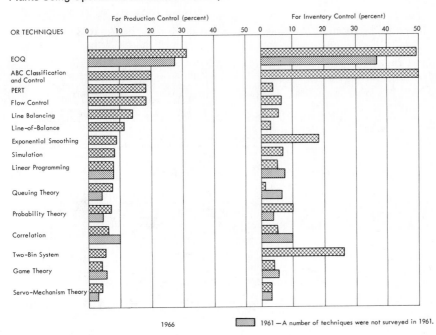

ABC analysis, and if your company is not using it, perhaps you had better investigate why.

It is especially interesting to observe how companies are forecasting sales. Although we have stressed quantitative methods, the majority of companies surveyed are using the sales manager's estimate and executive opinion as shown in Figure 25–6.

Figure 25–6
Basis for Sales Forecasting

FORECASTING TECHNIQUE	5-Year	Annual	Moving 12-Months	Moving 3-Months	Quarterly	Monthly	Use Technique for Any Time Period No. of Plants
Sales Manager's Estimate	112	255	72	66	98	92	
Adjusted by Latest Sales Information	30	81	45	62	92	135	
Executive Opinion	92	139	33	28	48	52	
Marketing Analysis	114	152	54	41	54	50	
Trend and Cycle Analysis	43	64	39	38	38	45	
Expected Share of the Market	94	157	32	21	42	32	
Correlation with Economic Indicator	55	74	18	16	22	23	
Exponential Smoothing	6	17	24	29	14	36	
Charts with Control Limits	16	39	18	17	22	33	
Other (Part history, material manager advises, backlog, stock control, contract analysis)	6	17	13	11	8	16	

Measuring P&IC's Effectiveness

How should the P&IC manager measure his department's performance? The chart in Figure 25-7 shows how companies in the APICS' study are

Figure 25-7
Measures of Effectiveness

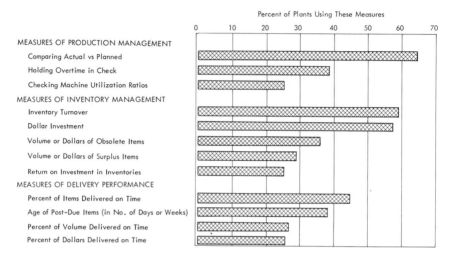

doing it. It is apparent that delivery of goods on time and inventory turnover are considered important measures of performance.

Measurement of Inventory Effectiveness. The most commonly used index of inventory efficiency is *turnover*. Turnover is the ratio of withdrawals to the average inventory on hand.

$$\text{Turnover} = \frac{\text{Cost of goods sold}}{\text{Average of total inventories}}$$

Since there are various classes of inventories, there are various turnover ratios. For example, there are ratios for finished goods, raw materials, and work in process. A ratio is meaningless unless compared with previous ratios or with norms which have been developed by others.

As the National Association of Accountants' bulletin[4] points out, the inventory turnover ratio is subject to accounting procedures. For example, a write-down of finished goods because of obsolescence could be charged against the cost of goods sold. This would normally imply an inefficient inventory management, but it would actually appear as an improved inventory turnover ratio.

---

[4] For an excellent discussion of this subject, see *Technical Inventory Management Research Report 40*, National Association of Cost Accountants, 505 Park Avenue, New York, New York 10032.

The inventory pricing method will affect the turnover ratio, but it can be minimized by calculating the ratio on the basis of number of items instead of dollars.

An aggregate turnover ratio can obscure the fact that some items are not moving at all while others are moving fast. In some situations an item-by-item study is best.

The inventory turnover ratio may be increased by reducing the average inventory. In fact, the best ratio would occur when practically no inventory was carried at all. This is contrary to the logic of the economic order quantity models which strive for an optimum quantity. A manager devoted to inventory turnover ratios can undo the purpose of the EOQ equations, that is, to keep enough inventory on hand so that the cost of frequent orders will not occur. In fact the inventory order quantity dictates its own turnover ratio. Considering this, the inventory turnover ratio should probably have limited use. At least it should not be the only measure of performance.

The ratio of inventory on hand to what is acceptable is another comparative ratio which will give a handle on inventory effectiveness.

As pointed out in the inventory chapter, inventory as a percent of assets can give an insight into inventory management effectiveness.

One way to measure inventory management would be to determine the costs of processing an order and storing the material with the objective of lowering these costs. The difficulty with this technique is ascertaining the cost data by which to make comparisons.

Logic for Management Problem Solving

An underlying theme has been the logic of problem solving and system designing. These points should be repeated here:

1. Become aware of the problem.
2. Define the problem.
3. Locate, evaluate, and organize information.
4. Discover relationships and formulate hypotheses.
5. Evaluate the hypotheses.
6. Apply the solution.

One should constantly review these steps until they become a familiar part of every problem-solving situation.

The P&IC manager will also want to become familiar with some recent developments in problem solving. Two which will be useful are the ideals[5] concepts of Gerald Nadler and those in *The Rational Manager*[6] by Charles Kepner and Benjamin Tregoe.

---

[5] Gerald W. Nadler, *Work Design: A Systems Concept* (Homewood, Ill.: Richard D. Irwin, Inc.).

[6] Charles Kepner, and Benjamin B. Tregoe, *The Rational Manager* (New York: McGraw-Hill).

Summary

The management of the P&IC department has two main thrusts. One is toward the plant where the attempt is to bring men, machines, and materials together to produce a product at an optimum cost. The other thrust is toward managing the internal operations of the department.

Both of these are extremely important, requiring the best of managerial skills. The functions of management are: planning, organizing, staffing, direction, control, and innovation. While all of these are important, one cannot exist without the others.

Control is of particular importance and here the servo-model plays the greatest part. To have control, it is essential to have feedback. To make adjustments to the system, it is necessary to measure. The P&IC manager should become sensitized to the measurements which will give him the best control possible.

QUESTIONS

25-1. In what respects is the production control manager a "manager"?
25-2. Discuss how you would organize the computer facilities for a job shop employing 500 employees.
25-3. Discuss the trend in the use of: (see Figure 25-4)
    a. Control boards.
    b. Computers.
    c. Edge notched cards.
25-4. Give three pieces of information you would want to improve the efficiency of a production control department.
25-5. How does the number of applications of operations research to production control (Figure 25-5) compare with the time you spend in studying them? What does this mean?

references

References

HANDBOOKS AND DICTIONARIES

ALJIAN, G. W. *Purchasing Handbook*. 2d ed. New York: McGraw-Hill Book Co., 1966.

AMERICAN PRODUCTION AND INVENTORY CONTROL SOCIETY. *APICS Bibliography* 4th ed. Robert G. Ames, ed. Washington: APICS, 1972.

——. *APICS Dictionary of Inventory Control Terms and Production Control Terms*. 3d ed. Richard C. Sherrill, ed. Chicago: APICS, 1970.

AMERICAN SOCIETY OF TOOL AND MANUFACTURING ENGINEERS. *Tool Engineers Handbook*, 2d ed. Frank W. Wilson, ed. New York: McGraw-Hill Book Co., 1959.

AMES, ROBERT G. *Bibliography of Articles, Books, and Films on Production and Inventory Control and Related Subjects*. 4th ed., Los Angeles: American Production and Inventory Control Society—Los Angeles Chapter, 1972.

CARSON, GORDON B., BOLZ, HAROLD A., and YOUNG, HEWITT H. *Production Handbook*. 3d ed., New York: Ronald Press Co., 1972.

GREENE, JAMES, H. *Production and Inventory Control Handbook*. American Production and Inventory Control Society, New York: McGraw-Hill Book Co., 1970.

IRESON, WILLIAM GRANT, AND GRANT, EUGENE L. *Handbook of Industrial Engineering and Management*. 2d ed. Englewood Cliffs, N.J.: Prentice-Hall, Inc., 1971.

MAYNARD, HAROLD B. *Handbook of Modern Manufacturing Management*. New York: McGraw-Hill Book Co., 1970.

——. *Industrial Engineering Handbook*, 3d ed. New York: McGraw-Hill Book Co., 1971.

O'BRIAN, JAMES G. *Scheduling Handbook*. New York: McGraw-Hill Book Co., 1969.

PRENTICE-HALL EDITORIAL STAFF. *Encyclopedic Dictionary of Production and Production Control*. Englewood Cliffs, N.J.: Prentice-Hall, Inc., 1964.

ZEYHER, LEWIS R. *Production Managers' Handbook of Formulae and Tables*. Englewood Cliffs, N.J.: Prentice-Hall, Inc., 1972.

APPLIED MATHEMATICS AND OPERATIONS RESEARCH

ACKOFF, R. L., and SASIENI, MAURICE W. *Fundamentals of Operations Research*. New York: John Wiley & Sons, Inc., 1968.

AITKEN, ALEXANDER CRAIG. *Determinants and Matrices*. 9th ed. Edinburgh: Oliver & Boyd; New York: Interscience Publishers, 1956.

CHURCHMAN, C. W., ACKOFF, R. L., and ARNOFF, E. L. *Introduction to Operations Research*. New York: John Wiley & Sons, Inc., 1957.

FABRYCKY, W. J., GHARE, P. M., and TORGERSEN, P. E. *Industrial Operations Research*. Englewood Cliffs, N.J.: Prentice-Hall, Inc., 1972.

HILLIER, FREDERICK S., and LIEBERMAN, GERALD J. *Introduction to Operations Research*. California: Holden-Day, Inc., 1967.

KAUFMANN, A. *Methods and Models of Operations Research*. Englewood Cliffs, N.J.: Prentice-Hall, Inc., 1963.

LEVIN, RICHARD I., and KIRKPATRICK, CHARLES A. *Quantitative Approaches to Management*. New York: McGraw-Hill Book Co., 1971.

RAU, JOHN G. *Optimization and Probability in Systems Engineering*. New York: Van Nostrand-Reinhold Co., 1970.

RICHMOND, SAMUEL B. *Operations Research for Management Decisions*. New York: The Ronald Press Co., 1968.

SPRINGER, CLIFFORD H., HERLIHY, ROBERT E., and BEGGS, ROBERT I. *Basic Mathematics*. Homewood, Ill.: Richard D. Irwin, Inc., 1965.

———. *Advanced Methods and Models*. Homewood, Ill.: Richard D. Irwin, Inc., 1965.

———. *Statistical Inference*. Homewood, Ill.: Richard D. Irwin, Inc., 1966.

———. *Probabilistic Models*. Homewood, Ill.: Richard D. Irwin, Inc., 1968.

TAHA, HAMDY, A. *Operations Research: An Introduction*. New York: Macmillan Co., 1971.

THEODORE, CHRIS A. *Applied Mathematics: An Introduction: Mathematical Analysis for Management*. Rev. ed. Homewood, Ill.: Richard D. Irwin, Inc., 1971.

THIERAUF, ROBERT J., and GROSSE, RICHARD A. *Decision Making through Operations Research*. New York: John Wiley & Sons, Inc., 1970.

WAGNER, HARVEY M. *Principles of Operations Research with Applications to Managerial Decisions*. Englewood Cliffs, N.J.: Prentice-Hall, Inc., 1969.

———. *Principles of Management Science with Applications to Executive Decisions*. Englewood Cliffs, N.J.: Prentice-Hall, Inc., 1970.

CHAPTER 1

BETHEL, LAWRENCE L., et al. *Production Control*. New York and London: McGraw-Hill Book Co., Inc., 1942.

BIEGEL, JOHN E. *Production Control: A Quantitative Approach*. Englewood Cliffs, N.J.: Prentice-Hall, Inc., 1971.

BOCK, ROBERT H., and HOLSTEIN, WILLIAM K. *Production Planning and Control, Text and Readings*. Columbus, Ohio: Charles E. Merrill Books, Inc., 1963.

BROWN, ROBERT GOODELL. *Management Decisions for Production Operations*. Hinsdale, Ill.: Dryden Press, 1971.

BUFFA, ELWOOD SPENCER, and TAUBERT, WILLIAM H. *Production-Inventory Systems: Planning and Control*. Homewood, Ill.: Richard D. Irwin, Inc., 1972.

CARROLL, PHIL. *Practical Production and Inventory Control*. New York: McGraw-Hill Book Co., 1966.

CORKE, D. K. *Production Control Is Management*. London: Edward Arnold Ltd., 1969.

DOOLEY, ARCH R., et al. *Casebooks in Production Management Operations Planning and Control*. New York: John Wiley & Sons, Inc., 1964.

EILON, SAMUEL. *Elements of Production Planning and Control*. New York: Macmillan Co., 1962.

ELMAGHRABY, SALAH E. *The Design of Production Systems*. New York: Reinhold Publishing Co., 1966.

GREENE, JAMES. *Operations Planning and Control*. Homewood, Ill.: Richard D. Irwin, Inc., 1967.

HOLT, CHARLES C., et al. *Planning Production, Inventories, and Work Force*. Englewood Cliffs, N.J.; Prentice-Hall, Inc., 1960.

HARVARD BUSINESS REVIEW. *Planning Series*. Reprints from *Harvard Business Review*.

KNOEPPEL, C. E. *Graphic Production Control*. New York: The Engineering Magazine Company, 1920.

KNOWLES, ASA, and THOMSON, ROBERT D. *Production Control*. New York: The Macmillan Co., 1943.

KOEPKE, CHARLES A. *Plant Production Control*. 3d ed. New York: John Wiley & Sons, Inc., 1961.

LANDY, THOMAS M. *Production Planning and Control*. New York: McGraw-Hill Book Co., Inc., 1950.

LOCKYER, K. G. *Production Control in Practice*. London: Pitman, 1966.

MACNIECE, E. H. *Production Forecasting, Planning and Control*. 3d ed. New York: John Wiley & Sons, Inc., 1961.

MAGEE, JOHN F. Boodman, David M. *Production Planning and Inventory Control*. 2d ed. New York: McGraw-Hill Book Co., 1967.

MCGARRAH, ROBERT E. *Production and Logistics Management: Text and Cases*. New York: John Wiley & Sons, Inc., 1963.

MIZE, JOE H., WHITE, CHARLES R., and BROOKS, GEORGE H. *Operations Planning and Control*. Englewood Cliffs, N.J.: Prentice-Hall, Inc., 1971.

MOORE, FRANKLIN G., and JABLONSKI, RONALD. *Production Control*. 3d ed. New York: McGraw-Hill Book Co., 1969.

NILAND, POWELL. *Production Planning, Scheduling, and Inventory Control*. New York: The Macmillan Co., 1970.

NORD, OLE C., ed. *Integrated Manufacturing Planning.* Sweden: Student-litteratur, 1969.

O'DONNELL, PAUL. *Production Control.* Englewood Cliffs, N.J.: Prentice-Hall, Inc., 1952.

PARTON, JAMES ALLAN, JR., and STERES, CHRIS P. *Production Control Manual.* New York: Conover-Mast Publications, 1955.

PLOSSL, GEORGE W., and WIGHT, OLIVER W. *Materials Requirements Planning by Computer.* American Production and Inventory Control Society, 1971.

————. *Production Planning and Inventory Control: Principles and Techniques.* Englewood Cliffs, N.J.: Prentice-Hall, Inc., 1967.

PRITZKER, ROBERT A., and GRING, ROBERT A. *Modern Approaches to Production Planning and Control.* New York: American Management Association, Inc., 1960.

RAGO, LOUIS J. *Production Analysis and Control.* Scranton, Pa.: International Textbook Co., 1963.

RAMLOW, DONALD E., and WALL, EUGENE H. *Production Planning and Control.* Englewood Cliffs, N.J.: Prentice-Hall, Inc., 1967.

REINFELD, NYLES V. *Production Control.* Englewood Cliffs, N.J.: Prentice-Hall, Inc., 1959.

RITCHIE, WILLIAM E. *Production and Inventory Control.* New York: Ronald Press Co., 1951.

SCHEELE, EVAN D., WESTERMAN, WILLIAM L., and WIMMERT, ROBERT J. *Principles and Design of Production Control Systems.* Englewood Cliffs, N.J.: Prentice-Hall, Inc., 1960.

TIRANTI, D. *Introduction to Production Control.* London: Chapman & Hall, 1946.

VAN DE MARK, ROBERT L. *Production Control Techniques.* Dallas, Texas, 1970.

————. *Production and Inventory Control Case Studies.* Grand Rapids, Mich.: Gilson Press, 1963.

VORIS, WILLIAM. *The Management of Production.* New York: Ronald Press Co., 1960.

————. *Production Control,* Rev. ed., Homewood, Ill.: Richard D. Irwin, Inc., 1961.

————. *Production Control: Text and Cases.* 3d ed. Homewood, Ill.: Richard D. Irwin, Inc., 1966.

WIGHT, OLIVER V. *Production and Inventory Control in the Computer Age: A Management Viewpoint.* Boston, Mass.: Cahners Publishing Co., Inc., 1974.

YATES, MORRIS LORD. *Production Control in an Engineering Factory.* Manchester, Eng.: Emmott, 1946.

CHAPTER 2

ACKOFF, RUSSELL L. *Scientific Method.* New York: John Wiley & Sons, Inc., 1962.

ALEXANDER, J. EUGENE, and BAILEY, J. MILTON. *Systems Engineering Mathematics*. Englewood Cliffs, N.J.: Prentice-Hall, Inc., 1962.

BLACK, MAX. *Critical Thinking: An Introduction to Logic and Scientific Method*. 2d ed. Englewood Cliffs, N.J.: Prentice-Hall, Inc., 1955.

BORING, EDWIN GARRIGUES, LANGFELD, H. S., and WELD, H. P. *Foundations of Psychology*. New York: John Wiley & Sons, Inc., 1948.

BRIERLEY, JOHN KEITH. *The Thinking Machine*. Rutherford, N.J.: Fairleigh Dickinson University Press, 1973.

CHURCHMAN, CHARLES W. *The Systems Approach*. New York: Delacorte Press, 1968.

———. *The Design of Inquiring Systems and Basic Concepts of Systems and Organizations*. New York: Basic Books, Inc., 1971.

DEWEY, JOHN. *How We Think*. Boston: D. C. Heath & Company, 1933, and paperback, Henry Regnery Co., Chicago, 1971.

DIMNET, ERNEST. *The Art of Thinking*. New York: Simon & Schuster, 1955, and paperback, Greenwich, Conn.: Fawcett World Library, 1971.

FLAGLE, CHARLES D., HUGGINS, WILLIAM H., and ROY, ROBERT H. *Operations Research and Systems Engineering*. Baltimore, Md.: Johns Hopkins Press, 1960.

FORRESTER, JAY WRIGHT. *Industrial Dynamics*. Cambridge, Mass.: M.I.T. Press, 1961.

———. *Principles of Systems*. Cambridge, Mass.: Wright-Allen, 1968.

GOODE, HENRY H., and MACHOL, ROBERT E. *System Engineering*. New York: McGraw-Hill Book Co., Inc., 1957.

GRABBE, EUGENE MUNTER, RAMO, SIMON, and WOOLDRIDGE, DEAN E. *Handbook of Automation, Computation and Control*. 3 vols. New York: John Wiley & Sons, Inc., 1958–61.

GREENE, JAMES H. "Industrial Communications—An Engineering Approach." *The Tool Engineer* 44 (March 1960): 75.

HALL, ARTHUR D. *A Methodology for Systems Engineering*. Princeton, N.J.: D. Van Nostrand Co., 1962.

MURPHY, GLENN. *Similitude in Engineering*. New York: Ronald Press Co., 1950.

RHEGG, THOMAS. "A Servo-System Analysis of an Industrial Organization." Unpublished Master's Thesis, West Lafayette, Ind.: Purdue University, 1963.

SUPPES, PATRICK. *Introduction to Logic*. Princeton, N.J.: D. Van Nostrand Co., 1959.

TRUXAL, JOHN G. *Control Engineers' Handbook*. New York: McGraw-Hill Book Co., 1958.

VINACKE, W. EDGAR. *The Psychology of Thinking*. New York: McGraw-Hill Book Co., 1952.

WASON, P. C., and JOHNSON-LAIRD, P. N. *Thinking and Reasoning*. Baltimore, Md.: Penguin Books, Inc., 1968.

CHAPTER 3

In addition to references listed here, see Chapter 1 references.

INTERNATIONAL BUSINESS MACHINES, INC. *Communications Oriented Production Information and Control System.* COPICS, White Plains, New York, 1974.
Vol. 1 Management Overview, System Req., Glossary, Index
Vol. 2 Customer Order Servicing Engineering and Production Data Control
Vol. 3 Forecasting, Master Production Schedule Planning
Vol. 4 Inventory Management
Vol. 5 Manufacturing Activity Planning, Order Release
Vol. 6 Plant Monitoring and Control, Plant Maintenance
Vol. 7 Purchasing and Receiving, Stores Control, Cost Planning and Control
Vol. 8 System Data Base

ANTHONY, ROBERT N. *Management Control Systems.* Rev. ed., Homewood, Ill.: Richard D. Irwin, Inc., 1972.

BOCCHINO, WILLIAM A. *Management Information Systems: Tools and Techniques.* Englewood Cliffs, N.J.: Prentice-Hall, Inc., 1972.

DONALD, A. G. *Management, Information and Systems.* Pergamon Press, 1967.

HODGE, BARTOW, and HODGSON, ROBERT N. *Management and the Computer in Information and Control.* New York: McGraw-Hill Book Co., Inc., 1969.

O'BRIEN, JAMES. *Management Information Systems: Concepts, Techniques, and Applications.* New York: Van Nostrand Reinhold Co., 1970.

CHAPTER 4

AYRES, R. V. *Technological Forecasting and Long Range Planning.* New York: McGraw-Hill Book Co., 1969.

BURR, IRVING. *Applied Statistical Methods.* New York: Academic Press, 1974.

CHOU, YA-LUN. *Probability and Statistics for Decision Making.* New York: Holt, Rinehart & Winston, Inc., 1972.

―――. *Statistical Analysis with Business and Economic Applications.* New York: Holt, Rinehart & Winston, Inc., 1969.

CROXTON, F. E., COWDEN, D. J., and BOLCH, B. *Practical Business Statistics.* 4th ed. Englewood Cliffs, N.J.: Prentice-Hall, Inc., 1969.

FERBER, ROBERT. *Statistical Techniques in Market Research.* New York: McGraw-Hill Book Co., 1949.

GRIFFEN, JOHN I. *Statistics Methods and Applications.* New York: Holt, Rinehart & Winston, Inc., 1962.

HOEL, P. G. *Elementary Statistics.* 3d ed. New York: John Wiley & Sons, Inc., 1971.

―――. *Introduction to Mathematical Statistics.* 4th ed. New York: John Wiley & Sons, Inc., 1971.

―――, and Jessen, Raymond J., *Basic Statistics for Business and Economics.* New York: John Wiley & Sons, Inc. 1971.

KIRKPATRICK, E. G. *Introductory Statistics and Probability for Engineering, Science and Technology.* Englewood Cliffs, N.J.: Prentice-Hall, Inc., 1974.

―――. *Quality Control for Managers and Engineers.* New York: John Wiley & Sons, Inc., 1970.

LYLE, PHILIP. *Regression Analysis of Production Costs and Factory Operations.* 3d ed. Edinburgh-Tweeddale Court, London: Oliver & Boyd, Ltd., 1957.

NEISWANGER, WILLIAM A. *Elementary Statistical Methods as Applied to Business and Economic Data.* Rev. ed. New York: The Macmillan Co., 1956.

NETER, JOHN, WASSERMAN, WILLIAM, and WHITMORE, G. A. *Fundamental Statistics for Business and Economics.* 4th ed. Boston: Allyn and Bacon, Inc., 1973.

SMITH, C. FRANK, and LEABO, D. A. *Basic Statistics for Business Economics.* 4th ed., Homewood, Ill.: Richard D. Irwin, Inc., 1972.

SMITH, LEE H., and WILLIAMS, DONALD R. *Statistical Analysis for Business: A Conceptical Approach.* Belmont California: Wadsworth Publishing Company, Inc., 1971.

WALKER, HELEN MARY, and LEV, JOSEPH. *Elementary Statistical Methods.* Rev. ed. New York: Holt, Rinehart & Winston, Inc., 1973.

CHAPTER 5

ABRAMSON, ADOLPH G., and MACK, RUSSELL H. *Business Forecasting in Practice: Principles and Cases.* New York: John Wiley & Sons, Inc., 1956.

AMERICAN PRODUCTION AND INVENTORY CONTROL SOCIETY. *Forecasting.* Washington, D.C.: APIC, 1973.

BASS, F. M., et al (eds.). *Mathematical Models and Methods in Marketing.* Homewood, Ill.: Richard D. Irwin, Inc., 1961.

BROWN, ROBERT GOODELL. *Smoothing, Forecasting, and Prediction of Discrete Time Series.* Englewood Cliffs, N.J.: Prentice-Hall, Inc., 1963.

————. *Statistical Forecasting for Inventory Control.* New York: McGraw-Hill Book Company, Inc., 1959.

CANTOR, GERRY. *Forecasting for Sales and Manufacturing.* New York: American Management Association, 1971.

CHISHOLM, ROGER K. and Whitaker, Gilbert R. *Forecasting Methods.* Homewood, Ill.: Richard D. Irwin, Inc., 1971.

COPULSKY, WILLIAM. *Practical Sales Forecasting.* New York: American Management Association, 1970.

CRISP, RICHARD D. *Market Research.* New York: McGraw-Hill Book Company, Inc., 1957.

ESTES, B. E. "What Management Expect of Forecasting." In *Sales Forecasting,* Special Report 16. New York: American Management Association, 1956.

MURDICK, ROBERT G., and SCHAEFER, ARTHUR E. *Sales Forecasting for Lower Costs and Higher Profits,* Englewood Cliffs, N.J.: Prentice-Hall, Inc., 1967.

WHEELWRIGHT, STEVEN C., and MAKRIDAKIS, SPYROS G. *Forecasting Methods for Management.* New York: John Wiley & Sons, Inc., 1973.

CHAPTER 6

ADAMS, RICHARD F. "A Procedure for Determining the Work-Units of the

Metalworking Machines." Unpublished MSIE thesis, West Lafayette, Ind.: Purdue University, 1951.

AMERICAN SOCIETY OF TOOL AND MANUFACTURING ENGINEERS. *Fundamentals of Tool Design.* Frank W. Wilson, ed. Englewood Cliffs, N.J.: Prentice-Hall, Inc., 1962.

————. *Handbook of Fixture Design.* New York: McGraw-Hill Book Company, Inc., 1962.

————. *Tool Engineers Handbook.* 2d ed. New York: McGraw-Hill Book Company, Inc., 1959.

ARNELL, ALVIN. *Standard Graphical Symbols: A Comprehensive Guide for Use in Industry, Engineering and Science.* New York: McGraw-Hill Book Company, Inc., 1963.

BEGEMAN, MYRON LOUIS. *Manufacturing Processes.* 6th ed. New York: John Wiley & Sons, Inc., 1969.

DEGARMO, ERNEST P. *Materials and Processes in Manufacturing.* 3d ed. New York: Macmillan Company, 1969.

DOYLE, LAWRENCE E. *Manufacturing Processes and Materials for Engineering.* 2d ed. Englewood Cliffs, N.J.: Prentice-Hall, Inc., 1969.

GREENE, JAMES H. "Process Planning—Organized Methods Pay Dividends." *The Tool Engineer* 4, no. 4, April 1958.

GREENWOOD, DOUGLAS C. *Engineering Data for Product Design.* New York: McGraw-Hill Book Company, Inc., 1961.

HEALY, WILLIAM L., and RAU, A. H. *Simplified Drafting Practice.* New York: John Wiley & Sons, Inc., 1957.

LASCOE, O. D., NELSON, C., and PORTER, H. W. *Machine Shop: Operations and Setup.* 4th ed. Chicago, Ill.: American Technical Society, 1973.

MELNITSKY, BENJAMIN. *Profiting from Industrial Standardization.* New York: Conover-Mast Publications, 1953.

STARR, MARTIN, K. *Product Design and Decision Theory.* Englewood Cliffs, N.J.: Prentice-Hall, Inc., 1963.

CHAPTER 7

AMERICAN SOCIETY OF TOOL AND MANUFACTURING ENGINEERS. *Manufacturing Planning and Estimating Handbook.* Frank W. Wilson, ed. New York: McGraw-Hill Book Co., 1963.

FISKE, WYMAN, P., and BECKETT, JOHN A. *Industrial Accountant's Handbook.* Englewood Cliffs: Prentice-Hall, Inc., 1957.

HENRICI, STANLEY B. *Standard Costs for Manufacturing.* 3d ed. New York: McGraw-Hill Book Co., 1960.

HORNGREN, CHARLES T. *Cost Accounting.* 3d ed. Englewood Cliffs, N.J.: Prentice-Hall, Inc., 1972.

HOUGHTON, PHILIP S. *Estimating and Planning for Engineering Production.* London: Blackie & Son, Ltd., 1950.

KNOEPPEL, CHARLES E. *Profit Engineering.* New York and London: McGraw-Hill Book Co., 1933.

MATZ, ADOLPH, and CURY, O. J. *Cost Accounting.* Cincinnati, Ohio: South Western Publishing Company, 1972.

MYER, JOHN. *Cost Accounting for Non-Accountants.* New York: Hawthorn Books, Inc., 1971.

NORDHOFF, WILLIAM A. *Machine Shop Estimating.* 2d ed. New York: McGraw-Hill Book Co., 1957.

PARSONS, C. W. S. *Estimating Machining Costs.* New York: McGraw-Hill Book Co., 1957.

RAUTENSTRAUCH, WALTER, and VILLERS, RAYMOND. *Budgetary Control.* New York: Funk & Wagnalls in association with *Modern Industry,* 1957.

SHILLINGLAW, GORDON. *Cost Accounting, Analysis and Control.* Rev. ed. Homewood, Ill.: Richard D. Irwin, Inc., 1972.

VANCE, L., and TAUSSING, R. *Accounting Principles and Control.* New York: Holt, Rinehart & Winston, Inc., 1972.

VAN SICKLE, CLARENCE L. *Cost Accounting Fundamentals and Procedures.* 2d ed. New York: Harper & Brothers, 1947.

CHAPTER 8

ABRUZZI, ADAM. *Work, Workers, and Work Measurement.* New York: Columbia University Press, 1956.

ANDRESS, FRANK J. "The Learning Curve as a Production Tool." *Harvard Business Review* 32: 87.

BARNES, RALPH M. *Motion and Time Study: Design and Measurement of Work.* 6th ed. New York: John Wiley & Sons, Inc., 1968.

———. *Work Sampling,* 2d ed. New York: John Wiley & Sons, Inc., 1957.

CARROLL, PHIL. *Time Study Fundamentals for Foremen.* 3d ed. New York: McGraw-Hill Book Company, 1972.

CURRIE, RUSSEL MACKENZIE. *Work Study.* London: Pitman, 1961.

HADDEN, ARTHUR A., and GENGER, VICTOR K. *Handbook of Standard Time Data for Machine Shops.* New York: Ronald Press Company, 1954.

HEILAND, ROBERT E., and RICHARDSON, WALLACE J. *Work Sampling.* New York: McGraw-Hill Book Co., 1957.

HUGHES, R. C., and GOLEM, H. G. *Production Efficiency Curve and Its Application.* San Diego, Calif.: Arts and Crafts Press, 1944.

KRICK, EDWARD V. *Methods Engineering: Design and Measurement of Work Methods.* New York: John Wiley & Sons, Inc., 1962.

MUNDEL, MARVIN E. *Motion and Time Study, Principles and Practice,* 4th ed. Englewood Cliffs, N.J.: Prentice-Hall, Inc., 1960.

NADLER, GERALD. *Work Design.* Homewood, Ill.: Richard D. Irwin, Inc., 1970.

———. *Work Systems Designs: The IDEALS Concept.* Homewood, Ill.: Richard D. Irwin, Inc., 1967.

NIEBEL, BENJAMIN W. *Motion and Time Study.* 5th ed. Homewood, Ill.: Richard D. Irwin, Inc., 1972.

NORDHOFF, W. A.   *Machine Shop Estimating.* 2d ed. New York: McGraw-Hill Book Co., 1960.

PAPPAS, FRANK F., and DINBERG, ROBERT A.   *Practical Work Standards.* New York: McGraw-Hill Book Co., Inc., 1962.

PARSONS, G. W. S.   "The 80% Learning Curve." *Modern Machine Shop.* March 1960.

CHAPTER 9

ALJIAN, GEORGE W.   *Purchasing Handbook.* 2d ed. New York: McGraw-Hill Book Co., 1966.

BAILEY, PETER J.   *Purchasing and Supply Management.* 2d ed. London: Chapman & Hall, 1969.

BARLOW, C. WAYNE.   *Purchasing for the Newly Appointed Buyer.* New York: American Management Association, 1970.

BRAND, GORDON T.   *The Industrial Buying Decision.* London: Associated Business Programmes, 1972.

CANTOR, JEREMIAH.   *Evaluating Purchasing Systems.* New York: American Management Association, 1970.

DOWST, SOMERBY R.   *Basics for Buyers.* Boston: Cahners Books, 1971.

ENGLAND, WILBUR B.   *The Purchasing System.* Homewood, Ill.: Richard D. Irwin, Inc., 1967.

———.   *Procurement: Principles and Cases.* 5th ed. Homewood, Ill.: Richard D. Irwin, Inc., 1970.

FABRYCKY, WOLTER J.   *Procurement and Inventory Systems.* New York: Reinhold, 1967.

HEDRICK, FLOYD D.   *Purchasing Management in the Smaller Company.* New York: American Management Association, 1971.

HEINRITZ, STEWART and FARRELL, PAUL.   *Purchasing: Principles and Applications.* 4th ed. Englewood Cliffs, N.J.: Prentice-Hall, Inc., 1965.

KOLLIOS, A. E. and STEMPEL, JOSEPH L.   *Purchasing and E.D.P.* New York: American Management Association, 1966.

LEE, LAMAR and DOBLER, DONALD W.   *Purchasing and Materials Management.* 2d ed. New York: McGraw-Hill Book Co., 1971.

NATIONAL ASSOCIATION OF PURCHASING AGENTS.   *Evaluation of Supplier Performance,* New York: NAPA, ———.

ROBINSON, PATRICK J.   *Industrial Buying and Creative Marketing.* Boston: Allyn and Bacon, 1967.

WEBSTER, FREDERICK E.   *Organizational Buying Behavior.* Englewood Cliffs, N.J.: Prentice-Hall, Inc., 1972.

WELLS, ROBERT.   *E.D.P. Applications for Purchasing Function.* New York: American Management Association, 1970.

WESTING, J. H., FINE, I. V., and LENZ, GARRY J.   *Purchasing Management Materials in Motion.* 3d ed. New York: John Wiley & Sons, Inc., 1969.

WILLETS, WALTER E.   *Fundamentals of Purchasing.* New York: Appleton-Century-Crofts, 1969.

CHAPTERS 10–13

ALFANDARY-ALEXANDER, MARK. *An Inquiry into Some Models of Inventory Systems.* Pittsburgh: University of Pittsburgh Press, 1962.

AMERICAN MANAGEMENT ASSOCIATION. *Company Approaches to Production Problems: Inventory, Warehousing, Traffic.* Manufacturing Series 220. New York: AMA, 1955.

————. *Key Consideration to Inventory Management.* H. Ford Dickie, ed. Manufacturing Series No. 207, New York: AMA, 1953.

AMERICAN PRODUCTION AND INVENTORY CONTROL SOCIETY. *Management of Lot Size Inventories.* Washington, D.C.: APICS, 1963.

AMMER, DEAN S. *Materials Management.* Homewood, Ill.: Richard D. Irwin, Inc., 1968.

ARROW, KENNETH JOSEPH, KARLIN, SAMUEL, and SCARF, HERBERT. *Studies in the Mathematical Theory of Inventory and Production.* Stanford, Calif.: Stanford University Press, 1958.

BAILY, P. J. *Design of Stock Control Systems and Records.* London: Gower Press, 1970.

————. *Purchasing and Supply Management.* 2d ed. London: Chapman & Hall.

BALLOT, ROBERT B. *Materials Management: A Results Approach.* New York: American Management Association, 1971.

BATTERSBY, ALBERT. *A Guide to Stock Control.* 2d ed. New York: Pitman Publishing Corp., 1970.

BRIGGS, ANDREW J. *Warehouse Operations Planning and Management.* New York: John Wiley & Sons, Inc., 1960.

BROWN, ROBERT G. *Statistical Forecasting for Inventory Control.* New York: McGraw-Hill Book Co., 1959.

————. *Decision Rules for Inventory Management.* New York: Holt, Rinehart and Winston, 1967.

————. *Smoothing, Forecasting and Prediction of Discrete Time Series.* Englewood Cliffs, N.J.: Prentice-Hall, Inc., 1963.

BUCHAN, JOSEPH, and KOENIGSBERG, ERNEST. *Scientific Inventory Management.* Englewood Cliffs, N.J.: Prentice-Hall, Inc., 1963.

EILON, SAMUEL, and LAMPKIN, WILLIAM. *Inventory Control Abstracts.* London: Oliver & Boyd, 1968.

ENRICK, NORBERT LLOYD. *Inventory Management; Installation, Operation, and Control.* San Francisco, California: Chandler Publishing Co., 1968.

FABRYCKY, W. J., and BANKS, JERRY. *Procurement and Inventory Systems: Theory and Analysis.* New York: Reinhold Publishing Corp., 1967.

FETTER, ROBERT B., and DALLECK, WINSTON C. *Decision Models for Inventory Management.* Homewood, Ill.: Richard D. Irwin, Inc., 1961.

FOX, JOHN J. *Inventory Management, Statistical Techniques for Inventory Management with UNIVAC Systems.* New York: Sperry Rand Corp., 1962.

GENERAL SERVICES ADMINISTRATION. *The Economic Order Quantity Principles and Application.* Washington, D.C.: U. S. Government Printing Office, 1966.

GREENE, JAMES H. *Production and Inventory Control Handbook*. New York: McGraw-Hill Book Co., 1970.

———, and COLLIER, JAMES A. "The Dynamics of Packaging." *Material Handling Engineering* 14 (May 1959): 96.

———, and RAYMOND, MURRAY. "Here's How Photography Can Eliminate Inventory Handling." *Flow* 13 (August 1958): 51.

HADLEY, GEORGE, and WHITIN, T. M. *Analysis of Inventory Systems*. Englewood Cliffs, N.J.: Prentice-Hall, Inc., 1963.

HANSSMANN, FRED. *Operations Research in Production and Inventory Control*. New York: John Wiley & Sons, Inc., 1962.

HOFFMAN, RAYMOND A. *Inventories: A Guide to Their Control, Costing and Effect upon Income and Taxes*. 2d ed. New York: Ronald Press, 1970.

———, and GUNDERS, HENRY. *Inventories, Control, Cost, and Effect upon Income Taxes*. 2d ed. New York: Ronald Press, 1970.

HOLT, CHARLES C. *Planning Production, Inventories, and Work Force*. Englewood Cliffs, N.J.: Prentice-Hall, Inc., 1960.

INTERNATIONAL BUSINESS MACHINES, INC. *Wholesale IMPACT—Advanced Principles and Implementation Reference Manual*. White Plains, N.Y.: IBM, 1969.

KILLEEN, LOUIS M. *Techniques of Inventory Management*. New York: American Management Association, 1969.

LEWIS, COLIN DAVID. *Scientific Inventory Control*. New York: American Elsevier Publishing Co., 1970.

LIPMAN, BURTON E. *How to Control and Reduce Inventory*. Englewood Cliffs, N.J.: Prentice-Hall, Inc., 1972.

MAGEE, JOHN F. *Physical Distribution Systems*. New York: McGraw-Hill Book Co., 1967.

———, and BOODMAN, DAVID M. *Production Planning and Inventory Control*. 2d ed. New York: McGraw-Hill Book Co., 1967.

MATTEIS, J. J. "An Economic Lot-Sizing Technique I: The Part Period Algorithm." *IBM Systems Journal* 7 (1968): 30–48.

MELNITSKY, BENJAMIN. *Industrial Storeskeeping Manual*. Philadelphia: Chilton Co., 1956.

———. *Management of Industrial Inventory*. New York: Conover-Mast Publications, 1951.

MENDOZA, A. G. "An Economic Lot-Sizing Technique II: Mathematical Analysis of the Part-Period Algorithm." *IBM Systems Journal* 7 (1968): 39–47.

MORRIS, ROBERT. Statement Studies. The Robert Morris Associates, *1973 Annual Statement Studies*, Philadelphia, Pa.

NATIONAL ASSOCIATION OF ACCOUNTANTS. *Techniques in Inventory Management*. Research Report No. 40. New York: NAA, 1964.

NADDOR, ELIEZER. *Inventory Systems*. New York: John Wiley & Sons, Inc., 1966.

NEUSCHEL, RICHARD F., and JOHNSON, H. TALLMAN. *How to Take Physical Inventory*. New York and London: McGraw-Hill Book Co., 1946.

NILAND, POWELL. *Production Planning, Scheduling, and Inventory Control.* New York: Macmillan, Inc., 1970.

PLOSSL, GEORGE W., and WIGHT, OLIVER W. *Material Requirements Planning by Computer.* Chicago: American Production and Inventory Control Society, 1971.

————. *Production and Inventory Control: Principles and Techniques.* Englewood Cliffs, N.J.: Prentice-Hall, Inc., 1967.

PRICHARD, JAMES W., and EAGLE, ROBERT H. *Modern Inventory Management.* New York: John Wiley & Sons, Inc., 1965.

PUTNAM, ARNOLD O., BOSLOW, E. ROBERT, and STILIAN, GABRIEL N. *Unified Operations Management.* New York: McGraw-Hill Book Co., 1963.

RAYMOND, MURRAY R. "The Use of Photographic Techniques in Making the Physical Inventory." Unpublished thesis for M.S.I.E., West Lafayette, Ind.: Purdue University, 1955.

REISMAN, ARNOLD. *Industrial Inventory Control.* New York: Gordon and Breach, 1972.

SCARF, HERBERT E., GILFORD, DOROTHY M., and SHELLEY, MAYNARD W. *Multistage Inventory Models and Techniques.* Stanford, Calif.: Stanford University Press, 1963.

SESPANIACK, LAWRENCE J. "An Application of Combinatorial Statistics to the Determination of the Order Point." Unpublished thesis for M.S.I.E., West Lafayette, Ind.: Purdue University, 1957.

STARR, MARTIN KENNETH, and MILLER, DAVID W. *Inventory Control: Theory and Practice.* Englewood Cliffs, N.J.: Prentice-Hall, Inc., 1962.

STOCKTON, R. STANSBURY. *Basic Inventory Systems: Concepts and Analysis.* Boston: Allyn and Bacon, Inc., 1965.

THOMAS, ADIN B. *Inventory Control in Production and Manufacturing.* Boston: Cahners Books, 1970.

————. *Stock Control in Manufacturing Industries.* London: Gorver Publications, 1968.

VAN DE MARK, R. L. *Inventory Control Techniques.* 2d ed. Dallas, Texas: Van de Mark, Inc., 1972.

————. *Managing Material Control,* Dallas, Texas: Van de Mark, Inc., ————.

————. *Production Control Techniques,* Dallas, Texas: Van de Mark, Inc., 1970.

————. *Production and Inventory Control Case Studies.* Dallas, Texas: Van de Mark, Inc., 1963.

————. *New Ideas in Materials Management.* Dallas, Texas: Van de Mark, Inc., 1963.

VAZSONYI, ANDREW. *Scientific Programming in Business and Industry.* New York: John Wiley & Sons, Inc., 1958.

WAGNER, HARVEY M. *Statistical Management of Inventory Systems.* New York: John Wiley & Sons, Inc., 1962.

WELCH, W. EVERT. *Tested Scientific Inventory Control.* Greenwich, Conn.: Management Publishing Corp., 1959.

WHITIN, THOMSON M. *The Theory of Inventory Management*. 2d ed. Princeton, N.J.: Princeton University Press, 1957.

CHAPTERS 14–15

AMERICAN MANAGEMENT ASSOCIATION. *PERT, A New Management Planning and Control Technique, Report No. 74*. ed. by Gabriel N. Stilian, et al. New York: AMA, 1962.

BATTERSBY, ALBERT. *Network Analysis for Planning and Scheduling*. New York: Saint Martin's Press, Inc., 1965.

BRUCE, ROBERT T., CHANDRUC, JEAN, and HORNBRUCH, FREDERICK W. *Practical Planning and Scheduling*. New London, Conn.: National Foremans' Institute, 1950.

CLARK, WALLACE. *The Gantt Chart, A Working Tool of Management*. 3d ed. London: Pitman, 1952.

CONWAY, RICHARD W., MAXWELL, WILLIAM L., and MILLER, LOUIS W. *Theory of Scheduling*. Reading, Mass.: Addison-Wesley Publishing Co., 1967.

EVARTS, HARRY F. *Introduction to PERT*. Boston: Allyn and Bacon, Inc., 1964.

FORD, LESTER R., and FULKERSON, D. R. *Flows in Networks*. Princeton, N.J.: Princeton University Press, 1962.

GREENE, JAMES H. "Control Charts—Key to Efficiency." *The Tool Engineer* 43, no. 3, September 1959.

HOROWITZ, JOSEPH. *Critical Path Scheduling—Management Control Through CPM and PERT*. New York: Ronald Press, 1967.

IVANNONE, ANTHONY L. *Management Program Planning and Control with PERT, MOST, and LOB*. Englewood Cliffs, N.J.: Prentice-Hall, Inc., 1967.

MARTINO, R. L. *Allocating and Scheduling Resources, Project Management and Control*. New York: American Management Association, 1965.

———. *Applied Operational Planning, Project Management and Control*. New York: American Management Association, 1964.

———. *Critical Path Networks*. New York: McGraw-Hill Book Co., 1970.

———. *Finding the Critical Path, Project Management and Control*. New York: American Management Association, 1964.

MILLER, ROBERT WALLACE. *Schedule, Cost and Profit Control with PERT*. New York: McGraw-Hill Book Co., 1963.

MODER, JOSEPH J. *Project Management with CPM and PERT*. New York: Reinhold Publishing Co., 1964.

———, and PHILLIPS, CECIL R. *Project Management with CPM and PERT*. 2d ed., New York: Van Nostrand-Reinhold Co., 1970.

MOORE, J. M., and WILSON, R. C. *A Review of Simulation Research in Job Shop Scheduling*. Washington, D.C.: Production and Inventory Management, American Production and Inventory Control Society, 1967.

MUTH, JOHN F., and THOMPSON, GERALD L. *Industrial Scheduling*. Englewood Cliffs, N.J.: Prentice-Hall, Inc., 1963.

National Aeronautics and Space Administration, Office of the Secretary of Defense, *DOD and NASA PERT COST, Systems Design*. Washington, D.C.: U.S. Government Printing Office, June, 1962.

Naval Research Logistics Quarterly, volume devoted to scheduling, vol. 15, no. 2, June 1968.

PERT Coordinating Group. *Supplemental No. 1 to DOD and NASA Guide PERT COST—Output Reports*. Washington, D.C.: Superintendent of Documents, U.S. Government Printing Office, March 1963.

Phillips, Cecil R., and Moder, Joseph J. *Manual of Critical Path Theory and Practice*. 2d ed. Baltimore, Maryland: Operations Research, Inc., 1962.

Putnam, Arnold O. *Critical Ratio Scheduling*. Proceedings of the American Production and Inventory Control, Washington, D. C., 1966.

Rice, William B. *Control Charts in Factory Management*. New York: John Wiley & Sons, Inc., 1947.

Riggs, J. L., and Heath, C. O. *Guide to Cost Reduction through Critical Path Scheduling*. Englewood Cliffs, N.J.: Prentice-Hall, Inc., 1966.

Smith, Martin R. *Short-Interval Scheduling: A Systematic Approach to Cost Reduction*. New York: McGraw-Hill Book Co., 1968.

Special Projects Office, Department of the Navy, Bureau of Naval Weapons, *PERT Summary Report, Phase 1*. Washington, D.C.: U.S. Government Printing Office, 1958.

———. *PERT Summary Report, Phase 2*. Washington, D.C., U.S. Government Printing Office, 1958.

———. *An Introduction to the PERT/COST System for Integrated Project Management*. Washington D.C.: U.S. Government Printing Office, 1961.

———. *PERT Guide for Management Use*. Washington, D.C.: U.S. Government Printing Office, June 1963.

Stires, David M., and Murphy, Maurice M. *Modern Management Methods PERT and CPM*. Boston: Materials Management Institute, 1963.

———, and Wenig, Raymond P. *PERT/COST*. Boston: Industrial Education Institute, 1964.

Wiest, Jerome D., and Levy, F. K. *A Management Guide to PERT/CPM*. Englewood Cliffs, N.J.: Prentice-Hall, Inc., 1969.

CHAPTER 16

Holt, C., et al. *Planning Production, Inventories, and Work Force*. Englewood Cliffs, N.J.: Prentice-Hall, Inc., 1960.

Jackson, J. R. "A Computing Procedure for a Line Balancing Problem." *Management Science* 2, no. 3, April 1956.

Kilbridge, M. D., and Wester, L. "A Heuristic Method of Assembly Line Balancing." *Journal of Industrial Engineering* 12, no. 4, July–August 1961.

———. "The Balance Delay Problem." *Management Science* 8, no. 1, October 1961.

———. "A Review of Analytical Systems of Line Balancing." *Operations Research* 10, no. 5, September–October 1962.

Moodie, C. L., and Young, H. H.   "A Heuristic Method of Assembly Line Balancing for Assumptions of Constant or Variable Work Element Times." *Journal of Industrial Engineering* 16, no. 1, January–February 1965.

Prenting, O., and Battaglin, M.   "The Precedence Diagram: A Tool for Analysis in Assembly Line Balancing." *Journal of Industrial Engineering* 15, no. 4, July–August 1964.

Wester, L., and Kilbridge, M.   "Heuristic Line Balancing: A Case." *Journal of Industrial Engineering* 13, no. 3, May–June 1962.

Young H. H.   "Optimization Models for Production Lines." *Journal of Industrial Engineering* 18 (January 1967): 70–78.

CHAPTER 17

Queueing Theory

Cooper, Robert S.   *Introduction to Queueing Theory.* New York: Macmillan, Inc. 1972.

Lee, A. M.   *Applied Queueing Theory.* New York: St. Martin's Press, 1970.

Morris, William T.   *Analysis for Materials Handling Management.* Homewood, Ill.: Richard D. Irwin, Inc., 1962.

Morse, Philip McCord.   *Queues, Inventories and Maintenance.* New York: John Wiley & Sons, Inc., 1958.

Panico, Joseph A.   *Queueing Theory: A Study of Waiting Lines for Business Economics and Science.* Englewood Cliffs, N.J.: Prentice-Hall, Inc., 1969.

Saaty, T. L.   *Elements of Queueing Theory.* New York: McGraw-Hill, 1961.

Takacs, Lajos.   *Introduction to Theory of Queues.* New York: Oxford Univerversity Press, 1962.

Simulation

Chortas, D. N.   *Systems and Simulation.* New York: Academic Press, 1965.

Emshoft, James R., and Sisson, Roger L.   *Design and Use of Computer Simulation Models.* New York: The Macmillan Co., 1970.

Evans, G. W., Wallace, G. F., and Sutherland, G. L.   *Simulation Using Digital Computers.* Englewood Cliffs, N.J.: Prentice-Hall, Inc., 1967.

Fishman, G. S.   *Concepts and Methods in Discrete Event Simulation.* New York: John Wiley & Sons, Inc., 1973.

Glickstein, Aaron, et al.   "Simulate Your Way to Sound Decisions." *Food Engineering* 35, no. 6, June 1963.

———.   *Simulation Procedures for Production Control in an Indiana Cheese Plant, Research Bulletin No. 757,* Lafayette, Indiana: Purdue University Agriculture Experiment Station, 1962.

Gordon, G.   *System Simulation.* Englewood Cliffs, N.J.: Prentice-Hall, Inc., 1969.

International Business Machines.   *General Purpose Simulation System/360 Introductory User's Manual.* White Plains, N.Y.: IBM, ———.

KIVIAT, P. J. VILLANUEVA, R., and MARKOWITZ, H. *The SIMSCRIPT II Programming Language.* Englewood Cliffs, N.J.: Prentice-Hall, Inc., 1969.

MARKOWITZ, HARRY M., HAUSNER, BERNARD, and KARR, HERBERT W. *SIMSCRIPT: A Simulation Programming Language.* Englewood Cliffs, N.J.: Prentice-Hall, Inc., 1963.

MEIR, ROBERT C., NEWELL, WILLIAM T., and PAZER, HAROLD L. *Simulation in Business and Economics.* Englewood Cliffs, N.J.: Prentice-Hall, Inc., 1969.

MIHRAM, G. A. *Simulation: Statistical Foundations and Methodology.* New York: Academic Press, 1972.

MIZE, JOE H., and COX, J. GRADY. *Essentials of Simulation.* Englewood Cliffs, N.J.: Prentice-Hall, Inc., 1968.

———— and HERRING, BRUCE E. *PROSIM.* Englewood Cliffs, N.J.: Prentice-Hall, Inc., 1971.

NAYLOR, THOMAS H., et al. *Computer Simulation Techniques.* New York: John Wiley & Sons, Inc., 1966.

PRITSKER, A. A. B., and KIVIAT, P. J. *Simulation with GASP II.* Englewood Cliffs, N.J.: Prentice-Hall, Inc., 1969.

RAND CORPORATION. *Digital Computer Simulations: Modeling Concepts.* RAND Memorandum RM 5378–PR (P. J. Kiviat), Santa Monica, Calif.: RAND Corp., August 1967.

REITMAN, J. *Computer Simulation Applications.* New York: John Wiley & Sons, Inc., 1971.

SCHMIDT, J. W., and TAYLOR, K. E. *Simulation and Analysis of Industrial Systems.* Homewood, Ill.: Richard D. Irwin, Inc., 1970.

SCHRIEBER, T. *A GPSS Primer.* Ann Arbor, Michigan: Ulrichs Books, Inc., 1972.

SMITH, W. NYE, ESTEY, ELMER E., and VINES, ELLSWORTH F. *Integrated Simulation.* 2d ed. Cincinnati, Ohio: South-western Publishing Co., 1974.

WYMAN, FORREST PAUL. *Simulation Modeling: A Guide to Using SIMSCRIPT.* New York: John Wiley & Sons, Inc., 1970.

CHAPTER 18

BLACKWELL, DAVID HAROLD, and GIRSHICK, M. A. *Theory of Games and Statistical Decisions.* New York: John Wiley & Sons, Inc., 1954.

BOWMAN, EDWARD H., and FETTER, ROBERT BARCLAY. *Analysis for Production and Operations Management.* 3d ed. Homewood, Ill.: Richard D. Irwin, Inc., 1967.

CHARNES, ABRAHAM, and COOPER, W. W. *Management Models and Industrial Applications of Linear Programming.* Vols. 1 and 2. New York: John Wiley & Sons, Inc., 1961.

CHATTO, KENNETH A. "An Application of Operations Research Methods to the Selection of a Processing Plan in a Meat Packing Plant." Unpublished MSIE thesis, West Lafayette, Ind.: Purdue University, 1955.

COOPER, WILLIAM WAGER, HENDERSON, A., and CHARNES, ABRAHAM. *An Introduction to Linear Programming.* New York: John Wiley & Sons, Inc., 1953.

DANTZIG, GEORGE BERNARD. *Linear Programming and Extensions.* 2d ed. Princeton, N.J.: Princeton University Press, 1965.

DEAN, BURTON V., SASIENI, MAURICE W., and GUPTA, SHIV K. *Mathematics for Modern Management.* New York: John Wiley & Sons, Inc., 1963.

DORFMAN, ROBERT. *Application of Linear Programming to the Theory of the Firm.* Berkeley, California: University of California Press, 1951.

————, SAMUELSON, PAUL A., and SOLOW, ROBERT M. *Linear Programming and Economic Analysis.* New York: McGraw-Hill Book Co., 1958.

DOTY, WILLIAM W. "An Introduction to the Application of Linear Programming to Industrial Engineering." Unpublished MSIE thesis West Lafayette, Ind.: Purdue University, 1954.

GALE, DAVID. *The Theory of Linear Economic Models.* New York: McGraw-Hill Book Co., 1960.

GASS, SAUL I. *An Illustrated Guide to Linear Programming.* New York: McGraw-Hill Book Co., 1970.

————. *Linear Programming: Methods and Applications.* 3d ed. New York: McGraw-Hill Book Co., 1969.

GREENE, JAMES H., et al. "Linear Programming in the Packing Industry," *Journal of Industrial Engineering*, Vol. X, No. 5, September–October 1959.

GREENWALD, DAKOTA ULRICH. *Linear Programming, An Explanation of the Simplex Algorithm.* New York: Ronald Press Co., 1957.

HADLEY, GEORGE. *Nonlinear and Dynamic Programming.* Reading, Mass.: Addison-Wesley Publishers, 1964.

————. *Linear Programming.* Reading, Mass.: Addison-Wesley Publishers, 1962.

KEMENY, J., et al. *Finite Mathematics with Business Applications.* 2d ed. Englewood Cliffs, N.J.: Prentice-Hall, Inc., 1972.

LEVIN, RICHARD L., and SAMONE, R. P. *Linear Programming for Management Decisions.* Homewood, Ill.: Richard D. Irwin, Inc., 1969.

LLEWELLYN, ROBERT W. *Linear Programming.* New York: Holt, Rinehart & Winston, Inc., 1964.

LOOMBA, N. PAUL. *Linear Programming: An Introduction Analysis.* New York: McGraw-Hill Book Co., 1964.

NAYLOR, THOMAS H., BYNE, EUGENE T., and VERNON, JOHN M. *Introduction to Linear Programming.* Englewood Cliffs, N.J.: Prentice-Hall, Inc., 1971.

REINFELD, NYLES V., and VOGEL, WILLIAM R. *Mathematical Programming.* Englewood Cliffs, N.J.: Prentice-Hall, Inc., 1958.

SIMMONARD, M. *Linear Programming, Management and Quantitative Methods.* Englewood Cliffs, N.J.: Prentice-Hall, Inc., 1966.

SIMMONS, DONALD M. *Linear Programming for Operations Research.* San Francisco, Calif.: Holden-Day, Inc., 1972.

SMYTHE, WILLIAM R., and JOHNSON, LYNWOOD A. *Introduction to Linear Programming with Applications.* Englewood Cliffs, N.J.: Prentice-Hall, Inc., 1966.

STOCKTON, R. STANSBURY. *Introduction to Linear Programming.* Homewood, Ill.: Richard D. Irwin, Inc., 1971.

CHAPTER 19

GRUENBERGER, FRED, and BABCOCK, DAVID. *Computing with Minicomputers,* Los Angeles, Calif.: Melville Publishing Co., ———.

IBM *Shop Floor Control Manual* # GH 20 0753 (White Plains, N.Y., International Business Machines) July 1971.

IBM *System–3; Shop Loading and Control Manual* # GH20 1240 (White Plains, N.Y., International Business Machines) September, 1972.

CHAPTER 20

For references to the Design of the Organization, see references for Chapter 25.

Design of Physical Facilities

APPLE, JAMES. *Plant Layout and Materials Handling.* 2d ed. New York: Ronald Press Co., 1963.

———. *Material Handling Systems Design.* New York: Ronald Press Co., 1972.

GREENE, JAMES H. "Is Current Layout Thinking Obsolete?" *Modern Materials Handling* 13 (December 1958): 70.

IMMER, JOHN R. *Layout Planning Techniques.* New York: McGraw-Hill Book Co., 1953.

JENKINS, CREED H. *Modern Warehouse Management.* New York: McGraw-Hill Book Co., 1968.

MOORE, JAMES M. *Plant Layout and Design.* New York: The Macmillan Co., 1962.

MUTHER, RICHARD. *Production-Line Technique.* New York and London: McGraw-Hill Book Co., 1944.

———. *Systematic Layout Planning.* Boston: Cahners Books, 1971.

———. and HAGANAS, KNUT. *Systematic Handling Analysis.* Boston: Cahners Books, 1969.

REED, RUDDELL, JR. *Plant Layout.* Homewood, Ill.: Richard D. Irwin, Inc., 1961.

SIMS, EUGENE R. *Planning and Managing Material Flow.* Boston: Cahners Books, 1968.

CHAPTER 21

AMERICAN MANAGEMENT ASSOCIATION, OFFICE MANAGEMENT DIVISION. *Organizing for Effective Systems Planning and Control.* New York: AMA, 1956.

BOCCHINO, WILLIAM A. *Management Information Systems: Tools and Techniques.* Englewood Cliffs, N.J.: Prentice-Hall, Inc., 1972.

GREENE, JAMES H. "How to Squeeze Profits from Paper Work." *Manufacturing and Industrial Engineering* 36, no. 5, May 1958.

HERRMANN, IRVIN A. *Manual of Office Reproductions.* New York: Office Publications Co., 1956.

KEYES, CARL. *Management Guide to Systems and Procedures*. Alhambra, Calif.: Tinnon-Brown/Borden Publishing Co., 1967.

LAZZARO, VICTOR. *Systems and Procedures: A Handbook for Business and Industry*. 2d ed. Englewood Cliffs, N.J.: Prentice-Hall, Inc., 1968.

NEUNER, JOHN J., and HAYNES, BENJAMIN R. *Office Management Principles and Practices*. 3d ed. Cincinnati: South-Western Publishing Co., 1953.

NEUSCHEL, RICHARD F. *Management by System*. 2d ed. New York: McGraw-Hill Book Co., 1960.

TERRY, GEORGE R. *Office Management and Control*. 6th ed. Homewood, Ill.: Richard D. Irwin, Inc., 1970.

CHAPTERS 22–23

AWAD, ELIAS M. *Business Data Processing*. Englewood Cliffs, N.J.: Prentice-Hall, Inc., 1971.

BLUMENTHAL, SHERMAN S. *Management Information Systems: A Framework for Planning and Development*. Englewood Cliffs, N.J.: Prentice-Hall, Inc., 1969.

BRIGHTMAN, RICHARD W. *Data Processing for Decision Making*. 2d ed. New York: Macmillan, Inc., 1971.

CASEY, ROBERT S., and PERRY, JAMES W. *Punched Cards, Their Applications to Science and Industry*. New York: Reinhold Publishing Co., 1951.

CHACKO, GEORGE K. *Computer-Aided Decision Making*. New York: American Elsevier Publishing Co., 1972.

CHAPIN, NED. *Computers: A Systems Approach*. New York: Reinhold Publishing Corp., 1971.

DAVIS, GORDON B. *Computer Data Processing*. 2d ed. New York: McGraw-Hill Book Co., 1973.

DEPARTMENT OF DEFENSE, *COBOL—1961*. Washington, D.C.: Superintendent of Documents, U.S. Government Printing Office, 1961.

FLORES, IVAN. *Data Structure and Management*. Englewood Cliffs, N.J.: Prentice-Hall, Inc., 1970.

———. *Computer Programming System/360*. Englewood Cliffs, N.J.: Prentice-Hall, Inc., 1971.

———. *Peripheral Devices*. Englewood Cliffs, N.J.: Prentice-Hall, Inc., 1973.

FORKNER, IRVINE, and McLEOD, RAYMOND. *Computerized Business Systems*. New York: John Wiley & Sons, Inc., 1973.

GLEIM, GEORGE A. *Electronic Data Processing Systems and Procedures*. Englewood Cliffs, N.J.: Prentice-Hall, Inc., 1971.

GREENE, JAMES H. "Computer Integration for Small Industry." *Systems Magazine* 22, no. 2, March–April 1958.

HODGE, BARTOW. *Management and the Computer in Information and Control Systems*. New York: McGraw-Hill Book Co., 1969.

IBM PERSONAL STUDY PROGRAM. *Punched Card Data Processing Principles*. Endicott, N.Y.: International Business Machines Company, 1961.

INTERNATIONAL BUSINESS MACHINES COMPANY. *Wholesale IMPACT—Advanced Principles and Implementation Reference Manual.* White Plains, N.Y.: IBM, 1969.

KELLY, JOSEPH F. *Computerized Management Information Systems.* New York: Macmillan, Inc., 1970.

KRAUSS, LEONARD I. *Computer-Based Management Information Systems.* New York: American Management Association, 1970.

LAZZARO, VICTOR. *Systems and Procedures: A Handbook for Business and Industry.* 2d ed. Englewood Cliffs, N.J.: Prentice-Hall, Inc., 1968.

LUCAS, HENRY C. *Computer Based Information Systems in Organizations.* Chicago: Science Research Associates, 1973.

MARTIN, EDLEY WAINRIGHT. *Computers and Information Systems.* Homewood, Ill.: Richard D. Irwin, Inc., 1973.

MARTINO, R. L. *Information Management.* New York: McGraw-Hill Book Co., 1970.

———. *M.I.S. Management Information Systems.* New York: McGraw-Hill Book Co., 1970.

McCRACKEN, DANIEL D. *A Guide to COBOL Programming.* New York: John Wiley & Sons, Inc., 1963.

O'BRIAN, JAMES JEROME. *Management Information Systems, Concepts, Techniques and Applications.* New York: Van Nostrand-Reinhold Co., 1970.

ORLICKY, JOSEPH A. *The Successful Computer System.* New York: McGraw-Hill Book Co., 1969.

SANDERS, DONALD H. *Computers in Business.* New York: McGraw-Hill Book Co., 1972.

SAXON, JAMES A. *COBOL, A Self-Instructional Manual.* Englewood Cliffs, N.J.: Prentice-Hall, Inc., 1963.

SILVER, GERALD A., and SILVER, JOAN B. *Data Processing for Business.* New York: Harcourt, Brace, Jovanovich, 1973.

STARR, MARTIN KENNETH. *Systems Management of Operations.* Englewood Cliffs, N.J.: Prentice-Hall, 1971.

WEISS, ERIC A. *Computer Usage; 360 Assembly Programming.* New York: McGraw-Hill Book Co., 1970.

CHAPTER 24

MILLER, ERNEST. *Conference Leadership.* New York: American Management Association, 1972.

WAGNER, RUSSELL, and ARNOLD, CARROLL C. *Handbook of Group Discussion.* Boston: Houghton Mifflin Co., 1944.

WEAVER, G. G., and BOLLINGER, E. W. *Visual Aids.* Princeton, N.J.: D. Van Nostrand Co., 1959.

WINFREY, ROBLEY. *Technical and Business Report Preparation.* 3d ed. Ames, Iowa: Iowa State University Press, 1962.

WITTLICH, WALTER W., and SCHULLER, CHARLES F. *Audio-Visual Materials.* New York: Harper & Brothers, 1951.

WOLFF, JACK L. *The Production Conference*. Boston: Houghton Mifflin Co., 1944.

CHAPTER 25

ABRAMOWITZ, IRVING. *Production Management: Concepts and Analysis for Production and Control*. New York: Ronald Press Co., 1967.

AMERICAN MANAGEMENT ASSOCIATION. *Guides to Effective Production Management*. New York: AMA, 1954.

ARGYRIS, CHRIS. *Personality and Organization*. New York, New York: Harper, 1957.

BARNARD, CHESTER. *The Functions of the Executive*. Cambridge, Mass.: Harvard University Press, 1938.

DALE, ERNEST. *Management Theory and Practice*. New York: McGraw-Hill Book Co., 1973.

DRUCKER, PETER. *The Practice of Management*. New York: Harper and Row, 1954.

FAYOL, HENRI. *General and Industrial Management*. Paris, France: Dunod, 1925.

HEIN, LEONARD W. *The Quantitative Approach to Managerial Decisions*. Englewood Cliffs, N.J.: Prentice-Hall, Inc., 1967.

HERZBERG, FREDERICK. *Work and Nature of Man*. Cleveland, Ohio: World Publishing Co., 1966.

KOONTZ, HAROLD, and O'DONNEL, CYRIL. *Principles of Management*. New York: McGraw-Hill Book Co., 1968.

LICKERT, RENSIS. *The Human Organization*. New York: McGraw-Hill Book Co., 1967.

MARCH, JAMES, and SIMON, HERBERT. *Organization*. New York: John Wiley & Sons, Inc., 1958.

MARTINO, ROCCO L. *Integrated Manufacturing Systems*. New York: McGraw-Hill Book Co., 1972.

MAYER, RAYMOND R. *Production Management*. New York: McGraw-Hill Book Co., 1968.

McGREGOR, DOUGLAS. *The Professional Manager*. New York: McGraw-Hill Book Co., 1967.

———. *Human Side of Enterprise*. New York: McGraw-Hill Book Company, 1960.

MOCKLER, ROBERT J. *Management Control Process*. New York: Appleton-Century-Crofts, Inc., 1972.

ODIORNE, G. *Management Decisions by Objectives*. Englewood Cliffs, N.J.: Prentice-Hall, Inc., 1968.

ROSS, JOEL E. *Management by Informative System*. Englewood Cliffs, N.J.: Prentice-Hall, Inc., 1970.

TERRY, GEORGE. *Principles of Management*. 6th ed. Homewood, Ill.: Richard D. Irwin, Inc., 1972.

TIMMS, HOWARD L.   *The Production Function in Business.* Homewood, Ill.: Richard D. Irwin, Inc., 1962.

WEINSTOCK, IRWIN T., and TORGERSON, PAUL E.   *Management: An Integrated Approach.* Englewood Cliffs, N.J.: Prentice-Hall, Inc., 1972.

ZEYHER, LEWIS R.   *Production Managers' Handbook for Formulae and Tables.* Englewood Cliffs, N.J.: Prentice-Hall, 1972.

index

Index

This book is set in 10 and 9 point Electra, leaded 2 points. Section and chapter numbers are set in 24 and 30 point Helvetica Medium and section and chapter titles are set in 24 and 18 point Helvetica Regular. The size of the type page is 27 × 46½ picas.

PATTERSON, D. W.